PERSONALITY AND PERSONAL GROWTH

PERSONALITY AND PERSONAL GROWTH
SECOND EDITION

ROBERT FRAGER
California Institute of Transpersonal Psychology

JAMES FADIMAN
Stanford University

1817

HARPER & ROW, PUBLISHERS, New York
Cambridge, Philadelphia, San Francisco,
London, Mexico City, São Paulo, Sydney

Sponsoring Editor: Susan Mackey
Project Editor: Pamela Landau
Designer: Michel Craig
Production Manager: William Lane
Photo Researcher: Mira Schachne
Compositor: Com Com Division of Haddon Craftsmen, Inc.
Printer and Binder: R. R. Donnelley & Sons Company
Art Studio: Fine Line Inc.

PERSONALITY AND PERSONAL GROWTH, Second Edition

Copyright © 1984 by Robert Frager and James Fadiman

Library of Congress Cataloging in Publication Data

Frager, Robert, 1940–
  Personality and personal growth.

  Rev. ed. of: Personality and personal growth /
James Fadiman. c1976
  Includes bibliographies and indexes.
  1. Personality. 2. Psychotherapy. 3. East Asia—
Religion. I. Fadiman, James, 1939–   . II. Fadiman,
James, 1939–   . Personality and personal growth.
III. Title. [DNLM: 1. Personality. 2. Psychological
theory. BF 698 F811p]
BF698.F67 1984   155.2   83–13014
ISBN 0–06–041964–4

To our wives: Ayhan and Dorothy
Our children: Ariel, Eddie, Renee, Maria
And
to our teachers

TEXT AND ILLUSTRATION CREDITS

We gratefully acknowledge the use of material from the following sources:

TEXT

Al-Ghazzali. *The Revival of Religious Sciences.* Reprinted by permission of Sufi Publishing Co. Ltd.
Orson Bean. *Me and the Orgone.* Reprinted by permission of St. Martin's Press, Inc.
J. H. Clarke. Illustration from "Yoga Aphorisms of Patanjali." This illustration first appeared in *New Society,* London, the weekly review of the Social Sciences.
A. Danielou. "The Six Main Centres of the Subtle Body" (illustration) from *Yoga: The Method of Re-Integration.* Reprinted by University Books Inc., a subsidiary of Lyle Stuart.
Erik Erikson. Reprinted from *Childhood and Society,* 2nd Edition, by Erik H. Erikson, by permission of W. W. Norton & Company, Inc. Copyright 1950, (c) 1963 by W. W. Norton & Company, Inc.
Sigmund Freud. "The Case of Katharina," from "Studies on Hysteria," Volume II, *The Standard Edition of the Complete Psychological Works of Sigmund Freud,* revised and edited by James Strachey. By permission of Sigmund Freud Copyrights Ltd., The Institute of Psychoanalysis, and The Hogarth Press Ltd.
James Holland and B. F. Skinner. Illustration from *The Analysis of Behavior: A Program for Self-Instruction.* Used by permission of McGraw-Hill Book Company.
Karen Horney. Reprinted from *Neurosis and Human Growth* by Karen Horney, M.D., by permission of W. W. Norton & Company, Inc. Copyright 1950 by W. W. Norton & Company, Inc. Copyright renewed 1978 by Renate Patterson, Brigitte Swarzenski, and Marianne Von Eckardt.
Ernest Jones. Excerpts from Chapter 4, "Fame and Suffering (1926–1933)" from *The Life and Work of Sigmund Freud, Volume 3: The Last Phase, 1919–1939,* by Ernest Jones, M.D., copyright © 1957 by Ernest Jones, Basic Books, Inc., Publishers, New York.
C. G. Jung. *Analytic Psychology: Its Theory and Its Practice,* Reprinted by permission of Random House, Inc. *C. G. Jung Letters: I,* edited by Gerhard Adler, in collaboration with Aniela Jaffe, trans. by R. C. F. Hull, Bollingen Series XCV (copyright © 1973 by Princeton University Press).
J. Kennett. *The Wild Goose.* By permission of the author.
Stanley Krippner. "The Plateau Experience: A. H. Maslow and Others," copyright *Journal of Transpersonal Psychology,* Volume 4, Number 2. Reprinted by permission of the Transpersonal Institute, 2637 Marshall Drive, Palo Alto, Calif. 94303.

PHOTOGRAPHS

CONTENTS

PREFACE

Why a second edition? The basic reason for a second edition is to improve the first edition by adding new material and rewriting the overall text. As students have become more sophisticated and demand more from a textbook, we have worked hard to improve each and every chapter, paying special attention to our students' requests to clarify the most puzzling areas. This is a student-driven text, designed by a generation of students for clarity and for personal value.

What do students want from a text and from a course in psychology? A small percentage wishes to emulate the professors, go on to graduate school, and do research and teaching. But the vast majority are interested in improving their understanding of human nature. The percentages were almost the same among psychology majors in a state school, an engineering college, an all-black college, and an avant-garde program in humanistic and transpersonal psychology.

As in our first edition, our aim is to focus on theories and concepts that have the clearest implications for personal understanding. We have stressed the value and usefulness of each theory because it is the positive aspects of a given theory that keep it as part of current psychological thought.

We have also retained the emphasis on experiential learning, because it met with such an enthusiastic response in the last edition.

Chapter exercises provide opportunities for students to personally experience major facets of each theory.

We have made three kinds of changes:

1. We have updated and revised every existing chapter. We have added new primary materials and references. We have also rewritten extensively along lines suggested by colleagues and students.

The opportunity to revise and improve one's work is a gift available only to writers of textbooks. We have taken full advantage of this opportunity and have had the pleasure (and pain) of reviewing and rewriting, sentence by sentence, section by section, more of the book than we would like to admit.

2. We have taken the material on women (an appendix in our first edition), expanded it, and integrated it into each chapter. At the time of the first edition, almost no text contained any references to the psychology of women, nor did the texts discuss the deficiencies of classical personality theories in that regard. We now feel there is enough known and written to integrate these concerns with the rest of the related materials. We still see it as a gap in most other texts.

3. We have added two new chapters—on Erik Erikson and Karen Horney. These two influential theorists were high second choices for our first edition. In the years that followed, the interest in their work has grown. We have been excited by the vitality of their ideas and have found that students have been pleased with these additions.

Although important new works have been published within almost every theory, we have found more significant new theoretical materials on the psychology of the body than for any other area. In the first edition, we saw this chapter as somewhat radical; but the role of these approaches in therapy and education in the past decade strongly supports our emphasis on this neglected area.

Interest in Eastern thought has continued unabated among students. There is a growing interest among faculty as well. We are pleased to see that a number of other personality texts have followed our example by including a chapter on non-Western thought as if it had always belonged there. It is now an accepted, although not universal, addition to the study of personality to consider cultural viewpoints beyond our own.

Our approach to teaching psychological theory is to focus on the original theory and the original theorist. Once students have reviewed the original and seminal positions, they are empowered to evaluate later variations and commentators with a critical eye.

Although it is tempting to take each theorist and attach to each the current research and cogent comments of the most sophisticated followers, we found it difficult not to pick that research and those commentators who supported our own subjective bias. Instead, we have attempted to encourage students to look at the original theorists and primary sources, and to draw their own conclusions, with the help of their instructors.

The improvements in this edition are due to students and instructors from all over the country who let us know what they wanted improved or simply shared with us better ideas than our own. Any mistakes are ours. Thank you all and please do help us improve this edition as well; such improvement benefits us all.

ACKNOWLEDGMENTS

With gratitude and humility we acknowledge the numerous people who have contributed to this edition. Their help was invaluable in our improving on the work of the first edition.

We are most grateful to our colleage Dr. Kathleen R. Speeth, who wrote the chapter on Karen Horney.

The students in the seminar on Personality and Personal Growth at the California Institute of Transpersonal Psychology went over each chapter line by line. Numerous and sophisticated criticisms and recommendations were a major resource for us in our work on this edition.

We are *grateful* to:

Aggie   Diane Moncrief
Richard Allen   Phyllis Moore

Sally Armin
Pat Baker
Junelle Barrett
Chayim Barton
Anne Bell
Michael Bennett
David Bishop
Diana Blakely
John Booth
William Brater
Emma Buckley
Marilyn Cohen
Virginia Dennehy
Iris Dillow
Dan Doucet
Bill Fitler
Lolly Font
Sandra Glickman
Bonnie L. Greenwell
Alan Javurek
Frances Javurek

Molly Moore-Sullivan
David O'Donaghue
John Prosise
Ronald Retzlaff
Chirs Satris
Nancy Scheinfeld
Michael Smith
Laura Sosnowski
John Spurr
Ginny Stafford
Alan Strachan
John Van Ness
Marianna Baldwin
Ellen Waldman
Christopher White
Judith Whitman-Small
Jody Zeman

We wish to thank Kim Schnurpfeil for her extensive criticism of numerous manuscript chapters.

Our manuscript chapters were typed and corrected compassionately and sensitively by Bonnie Miller, Linda Starr, and Nuriya White.

We are grateful to the following collegues for their professional criticism of the following chapters: Jung: June Singer; Yoga: Swami Sivananda Radha.

We'd also like to thank many psychology teachers across the country who have used our text and given us both encouraging and critical feedback.

Special thanks to Professor Robert Jones, Diablo University; Professor Robert E. Francis, North Shore Community College; Professor Eugene Mathis, Western Illinois University; Professor Solomon Schuck, Monmouth College, who viewed the entire manuscript and made many helpful suggestions.

Robert Frager
James Fadiman

INTRODUCTION

Why did we write this book? We found that students are no longer satisfied with the same personality course that we took as undergraduates. And, frankly, both of us have found that the changing values and interests of our students have supported similar tendencies in our own intellectual development.

We have both been deeply influenced by the growth movement, by experiences with encounter groups, and by exposure to many of the attitudes and values prevalent in the human potential subculture. We have also been personally involved with various Eastern disciplines, with their practical techniques and the various gurus and spiritual guides with whom we have come in contact. At the same time, both of us have remained concerned with academic psychology, with teaching, publishing, and the other intellectual pursuits within academia. Yet we have found that our teaching and our writing have been very much affected by these other influences in our lives. We have included more and more experiential material in our courses, and we have experimented with a wide variety of formats in an attempt to break out of the rigid and passive roles inherent in many of the traditional models of learning.

We have written this textbook to meet student interest in psychology as a body of knowledge that is of practical use in understanding human nature. Psychology has become more popular on campuses across the country in the past ten years not because of the improved quality of psychology research, but because many students are hoping to find within psychology, structure, concepts, theories, and perspectives that will facilitate their own growth and their capacity to adjust to a rapidly changing, diverse society. We confess that, along with our students, we have found many of the current textbooks too technical, too ponderous, or too much concerned with arid academic abstractions to be of much personal value or interest.

BACKGROUND

The terms *personality* and *personality theory* have become limited to a number of theoretical systems integrated into contemporary academic psychology. The standard personality texts all deal with the same dozen or so theories and theorists. They refer to the same experimental studies and the same body of material, and they reflect a clearly understood and generally accepted academic perspective.

In recent years two new approaches to human nature and functioning have become increasingly important: the human potential movement and Eastern growth disciplines. The impact of these forces on our own thinking has served to expand the limits and range of our approach to personality theory.

The human potential movement, founded in part by Esalen Institute in California and National Training Laboratories in Maine, is now a widely accepted cultural force. New institutions, known as growth centers, exist in most major cities, centers which generally offer intensive and powerful weekend or week-long workshops in various kinds of encounter groups, body-oriented work, meditation, spiritual disciplines, and other experiential systems. More and more colleges and universities now offer experientially oriented courses that stress personal involvement and emotional experience.

The intensive small group experiences that are one of the major innnovations of the human potential movement often result in rapid and extensive personality change. Group leaders and participants generally believe that these changes are beneficial and long lasting. Beyond this consensus, there is little agreement among group leaders and others in this movement concerning personality structure, dynamics, or change. Along with the emphasis on direct experiential learning, there has developed an antitheoretical and anticonceptual bias and a deliberate disregard of academic psychology as being old-fashioned or irrelevant. Those in the growth movement generally espouse a fundamental humanistic belief in the individual's capacity for purposeful, positive growth. This belief has become an almost unchallengeable axiom that has not been clearly understood, researched, or documented. The human potential movement has, however, contributed an innovative vitality to psychotherapy and developed a wide range of effective techniques for interpersonal communication, emotional expression, and body awareness. While those concerned with the growth movement have tended to ignore academic psychology, so too have academic psychologists tended to remain ignorant of the movement's very real and important achievements.

It is possible to view the major developments within the growth movement in theoretical terms without losing sight of the goals of self-exploration. As this book was being structured, we realized that the sections in our original outline that discussed the human growth movement became, one by one, subheadings in chapters having solid and congruent intellectual frameworks. For example, the chapter on Perls places the experiential aspects of Gestalt therapy on much firmer theoretical grounds by tracing its antecedents from phenomenology, holism, psychoanalysis, Reich, and Gestalt psychology. While those in the growth movement have steadfastly refused to discuss intellectual antecedents, this does not mean that their positions lack such a foundation. We are attempting to restore the balance necessary for theories to continue to develop beyond their initial charismatic innovators.

The second new perspective on human nature has been provided mainly from Eastern philosophies. Many of the Eastern systems include a theory of personality structure and fundamental rules for behavior and character change. These systems cover many of the same topics as Western personality theories, and they have influenced many of the theories and techniques current in the human potential movement. They tend to deal more explicitly with transpersonal and religious experience and with the role of values and morals in human behavior.

We have chosen to focus our discussion on three particular aspects of the great Eastern traditions of Buddhism, Hinduism, and Islam. Zen, Yoga, and Sufism represent those aspects of each tradition that are most concerned with direct experience and personal growth. They are also among the best known and most influential Eastern disciplines in the West. These disciplines have been summarized and discussed using the same theoretical structure employed for the Western theories.

AN APPROACH TO PERSONALITY THEORY

We believe that each of the theories we have presented in this book has something of unique value and relevance. Each major theorist has isolated and clarified certain particular aspects of human nature. We feel that each theorist is essentially "correct" in the area he has looked at most carefully. The only error that most have made is to argue that they have the very best single overall answer. The major disagreements among personality theorists often seem to resemble the story of the blind men and the elephant. A theory that is based on the study of psychopathology may lack the conceptual tools and the empirical data to deal adequately with the varieties of transpersonal experience. A theory that is primarily concerned with conscious phenomena may not be adequate in explaining dreams and other forms of symbolism. We believe that each theorist has a firm grasp on one part of the whole, but, at times, instead of acknowledging that it is only a part, each tries to convince the others that the portion he holds is either the most important part or that it is the whole elephant.

Each chapter discusses a theory or perspective that adds to our general knowledge of human behavior. We are particularly concerned with the relevance of each theory for understanding human potential and enhancing personal growth and development. We are convinced that in addition to our innate biological pattern of growth and development, each individual possesses a tendency for psychological development. This has been described by various psychologists as a tendency toward self-actualization, an urge for self-understanding, a need to improve one's awareness and effectiveness—all in order to gain more joy and satisfaction from life.

We have tried to approach each theory as positively and as sympathetically as possible. Each chapter has been read and evaluated by theorists and practitioners from each system; they have helped us in insuring that our treatment is relatively comprehensive and unbiased. We have avoided as much as possible the tendency to criticize or belittle the accomplishments of each theory. Instead, we have tried to highlight the strengths and the effectiveness of each theoretical approach. We have sought to be neither one-sidedly partisan nor unthinkingly eclectic. Our bias has been most pronounced in our choice of theorists. We have included those theorists whose importance and utility is evident to us, and we have left out many well-known theories that seemed less useful and less congruent with the overall aim of this book.

STRUCTURE OF EACH CHAPTER

Each chapter follows this outline:

Personal History
Intellectual Antecedents
Major Concepts

Dynamics
Psychological growth
Obstacles to growth
Structure
Body
Social relationships
Will
Emotions
Intellect
Self
Therapist (or teacher)
Evaluation
The Theory Firsthand
Exercises
Annotated Bibliography

We begin each chapter with a discussion of the personal history and the intellectual antecedents of the theorist. We have tried to indicate the major influences on each theorist's thinking, influences rooted in their childhood experiences or adult lives. The main portion of each
chapter deals with theory. The first section is a summary of the major concepts. Next is a section on psychological development and obstacles to growth. The third section deals with structure. We have described how each theory deals with the following seven categories: the body,
social relationships, will, emotions, intellect, self, and the therapist or teacher. Most theoretical
systems have something of relevance for each category. Whenever a category is not a significant part of a theory, we have left it out. For other theories, one or another category forms such
a major part of the theory that we have included it under major concepts rather than under
structure. We have tried to be consistent, to help readers compare and contrast different theories, but not to be so rigid as to be unfair to the theory.

The next section of each chapter is an evaluation of the theory. As indicated earlier, we
have tried to evaluate each theory sympathetically and constructively, in view of its strengths
rather than in terms of what it may leave out. Next is an extended passage taken from the theorist's writings or a description of the theorist's therapeutic or growth system in operation. We
feel it is important for the reader to be directly exposed to the style and the "feeling" of each
theorist. We have also added a number of quotations in the margin of each chapter. We have
found that theorists often have unique and fascinating ways of phrasing their ideas and arguments. Thus the use of these quotes has allowed us to present an author's point of view in a
very direct way without making the text itself too cumbersome. From time to time a marginal
quote may be in sharp distinction to the point of view of the theorist. They serve to add a dimension of contrast and commentary without interrupting the ongoing presentation within the
text proper.

The next part of each chapter consists of exercises suitable for either individual or class
use. We want you to have the opportunity to "taste" at least some aspects of each theory experientially. We find that experiential and intellectual learning are complementary rather than con-
tradictory processes, and we believe that personal experience of the meaning of an author's
concepts can add a dimension of immediacy and interest to each theory.

We are aware that for some of you the notion of exercises at the end of each chapter recalls the seemingly endless "projects" that you have been required to do from grammar school on. While we too drew crayon maps of the routes of the explorers and divided up plastic fruit in order to discover the reality of fractions, we are making a different kind of offer. The exercises have all been tried out and been found helpful by students in our courses. The rationale behind the exercises is to let you experience for yourself what you have been reading. The results have been, in many cases, that students have become more impressed with the power, utility, or validity of a theory through experiencing some aspect of it for themselves.

Finally, each chapter concludes with an annotated bibliography. Our presentation of each theorist is really only a bare introduction to a complex system of thought. We hope that you will pursue those theories that you find most interesting and valuable, and we have tried to facilitate this next step by suggesting those books that we have found most valuable in understanding each theory.

LIFE HISTORY QUESTIONNAIRE

We approach any body of material already primed to accept or reject parts of it. We are to some extent developed and conditioned by past experience.

Before reading this book it may be useful for you to begin to observe some of the major forces that have inclined you to develop as you are. As we proceed you may find that reexamining your answers in terms of various theories may shed light on the theories as well as on yourself. Answer the questions as freely and as fully as you feel will be helpful to you, since this exercise is designed for your own use.

1. Nicknames you prefer (reasons for preference).
2. Ethnic and/or religious identification. If different from your family, comment on the differences.
3. Describe your siblings.
4. Describe your parents (step-parents).
5. Who in your family do you most resemble? How?
6. What's your current life situation—job, living with whom, and so forth?
7. Do you have any recurring dreams/daydreams?
8. What men or women of the past or present do you appreciate and admire most? Why? Whom might you consider an "ideal model"?
9. What books (poems, works of art) have influenced you most? When and how?
10. What events or inner experiences give or have given you the greatest joy? The greatest sorrow?
11. What occupation would interest you the most if you could become whatever you wanted?
12. Is there anything about yourself that you would like to change?
13. What is there about yourself that you especially like?

PERSONALITY AND PERSONAL GROWTH

PART ONE

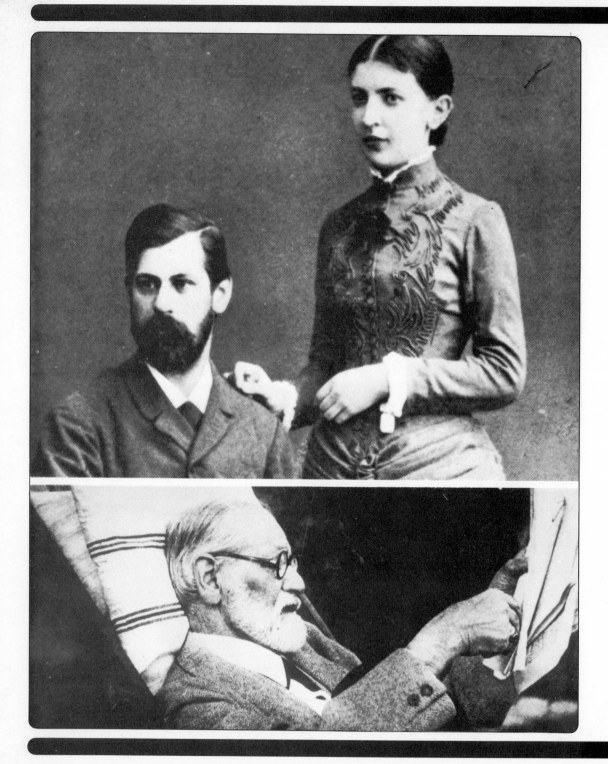

CHAPTER 1
SIGMUND FREUD AND PSYCHOANALYSIS

Sigmund Freud's work, originating in the disciplines of biology, neurology, and psychiatry, proposed a new understanding of personality that profoundly affected Western culture. His view of the human situation, striking violently against the prevailing opinions of his era, offered a complex and compelling way to understand normal and abnormal functioning.

Freud explored areas of the psyche that were discreetly obscured by Victorian morality and philosophy. He devised new approaches to treat the mentally ill. His work contradicted cultural, religious, social, and scientific taboos. His writings, his personality, and his determination to extend the boundaries of his work kept him the center of an intense, shifting circle of friends, disciples, and critics. Freud was constantly rethinking and revising his earlier ideas. Interestingly, his most strenuous critics included those he had personally supervised at various stages in their careers.

It is not possible to discuss all of Freud's contributions in a single chapter. Therefore, what follows is a deliberate simplification of a complex, intricately connected but incomplete system. It is an overview intended to make later exposure to Freudian ideas more intelligible and to allow a better understanding of other theorists whose works are heavily influenced by Freud.

PERSONAL HISTORY

Sigmund Freud was born on May 6, 1856, in Freiberg in Moravia (now Czechoslovakia). When he was 4 years old, his family suffered financial setbacks and moved to Vienna. He remained a resident of Vienna until 1938, when he emigrated to England where he died one year later.

During his childhood he excelled as a student. Despite the limited financial position of his family, which forced all eight members to live in a crowded apartment, Freud, the eldest child, had his own room and even an oil lamp to study by. The rest of the family made do with candles. In *gymnasium* he continued his excellent academic performance. "I was at the top of my class for seven years. I enjoyed special privileges there and was required to pass scarcely any examinations" (Freud, 1935, p. 9).

Because he was Jewish, all professional careers except medicine and law were closed to him—such was the prevailing anti-Semitic climate of the times. Influenced by the works of Darwin and Goethe, he chose to enter the Faculty of Medicine at the University of Vienna in 1873.

His experiences at the University of Vienna, where he was treated as both an "inferior and an alien" because of being Jewish, strengthened his capacity to withstand criticism. "At an early age I was made familiar with the fate of being in the opposition and being put under the ban of the 'compact majority.' The foundations were thus laid for a certain degree of independence of judgement" (Freud, 1935, p. 11). He remained a medical student for eight years, three more than

Sigmund Freud, by the power of his writings and by the breadth and audacity of his speculations, revolutionized the thought, the lives, and the imagination of an age. . . . It would be hard to find in the history of ideas, even in the history of religion, someone whose influence was so immediate, so broad, or so deep. [Wolheim, 1971, p. ix]

He was profoundly a Jew, not in a doctrinal sense, but in his conception of morality, in his love of the skeptical play of reason, in his distrust of illusion, in the form of his prophetic talent . . . [Bruner, 1956, p. 344]

customary. During these years he worked in the physiological labora-tory of Dr. Ernst Brücke. Some of Freud's faith in the biological origins of consciousness may be traced to Brücke's own positions. Brücke once took a formal oath to abide by the following proposition:

> No other forces than the common physical and chemical ones are active within the organism. In those cases which cannot at present be explained by these forces one either has to find the specific way or form of their action by means of the physical-mathematical method or to assume new forces equal in dignity to the chemical-physical forces inherent in matter, reducible to the force of attraction and repulsion. [In Rycroft, 1972, p. 14]

Freud did independent research in histology[1] and published arti-cles on anatomy and neurology. At the age of 26, Freud received his medical degree. He continued his work under Brücke for a year and lived at home with his family. He aspired to fill the next open position in the laboratory, but Brücke had two excellent assistants ahead of Freud. "The turning point came in 1882, when my teacher, for whom I felt the highest possible esteem, corrected my father's generous im-providence by strongly advising me, in view of my bad financial posi-tion, to abandon my theoretical career" (Freud, 1935, p. 13). In addi-tion, Freud had fallen in love and realized that if he ever were to marry, he would need a better-paying position.

Although he moved reluctantly to a private practice, his primary interests remained in scientific exploration and observation. Working first as a surgeon, then in general medicine, he became a "house physi-cian" at the principal hospital in Vienna. He took a course in psychia-try that furthered his interest in the relationships between mental symptoms and physical disease. By 1885 he had established himself in the prestigious position of lecturer at the University of Vienna. His ca-reer began to look promising.

From 1884 to 1887 Freud did some of the first research with co-caine. At first he was impressed with its properties. "I have tested this effect of coca, which wards off hunger, sleep, and fatigue and steels one to intellectual effort, some dozens of times on myself . . ." (Freud, 1963, p. 11). He wrote of its possible uses for both physical and mental distur-bances. Briefly an advocate, he later became concerned with its addict-ing properties and discontinued the research (Byck, 1975).

With Brücke's backing, Freud obtained a travel grant and went to Paris to work under Charcot. Charcot demonstrated that it was possible to induce or relieve hysterical symptoms with hypnotic sug-gestion. Freud realized that in hysteria patients exhibit symptoms that are anatomically impossible. For example, in "glove anesthesia" a person will have no feeling in his or her hand, but will have normal sensations in the wrist and arm. Because the nerves run continuously

Neither at that time, nor indeed in my later life, did I feel any particular predilection for the career of a physician. I was moved, rather by a sort of curiosity, which was however, directed more towards human concerns than towards natural objects; nor had I grasped the importance of observation as one of the best means of gratifying it. [Freud, 1935, p. 10]

"I sometimes come out of his lectures [Charcot's] . . . with an entirely new idea about perfection . . . no other human being has ever affected me in the same way." [In E. Freud, 1961, pp. 184–185]

---

[1]The study of the minute structure of animal and vegetable tissues.

from the shoulder into the hand, there can be no physical cause for this symptom. It became clear to Freud that hysteria was a disorder whose genesis required a psychological explanation. Charcot saw Freud as a capable and understanding student and gave him permission to translate Charcot's papers into German upon Freud's return to Vienna.

His work in France increased his interest in hypnosis as a therapeutic tool. With the cooperation of the distinguished older physician Breuer, Freud explored the dynamics of hysteria (1895). Their findings were summarized by Freud: "The symptoms of hysterical patients depend upon impressive, but forgotten scenes of their lives (traumata). The therapy founded thereon was to cause the patients to recall and reproduce these experiences under hypnosis (catharsis) . . ." (1914, p. 13). He found, however, that hypnosis was not as effective as he had hoped. It did not allow the patient or the therapist to work with the resistance to recalling the traumatic memories. Eventually, Freud abandoned it altogether in favor of encouraging his patients to speak freely and to report whatever their thoughts were, regardless of the apparent relationship—or lack of relationship—to their symptoms.

Even a superficial glance at my work will show how much I am indebted to the brilliant discoveries of Freud. [Jung, 1906; In McGuire, 1974]

In 1896 Freud first used the term *psychoanalysis* to describe his methods. His own self-analysis began in 1897. By 1900 he had published *The Interpretation of Dreams,* considered by many to be his most important work, although at the time it received almost no attention. Freud followed it the next year with another major book, *The Psychopathology of Everyday Life.* Gradually, a circle of interested physicians formed around Freud; it included Alfred Adler, Sandor Ferenczi, Carl Gustav Jung, Otto Rank, Karl Abraham, and Ernest Jones. The group established a society. Papers were written, a journal was published, and the psychoanalytic movement began to expand.

As I stepped on to the platform at Worcester to deliver my "Five Lectures" upon psychoanalysis it seemed like some incredible daydream: psychoanalysis was no longer a product of delusion, it had become a valuable part of reality. [Freud, 1925a, p. 104]

In 1910 Freud was invited to America to deliver lectures at Clark University. His works were being translated into English. People were becoming interested in the theories of Dr. Sigmund Freud.

Freud spent his life developing, extending, and clarifying psychoanalysis. He tried to retain control over the psychoanalytic movement by ejecting members who disagreed with his views and by demanding an unusual degree of loyalty to his own position. Jung, Adler, and Rank, among others, left after repeated disagreements with Freud on theoretical issues. Each later founded a separate school of thought.

Freud wrote extensively. His collected works fill 24 volumes and include essays concerning the fine points of clinical practice, a series of lectures outlining the full theory, and specialized monographs on religious and cultural questions. He attempted to build a structure that would outlive him, one that might eventually reorient all of psychiatry. He was compelling and tyrannical. He feared that analysts who deviated from the procedures he established might dilute the power and the possibilities of psychoanalysis. Above all he wanted to prevent the distortion and misuse of psychoanalytic theory. When, for example, in 1931 Ferenczi suddenly changed his procedures, making the analytic situation one in which affection might be more freely expressed, Freud wrote him as follows:

> I see that the differences between us have come to a head in a technical detail which is well worth discussing. You have not made a secret of the fact that you kiss your patients and let them kiss you. . . . Now when you decide to give a full account of your technique and its results you will have to choose between two ways; either you relate this or you conceal it. The latter, as you may well think, is dishonorable. . . .
>
> Now I am assuredly not one of those who from prudishness or from consideration of bourgeois convention would condemn little erotic gratifications of this kind. And I am also aware that in the time of the Nibelungs a kiss was a harmless greeting granted to every guest. I am further of the opinion that analysis is possible even in Soviet Russia where so far as the State is concerned there is full sexual freedom. But that does not alter the facts that we are not living in Russia and that with us a kiss signifies a certain erotic intimacy. We have hitherto in our techniques held to the conclusion that patients are to be refused erotic gratifications. . . .
>
> Now picture what will be the result of publishing your technique. There is no revolutionary who is not driven out of the field by a still more radical one. A number of independent thinkers in matters of technique will say to themselves: why stop at a kiss? Certainly one gets further when one adopts "pawing" as well, which after all doesn't make a baby. And then bolder ones will come along who go further to peeping and showing—and soon we shall have accepted in the technique of analysis the whole repertoire of demiviergerie and petting-parties, resulting in an enormous increase of interest in psychoanalysis among both analysts and patients. The new adherent, however, will easily claim too much of this interest for himself, the younger of our colleagues will find it hard to stop at the point they originally intended, and God the Father Ferenczi gazing at the lively scene he has created will perhaps say to himself: maybe after all I should have halted in my technique of motherly affection *before* the kiss. [Quoted in Jones, 1955, pp. 163–164]

As Freud's work became more generally available, the criticisms increased. In 1933 the Nazis burned a pile of Freud's books in Berlin. Freud commented on the event. "What progress we are making. In the Middle Ages they would have burnt me, nowadays they are content with burning my books" (Jones, 1957).

Perpetually embroiled in battles over the validity or utility of his work, he continued to write. His last book, *An Outline of Psycho-Analysis* (1940), begins with a blunt warning to critics. "The teachings of psycho-analysis are based on an incalculable number of observations and experiences, and only someone who has repeated those observa-

No one who, like me, conjures up the most evil of those half-tamed demons that inhabit the human breast, and seeks to wrestle with them, can expect to come through the struggle unscathed. [Freud, 1905b]

tions on himself and others is in a position to arrive at a judgment of his own upon it" (p. 1).

Freud's last years were difficult ones. From 1923 on he was in ill health, suffering from cancer of the mouth and jaws. He was in almost continual pain and had a total of 33 operations to halt the spreading cancer. When the Germans took over Austria in 1938, Freud was granted permission to leave for London. He died there a year later.

Freud's success can be judged not only by the continued interest and debate over aspects of psychoanalytic theory, but, to a greater extent, by his ideas that have become part of the common heritage of the West. We are all in Freud's debt for uncovering the world that moves beneath conscious awareness.

MAJOR CONCEPTS

> One evening last week when I was hard at work, tormented with just that amount of pain that seems to be the best state to make my brain function, the barriers were suddenly lifted, the veil was drawn aside, and I had a clear vision from the details of the neuroses to the conditions that make consciousness possible. Everything seemed to connect up, the whole worked well together, and one had the impression that the thing was really a machine and would soon go by itself . . . all that was perfectly clear, and still is. Naturally I don't know how to contain myself for pleasure. [Freud, letter to Fliess, Oct. 20, 1895; in Bonaparte, 1954]

Many of the most puzzling and seemingly arbitrary turns of psychoanalytic theory, . . . are either hidden biological assumptions, or result directly from such assumptions. . . . [Holt, 1965, p. 94]

Underlying all of Freud's thinking is the assumption that the body is the sole source of all mental energy. He looked forward to the time when all mental phenomena might be explained with direct reference to brain physiology (Sulloway, 1979).

Psychic Determinism

Freud assumed that there were no discontinuities in mental life and that all thought and all behavior have meaning. He contended that *nothing* occurs randomly, least of all mental processes. There is a cause for every thought, feeling, memory, or action. Every mental event is brought about by conscious or unconscious intention and is determined by the events that have preceded it. It appears that many mental events occur spontaneously; however, Freud began to search out and describe the hidden links that join one conscious event to another.

Conscious, Unconscious, Preconscious
Conscious

"The starting point for this investigation is provided by a fact without parallel, which defies all explanation or description—the fact of consciousness. Nevertheless, if anyone speaks of consciousness, we know immediately and from our most personal experience what is meant by it" (Freud, 1940, p. 14). The conscious is only a small portion of the mind; it includes everything that we are aware of in any given moment. Although Freud was interested in the mechanisms of consciousness, he was far more interested in the less exposed and explored areas of consciousness, which he labeled the *preconscious* and the *unconscious*.

Unconscious

When a conscious thought or feeling seems to have no relation to the thoughts and feelings that preceded it, Freud suggested that the connections were present but unconscious. Once the unconscious links are found, the apparent discontinuity is resolved. "We call a psychical process unconscious whose existence we are obliged to assume—we infer it from its effects—but of which we know nothing" (Freud, 1933, p. 70).

Within the unconscious are instinctual elements, which have never been conscious and which are never accessible to consciousness. In addition, there is material that has been barred from consciousness, censored, and repressed. This material is not forgotten or lost, but it is not allowed to be remembered. The thought or memory still affects consciousness, but only indirectly.

There is a liveness and an immediacy to unconscious material. Memories that are decades old, when released into consciousness have lost none of their emotional force. "We have found by experience that unconscious mental processes are in themselves 'timeless.' That is to say to begin with: they are not arranged chronologically, time alters nothing in them, nor can the idea of time be applied to them" (Freud, 1920; in Fodor & Gaynor, 1958, p. 162).

Preconscious

Strictly speaking, the preconscious is a part of the unconscious, but a part that is easily capable of becoming conscious. Those portions of memory that are accessible are part of the preconscious. This might include memories of everything you did yesterday, your middle name, all the streets you have ever lived on, the date of the Norman conquest, your favorite foods, the smell of fall leaves burning, the oddly shaped birthday cake you had on your tenth birthday, and a host of other past experiences. The preconscious is like a holding area for the memories that the consciousness needs in order to perform its functions.

Drives or Impulses[2]

Impulses are pressures to act without conscious thought toward particular ends. Such impulses are "the ultimate cause of all activity"

There is no need to characterize what we call "conscious." It is the same as the consciousness of philosophers and of everyday opinion. [Freud, 1940, p. 16]

Certain inadequacies of our psychic functions and certain performances which are apparently unintentional prove to be well motivated when subjected to psychoanalytic investigation. [Freud, 1901]

---

[2]From the German *Trieb* incorrectly translated in most editions and most textbooks as "instinct" (Bettelheim, 1982, pp. 87–88).

(Freud, 1940, p. 5). Freud labeled the physical aspects of impulses, needs, and the mental aspects of impulses, wishes. These needs and wishes propel people to take action.

There can be no question of restricting one or the other basic impulses to a single region of the mind. They are necessarily present everywhere. [Freud, 1940]

All impulses have four components: a *source*, an *aim*, an *impetus*, and an *object*. The *source*, where the need arises, may be a part or all of the body. The *aim* is to reduce the need until no more action is necessary; it is to give the organism the satisfaction it now desires. The *impetus* is the amount of energy, force, or pressure that is used to satisfy or gratify the impulse; this is determined by the strength of urgency of the underlying need. The *object* of an impulse is whatever thing or action or expression allows satisfaction of the original aim.

Consider the way these components appear in a thirsty person. The body dehydrates until it needs more liquids; the source is the growing need for fluids. As the need becomes greater, it may become conscious as "thirst." As this thirst is unsatisfied, it becomes more pronounced; as the intensity rises, so does the impetus or energy available to do something to relieve the thirst. The aim is to reduce the tension. The object is not simply a liquid—milk, water, or beer—but all acts that go toward reducing the tension. These might include getting up, going to the kitchen, choosing between alternative drinks, preparing a drink, and drinking it.

Although the initial seeking reactions might be instinctual, the critical point to remember is that the impulse can be fully or partially satisfied in a number of ways. The capacity to satisfy needs in animals is often limited by a pattern of stereotyped behavior. Human impulses only *initiate* the need for action; they do not predetermine the particular action or how it will be completed. The number of solutions open to an individual is a summation of his or her initial biological urge, the mental "wish" (which may or may not be conscious), and a host of prior ideas, habits, and available options.

Freud assumes that the normal, healthy, mental, and behavioral pattern is aimed at reducing tension to previously acceptable levels. A person with a need will continue seeking activities that can reduce this original tension. The complete cycle of behavior from relaxation to tension and activity and back to relaxation is called a *tension-reduction* model. Tensions are resolved by returning the body to the level of equilibrium that existed before the need arose.

Many thoughts and behaviors, however, do not seem to reduce tension; in fact, they create and maintain tension, stress, or anxiety. These behaviors may indicate that the direct expression of an impulse has been redirected or blocked.

Basic Impulses

Freud developed two descriptions of the basic impulses. The early model described two opposing forces, the sexual (or, more generally, the erotic, physically gratifying) and the aggressive or the destructive. His later, more global, descriptions saw these forces as either life supporting or death (and destruction) encouraging. Both formulations presupposed a biological, ongoing, and unresolvable pair of conflicts. This basic antagonism is not necessarily visible in mental life because most of our thoughts and actions are evoked not by one of these instinctual forces in isolation but by both in combination.

Freud was impressed with the diversity and complexity of behavior that arises from the fusion of the basic drives. For example, Freud writes: "The sexual impulses are remarkable for their plasticity, for the facility with which they can change their aims, for their interchangeability—for the ease with which they can substitute one form of gratification for another, and for the way in which they can be held in suspense . . ." (1933, p. 97). The impulses are the channels through which the energy can flow. This energy obeys laws of its own.

Libido and Aggressive Energy

Each of these generalized impulses has a separate source of energy. Libido (from the Latin word for wish or desire) is the energy available to the life impulses. "Its production, increase or diminution, distribution and displacement should afford us possibilities for explaining the psychosexual phenomena observed" (Freud, 1905a, p. 118).

One characteristic of libido is its "mobility," the ease with which it can pass from one area of attention to another. Freud pictured the volatile nature of emotional responsiveness as a flow of energy, flowing in and out of areas of immediate concern.

The energy of the aggressive or the death impulse has no special name. It has been assumed to have the same general properties as libido, although Freud did not make this clear.

A person falls ill of a neurosis if his ego has lost the capacity to allocate his libido in some way. [Freud, 1916]

Cathexis

Cathexis is the process by which the available libidinal energy in the psyche is attached to or invested in a person, idea, or thing. Libido that has been cathected is no longer mobile and can no longer move to new objects. It is rooted in whatever part of the psyche has attracted and held it.

The original German word, *Besetzung,* means both to occupy and to invest. If you imagine your store of libido as a given amount of money, cathexis is the process of investing it. Once a portion has been invested or cathected, it remains there leaving you with that much less to invest elsewhere.

Psychoanalytic studies of mourning, for example, interpret the disinterest in normal pursuits and the excessive preoccupation with the recently deceased as a withdrawal of libido from usual relationships and an extreme or "hypercathexis" of the lost person.

There are certain pathological conditions which seem to leave us no alternative but to postulate that the subject draws on a specific quantity of energy which he distributes in variable proportions in his relationships with objects and with himself. [LaPlanche and Pontalis, 1973, p. 65]

Psychoanalytic theory is concerned with understanding where libido has been inappropriately cathected. Once released or redirected, this same energy is then available to satisfy other current needs. The need to release bound energies is also found in the ideas of Rogers and Maslow, as well as in Buddhism and Sufism. Each of these theories comes to different conclusions about the source of psychic energy, but all agree with the Freudian contention that the identification and channeling of psychic energy is a major issue in understanding personality.

Structure of the Personality

Freud's observations of his patients revealed an unending series of psychic conflicts and compromises. Impulse was pitted against impulse; social prohibitions blocked biological drives, and ways of coping often conflicted with one another. He attempted to order this seeming chaos by proposing three basic structural components of the psyche: the id, the ego, and the superego.[3]

The Id

The id is the original core out of which the rest of the personality emerges. It is biological in nature and contains the reservoir of energy for all parts of the personality. Although the other parts of consciousness develop out of the id, the id itself is formless and unorganized. "The logical laws of thought do not apply in the id" (Freud, 1933, p. 73). Moreover, the id is not modified as one grows and matures. The id is not changed by experience because it is not in contact with the external world. Its goals are to reduce tension, to increase pleasure, and to minimize discomfort. The id strives to do this through reflex actions (automatic reactions such as sneezing or blinking) and the psychological processes of the other portions of the mind.

In the id there is nothing corresponding to the idea of time, no recognition of the passage of time, and (a thing which is very remarkable and awaits adequate attention in philosophic thought) no alteration of mental processes by the passage of time . . . . Naturally the id knows no values, no good and evil, no morality. [Freud, 1933, p. 74]

The id may be likened to a blind king who has absolute power and authority but who must rely on trusted counselors, such as the ego, to tell him how and where to use these powers.

The contents of the id are almost entirely unconscious. They include primitive thoughts that have never been conscious and thoughts that have been denied and found unacceptable to consciousness. Freud stressed that experiences which have been denied or repressed still have the power to affect a person's behavior with undiminished intensity and without any conscious control.

---

[3]Although id, ego, and superego have become accepted technical terms, Freud's words for each were simple and direct. Id simply means "it" or the impersonal, ego means "I," and superego means "above I." It is too late to correct the damage done by the initial translator who made Freud, in English, deliberately obscure (Bettelheim, 1982, p. 80–81).

The Ego

The ego is that portion of the psyche which is in contact with external reality. It develops out of the id, as the infant becomes aware of its own identity, to serve and placate the id's repeated demands. Like the bark of a tree, it protects the id but draws energy from the id in order to accomplish this. It has the task of insuring the health, safety, and sanity of the personality. Freud describes its several functions both in relation to the outside world and to the inner world whose urges it strives to satisfy.

> The principal characteristics of the ego are these. In consequence of the relation which was already established between sensory perception and muscular action, the ego is in control of voluntary movement. It has the task of self-preservation. As regards *external* events, it performs that task by becoming aware of the stimuli from without, by storing up experiences of them (in the memory), by avoiding excessive stimuli (through flight), by dealing with moderate stimuli (through adaptation), and finally by learning to bring about appropriate modifications in the external world to its own advantage (through activity). As regards *internal* events, in relation to the id, it performs that task by gaining control over the demands of the instincts, by deciding whether they shall be allowed to obtain satisfaction, by postponing that satisfaction to times and circumstances favorable in the external world or by suppressing their excitations completely. Its activities are governed by considerations of the tensions produced by stimuli present within it or introduced into it. The raising of these tensions is in general felt as *unpleasure* and their lowering as *pleasure*. . . . The ego pursues pleasure and seeks to avoid unpleasure. [1940, pp. 2–3]

Thus the ego is originally created by the id in an attempt to cope with the need to reduce tension and increase pleasure. However, to do this, the ego must in turn control or modulate the id's impulses so that the individual can pursue realistic approaches to life.

An example might be that of dating. The id feels tension arising from unfulfilled sexual arousal and would reduce this tension through immediate and direct sexual activity. The ego must determine how much sexual expression is possible and how to establish situations where sexual contact will be most fulfilling. The id is responsive to needs, whereas the ego is responsive to opportunities.

. . . we might say that the ego stands for reason and good sense while the id stands for the untamed passions. [Freud, 1933]

The Superego

This last part of the structure develops not from the id but from the ego. It serves as a judge or censor over the activities and thoughts of the ego. It is the repository of moral codes, standards of conduct, and those constructs that form the inhibitions for the personality. Freud describes three functions of the superego: conscience, self-observation, and the formation of ideals. As conscience, the superego acts both to

[The superego] is like a secret police department, unerringly detecting any trends of forbidden impulses, particularly of an aggressive kind, and punishing the individual inexorably if any are present. [Horney, 1939, p. 211]

restrict, prohibit, or judge conscious activity; but it also acts unconsciously. The unconscious restrictions are indirect, appearing as compulsions or prohibitions. "The sufferer . . . behaves as if he were dominated by a sense of guilt, of which he knows nothing" (Freud, 1907, p. 123).

The superego develops and elaborates and maintains the moral code of an individual. The child learns that not only does he or she have to know the real constraints in a situation, but also to incorporate the moral views of his or her parents before being able to act to obtain pleasure or reduce pain. Thus the superego is not merely based on the behavior of the parents. "A child's superego is in fact constructed on the model, not of its parents but of its parents' superego; the contents which fill it are the same and it becomes the vehicle of tradition and all the time resisting judgments of value which have propagated themselves in this manner from generation to generation" (Freud, 1933, p. 39).

Relationship Between the Three Subsystems

The overarching goal of the psyche is to maintain—and when that is lost, to regain—an acceptable level of dynamic equilibrium that maximizes pleasure and minimizes tension. The energy that is used originates in the id, which has a primitive, instinctual nature. The ego, arising from the id, exists to deal realistically with the basic drives of the id. It also mediates between the forces that operate on the id, the superego, and the demands of external reality. The superego, arising from the ego, acts as a moral brake or counterforce to the practical concerns of the ego. It sets out a series of guidelines that define and limit the flexibility of the ego.

The id is entirely unconscious, the ego and the superego partly so. "Certainly large portions of the ego and superego can remain unconscious, are, in fact, normally unconscious. That means to say that the individual knows nothing of their contents, and that it requires an expenditure of effort to make him conscious of them" (Freud, 1933, p. 69).

The practical goal of psychoanalysis, in these terms, is to strengthen the ego, to make it independent of the overly strict concerns of the superego, and to increase its capacity to deal with material formerly repressed or hidden in the id.

Psychosexual Stages of Development

As an infant becomes a child, a child an adolescent, and an adolescent an adult, there are marked changes in what is desired and how those desires are satisfied. The shifting modes of gratification and the physical areas of gratification are the basic elements in Freud's description of the developmental stages. Freud uses the term *fixation* to describe what occurs when a person does not progress normally from stage to stage but remains overly involved with a particular stage. A person fixated in a particular stage will prefer to gratify his or her needs in simpler or more childlike ways, rather than in the most adult mode that would result from normal development.

Psychoanalysis is the first psychology to take seriously the whole human body as a place to live in. . . . Psychoanalysis is profoundly biological. . . . [Le Barre, 1968]

The Oral Stage

Beginning at birth, both needs and gratification are focused predominantly around the lips, tongue, and, somewhat later, the teeth. The basic drive of the infant is not social or interpersonal; it is simply to take in nourishment, to relieve the tensions of hunger and thirst. During feeding the child is also soothed, cuddled, rocked, and fondled. The child associates both pleasure and the reduction of tension with the feeding process.

The mouth is the first area of the body that the infant can control; most of the libidinal energy available is directed or focused on this one area. As the child matures, additional areas of the body develop and become important sites of gratification. However, some energy remains permanently affixed or cathected to the means for oral gratification. In adults there are many well-developed oral habits and a continued interest in maintaining oral pleasures. Eating, sucking, chewing, smoking, biting, and licking or smacking one's lips are physical expressions of these interests. Constant nibblers, smokers, and those who often overeat may be people who are partially fixated in the oral stage, people whose psychological maturation may be incomplete.

The late oral stage, after teeth have appeared, includes the gratification of the aggressive instincts. Biting the breast, which causes the mother pain and leads to the actual withdrawal of the breast, is an example of this kind of behavior. Adult sarcasm, tearing at one's food, and gossip have been described as being related to this developmental stage.

It is normal to retain some interest in oral pleasures. It can be looked upon as pathological only if it is a dominant mode of gratification, that is, if a person is excessively dependent on oral habits to relieve anxiety or tension.

The Anal Stage

As the child grows, new areas of tension and gratification are brought into awareness. Between 2 and 4, children generally learn to control the anal sphincter and the bladder. The child pays special attention to urination and defecation. Toilet training fans a natural interest in self-discovery. The rise in physiological control is coupled with the realization that such control is a new source of pleasure. In addition, children quickly learn that the rising level of control brings them attention and praise from their parents. The reverse is also true: The parents' concern over toilet training allows the child to demand attention both by successful control and by "mistakes."

Adult characteristics that are associated with partial fixation at the anal stage are orderliness, parsimoniousness, and obstinacy. Freud observed that these three traits are usually found together. He speaks of the "anal character" whose behavior is closely linked to difficult experiences suffered during this time in childhood.

Part of the confusion that can accompany the anal stage is the apparent contradiction between lavish praise and recognition on the one hand, and the idea that toilet behavior is "dirty" and should be kept a secret on the other. The child does not initially understand that his or her bowel movements and urine are not valued. Small children love to watch the action of the toilet bowl as it flushes, often waving or saying good-bye to their evacuations. It is not unusual for a child to offer part of a bowel movement to a parent as a gift. Having been praised for producing it, the child may be surprised and confused if the parents react with disgust at the gift. Few areas of contemporary life are as saddled with prohibitions and taboos as toilet training and behaviors typical of the anal stage.

The Phallic Stage

Starting as early as age 3, the child moves into the phallic stage, which focuses on the genital areas of the body. Freud maintained that this stage is best characterized as phallic since it is the period when a child either becomes aware of having a penis or lacking one. This is the first stage that children become conscious of sexual differences.

Freud tried to understand the tensions a child experiences when he or she feels "sexual" excitement, that is, pleasure from the stimulation of the genital areas. This excitement is linked in the child's mind with the close physical presence of his or her parents. The craving for this contact becomes increasingly more difficult for the child to satisfy; the child is struggling for the intimacy that the parents share with one another. This stage is characterized by the child wanting to get into bed with the parents and becoming jealous of the attention the parents give to each other instead of to the child. Freud concluded from his observations that during this period both males and females develop fears about sexual issues.

Freud saw children in the phallic stage reacting to their parents as potential threats to the fulfillment of their needs. Thus for the boy who wishes to be close to his mother, the father takes on some of the attributes of a rival. At the same time, the boy still wants his father's love and affection, for which his mother is seen as a rival. The child is in the untenable position of wanting and fearing both parents.

In boys, Freud called the conflict situation the Oedipal complex, after the play by Sophocles. In the Greek tragedy Oedipus kills his father (not knowing his father's true identity) and later marries his mother. When he is eventually made aware of who he has killed and who he has married, Oedipus disfigures himself by tearing out both his eyes. Freud believed that every male child reenacts a similar inner drama. He wishes to possess his mother and wishes to kill his father to achieve this end. He also fears his father and is afraid that he will be castrated by him, reducing the child to a sexless being. The anxiety around castration, the fear and love for his father, and the love and sexual desire for his mother can never be fully resolved. In childhood the entire complex is repressed. Among the first tasks of the developing superego are keeping this disturbing conflict out of consciousness, protecting the child from acting it out, preventing the child from any thought of it.

For girls the problem is similar, but its expression and solution take a different turn. The girl wishes to possess her father and sees her mother as the major rival. Whereas boys repress their feelings partly out of fear of castration, the girl's need to repress her desires is less severe, less total. The difference in intensity allows the girl to "remain in the Oedipus situation for an indefinite period. She only abandons it late in life, and then incompletely" (Freud, 1933, p. 129).

Whatever form the resolution of the struggle actually takes, most children seem to modify their attachment to their parents somewhere after 5 years of age and turn to relationships with peers, school activities, sports, and other skills. This time, from age 5 to 6 until the onset of puberty, is called the *latency period,* a time when the unresolvable sexual desires of the phallic stage are not attended to by the ego and are successfully repressed by the superego. "From then on, until puberty, it goes through the so-called latency period, in which, normally, sexuality makes no progress; on the contrary, the sexual strivings diminish in strength, and much that the child practiced or knew before is given up and forgotten. In this period, after the early blooming of sexual life has withered, are built up such attitudes of the ego as shame, disgust, and morality, designed to stand against the later storms of puberty and to direct the paths of the freshly-awakened sexual desires" (Freud, 1926, p. 216).

The Genital Stage
The final stage of biological and psychological development occurs with the onset of puberty and the consequent return of libidinal energy to the sexual organs. Now boys and girls are made aware of their separate

So you too are aware that the Oedipus complex is at the root of religious feeling. Bravo! [Freud, letter to Jung, 1913; in McGuire, 1974]

sexual identities and begin to look for ways to fulfill their erotic and interpersonal needs.

THE PSYCHOLOGY OF WOMEN

Freud's ideas about women were based heavily on biological differences between men and women. Here we will consider his views on female development.

The desire for a penis and a girl's related realization that she is "lacking" is a critical juncture in female development. According to Freud: "The discovery that she is castrated is a turning point in a girl's growth. Three possible lines of development diverge from it: one leads to sexual inhibition and to neurosis, the second to a modification of character in the sense of masculinity complex, and the third to normal feminity" (1933, p. 126).

This theory has, according to Freud, substantial implications for the development of the female personality. The girl's penis envy persists as a feeling of inferiority and a predisposition to jealousy; her perpetual desire for a penis or "superior endowment" is, in the mature woman, converted to the desire for a child, particularly for a son "who brings the longed-for-penis with him" (Freud, 1933). The woman is never decisively forced to renounce her Oedipal strivings out of castration anxiety. As a consequence, the woman's superego is less developed and internalized than the man's.

Freud asserts that women "have the hope of someday obtaining a penis in spite of everything. . . . I cannot escape the notion (though I hesitate to give it expression) that for women the level of what is ethically normal is different from what it is in men. . . . We must not allow ourselves to be deflected from such conclusions by the denials of the feminists, who are anxious to force us to regard the two sexes equal in position and worth" (Freud, 1925, p. 258).

Freud viewed the little girl as a creature in whom phallic strivings were extremely important but inevitably unsatisfied, thus dooming the girl to feelings of perpetual deficiency and inferiority. Yet in spite of such assertions (which have, not surprisingly, received enormous attention in feminist critiques of Freud's work), Freud frequently stated that he never really felt that he understood women or the psychology of women. He, in fact, reiterated time and again the tentative nature and value of his own portrayal of female sexuality and its vicissitudes.

Perhaps the most striking weak point of Freud's theory is one that appears remarkably obvious. Female sexuality is assumed by Freud to constitute disappointed *male* sexuality, rather than the outcome of distinctly female tendencies. Given this rather central bias, many of

Freud's conclusions about the nature of female sexuality and female psychology seem questionable. In fact, some of the phenomena that Freud observed and attempted to describe seem a good deal more plausible when they are stripped of their disappointed-male bias.

The assumption is made, for example, in most early psychoanalytic writing that a little girl's lack of a penis leads not only to envy of the boy's penis and *feelings* of inferiority, but also to *actual* inferiority vis-à-vis men—that is, inferiority in terms of a woman's sense of justice, intellectual curiosity, capacity to implement her ideas independent of a man's approval, and so forth. A common feminist approach to this kind of reasoning is angry rejection of the whole postulated series of events, beginning with penis envy. The notion that penis envy may be a very real and commonly observed clinical phenomenon is dismissed because it is so intimately connected, in the minds of many people, with the assumption of generalized female inferiority. This seems unfortunate; for, as Karen Horney (1926) has suggested, penis envy may be a natural experience for females in the same way that envy of pregnancy, childbirth, motherhood, and suckling is a natural experience for males. Even more important, *experiencing envy* does not doom the little girl to perpetual inferiority. Rather, its occurrence, says Horney, may present her with a complex set of feelings, the working through and mastery of which are central to her growth and development as a mature—certainly not inferior—human being.

Here is an instance, then, where we may usefully reexamine a traditional psychoanalytic concept, one that has, in fact, received a major portion of feminist hostility toward psychoanalytic theory. Instead of eliminating the whole notion of penis envy (and explaining away its frequent clinical manifestations), we may reevaluate the idea that women feel inferior *as a result of penis envy*. The recurrent anger in the feminist literature at having had inferiority feelings suggests that Freud's observations about feelings of inferiority might be reexamined, even if his idea of how they originated does not seem realistic. Learning how to deal (in productive ways) with feelings of envy or of insecurity or of being different from other people is, after all, central to the challenge of growing up.

Ernest Jones, Freud's biographer, was one of the first psychoanalysts who argued that "the little girl's Oedipal attachment develops out of her intrinsic, innate femininity undergoing its own maturation processes" (In Fliegel, 1973, p. 387). He also suggested that castration anxiety derives from a basic fear of loss of sexuality and that this fear poses as much threat to the little girl as to the little boy (Jones, 1929). (See Horney, pp. 126–129, for additional considerations of Freud's position.)

. . . though anatomy, it is true, can point out the characteristics of maleness and femaleness, psychology cannot. For psychology the contrast between the sexes fades away into activity and passivity, in which we far too readily identify activity with maleness and passivity with femaleness . . . [Freud, 1930]

DYNAMICS

Psychological Growth
Psychoanalysis

Freud's intention, from his earliest writings, was to better understand those aspects of mental life that were obscure and apparently unreachable. He called the theory and the therapy psychoanalysis. "Psychoanalysis is the name (1) of a procedure for the investigation of mental processes which are almost inaccessible in any other way, (2) of a method (based upon that investigation) for the treatment of neurotic disorders and (3) of a collection of psychological information obtained along those lines, which is gradually being accumulated into a new scientific discipline" (Freud, 1923, p. 234).

The more psychoanalysis becomes known, the more will incompetent doctors dabble in it and naturally make a mess of it. This will then be blamed on you and your theory. [Jung, letter to Freud, 1906; in McGuire, 1974]

The goal of psychoanalysis is to liberate previously inaccessible unconscious materials so they may be dealt with consciously. Freud believed that the unconscious material remained unconscious only with considerable and continual expenditure of libido. As this material is made accessible, energy is released that can be used by the ego for healthier pursuits.

The release of blocked materials can minimize self-destructive attitudes. The need to be punished or the need to feel inadequate can be reevaluated, for example, by bringing into awareness those early events or fantasies that led to the need. People may then be freed from the suffering they perpetually bring upon themselves. For example, many, if not most, Americans feel that their sexual organs are not the right size: penises are too short or too thin; breasts are too flabby, too tiny, too large, not well formed, and so forth. Most of these beliefs arise during the teen-age years or earlier. The unconscious residues of these attitudes are visible in worries over sexual adequacy, desirability, premature ejaculation, frigidity, and a host of related symptoms. If these unexpressed fears are explored, exposed, and relieved, there can be a rise in available sexual energy as well as a lowering of overall tension.

There is still no acceptable evidence to support the view that psychoanalysis is an effective treatment. [Rachman & Wilson, 1980, p. 76]

Psychoanalysis suggests that it is possible, but difficult, to come to terms with the recurring demands of the id. "The analysis aims at laying bare the complexes which have been repressed as a result of the painful feelings associated with them, and which produce signs of resistance when there is an attempt to bring them into consciousness" (Freud, 1906, p. 109). "One of the tasks of psychoanalysis, as you know, is to lift the veil of amnesia which shrouds the earliest years of childhood and to bring the expressions of infantile sexual life which are hidden behind it into conscious memory" (Freud, 1933, p. 28). The goals as described by Freud assume that if one is freed from the inhibitions of the unconscious, the ego establishes new levels of satisfaction in all areas of functioning. Thus the resolution of anxieties rooted in early childhood frees blocked or displaced energy for more realistic and complete gratification of ones needs.

Dreams and Dreamwork

In listening to the free associations of his patients, as well as in his own self-analysis, Freud began to scrutinize the reports and memories of dreams. In what has been described as his most important book, *The Interpretation of Dreams* (1900), he writes how dreams help the psyche protect and satisfy itself. Incessant obstacles and unmitigated desires fill daily life. Dreams are a partial balance both physically and psychologically between instinctual urges and real-life limitations. Dreaming is a way of channeling unfulfilled desires through consciousness without arousing the physical body. "A structure of thoughts, mostly very complicated, which has been built up during the day and not brought to settlement—a day remnant—clings firmly even during night to the energy which it has assumed . . . and thus threatens to disturb sleep. This day remnant is transformed into a dream by the dream-work and in this way rendered harmless to sleep" (Freud, 1905; in Fodor & Gaynor, 1958, pp. 52–53).

More important than the biological value of dreams are the psychological effects of *dreamwork*. Dreamwork is "the whole of the operations which transform the raw materials of the dream—bodily stimuli, day's residues, dream-thoughts—so as to produce the manifest dream" (LaPlanche and Pontalis, 1973, p. 125). A dream does not simply appear; it is developed to meet specific needs, although these are not clearly described by the dream's manifest content.

Almost every dream can be understood as a *wish-fulfillment*. The dream is an alternative pathway to satisfy the desires of the id. While awake the ego strives to allow pleasure and reduce tension. During sleep unfulfilled needs are sorted, combined, and arranged so that the dream sequences allow additional satisfaction or tension reduction. For the id, it is unimportant whether satisfaction occurs in physical sensory reality or in internal imagined dream-reality. In both cases accumulated energies are discharged. The dream plays out, on at least two levels, current incidents that are unresolved or that are part of larger, older patterns that have never been resolved.

Repetitive dreams may occur when a daytime event triggers the same kind of anxiety that led to the original dream. For example, an active, happily married woman in her sixties still dreams, from time to time, of going to take a college exam. She arrives at the classroom but it is empty. The examination is over, she arrived too late. She has this dream when she is anxious over some current difficulty; however, her anxiety is related neither to college nor to examinations, both of which she left behind many years ago.

Many dreams do not appear to be satisfying; some are depressing,

We recognize the soundness of the wish-fulfillment theory up to a certain point, but we go beyond it. In our view it does not exhaust the meaning of the dream. [Jung, letter to Freud, 1913; in McGuire, 1974]

A dream then, is a psychosis, with all the absurdities, delusions and illusions of a psychosis. No doubt it is a psychosis which has only a short duration, which is harmless and even performs a useful function. [Freud, 1940]

Dreams are not to be likened to the unregulated sounds that rise from a musical instrument struck by the blow of some external force instead of a player's hand; they are not meaningless, they are not absurd; they do not imply that one portion of our store of ideas is asleep while another portion is beginning to wake. On the contrary, they are psychical phenomena of complete validity—fulfillment of wishes; they can be inserted into the chain of intelligible waking mental acts; they are constructed by a highly complicated activity of the mind. [Freud, 1900]

Dreams are the true interpreters of our inclinations, but art is required to sort and understand them. [Montaigne, 1553–1592, *Essays*]

Dreams are real while they last—can we say more of life? [Havelock Ellis]

some disturbing, some frightening, and many simply obscure. Many dreams seem to be the reliving of past events, whereas a few appear to be prophetic. Through the detailed analysis of dozens of dreams, linking them to events in the life of the dreamer, Freud was able to show that dreamwork is a process of selection, distortion, transformation, inversion, displacement, and other modifications of an original wish. These changes render the modified wish acceptable to the ego even if the original wish is totally unacceptable to waking consciousness. Freud suggested reasons for the permissiveness in dreams where we act beyond the moral restrictions of our waking lives. In dreams we kill, maim, or destroy enemies, relatives, or friends; we have sexual liaisons, act out perversions, and take as sexual partners a wide range of people. In dreams we combine people, places, and occasions impossible in our waking world.

Dreams attempt to fulfill wishes, but they are not always successful. "Under certain conditions, the dream can only achieve its end in a very incomplete way, or has to abandon it entirely; an unconscious fixation to the trauma seems to head the list of these obstacles to the dream functions" (Freud, 1933, p. 29).

Within the context of psychoanalysis, the therapist aids the patient in interpreting dreams to facilitate the recovery of unconscious material. Freud made certain generalizations about special kinds of dreams (e.g., falling dreams, flying dreams, swimming dreams, and dreams about fire) but he makes it clear that for any specific case the general rules may not be valid, and that an individual's associations in his or her own dreams are more important than any preconceived set of rules of interpretation.

Critics of Freud often suggest that he overinterpreted the sexual components of dreams to conform to his overall theory. Freud's rejoinder is clear. "I have never maintained the assertion which has often been ascribed to me that dream-interpretation shows that all dreams have a sexual content or are derived from sexual motive forces" (Freud, 1925a, p. 47). What he stressed was that dreams are neither random nor accidental but are a way to satisfy unfulfilled wishes.

Sublimation

 Sublimation is the process whereby energy originally directed toward sexual or aggressive goals is redirected toward new aims—often artistic, intellectual, or cultural goals. Sublimation has been called the "successful defense" (Fenichel, 1945). The original energy might be thought of as a river that floods, destroying homes and property. To prevent this, a dam is built. The destruction can no longer occur, but the pressure builds up behind the dam, threatening far worse damage should it ever burst. Sublimation is the building of diversionary channels, which in turn may be used to generate electric power, irrigate formerly arid areas, create parks, and open up other recreational opportunities. The original energy of the river has been successfully diverted into socially acceptable or culturally sanctioned channels.

The sublimated energy is responsible for what we call civilization. Freud argues that the enormous energy and complexity of civilization is the result of the desire to find acceptable and sufficient avenues for suppressed energy. Civilization encourages the transcendence of the original drives and, in some cases, the alternative goals can be more satisfying to the id than the satisfaction of the original urges.

Energy sublimated reduces the original drives. This transformation "places extraordinarily large amounts of force at the disposal of civilized activity, and it does this in virtue of its especially marked characteristic of being able to displace its aim without materially diminishing its intensity" (Freud, 1908, p. 187).

> The forces that can be employed for cultural activities are thus to a great extent obtained through the suppression of what are known as the *perverse* elements of sexual excitation. [Freud, 1908]

Obstacles to Growth
Anxiety

The major problem for the psyche is how to cope with anxiety. Anxiety is triggered by an expected or foreseen increase in tension or displeasure; it can develop in any situation (real or imagined) when the threat to some part of the body or psyche is too great to be ignored, mastered, or discharged.

> Anxiety makes repression and not, as we used to think, the other way round. [Freud, 1933, p. 69]

Prototypical situations, situations that cause anxiety, include the following:

1. Loss of a desired object—for example, a child deprived of a parent, a close friend, or a pet.
2. Loss of love—for example, rejection, failure to win back the love or approval of someone who matters to you.
3. Loss of identity—for example, castration fears, loss of face, public ridicule.
4. Loss of love for self—for example, superego disapproval of acts or traits, acts which result in guilt or self-hate.

The threat of these and other events causes anxiety. There are two general ways to decrease the anxiety. The first is to deal with the situation directly. We resolve the problems, overcome obstacles, either confront or run from threats, and come to terms with problems to minimize their impact. In these ways we are working to eliminate difficulties, lowering the chances of their future recurrence, and also decreasing the prospects of additional anxiety in the future. In Hamlet's words, we "take up arms against a sea of trouble and by opposing end them."

The alternative approach defends against the anxiety by distorting or denying the situation itself. The ego protects the whole personality against the threat by falsifying the nature of the threat. The ways

> If the ego is obliged to admit its weakness, it breaks out into anxiety—realistic anxiety in regarding the face of the external world, moral anxiety regarding the super-ego, and neurotic anxiety regarding the strength of the passions in the id. [Freud, 1933]

in which the distortions are accomplished are called the *defense mechanisms*.

Defense Mechanisms

The major defense mechanisms described here are repression, denial, rationalization, reaction formation, projection, isolation, and regression (A. Freud, 1936; Fenichel, 1945). Sublimation, described earlier, is a successful defense; it actually resolves and eliminates the tension. All the other defenses block direct expression of instinctual needs. Although any of these mechanisms can be found in healthy individuals, their presence is an indication of possible neurotic or excessive concerns.

Repression. "The essence of repression lies simply in turning something away, and keeping it at a distance, from the consciousness" (Freud, 1915, p. 147). Repression forces a potentially anxiety-provoking event, idea, or perception away from consciousness, thus precluding any possible resolution. Unfortunately, the repressed element is still part of the psyche, although unconscious, and still remains active. "Repression is never performed once and for all but requires a constant expenditure of energy to maintain the repression, while the repressed constantly tried to find an outlet" (Fenichel, 1945, p. 150). Hysterical symptoms are often found to have originated in earlier repression. Some psychosomatic ailments such as asthma, arthritis, and ulcers may be linked to repression. Excessive lassitude, phobias, and impotence or frigidity may also be derivatives of repressed feelings. If, for example, you have strongly ambivalent feelings about your father, you might love him and at the same time wish he were dead. The desire for his death, the accompanying fantasies, and your resulting feelings of guilt and shame might all be unconscious because both your ego and your superego would find the idea unacceptable. Should your father actually die, this complex would be still more rigidly repressed. To admit to the feelings would mean you would feel pleasure at his death, a feeling even more unacceptable to your superego than the original resentment or hostility. In this situation you might appear unaffected or unmoved by his death, the repression withholding your genuine and appropriate grief and loss as well as your unexpressible hostility.

Denial. Denial is the attempt to not accept into reality an event that disturbs the ego. Adults have a tendency to "daydream" that certain events are not so, that they didn't really happen. This flight into fantasy can take many forms, some of which seem absurd to the objective observer. The following story is an illustration:

> A woman was brought into court at the request of her neighbor. This
> neighbor charged that the woman had borrowed and damaged a valuable

vase. When it came time for the woman to defend herself, her defense was threefold: "In the first place, I never borrowed the vase. Secondly, it was chipped when I took it. Finally, your honor, I returned it in perfect condition."

The remarkable capacity to remember events incorrectly is the form of denial found most often in psychotherapy. The patient recalls vividly one version of an incident, then at a later time may recall the incident differently and be suddenly aware that the first version was a defensive fabrication.

Freud did not claim that his clinical observations were entirely original. In fact, he quotes Darwin's and Nietzsche's observations about themselves (1901, p. 148). Darwin, in his autobiography, noted:

"People are in general not candid over sexual matters. They do not show their sexuality freely, but to conceal it they wear a heavy overcoat woven of a tissue of lies, as though the weather were bad in the world of sexuality." [Freud in Malcolm, 1980]

> I had during years followed a golden rule, namely, whenever I came across a published fact, a new observation or idea, which ran counter to my general results, I made a memorandum of it without fail and at once; for I had found by experience that such facts and ideas were far more apt to slip the memory than favorable ones.

Nietzsche commented on a different aspect of the same process:

> "I have done that", says my memory. "It is impossible that I should have done it", says my pride, and it remains inexorable. Finally my memory yields.

Rationalization. Rationalization is the process of finding acceptable reasons for unacceptable thoughts or actions. It is a process whereby a person presents an explanation that is either logically consistent with or ethically acceptable for an attitude, action, idea, or feeling that arises from other motivating sources. We use it to justify our behavior when in fact the reasons for our actions are not commendable or not even understood by us. The following statements might be rationalizations; the statements in parentheses are possible unexpressed feelings.

> "I'm only doing this for your own good." (I want to do this to you. I don't want it done to me. I even want you to suffer a little bit.)
> "The experiment was a logical continuation of my prior work." (It started as a mistake but I was lucky it worked out.)
> "I think I'm in love with you." (I'm turned on to your body; I want to get you more relaxed.)

Rationalization is a way of accepting pressure from the superego; it disguises our motives, rendering our actions morally acceptable. As an obstacle to growth, it prevents the person who is rationalizing (or anyone else!) from working with, observing, and understanding the genuine, less commendable motivating forces. Viewed from outside, as in the following story by Idries Shah, its foolish aspect is obvious.

CHEESE FOR CHOICE

"I have chosen," said the mouse, "to like cheese. Such an important decision, needless to say, cannot be arrived at without a sufficient period of careful deliberation. One does not deny the immediate, indefinable aesthetic attraction of the substance. Yet this in itself is possible only to the more refined type of individual—as an example, the brutish fox lacks the sensitive discrimination even to approach cheese.

"Other factors in the choice are not less susceptible to rational analysis: which is, of course, as it should be.

"The attractive colour, suitable texture, adequate weight, interestingly different shapes, relatively numerous places of occurrence, reasonable ease of digestion, comparative abundance of variety in nutritional content, ready availability, considerable ease of transport, total absence of side-effects—these and a hundred other easily defined factors abundantly prove my good sense and deep insights, consciously exercised in the making of this wise and deliberate choice." [1972, p. 138]

Reaction Formation. This mechanism substitutes behaviors or feelings that are diametrically opposed to the actual wish; it is an explicit and usually unconscious inversion of the wish.

Like other defense mechanisms, reaction formations are developed first in childhood. "As the child becomes aware of sexual excitement which cannot be fulfilled, the sexual 'excitations' evoke opposing mental forces which, in order to suppress this unpleasure effectively, build up the mental dams of disgust, shame and morality" (Freud, 1905a, p. 178). Not only is the original idea repressed, but any shame or self-reproach that might arise by admitting such thoughts is also excluded from awareness.

Unfortunately, the side effects of reaction formations may cripple social relationships. The principal identifying characteristics of reaction formation are its excessiveness, its rigidity, and its extravagance. The urge being denied must be obscured again and again and again.

The following letter was written to a researcher from an antivivisectionist. It is a clear example of one feeling—compassion toward all living things—used to disguise another feeling—a desire to harm and torture.

> I read [a magazine article] . . . on your work on alcoholism. . . . I am surprised that anyone who is as well educated as you must be to hold the position that you do would stoop to such a depth as to torture helpless little cats in the pursuit of a cure for alcoholics. . . . A drunkard does not want to be cured—a drunkard is just a weak-minded idiot who belongs in the gutter and should be left there. Instead of torturing helpless little cats why not torture the drunks or better still exert your would-be noble effort toward getting a bill passed to *exterminate* the drunks. . . . My greatest wish is that you have brought home to you a torture that will be a thousandfold greater than what you have, and are doing to the little animals. . . . If you are an example of what a noted psychiatrist should be I'm glad I am just an ordinary human being without letters after my

The person who has built up reaction-formations does not develop certain defense mechanisms for use when an instinctual danger threatens; he has changed his personality structure as if this danger were continually present, so that he may be ready whenever the danger occurs. [Fenichel, 1945]

name. I'd rather be just myself with a clear conscience, *knowing I have not hurt any living creature,* and can sleep without seeing frightened, terrified dying cats—because I know they must die after you have finished with them. No punishment is too great for you and I hope I live to read about your mangled body and long suffering before you finally die—and I'll laugh long and loud. [Masserman, 1961, p. 38]

Reaction formations may be evident in any excessive behavior. The housewife who is continually cleaning her home may, in reality, be concentrating her awareness on being with and examining dirt. The parent who cannot admit his or her resentment of the children "may interfere so much in their lives, under the pretext of being concerned about their welfare and safety, that [the] overprotection is really a form of punishment" (Hall, 1954, p. 93). Reaction formation masks parts of the personality and restricts a person's capacity to respond to events; the personality may become relatively inflexible.

Projection. The act of attributing to another person, animal, or object the qualities, feelings, or intentions that originate in one's self, is called *projection.* It is a defense mechanism whereby the aspects of one's own personality are displaced from within the individual onto the external environment. The threat is treated as if it were an external force. A person can therefore deal with actual feelings, but without admitting or being aware of the fact that the feared idea or behavior is his or her own. The following statements might be projections; the statement in parentheses might be the actual unconscious feeling.

1. "All men/women want is one thing." (I think about sex a lot.)
2. "You can never trust a wop/spic/nigger/wasp/honkie/college boy/woman/priest." (I want to take unfair advantage of others sometimes.)
3. "I know you're mad at me." (I'm mad at you.)

Whenever we characterize something "out there" as evil, dangerous, perverted, and so forth, without acknowledging that these characteristics might also be true for us, we are probably projecting. It is equally true that when we see others as being powerful, attractive, capable, and so forth, without appreciating the same qualities in ourselves, we are also projecting. The critical variable in projection is that we do not see in ourselves what seems vivid and obvious in another.

Research into the dynamics of prejudice has shown that people who tend to stereotype others also display little insight into their own feelings. People who deny having a specific personality trait are more critical of that trait when they see it in or project it onto others (Sears, 1936).

Isolation. Isolation is a way of separating the anxiety-arousing parts of the situation from the rest of the psyche. It is the act of partitioning it off, so that there is little or no emotional reaction connected to the event.

The result is that when a person discusses problems that have been isolated from the rest of the personality, the events are recounted with no feeling, as if they had happened to a third party. This arid approach can become a dominant style of coping. A person may withdraw more and more into ideas, having less and less contact with his or her own feelings.

Children may play at this, dividing their identities into good and bad aspects. They may take a toy animal and have it say and do all types of forbidden things. The animal's personality may be tyrannical, rude, sarcastic, and unreasonable. A child may display, through the animal, behaviors that parents would not allow under normal circumstances.

Freud writes that the normal prototype of isolation is logical thinking, which also tries to detach the content from the emotional situation in which it is found. Isolation is a defense mechanism only when it is used to protect the ego from accepting anxiety-ridden aspects of situations or relationships.

Regression. Regression is a reversion to an earlier level of development or to a mode of expression that is simpler and more childlike. It is a way of alleviating anxiety by withdrawing from realistic thinking into behaviors that have, in earlier years, reduced anxiety. Linus, in the Charlie Brown comic strip, always returns to a safe psychological situation when he is under stress; he feels secure when he is holding his blanket.

Regression is a more primitive way of coping. Although it reduces anxiety, it often leaves unresolved the source of the initial anxiety. Calvin Hall's extensive list of regressive behaviors offers you a chance to see if it includes any behaviors of your own.

> Even healthy, well-adjusted people make regressions from time to time in order to reduce anxiety, or, as they say, to blow off steam. They smoke, get drunk, eat too much, lose their tempers, bite their nails, pick their noses, break laws, talk baby talk, destroy property, masturbate, read mystery stories, go to the movies, engage in unusual sexual practices, chew gum and tobacco, dress up as children, drive fast and recklessly, believe in good and evil spirits, take naps, fight and kill one another, bet on the horses, daydream, rebel against or submit to authority, gamble, preen before the mirror, act out their impulses, pick on scapegoats, and do a thousand and one other childish things. Some of these regressions are so commonplace that they are taken to be signs of maturity. Actually they are all forms of regression used by adults. [1954, pp. 95–96]

Summary of the Defense Mechanisms. The defenses described here are ways the psyche has to protect itself from internal or external tension. The defenses avoid reality (repression), exclude reality (denial), redefine reality (rationalization), or reverse reality (reaction formation). They place inner feelings on the outer world (projection), partition reality (isolation), or withdraw from reality (regression). In every case libidinal energy is necessary to maintain the defense, effectively limiting the flexibility and strength of the ego. "They tie up psychological energy which could be used for more effective ego activities. When a defense becomes very influential, it dominates the ego and curtails its flexibility and its adaptability. Finally, if the defenses fail to hold, the ego has nothing to fall back upon and is overwhelmed by anxiety" (Hall, 1954, p. 96).

STRUCTURE

Energy
At the center of Freud's theories is his concept of energy flow. It is the link between his concepts of the unconscious, psychological development, personality, and neurosis. "His theories on instincts deal with the *source* of energy; his theories on psychosexual development, fixation, and regression deal with the *diversion* of energy; and his theories of the id, ego, and superego deal with *conflicts* of energy" (Cohen, 1982, p. 4).

Body
Freud developed his theories based on physical and biological assumptions. Basic drives arise from somatic sources; libidinal energy is derived of physical energy; responses to tension are both mental and physical. The body is the core of experience. As Sulloway points out, "It was Freud's continued appeal to biological assumptions that justified his personal conviction that he had finally created a universally valid theory of human thought and behavior" (1979, p. 419).

> The ego is first and foremost a body ego. [Freud, 1927]

Moreover, the primary focuses of energy are through the various forms of sexual expression (oral, anal, genital). Full maturity is partially defined as full genital sexuality in terms of capacity and quality of expression. Many of Freud's critics never looked at his full theory, but instead became obsessed with his reintroduction of physical and sexual concerns into the fields of so-called mental functioning.

In spite of Freud's recognition of the centrality of the body, his own writings on therapy almost totally ignore it. Perhaps the cultural denial of the body that characterized the age in which he lived colored his own apparent lack of interest in gestures, postures, and physical expressions exhibited by his patients. Many of the later Freudians, such as Erikson and Perls, as well as those theorists who broke from

Freud, such as Jung and Reich, paid more attention to the actual physical body but less attention to the biological theories about it.

Social Relationships

The all-inclusive nature of sex energy has not yet been correctly understood by psychologists. In fact, the very term *reproductive* or *sex energy* is a misnomer. Reproduction is but one of the aspects of the life energy, of which the other theater of activity is the brain. [Gopi Krishna, 1974]

Adult interactions and relationships are greatly influenced by early childhood experiences. The first relationships, those that occur within the nuclear family, are the defining ones; all later relationships relate in various ways back to the ways those initial relationships were formed and maintained. The basic patterns of child-mother, child-father, and child-sibling are the prototypes against which later encounters are unconsciously measured. Later relationships are, to some degree, recapitulations of the dynamics, tensions, and gratifications that occurred within the original family.

Our choices in life—lovers, friends, bosses, even our enemies—are derivatives of the parent-child bonds. The natural rivalries are recapitulated in our sex roles and in the way we accommodate the demands of others. Over and over again, we play out the dynamics begun in our homes, frequently picking as partners people who reawaken in us unresolved aspects of our early needs. For some these are conscious choices, for others it is done in ignorance of the underlying dynamics.

I confess that plunging into sexuality in theory and practice is not to my taste. But what have my taste and feeling about what is seemly and what is unseemly to do with the question of what is true? [Breuer in Sulloway, 1979, p. 80]

People shy away from this aspect of Freudian theory because it suggests that one's future choices are already circumscribed. The issue turns on the question of how much childhood experience determines adult choices. For example, one critical period in developing relationships occurs during the phallic stage when both sexes first confront their growing erotic feelings toward their parents and the concomitant inability to gratify these urges. However, even as the resulting Oedipal complications are resolved, those dynamics continue to affect later relationships.

Relationships are built on a foundation of the residual effects of intense early experiences. Teen-age, young adult, and adult dating, and friendship and marriage patterns are a reworking of unresolved facets of childhood beginnings.

Will

The will was not a topic of major concern to Freud. In an early work (1894) he wrote that it was through an effort of the will that anxiety-provoking events could be repressed, though the repression was not always totally successful. "At least in a number of cases the patients themselves inform us that their phobia or obsession made its first appearance after the effort of will had apparently succeeded in its aim. 'Something very disagreeable happened to me once and I tried very hard to put it away from me and not to think about it any more. I succeeded at last; but then I got this other thing [obsession] which I have not been able to get rid of since' " (Freud, 1894, pp. 52–53).

In cases of overpowering obsessions, the patient may experience a "paralysis" of the will. A person is unwilling or unable to make any meaningful decisions because he or she is caught between an excessive need for approval and a fear of being opposed or threatened.

One later analyst has extended psychoanalytic theory to give a fuller description of the will (Farber, 1966), but it has not been a central theoretical interest within the psychoanalytic movement.

Emotions

What Freud uncovered, in an age that had worshiped reason and denied the value and the power of emotion, was that we are not primarily rational animals, but are driven by powerful emotional forces whose genesis is unconscious. Emotions are the avenues for the release of tension and the appreciation of pleasure. Emotions may also serve the ego by helping it to keep certain memories or situations out of awareness. For example, strong emotional reactions may actually mask a childhood trauma. A phobic reaction effectively prevents a person from approaching an object or class of objects that might trigger a more threatening source of anxiety.

It was through observing emotional responses, their appropriate and inappropriate expressions, that Freud found clues which were the keys to uncovering and understanding the motivating forces within the unconscious.

Intellect

The intellect is one of the tools available to the ego. The person who is most free is the one who is able to use reason when it is expedient and whose emotional life is open to conscious inspection. Such a person is not driven by unfulfilled remnants of past events, but can respond directly to each situation, balancing his or her individual preferences against the restrictions imposed by the culture.

The most striking and probably the strongest emotional force in Freud was his passion for truth and his uncompromising faith in reason; for him, reason was the only human capacity that could help to solve the problem of existence or at least ameliorate the suffering that is inherent in human life.

For Freud, as for the age in which he lived, the impact of Darwin's work cannot be underestimated. To prove through the use of reason that one was higher than the beasts was an unquestioned goal of the time. Much of the resistance to Freud's work arose from his evidence that people were in fact less reasonable, more emotional, more irrational, and more like animals than anyone had suspected. Freud's own hope and personal belief was that reason was primary and that the intellect was the most, if not the only, important tool that consciousness possessed to control its darker sides.

Reason, so Freud felt, is the only tool—or weapon—we have to make sense of life, to dispense with illusions . . . to become independent of fettering authorities, and thus to establish our own authority. [Fromm, 1959]

What Freud realized was that any aspect of unconscious existence, raised into the light of consciousness, might be dealt with rationally. "Where id is, there let ego be" (Freud, 1933, p. 80). Where the irrational instinctual urges dominate, let them be exposed, moderated, and dominated by the ego. If the original drive is not to be suppressed, it becomes the task of the ego, using the intellect, to devise safe and sufficient ways of satiation. The use of intellect depends entirely on the capacity and strength of the ego.

Self

The self is the total being: the body, the instincts, the conscious and unconscious processes. A self independent of the body or detached from it has no place in Freud's biological beliefs. When such metaphysical questions were raised, Freud asserted that they were not within his province as a scientist.

Therapist/Therapy

We have been chiefly concerned with Freud's general theory of personality. Freud himself, however, was involved with the practical applications of his work—the practice of psychoanalysis. The aim of psychoanalysis is to help the patient establish the best possible level of ego functioning, given the inevitable conflicts arising from the external environment, the superego, and the relentless instinctual demands of the id. Kenneth Colby, a former training analyst, describes the goal of the analytic procedure:

> In speaking of the goal of psychotherapy, the term "cure" frequently intrudes. It requires definition. If by "cure" we mean relief of the patient's current neurotic difficulties, then that is certainly our goal. If by "cure" we mean a lifelong freedom from emotional conflict and psychological problems, then that cannot be our goal. Just as a person may suffer pneumonia, a fracture, and diabetes during his lifetime and require particular medication and separate treatment for each condition, so another person may experience at different times a depression, impotence, and a phobia, each requiring psychotherapy as the condition arises. Our aim is to treat the presenting problems, hoping that the work will strengthen the patient against further neurotic difficulties but realizing that therapy cannot guarantee a psychological prophylaxis. [1951, p. 4]

The Role of the Psychoanalyst

The therapist's task is to help the patient recall, recover, and reintegrate unconscious materials in order that the patient's present life can become more satisfying. Freud says, "We pledge him to obey the *fundamental rule* of analysis which is henceforward to govern his behavior towards us. He is to tell us not only what he can say intentionally and willingly, what will give him relief like a confession, but everything else as well that comes into his head, even if it is *disagreeable* for him to say it, even if it seems to him *unimportant* or actually *nonsensical*" (1940, p. 31).

The analyst is supportive of these disclosures, and neither critical nor approving of their content. The analyst takes no moral position but serves as a blank screen for the patient's opinions. The therapist presents as little as possible of his or her personality to the patient. This gives the patient the freedom to treat the analyst in a host of ways, transferring to the therapist attitudes, ideas, even physical characteristics that actually belong to persons in the patient's past. This *transference* is critical to the therapeutic process because it brings past events into a new context, one that can be dealt with in the therapy. For example, if a female patient starts to treat a male therapist as she treats her father—outwardly submissive and deferential, but covertly hostile and disrespectful—the analyst can clarify these feelings for the patient. He can point out that he, the therapist, is not the cause for the feelings, but that they originate within the patient herself, and may reflect aspects of her relationship with her father that she may have repressed.

To aid the patient in making these connections, the analyst interprets some of what the patient is saying back to the patient, suggesting links that the patient may or may not have previously acknowledged. This process of interpretation is a matter of intuition and clinical experience.

In all psychoanalytic procedures the patient is never pressured to uncover material, but is encouraged to allow material to emerge as the ongoing analytic process makes it possible. Freud saw the analysis as a natural process; the energy that had been repressed slowly emerges into consciousness where it can be used by the developing ego. "Whenever we succeed in analyzing a symptom into its elements, in freeing an impulse from one nexus, it does not remain in isolation, but immediately enters into a new one" (Freud, 1919, p. 161).

The task of the therapist is to expose, explore, and isolate the component impulses that have been denied or distorted by the patient. Reforming or establishing newer and healthier habits occurs without the intrusion of the therapist. "The psychosynthesis is thus achieved during analytic treatment without our intervention, automatically and inevitably" (Freud, 1919, p. 161).

Limitations of Psychoanalysis

Analysis is not for everyone, nor does the proper application of its procedures inevitably lead to improvement. Freud says: "The field of application of analytic therapy lies in the transference neuroses—phobias, hysteria, obsessional neurosis—and further, abnormalities of charac-

To stand firm against this general assault by the patient the analyst requires to have been fully and completely analyzed himself. . . . The analyst himself, on whom the fate of so many people depends, must know and be in control of even the most recondite weaknesses of his own character; and this is impossible without a fully completed analysis. [Ferenczi, 1955]

The concept of Transference . . . contends that the observation, understanding and discussion of the patient's emotional reactions to the psychoanalytical situation constitute the most direct ways of reaching an understanding of his character structure and consequently of his difficulties. It has become the most powerful, and indeed the indispensable, tool of analytical therapy. [Horney, 1939, pp. 33–34]

It almost looks as if analysis were the third of those "impossible" professions in which one can be sure beforehand of achieving unsatisfying results. The other two, which have been known much longer, are education and government. [Freud, 1937]

ter which have been developed in place of these diseases. Everything differing from these, narcissistic and psychotic conditions, is unsuitable to a greater or less extent" (1933, p. 155).

Some analysts have said that it is the patients who are already functioning well, whose ego structure is healthy and intact, who make the best candidates for psychoanalysis. Although Freud did see that psychoanalysis could help explain and understand the whole of human consciousness, he gently chided those who might believe that psychoanalytic psychotherapy was the ultimate cure. "Psychoanalysis is really a method of treatment like others. It has its triumphs and its defeats, its difficulties, its limitations, its indications. . . . I should like to add that I do not think our cures can compete with those of Lourdes. There are so many more people who believe in the miracles of the Blessed Virgin than in the existence of the unconscious" (1933, p. 152).

EVALUATION

We have presented an overview of the vast and complex theoretical structure that Freud developed. We have not, in this chapter, attempted to add to it the numerous shadings and elaborations of his followers, disciples, detractors, critics, and clients. We have tried to organize and simplify the outlines of what was, at its inception, a radical and innovative point of view. Freud threw down a gauntlet that few thinkers have been able to refuse. Most of the other theorists in this book acknowledge their debt to Freud, those who agreed with him as well as those who repeatedly opposed him.

Freud's ideas have influenced psychology, literature, art, anthropology, sociology, and medicine. Many of his ideas, such as the importance of dreams and the vitality of the unconscious processes, are widely accepted. Other facets of his theory, such as the relationship between the ego, the id, and the superego, or the role of the Oedipal complex in adolescent development, are extensively debated. Still other parts of his work, including his analysis of female sexuality and his theories on the origins of civilization, have been generally criticized.

Our position is to recognize that there are times in a person's life when Freud's picture of the role of conscious and unconscious seems like a personal revelation. The stunning impact of his thinking illuminates an aspect of your own or someone else's character and sends you scurrying after more of his books. There are other times when he does not seem to be of use, when his ideas seem distant, convoluted, and not relevant to your experience.

At either time, Freud is a figure to be dealt with. His work evokes a personal response. As we looked over his books, accumulated over the years, we reread our own marginal notes, some of praise and some of damnation. He cannot be treated lightly because he discussed and described issues that arise in everyone's life.

Whatever your response to Freud's ideas, Freud's advice would be to regard your response as an indicator of your own state of mind, as well as a reasoned reaction to his work. In the words of the poet W. H. Auden about Freud: "If often he was wrong and at times absurd, to us he is no more a person now, but a whole climate of opinion" (1945).

Implications for Personal Growth

It is possible to examine your own inner world for clues to your own behavior; however, it is an extremely difficult task because you have, with varying degrees of success, hidden these same clues away from yourself.

Freud suggests that all behavior is linked together, that there are no psychological accidents—that some of your choices of persons, places, foods, and amusements stem from experiences you do not or will not remember—that all thoughts, all behaviors have meaning.

If your memory for past events is actually a mixture of accurate remembrances plus slanted, skewed, and distorted ones, how can you ever know what actually happened?

Here is an example from one author's childhood:

> I recall with the clarity of personal suffering being forced to eat hot breakfast cereal for a lengthy period in my childhood. I recall it vividly and viscerally. I can evoke the dining room, my place, the table, the feeling of revulsion in my throat, the delaying strategies, waiting until the adults tired of me and left me in solitude with my half-completed bowl of now cold caking cereal; my attempts to kill the taste with all the sugar I could overpower it with, and so forth, are still clear to me. To this day I cannot look a bowl of hot oatmeal in the face without this rush of childhood memories going through me. I "know" that I went through months of fighting with my mother over this issue. Several years ago, I discussed it with her. She recalled it clearly, but she "knew" that it was a brief set of events, a few days, perhaps a week or two at best, and she was surprised that I had any memory of it at all. I was left to decide—her memory against mine, my hot-cereal phobia against her sensible, conscious mothering.

What emerged was the realization that neither of us was consciously lying to one another, yet our stories were conspicuously different. There might be no way of ever knowing the actual events. The historical truth was not available; only the memories remained, and those were colored on both sides by the selective repressions and distortions, elaborations and projections that Freud described.

Freud does not suggest any way out of the dilemma; what he does open up is the realization that your memory or your version of your own past holds clues to your own ways of acting and being. It is not simply a record of past events laid out in neat little rows for objective examination.

Psychoanalytic theory offers a set of tools for personal analysis. The tools, which include patient self-examination, reflection, dream analysis, and noting recurrent patterns of thought and behavior, are to be used as you wish. Freud has written of how he used the tools, what he discovered, and what he concluded from his discoveries. Although his conclusions are still a question of debate, his tools are at the core of a dozen other systems and may be the most lasting of his contributions to the study of personality.

THE THEORY FIRSTHAND

The following material comes from one of Freud's early works. Most of it is self-explanatory. It is a glimpse of the way Freud worked with information, the way he pieced together a coherent picture of the cause of a single symptom from a few items of information.

In the summer vacation of the year 189– I made an excursion into the Hohe Tauern[1] so that for a while I might forget medicine and more particularly the neuroses. I had almost succeeded in this when one day I turned aside from the main road to climb a mountain which lay somewhat apart and which was renowned for its views and for its well-run refuge hut. I reached the top after a strenuous climb and, feeling refreshed and rested, was sitting deep in contemplation of the charm of the distant prospect. I was so lost in thought that at first I did not connect it with myself when these words reached my ears: "Are you a doctor, sir?" But the question was addressed to me, and by the rather sulky-looking girl of perhaps eighteen who had served my meal and had been spoken to by the landlady as "Katharina." To judge by her dress and bearing, she could not be a servant, but must no doubt be a daughter or relative of the landlady's.

Coming to myself I replied: "Yes, I'm a doctor: but how did you know that?"

"You wrote your name in the Visitors' Book, sir. And I thought if you had a few moments to spare . . . The truth is, sir, my nerves are bad. I went to see a doctor in L——about them and he gave me something for them; but I'm not well yet."

So there I was with the neuroses once again—for nothing else could very well be the matter with this strong, well-built girl with her unhappy look. I was interested to find that neuroses could flourish in this way at a height of over 6,000 feet; I questioned her further therefore. I report the conversation that followed between us just as it is impressed on my memory and I have not altered the patient's dialect.[2]

"Well, what is it you suffer from?"

"I get so out of breath. Not always. But sometimes it catches me so that I think I shall suffocate."

This did not, at first sight, sound like a nervous symptom. But soon it

[1][One of the highest ranges in the Eastern Alps.]
[2][No attempt has been made in the English translation to imitate this dialect.]

occurred to me that probably it was only a description that stood for an anxiety attack: she was choosing shortness of breath out of the complex of sensations arising from anxiety and laying undue stress on that single factor

"Sit down here. What is it like when you get 'out of breath'?"

"It comes over me all at once. First of all it's like something pressing on my eyes. My head gets so heavy, there's a dreadful buzzing, and I feel so giddy that I almost fall over. Then there's something crushing my chest so that I can't get my breath."

"And you don't notice anything in your throat?"

"My throat's squeezed together as though I were going to choke."

"Does anything else happen in your head?"

"Yes, there's a hammering, enough to burst it."

"And don't you feel at all frightened while this is going on?"

"I always think I'm going to die. I'm brave as a rule and go about everywhere by myself—into the cellar and all over the mountain. But on a day when that happens I don't dare to go anywhere; I think all the time someone's standing behind me and going to catch hold of me all at once."

So it was in fact an anxiety attack, and introduced by the signs of a hysterical "aura"[1]—or, more correctly, it was a hysterical attack the content of which was anxiety. Might there not probably be some other content as well?

"When you have an attack do you think of something? and always the same thing? or do you see something in front of you?"

"Yes. I always see an awful face that looks at me in a dreadful way, so that I'm frightened."

Perhaps this might offer a quick means of getting to the heart of the matter.

"Do you recognize the face? I mean, is it a face that you've really seen some time?"

"No."

"Do you know what your attacks come from?"

"No."

"When did you first have them?"

"Two years ago, while I was still living on the other mountain with my aunt. (She used to run a refuge hut there, and we moved here eighteen months ago.) But they keep on happening."

Was I to make an attempt at analysis? I could not venture to transplant hypnosis to these altitudes, but perhaps I might succeed with a simple talk. I should have to try a lucky guess. I had found often enough that in girls anxiety was a consequence of the horror by which a virginal mind is overcome when it is faced for the first time with the world of sexuality.[2]

So I said: "If you don't know, I'll tell you how *I* think you got your attacks. At that time, two years ago, you must have seen or heard some-

---

[1] [The premonitory sensations preceding an epileptic or hysterical attack.]

[2] I will quote here the case in which I first recognized this causal connection. I was treating a young married woman who was suffering from a complicated neurosis and, once again, was unwilling to admit that her illness arose from her married life. She objected that while she was still a girl she had had attacks of anxiety, ending in fainting fits. I remained firm. When we had come to know each other better she suddenly said to me one day: "I'll tell you now how I came by my attacks of anxiety when I was a girl. At that time I used to sleep in a room next to my parents'; the door was left open and a nightlight used to burn on the table. So more than once I saw my father get into bed with my mother and heard sounds that greatly excited me. It was then that my attacks came on."

thing that very much embarrassed you, and that you'd much rather not have seen."

"Heavens, yes!" she replied, "that was when I caught my uncle with the girl, with Franziska, my cousin."

"What's this story about a girl? Won't you tell me all about it?"

"You can say *anything* to a doctor, I suppose. Well, at that time, you know, my uncle—the husband of the aunt you've seen here—kept the inn on the ———kogel.[1] Now they're divorced, and it's my fault they were divorced, because it was through me that it came out that he was carrying on with Franziska."

"And how did you discover it?"

"This way. One day two years ago some gentlemen had climbed the mountain and asked for something to eat. My aunt wasn't at home, and Franziska, who always did the cooking, was nowhere to be found. And my uncle was not to be found either. We looked everywhere, and at last Alois, the little boy, my cousin, said: 'Why, Franziska must be in Father's room!' And we both laughed; but we weren't thinking anything bad. Then we went to my uncle's room but found it locked. That seemed strange to me. Then Alois said: 'There's a window in the passage where you can look into the room.' We went into the passage; but Alois wouldn't go to the window and said he was afraid. So I said: 'You silly boy! I'll go. I'm not a bit afraid.' And I had nothing bad in my mind. I looked in. The room was rather dark, but I saw my uncle and Franziska; he was lying on her."

"Well?"

"I came away from the window at once, and leant up against the wall and couldn't get my breath—just what happens to me since everything went blank, my eyelids were forced together and there was a hammering and buzzing in my head."

"Did you tell your aunt that very same day?"

"Oh no, I said nothing."

"Then why were you so frightened when you found them together? Did you understand it? Did you know what was going on?"

"Oh no. I didn't understand anything at that time. I was only sixteen. I don't know what I was frightened about."

"Fräulein Katharina, if you could remember now what was happening in you at that time, when you had your first attack, what you thought about it—it would help you."

"Yes, if I could. But I was so frightened that I've forgotten everything."

(Translated into the terminology of our "Preliminary Communication" [p. 12], this means: "The affect itself created a hypnoid state, whose products were then cut off from associative connection with the ego-consciousness.")

"Tell me, Fräulein. Can it be that the head that you always see when you lose your breath is Franziska's head, as you saw it then?"

"Oh no, she didn't look so awful. Besides, it's a man's head."

"Or perhaps your uncle's?"

"I didn't see his face as clearly as that. It was too dark in the room. And why should he have been making such a dreadful face just then?"

"You're quite right."

(The road suddenly seemed blocked. Perhaps something might turn up in the rest of her story.)

---

[1][The name of the "other" mountain.]

"And what happened then?"

"Well, those two must have heard a noise, because they came out soon afterwards. I felt very bad the whole time. I always kept thinking about it. Then two days later it was a Sunday and there was a great deal to do and I worked all day long. And on the Monday morning I felt giddy again and was sick, and I stopped in bed and was sick without stopping for three days."

We [Breuer and I] had often compared the symptomatology of hysteria with a pictographic script which has become intelligible after the discovery of a few bilingual inscriptions. In that alphabet being sick means disgust. So I said: "If you were sick three days later, I believe that means that when you looked into the room you felt disgusted."

"Yes, I'm sure I felt disgusted," she said reflectively, "but disgusted at what?"

"Perhaps you saw something naked? What sort of state were they in?"

"It was too dark to see anything; besides they both of them had their clothes on. Oh, if only I knew what it was I felt disgusted at!"

I had no idea either. But I told her to go and tell me whatever occurred to her, in the confident expectation that she would think of precisely what I needed to explain the case.

Well, she went on to describe how at last she reported her discovery to her aunt, who found that she was changed and suspected her of concealing some secret. There followed some very disagreeable scenes between her uncle and aunt, in the course of which the children came to hear a number of things which opened their eyes in many ways and which it would have been better for them not to have heard. At last her aunt decided to move with her children and niece and take over the present inn, leaving her uncle alone with Franziska, who had meanwhile become pregnant. After this, however, to my astonishment she dropped these threads and began to tell me two sets of older stories, which went back two or three years earlier than the traumatic moment. The first set related to occasions on which the same uncle had made sexual advances to her herself, when she was only fourteen years old. She described how she had once gone with him on an expedition down into the valley in the winter and had spent the night in the inn there. He sat in the bar drinking and playing cards, but she felt sleepy and went up to bed early in the room they were to share on the upper floor. She was not quite asleep when he came up; then she fell asleep again and woke up suddenly "feeling his body" in the bed. She jumped up and remonstrated with him: "What are you up to, Uncle? Why don't you stay in your own bed?" He tried to pacify her: "Go on, you silly girl, keep still. You don't know how nice it is"—"I don't like your 'nice' things; you don't even let one sleep in peace." She remained standing by the door, ready to take refuge outside in the passage, till at last he gave up and went to sleep himself. Then she went back to her own bed and slept till morning. From the way in which she reported having defended herself it seems to follow that she did not clearly recognize the attack as a sexual one. When I asked her if she knew what he was trying to do to her, she replied: "Not at the time." It had become clear to her much later on, she said; she had resisted because it was unpleasant to be disturbed in one's sleep and "because it wasn't nice."

I have been obliged to relate this in detail, because of its great importance for understanding everything that followed.—She went on to tell me of yet other experiences of somewhat later date: how she had once again had to defend herself against him in an inn when he was completely drunk, and similar stories. In answer to a question as to whether on these occasions she had felt anything resembling her later loss of breath, she answered with decision that she had every time felt the pressure on her eyes and chest, but with nothing like the strength that had characterized the scene of discovery.

Immediately she had finished this set of memories she began to tell me a second set, which dealt with occasions on which she had noticed something between her uncle and Franziska. Once the whole family had spent the night in their clothes in a hay loft and she was woken up suddenly by a noise; she thought she noticed that her uncle, who had been lying between her and Franziska, was turning away, and that Franziska was just lying down. Another time they were stopping the night at the inn at the village of N———; she and her uncle were in one room and Franziska in an adjoining one. She woke up suddenly in the night and saw a tall white figure by the door, on the point of turning the handle: "Goodness, is that you, Uncle? What are you doing at the door?"—"Keep quiet. I was only looking for something."—"But the way out's by the *other* door."—"I'd just made a mistake". . . and so on.

I asked her if she had been suspicious at that time. "No, I didn't think anything about it; I only just noticed it and thought no more about it." When I enquired whether she had been frightened on these occasions too, she replied that she thought so, but she was not so sure of it this time.

At the end of these two sets of memories she came to a stop. She was like someone transformed. The sulky, unhappy face had grown lively, her eyes were bright, she was lightened and exalted. Meanwhile the understanding of her case had become clear to me. The later part of what she had told me, in an apparently aimless fashion, provided an admirable explanation of her behaviour at the scene of the discovery. At that time she had carried about with her two sets of experiences which she remembered but did not understand, and from which she drew no inferences. When she caught sight of the couple in intercourse, she at once established a connection between the new impression and these two sets of recollections, she began to understand them and at the same time to fend them off. There then followed a short period of working-out, of "incubation," after which the symptoms of conversion set in, the vomiting as a substitute for moral and physical disgust. This solved the riddle. She had not been disgusted by the sight of the two people but by the memory which that sight had stirred up in her. And, taking everything into account, this could only be the memory of the attempt on her at night when she had "felt her uncle's body."

So when she had finished her confession I said to her: "I know now what it was you thought when you looked into the room. You thought: 'Now he's doing with her what he wanted to do with me that night and those other times.' That was what you were disgusted at, because you remembered the feeling when you woke up in the night and felt his body."

"It may well be," she replied, "that that was what I was disgusted at and that that was what I thought."

"Tell me just one thing more. You're a grown-up girl now and know all sorts of things . . ."

"Yes, now I am."

"Tell me just one thing. What part of his body was it that you felt that night?"

But she gave me no more definite answer. She smiled in an embarrassed way, as though she had been found out, like someone who is obliged to admit that a fundamental position has been reached where there is not much more to be said. I could imagine what the tactile sensation was which she had later learnt to interpret. Her facial expression seemed to me to be saying that she supposed that I was right in my conjecture. But I could not penetrate further, and in any case I owed her a debt of gratitude for having made it so much easier for me to talk to her than to the prudish ladies of my city practice, who regard whatever is natural as shameful.

Thus the case was cleared up.—But stop a moment! What about the recurrent hallucination of the head, which appeared during her attacks and struck terror into her? Where did it come from? I proceeded to ask her about it, and, as though *her* knowledge, too, had been extended by our conversation, she promptly replied: "Yes, I know now. The head is my uncle's head—I recognize it now—but not from *that* time. Later, when all the disputes had broken out, my uncle gave way to a senseless rage against me. He kept saying that it was all my fault: if I hadn't chattered, it would never have come to a divorce. He kept threatening he would do something to me; and if he caught sight of me at a distance his face would get distorted with rage and he would make for me with his hand raised. I always ran away from him, and always felt terrified that he would catch me some time unawares. The face I always see now is his face when he was in a rage."

This information reminded me that her first hysterical symptom, the vomiting, had passed away; the anxiety attack remained and acquired a fresh content. Accordingly, what we were dealing with was a hysteria which had to a considerable extent been abreacted. And in fact she had reported her discovery to her aunt soon after it happened.

"Did you tell your aunt the other stories—about his making advances to you?"

"Yes. Not at once, but later on, when there was already talk of a divorce. My aunt said: "We'll keep that in reserve. If he causes trouble in the Court, we'll say that too.""

I can well understand that it should have been precisely this last period—when there were more and more agitating scenes in the house and when her own state ceased to interest her aunt, who was entirely occupied with the dispute—that it should have been this period of accumulation and retention that left her the legacy of the mnemic symbol [of the hallucinated face].

I hope this girl, whose sexual sensibility had been injured at such an early age, derived some benefit from our conversation. I have not seen her since.[1] [Breurer and Freud, 1895, pp. 125–134]

EXERCISES

Early Memories
Freud found that early memories were often indicative of current personal issues. This exercise is a way for you to begin to evaluate that idea.

[1](*Footnote added* 1924:) I venture after the lapse of so many years to lift the veil of discretion and reveal the fact that Katharina was not the niece but the daughter of the landlady. The girl fell ill, therefore, as a result of sexual attempts on the part of her own father. Distortions like the one which I introduced in the present instance should be altogether avoided in reporting a case history. From the point of view of understanding the case, a distortion of this kind is not, of course, a matter of such indifference as would be shifting the scene from one mountain to another.

1. Divide into pairs. Within each couple decide who will be the speaker and who will be the recorder. You will trade roles so don't worry about who goes first.
2. (For speaker) Sit so you are not looking at the recorder. You are to take 5 minutes to recall your earliest memory or any very early memory. Tell it to the person who is the recorder. The more clearly and vividly you can recall it, the more you may gain from this exercise. If you recall other memories that link up to the one you are describing, feel free to mention them.
3. (For recorder) Your task is to take notes while your partner talks about past memories. Pay attention to the importance your partner puts on any aspect of a memory. If you wish, use the Freudian terms (id, ego, projection, etc.) described in this chapter as you record.
4. After 5 minutes stop and without discussing the exercise switch roles. Again the person who is the speaker relates memories while the partner writes them down.
5. At the end of 5 minutes stop and think about what you have said and what you have heard.
6. Discuss your notes with each other. Point out the implications and connections you observe. Note differences in feelings expressed by your partner. Be aware of possible defense mechanisms distorting or disguising the memories.
7. Try to relate aspects of the memories to current events in your life or how you react now to situations similar to ones you have recalled.

Are There Patterns in Your Life?

Freud suggests that our current relationships are related to our relationships with our parents. Here is a way to investigate the possibility.

I

1. Make a list of some of the people you have liked or loved most in your life—excluding your parents. List men and women separately.
2. List the desirable and the undesirable aspects of their personalities.
3. Notice, reflect on, or write up the similarities and differences in your lists. Do many of the men share certain traits while the women share other traits? Is there a particular type of person you enjoy?

II

1. List the desirable and undesirable characteristics of your parents as they are right now.
2. List the desirable and undesirable characteristics of your parents as you saw them when you were growing up.

III

1. Compare and contrast the list of attributes of your parents with those of your friends.
2. Consider, discuss, or write up any relationships between the qualities of your parents and your friends.

Dream Journal

1. Keep a pad of paper by your bed. In the morning, *before* you do anything else, make a few notes about your dreams. (Even if you have never remembered dreams before, this procedure will probably help you to recall them. Groups of students given this as a forced assignment were all recalling dreams regularly within a few days.)
2. Later in the day write up your dream fully.
3. Try to understand what various segments of your dreams might mean. Pay attention to those fragments that seem to be part of your "day residue." Are there any parts to the dream that reflect your own desires or attitudes toward others? Do your dreams seem to be meaningful for you?

    What are your associations with particular aspects of your dreams? See if these associations point to possible meanings of the dream. How might the dreams constitute attempts at "wish-fulfillment"?
4. Keep this journal for several weeks, As you read other parts of this text, you will learn about other ways of looking at dreams. From time to time, go over your dream book and see if you can make new interpretations. Can you notice any recurrent themes or patterns in your dreams?

Defense Mechanisms

1. Recall a time or an event that was psychologically painful; perhaps the death of a close friend or relative or a time when you were deeply humiliated, beaten up, or caught in a crime.
2. Notice first your disinterest in recalling the events clearly, your resistance to even thinking about it. "I don't want to do this. I can skip that exercise, it's easy to understand. Why should I think about that again?"
3. If you can, overcome your initial defenses with an act of will and recall the event. You may be aware of strong feelings all over again.
4. If it is difficult to stay focused on the memory, notice instead the ways your mind keeps sending your attention away on side trips. Can you begin to see how you avoid psychic tension?

Psychosexual Stages
The following exercises will give you a chance to experience the ideas, attitudes, and feelings of each developmental stage.

Oral
Go to a drugstore and buy a baby bottle with a nipple. Fill it with milk, water, or fruit juice.

Either alone or with other members of this class drink from the bottle. Be aware of your reactions. Does the drinking or even the thought of drinking from a bottle bring up any memories, any feelings? If you go ahead and do it, what postures are you most comfortable in? Allow yourself to experience your undampened reactions to this experiment.

Compare your reactions with others. Are there experiences common to men? Women?

Anal

Try to become more aware of the way privacy is built into bathroom architecture, public lavatories, your bathroom at home. Notice your own behavior in a school's men's or women's room. Do you strive to remain isolated, not meeting anyone's eyes or really even looking at anyone else?

Can you imagine urinating in public? In a park? By the side of the highway? In a forest?

Many people have very strongly conditioned toilet behaviors. Some people must read while sitting on a toilet. What might be the purpose of this behavior?

Share some of your observations with others. Become aware of your resistance to talking about aspects of this exercise.

Phallic

Can you remember your initial memories of your sex organs? Can you recall what your parents said to you about them? (Women) Can you recall any thoughts or ideas you had about boys and their penises? (Men) Can you ever recall fearing that you might lose your penis?

If you have no memories of these kinds of feelings, is that sufficient reason to assume that there were no such feelings at the time?

Genital

1. Write up the misinformation you had about sexual matters that has been subsequently corrected. (Examples: You were brought by the stork, or found at the supermarket. Every time you have intercourse it leads to pregnancy.)
2. Did your early sexual experiences change your attitudes or beliefs about your own sexuality? Did they reinforce previously held beliefs? How did you feel about your first sexual experience? Do you feel differently now? Can you relate your present attitudes about sexual matters to earlier attitudes or beliefs?

ANNOTATED BIBLIOGRAPHY

Books by Freud

Freud, Sigmund. *The interpretation of dreams.* Standard edition (Vols. 4, 5). (Originally published, 1900.)* Freud said of it in 1931: "It contains, even according to my present-day judgment, the most valuable of all the discoveries it has been my good fortune to make." We agree. The best of Freud; read it to appreciate his intuitive genius and his writing style.
———. *Introductory lectures on psychoanalysis.* Standard edition (Vols. 15, 16). (Originally published, 1916–1917.) Two courses of lectures given at the University of Vienna. The first part of the book assumes no knowledge of the subject; the second part assumes you are familiar with the first. Lectures to and for students.

*The date in parentheses after each reference by Freud is the original date of publication in German. When possible, references have been listed as they appear in James Strachey (Ed), *The Standard Edition of the Complete Psychological Works of Sigmund Freud* (Vols. 1–24). London: Hogarth Press, 1953–1966. Other editions are mentioned only if used for citations in the text. Most of Freud's writings are available in a variety of inexpensive editions.

———. *A general selection from the works of Sigmund Freud.* (John Rickman, Ed.). New York: Doubleday, 1957. A good set of readings taken from different parts of Freud's work. There are other collections that may be as good. We like this one.

———. *Three case histories.* New York: Collier Books, 1963. Three cases that Freud analyzed. He presents material from the cases, interweaving it with his developing theory. As close to seeing Freud in action as can be gleaned from his writings.

Books About Freud and His Ideas

Engleman, Edmund. *Berggasse 19: Sigmund Freud's home and offices, Vienna, 1938.* Chicago: University of Chicago Press, 1981. A collection of photos of Freud's working and living spaces with a short moving essay about the man.

Hall, Calvin S. A *A primer of Freudian psychology.* New York: New American Library (Mentor Books), 1954. A short, readable, and lucid exposition of the major features of Freud's theories. It is compact and accurate. The best easy introduction available.

Hall, Calvin, & Lindzey, Gardner. The relevance of Freudian psychology and related viewpoints for the social sciences. In *The handbook of social psychology* (2nd ed.). G. Lindzey & E. Arronson (Eds.), Menlo Park, Calif: Addison-Wesley, 1968. An intermediate-level summary of psychoanalytic thinking with emphasis on its relevance to social psychology. A theoretical rather than clinical focus.

Jones, Ernest. *The life and work of Sigmund Freud* (Lionel Trilling, Ed.). New York: Doubleday, 1963. A short version of the three-volume standard biography of Freud. Readable and fascinating.

Rapaport, David. The structure of psychoanalytic theory. In S. Koch (Ed.), *Formulations of the person and the social context* (Vol. 3). Psychology: The study of a science. New York: McGraw-Hill, 1959. Among the most sophisticated and complete theoretical statements of psychoanalytic thinking. Not for the faint-hearted.

Sulloway, Frank J. *Freud, biologist of the mind: Beyond the psychoanalytic legend.* New York: Basic Books, 1979. Suggests that Freud was more aligned with biology than with psychology. A more human, less heroic view of him than usual, solidly based on historical documents. Disagrees with Jones on matters of fact and opinion. Endless references.

Psychoanalytic Books About Women

Mitchell, Juliet. *Psychoanalysis and feminism.* New York: Pantheon, 1974. Mitchell explores at length the usefulness of psychoanalytic theory in contributing to an understanding of women's psychology in Western, male-dominated society. Mitchell is strongly and openly a feminist, and it is as a feminist that she examines psychoanalysis as put forth by Freud and various theorists since Freud. A critique of various feminist critiques of these same theories—psychoanalysis in particular—is offered.

Ruitenbeck, Hendrik M. (Ed.) *Psychoanalysis and female sexuality.* New Haven, Conn.: College and University Press, 1966. A collection of psychoanalytic papers on female sexuality. Included are essays by Jones, Thompson, Horney, Freud, Greenacre, Riviere, and, somewhat surprisingly, Maslow.

REFERENCES

Auden, W. H. *The collected poems of W. H. Auden.* New York: Random House, 1945.

Bettelheim, Bruno. Reflections: Freud and the soul. *The New Yorker.* March 1, 1982, pp. 52–93.

Bonaparte, Maria (ed.) The origins of psychoanalysis: Letters to Wilhelm Fliess. London: Imago, 1954.

Breuer, Joseph, & Freud, Sigmund. *Studies in Hysteria.* Standard edition (Vol. 2). (Originally published, 1895.).

Bruner, Jerome. Freud and the image of man. *Partisan Review,* 1956, *23;* 340–347.

Byck, Robert (Ed.). *Cocaine papers by Sigmund Freud.* New York: New American library, 1975.

Cohen, Marilyn. Putting energy back into Freud. California Institute of Transpersonal Psychology. Unpublished, 1982.

Colby, Kenneth Mark. *A primer for psychotherapists.* New York: Ronald Press, 1951.

Farber, Leslie H. *The ways of the will: Essays toward a psychology and psycho-pathology of will.* New York: Harper & Row, 1966.

Fenichel, Otto. *The psychoanalytic theory of neurosis.* New York: Norton, 1945.

Fliegel, Zenia Odes. Feminine psychosexual development in Freudian theory; a historical reconstruction. *The Psychoanalytic Quarterly,* 1973, 42(3), 385–408.

Fodor, Nandor, & Gaynor, Frank. *Freud: Dictionary of psychoanalysis.* New York: Fawcett Books, 1958.

Freud, Anna. *The ego and the mechanisms of defense.* London: Hogarth Press, 1936.

Freud, Ernst. *Letters of Sigmund Freud.* New York, Basic Books, 1961.

Freud, Sigmund. *The neuro-psychoses of defense.* Standard edition (Vol. 3). (Originally published, 1894.)

———. *The interpretation of dreams.* Standard edition (Vols. 4–5). (Originally published, 1900.)

———. *The psychopathology of everyday life.* Standard edition (Vol. 6). (Originally published, 1901.)

———. Three essays on the theory of sexuality. Standard edition (Vol. 7). (Originally published, 1905a.)

———. Fragment of an analysis of a case of hysteria. Standard edition (Vol. 8). (Originally published, 1905b.)

———. Psycho-analysis and the establishment of the facts in legal proceedings. Standard edition (Vol. 9). (Originally published, 1906.)

———. Obsessive actions and religious practices. Standard edition (Vol. 9). (Originally published, 1907.)

———. "Civilized" sexual morality and modern nervous illness. Standard edition (Vol. 9). (Originally published, 1908.)

———. Notes upon a case of obsessional neurosis. Standard edition (Vol. 10). (Originally published, 1909.)

———. Five lectures on psycho-analysis. Standard edition (Vol. 11). (Originally published, 1910.)

———. Formulations on the two principles of mental functioning. Standard edition (Vol. 12). (Originally published, 1911.)

———. On the history of the psycho-analytic movement. Standard edition (Vol. 14). (Originally published, 1914.)

———. Repression. Standard edition (Vol. 14). (Originally published, 1915.)

————. Introductory lectures on psycho-analysis (part III). Standard edition (Vol. 16). (Originally published, 1916.)

————. On the transformations of instinct, as exemplified in anal eroticism. Standard edition (Vol. 17). (Originally published, 1917.)

————. Lines of advance in psycho-analytic therapy. Standard edition (Vol. 17). (Originally published, 1919.)

————. Beyond the pleasure principle. Standard edition (Vol. 18). (Originally published, 1920.)

————. Two encyclopedia articles. Standard edition (Vol. 18). (Originally published, 1923.)

————. *An autobiographical study.* Standard edition (Vol. 20). (Originally published, 1925a). Also, *Autobiography.* New York: Norton, 1935. York: Norton, 1935.

————. The question of lay analysis. Standard edition (Vol. 20). (Originally published, 1926.)

————. Some psychical consequences of the anatomical distinctions between the sexes. Standard edition (Vol. 19). (Originally published, 1925b.)

————. *Civilization and its discontents.* Standard edition (Vol. 21). (Originally published, 1930.)

————. *New introductory lectures on psycho-analysis.* Standard edition (Vol. 22). (Originally published, 1933.) Also, New York: Norton, 1949.

————. Analysis terminable and interminable. Standard edition (Vol. 23). (Originally published, 1937.)

————. *An outline of psycho-analysis.* Standard edition (Vol. 23). (Originally published, 1940.) Also, New York: Norton, 1949.

————. *The origins of psychoanalysis* (including 1895, A project for a scientific psychology), London: Hogarth Press, 1950.

————. *The cocaine papers.* Zurich: Duquin Press, 1963 (Papers not found in the Standard edition, originally published 1884–1887.)

Fromm, Erich. *Sigmund Freud's mission: An analysis of his personality and influence.* New York: Harper & Row, 1959.

Hall, Calvin S. *A primer of Freudian psychology.* New York: New American Library (Mentor Books), 1954.

Halt, Robert R. A review of some of Freud's biological assumptions and their influence on his theories. In Norman S. Greenfield & William C. Lewis (Eds.), *Psychoanalysis and current biological thought.* Madison: University of Wisconsin Press, 1965.

Horney, Karen. The flight from womanhood. In Harold Kelman (Ed.), *Feminine Psychology.* New York: Norton, 1967. (Originally published, 1926.)

————. *New ways in psychoanalysis.* New York: Norton, 1939.

Jones. Ernest. The early development of female sexuality. In H. Ruitenbeck (Ed.), *Psychoanalysis and female sexuality.* New Haven, Conn.: College and University Press, 1966. (Originally published, 1927.)

————. *The life and work of Sigmund Freud* (3 vols.). New York: Basic Books, 1953, 1955, 1957.

Krishna, Gopi. *Higher consciousness: The evolutionary thrust of kundalini.* New York: Julian Press, 1974.

Le Barre, Weston. Personality from a psychoanalytic viewpoint. In E. Norbeck, D. Price-Williams, & W. McCord (Eds.), *The study of personality: An interdisciplinary appraisal.* New York: Holt, Rinehart and Winston, 1968, pp. 65–87.

La Planche, J., & Pontalis, J. B. *The language of psychoanalysis.* (Donald Nicholson-Smith, Trans.). New York: Norton, 1973.

Lauzan, Gerard. *Sigmund Freud: The man and his theories.* (Patrick Evans, Trans.). New York: Fawcett, 1962.

McGuire, William (Ed.). *The Freud/Jung letters.* Bollingen Series XCIV. Princeton, N.J.: Princeton University Press, 1974.

Malcolm, Janet. The impossible profession. *The New Yorker,* part I, November 24; part II, December 1, 1980.

Masserman, Jules H. *Principles of dynamic psychiatry* (2nd ed.). Philadelphia: Saunders, 1961.

Rachman, S. J., & Wilson, G. T. *The effects of psychological therapy* (2nd ed.). New York: Pergamon Press, 1980.

Rycroft, Charles. *Wilhelm Reich.* New York: Viking, 1972.

Sears, Robert T. Experimental studies of projection: I. Attributions of traits. *Journal of Social Psychology,* 1936, 7, 151–163.

Shah, Idries. *The magic monastery.* New York: Dutton, 1972.

Wollheim, Richard. *Sigmund Freud.* New York: Viking Press, 1971.

CHAPTER 2
CARL GUSTAV JUNG
AND
ANALYTIC PSYCHOLOGY

Jungian psychology focuses on establishing and fostering the relationship between the conscious and the unconscious processes and improving the dynamic interchange between them. Dialogue between the conscious and unconscious aspects of the psyche enriches the person, as the unconscious is heard and understood in consciousness. Without this dialogue, unconscious processes can weaken and jeopardize the personality.

One of Jung's central concepts is *individuation,* his term for a process of personal development that involves establishing a connection between the ego and the self. The ego is the center of consciousness; the self is the center of the total psyche, including both consciousness and the unconscious. For Jung, there is constant interplay between consciousness and the unconscious. The two are not separate; they are two aspects of a single system. Individuation is a process of developing wholeness through integrating all the various parts of the psyche.

Whereas Jung by no means ignored the negative, maladaptive side of human nature, his greatest efforts were devoted to investigating the farther reaches of human aspiration and achievement. Jung's analysis of human nature includes investigations of Eastern and Western religions, alchemy, parapsychology, and mythology. His initial impact was greater on philosophers, folklorists, and writers than on psychologists or psychiatrists. Today, however, growing concern with human consciousness and human potential has caused a resurgence of interest in Jung's ideas.

> I can only hope and wish that no one becomes "Jungian" . . . I proclaim no cut-and-dried doctrine and I abhor "blind adherence." I leave everyone free to deal with the facts in his own way, since I also claim this freedom for myself. [Jung, 1973, p. 405]

PERSONAL HISTORY

Carl Gustav Jung was born in Switzerland on July 26, 1875. His father and several close relatives were pastors, and thus even as a child Jung was deeply concerned with religious and spiritual questions. In his autobiography, *Memories, Dreams, Reflections* (1961), Jung relates two extremely powerful early experiences that strongly influenced his attitude toward religion. Between ages 3 and 4 he dreamed of a terrifying phallic image standing on a throne in an underground chamber. The dream haunted Jung for years. It was not until many years later that he realized the image was a ritual phallus; it represented a hidden, "subterranean God" that was more frightful yet much more real and powerful for Jung than Jesus and the church.

The second experience occurred when Jung was 12. He came out of school at noon and saw the sun sparkling on the roof of the Basel church. He reflected on the beauty of the world, the splendor of the church, and the majesty of God sitting high up in the sky on a golden throne. Jung then was suddenly gripped with terror at where his thoughts were leading, and he refused to let himself pursue his train of thought, which he felt was highly sacrilegious. He struggled desperately for several days to suppress the forbidden thought. Finally, Jung allowed himself to complete his thought; he saw the beautiful cathedral and God seated on his throne high above the world, and from under the throne came an enormous turd which fell on the cathedral roof, shattered it, and broke the walls of the cathedral.

In some ways it may be hard for us today to imagine the terrifying power of Jung's vision. Given the conventional pietism and lack of psychological sophistication in 1887, such thoughts were not merely unutterable, they were unthinkable. However, following his vision, Jung felt an enormous relief and a sense of grace instead of the expected damnation. He interpreted his experience as a trial sent by God to show him that fulfilling the will of God may even cause one to go against the church or the most sacred of traditions. From that time on, Jung felt far removed from the conventional piety of his father and his pastoral relatives. He saw how most people cut themselves off from direct religious experience by remaining bound by the letter of church convention instead of seriously considering the spirit of God as a living reality.

Partly as a result of his inner experiences, Jung felt himself isolated from other people; sometimes he felt almost unendurably lonely. School bored him; however, he developed a passion for reading, an "absolute craving . . . to read every scrap of printed matter that fell into my hands" (Jung, 1961, p. 30).

When it came time to enter the university, Jung chose to study medicine as a compromise between his interests in both science and humanities. He became attracted to psychiatry as the study of "diseases of the personality" (although in those days psychiatry was relatively undeveloped and undistinguished); he realized that psychiatry in particular involved both scientific and humanistic perspectives. Jung also developed an interest in psychic phenomena and investigated the messages received by a local medium for his thesis, "On the psychology and pathology of so-called occult phenomena."

In 1900 Jung became an intern at the Burghölzli Medical Hospital in Zurich, one of the most progressive psychiatric centers in Europe. Zurich became his permanent home.

In 1904 Jung set up an experimental laboratory at the Psychiatric Clinic and developed the word association test for psychiatric diagnostic purposes. In this test the subject is asked to respond to a standard list of stimulus words; any inordinate delay between the stimulus and the response is taken as an indicator of emotional stress related in some way to the stimulus word. Jung also became skillful at interpreting the psychological meanings behind the various associations produced. In 1905, at age 30, he became lecturer in psychiatry at the University of Zurich and senior physician at the Psychiatric Clinic.

Despite the strong criticisms leveled at Freud in scientific and academic circles, Jung became convinced of the value of Freud's work.

Nobody could rob me of the conviction that it was enjoined upon me to do what God wanted and not what I wanted . . . often I had the feeling that in all decisive matters I was no longer among men but was alone with God. [Jung, 1961, p. 48]

Freud was the first man of real importance I had encountered. [Jung, 1961, p. 149]

He sent Freud copies of his articles and of his first book, *The Psychology of Dementia Praecox* (1907), following which Freud invited him to Vienna. At their first meeting, the two men talked virtually without pause for 13 hours. They corresponded weekly after that, and Freud came to consider Jung his logical successor.

Despite their close friendship, the two men had fundamental disagreements. Jung was never able to accept Freud's insistence that the causes of repression are always sexual trauma. Freud, for his part, was always uneasy with Jung's interest in mythological, spiritual, and occult phenomena. The two men had a clear break (1912) when Jung published *Symbols of Transformation,* which included his analysis of libido as generalized psychic energy as well as other ideas that varied from Freud. The break was a painful, traumatic one for Jung, but he was determined to stand behind his own convictions.

Jung gradually developed his own theories of unconscious processes and dream-symbol analysis. He came to realize that his procedures for analyzing the dream symbols of his patients could also be applied to the analysis of other forms of symbolism—that he held a key to the interpretation of myths, folktales, religious symbols, and art.

Dreams bring to light material which cannot have originated either from the dreamer's adult life or from his forgotten childhood. We are obliged to regard it as part of the *archaic heritage* which a child brings with him into the world, before any experience of his own, influenced by the experiences of his ancestors. We find the counterpart of this philogenetic material in the earliest human legends and in surviving customs. [Freud, 1964, p. 177]

His interest in fundamental psychological processes turned Jung to the study of the ancient Western traditions of alchemy and Gnosticism (a Hellenistic religious and philosophical tradition), and also to the investigation of non-European cultures. Jung made two trips to Africa, and he traveled to New Mexico to visit the Pueblo Indians. Jung also went to India, and he was a serious student of Indian, Chinese, and Tibetan thought.

In 1944, when he was 69, Jung nearly died following a severe heart atack. In the hospital he experienced a powerful vision in which he seemed to be floating high in space, 1,000 miles above the earth, with Ceylon below his feet, India lying ahead of him, and the desert of Arabia off to the left. Jung then entered a great block of stone that was also floating in space. A temple had been hollowed out of the giant block; and as he approached the steps leading to the entrance Jung felt that everything was left behind him, and all that remained of his earthly existence was his own experience, his life's history. He saw his life as part of a great historical matrix of which he had never before been aware. Before he could enter the temple, Jung was confronted by his doctor, who told him he had no right to leave the earth at that time. At that moment, the vision ceased.

For weeks after, as Jung gradually recovered from his illness, he was weak and depressed by day but would awaken each night around midnight with a feeling of deep ecstasy, feeling as if he were floating in a bliss-filled world. His nightly visions would last for about an hour and then he would again fall asleep.

After he recovered, Jung entered a highly productive period in which he wrote many of his most important works. His visions gave him the courage to formulate some of his most original ideas. These experiences also changed Jung's personal outlook to a more deeply affirmative attitude toward his own destiny. "I might formulate it as an affirmation of things as they are: an unconditional 'yes' to that which is, without subjective protests—acceptance of the conditions of existence as I see them and understand them, acceptance of my own nature, as I happen to be. . . . In this way we forge an ego that does not break down when incomprehensible things happen; an ego that endures the truth, and that is capable of coping with the world and with fate" (Jung, 1961, p. 297).

Jung died on June 6, 1961, at the age of 86, after a lifetime of clinical practice, research, and writing.

INTELLECTUAL ANTECEDENTS

Freud

Although Jung was already a practicing psychiatrist before he met Freud, Freud's theories were clearly among the strongest influences on his thinking. Freud's *The Interpretation of Dreams* (1900) inspired Jung to attempt his own approach to dream and symbol analysis. Freud's theories of unconscious processes also gave Jung his first glimpse into the possibilities of systematically analyzing the dynamics of mental functioning, rather than relying on the superficial classification schemes that typified psychiatry at that time. Jung acknowledged the validity of Freud's achievements in the area of psychopathology; however, he felt that his own theoretical efforts could be devoted more to issues concerning positive growth and individuation.

Jung has written that "Freud's greatest achievement probably consisted in taking neurotic patients seriously and entering into their peculiar individual psychology. He had the courage to let the case material speak for itself, and in this way was able to penetrate into the real psychology of his patients. . . . By evaluating dreams as the most important source of information concerning the unconscious processes, he gave back to mankind a tool that had seemed irretrievably lost" (1961, pp. 168–169).

Jung's conception of the personal unconscious is similar to the unconscious in psychoanalytic theory. The personal unconscious is composed of forgotten memories, repressed experiences, and subliminal perceptions.

Jung also formulated the concept of the collective unconscious, also known as the impersonal or transpersonal unconscious. Its contents are universal and not rooted in our personal experience. This con-

To understand is my one great passion. But I also possess the physician's instinct. I would like to help people. (Jung, 1961, p. 322)

When people say I am wise, or a sage, I cannot accept it. A man once dipped a hatful of water from a stream. What did that amount to? I am not that stream. I am at the stream, but I do nothing. [Jung, 1961, p. 355]

The unconscious is on no account an empty sack in which the refuse of consciousness is collected . . . it is the whole other half of the living psyche. [Jung, 1973, p. 143]

cept is perhaps Jung's greatest departure from Freud as well as his major contribution to psychology. (See the section on Major Concepts.)

Literature

Jung was extremely well read in philosophy and literature. As a young man he was deeply impressed by Goethe. Goethe's *Faust* was a major influence on Jung's conceptualization of the search for individual development and provided insight into the power of evil and its relation to growth and self-insight.

Nietzsche also had a profound effect on him. Jung felt that Nietzsche's work possessed great psychological insight even though his fascination with power tended to overshadow his portrait of the mature and free human being. Jung saw Nietzsche and Freud as representatives of the two greatest themes in Western culture—power and eros. However, he felt that both men had become so deeply involved with these two vital themes that they were almost obsessed by them.

Alchemy

Jung searched for Western traditions that dealt with the development of consciousness. He was especially interested in the symbols and concepts used to describe this process. Jung discovered the Western alchemical literature, long ignored as magical, prescientific nonsense. He interpreted the alchemical treatises as representations of inner change and purification disguised in chemical and magical metaphors. The transformation of base metals into gold, for example, can be seen as a metaphor for the reformation of the personality and consciousness in the process of individuation. "Only after I had familiarized myself with alchemy did I realize that the unconscious is a process, and that the psyche is transformed or developed by the relationship of the ego to the content of the unconscious" (Jung, 1936, p. 482).

Eastern Thought

The Golden Flower is a mandala symbol which I have often met with in the material brought me by my patients. It is drawn either seen from above as a regular geometric ornament, or as a blossom growing from a plant. The plant is frequently a structure in brilliant fiery colours growing out of a bed of darkness, and carrying the blossom of light at the top . . . [Jung in Wilhelm & Jung, 1962, p. 101]

In pursuing his researches into myth and symbolism, Jung developed his own theories concerning individuation or personality integration. Jung subsequently became deeply impressed with various Eastern traditions that provided the first outside confirmation of many of his own ideas, especially his concept of individuation.

Richard Wilhelm, a German scholar who lived in China for many years, sent Jung the manuscript of his translation of an ancient Chinese spiritual text phrased in alchemical terms (*The Secret of the Golden Flower*, 1962). Jung discovered that Eastern descriptions of spiritual growth, inner psychic development, and integration closely corresponded to the process of individuation that he had observed in his Western patients.

The Eastern concept of the mandala also strongly influenced Jung's thought. Mandala is the Sanskrit word for circle or a circular design or diagram frequently used in meditation and other spiritual practices. Jung found that his analysands spontaneously produced mandala drawings even though they were completely unfamiliar with Eastern art or philosophy. For Jung, the mandala symbolizes the process of individuation; it tends to appear in the drawings of analysands who have made considerable progress in their own personal growth. The center of the drawing stands for the self, which comes to replace the limited ego as the center of the personality; and the circular diagram as a whole represents the balance and order that develops in the psyche as the individuation process progresses.

Jung was also careful to point out important differences between Eastern and Western paths of individuation. The social and cultural framework in which the process of growth takes place differs greatly in the East and the West, as do the prevailing attitudes toward the concept of individuation and those who actively seek this goal. The desirability of inner development and enlightenment is widely accepted in the East, where there are clearly recognized paths and techniques for facilitating the process.

However, Jung believed that such systematization of growth processes had its own dangers.

> Centuries ago Yoga congealed into a fixed system, but originally the mandala symbolism grew out of the unconscious just as individually and directly as it does with Western man today. . . . Yoga, however, as we know it today, has become a method of spiritual training which is drilled into the initiands from above . . . that is the exact opposite of what I do. [Jung, 1973, pp. 196–197]

Jung sought to develop his own theories first, and carefully avoided imitating Eastern thinking. After returning from his trip to India, Jung wrote,

> I studiously avoided all so-called "holy men." I did so because I had to make do with my own truth, not accept from others what I could not attain on my own. I would have felt it as a theft had I attempted to learn from the holy men and to accept their truth for myself. [Jung, 1961, p. 275]

Jung has argued that Eastern paths to individuation, such as Yoga and Buddhism, are generally unsuitable for Westerners. He felt that the cultural contexts and attitudes related to these practices are in many ways alien to those born and raised in the West. Those Westerners who have pursued Eastern disciplines have tended to deny their Western heritage, attempting to imitate as much of Eastern culture as possible and cutting themselves off from important parts of their own psyches.

Jung's observations may have been more true for his day than ours (as thousands of Westerners today are pursuing Eastern spiritual disciplines in a serious, balanced, and grounded manner). The dated nature of Jung's attitude toward Eastern thought is clear in his fore-

Follow that will and that way which experience confirms to be your own, i.e. the true expression of your individuality. [Jung in Serrano, 1966, p. 83]

word to D. T. Suzuki's *Introduction to Zen Buddhism*. "Great as is the value of Zen Buddhism for the understanding of the religious transformation process, its use among Western people is very improbable. The spiritual conceptions necessary to Zen are missing in the West" (Jung in Suzuki, 1964). Jung's emphasis on our need to retain our connection with the deep psychic roots of our Western heritage merits serious consideration as so many people turn East for spiritual guidance.

MAJOR CONCEPTS

The Attitudes: Introversion and Extraversion

Among all of Jung's concepts, *introversion* and *extraversion* have probably gained widest general use. Jung found that each individual can be characterized as being either primarily inwardly or outwardly oriented. Introverts' energy flows more naturally toward their inner world, while extraverts' energy is more focused on the outer world.

The path to wholeness is made up of fateful detours and wrong turnings. (Jung, 1961, p. 325)

No one is a pure introvert or a pure extravert. Jung compared these two processes to the heartbeat—there is a rhythmic alternation between the cycle of contraction (introversion) and the cycle of expansion (extraversion). However, each individual tends to favor one or the other attitude and operates more often in terms of the favored attitude.

At times introversion is more appropriate; at other times extraversion is more suitable. The two are mutually exclusive; you cannot hold both an introverted and an extraverted attitude concurrently. Neither one is better than the other. The ideal is to be flexible and to be able to adopt either attitude when it is most appropriate—to operate in terms of a dynamic balance between the two and not develop a fixed way of responding to the world.

Introverts are interested primarily in their own thoughts and feelings, in their inner world. They tend to be deeply introspective. One danger for such people is that they may become too immersed in their inner world, losing touch with the outer environment. The absent-minded professor is a clear, if stereotypic, example.

Extraverts are concerned with the outer world of people and things; they tend to be more social and more aware of what is going on around them. They need to guard against becoming dominated by externals and alienated from their internal processes. Riesman (1950) discusses this tendency in his description of other-directed individuals, who rely almost completely on the ideas and opinions of others rather than develop their own opinions.

Introverts see the world in terms of how it affects them, whereas extraverts are more concerned with their impact upon the world.

The Functions: Thinking, Feeling, Sensation, Intuition

Jung identified four fundamental psychological functions: thinking, feeling, sensation, and intuition. Each function may be experienced in an introverted or extraverted fashion. Generally, two of the functions are more conscious, developed, and dominant; the other two are less conscious and less developed.

Thinking and feeling are alternative ways of forming judgments and making decisions. *Thinking* is concerned with objective truth, with judgments derived from impersonal, logical criteria. Consistency and abstract principles are highly valued. Thinking types (those individuals in whom the thinking function predominates) are the greatest planners; they do, however, tend to hold on to their plans and theories even when confronted by new and contradictory evidence.

Feeling is making decisions according to one's value judgments, for instance, good or bad, right or wrong, agreeable or disagreeable (as opposed to decision making according to criteria of logic or efficiency, as in thinking). Feeling types are oriented to the emotional aspects of experience. They prefer strong intense emotions, even negative ones, to "bland" experiences.

Jung classifies sensation and intuition together as ways of gathering information, as opposed to ways of making decisions. *Sensation* refers to a focus on direct experience, perception of details, concrete facts: what one can see, touch, smell. Tangible concrete experience is given priority over discussion or analysis of experience. Sensing types tend to respond to the immediate situation and deal effectively and efficiently with all sorts of crises and emergencies. They generally work better with tools and materials than any of the other types.

Intuition is a way of processing information in terms of past experience, future goals, and unconscious processes. The implications of experience (what *might* happen, what is possible) are more important to intuitives than the actual experience itself. Strongly intuitive people add meaning to their perceptions so rapidly that they often cannot separate their interpretations from the raw sensory data. Intuitives process information quickly, automatically relating past experience and relevant information to immediate experience. Because their processing often includes unconscious material, their thinking appears to proceed by leaps and bounds.

For the individual, a combination of all four functions results in a well-rounded approach to the world. "In order to orient ourselves, we must have a function which ascertains that something is there (sensation); a second function which establishes *what* is (thinking); a third function which states whether it suits us or not, whether we wish to accept it or not (feeling); and a fourth function which indicates where it came from and where it is going (intuition)" (Jung, 1942, p. 167).

Unfortunately, no one develops all four functions equally well. Everyone has one very strong dominant function and one partially developed auxiliary function. The other two functions are generally unconscious and operate with considerably less effectiveness. The more

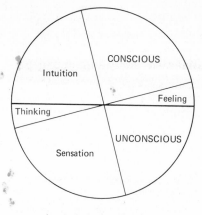
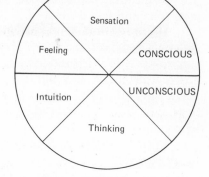

1a. An intuitive-feeling type
(intuition strongly developed; feeling less so)

1b. A sensation-feeling type
(both sensation and feeling well developed)

Figure 2.1 Examples of Jung's Functional Typology. Functions above the horizontal line are the better-developed, more conscious functions, and those below the line less developed, less conscious.

developed and conscious the dominant and auxiliary functions, the more deeply unconscious are their opposites. (See Figure 2.1.)

Our function type indicates our relative strengths and weaknesses and the style of activity we tend to prefer. Jung's typology is especially useful in relating to others, in helping us understand social relationships; it describes how people perceive in alternate ways and use different criteria in acting and making judgments. For example, intuitive-feeling speakers will not have the same logical, tightly organized, and detailed lecture style as thinking-sensation lecturers. The talks of the former are more likely to ramble, to give the sense of an issue by approaching it from many different angles, rather than developing it systematically.

Jung has called the least developed function in each individual the "inferior function." This function is the least conscious and the most primitive, or undifferentiated. It can represent a seemingly demonic influence for some people because they have so little understanding of or control over it. For example, strongly intuitive types may find that sexual impulses seem mysterious or even dangerously out of control because they are so much out of touch with their sensation function. Because it is less consciously developed, the inferior function may also serve as a way into the unconscious.

Collective Unconscious

Our unconscious mind, like our body, is a storehouse of relics and

Jung writes that we are born with a psychological heritage, as well as our biological heritage. Both are important determinants of behavior and experience. "Just as the human body represents a whole museum of organs, each with a long evolutionary period behind it, so we should expect to find that the mind is organized in a similar way. It can no more be a product without history than is the body in which it exists" (Jung, 1964, p. 67).

The collective, or transpersonal, unconscious includes psychic materials that do not come from personal experience. Some psychologists, such as Skinner, implicitly assume that each individual is born like a blank slate, a tabula rasa; consequently, all psychological development can come only from personal experience. Jung postulates that the mind of the infant already possesses a structure that molds and channels all further development and interaction with the environment. This basic structure is essentially the same in all infants. Although we each develop differently and become unique individuals, the collective unconscious is common to all people and is therefore one (Jung, 1951).

> The collective unconscious contains the whole spiritual heritage of mankind's evolution, born anew in the brain structure of every individual. His conscious mind is an ephemeral phenomenon that accomplishes all provisional adaptations and orientations. . . . The unconscious, on the other hand, is the source of the instinctual forces of the psyche. . . . All the most powerful ideas in history go back to archetypes. [Jung in Campbell, 1971, p. 45]

Jung's approach to the collective unconscious can be seen in the following passage from a letter to one of his analysands:

> You trust your unconscious as if it were a loving father. But it is *nature* and cannot be made use of as if it were a reliable human being. It is *inhuman* and it needs the human mind to function usefully for man's purposes. . . . It always seeks its collective purposes and never your individual destiny. Your destiny is the result of the collaboration between the conscious and the unconscious. [Jung, 1973, p. 283, italics his]

Archetype

Within the collective unconscious are psychic structures, or archetypes. These are forms, without content of their own, that serve to organize or channel psychological material. They are somewhat like dry stream beds whose shape determines the characteristics of a river once water begins flowing through them.

Archetypes form the infrastructure of the psyche. Archetypal patterns are similar to the patterns found in crystal formation. No two snowflakes are exactly alike; however, every single snowflake has the same basic six-pointed structure. Similarly, the contents and experiences of each individual's psyche are unique, but the general patterns

memories of the past. [Jung, 1968, p. 44]

It [the collective unconscious] is more like an atmosphere in which we live than something that is found *in* us. It is simply the unknown quantity in the world. [Jund, 1973, p. 433]

It is essential to insist that archetypes are not mere names, or even philosophical concepts. They are pieces of life itself—images that are integrally connected to the living individual by the bridge of the emotions. [Jung, 1964, p. 96]

that these experiences fall into are determined by universal parameters and generating principles, which Jung called archetypes.

Jung also calls archetypes "primordial images" because they often correspond to mythological themes that reappear in the folktales and legends of many different times and cultures. The same themes can be found in the dreams and fantasies of many individuals. According to Jung, the archetypes, as structural forming elements in the unconscious, give rise both to individual fantasy lives and to the mythologies of a people. They tend to appear as certain regularities—recurring types of situations and figures. Archetypal situations include "the hero's quest," "the night-sea journey," and "the battle for deliverance from the mother." Archetypal figures include the divine child, the double, the old sage, and the primordial mother.

Primordial means "first" or "original"; therefore a primordial image refers to the earliest development of the psyche. Man inherits these images from his ancestral past, a past that includes all of his human ancestors as well as his prehuman or animal ancestors. [Jung in Hall & Nordby, 1973, p. 39]

In *Hero with a Thousand Faces* (1949), Joseph Campbell, a Jungian scholar, outlines the basic archetypal themes and patterns in the stories and legends of heroes found in cultures throughout history. The story of Oedipus is a good illustration of an archetypal situation that deals with a son's deep love for his mother and conflict with his father. The same basic situation can be found as a theme in many myths and legends and also as a psychological pattern in many individuals. There are many other related situations, such as the daughter's relationship to her parents, parents' relationship to children, relationships between man and woman, brothers, sisters, and so forth.

> The term "archetype" is often misunderstood as meaning certain definite mythological images or motifs. But these are nothing more than conscious representations. . . . The archetype is a tendency to form such representations of a motif—representations that can vary a great deal in detail without losing their basic pattern. There are, for instance, many representations of the motif of the hostile brethren, but the motif itself remains the same. [Jung, 1964, p. 67]

A wide variety of symbols can be associated with a given archetype. For example, the mother archetype embraces not only each individual's real mother but also all mother figures and nurturant figures. This includes women in general, mythical images of women (such as Venus, Virgin Mary, Mother Nature), and supportive and nurturant symbols, such as the church and paradise. The mother archetype includes not only positive features but also negative ones, such as the threatening, domineering, or smothering mother. In the Middle Ages, for example, this aspect of the archetype was crystallized into the image of the witch.

Jung has written that "the contents of an archetype may be integrated into consciousness but they themselves cannot. Archetypes then cannot be done away with through integration any more than by a refusal to admit their contents to enter consciousness. The ar-

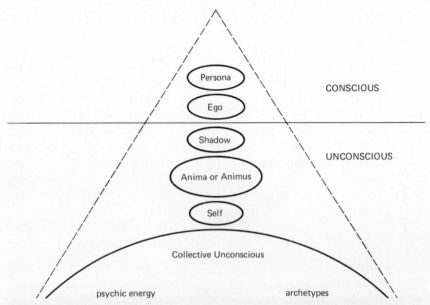

Figure 2.2 The Structure of the Personality. This diagram depicts the order in which the major archetypes generally appear in Jungian analysis. However, any two-dimensional representation of Jungian theory is bound to be misleading or even inaccurate. The self, for example, is more deeply unconscious than the other structures of the personality, but, at the same time, it is also the center of the total personality. (Courtesy Thomas Parker.)

chetypes remain a source for the channeling of psychic energies throughout the entire lifetime and must be continually dealt with" (Jung, 1951, p. 20).

Each of the major structures of the personality are archetypes. These include the *persona,* the *ego,* the *shadow,* the *anima* (in men), the *animus* (in women), and the *self.*

The Ego

The ego is the center of consciousness and one of the major archetypes of the personality. The ego provides a sense of consistency and direction in our conscious lives. It tends to oppose whatever might threaten this fragile consistency of consciousness and tries to convince us that we must always consciously plan and analyze our experience.

The ego wants explanations always in order to assert its existence. [Jung, 1973, p. 427]

According to June, the psyche at first consists only of the unconscious. Similar to Freud's view, the ego arises from the unconscious and brings together various experiences and memories, developing the division between unconscious and conscious. There are no unconscious elements in the ego, only conscious contents derived from personal experience. We are led to believe that the ego is the central element of the entire psyche, and we come to ignore the other half of the psyche, the unconscious.

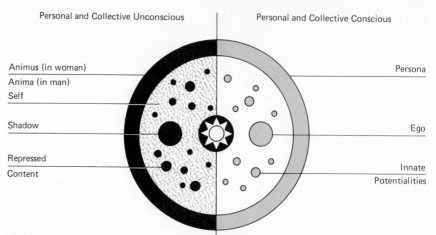

Personal and Collective Unconscious   Personal and Collective Conscious

Animus (in woman)

Anima (in man)

Self

Shadow

Repressed

Content

Persona

Ego

Innate

Potentialities

Figure 2.3 General Scheme of the Psyche. (Adapted from Harding, 1965.)

The Persona

Our persona is the appearance we present to the world. It is the character we assume; through it, we relate to others. The persona includes our social roles, the kind of clothes we choose to wear, and our individual styles of expressing ourselves. The term *persona* comes from the Latin, meaning "mask," "false face," the mask worn by an actor on the Roman stage through which he spoke (*per-sonare,* "to sound through"). We have to appear in something that defines our roles in order to function socially at all. Even those who try to reject such adaptive devices can only put on others representing rejection. The words *person* and *personality* are also related.

The persona has both positive and negative aspects. A dominant persona can smother the individual, and those who identify with their persona tend to see themselves only in terms of their superficial social roles and facade. Jung also called the persona the "conformity archetype." However, the persona is not all negative. It serves to protect the ego and the psyche from the varied social forces and attitudes that impinge on us. The persona is also a valuable tool for communication. In Greek drama, the actors' boldly drawn masks informed the entire audience clearly, if somewhat stereotypically, of the character and the attitudes of the role each actor was playing. The persona can often play a leading role in our positive development. As we begin to act a certain way, to play a role, our ego gradually alters in that direction.

Symbols commonly used for the persona include objects we use to cover ourselves (clothing, veils), symbols of an occupational role (tools, briefcase), and status symbols (car, house, diploma). These symbols have all been found in dreams as representations of the persona. In dreams, for example, someone with a strong persona may appear overdressed, or constricted by too much clothing. A person with a weak persona might appear naked and exposed. One possible expression of an extremely inadequate persona would be to have no skin.

The Shadow

The shadow is an archetypal form that serves as the focus for material that has been repressed from consciousness; its contents include those tendencies, desires, memories, and experiences that are rejected by the individual as incompatible with the persona and contrary to social standards and ideals. The stronger our persona and the more we identify with it, the more we deny others parts of ourselves. The shadow represents what we consider to be inferior in our personality and also that which we have neglected and never developed in ourselves. In dreams, shadow figures may appear as an animal, as a dwarf, as a vagrant, or as any other low-status figure.

In his work on repression and neurosis, Freud focused primarily on what Jung calls the shadow. Jung found that the repressed material becomes organized and structured around the shadow, which becomes, in a sense, a negative self, the shadow of the ego. The shadow is often experienced in dreams as a dark, primitive, hostile, or repellent figure because the contents of the shadow were forcibly pushed out of consciousness and appear antagonistic to the conscious outlook. If the material from the shadow is allowed back into consciousness, it loses much of its frightening and dark nature.

The shadow is most dangerous when unrecognized. Then the individual tends to project his or her unwanted qualities onto others or to become dominated by the shadow without realizing it. The more the shadow material is made conscious, the less it can dominate. But the shadow is an integral part of our nature, and it can never be simply eliminated. A person who appears to be without a shadow is not a full individual but a two-dimensional caricature who denies the mixture of good and evil and the ambivalence that are present in all of us.

How can I be substantial without casting a shadow? I must have a dark side too if I am to be whole; and by becoming conscious of my shadow I remember once more that I am a human being like any other. [Jung, 1931c, p. 59]

There was a man
who was so disturbed
by the sight of his own shadow
and so displeased with his own footsteps
that he determined to get rid of both.

The method he hit upon was to run away from them.
So he got up and ran.

But every time he put his foot down
there was another step,
while his shadow kept up with him
without the slightest difficulty.

He attributed his failure
to the fact that he was not running fast enough.
So he ran faster and faster, without stopping,
until he finally dropped dead.

He failed to realize
that if he merely stepped into the shade,
his shadow would vanish,
and if he sat down and stayed still,
there would be no more footsteps.

CHUAN TZU

Each repressed portion of the shadow represents a part of ourselves. To the extent that we keep this material unconscious, we limit ourselves. As the shadow is made more conscious, we repossess previously repressed parts of ourselves. Also, the shadow is not simply a negative force in the psyche. It is a storehouse for considerable instinctual energy, spontaneity, and vitality, and it is a major source of our creative energies. Like all archetypes, the shadow is rooted in the collective unconscious, and it can allow the individual access to much of the valuable unconscious material that is rejected by the ego and the persona.

Just when we think we understand it, the shadow will appear in another form. Dealing with the shadow is a lifelong process of looking within and honestly reflecting on what we see there.

The following passage from one of Jung's letters provides a clear illustration of Jung's approach to the shadow and to the unconscious in general.

It is a very difficult and important question, what you call the technique of dealing with the shadow. There is, as a matter of fact, no technique at all, inasmuch as technique means that there is a known and perhaps even prescribable way to deal with a certain difficulty or task. It is rather a dealing comparable to diplomacy or statesmanship. There is, for instance, no particular technique that would help us to reconcile two political parties opposing each other. It can be a question of good will, or diplomatic cunning or civil war or anything. If one can speak of a technique at all, it consists solely in an attitude. First of all, one has to accept and to take seriously into account the existence of the shadow. Secondly, it is necessary to be informed about its qualities and intentions. Thirdly, long and difficult negotiations will be unavoidable. . . .

Nobody can know what the final outcome of such negotiations will be. One only knows that through careful collaboration the problem itself becomes changed. Very often certain apparently impossible intentions of the shadow are mere threats due to an unwillingness on the part of the ego to enter upon a serious consideration of the shadow. Such threats diminish usually when one meets them seriously. Pairs of opposites have a natural tendency to meet on the middle line, but the middle line is never a compromise thought out by the intellect and forced upon the fighting parties. It is rather a result of the conflict one has to suffer. Such conflicts are never solved by a clever trick or by an intelligent invention but by enduring them. As a matter of fact, you have to heat up such conflicts until they rage in full swing so that the opposites slowly melt together. It is a sort of alchemistic procedure rather than a rational choice and decision. The suffering is an indispensable part of it. Every real solution is only reached by intense suffering. The suffering shows the degree in which we are intolerable to ourselves. "Agree with thine enemy" outside and inside! That's the problem! Such agreement should violate yourself as little as your enemy. I admit it is not easy to find the right formula, yet if you find it you have made a whole of yourself and this, I think, is the meaning of human life. [1973, p. 234]

Anima and Animus

Jung postulated an unconscious structure that represents the contra-sexual part of the psyche of each individual; he calls this the *anima* in man and the *animus* in woman. This basic psychic structure serves as a focus for all the psychological material that does not fit with an individual's conscious self-image as a man or woman. Thus to the extent that a woman defines herself in feminine terms, her animus will include those unrecognized tendencies and experiences that she has defined as masculine.

> Every man carries within him the eternal image of woman, not the image of this or that particular woman, but a definitive feminine image. This image is . . . an imprint or "archetype" of all the ancestral experiences of the female, a deposit, as it were, of all the impressions ever made by woman. . . . Since this image is unconscious, it is always unconsciously projected upon the person of the beloved, and is one of the chief reasons for passionate attraction or aversion. [Jung, 1931b, p. 198]

According to Jung, the child's opposite sex parent is a major influence on the development of the anima or animus, and all relations with the opposite sex, including parents, are strongly affected by the projection of anima or animus fantasies. This archetype is one of the most influential regulators of behavior. It appears in dreams and fantasies as figures of the opposite sex, and it functions as the primary mediator between unconscious and conscious processes. It is oriented primarily toward inner processes, just as the persona is oriented to the outer processes. It is a source of projections, a source of image making, and a door to creativity in the psyche. (It is not surprising then that male writers and artists have depicted their muses as female goddesses.)

The Self

Jung has called the self the *central archetype,* the archetype of psychological order, and the totality of the personality. According to Jung, "conscious and unconscious are not necessarily in opposition to one another, but complement one another to form a totality, which is the *self*" (Jung, 1928b, p. 175). Jung discovered the self archetype only after his investigations of the other structures of the personality. The self is often depicted in dreams or images impersonally (as a circle, mandala, crystal, or stone) or personally (as a royal couple, a divine child, or as some other symbol of divinity). These are all symbols of wholeness, unification, reconciliation of polarities, or dynamic equilibrium—the goals of the individuation process.

The self is a deep inner guiding factor, which can seem quite different, even alien, from the ego and consciousness. "The self is not only the centre, but also the whole circumference which embraces both conscious and unconscious; it is the centre of this totality, just as the ego is the centre of consciousness" (Jung, 1936b, p. 41). It may first appear in dreams as an insignificant image, a dot or a flyspeck, because the self is so unfamiliar and undeveloped in most people. The development of the self does not mean that the ego is dissolved. The ego remains the center of consciousness but becomes linked to the self as the result of a long arduous process of understanding and accepting unconscious processes. The ego no longer seems the center of the personality, but rather one of many structures within the psyche.

> The archetype of the individual is the Self. The Self is all-embracing. God is a circle whose center is everywhere and whose circumference is nowhere. (Jung in McGuire & Hull, 1977, p. 86)

> The ego receives the light from the Self. Though we know of this Self, yet it is not known. . . . Although we receive the light of consciousness from the Self and although we know it to be the source of our illumination, we do not know whether it possesses anything we would call consciousness. . . . If the Self could be wholly experienced, it would be a limited experience, whereas in reality its experience is unlimited and endless. . . . If I were one with the Self I would have knowledge of everything, I would speak Sanskrit, read cuneiform script, know the events that took place in pre-history, be acquainted with the life of other planets, etc. [Jung, 1975, pp. 194–195]

Symbols

"The symbol has a very complex meaning because it defies reason; it always presupposes a lot of meanings that can't be comprehended in a single logical concept. The symbol has a future. The past does not suffice to interpret it, because germs of the future are included in every actual situation. That's why, in elucidating a case, the symbolism is spontaneously applicable, for it contains the future" (Jung in McGuire & Hull, 1977, p. 143).

According to Jung, the unconscious expresses itself primarily through symbols. Although no specific symbol or image can ever fully represent an archetype (which is a form without specific content), the more closely a symbol conforms to the unconscious material organized around an archetype, the more it evokes a strong, emotionally charged response.

Jung is concerned with two kinds of symbols: individual and collective. By individual symbols Jung means "natural" symbols that are spontaneous productions of the individual psyche, rather than images or designs created deliberately by an artist. In addition to the personal symbols found in an individual's dreams or fantasies, there are also important collective symbols, which are often religious images, such as the cross, the six-pointed Star of David, and the Buddhist wheel of life.

As a plant produces its flower, so the psyche creates its symbols. [Jung, 1964, p. 64]

Symbolic terms and images represent concepts that we cannot clearly define or fully comprehend. For Jung, a sign *stands for* something else; a symbol, such as a tree, *is* something in itself—a dynamic, living thing. The symbol represents the individual's psychic situation, and it *is* that situation at a given moment.

> What we call a symbol is a term, a name, or even a picture that may be familiar in daily life, yet that possesses specific connotations in addition to its conventional and obvious meaning. It implies something vague, unknown, or hidden from us. . . . Thus a word or an image is symbolic when it implies something more than its obvious and immediate meaning. It has a wider "unconscious" aspect that is never precisely defined or fully explained. [Jung, 1964, pp. 20–21]

Dreams

For Jung, dreams play an important complementary (or compensatory) role in the psyche. The widely varied influences we are exposed to in our conscious life tend to distract us and to mold our thinking in ways that are often unsuitable to our personality and individuality. "The general function of dreams is to try to restore our psychological balance by producing dream material that re-establishes, in a subtle way, the total psychic equilibrium" (Jung, 1964, p. 50).

Jung approached dreams as living realities that must be experienced and observed carefully to be understood. He tried to uncover the significance of dream symbols by paying close attention to the form and content of the dream, and he gradually moved away from the psychoanalytic reliance on free association in dream analysis. "Free association will bring out all my complexes, but hardly ever the meaning of a dream. To understand the dream's meaning I must stick as close as possible to the dream images" (Jung, 1934, p. 149). In analysis Jung would continually bring his patients back to the dream images and ask them, "What does the *dream* say?" (Jung, 1964, p. 29).

The image is a condensed expression of the psychic situation as a whole, not merely, nor even predominantly, of unconscious contents pure and simple. [Jung, 1921, p. 442]

Because the dream deals with symbols that have more than one meaning, there can be no simple, mechanical system for dream interpretation. Any attempt at dream analysis must take into account the attitudes, experience, and background of the dreamer. It is a joint venture between analyst and analysand. The dreamer interprets the dream with the help and guidance of the analyst. The analyst may be vitally helpful, but in the end only the dreamer alone can "know" what the dream means.

More important than cognitive understanding of dreams is the act of experiencing the dream material and taking this material seriously. One Jungian analyst has pointed out the importance of "befriending" our dreams and treating them not as isolated events but as communications from ongoing unconscious processes. "It is necessary that the unconscious make known its own direction and we must allow it an equal voice with that of the ego, if each side is to be able to adapt to the other. As the ego listens, and the unconscious is encouraged to participate in the dialogue, the unconscious position is transformed from that of an adversary to that of a friend with a somewhat differing but complementary point of view" (Singer, 1972, p. 283).

JUNG'S PSYCHOLOGY OF WOMEN

Jungian psychology incorporates an extensive psychology of the feminine, but substantially less in the way of a psychology of women. Jung, in fact, notes: "It is a foregone conclusion among the initiated that men understand nothing of women's psychology as it actually is, but it is astonishing to find that women do not know themselves" (in Harding, 1970, p. xv).

Jung asserts that a woman's psyche is different in very basic ways from the male psyche; this is manifested in the differences between the masculine ego and the feminine ego as well as between animus and anima. The feminine ego is the adaptively organized image of the self that a woman presents to the world. It is essentially a socially determined aspect of the personality. Differences between masculine and feminine egos are largely determined by cultural norms and role distinctions. The soul image is a more deeply unconscious image than the ego; in a woman it is called the animus, in a man the anima. The animus and anima are sexually determined images that derive from the child's early experiences with persons of the opposite sex, the archetypal structuring of emotional life, and from repressed opposite-sex tendencies that have been repressed from consciousness. The animus may be pathologically dominated by identification with archetypal images (for example, the bewitched prince, the romantic poet, the ghostly lover, the marauding pirate), and/or by an extreme father fixation. For a woman, the process of psychological development entails entering into a dialogue between her ego and her animus. The animus is initially viewed as a wholly separate personality. As the animus and its influence on the individual is recognized, the animus begins to assume the role of liaison between conscious and unconscious until it gradually becomes integrated into the self. The quality of this union of opposites (in this case, masculine and feminine) Jung views as the major determinant of female personality functioning. A similar process occurs between the anima and masculine ego in the male.

Jung, like Freud, stressed the essentially bisexual nature of every individual, although Jung attached less weight to the strictly biological nature of the sexual differentiation that the developing personality undergoes. The attributes of feminine persona and animus are clearly distinguishable from parallel attributes in the masculine persona and anima. The anima, according to Jung, has an erotic, emotional, receptive character whereas the animus is primarily rationalizing and active. These varying natures of animus and anima complement the varying natures of feminine and masculine egos.

Esther Harding, a Jungian analyst, describes a certain kind of feminine persona as a composite of ways of acting that are fundamentally feminine. These ways (although not, she says, *inferior* to masculine ways) tend to be dependent, receptive, coy, winsome, nonaggressive, naive, and unreflective (Harding, 1970). These characteristics are, however, only part of any woman's identity. As the woman begins to render conscious her unconscious animus, she begins to develop qualities that are called masculine: self-assertiveness, independence, forcefulness, and capacities for logical and analytic thinking. Her basic feminine nature expresses what is called the yin principle in Eastern traditions, but she only becomes an integrated, psychologically developed individual when she claims the masculine yang principle that resides in her unconscious animus. If she does not recognize and become familiar with her own animus, the woman remains expressive only of the yin side of herself; she never accepts her unconscious "masculine" side as part of herself but perpetually projects it onto the various men in her life.

DYNAMICS

Psychological Growth
Individuation

According to Jung, every individual possesses a tendency toward individuation, or self-development. "Individuation means becoming a single, homogeneous being, and, insofar as 'individuality' embraces our innermost, last, and incomparable uniqueness, it also implies becoming one's own self. We could therefore translate individuation as 'coming to selfhood' or 'self-realization' " (Jung, 1928b, p. 171).

> Individuation is a natural process. It is what makes a tree turn into a tree; if it is interfered with, then it becomes sick and cannot function as a tree, but left to itself it develops into a tree. This is individuation. . . . Consciousness is a part of it, perhaps, yes, but that depends on how much consciousness there is naturally there. Consciousness can also block individuation by not allowing what is in the unconscious to develop. [Jung in McGuire & Hull, 1977, p. 210]

Everything that happens
to us, properly
understood, leads us
back to ourselves; it is as
though there were some
unconscious guidance
whose aim it is to deliver
us from all this and
make us dependent on
ourselves. [Jung, 1973,
p. 78]

Individuation is a process of developing wholeness and thus moving toward greater freedom. This includes development of a dynamic relationship between the ego and the self, along with the integration of the various parts of the psyche: the ego, persona, shadow, anima or animus, and the other unconscious archetypes. As people become more individuated, these archetypes may be seen as expressing themselves in more subtle and complex ways.

> The more we become conscious of ourselves through self-knowledge, and act accordingly, the more the layer of the personal unconscious that is superimposed on the collective unconscious will be diminished. In this way there arises a consciousness which is no longer imprisoned in the petty, oversensitive, personal world of objective interests. This widened consciousness is no longer that touchy, egotistical bundle of personal wishes, fears, hopes, and ambitions which always has to be compensated or corrected by unconscious countertendencies; instead, it is a function of relationship to the world of objects, bringing the individual into absolute, binding, and indissoluble communion with the world at large. [Jung, 1928b, p. 176]

As an analyst, Jung found that those who came to him in the first half of life were relatively uninvolved with the inner process of individuation; they tended to be concerned primarily with emergence as an individual, external achievement, and the attainment of the goals of the ego. Older patients, who had fulfilled such goals reasonably well, tended to develop different aims: to become concerned with integration rather than achievement and to seek harmony with the totality of the psyche.

> The individuated human being is just ordinary, therefore almost invisible. . . . His feelings, thoughts, etc., are just anybody's feelings, thoughts, etc.—quite ordinary, as a matter of fact, and not interesting at all. . . . He will have no need to be exaggerated, hypocritical, neurotic, or any other nuisance. He will be "in modest harmony with nature." . . . No matter whether people think they are individuated or not, they are just what they are: in the one case a man plus an unconscious nuisance disturbing to himself—or, without it, unconscious of himself; or in the other case, conscious. The criterion is consciousness. [Jung, 1975, p. 377]

From the point of view of the ego, growth and development consist of integrating new material into one's consciousness; this includes the acquisition of knowledge of the world and of oneself. Growth, for the ego, is essentially the expansion of conscious awareness. However, individuation is the development of the self, and from the point of view of the self, the goal is the union of consciousness with the unconscious.

Unveiling the Persona Early in the individuation process it is necessary to recognize the unveiling of the persona and to view it as a useful tool rather than as a permanent part of oneself. Although the persona has important protective functions, it is also a mask that hides the self and the unconscious.

> When we analyze the persona we strip off the mask, and discover that what seemed to be individual is at bottom collective; in other words, that the persona was only a mask for the collective psyche. Fundamentally the persona is nothing real: it is a compromise between individual and society as to what a man should appear to be. He takes a name, earns a title, represents an office, he is this or that. In a certain sense all this is real, yet in relation to the essential individuality of the person concerned it is only secondary reality, a product of compromise, in making which others often have a greater share than he. [Jung, 1928b, p. 156]

Confronting the Shadow When we look beyond mere appearances, we are forced to confront the shadow. We can become free of the shadow's influence to the extent that we accept the reality of the dark side and simultaneously realize that we are more than the shadow.

Confronting the Anima or Animus A further step is to confront the anima or animus. This archetype must be dealt with as a real person or persons that one can communicate with and learn from. Jung would ask the anima figures that appeared to him about the interpretation of dream symbols, like an analysand consulting an analyst. The individual also becomes aware that the anima or animus figures have considerable autonomy and that they are likely to influence or even dominate those who ignore them or who blindly accept their images and projections as their own personal productions.

Developing the Self The goal and culmination of the individuation process is the development of the self. "The self is our life's goal, for it is the completest expression of that fateful combination we call individuality . . ." (Jung, 1928b, p. 238). The self replaces the ego as the midpoint of the psyche. Awareness of the self brings unity to the psyche and helps to integrate conscious and unconscious material. The ego is still the center of consciousness, but it is no longer seen as the nucleus of the entire personality.

Jung writes that "one must be what one is; one must discover one's own individuality, that centre of personality, which is equidistant between the conscious and the unconscious; we must aim for that ideal point towards which nature appears to be directing us. Only from that point can one satisfy one's needs" (in Serrano, 1966, p. 91).

It is necessary to keep in mind that although it is possible to describe individuation in terms of stages, the individuation process is con-

Individuation means precisely the better and more complete fulfillment of the collective qualities of the human being . . . [Jung, 1928b, pp. 173–174]

Treat her [the anima] as a person, if you like as a patient or a goddess, but above all treat her as something that does exist . . . you must talk to this person in order to see what she is about and to learn what her thoughts and character are. [Jung, 1973, p. 461]

The unconscious mind of man sees correctly even when conscious reason is blind and impotent. [Jung, 1952b, p. 386]

siderably more complex than the simple progression outlined here. All the steps listed overlap, and one continually returns to old problems and issues (hopefully from a different perspective). Individuation might be represented as a spiral in which one keeps confronting the same basic questions, each time in a finer form. (This concept is closely related to the Zen Buddhist conception of enlightenment, in which one individual never finishes a personal *koan*, or spiritual problem, and the searching itself is seen as identical with the goal.)

Obstacles to Growth

Individuation consciously undertaken is a difficult task, and the individual must be relatively psychologically healthy to handle the process. The ego must be strong enough to undergo tremendous changes, to be turned inside out in the process of individuation.

> One could say that the whole world with its turmoil and misery is in an individuation process. But people don't know it, that's the only difference. . . . Individuation is by no means a rare thing or a luxury of the few, but those who know that they are in such a process are considered to be lucky. They get something out of it, provided they are conscious enough. [Jung, 1973, p. 442]

This process is especially difficult because it is an individual enterprise, often carried out in the face of the rejection or at best indifference of others. Jung writes that "nature cares nothing whatsoever about a higher level of consciousness; quite the contrary. And then society does not value these feats of the psyche very highly; its prizes are always given for achievement and not for personality, the latter being rewarded for the most part posthumously" (1931a, p. 394).

Each stage in the individuation process is accompanied by difficulties. First is the danger of identification with the persona. Those who identify with the persona may try to become too "perfect," unable to accept their mistakes or weaknesses, or any deviations from their idealized self-concept. Those *fully* identified with the persona will tend to repress all those tendencies that do not fit and project them onto others; the job of acting out aspects of the repressed negative identity will be assigned to other people.

The shadow can also become a major obstacle to individuation. People who are unaware of their shadows can easily act out harmful impulses without ever recognizing them as wrong, or without even becoming aware of their own negative feelings. The initial impulses to harm or do wrong are often instantly justified by rationalizations when someone has never acknowledged the presence of such impulses in himself or herself. Ignorance of the shadow may also result in an attitude

Filling the conscious mind with ideal conceptions is a characteristic feature of Western theosophy. . . . One does not become enlightened by imagining figures of light, but by making the darkness conscious. [Jung, 1954a, pp. 265–266]

of moral superiority and projection of the shadow onto others. For example, those most in favor of censorship of pornography tend to be fascinated by the materials they want to ban; they may even convince themselves of the need to study carefully all the available pornography in order to be effective censors.

Confronting the anima or animus brings with it the whole problem of relating to the collective unconscious. The anima may bring on sudden emotional changes or moodiness in a man. The animus often manifests itself as irrational, rigidly held opinions in the woman. (We should remember that Jung's discussion of anima and animus is not a description of masculinity and femininity in general. The content of the anima or animus is the complement of our conscious conception of ourselves as masculine or feminine, which, in most people, is strongly determined by cultural values and socially defined sex roles.)

Once the individual is exposed to collective material, there is a danger of becoming engulfed by the unconscious. According to Jung, this can take one of two forms. First is the possibility of ego inflation, in which the individual claims all the virtues of the collective psyche. The other reaction is that of ego impotence; the person feels that he or she has no control over the collective psyche and becomes acutely aware of unacceptable aspects of the unconscious—irrationality, negative impulses, and so forth.

As in many myths and fairy tales, the greatest obstacles are those found closest to the goal. When the individual deals with the anima and animus, tremendous energy is unleashed. This energy can be used to build up the ego instead of developing the self. Jung has referred to this as identification with the archetype of the mana-personality. (*Mana* is a Melanesian word for the energy or power that emanates from people, objects, or supernatural beings, energy that has an occult or bewitching quality.) The ego identifies with the archetype of the wise man or wise woman, the sage who knows everything. (This syndrome is not uncommon among older university professors, for example.) The mana-personality is dangerous because it is an exaggeration of power. Individuals stuck at this stage try to be both more and less than they really are: more, because they tend to believe they have become perfect, holy, or even godlike; but actually less, because they have lost touch with their essential humanity and the fact that no one is perfectly wise, infallible, and flawless.

Jung saw temporary identification with the archetype of the self or the mana-personality as being almost inevitable in the individuation process. The best defense against the development of ego inflation is to remember one's essential humanity, to stay grounded in the reality of what one can and must do, not what one "should" do or be.

Not perfection, but completeness is what is expected of you. [Jung, 1973, p. 97]

STRUCTURE

Body

In his voluminous writings Jung did not deal explicitly with the role of the body, but chose to direct his efforts to analyzing the psyche. He has argued that physical processes are relevant to us only to the extent that they are represented in the psyche. The physical body and the external world can be known only as psychological experiences. "I'm chiefly concerned with the psyche itself, therefore I'm leaving out body and spirit. . . . Body and spirit are to me mere aspects of the reality of the psyche. Psychic experience is the only immediate experience. Body is as metaphysical as spirit" (Jung, 1973, p. 200).

Psyche and body are not separate entities, but one and the same life. [Jung, 1917, p. 113]

Social Relationships

Social interaction is important in the formation and development of the major personality structures: persona, shadow, and anima or animus. The contents of social experiences help determine the specific images and symbols associated with each structure; at the same time, these basic archetypal structures mold and guide our social relationships.

Jung stressed that individuation is essentially a personal endeavor; however, it is also a process that develops through relationships with other people. "As nobody can become aware of his individuality unless he is closely and responsibly related to his fellow beings, he is not withdrawing to an egoistic desert when he tries to find himself. He only can discover himself when he is deeply and unconditionally related to some, and generally related to a great many, individuals with whom he has a chance to compare, and from whom he is able to discriminate himself" (Jung in Serrano, 1966, pp. 83–84).

Individuation does not isolate, it connects. I never saw relationships thriving on unconsciousness. [Jung, 1973, p. 504]

Will

Jung defines the will as the energy that is at the disposal of consciousness or the ego. The development of the will is associated with learning cultural values, moral standards, and the like. Will has power only over conscious thought and action and cannot directly affect instinctual or other unconscious processes, although it has substantial indirect power over them through conscious processes.

Jung felt that individual will is a relatively recent human development. In primitive cultures, rituals (such as hunting dances) work tribal members into a state of action, a state that substitutes for our modern willpower. ". . . The will was practically nonexistent and it needed all the ceremonial which you observe in primitive tribes to bring up something that is an equivalent to our word 'decision.' Slowly through the ages we have acquired a certain amount of willpower. We could detach so much energy from the energy of nature, from the original unconsciousness, from the original flow of events, an amount of energy we could control" (Jung in McGuire & Hull, 1977, p. 103).

Emotions

Jung has stressed the central role that the study of the emotions must play in psychology. "Psychology is the only science that has to take the factor of value (i.e., feeling) into account, because it is the link between psychical events and life. Psychology is often accused of not being scientific on this account; but its critics fail to understand the scientific and practical necessity of giving due consideration to feeling" (Jung, 1964, p. 99).

Psychic material that is directly related to the archetypes tends to arouse strong emotions and often has an awe-inspiring quality. When Jung discusses symbols, he is not writing about lifeless words or empty forms, but about powerful, living realities by which men and women live their lives, and for which many have died. According to Jung, emotion accompanies all psychic changes. It is the force behind the process of individuation. "Emotion is the chief source of consciousness" (Jung, 1954b, p. 96).

> Psychic development cannot be accomplished by intention and will alone; it needs the attraction of a symbol. . . . [Jung, 1928a, p. 25]

Intellect

For Jung, the intellect refers to directed, conscious thought processes. Jung distinguishes intellect from intuition, which draws strongly on unconscious material. The intellect has a limited, although important, role in psychological functioning. Jung stressed that purely intellectual understanding could not be complete. "A psychology that satisfies the intellect alone can never be practical, for the totality of the psyche can never be grasped by intellect alone" (Jung, 1917, p. 117).

> In my medical experience as well as in my own life I have again and again been faced with the mystery of love, and have never been able to explain what it is. [Jung, 1961, p. 353]

Therapist

Jung emphasized that therapy is a joint effort between analyst and analysand working together as equals. Because the two form a dynamic unit, the analyst must also be open to change as a result of the interaction. Jung felt that therapy is primarily a matter of the unconscious of the analyst interacting with the unconscious of the analysand, who can go no further in therapy than the analyst has gone.

> A therapist who has a neurosis does not deserve the name, for it is not possible to bring the patient to a more advanced stage than one has reached oneself. [Jung, 1973, p. 95]

> It is a remarkable thing about psychotherapy: you cannot learn any recipes by heart and then apply them more or less suitably, but can cure only from one central point; and that consists in understanding the patient as a psychological whole and approaching him as a human being, leaving aside all theory and listening attentively to whatever he has to say. [Jung, 1973, p. 456]

Jung tried to avoid reliance on theory and on specific techniques in the process of therapy, as he believed that this tends to make the analyst mechanical and out of touch with the analysand. For Jung, the aim of therapy is to attempt to deal with the whole individual through a genuine relationship, without trying to patch up individual parts of the psyche as if the analysand were a car with carburetor trouble.

Jung generally saw people only once or twice a week. He tried to foster a sense of autonomy in analysands and would often give them homework, such as analyzing their own dreams. He would also insist that clients take occasional vacations from analysis in order to avoid becoming dependent on him and on the analytic sessions.

Jung has outlined two major stages of the therapeutic process, each of which has two parts. First comes the *analytic stage*. It consists initially of *confession,* in which the individual begins to recover unconscious material. Ties of dependency on the therapist tend to develop at this stage. Next comes *elucidation* of the confessional material, where greater familiarity and understanding of psychic processes develops. The person remains dependent on the therapist.

The second stage of therapy is the *synthetic*. First comes *education,* in which Jung stressed the need to move from psychological insight to actual new experiences that result in individual growth and the formation of new habits. The final part is the *transformation*. The analysand-analyst relationship is integrated and dependency is reduced as the relationship becomes transformed. The individual experiences a highly concentrated individuation process, although archetypal material is not necessarily confronted. This is a stage of self-education in which the individual takes more and more responsibility for his or her own development.

EVALUATION

An Open System of Psychology

Jung has often been criticized for his lack of a coherent, clearly structured system of thought. His writing often seems to ramble off on tangents rather than presenting ideas in a formal, logical, or even systematic fashion. Also, Jung often uses varying definitions for the same terms at different times. He was aware of this difficulty in his writing but did not see it as necessarily a drawback. Jung believed that life rarely follows the logical coherent pattern that has become standard for scientific and academic writing, and his own style may be closer to the rich complexity of psychological reality.

Jung deliberately developed an open system, one that could admit new information without distorting it to fit an inclusive theoretical structure. He never believed that he knew all the answers or that new information would merely confirm his theories. Consequently, his theorizing lacks a tight logical structure that categorizes all information in terms of a small number of theoretical constructs.

Any of my pupils could give you so much insight and understanding that you could treat yourself if you don't succumb to the prejudice that you receive healing through others. In the last resort every individual alone has to win his battle, nobody else can do it for him. [Jung, 1973, p. 126]

The main interest of my work is not concerned with the treatment of neuroses but rather with the approach to the numinous. But the fact is that the approach to the numinous is the real therapy and inasmuch as you attain to the numinous experiences you are released from the curse of pathology. [Jung, 1973, p. 377]

The serious problems in life, however, are never fully solved. If ever they should appear to be so it is a sure sign that something has been lost. The meaning and purpose of a problem seem to lie not in its solutions but in our working at it incessantly. [Jung, 1931a, p. 394]

Religion and Mysticism

Because he dealt with religion, alchemy, spirituality, and the like, some critics have labeled Jung a mystic rather than a scientist. But it is clear that Jung's attitude was always that of an investigator rather than that of a believer or disciple. He viewed mystical belief systems as important expressions of human ideals and aspirations, as data that should not be ignored by anyone concerned with the full range of human thought and behavior.

> I am a researcher and not a prophet. What matters to me is what can be verified by experience. But I am not interested at all in what can be speculated about experience without any proof. [Jung, 1973, p. 203]

The Analysis of Symbols

Jung's recognition of the psychological importance of symbols and his detailed analysis of symbols and their interpretations are his most important contributions to psychology. Jung was centrally concerned with the complexity of symbolism and with the need to analyze symbols without oversimplifying. He was drawn to mythology, folklore, and alchemy because they provided various contexts that shed light upon the complex symbolic productions he came upon in analysis.

Jung's writing is difficult to comprehend but perhaps more valuable because of the richness of his thinking. His flexibility and open-mindedness, his concern for the deeper truths of human existence, give Jung's work a breadth and complexity virtually unmatched in psychology.

THE THEORY FIRSTHAND

Word Association

Jung's first introduction to depth psychology was a result of his experiments with word associations. He developed great expertise at interpreting associations; his intuitive abilities were often astonishing.

> Many years ago, when I was quite a young doctor, an old professor of criminology asked me about the experiment [in word association] and said he did not believe it. I said: "No, Professor? You can try it whenever you like." He invited me to his house and I began. After ten words he got tired and said: "What can you make of it? Nothing has come of it." I told him he could not expect a result with ten or twelve words; he ought to have a hundred and then we would see something. He said: "Can you do something with these words?" I said: "Little enough, but I can tell you something. Quite recently you have had worries about money, you have too little of it. You are afraid of dying of heart disease. You must have studied in France, where you had a love affair, and it has come back to your mind, as often, when one has thoughts of dying, old sweet memories come back from the womb of time." He said: "How do you know?" Any child could have seen it! He was a man of 72 and he had associated *heart* with *pain*—fear that he would die of heart failure. He associated *death* with *to die*—a natural reaction—and with

money he associated *too little,* a very usual reaction. Then things became rather startling to me. To *pay,* after a long reaction time, he said *La Semeuse,* though our conversation was in German. That is the famous figure on the French coin. Now why on earth should this old man say *La Semeuse?* When he came to the word *kiss* there was a long reaction time and there was a light in his eyes and he said: *Beautiful.* Then of course I had the story. He would never have used French if it had not been associated with a particular feeling, and so we must think why he used it. Had he had losses with the French franc? There was no talk of inflation and devaluation in those days. That could not be the clue. I was in doubt whether it was money or love, but when he came to *kiss/beautiful* I knew it was love. He was not the kind of man to go to France in later life, but he had been a student in Paris, a lawyer, probably at the Sorbonne. It was relatively simple to stitch together the whole story. [Jung, 1968, p. 57]

Dream Analysis
The following is an example of Jung's approach to dream analysis.

> . . . [T]oday I am going to contradict myself and break all my rules. I am going to interpret a single dream, not one out of a series; moreover I do not know the dreamer, and further, I am not in possession of the associations. Therefore I am interpreting the dream arbitrarily. There is a justification for this procedure. If a dream is clearly formed of *personal* material you have to get the individual associations; but if the dream is chiefly a *mythological* structure—a difference which is obvious at once—then it speaks a universal language, and you or I can supply parallels with which to construct the context as well as anybody else, always provided we possess the necessary knowledge. For instance, when the dream takes up the hero-dragon conflict, everybody has something to say about it, because we have all read fairy tales and legends and know something of heroes and dragons. On the collective level of dreams there is practically no difference in human beings, while there is all the difference on the personal level.

Everything men assert about God is twaddle, for no man can know God. [Jung, 1975, p. 377]

> My colleague was an alienist at a clinic, and the patient was a distinguished young Frenchman, twenty-two years of age, highly intelligent, and very aesthetic. He had travelled in Spain and had come back with a depression which was diagnosed as manic-depressive insanity, depressive form. The depression was not very bad, but bad enough for him to be sent to the clinic. After six months he was released from confinement, and a few months later he committed suicide. He was no longer under the depression, which was practically cured; he committed suicide apparently in a state of calm reasoning. We shall understand from the dream why he committed suicide. This is the dream, and it occurred at the beginning of the depression:
>
> *Underneath the great cathedral of Toledo there is a cistern filled with water which has a subterranean connection with the river Tagus, which skirts the city. This cistern is a small dark room. In the water there is a huge serpent whose eyes sparkle like jewels. Near it there is a golden bowl containing a golden dagger. This dagger is the key to Toledo, and its owner commands full power over the city. The dreamer knows the serpent to be the friend and protector of B— C—, a young friend of his who is present.*

B— C— puts his naked foot into the serpent's jaws. The serpent licks it in a friendly way and B— C— enjoys playing with the serpent; he has no fear of it because he is a child without guilt. In the dream B— C— appears to be about the age of seven; he had indeed been a friend of the dreamer's early youth. Since this time, the dream says, the serpent has been forgotten and nobody dared to descend into its haunts.

This part is a sort of introduction, and now the real action begins.

The dreamer is alone with the serpent. He talks to it respectfully, but without fear. The serpent tells the dreamer that Spain belongs to him as he is B— C—'s friend, and asks him to give back the boy. The dreamer refuses to do this and promises instead that he himself will descend into the darkness of the cave to be the friend of the serpent. But then he changes his mind, and instead of fulfilling his promise he decides to send another friend, a Mr S—, to the serpent. This friend is descended from the Spanish Moors, and to risk the descent into the cistern he has to recover the original courage of his race. The dreamer advises him to get the sword with the red hilt which is to be found in the weapons factory on the other bank of the Tagus. It is said to be a very ancient sword, dating back to the old Phocaeans.* S— gets the sword and descends into the cistern, and the dreamer tells him to pierce his left palm with the sword. S— does so, but he is not able to keep his countenance in the powerful presence of the serpent. Overcome by pain and fear, he cries out and staggers upstairs again without having taken the dagger. Thus S— cannot hold Toledo, and the dreamer could do nothing about it and had to let him stay there as a mere wall decoration.

That is the end of the dream. The original of course is in French. Now for the context. We have certain hints as to these friends. B— C— is a friend of the dreamer's early youth, a little bit older than himself, and he projected everything that was wonderful and charming into this boy and made him a sort of hero. But he lost sight of him later; perhaps the boy died. S— is a friend of more recent date. He is said to be descended from the Spanish Moors. I do not know him personally, but I know his family. It is a very old and honourable family from the South of France, and the name might easily be a Moorish name. The dreamer knew this legend about the family of S—.

As I told you, the dreamer had recently been to Spain and of course had seen Toledo, and he had the dream after he got back and had been taken to the clinic. He was in a bad state, practically in despair, and he could not help telling the dream to his doctor. . . .

We make no mistake when we assume that the dreamer has picked out Toledo for a particular reason—both as the object of his trip and of his dream; and the dream brings up material which practically everybody would have who had seen Toledo with the same mental disposition, the same education and refinement of aesthetic perception and knowledge. Toledo is an extremely impressive city. It contains one of the most marvelous Gothic cathedrals of the world. It is a place with an immensely old tradition; it is the old Roman Toletum, and for centuries has been the seat of the Cardinal Archbishop and Primate of Spain. From the sixth to the eighth century it was the capital of the Visigoths; from the eighth to the eleventh it was a provincial capital of the Moorish kingdom; and from the eleventh to the sixteenth century it was the capital of Castile.

But we must not forget that only a very few people are artists in life; that the art of life is the most distinguished and rarest of all the arts. [Jung in Campbell, 1971, p. 19]

The cathedral of Toledo, being such an impressive and beautiful building, naturally suggests all that it represents: the greatness, the power, the splendour, and the mystery of medieval Christianity, which found its essential expression in the Church. Therefore the cathedral is the embodiment, the incarnation, of the spiritual kingdom, for in the Middle Ages the world was ruled by the Emperor *and* by God. So the cathedral expresses the Christian philosophy or *Weltanschauung* of the Middle Ages.

The dream says that underneath the cathedral there is a mysterious place, which in reality is not in tune with a Christian church. What is beneath a cathedral of that age? There is always the so-called under-church or crypt. You have probably seen the great crypt at Chartres; it gives a very good idea of the mysterious character of a crypt. The crypt at Chartres was previously an old sanctuary with a well, where the worship of a virgin was celebrated—not of the Virgin Mary, as is done now—but of a Celtic goddess. Under every Christian church of the Middle Ages there is a secret place where in old times the mysteries were celebrated. What we now call the sacraments of the Church were the mysteria of early Christianity. In Provencal the crypt is called *le musset,* which means a secret; the word perhaps originates from *mysteria* and could mean mystery-place. In Aosta, where they speak a Provencal dialect, there is a *musset* under the cathedral.

The crypt is probably taken over from the cult of Mithras. In Mithraism the main religious ceremony took place in a vault half sunk into the earth, and the community remained separated in the main church above. There were peepholes so that they could see and hear the priests and the elect ones chanting and celebrating their rites below, but they were not admitted to them. That was a privilege for the initiates. In the Christian church the separation of the baptistry from the main body of the building derives from the same idea, for baptism as well as the communion were mysteria of which one could not speak directly. One had to use a sort of allegorical allusion so as not to betray the secrets. The mystery also attached to the name of Christ, which therefore was not allowed to be mentioned; instead, he was referred to by the name of Ichthys, the Fish. . . .

The idea of the crypt or mystery-place leads us to something below the Christian *Weltanschauung,* something older than Christianity, like the pagan well below the cathedral at Chartres, or like an antique cave inhabited by a serpent. The well with the serpent is of course not an actual fact which the dreamer saw when he travelled in Spain. This dream-image is not an individual experience and can therefore only be paralleled by archaeological and mythological knowledge. I have to give you a certain amount of that parallelism so that you can see in what context or tissue such a symbolical arrangement appears when looked at in the light of comparative research work. You know that every church still has its baptismal font. This was originally the piscina, the pond, in which the initiates were bathed or symbolically drowned. After a figurative death in the baptismal bath they came out transformed *quasi modo geniti,* as reborn ones. So we can assume that the crypt or baptismal font has the meaning of a place of terror and death and also of rebirth, a place where dark initiations take place.

The serpent in the cave is an image which often occurs in antiquity. It is important to realize that in classical antiquity, as in other civilizations, the serpent not only was an animal that aroused fear and represented danger, but also signified healing. Therefore Asklepios, the god of physicians, is connected with the serpent; you all know his emblem which is still in use. In the temples of Asklepios, the Asklepieia, which were the ancient clinics, there was a hole in the ground, covered by a stone, and in that hole lived the sacred serpent. There was a slot in the stone through which the people who came to the place of healing threw down the fee for the doctors. The snake was at the same time the cashier of the clinic and collector of gifts that were thrown down into its cave. During the great pestilence in the time of Diocletian the famous serpent of the Asklepieion at Epidaurus was brought to Rome as an antidote to the epidemic. It represented the god himself.

The serpent is not only the god of healing; it also has the quality of wisdom and prophecy. The fountain of Castalia at Delphi was originally inhabited by a python. Apollo fought and overcame the python, and from that time Delphi was the seat of the famous oracle and Apollo its god, until he left half his powers to Dionysus, who later came in from the East. In the underworld, where the spirits of the dead live, snakes and water are always together, as we can read in Aristophanes' *The Frogs*. The serpent in legend is often replaced by the dragon; the Latin *draco* simply means snake. A particularly suggestive parallel to our dream symbol is a Christian legend of the fifth century about St Sylvester:† there was a terrible dragon in a cave under the Tarpeian rock in Rome to whom virgins were sacrificed. Another legend says that the dragon was not a real one but artificial, and that a monk went down to prove it was not real and when he got down to the cave he found that the dragon had a sword in his mouth and his eyes consisted of sparkling jewels.

Very often these caves, like the cave of Castalia, contain springs. These springs played a very important role in the cult of Mithras, from which many elements of the early Church originated. Porphyry relates that Zoroaster, the founder of the Persian religion, dedicated to Mithras a cave containing many springs. Those of you who have been to Germany and seen the Saalburg near Frankfurt will have noticed the spring near the grotto of Mithras. The cult of Mithras is always connected with a spring. There is a beautiful Mithraeum in Provence which has a large piscina with wonderful crystal-clear water, and in the background a rock on which is carved the Mithras Tauroktonos—the bull-killing Mithras. These sanctuaries were always a great scandal to the early Christians. They hated all these natural arrangements because they were no friends of nature. In Rome a Mithraeum has been discovered ten feet below the surface of the Church of San Clemente. It is still in good condition but filled with water, and when it is pumped out it fills again. It is always under water because it adjoins a spring which floods the interior. The spring has never been found. We know of other religious ideas in antiquity, for instance of the Orphic cult, which always associate the underworld with water.

This material will give you an idea that the serpent in the cave full of water is an image that was generally known and played a great role in antiquity. As you have noticed, I have chosen all my examples exclusively from antiquity; I could have chosen other parallels from other civilizations, and you would find it was the same. The water in the depths represents the unconscious. In the depths as a rule is a treasure guarded by a serpent or a dragon; in our dream the treasure is the golden bowl with the dagger in it. In order to recover the treasure the dragon has to be overcome. The treasure is of a very mysterious nature. It is connected with the serpent in a strange way; the peculiar nature of the serpent denotes the character of the treasure as though the two things were one. Often there is a golden snake with the treasure. Gold is something that everyone is seeking, so we could say that it looks as if the serpent himself were the great treasure, the source of immense power. In early Greek myths, for instance, the dweller in the cave is a hero, such as Cecrops, the founder of Athens. Above he is half man and half woman, a hermaphrodite, but the lower part of his body is a serpent; he is clearly a monster. The same is said of Erechtheus, another mythical king of Athens.

That prepares us a little for understanding the golden bowl and the dagger in our dream. If you have seen Wagner's *Parsifal* you know that the bowl corresponds to the Grail and the dagger to the spear and that the two belong together; they are the male and the female principle which form the union of opposites. The cave or underworld represents a layer of the unconscious where there is no discrimination at all, not even a distinction between the male and the female, which is the first differentiation primitives make. They distinguish objects in this way, as we still do occasionally. Some keys, for instance, have a hole in the front, and some are solid. They are often called male and female keys. You know the Italian tiled roofs. The convex tiles are placed above and the concave ones underneath. The upper ones are called monks and the under ones the nuns. This is not an indecent joke to the Italians, but the quintessence of discrimination.

When the unconscious brings together the male and the female, things become utterly indistinguishable and we cannot say any more whether they are male or female, just as Cecrops came from such a mythical distance that one could not say whether he was man or woman, human or serpent. So we see that the bottom of the cistern in our dream is characterized by a complete union of opposites. This is the primordial condition of things, and at the same time a most ideal achievement, because it is the union of elements eternally opposed. Conflict has come to rest, and everything is still or once again in the original state of indistinguishable harmony. You find the same idea in ancient Chinese philosophy. The ideal condition is named Tao, and it consists of the complete harmony between heaven and earth. [The] Figure represents the symbol for Tao. On one side it is white with a black spot, and on the other it is black with a white spot. The white side is the hot, dry, fiery principle, the south; the black side is the cold, humid, dark principle, the north. The condition of Tao is the beginning of the world where nothing has yet begun—and it is also the condition to be achieved by the attitude of superior wisdom. The idea of the union of the two opposite principles, of male and female, is an archetypal image. . . .

When the dreamer comes to these symbols he reaches the layer of com-

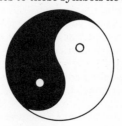

plete unconsciousness, which is represented as the greatest treasure. It is the central motif in Wagner's *Parsifal* that the spear should be restored to the Grail because they belong eternally together. This union is a symbol of complete fulfillment—eternity before and after the creation of the world, a dormant condition. That is probably the thing which the desire of man is seeking. That is why he ventures into the cave of the dragon, to find that condition where consciousness and the unconscious are so completely united that he is neither conscious nor unconscious. Whenever the two are too much separated, consciousness seeks to unite them again by going down into the depths where they once were one. Thus you find in Tantric Yoga or Kundalini Yoga an attempt to reach the condition where Shiva is in eternal union with Shakti. Shiva is the eternally unextended point, and he is encircled by the female principle, Shakti, in the form of a serpent. . . .

The bowl is a vessel that receives or contains, and is therefore female. It is a symbol of the body which contains the anima, the breath and liquid of life, while the dagger has piercing, penetrating qualities and is therefore male. It cuts, it discriminates and divides, and so is a symbol of the masculine Logos principle.

In our dream the dagger is said to be the key to Toledo. The idea of the key is often associated with the mysteries in the cave. . . .

The ancient mystery cults are always connected with psychopompic deities. Some of these deities are equipped with the keys to the underworld, because as the guardians of the door they watch over the descent of the initiates into the darkness and are the leaders into the mysteries. Hecate is one of them.

In our dream the key is the key to the city of Toledo, so we have to consider the symbolic meaning of Toledo and of the city. As the old capital of Spain, Toledo was a very strong fortification and the very ideal of a feudal city, a refuge and stronghold which could not easily be touched from outside. The city represents a totality, closed in upon itself, a power which cannot be destroyed, which has existed for centuries and will exist for many centuries more. Therefore the city symbolizes the totality of man, an attitude of wholeness which cannot be dissolved.

The city as a synonym for the self, for psychic totality, is an old and well-known image. We read for instance in the Oxyrhynchus sayings of Jesus:‡ 'A city built up on the top of a high hill and stablished, can neither fall nor be hid.' And: 'Strive therefore to know yourselves, and ye shall be aware that ye are the sons of the almighty Father; and ye shall know that ye are in the city of God and ye are the city'. There is a Coptic treatise in the Codex Brucianus in which we find the idea of the Monogenes or only son of God, who is also the Anthropos, Man.§ He is called the city with the four gates. The city with the four gates symbolizes the idea of totality; it is the individual who possesses the four gates to the world, the four psychological functions, and so is contained in the self. The city with the four gates is his indestructible wholeness— consciousness and the unconscious united.

So these depths, that layer of utter unconsciousness in our dream, contain at the same time the key to individual completeness and wholeness, in other words to healing. The meaning of 'whole' or 'wholeness' is to make holy or to heal. The descent into the depths will bring healing. It is the way to the total being, to the treasure which suffering mankind is forever seeking, which is hidden in the place guarded by terrible danger. This is the place of primordial unconsciousness and at the same time the place of healing and redemption, because it contains the jewel of wholeness. It is the cave where the dragon of chaos lives and it is also the indestructible city, the magic circle or *temenos,* the sacred precinct where all the split-off parts of the personality are united.

The use of a magic circle or mandala, as it is called in the East, for healing purposes is an archetypal idea. When a man is ill the Pueblo Indians of New Mexico make a sand-painting of a mandala with four gates. In the centre of it they build the so-called sweat-house or medicine-lodge, where the patient has to undergo the sweat-cure. On the floor of the medicine-lodge is painted another magic circle—being thus placed in the centre of the big mandala—and in the midst of it is the bowl with the healing water. The water symbolizes the entrance to the underworld. The healing process in this ceremony is clearly analogous to the symbolism which we find in the collective unconscious. It is an individuation process, an identification with the totality of the personality, with the self. In Christian symbolism the totality is Christ, and the healing process consists of the *imitatio Christi.* The four gates are replaced by the arms of the cross.

The serpent in the cave in our dream is the friend of B— C—, the hero of the dreamer's early days, into whom he projected everything he wanted to become and all the virtues to which he was aspiring. That young friend is at peace with the serpent. He is a child without guile, he is innocent and knows as yet of no conflict. Therefore he has the key to Spain and the power over the four gates. [Jung, 1968, pp. 124–138]

*[The people of ancient Phocaea, on the western coast of Asia Minor, founded Massilia (Marseilles) and colonies on the east coast of Spain.]

†[*Symbols of Transformation,* pars. 572f.]

‡[*New Sayings of Jesus and Fragment of a Lost Gospel,* ed. by Grenfell and Hunt, pp. 36 and 15.]

§[It is MS. Bruce 96, Bodleian Library, Oxford. Cf. *Psychology and Alchemy,* par. 138f.]

EXERCISES

Dream Symbolism

This is an exercise in evoking some of the provocative and emotional power of symbols. The following passage is from an actual dream experience, rewritten very slightly. To experience it most fully, have someone else read the passage to you. First, relax and close your eyes. (Note to the reader: Read slowly and expressively; / means pause; // means a longer pause.)

We are . . . fully justified in speaking of an unconscious psyche. It is not directly accessible to observation—otherwise it would not be conscious . . . [Jung in Campbell, 1971, p. 28]

In your dream you have been told to enter a cave and search for something that is valuable to you. You are entering the cave. / It is damp, stone-damp and there are wet places as you walk. You feel uneasy as you walk on, you are looking for something but you don't know what. /

At the end of a long passage you see a jewel—a jewel as large as your hand. It is resting on something reflecting light all around it. You know that this is what you have been told to find.

As you move toward the jewel you see that blocking the entire passageway is a thick spider's web. / You stop, terrified. You have always been afraid of spiders, but never have you seen one this huge or this frightening. You don't know what to do. //

After a while you go onto your knees and finally onto your stomach.

You move very slowly toward the web. There is a small space near the floor where you may be able to slip through without disturbing the web. Sweating with fear and effort you move slowly / slowly through this gap. //

Once through you lie still a moment trembling with relief. Then you stand and walk toward the jewel. You pick it up, impressed with its weight and its beauty. The possession of the jewel seems to fill you with energy.

You turn back toward the web. Holding this large jewel you know you cannot slip back under the web. The spider sits at the center of the web, its legs arching and retracting. A wave of the old fear runs through you. /

You advance on the spider, and taking the jewel in both hands like a short sword, you slash down on the spider killing it. / Then you use the jewel to cut through the web. / You walk back toward the cave entrance.

Outside the cave is a vast empty meadow. You walk out into it holding the jewel—not sure what the use of this jewel is now that you are free from the spider. As the sunlight plays over the surface of the jewel it begins to change its form. It becomes softer and then seems to turn into a kind of cake or bread. /

Without fully understanding, you take the jewel and begin to eat it. It is delicious and each bit seems to fill you with energy and good feeling. // As you are finishing, you see around the meadow people are appearing and beginning to dance. All of the people come toward you and you join in the dance. // All of you are dancing as the dream ends.

The person who dreamed this then reported: "I emerged from this dream feeling relaxed and confident about my whole life. Also I did not seem to have my usual feelings about spiders. I still didn't like them but it was hard for me to bring on the usual kind of blind panic I always had experienced if I so much as thought about them." (Personal communication)

1. You may wish to write down your feelings during the experience, or, if others were participating at the same time, to share your experiences.
2. Did you feel you needed to modify the dream sequence to suit your own needs or experiences? In what ways was the dream symbolism appropriate, in what ways inappropriate to you?
3. Some people might object to certain aspects of the dream (for example, the killing, the jewel turning into a cake). If you have such objections, discuss them.
4. In what ways does the dream and your own experiences with it fit with Jung's theories?

Active Imagination

It is possible to engage the unconscious in dialogue with the ego through the imagination as well as through dreams. Active imagination refers to any conscious effort to produce material directly related to unconscious processes, to relax our usual ego controls without allowing the unconscious to take over completely. Active imagination is not a single technique or method of dealing with the unconscious, but will differ for each individual. Some people can use drawing or painting most profitably, others prefer to explore conscious imagery, or fantasy, or some other form of expression.

Media

Jung himself used many different media in dealing with his unconscious. He designed his retreat house in Bollingen according to his inner needs, and as he himself grew, he added new wings to the house. Jung also painted murals on the walls at Bollingen; he inscribed manuscripts in Latin and high German script, illustrated his own manuscripts, and also carved in stone.

Many modern media are also available to us today. Still and motion picture photography offer many possibilities, including a wide range of darkroom techniques for special effects. Tape recording, multiple-voice recording, and videotape are also potential vehicles for active imagination, as are traditional and electronic music.

Drawing

Start a "doodle diary," a daily collection of sketches and drawings. As the diary progresses, you will be able to see how major changes in your psychological life are related to your drawings. As you draw, you will probably find that certain colors or forms are associated with certain emotions and certain people, and your drawings will become a clearer medium for self-expression.

Another approach to drawing is to sit down with pad and crayons and ask your unconscious a question. Then let your imagination find an image; put the image on paper. Do not *think* an answer.

Conscious Imagining

Start with a dream image or any image that is particularly powerful or meaningful for you. Contemplate it and observe how it begins to change or unfold. Don't try to make anything happen, just observe what seems to occur spontaneously. Hold to your first image and try and avoid impatient jumping from one subject to another.

You can eventually choose to step into the picture yourself and to address the image and listen to what it has to say.

Persona Exercise

List your favorite articles of clothing, jewelry, or other possessions that you generally carry with you: a purse, backpack, and so forth. Choose the one article that you feel most represents *you,* that somehow is an integral part of your self-image. Choose something that you wear or carry most of the time.

1. Go without it for a week and note your reactions to its absence.
2. Lend it to a friend. How does it feel to see it worn or used by someone else?

Anima/Animus and Shadow

List all the qualities you admire in the person you love most. Then list all those qualities you hate in the person you dislike most.

The first list contains your anima or animus projections—those qualities you have inside you that you can develop. The second list contains your shadow projections—those qualities that you must confront within yourself.

Dream Journal

Keep a journal of the dreams you have each night. Review the dreams at the end of each week, looking for recurrences of patterns or symbolism. You can also experiment with different ways of recording your dreams. You can tape them as you wake up, write them out; or you can sketch the symbols and images of your dreams.

ANNOTATED BIBLIOGRAPHY

Jung, C. G. *Memories, dreams, reflections.* New York: Random House (Vintage Books), 1961. An autobiography that helps place Jung's many-faceted thinking in perspective and provides an excellent introduction to Jung's thought. Includes a glossary with discussions of Jung's major concepts.

––––––, (Ed.). *Man and his symbols.* London: Aldus Books, 1964. Contains an extremely clear essay by Jung, "Approaching the Unconscious." The book is profusely illustrated, one of the best integrations of text and pictures in psychology. There is an inexpensive Dell paperback edition, but the Doubleday hardcover edition has more photos, many in color.

––––––. *Analytic psychology: Its theory and practice.* New York: Pantheon Books, 1968. A clear account of Jung's theories, transcripts of a series of lectures he gave in London.

––––––. *Collected works* (H. Read, M. Fordham, & G. Adler, Eds.). Princeton N.J.: Princeton University Press.* For those seriously interested in exploring Jung in depth, this includes virtually all of Jung's writings.

Many of Jung's essays are now available in paperback editions. Of special interest: *Two Essays on Analytical Psychology,* an overview of the entire theoretical system, and *Psychological Types,* especially Chapter 10, "General Descriptions of Types," and Chapter 11, "Definitions," both of which describe the major Jungian concepts.

Good Secondary Sources

Dry, Avis. *The psychology of Jung.* New York: Wiley, 1961.

Fordham, Frieda. *An introduction to Jung's psychology.* London: Penguin Books, 1953.

Hall, C., & Nordby, V. *A primer of Jungian psychology.* New York: New American Library (Mentor Books), 1973. Clear and well-written overview of Jungian psychology.

Jacoby, Jolande. *Complex, archetype, symbol in the psychology of C. G. Jung.* New York: Pantheon Books, 1959.

Serrano, M. *C. G. Jung and Hermann Hesse: A record of two friendships.* London: Routledge & Kegan Paul, 1966. Includes some fascinating conversations between Jung and Serrano, a Chilean poet and novelist who lived in India for several years.

Singer, June. *Boundaries of the soul: The practice of Jung's psychology.* New York: Doubleday, 1972. An excellent account of the dynamics of Jungian theory and therapy, by a modern Jungian analyst.

REFERENCES

Adler, G. *Studies in analytical psychology.* New York: Norton, 1918.

Campbell, Joseph. *Hero with a thousand faces.* New York: Harcourt Brace Jovanovich, 1949.

*All Jung references, unless otherwise noted, are from the *Collected Works of C. G. Jung* (H. Read, M. Fordham, & G. Adler, Eds.), published under the sponsorship of Bollingen Foundation. English edition, London: Routledge & Kegan Paul; American edition volumes issued 1953–1967, Pantheon Books; 1967 on, Princeton University Press. Dates of first publication are given in parentheses after the titles; multiple dates indicate important revisions in both the Swiss and the Anglo-American editions.

_____ (Ed.). *The portable Jung.* New York: Viking Press, 1971.

Dry, Avis. *The psychology of Jung.* New York: Wiley, 1961.

Evans, R. *Conversations with Carl Jung.* New York: Van Nostrand, 1964.

Fordham, Frieda. *An introduction to Jung's psychology.* London: Penguin Books, 1953.

Freud, Sigmund. *An outline of psychoanalysis,* Standard edition, (Vol. 23). London: Hogarth Press and Institute of Psychoanalysis, 1964.

Glover, E. *Freud or Jung?* New York: Norton, 1950.

Hall, C. & Nordby, V. *A primer of Jungian psychology.* New York: New American Library (Mentor Books), 1973.

Harding, M. E. *The "I" and the "Not-I."* New York: Bollingen, 1965.

_____. The way of all women. New York: C. G. Jung Foundation for Analytical Psychology, 1970.

Jacobs, H. *Western psychotherapy and Hindu-sadhana.* London: Allen & Unwin, 1961.

Jacoby, Jolande. *Complex, archetype, symbol in the psychology of C. G. Jung.* New York: Pantheon Books, 1959.

Jung, C. G. The psychology of dementia praecox. In *Collected works.* (Vol. 3). (Originally published, 1907.)

_____. The transcendent function. In *Collected works* (Vol. 8). (Originally published, 1913.)

_____. Symbols of transformation. In *Collected works* (Vol. 5). (Originally published, 1912.)

_____. The psychology of the unconscious. In *Collected works* (Vol. 7). (Originally published, 1917.)

_____. Psychological types. In *Collected works* (Vol. 6). (Originally published, 1921.)

_____. On psychic energy. In *Collected works* (Vol. 8). (Originally published, 1928a.)

_____. The relations between the ego and the unconscious. In *Collected works* (Vol. 7). (Originally published, 1928b.)

_____. The stages of life. In *Collected works* (Vol. 8). (Originally published, 1931a.)

_____. Marriage as a psychological relationship. In *Collected works* (Vol. 17). (Originally published, 1931b.)

_____. Problems of modern psychotherapy. In *Collected works* (Vol. 16). (Originally published, 1931c.)

_____. *Modern man in search of a soul.* New York: Harcourt Brace Jovanovich, 1933.)

_____. The practical use of dream analysis. In *Collected works* (Vol. 16). (Originally published, 1934.)

_____. The concept of the collective unconscious. In *Collected works* (Vol. 9, part 1). (Originally published, 1936a.)

_____. Individual dream symbolism in relation to alchemy. In *Collected works* (Vol. 12). (Originally published, 1936b.)

_____. The archetypes and the collective unconscious. In *Collected works* (Vol. 9, part 1). (Originally published, 1936c.)

_____. Psychology and religion. In *Collected works* (Vol. 2). (Originally published, 1938.)

_____. Conscious, unconscious, and individuation. In *Collected works* (Vol. 9, part 1). (Originally published, 1939.)

_____. A psychological approach to the dogma of the Trinity. In *Collected works* (Vol. 11). (Originally published, 1942.)

_____. The relations between the ego and the unconscious. In *Collected works* (Vol. 7). (Originally published, 1945.)

_____. Instinct and the unconscious. In *Collected works* (Vol. 8). (Originally published, 1948.)

_____. A study in the process of individuation. In *Collected works* (Vol. 9, part 1). (Originally published, 1950.)

_____. Aion. In *Collected works* (Vol. 9, part 2). (Originally published, 1951.)

_____. Symbols of transformation. In *Collected works* (Vol. 5). (Originally published, 1952a.)

_____. Answer to Job. In *Collected works* (Vol. 12). (Originally published, 1952b.)

_____. The philosophical tree. In *Collected works* (Vol. 13). (Originally published, 1954a.)

_____. Psychological aspects of the mother archetype. In *Collected works* (Vol. 9, part 1). (Originally published, 1954b.)

_____. The undiscovered self (present and future). In *Collected works* (Vol. 10). (Originally published, 1957.)

_____. *Memories, dreams, reflections.* New York: Random House, 1961.

_____. *Analytical psychology: Its theory and practice.* New York: Random House, 1968.

_____. *Letters* (G. Adler, Ed.). Princeton, N.J.: Princeton University Press, 1973.

_____ (Ed.). *Man and his symbols.* New York: Doubleday, 1964.

_____. *Letters, Vol. II: 1951–61.* Princeton, N.J.: Princeton University Press, 1975.

McGuire, W. (Ed.). *The Freud-Jung letters: The correspondence between Sigmund Freud and C. G. Jung.* Princeton, N.J.: Princeton University Press, 1974.

McGuire, W., & Hull, R. F. C. (Eds.). *C. G. Jung speaking,* Princeton, N.J.: Princeton University Press, 1977.

Neumann, E. *The origins and history of consciousness.* Princeton, N.J.: Princeton University Press, 1954.

Progoff, I. *Jung's psychology and its social meaning.* New York: Julian Press, 1953.

Riesman, D. *The lonely crowd.* New Haven, Conn.: Yale University Press, 1950.

Serrano, M. *C. G. Jung and Hermann Hesse.* London: Routledge & Kegan Paul, 1966.

Singer, J. *Boundaries of the soul: The practice of Jung's psychology.* New York: Doubleday, 1972.

Suzuki, D. T. *An introduction to Zen Buddhism.* New York: Grove Press, 1964.

Whitmont, E. *The symbolic quest.* New York: Putnam, 1969.

Wilhelm, R., & Jung, C. G. *The secret of the golden flower.* London: Routledge & Kegan Paul, 1962.

CHAPTER 3
ALFRED ADLER AND INDIVIDUAL PSYCHOLOGY

Alfred Adler was the founder of the holistic system of Individual Psychology, which emphasizes an approach to understanding each person as an integrated totality within a social system. His followers established centers throughout Europe, England, and the United States, and many of his original ideas have become widely accepted in psychology and psychotherapy today. Adler's major principles are holism, the unity of the individual's style of life, social interest or community feeling, and the importance of goal-directedness of behavior. Adler argued that goals and expectations have a greater influence on behavior than past experiences; he believed that everyone is motivated primarily by the goal of superiority or conquest of the environment. He also stressed the effect of social influences on each individual and emphasized the importance of social interest: a sense of community, cooperation, and concern for others. Adler felt that life is essentially a movement toward better adaptation to the environment. The basic goal for human beings is to move from an inferior life situation to a superior one.

Adler's individual psychology is similar to behaviorism in its stress on overt behavior and its consequences, and in his unwillingness to develop abstract concepts unrelated to actual behavior. In contrast to all the other psychological theories covered in this text, individual psychology is not a *depth* psychology—that is, it does not postulate intangible forces and constructs deep within the psyche. Adler developed a *context* psychology in which behavior is understood in terms of its larger context, a context that the individual generally is not aware of.

PERSONAL HISTORY

Alfred Adler was born in a suburb of Vienna on February 7, 1870, the son of a middle-class Jewish merchant. As a child he suffered from a number of serious illnesses, including rickets. He also suffered from an extremely jealous rivalry with his older brother. Adler struggled hard to overcome his physical weakness. Whenever possible, young Alfred liked to run outside and play away from home with the other children, with whom he was popular. From them he seemed to have gained a sense of equality and self-esteem he did not find at home. These experiences can be seen later in Adler's stress on the community sharing of feelings and values, which he called social interest, and through which Adler believed a person could find his or her potential as a productive member of society.

During his sickly youth Adler developed the habit of reading widely. In his adult years his knowledge of and familiarity with literature, the Bible, psychology, and German philosophy made him popular in Viennese society and later as a lecturer throughout the world.

As a child, Adler was closely confronted with death on several occasions. His younger brother died in the bed they shared when Adler was 3 years old. In addition, Adler twice narrowly escaped being killed

The hardest things for human beings to do is to know themselves and change themselves. [Adler, 1928, p.11]

in street accidents; and at the age of 5, he contracted a severe case of pneumonia. The family physician believed the case to be hopeless, but another doctor managed to save him. Adler decided to become a doctor after he recovered.

At 18, Adler entered the University of Vienna to study medicine. He was deeply interested in socialism and attended a number of political meetings. It was at one of these meetings that he met his wife, Raissa Epstein, a student from Russia who was attending the University of Vienna.

Adler received his medical degree in 1895. He established a practice first in ophthalmology and then in general medicine. Because of his growing interest in nervous system functioning and adaptation, Adler's professional interests later shifted to neurology and psychiatry.

Freud formed his original circle in 1922 by inviting Adler and three other junior colleagues to meet with him one evening a week. This group developed into the Vienna Psychoanalytic Society. Adler eventually became its president and coeditor of one of its journals, just one year before his resignation in 1911.

By 1911 Adler's theoretical differences had become unacceptable to Freud and to many other members of the society. Adler resigned as president and left the society along with nine of the other 23 members. He founded his own organization, the Association for Individual Psychology, which gradually spread throughout Europe.

Adler and his followers became active in the field of education, especially in teacher training, because Adler believed it was extremely important to work with those who shaped the minds and characters of the young. Adler and his associates also established child guidance centers in the public schools where children and their families could receive counseling. By the 1930s there were 30 such clinics in Vienna alone.

> All neurotic symptoms are safeguards of persons who do not feel adequately equipped or prepared for the problems of life . . . [Adler, 1964b, p. 95]

Adler published numerous papers and monographs and also began to devote a great deal of time to lecture tours throughout Europe and in the United States. In 1928 he lectured at the New School for Social Research in New York, and a year later returned to give a series of lectures and clinical demonstrations. Adler left Vienna because of the rise of Nazism. He settled in the United States and accepted a post in medical psychology at the Long Island Medical College in 1932. Adler died in Scotland in 1937, at the age of 67, while on a European lecture tour.

INTELLECTUAL ANTECEDENTS

Evolution

Adler was strongly influenced by Darwin's theory of evolution, as were most of his contemporaries. His theory of individual psychology is

Individual Psychology stands firmly on the ground of evolution and in the light of evolution regards all human striving as a struggle for perfection. [Adler, 1964a, pp. 36–37]

based on the premise that adaptation to the environment is the most fundamental aspect of life.

Most psychology theorists are primarily concerned with intrapsychic dynamics; in contrast, Adler was an "ecological psychologist," dealing with relations between individual and environment. Adler's early book on organ inferiorities and compensation was largely an application of the Darwinian point of view toward medicine. It was considered a psychological complement to psychoanalytic theory and was well received by Freud. Adler's later work can be viewed as a refutation of Social Darwinism, which emphasized the survival of the fittest and the elimination of the unfit. Adler believed that organic inferiority can stimulate us to superior attainments, instead of necessarily causing defeat in the struggle of life. Also, Adler argued that cooperation and community feeling are more important than competitive struggle in the process of human evolution.

Psychoanalysis

Adler had begun his own theoretical work and had already published papers in the areas of social medicine and education before he met Freud. Although he never really accepted the concepts of libido or the Oedipal complex, Adler was profoundly influenced by psychoanalytic theory, especially the importance of the mother-child relationships, the role of psychological development in the first six years, the interpretation of neurotic symptoms, and the analysis of dreams.

Freud considered Adler to have been his pupil, which Adler consistently denied. Rather than building upon psychoanalytic theory, Adler developed his own theoretical position in response to Freud's views.

Adler disagreed with Freud on several major points. He could never accept Freud's theory that the repressed unconscious sexual material of childhood was the core of all neuroses. Adler saw sexuality as an expression of one's personality and not its fundamental motivator, opposing Freud's assertion of the primacy of the libido. Adler suggested a different fundamental drive, the drive for power. He saw this as the child striving to become strong and take power to dominate others. The major biological fact for Adler was not the child's instinctive sexual behavior, but the child's smallness and helplessness in relation to the surrounding adult world. According to Adler, children's early attempts to adapt to their environment may easily result in choosing the exercise of power over others as a means to gain self-esteem and to achieve success.

Nietzsche

Adler was also affected by Nietzsche's powerful writings, as were virtually all intellectuals of his generation. However, he was not a superficial imitator of Nietzsche as some critics have maintained. Although his earliest conceptualization of the aggressive instincts did have much in common with Nietzsche's will to power, Adler's later formulation of the striving for superiority is a much broader concept than striving for power; it emphasizes the role of creative growth and development. In addition, Adler's concept of social interest is in basic contradiction to Nietzsche's ideas.

The Philosophy of "As If"

Adler was significantly influenced by the writing of Hans Vaihinger, a philosopher who proposed that there are social "fictions" that have no basis in reality but become critical determinants of human behavior. Vaihinger believed that people, confronted by a welter of facts and experiences, create systems to organize and systematize their experiences; they then assume that these systems are true. These fictions become some of the most important influences on our behavior. Vaihinger argued that people are more affected by their *expectations* than their actual experiences. He called this approach "fictionalism," or "the philosophy of 'as if.' " In *The Neurotic Constitution* (1912) Adler suggests that all human behavior, thought, and feeling proceed along "as if " lines. Beginning in childhood, we all attempt to adapt our environment and overcome any felt weakness. We create for ourselves an idealized goal of perfect adaptation, then struggle toward it, "as if" the goal equals success, happiness, security.

Holism

Fifteen years after his exposure to Vaihinger, Adler's thinking was affected by the holistic philosophy of Jan Smuts. Smuts was a South African military leader, statesman, and philosopher whose work on holism influenced many contemporary thinkers. The two men corresponded and Adler was instrumental in having Smuts's work published in Europe. Smuts wrote that whole systems often have properties that are distinct from the properties of their parts; that there is an impulse toward increasing organization, toward wholeness in every individual. Adler found in holistic philosophy a confirmation of many of his own ideas and an important philosophical basis for individual psychology.

When asked to what he attributed his success in diagnosis in fields other than his own, Adler would say with a sly twinkle: "Perhaps because I happened to notice that there was a patient behind the disease." [Bottome, 1957, p. 146]

MAJOR CONCEPTS

Inferiority and Compensation

Adler's monograph on organ inferiority, which first appeared in 1907, attempted to explain why illness affects people in different ways. At the time, Adler wrote as a physician who was concerned primarily with physiological processes. He suggested that in each individual certain organs are somewhat weaker than others, which makes the person more susceptible to illnesses and diseases involving these weaker organs. Adler also noted that people with severe organic weaknesses will

The important thing is not what one is born with, but what use one makes of that equipment. [Adler, 1964b, p. 86]

often try to compensate for them, and a previously weak organ may become strongly developed as a result of training and exercise, often resulting in the individual's greatest skill or strength.

> In almost all outstanding people we find some organ imperfection; and we gather the impression that they were sorely confronted at the beginning of life but struggled and overcame their difficulties. [Adler, 1931, p. 248]

Adler extended his investigation of organ inferiority to the study of the psychological sense of inferiority. He coined the term *inferiority complex,* and he claimed that all children are deeply affected by a sense of inferiority, which is an inevitable consequence of the child's size and lack of power. Adler believed that the life experiences of all children involve feelings of weakness, inadequacy, and frustration. Children are relatively small and helpless in the world of adults. Their own wants become secondary to the desire to control their own activities and to become free from being dominated by others. From this perspective, power is seen as the first good and weakness as the first evil. The struggle to attain power is the first compensation for a sense of inferiority.

Inferiority feelings are not in themselves abnormal. They are the cause of all improvements in the position of mankind. [Adler, 1956, p. 117]

A strong sense of inferiority will impede positive growth and development, whereas moderate feelings of inferiority can motivate the individual to constructive achievements. "He [the child] realizes at an early age that there are other human beings who are able to satisfy their urges more completely, and are better prepared to live . . . he learns to over-value the size and stature which enable one to open a door, or the ability to move heavy objects, or the right of others to give commands and claim obedience to them. A desire to grow, to become as strong or even stronger than all others, arises in his soul" (Adler, 1928, p. 34).

Aggression and Striving for Superiority

In his early writings Adler emphasized the importance of aggression and striving for power. He did not equate aggression with hostility, but rather meant aggression in the sense of strong initiative in overcoming obstacles, as in an aggressive salesman, for example. Adler asserted that human aggressive tendencies have been crucial in individual and species survival. Aggression may manifest itself in the individual as the will to power, a phrase of Nietzsche's that Adler used. Adler pointed out that even sexuality is often used to satisfy the urge for power.

In his later theorizing, Adler viewed aggression and the will to power as manifestations of a more general motive, the goal of superiority or perfection—that is, motivation to improve ourselves, to develop our own capacities and potential. "The striving for perfection is innate in the sense that it is a part of life, a striving, an urge, a something without which life would be unthinkable" (Adler, 1956, p. 104).

The goal of superiority can take either a positive or a negative direction. When the goal includes social concerns and interest in the welfare of others, it develops in a constructive and healthy direction. It takes the form of a striving to grow, to develop one's skills and abilities, and to work for a superior way of living. However, some people strive for *personal* superiority; they try to achieve a sense of superiority by dominating others rather than by becoming more useful to others. For Adler, striving for personal superiority is a neurotic perversion, the result of a strong sense of inferiority and a lack of social interest. It generally fails to bring the recognition and personal satisfaction that the individual is seeking.

The goal of superiority has its roots in the evolutionary process of continual adaptation to the environment. All species must evolve toward more effective adaptation or else suffer extinction, and thus each individual is driven to strive toward a more perfect relationship with the environment. "If this striving were not innate to the organism, no form of life could preserve itself. The goal of mastering the environment in a superior way, which one can call the striving for perfection, consequently also characterizes the development of man" (Adler, 1964b, p. 39).

Everyone wants to be a worthy human being. According to Adler the "supreme law" of life is that "the sense of worth of the self shall not be allowed to be diminished" (Adler, 1956, p. 358).

> The feeling of personal worth can only be derived from achievement, from the ability to overcome . . . [Adler, 1964b, p. 91]

> To live means to develop. [Adler, 1964b, p. 31]

Life Goals

Adler viewed the goal of mastering the environment as being too abstract to satisfy the need for a direction in life; thus each individual develops a more specific life goal that serves as a focus for achievement. Each individual's life goal is influenced by personal experiences, values, attitudes, and personality. The life goal is not a clear and consciously chosen aim. As adults we may have definite, logical reasons for our choice of a career. However, the life goals that guide and motivate us were first formed early in childhood and remain somewhat obscured from consciousness. For example, Adler mentions that many physicians chose their careers in childhood, as he did, as a means of coping with their insecurity concerning death.

The formation of life goals begins in childhood as compensation for feelings of inferiority, insecurity, and helplessness in an adult world. Life goals generally serve as a defense against feelings of impotence, as a bridge from the unsatisfying present to a bright, powerful, and fulfilling future. They are always somewhat unrealistic and may become neurotically overinflated if inferiority feelings are very strong. For the neurotic, there is generally a large gap between conscious aims

> The goal of superiority with each individual is personal and unique. It depends upon the meaning he gives to life. This meaning is not a matter of words. It is built up in his style of life and runs through it. . . . [Adler, 1956, p. 181]

and unconscious, self-defeating life goals. Fantasies of personal superiority and self-esteem are given more attention than goals involving real achievement.

Man is but a drop of water . . . but a very conceited drop. [Adler in Way, 1950, p. 167]

Life goals provide direction and purpose for our activities; they enable an outside observer to interpret various aspects of thought and behavior in terms of these goals. For example, someone who strives for superiority by seeking personal power will develop various character traits necessary to attain this goal—traits such as ambition, envy, and distrust. Adler points out that these character traits are neither innate nor unalterable, but were adopted as integral facets of the individual's goal orientation. "They are not primary but secondary factors, forced by the secret goal of the individual, and must be understood teleologically" (Adler, 1956, p. 219).

Style of Life

Adler emphasized the need to analyze each individual as a unified totality. The life-style is the unique way that an individual chooses to pursue his or her life goal. It is an integrated style of adapting to and interacting with life in general.

The foremost task of Individual Psychology is to prove this unity in each individual—in his thinking, feeling, acting; in his so-called conscious and unconscious—in every expression of his personality. [Adler, 1964b, p. 69]

According to Adler, the key to understanding a person's behavior is the hidden purpose to which all energies are directed. This purpose reveals all, not the external fact or situation. For example, if I believe that my father mistreated me and go on to blame a life of failure on that, it does not matter what he did in reality; if I think so and believe it, it is so, psychologically, because I have made it so to fit my style of life.

> It is, as we have already seen, in the first four or five years of life that the individual is establishing the unity of his mind and constructing the relationship between mind and body. He is taking his hereditary material and the impressions he receives from the environment and is adapting them to his pursuit of superiority. By the end of the fifth year his personality has crystallized. The meaning he gives to life, the goal he pursues, his style of approach, and his emotional disposition are all fixed. They can be changed later; but they can be changed only if he becomes free from the mistake involved in his childhood crystallization. Just as all his previous expressions were coherent with his interpretation of life, so now, if he is able to correct the mistake, his new expressions will be coherent with his new interpretation. [Adler, 1931, p. 34]

Seemingly isolated habits and behavior traits gain their meaning from the full context of the individual's life and goals, and thus psychological and emotional problems cannot be treated as isolated issues. The whole style of life is involved because a given symptom or trait is but an expression of the unified life-style of the individual.

The science of Individual Psychology developed out of the effort to understand that mysterious creative power of life which expresses itself in the desire to develop, to strive, to achieve. . . . This power is *teleological,* it expresses itself in the striving after a goal, and, in this striving, every bodily and psychological movement is made to cooperate. It is thus absurd to study bodily movements and mental conditions abstractly without relation to an individual whole. [Adler, 1956, p. 92]

The Schema of Apperception

As part of the life-style, each individual develops a conception of self and of the world. Adler called this the *schema of apperception.* Apperception is a psychological term that refers to perception involving a subjective interpretation of what is perceived.

Adler emphasized that it is one's conception of the world that determines behavior. If someone believes that a coil of rope in a dark corner is a snake, his or her fear can be as intense as if a snake were actually present. Adler reminds us that "our senses do not receive actual facts, but merely a subjective image of them, a reflection of the external world" (Adler, 1956, p. 182). The schema of apperception is generally self-reinforcing. For example, when we are afraid, we are more likely to perceive threats in the environment, which reinforces our original belief that the environment is a threatening one.

The Creative Power of the Individual

Adler pointed out that we respond actively and creatively to the various influences affecting our lives. We are not inert objects, passively accepting all outside forces; we actively seek out certain experiences and reject others. We selectively codify and interpret experience, developing an individualized schema of apperception and forming a distinct pattern of relating to the world.

At the core of Adler's model of human nature, creativity is the capacity to formulate (consciously or unconsciously) goals and the means of achieving them. This culminates in the development of a life plan, which organizes one's life into a self-consistent life-style.

For Adler, this process of the formation of a life goal, life-style, and schema of apperception is essentially a creative act. It is the creative power of the personality, or of the self, that guides and directs the individual's response to the environment. Adler attributes to the individual uniqueness, awareness, and control over his or her own destiny—qualities he felt that Freud did not sufficiently stress in his conception of human nature. Adler emphasized that we are not powerless pawns of external forces. We mold our own personalities. "Every individual represents both a unity of personality and the individual fashioning of that unity. The individual is thus both the picture and the artist. He is the artist of his own personality . . ." (Adler, 1956, p. 177).

The individual as a complete being cannot be dragged out of his connection with life. . . . For that reason experimental tests, which at the best deal only with partial aspects of the individual's life, can tell us nothing about his character. . . . [Adler, 1964a, p. 39]

You find what you planned to find. [Adler, 1964b, p. 100]

Each individual arrives at a concrete goal of overcoming through his creative power, which is identical with the self. [Adler, 1956, p. 180]

It is futile to attempt to establish psychology on the basis of drives alone, without taking into consideration the creative power of the child which directs the drive, molds it into form, and supplies it with a meaningful goal. [Adler, 1956, p. 177]

Social Interest

Although Adler's theories have been oversimplified by many critics solely emphasizing aggression and striving for personal power, Adler's later writings are centrally concerned with the concept of social interest. (A better translation of his original German term, *Gemeinschaftsgefühl,* might be "community feeling.") By social interest, Adler means "the sense of human solidarity, the connectedness of man to man ... the wider connotation of a 'sense of fellowship in the human community' " (Wolfe in Adler, 1928, p. 32n). Community feeling refers to the interest we take in others not simply to serve our own purposes, but "an interest in the interests" of others.

All failures . . . are products of inadequate preparation in social interest. They are all non-cooperative, solitary beings who run more or less counter to the rest of the world; beings who are more or less asocial if not antisocial. [Adler, 1964b, p. 90]

From his holistic perspective, Adler saw the individual not only as a unified whole, but also as a part of larger wholes—family, community, society, humanity. Our lives and all our activities are carried out within a social context.

> Any man's value is determined by his attitude toward his fellow man, and by the degree in which he partakes of the division of labor which communal life demands. His affirmation of this communal life makes him important to other human beings, makes him a link in a great chain which binds society, the chain which we cannot in any way disturb without also disturbing human society. [Adler, 1928, p. 121]

In one sense all human behavior is social because, Adler argues, we develop in a social environment and our personalities are socially formed. Social interest is more than concern for one's immediate community or society. It includes feelings of kinship with all humanity and relatedness to the whole of life. Social interest in its broadest sense refers to concern for "the ideal community of all mankind, the ultimate fulfillment of evolution" (Adler, 1964b, p. 35).

Cooperation

One important aspect of social interest is the development of cooperative behavior. From an evolutionary point of view, the ability to cooperate in food gathering, hunting, and defense against predators has been one of the most important factors in the survival of the human race and the most effective form of adaptation to the environment.

The only individuals who can really meet and master the problems of life, however, are those who show in their striving a tendency to enrich all others, who go ahead in such a way that others benefit also. [Adler, 1956, p. 255]

Adler believed that only through cooperation with others and operating as a valuable, contributing member of society can we overcome our actual inferiorities or our sense of inferiority. He wrote that those who have made the most valuable contributions to humanity have been the most cooperative individuals, and the works of the great geniuses have always been oriented in a social direction (Adler, 1931). On the other hand, a lack of cooperation and a resulting sense of inadequacy and failure are at the root of all neurotic or maladaptive styles of life.

Adler believed that "if a person cooperates, he will never become a neurotic" (Adler, 1964b, p. 193).

ADLER'S PSYCHOLOGY OF WOMEN

Alfred Adler made the fairly radical suggestion that psychological differences between the sexes are entirely the result of cultural attitudes. He also pointed out that a culture's attitudes toward differences between men and women are among the attitudes that most profoundly affect an individual's development from birth. He condemned society's conception of women in which, he suggested, women are viewed as inferior in order to perpetuate societal systems of male domination and male privilege. He suggested that a "girl comes into the world with a prejudice sounding in her ears which is designed only to rob her of her belief in her own value, to shatter her self-confidence, and destroy her hope of ever doing anything worthwhile. . . . The obvious advantages of being a man (in our society) have caused severe disturbances in the psychic development of women" (Adler, 1973, pp. 41–42).

DYNAMICS

Psychological Growth

Psychological growth is primarily a matter of moving from a self-centered goal of personal superiority to an attitude of constructive mastery of the environment and socially useful development. Constructive striving for superiority plus strong social interest and cooperation are the basic traits of the healthy individual.

Life Tasks

Adler discusses three major life tasks that confront each individual: work, friendship, and love. They are determined by the basic conditions of human existence. "These three main ties are set by the facts that we are living in one particular place in the universe and must develop with the limits and possibilities which our circumstances set us; that we are living among others of our own kind to whom we must learn to adapt ourselves; and that we are living in two sexes with the future of our race dependent on the relations of these two sexes" (Adler, 1931, p. 264).

Work includes all those activities that are useful to the community, not simply those occupations for which we receive an income. For Adler, work provides a sense of satisfaction and self-worth only to the extent that it benefits others. The importance of our work is ultimately based upon our dependence on the physical environment. "We are living on the surface of this planet, with only the resources of this planet, with the fertility of its soil, with its mineral wealth, and with its climate and atmosphere. It has always been the task of mankind to find the right answer to the problem these conditions set us . . . it has always been necessary to strive for improvement and further accomplishments" (Adler, 1956, p. 131).

Friendship is an expression of our membership in the human race and our constant need to adapt to and interact with others of our species. Our specific friendships provide essential links to our communities because no individual ever relates to society in the abstract. Friendly, cooperative endeavor is also an important element in constructive work.

Love is discussed by Adler in terms of heterosexual love. It involves a close union of mind and body and the utmost cooperation between two people of the opposite sex. Love is based on the fact that each human being is a member of one sex and not the other, and that intimacy between the sexes is essential to the continuance of our species. Adler writes that the close bond of marriage represents the greatest challenge to our ability to cooperate with another human being, and a successful marriage creates the best environment for promoting cooperation and social interest in children.

Adler stressed that these three tasks (work, friendship, and love) are always interrelated. "A solution of one helps toward the solution of the others, and indeed we can say that they are all aspects of the same situation and the same problem—the necessity for a human being to preserve life and to further life in the environment in which he finds himself" (Adler, 1956, p. 133).

Obstacles to Growth
Organ Inferiority, Pampering, and Neglect

Adler specifies three childhood situations that tend to result in isolation, a lack of social interest, and the development of a noncooperative style of life based on an unrealistic goal of personal superiority. These are organ inferiority, pampering, and neglect.

Children who suffer from illnesses or disease tend to become strongly self-centered. They withdraw from interaction with others out of a sense of inferiority and inability to compete successfully with other children. Adler does point out, however, that those children who overcome their difficulties tend to overcompensate for their original weakness and develop their abilities to an unusual degree.

Pampered or spoiled children also have difficulties in developing a sense of social interest and cooperation. They lack confidence in their own abilities because others have always done things for them. Rather than cooperate with others, they tend to make one-sided demands on friends and family. Social interest is usually minimal, and Adler found that pampered children generally have little genuine feeling for the parents they manipulate so well.

Neglect is the third situation that tends to strongly impede a child's development. A neglected or unwanted child has never known love and cooperation in the home, and therefore finds it extremely difficult to develop these capacities. Such children have no confidence in their ability to be useful and to gain affection and esteem from others. They tend to become cold and hard as adults. "The traits of unloved children in their most developed form can be observed by studying the biographies of all the great enemies of humanity. Here the one thing that stands out is that as children they were badly treated. Thus they developed hardness of character, envy and hatred; they could not bear to see others happy" (Adler, 1956, p. 371).

Striving for Personal Superiority

When inferiority feelings predominate or when social interest is underdeveloped, individuals tend to seek personal superiority because they lack confidence in their ability to function effectively and to work constructively with others. The trappings of success, prestige, and esteem become more important than concrete achievements. Such individuals contribute nothing of real value to society and become fixed in self-centered behavior patterns that inevitably lead to a sense of failure. "They have turned away from the real problems of life and are engaged in shadow-fighting to reassure themselves of their strength" (Adler, 1956, p. 255).

No act of cruelty has ever been done which has not been based upon a secret weakness. The person who is really strong has no inclination to cruelty. [Adler, 1956, p. 390]

STRUCTURE

Body

The body is a major source of inferiority feelings in the child, who is surrounded by those who are bigger and stronger and who function more effectively physically. Adler has also pointed out that what is most important is our attitude toward our bodies (Adler, 1964b). Many attractive men and women have never resolved childhood feelings of ugliness and unacceptability, and they still behave as if they were unattractive. On the other hand, through compensation, those who have physical deficiencies may strive hard and develop their bodies to a greater than average extent.

Social Relationships

Social relationships are of central importance in Adler's theories. They are a direct expression of social interest and are essential in developing a fulfilling, constructive life-style. (For a more complete discussion, see the paragraph on friendship under Psychological Growth.)

Will

Will is, for Adler, another name for striving for superiority and actualizing life goals. As such, it is a central element in his theory.

Emotions

Adler writes of two kinds of emotions: socially disjunctive emotions, which are related to individual goal attainment, and socially conjunctive emotions, which tend to promote social interaction. Disjunctive emotions, such as anger, fear, or disgust, are intended to bring about a positive change in the life situation of the individual, although sometimes at the expense of others. They result from a sense of failure or inadequacy and serve to mobilize the individual's strength to make fresh efforts (Adler, 1956). Conjunctive emotions tend to be socially oriented, as in the desire to share our joy and laughter with others. The emotion of sympathy is "the purest expression of social interest" and reveals the extent to which we can relate to others (Adler, 1956, p. 228).

Intellect

Adler distinguishes between reason and intelligence. Neurotics, criminals, and others who have failed to function successfully in society are often quite intelligent; frequently, they give perfectly logical arguments and justifications for their behavior. However, Adler has called this kind of intelligence "personal intelligence," or thinking that is bounded by the individual's goal of personal superiority rather than by socially useful considerations. Reason is "the kind of intelligence which contains social interest and which is thus limited to the generally useful" (Adler, 1956, p. 150). Reason is in accord with common sense, that is, basic cultural attitudes and values.

Self

The self *is* the individual's style of life. It is the personality viewed as an integrated whole.

> In real life we always find a confirmation of the melody of the total self, of the personality, with its thousandfold ramifications. If we believe that the foundation, the ultimate basis of everything has been found in character traits, drives, or reflexes, the self is likely to be overlooked. Authors who emphasize a part of the whole are likely to attribute to this part all the aptitudes and observations pertaining to the self, the individual. They show "something" which is endowed with prudence, determination, volition, and creative power without knowing that they are actually describing the self, rather than drives, character traits, or reflexes. [Adler, 1956, p. 175]

For Adler, the self is a dynamic, unitary *principle* rather than a structure to be found within the psyche. "[In Adlerian psychology] the self is not considered as an entity. . . . There is literally no self to actualize but through transactions with its world" (Ansbacher, 1971, p. 60). Adler's position concerning the self strongly resembles the concept of "selflessness" in Buddhist psychology.

Therapist

The aim of Adlerian psychotherapy is to help the individual reconstruct assumptions and goals in accord with greater social usefulness. Adler defines three major aspects of therapy: understanding the specific life-style of the patient, helping patients understand themselves, and strengthening social interest.

Understanding the Life-Style

Because the life-style forms a basically consistent whole, the therapist looks for themes that run through the individual's behavior. In order to determine their life-style, Adler always asked patients for their earliest memories, the most salient events from early childhood. "There are no 'chance memories'; out of the incalculable number of impressions which meet an individual, he chooses to remember only those which he feels, however darkly, to have a bearing on his situation" (Adler, 1931, p. 73).

Adler assumed that the patient's life plan had developed under negative conditions, so the therapist should be sensitized to look for organ inferiority, pampering, or neglect in childhood.

Adler also emphasized the importance of expressive behavior, including posture and intonation. "I have found it of considerable value to conduct myself as during pantomime, that is, for a while not to pay any attention to the words of the patient, but instead to read his deeper intention from his bearing and his movements within a situation" (Adler, 1956, p. 330).

> There must be uncovered, step by step, the unattainable goal of superiority over all; the purposive concealment of this goal; the all-dominating, direction-giving power of the goal; the patient's lack of freedom and his hostility toward mankind, which are determined by the goal. [Adler, 1956, p. 333]

Promoting Self-Understanding

Adler viewed the major problem of most patients as being their erroneous schema of apperception determined by an unattainable and unrealistic goal of superiority over all others. One of the major tasks of the therapist is to help patients understand their own life-style, including their basic approach to life. Only after self-understanding is reached can people correct their nonadaptive style of life. "A patient has to be brought into such a state of feeling that he likes to listen, and wants to understand. Only then can he be influenced to live what he has understood" (Adler, 1956, p. 335). This approach will succeed only when the therapist's explanation is clear and detailed and speaks directly to the experience of the patient.

> Even when a patient lies it is of value to me . . . it is *his* lie and nobody else's! What he cannot disguise is his own originality. [Adler in Bottome, 1957, p. 162]

Self-understanding is learning to see the mistakes we are making in coping with daily situations. It involves gaining a better understanding of how the world is run and of our place in it. Adler stresses the importance of learning to understand the consequences of our behavior rather than learning more about our inner experience.

Adler emphasized that success in therapy is always up to the patient. "The actual change in the nature of the patient can only be his own doing. . . . One should always look at the treatment and the cure not as the success of the consultant but as the success of the patient. The adviser can only point out the mistakes, it is the patient who must make the truth living" (Adler, 1956, p. 336).

Psychotherapy is an exercise in cooperation and a test of cooperation. We can succeed only if we are genuinely interested in the other. [Adler, 1956, p. 340]

Strengthening Social Interest

Therapy is a cooperative enterprise between therapist and patient, a supportive relationship that helps the patient develop cooperation and social interest. "The task of the physician or psychologist is to give the patient the experience of contact with a fellow man, and then to enable him to transfer this awakened social interest to others" (Adler, 1956, p. 341).

Adler pointed out that the therapist often has to provide the care, support, and sense of cooperation that the patient never received from his or her own parents. Adler was convinced that concern for self rather than for others is at the core of most psychological problems. He felt that the major task of the therapist is gradually to guide the patient away from exclusive interest in self toward working constructively for others as a valuable member of the community. In caring for the patient the therapist serves as a model of social interest.

I tell [patients] "You can be cured in fourteen days if you follow this prescription. Try to think every day how you can please someone." [Adler, 1956, p. 347]

The Role of the Therapist

Adler stressed the importance of establishing a sense of equality between patient and therapist. He preferred facing the person to sitting behind a reclining patient as Freud did. Adler also emphasized engaging in a free discussion, not free association. His beliefs and attitudes concerning the therapeutic relationship seem to foreshadow the work of Carl Rogers.

> We can succeed only if we are genuinely interested in the other. We must be able to see with his eyes and listen with his ears. He must contribute his part to our common understanding. . . . Even if we felt we'd understood him we should have no witness that we were right unless he also understood. [Adler, 1929, p. 340]

EVALUATION

Adler's theories have had a great impact on humanistic psychology, psychotherapy, and personality theory. Many of his concepts have been integrated into other schools than his own. Adler's stress on social interest provided a major social orientation to psychotherapy; and his concern with conscious, rational processes provided the first ego psychology. In fact, it has been suggested that "neo-Adlerian" is a more accurate term than neo-Freudian for theorists such as Erich Fromm, Karen Horney, and Harry Stack Sullivan (Wittels, 1939). It is astonishing that Adler's thoughts have had such an influence on so many other eminent psychologists, yet he is relatively unknown outside the field.

Viktor Frankl and Rollo May, noted existential analysts, have regarded Adler as an influential precursor to existential psychiatry (Frankl, 1970; May, 1970), and Adler's interest in holism, goal-directedness, and the role of values in human behavior anticipated many of the developments of humanistic psychology. Abraham Maslow wrote, "For me Alfred Adler becomes more and more correct year by year. As the facts come in, they give stronger and stronger support to his image of man" (1970, p. 13).

However, Adler has generally failed to receive credit for his accomplishments. His original achievements are often seen as derivatives of psychoanalytic theory or self-evident or trivial. In his survey of major psychiatric schools of thought, Ellenberger writes:

> It would not be easy to find another author from which so much has been borrowed from all sides without acknowledgment than Alfred Adler. His teaching has become . . . a place where anyone and all may come and draw anything without compunction. An author will meticulously quote the source of any sentence he takes from elsewhere, but it does not occur to him to do the same whenever the source is individual psychology; it is as if nothing original could ever come from Adler. [1970, p. 645]

One reason for Adler's relative lack of popularity lies in his writing style. He was an excellent speaker and much preferred lecturing to writing. His writing is not always precise, and his theorizing tends to be phrased in a simple, commonsensical manner that often seems superficial or shallow. Adler was more interested in practice than in theory. He was at his best in dealing with actual case materials; thus his work has tended to be most popular among teachers, social workers, clinical practitioners, and others who require practical psychological skills in their professional work.

Many of Adler's pioneering ideas have become so well accepted that they are taken for granted today. Adler is virtually the father of psychosomatic medicine in his pioneering work on the interaction of psychological and physical elements in organ inferiority. Adler's seminal contributions to the development of modern psychology include the inferiority complex, the role of power and aggression in human behavior, the concept of unity of the personality, and the significance of nonsexual factors in development.

THE THEORY FIRSTHAND

The following passage provides an example of Adler's analytic methods. Adler discusses the theoretical importance of first memories and then demonstrates his technique of analyzing them.

Early recollections have especial significance. To begin with, they show the style of life in its origins and in its simplest expressions. We can judge from them whether the child was pampered or neglected; how far he was training for cooperation with others; with whom he preferred to cooperate; what problems confronted him, and how he struggled against them. In the early recollections of a child who suffered from difficulties in seeing and who trained himself to look more closely, we shall find impressions of a visual nature. His recollections will begin, "I looked around me . . . ," or he will describe colors and shapes. A child who had difficulties of movement, who wanted to walk or run or jump, will show these interests in his recollections. Events remembered from childhood must be very near to the main interest of the individual; and if we know his main interest we know his goal and his style of life. It is this fact which makes early recollections of such value in vocational guidance. We can find, moreover, the child's relations towards his mother, his father and the other members of the family. It is comparatively indifferent whether the memories are accurate or inaccurate; what is of most value about them is that they represent the individual's judgment, "Even in childhood, I was such and such a person," or, "Even in childhood, I found the world like this."

Most illuminating of all is the way he begins his story, the earliest incident he can recall. The first memory will show the individual's fundamental view of life; his first satisfactory crystallization of his attitude. It offers us an opportunity to see at one glance what he has taken as the starting point for his development. I would never investigate a personality without asking for the first memory. Sometimes people do not answer, or profess that they do not know which event came first; but this itself is revealing. We can gather that they do not wish to discuss their fundamental meaning, and that they are not prepared for cooperation. In the main people are perfectly willing to discuss their first memories. They take them as mere facts, and do not realize the meaning hidden in them. Scarcely anyone understands a first memory; and most people are therefore able to confess their purpose in life, their relationship to others and their view of the environment in a perfectly neutral and unembarrassed manner through their first memories. Another point of interest in first memories is that their compression and simplicity allows us to use them for mass investigations. We can ask a school class to write their earliest recollections; and, if we know how to interpret them, we have an extremely valuable picture of each child.

Let me, for the sake of illustration, give a few first memories and attempt to interpret them. [Adler had members of the audience write down their first memories on slips of paper and hand them to him.] I know nothing else of the individuals than the memories they tell—not even whether they are children or adults. The meaning we find in their first memories would have to be checked by other expressions of their personality; but we can use them as they stand for our training, and for sharpening our ability to guess. We shall know what might be true, and we shall be able to compare one memory with another. In especial we shall be able to see whether the individual is training towards cooperation or against it, whether he is courageous or discouraged, whether he wishes to be supported and watched, or to be self-reliant and independent; whether he is prepared to give or anxious only to receive.

"Since my sister . . ." It is important to notice which people in the environment occur in first memories. When a sister occurs, we can be pretty sure that the individual has felt greatly under her influence. The sister has thrown a shadow over the other child's development. Generally we find a rivalry between the two, as if they were competing in a race; and we can understand that such a rivalry offers additional difficulties in development. A child cannot extend his interest to others as well when he is occupied with rivalry as when he can cooperate on terms of friendship. We shall not jump to conclusions, however: perhaps the two children were good friends.

"Since my sister and I were the youngest in the family, I was not permitted to attend [school] until she (the younger) was old enough to go." Now the rivalry becomes evident. My sister has hindered me! She was younger, but I was forced to wait for her. She narrowed my possibilities! If this is really the meaning of the memory, we should expect this girl or boy to feel, "It is the greatest danger in my life when some one restricts me and prevents my free development." Probably the writer is a girl. It seems less likely that a boy would be held back till a younger sister is ready to go to school.

"Accordingly we began on the same day." We should not call this the best kind of education for a girl in her position. It might well give her the impression that, because she is the older, she must stay behind. In any case, we see that this particular girl has interpreted it in this sense. She feels that she is slighted in favor of her sister. She will accuse some one of this neglect; and probably it will be her mother. We should not be surprised if she leaned more towards her father, and tried to make herself his favorite.

"I recall distinctly that mother told every one how lonely she was on our first day at school. She said, 'I ran out to the gate many times that afternoon and looked for the girls. I just thought they would never come.' " Here is a description of the mother; and a description which does not show her behaving very intelligently. It is the girl's portrait of her mother. "Thought we should never come"—the mother was obviously affectionate, and the girls knew of her affection; but at the same time she was anxious and tense. If we could speak to this girl, she could tell us more of the mother's preference for the younger sister. Such a preference would not astonish us, for the youngest child is almost always pampered. From the whole of this first memory, I should conclude that the older of the two sisters felt hindered through the rivalry of the younger. In later life we should expect to find marks of jealousy and fear of competition. It would not surprise us to find her disliking women younger than herself. Some people feel too old all through their lives, and many jealous women feel inferior towards members of their own sex who are younger than they. [Adler, 1931, pp. 74–78]

EXERCISES

Goals

Set aside 15 minutes for this exercise. Sit down with four pieces of paper and a pen or pencil. Write at the top of the first sheet, "What are my lifetime goals?" Take 2 minutes to answer this question. Put down whatever comes into your mind, no matter how general and abstract, or how trivial it may seem. You may want to include personal, family, career, social, community, or spiritual goals. Then give yourself an additional 2 minutes to go over your list and make any additions or alterations. Set aside this first sheet.

Take your second sheet and write at the top, "How would I like to spend the next three years?" Take 2 minutes to answer this question. Then take 2 more minutes to go over your list. This should help you pinpoint your goals more specifically than the first question. Again set aside this list.

For a different perspective on your goals, write on your third sheet, "If I knew my life was to end six months from today, how would I live until then?" The purpose of this question is to find out if there are things that are important to you that you are not doing or even considering now. Again write for 2 minutes; go back over your answers for another 2 minutes, and set this sheet aside.

On a fourth piece of paper, write down the three goals you consider most important out of all the goals you have listed.

Compare your lists. Are there any themes running through the various goals you have given? Are most of your goals in one category, such as social or personal? Are there some goals that appear on all of the first three lists? Do the goals you have chosen as most important differ in some way from the other goals on your lists?

Although this method of analyzing life goals does not fully uncover the unconscious life goals that Adler discussed, it can be a powerful way of discovering the relationship between your goals and your daily activities. It is also a useful exercise to repeat every six months or so in order to see what changes may have occurred. (Adapted from Alan Lakein, 1974.)

Cooperation

In order to understand more clearly what Adler means by cooperation and social interest, for one week devote as much time as you can to helping others. Keep a record of your choices and how they made you feel. Resolve that you will not refuse any reasonable requests from others, even if they take up some of your valuable time, energy, or some money. (If you want to make the exercise more demanding, let all your friends know that you are carrying out this exercise and you will be available to serve them for a week.) Don't simply wait for someone to ask you, but actively look for opportunities to offer your help to others.

At the end of the week, review your experiences. How did other people react to you? What were your reactions to helping others? What did you learn from the exercise?

ANNOTATED BIBLIOGRAPHY

Adler, A. *The individual psychology of Alfred Adler: A systematic presentation in selections from his writings* (H. L. Ansbacher & Rowena R. Ansbacher, Eds.) New York: Harper & Row, 1956. The best introduction to Adler's work; it includes materials that are not available elsewhere in English. Two major sections: personality theory and abnormal psychology.

_____. *Superiority and social interest: A collection of later writings*. (H. L. Ansbacher & Rowena Ansbacher, Eds). New York: Viking Press, 1964. Includes sections on theory, case studies, religion, and various applications of individual psychology. Also, an essay on the increasing recognition of Adler, a biography, and a definitive bibliography of Adler's writings.

_____. *The practice and theory of individual psychology*. London: Routledge & Kegan Paul, 1929. A collection of essays and discussions on neurosis and psychological problems, including considerable case material.

_____. *What life should mean to you*. Boston: Little, Brown, 1931. A clearly written exposition of Adler's basic concepts, for the layperson.

Dreikurs, R. *Psychology in the classroom: A manual for teachers*. New York: Harper & Row, 1957. An application of Adler's theories to education, including extensive case material.

REFERENCES

Ackerknecht, Lucy. Recent influences of Adlerian psychology on general psychology. Manuscript, n. d.

Adler, A. *Understanding human nature*. London: Allen & Unwin, 1928.

_____. *The neurotic constitution*. New York: Moffat, Yard, 1912.

_____. *The practice and theory of individual psychology*. London: Routledge & Kegan Paul, 1929.

_____. *The science of living*. London: Allen & Unwin, 1930.

_____. *What life should mean to you*. Boston: Little, Brown, 1931.

_____. *The individual psychology of Alfred Adler: A systematic presentation in selections from his writings*. (H. L. Ansbacher & Rowena Ansbacher, Eds.). New York: Harper & Row, 1956.

_____. *Social interest: A challenge to mankind*. New York: Capricorn Books, 1964a.

_____. *Superiority and social interest: A collection of later writings* (H. L. Ansbacher & Rowena Ansbacher, Eds.). New York: Viking Press, 1964b.

_____. Sex. In *Psychoanalysis and women,* Jean Miller (Ed.). Baltimore: Penguin, 1973.

Ansbacher, H. Alfred Adler and humanistic psychology. *Journal of Humanistic Psychology,* 1971, *2,* 53–63.

_____. The Adlerian and Jungian schools. [Part]A: Individual psychology. In S. Arieti (Ed.), *American handbook of psychiatry*. New York: Basic Books, 1974.

Bottome, Phyllis. *Alfred Adler: A portrait from life*. New York: Vanguard Press, 1957.

Dreikurs, R. *Fundamentals of Adlerian psychology*. New York: Greenberg, 1950.

_____. *Psychology in the classroom: A manual for teachers*. New York: Harper & Row, 1957.

Ellenberger, H. *The discovery of the unconscious: The history and evolution of dynamic psychiatry*. New York: Basic Books, 1970.

Frankl, V. Tributes to Alfred Adler on his hundredth birthday. *Journal of Individual Psychology,* 1970, *26,* 12.

Hall, C., & Lindzey, G. *Theories of personality*. New York: Wiley, 1957.

Lakein, A. *How to get control of your time and your life.* New York: New American Library, 1974.

Maslow, A. Tributes to Alfred Adler on his hundredth birthday. *Journal of Individual Psychology,* 1970, *26,* 13.

May, R. Tributes to Alfred Adler on his hundredth birthday. *Journal of Individual Psychology,* 1970, *26,* 13.

Orgler, Hertha. *Alfred Adler: The man and his work.* London: Daniel, 1939.

Way, L. *Adler's place in psychology.* London: Allen & Unwin, 1950.

Wittels, F. The neo-Adlerians. *American Journal of Sociology,* 1939, *45,* 433–445.

CHAPTER 4
KAREN HORNEY AND THE PSYCHOLOGY OF WOMEN

Karen Horney was a pioneer in the exploration of the social and cultural aspects of personality. Although she was a practicing psychoanalyst and revered Freud's revolutionary clinical observations and insights, she was one of the first of Freud's followers to openly and cogently disagree with many of his fundamental assumptions.

Horney rejected Freud's impulse-oriented theoretical stance and questioned the universality of key Freudian concepts. These included the Oedipus complex, the opposition of the life and death impulses, and the overriding importance of sexual factors in neurosis. Her work on the psychology of women foreshadowed the current recognition of a feminine psychology. Against the sober pessimism of psychoanalytic theory she developed and promulgated an open, optimistic, and self-actualizing view of the human condition.

For Horney, neurosis was the product of cultural influences—that is, the economic, social, and educational environmental forces. It is not, as Freud assumed, the product of dammed-up impulses in a restrictive environment. In developing her belief that everyone has the capacity for personal growth, she popularized psychoanalytic insights and attempted to demystify the therapeutic process. Her own approach to clients emphasized the analysis of current conflicts, needs, and attempted solutions to restore a true sense of self and assure continued individual growth.

PERSONAL HISTORY

The first daughter and second child of Berndt and Clothilde Danielson, Karen Horney was born in Hamburg, Germany, on September 16, 1885. Her family was Protestant, comfortably well-off, and settled, but with one significant difference: her father was the captain of a commercial ship and sometimes took his young daughter with him on long voyages. These unusual experiences may have contributed to her later cross-cultural sensitivity. But the trips were only brief punctuations in the more usual situation of living at home with her mother and older brother, Berndt, father's namesake and mother's favorite.

As a student, Karen Danielson's performance was outstanding. Even though it was rare for a girl to study medicine in her day, she decided at the age of 12, against her father's strong opposition, to prepare for medical school. Her interest in psychological self-study was also precocious; at the age of 13 she began a diary that she kept continuously until she completed psychoanalysis 10 years later.

At 21 Karen Danielson went to Berlin to medical school. She married Oscar Horney, a young Berlin lawyer, two years later. After receiving her M.D. degree in 1911, she joined the Berlin Psychoanalytic Society and went into analysis with a staunch Freudian, Karl Abraham.

Soon she became a practicing psychoanalyst herself, then a training analyst at the Berlin Psychoanalytic Institute, founded in 1920. She also raised three daughters (Kelman, 1971).

Horney studied and practiced in Berlin in the ferment of the very beginnings of psychoanalysis. Freud was still generating startling insights in Vienna and evolving his theories of anxiety, defense mechanisms, the unconscious, and the id-ego-superego map of the mind. Horney participated by writing several articles of theoretical importance, including several on the psychology of women. From the beginning of her career, she felt the female was inadequately understood by her male colleagues. She also participated in a famous discussion of lay analysis with Freud himself in which she was, as usual, on the side of the laity.

At this time there was also a political ferment occurring in Germany. A polarity was emerging in which the Second Reich under the domination of the kaiser was evolving into what would ultimately become Fascism, countered by a movement toward Marxism. With her colleagues Erich Fromm and Wilhelm Reich, Horney chose the Marxist left.

In 1932, on the invitation of Franz Alexander, Horney came to the United States to become Associate Director of the Chicago Psychoanalytic Institute. She had separated from her husband before emigrating to America. The association with Alexander did not work out and two years later, in 1934, Horney moved again, this time to New York. She settled down to clinical work and active participation in the New York Psychoanalytic Society and Institute.

After two decades of classical psychoanalytic practice, Horney began to author books that criticized and revised the Freudian view of human growth, the nature of neurosis, and the technique of psychotherapy. Although she had published several articles in Germany, her first book, *The Neurotic Personality of Our Time,* appeared in the United States in 1937, also the year of her divorce. *New Ways in Psychoanalysis,* a point-by-point revision of Freud's theory, appeared in 1939, the year of Freud's death.

The publication of this book, as well as her outspoken criticisms of the way analysis was being taught, shocked the more orthodox of her colleagues into direct action. In a tempestuous meeting of the New York Psychoanalytic Society in 1941 she was officially demoted. After the vote, she rose and, with a number of her supporters, walked out of the meeting. Three days later the group sent this letter of resignation to the Society:

> For the last few years it has become gradually more apparent that the scientific integrity of the New York Psychoanalytic Society has steadily

deteriorated. Reverence for dogma has replaced free inquiry; academic freedom has been abrogated; students have been intimidated; scientific sessions have degenerated into political machinations.

When an instructor and training analyst is disqualified solely because of scientific convictions, any hopes we may have harbored for improvement in the politics of the Society have been dispelled.

We are interested only in the scientific advancement of psychoanalysis in keeping with the courageous spirit of its founder, Sigmund Freud. This obviously cannot be achieved within the framework of the New York Psychoanalytic Society as it is now constituted.

Under the circumstances we have no alternative but to resign, however much we may regret the necessity for this action. [In Rubins, 1978, p. 240]

In September of that year, Horney and 20 other analysts formed the Association for the Advancement of Psychoanalysis.

From that crucial year until the end of her life, Horney was involved in personal and political struggles within the psychoanalytic world and with debates involving articles and rebuttals in the respective journals of the two competing organizations. She raised her children, took up painting, and maintained a wide circle of friends that included dramatists, theologians, philosophers, and anthropologists.

Apart from the clinical psychoanalytic articles, Horney wrote a remarkable series of books designed for the public that were not at all to the taste of her more orthodox colleagues. Some books were never reviewed in professional journals and some were roundly attacked when they were given any official recognition. Horney continued to express her own developing ideas and theories as they evolved from her clinical experience. The social and economic upheavals in Germany as well as the enormous personal changes in her own life (her marriage, separation, and move to America) sensitized her to the importance and impact of social factors on personality. She brought to the psychoanalytic movement a new awareness of the need to include the effects of the family and the society in understanding the genesis and maintenance of neurosis.

With her writings Horney opened up a new set of possibilities for all persons, men and women, who were concerned with self-understanding. She was never comfortable with the Freudian idea of biological determinism, which ignored cultural issues and indirectly denigrated her for being a woman. She became the first major psychoanalytic writer who dared to suggest that although the therapist was valuable, it was possible to gain the insights attained within psychoanalysis outside it—through self-analysis (1942).

As she became friends with the Zen teacher D. T. Suzuki, she became interested in Eastern thought. She even traveled to Japan and stayed in Zen monasteries. Deeply drawn to the study of Zen practice, she explored the uses of meditation and the methods of helping others as utilized by the *roshi,* or teacher.

Karen Horney died in New York City on December 4, 1952. She was 67. Four years later her students and admirers organized themselves into the American Academy of Psychoanalysis, which has been active since that time. Her books have never been out of print. They continue to educate each new generation in the optimistic possibilities inherent in her view of human functioning.

INTELLECTUAL ANTECEDENTS

Sigmund Freud and Psychoanalysis

Horney deeply acknowledged her debt to Freud. She heartily accepted the theory of psychic determinism on which psychoanalysis is founded as well as Freud's emphasis on the importance of unconscious motivation and the primacy of emotional over rational forces in the mind. She agreed with the basic Freudian insight that adult neurosis is due to the persistence of childhood influences. She also accepted the doctrine of repression and resistance as well as the basic idea of neurotic conflict. In her psychotherapeutic work she used the basic Freudian techniques of free association, dream interpretation, and analysis of transference.

Her own work, although original, was derived from her reactions to traditional psychoanalytic thinking. Rejecting the biological, genetic, and mechanistic orientation, she opted for a social and interpersonal one, which was her response to a Freudian emphasis that made no sense to her. Her exploration of the feminine was a reaction to the Freudian dictum, "Anatomy is destiny." She viewed the orthodox explanations as simplistic, culture-bound, and theoretically inadequate. Her own nondirective method of doing therapy was a reaction to the standard practices of nondirectness and the avoidance of evaluative positions on the moral issues in a client's life.

> . . . the system of theories which Freud has gradually developed is so consistent that when one is once entrenched in them it is difficult to make observations unbiased by his way of thinking. [Horney, 1939, pp. 7–8]

Hegel and Dialectical Materialism

Horney grew up in Germany at a time when the ideas of Hegel (1770–1831) were widely discussed. He proposed that the natural sequence of ideas—the thought process itself—moves in a three-beat rhythm called the *dialectic.* One has an idea or a *thesis.* Then one proceeds to develop its opposite or the *antithesis.* Finally, the mind recognizes the relationship between the thesis and antithesis and weaves them into a *synthesis.* This synthesis is the thesis of the next cycle. Karl Marx took the idealism of Hegel and formulated the doctrine of dialectical materialism, which proposes that the social development of a culture also moves from thesis to antithesis (in this case, revolution) to synthesis.

In Horney's work we see the rejection of Freud's dualism, the endless and static opposition of forces (sexual vs. aggressive or life vs. death), and her espousal of an integration of psychological material in a continual recurring cycle of growth.

Other Intellectual Influences

Horney's idea that the origin of neurosis is not the frustration of instinctual drives, but rather the alienation from the real center of our being, comes at least in part from the existentialists. Horney's understanding of the despair that one feels when cut off from the real self reflects Kierkegaard's works. She was also influenced by Adler, whose theory of the striving for power and superiority may be the root of Horney's more extensive concept of "the search for glory." She learned about human nature from such diverse sources as the innovative theater of Max Reinhardt, the philosophy of Georg Simmel, and the discoveries of contemporary anthropologists. She saw in anthropological reports the evidence to support her own perspective: that culture was the critical factor in personality development and that different cultures could and did produce radically different kinds of persons.

MAJOR CONCEPTS

The Real Self

There is, says Horney, "a central inner force, common to all human beings and yet unique in each, which is the deep source of growth" (1950, p. 17). This is the *real self,* the inborn potential, the core of the personality. This real self is sharply different from the Freudian ego that must borrow its energy from a primitive id to maintain a precarious balance between impulses, environmental conditions, and moral prohibitions.

Given the proper conditions "the human individual . . . will develop then the clarity and depth of his own feelings, thoughts, wishes, interests; the ability to tap his own resources, the strength of his will power . . . the faculty to express himself and to relate himself to others with his spontaneous feelings. . . . In short, he will grow substantially undiverted toward self-realization" (1950, p. 17).[1]

These proper conditions include family warmth, to give an individual inner security and inner freedom; the goodwill of others, to encourage mature and fulfilling behavior; and "healthy friction with the wills and wishes of others" (1950, p. 18), to develop inner strength.

The search for unity is one of the strongest motivating forces for human beings and it is even more important for the neurotic. [Horney, 1950, p. 240]

Safety

Contrary to Freud, who saw humans as being driven by sexual urges, Horney perceived the sexual urge to be a manifestation of a more fun-

---

[1]Although Horney was sensitive to feminine issues, she published at a time when the use of *he* and *his* was the usual way of referring to an indefinite person.

damental need, the need to be loved. Being loved can be nonsexual and can satisfy the wish to be accepted. It is this wish to be accepted that Horney suggests is the most visible sign of the need for *safety*. People "are not ruled by the pleasure principle alone but by two guiding principles: safety and satisfaction. . . . People can renounce food, money, attention, and affection as long as they are only renouncing satisfaction, but they cannot renounce these things if without them they would feel in danger of destitution or starvation or of being helplessly exposed to hostility, in other words, if they would lose their feelings of safety" (1950, p. 73).

It is the drive to be safe that precedes the satisfaction of pleasure. One cannot enjoy the pleasures of food, rest, or even sex if one is afraid. Thus, the drive to eliminate situations that might lead to fear or anxiety is the goal of healthy *and* of neurotic behavior.

The Idealized Self

The child given insufficient safety within the family will imagine being the kind of person who is never anxious or afraid. Gradually, this fantasy evolves into an *idealized self*. The child then attempts to become this fantasy and begins a process of alienation or denial of the real self. In so doing an inner bargain, a pact with the Devil or a Faustian agreement, is made in which the part that is genuine is disowned in favor of a façade. Protective in nature rather than creative, and compulsive rather than spontaneous, this contrived self is manipulative, guarded, and lacking in its capacity to include or express genuine feelings.

In a letter to Horney, one of her patients described the process.

> How is it possible to lose a self? The treachery, unknown and unthinkable, begins with our secret, psychic death in childhood—if and when we are not loved and are cut off from our spontaneous wishes. . . . It is a perfect double crime in which . . . the tiny self gradually and unwittingly takes part. He has not been accepted for himself, *as he is*. Oh, they love him, but they want him or force him or expect him to be different! Therefore *he must be unacceptable*. He himself learns to believe it and at last even takes it for granted. He has truly given himself up. No matter now whether he obeys them, whether he clings, rebels or withdraws—his behavior and his performance is all that matters. His center of gravity is in them, not in himself—yet if he so much as noticed it he would think it natural enough. And the whole thing is entirely plausible; all invisible, automatic and anonymous. . . . He has been rejected, not only by them but by himself. [1949, p. 3]

Neurotic Trends

Many people do not feel safe either as children or as adults. This feeling develops in various ways, "but when summarized, they all boil down to the fact that the people in the environment are too wrapped up in their own neuroses to be able to love the child, or even to conceive of him as the particular individual he is; their attitudes toward him are determined by their own neurotic needs and responses. In simple words, they may be dominating, overprotective, intimidating, irritable, overexacting, overindulgent, erratic, partial to other siblings, hypocritical, indifferent, etc. It is never a matter of just a single factor, but always the whole constellation that exerts the untoward influence on a child's growth" (Horney, 1950, p. 18).

This thwarted development is called *neurosis*. For Horney there are three paths that an individual may take to regain the feeling of safety and the capacity of satisfaction. One may move toward others, move away from others, or move against others as attempts to escape a feeling of inner anxiety and loss of acceptance. To the extent that these tendencies distort either inner reality (lying to oneself) or outer reality, they will be unsuccessful. However, they can also become compulsive, dominant trends as a person unconsciously attempts to resolve inner conflicts by creating artificial harmony.

Moving Toward People: Compulsive Compliance

Someone in whom this trend predominates is self-effacing and has a continual need for love and approval. This type of person "needs such acceptance in whatever form it is available: attention, approval, gratitude, affection, love, sex . . . the self-effacing type measures his value in the currency of love. . . . He is worth as much as he is liked, needed, wanted, or accepted" (Horney, 1950, p. 227).

To be loved and to have a partner whom one can love is a vital part of the solution to the problem of feeling safe. This type needs someone to help, to take care of, or to perform for. In order to be loved, one's own needs must be submerged; assertiveness, criticism of others, and getting one's own way must be repressed in favor of idealized lovableness.

Sacrifice is another theme. The self-effacing person does not like to win—at games or in any situation where winning might offend or displease someone else. Success frightens this individual and he or she will often devalue or deny his or her own achievements. What is important to this person is to be useful to others, to support others' goals. "While curtailed in any pursuit on his own behalf, he is not only free to do things for others but, according to his inner dictates, should be the ultimate of helpfulness, generosity, considerateness, understanding, sympathy, love and sacrifice. In fact, love and sacrifice in his mind are closely intertwined: he should sacrifice everything for love—love is sacrifice" (Horney, 1950, p. 220).

Moving Against Others: Compulsive Aggression

Although there is just as much basic anxiety driving the aggressive person as anyone else, he or she will make every effort to mask any evidence of weakness or fear. The compulsive needs of this type are to dominate and control others, to exploit and outsmart them, and to prevail on them. This domination results in a philosophy of the jungle that is often rationalized as realism. Consciously, such a person feels tough-minded, hard-driving, efficient, and comparatively uninhibited. Actually, however, what appears as expansiveness and lust for life is an insatiable need to appear big and tough, acquired at the price of the ruthless disregard for the feelings and rights of others, which isolates the individual from humanity and from tender feelings within. Horney describes this individual as follows:

> He glorifies and cultivates in himself everything that means mastery. Mastery with regard to others entails the need to excel and to be superior in some way. He tends to manipulate or dominate others and to make them dependent upon him. . . . Whether he is out for adoration, respect, or recognition, he is concerned with their subordinating themselves to him and looking up to him. He abhors the idea of his being compliant, appeasing, or dependent . . .
>
> Mastery with regard to himself means that he is his idealized proud self. Through will power and reason he is the captain of his soul. . . . It disturbs him inordinately to recognize a conflict within himself, or any problem that he cannot solve (master) right away. Suffering is felt as a disgrace to be concealed. . . . Nothing should push him around. . . . He abhors being helpless toward anything in himself as much as or more than being helpless toward any external factor. [1950, pp. 214–215]

Moving Away from People: Compulsive Detachment

The predominance of this trend is seen in the world's outsiders, those who draw a kind of magic circle around themselves that no one may actually penetrate. Estranged from himself or herself as well as from others, this person restricts personal needs to maintain self-sufficiency, even eating and drinking less than others. The need for privacy and independence makes a kind of hypersensitivity to any demands, requests, or even influences from outside, which are felt as intrusive, coercive, and dominating.

> Another characteristic of a resigned person is his hyper-sensitivity to influence, pressure, coercion or ties of any kind. This is a relevant factor too in his detachment. Even before he enters into a personal relationship or a group activity the fear of a lasting tie may be aroused. And the question as to how he can extricate himself may be present from the very beginning. When this type of person is contemplating marriage, for example, this fear may grow into panic.
>
> What he resents and sees as coercion varies. It may be any contract, such as signing a lease or any long-term engagement. It may be any physical pressure, even collars, girdles, shoes. It may be an obstructed view. He may resent anything that others expect, or might possibly expect, from him—like Christmas presents, letters, or paying his bills at certain times. This resistance may extend to institutions, traffic regulations, conventions, government interference. He does not fight all of this because he is no fighter; but he rebels inwardly and may consciously or uncon-

sciously frustrate others in his own passive way by not responding or by forgetting. [Horney, 1950, p. 266]

Within this splendid isolation the individual feels unique, special, and secretly important. His or her efforts are negatively oriented: *not* to need anybody, *not* to be involved, *not* to be influenced by others are the goals. All feelings, whether positive or negative, are suppressed in favor of detached observation, for any attachment might endanger the compulsion to avoid relationships. This person is an onlooker who lives "as if he were sitting in the orchestra and observing a drama acted on the stage . . ." (Horney, 1950, p. 261).

Neurotic Claims

One simply cannot be unrealistic about oneself and remain entirely realistic in other respects. [Horney, 1950, p. 31]

Having forgotten the real self and having identified with the idealized self, individuals must maintain the illusion of who they are by diminishing their faults and exaggerating their importance. We have all had the experience of observing other people blatantly denying something they did. It is not lying, because lying suggests that the person is aware of the lie; rather, it is a compulsive reframing of reality to protect the idealized image from being exposed as fraudulent. As the significant person one wishes to be, it is easy to understand why one might demand to be treated with special care and consideration, to be an exception to the rules, to be given special privileges.

Imagination plays a crucial role in this neurotic process. The person puffs up his or her desirable qualities and downplays or ignores the difficulties his or her weaknesses cause for others. However, it is the imagined self, *not the actual self,* that must be honored and given its reward; he or she feels entitled to whatever is desired. Each neurotic trend has different neurotic claims. The self-effacing type (the mover toward people), who needs above everything else to be lovable, will claim the right to be loved regardless of callous, hurtful, or objectionable behavior. For the person driven to mastery (the mover against people), the idealized self must always be right. The individual claims immunity from criticism, regardless of the cruelty or oppression of his or her acts. The person who has been driven into self-sufficiency (the mover away from people) will claim that others make no demands on him or her, must need nothing, and indeed should go away and disappear when told to do so.

THE PSYCHOLOGY OF WOMEN

Horney's exploration of the psychological meaning of the important events in a woman's life is intrinsically worthwhile and historically significant in the reorientation of social values toward the equality of women.

Throughout her life, Karen Horney attempted to counteract the deficiency in psychoanalytic theory brought about by Freud's failure to understand female development. In his paper on infantile genital organization (1923), Freud asserted that for both sexes only one genital, the male one, is important. In this paper he asserted "the primacy of the phallus" for men and women. At about the same time Horney presented the first of her own papers on the feminine. In it she stated, ". . . an assertion that one half of the human race is discontented with the sex assigned to it and can overcome this discontent only in favorable circumstances . . . is decidedly unsatisfying" (1967, p. 38).

In 1926 she wrote a paper that gently but directly opposed the emerging Freudian position. The one-sidedness of the psychoanalytic position is understandable because, as she points out, "Psychoanalysis is the creation of a male genius and almost all those who have developed his ideas have been men" (1967, p. 54). Freud had made efforts to account for the patterns of psychological growth in little girls, but always in terms of a felt lack of male genitals. Horney would not see girls merely as castrated boys—pseudomales who lack a penis and are bound to suffer for it, psychologically, their whole lives.

The concept of penis envy was based on clinical observations that were undoubtedly accurate: women did remember the childhood wish to have a penis. But to Horney that was only half of the story. The other half had been neglected because of the male-oriented preconceptions of the observers. Horney's female clients did recall wanting to have a penis. However, these women were less interested in having the male organ than in having the *rights* and *privileges* they saw being accorded to their fathers and brothers. They did indeed feel cheated and they actually were because the culture favored males and was controlled by men. Whereas Freud saw anatomy as destiny, and therefore assumed that a girl wanted a physiological penis, Horney saw that a girl wished for much more: she wanted the cultural advantages that were given to men. Paralleling women's childhood envy of males, Horney's male patients routinely recalled their envy of the female genital functions of pregnancy and childbirth, the female breast, and the female cultural advantage of not having to compete. Thus both sexes yearned for the advantages of the other; but the yearning of women was more obvious in a culture in which they were truly socially inferior.

In addition to studying penis envy in girls, Horney contributed to the understanding of masochism in women. Masochistic attitudes appear in fantasies of pleasure involving suffering, or the importation of suffering into situations in which others would not find it. People with masochistic character structures feel weak, helpless, and emotionally dependent. They see themselves as inferior, hide their aggressions, and tend to feel abused. Covertly, they use their weaknesses as a way of manipulating others.

At this point, I, as a woman, ask in amazement, and what about motherhood? And the blissful consciousness of bearing a new life within oneself? And the ineffable happiness of the increasing expectation of the appearance of this new being? And the joy when it finally makes its appearance and one holds it for the first time in one's arms? And the deep pleasurable feeling of satisfaction in suckling it and the happiness of the whole period when the infant needs her care? [Horney, 1967, p. 60]

Like Freud, Horney found that this particular type of personality structure was far more frequently found in women than in men. Rejecting biological reasons for this difference between the sexes, she pointed instead to significant cultural factors that might drive women into such symptoms. In the first decades of this century, women were frustrated by the lack of possibilities of career advancement imposed by the number of children they had, child rearing being the traditional avenue to esteem by self and society for a woman. There were also social conventions restricting women to jobs such as schoolteaching and charity work that emphasized sentiment and emotion rather than intellectual creativity. Horney realized the subtle and pervasive attitudes among men and women alike, first noted by the philosopher George Simmel (in Horney, 1967, p. 58), that social attitudes assumed male superiority and stereotyped women as *just a little* inferior. The very fabric of Western culture was based on such almost invisible, because seemingly self-evident, preconceptions. Data on American Indian society and Trobriand Islanders (Mead, 1949) indicated that this denigration of females was a cultural, not a biological, event. Little girls in these cultures did not seem to be particularly masochistic. Thus on the basis of anthropological evidence unavailable to Freud in his early period of theory-building, Horney suggested that far from being woman's biological destiny, masochism was a learned pattern of cultural behavior (Horney 1935).

Horney (1934) also collected observations of adolescent girls whose adjustment became abnormal at the onset of menstruation. She grouped these difficulties into four major types:

1. A girl who worked and played well as a preadolescent might become boy-crazy and have no concentration left for her schoolwork.
2. A girl might suddenly lose interest in everything except some mental or religious problem.
3. A girl might suddenly develop a preference for homosexuality.
4. A girl might show a sudden slackening of interest in everything, as if caring about nothing and renouncing all intense concerns was required of her.

Horney noticed that the four behavior patterns, seemingly different, had the same common denominator: deeply repressed rage at the mother and generalized toward other females and, finally (although unconsciously), in the adolescent girl, at herself. Each of the four character changes was actually a safety measure to prevent competition and aggressive confrontation with other females.

Menstruation was another topic that had been neglected by earlier psychoanalytic thinkers. Based upon observations of many women in therapy, Horney suggested that premenstrual tension was related to conflicting unconscious tendencies involving the wish for a child. She was the first to note that functional female disorders, such as menstrual cramps and vaginal infections, were a regular occurrence in disturbed women, regardless of the nature of their neurotic symptoms (1931a). She also observed that, specifically, frigidity was not a natural feminine attitude, as was commonly believed, but a sign of psychological problems (1926b). The sexual feelings of women are much more closely related to their emotional lives than is true of men so that neurotic conflicts are more likely to appear as sexual dysfunction.

Horney made other significant contributions to the psychology of women. She studied the origins and traditions of the fear of women in ancient and modern cultures (1932a), and examined the patterns of distrust between the sexes (1931b). Analyzing the problems of contemporary marriage (1932b), she described how the unconscious expectation that the spouse can be a substitute for the beloved parent can only lead to disappointment. She argued that the Freudian view that men were more polygamous was without clinical substantiation and was even (perhaps) a masculine rationalization. Being a psychoanalyst, a wife, and a mother, she explored maternal conflicts, the meaning of pregnancy and childbirth.

Her contribution is well described in her own words in an early paper (1926) that foreshadowed her later work:

> In the foregoing discussion I have put a construction upon certain problems of feminine psychology, which in many points differs from current views. It is possible and even probable that the picture I have drawn is one-sided from the opposite point of view. But my primary intention in this paper was to indicate a possible source of error arising out of the sex of the observer, and by so doing, to make a step forward toward the goal that we are all striving to reach: to get beyond the subjectivity of the masculine or the feminine standpoint and to obtain a picture of the mental development of woman that will be more true to the facts of her nature—with its specific qualities and its differences from that of man—than any we have hitherto achieved. [1967, p. 70]

DYNAMICS

Psychological Growth

Normal human development in a healthy interpersonal setting, with sensitivity and attention for the child's real needs, results in the natural fulfillment of his or her potential. This tendency to evolve toward what we are destined to become is intrinsic in all humanity as well as in all living things.

In the person who is evolving toward inner harmony the forces that are distorted in the neurotic (toward people, against people, away from people) become harmonized. "Most of us want and appreciate af-

. . . Always, everywhere, the man strives to rid himself of his dread of women by objectifying it. "It is not," he says, "that I dread her; it is that she herself is malignant, capable of any crime, a beast of prey, a vampire, a witch, insatiable in her desires. She is the very personification of what is sinister." May not this be one of the principal roots of the whole masculine impulse to creative work—the never ending conflict between his longing for the woman and his dread of her? [Horney, 1967, p. 135]

fection, self-control, modesty, consideration of others. . . . Self-sufficiency, independence and guidance through reason are generally regarded as valuable goals" (Horney, 1942, p. 56). It is the development of the real self, the forgotten self, that is the mark of psychological growth. This requires no effort of will, only the absence of hindrances.

> The difference, then, between healthy strivings and neurotic drives for glory is one between spontaneity and compulsion; between recognizing and denying limitations; between a focus on a vision of a glorious end product and a feeling of evolution; between seeming and being, fantasy and truth. [Horney, 1950, p. 38]

Obstacles to Growth
Basic Anxiety

Normal growth toward self-actualization of the real self can be distorted and blocked by factors in one's childhood environment. If in the early years a child's real needs are ignored or given too little respect, or if the parents are untrustworthy, the child may develop *basic anxiety,* a diffuse, uncertain sense of isolation and helplessness in a potentially hostile world (Horney, 1945). Neurotic processes arise out of the need to fend off awareness of this basic anxiety. The following description of basic anxiety, as Horney observed it over and over again, underscores the extraordinary lengths people go to avoid experiencing this anxiety.

> Basic anxiety is that the environment is dreaded as a whole because it is felt to be unreliable, mendacious, unappreciative, unfair, unjust, begrudging and merciless. According to this concept the child not only fears punishment or desertion because of forbidden drives, but he feels the environment as a menace to his entire development and to his most legitimate wishes and strivings. He feels in danger of his individuality being obliterated, his freedom taken away, his happiness prevented. In contrast to the fear of castration this fear is not fantasy, but is well founded on reality. In an environment in which the basic anxiety develops, the child's free use of energies is thwarted, his self-esteem and self-reliance are undermined, fear is instilled by intimidation and isolation, his expansiveness is warped through brutality, standards or overprotective "love."
>
> The other essential element in the basic anxiety is that a child is rendered helpless to defend himself adequately against infringements. Not only is he biologically helpless and dependent on the family, but every kind of self-assertion is discouraged. He is usually too intimidated to express his resentment or his accusations, and when he does express them he is made to feel guilty. The hostility which has to be repressed precipitates anxiety, because hostility is a danger when directed against someone on whom one feels dependent. [1939, pp. 75–76]

Basic Conflict

A child with basic anxiety is in conflict between his or her actual dependence on the parents and the need to rebel against insensitive parenting, thereby preserving the real self. Anger and aggression must be repressed because of the situation of dependence. The child is thus rendered unaware of real dangers to the self and produces an indiscriminate compliance. Thus the child's helplessness actually increases. Compliance is necessary, yet it produces a defenselessness that in turn fosters a process by which the child loses touch with self-love within, identifying instead with the idealized self constructed in response to family requirements.

Horney (1937) describes four ways to minimize the conflict and to escape from basic anxiety: to rationalize it, deny it, narcotize it, or to avoid situations, thoughts, and feelings that might bring it into awareness.

Rationalization— To turn basic anxiety into "rational" fears. One worries unrealistically about situations over which one has little control. Examples might include excessive concern for one's children's health, earthquakes, car accidents, or if one will lose one's job. The topics picked may be sensible but the quality of the concern is excessive, compulsive, and desperate.

Denial—(two forms)

1. To exclude the anxiety from consciousness; to be unaware of it. What appears are the physical symptoms, such as nervous twitching, sweating, accelerated heartbeat, and so on; and/or the mental symptoms, such as feeling restless, being rushed or agitated, or being immobile and unable to function.
2. To consciously override the anxiety. One "pulls oneself together." It is the act of being brave; recognizing the fear and acting anyway. It has practical value in that it does allow a person to function in spite of fears, but the underlying personality dynamics remain unchanged. The control over the fear cannot be relaxed.

Narcotization—To lower general awareness of anxiety and other feelings by external means. These might include the obvious use of drugs or alcohol as well as less obvious behaviors of incessant social activities (to avoid facing loneliness), excessive work and the inability to take leisure time, excessive sleep without feeling rested, or excessive sexual activities (to avoid feeling unacceptable).

Inhibition—To avoid parts of experiences that trigger awareness of basic anxiety. Inhibition consists of an inability or unwillingness to feel, think, or do certain things. Its function is to avoid the anxiety that could arise if the person did feel, think, or do these things.

The Search for Glory

In the neurotic the energy of self-realization is turned toward self-idealization—that is, the maintenance of the ideal self. Self-glorification promises feelings of superiority and significance to compensate for the actual feelings of fear and lack of acceptance. Horney calls the search to justify and substantiate the idealized self the *search for glory*. One idealizes the neurotic trend that one has developed to cope with anxiety. "Compliance becomes goodness, love, saintliness; aggressiveness becomes strength, leadership, heroism, omnipotence; aloofness becomes wisdom, self-sufficiency, independence. What—according to his particular solution—appears as shortcomings or flaws are always dimmed out or retouched" (Horney, 1950, p. 22). In the search for glory, doing a task is colored by the neurotic need for perfection; ambition becomes an insatiable drive for greater and greater success, whereas working with others is oriented toward vindictive triumph. According to Horney the neurotic process is a set of compulsive and conflicting drives to actualize and maintain the fictional idealized self. This hoped-for glorious version of one's self is substituted for the lost or hidden real self. Lacking an authentic sense of identity, the neurotic person strains to "be somebody." This struggle gradually becomes the primary use of psychic energy; any interest in self-development fades before the compulsion to become special, superior, and untouchable.

Much of the search for glory takes place in the imagination where the hoped-for ideal being can be seen, praised, and respected. The neurotic's inner life is filled with visions of unattainable success as well as fantasies of devastating failures. Ongoing activities and interactions display an actual disregard for the real self and look, indeed, self-destructive to an outside observer.

This strange imbalance occurs because the neurotics not only strive to glorify their false portraits of themselves, but at the same time they also hate themselves. To the same degree that they have invested in an idealized, dazzling self-image, they correspondingly despise their actual being and attainments. The neurotic enhancement of the false self and the devaluation of the real self Horney summarized in the concept of the pride system.

The Pride System

To monitor their success, neurotics must inevitably engage in comparing themselves to others. There is always the possibility of shame and humiliation rather than the sought-after vindictive triumph that will signal that the idealized self is for the moment safe. The pride system is made up not only of the idealized image of the self and whatever defenses are necessary to maintain it, but it also consists of a central conflict between this idealization and hate directed toward the real self.

Constant demands for surpassingly high standards of performance make a "tyranny of shoulds" (Horney, 1950), torments of
self-recriminations, and feelings of hopelessness. The pursuit of the
ideal self leads inevitably away from truth, dignity, and vitality into
a morass of neurotic ambitions and conflicts that are accompanied by
feelings of futility, vulnerability, and failure.

THE PROCESS OF PSYCHOTHERAPY

Although Horney is most widely known for her popular books, her
daily work was psychoanalytic psychotherapy. Her theory of personality development, recognition of safety needs, the role of anxiety, the
idealized self, and the neurotic trends all arose from sensitive interaction with her clients.

> A crescendo of observation opened my eyes to the significance of such con-
> flicts. What first struck me most forcibly was the blindness of patients
> towards obvious contradictions within themselves. When I pointed these
> out they became elusive and seemed to lose interest. After repeated expe-
> riences of this kind, I realized that the elusiveness expressed a profound
> aversion to tackling these contradictions. Finally, panic reactions in re-
> sponse to a sudden recognition of a conflict showed me I was working with
> dynamite. Patients had good reason to shy away from these conflicts: they
> dreaded their power to tear them to pieces" (Horney, 1945, p. 15).
>
> "According to my slant on neurosis," says Horney, "the main neurotic
> disturbances are the consequences of the neurotic trends. Hence my main
> objective in therapy is, after having recognized the neurotic trends, to
> discover in detail the functions they serve and the consequences they
> have on the patient's personality and his life" (Horney, 1939, p. 281). In
> an even larger perspective the aim of psychotherapy in Horney's view
> is the restoration of the constructive forces inherent in the individual
> so that his or her life can become an expression of the real self.
>
> In order to arrive at a rough estimate of the difficulties of the therapeu-
> tic process we must consider what it involves for the patient. Briefly, he
> must overcome all those needs, drives, or attitudes which obstruct his
> growth: only when he begins to relinquish his illusions about himself and
> his illusory goals has he a chance to find his real potentialities and to
> develop them. Only to the extent to which he gives up his false pride can
> he become less hostile to himself and evolve a solid self-confidence. Only
> as his shoulds lose their coercive power can he discover his real feelings,
> wishes, beliefs, and ideals. Only when he faces his existing conflicts has
> he the chance for a real integration—and so forth. [Horney, 1950, p. 334]

This objective is accomplished through the therapist's emphasis
on present-day problems, conflicts, anxieties, and defenses. Although
such an exploration into personal motivations inevitably mobilizes important memories, relating these memories to present problems is not
considered as valuable as relating the character trends to each other
and thus delineating opposing tendencies and unconscious conflicts.

The subjective value of each trend in the character and its life toll must be acknowledged in specific detail.

Every piece of analytic work well done changes these conditions in that it makes a person less helpless, less fearful, less hostile, and less alienated. . . . [Horney, 1945, p. 19]

In the process of self-discovery there are always moments of painful awareness when accepting the truth about oneself, instead of the ideal image, and times of anxiety when unconscious conflicts come into conscious awareness. The personal bravery required to sustain this oftentimes painful process is easier to accomplish in the context of a trusting relationship in which the therapist supports, guides, and helps the patient. Thus Horney recommended that the analyst and the patient sit face to face so that the therapist could be seen, could be supportive, and could be fully participatory during the therapeutic process.

Observation and critical intelligence are no substitute for that inner certainty with reference to others which is possessed by a person who is realistically aware of himself as himself and others as themselves, and who is not swayed in his estimate of them by all kinds of compulsive needs. [Horney, 1950, p. 295]

Horney's psychotherapeutic tools are basically Freudian. They include free association, interpretation, the analysis of dreams, and the sensitive appreciation of patterns of interaction between patient and therapist. For Horney the analyst must not be merely passive, but must question, probe, and directly influence the patient to make real-life changes after insight into problems has been attained. Horney taught that the analyst should deliberately conduct the psychotherapeutic process and not leave its direction up to the patient's free associations. The analyst's direction must necessarily involve value judgments.

As analysis proceeds, motivation to live fully and happily should increase, in Horney's view, because her method of exposing neurotic conflicts allows patients to get detailed and compelling insights into their actual suffering. For Horney the goal of therapy was beyond simple insight. As neurotic conflicts are banished through insight, an individual becomes increasingly able to solve life's problems without outside support, reducing by stages the dependence upon the analyst. At the completion of therapy he or she will have regained the courage and the capacity to recognize and to actualize the real self.

EVALUATION

Karen Horney belongs among the social and cultural left wing of Freud's followers, along with Erich Fromm, Harry Stack Sullivan, and Wilhelm Reich. In emphasizing the constructive, evolutionary nature of human development and the great modifiability of human nature, Horney rejected the orthodox, genetic position that "anatomy is destiny" in favor of a more optimistic stance.

Horney contributed much to the understanding of women's problems and prospects. Not only did she work to dispel male-oriented myths about female psychodynamics, but she also gave needed attention to such previously neglected, but centrally important, topics as frigidity, menstruation, pregnancy, childbirth, and motherhood.

She possessed an optimism about a person's inner capacities that extended even to the possibility that self-analysis was possible. In her books she examined the structure of personality and offered solutions to basic neurotic conflicts. Her books, written directly to the public and unfiltered by the psychoanalytic establishment, continue to influence the psychological climate. A constant theme in her writings is a hopeful trust in humanity and our abilities to change.

"Albert Schweitzer uses the terms 'optimistic' and 'pessimistic' in the sense of 'world and life affirmation' and 'world and life negation.' Freud's philosophy, in this deep sense, is a pessimistic one. Ours, with all its cognizance of the tragic element in neurosis, is an optimistic one" (Horney, 1950, p. 378).

THE THEORY FIRSTHAND

The following excerpt outlines and illustrates Horney's concept of "the tyranny of the should," the process by which compulsive neurotic trends construct, support, and maintain a fictional, idealized image.

> We have discussed so far chiefly how the neurotic tries to actualize his idealized self with regard to the *outside world*: in achievements, in the glory of success or power or triumph. Neurotic claims, too, are concerned with the world outside himself: he tries to assert the exceptional rights to which his uniqueness entitles him whenever, and in whatever ways, he can. His feeling entitled to be above necessities and laws allows him to live in a world of fiction as if he were indeed above them. And whenever he falls palpably short of being his idealized self, his claims enable him to make factors outside himself responsible for such "failures."
>
> We shall now discuss that aspect of self-actualization, briefly mentioned in the first chapter, in which the focus is *within himself*. Unlike Pygmalion, who tried to make another person into a creature fulfilling his concept of beauty, the neurotic sets to work to mold himself into a supreme being of his own making. He holds before his soul his image of perfection and unconsciously tells himself: "Forget about the disgraceful creature you actually *are;* this is how you *should* be; and to be this idealized self is all that matters. You should be able to endure everything, to understand everything, to like everybody, to be always productive"—to mention only a few of these inner dictates. Since they are inexorable, I call them "the tyranny of the should."
>
> The inner dictates comprise all that the neurotic should be able to do, to be, to feel, to know—and taboos on how and what he should not be. I shall begin by enumerating some of them out of context, for the sake of a brief survey. (More detailed examples will follow as we discuss the characteristics of the shoulds.)
>
> He should be the utmost of honesty, generosity, considerateness, justice, dignity, courage, unselfishness. He should be the perfect lover, husband, teacher. He should be able to endure everything, should like everybody, should love his parents, his wife, his country; or, he should not be attached to anything or anybody, nothing should matter to him, he should never feel hurt, and he should always be serene and unruffled.

He should always enjoy life; or, he should be above pleasure and enjoyment. He should be spontaneous; he should always control his feelings. He should know, understand, and foresee everything. He should be able to solve every problem of his own, or of others, in no time. He should be able to overcome every difficulty of his as soon as he sees it. He should never be tired or fall ill. He should always be able to find a job. He should be able to do things in one hour which can only be done in two to three hours.

This survey, roughly indicating the scope of inner dictates, leaves us with the impression of demands on self which, though understandable, are altogether too difficult and too rigid. If we tell a patient that he expects too much of himself, he will often recognize it without hesitation; he may even have been aware of it already. He will usually add, explicitly or implicitly, that it is better to expect too much of himself than too little. But to speak of too high demands on self does not reveal the peculiar *characteristics of inner dictates*. These come into clear relief under closer examination. They are overlapping, because they all result from the necessity a person feels to turn into his idealized self, and from his conviction that he can do so.

What strikes us first is the same *disregard for feasibility* which pervades the entire drive for actualization. Many of these demands are of a kind which no human being could fulfill. They are plainly fantastic, although the person himself is not aware of it. He cannot help recognizing it, however, as soon as his expectations are exposed to the clear light of critical thinking. Such an intellectual realization, however, usually does not change much, if anything. Let us say that a physician may have clearly realized that he cannot do intensive scientific work in addition to a nine-hour practice and an extensive social life; yet, after abortive attempts to cut down one or another activity, he keeps going at the same pace. His demands that limitations in time and energies should not exist for him are stronger than reason. Or take a more subtle illustration. At an analytic session a patient was dejected. She had talked with a friend about the latter's marital problems, which were complicated. My patient knew the husband only from social situations. Yet, although she had been in analysis for several years and had enough understanding of the psychological intricacies involved in any relationship between two people to know better, she felt that she should have been able to tell her friend whether or not the marriage was tenable.

I told her that she expected something of herself which was impossible for anybody, and pointed out the multitude of questions to be clarified before one could even begin to have a more than dim impression of the factors operating in the situation. It turned out then that she had been aware of most of the difficulties I had pointed out. But she had still felt that she *should* have a kind of sixth sense penetrating all of them.

Other demands on self may not be fantastic in themselves yet show a complete *disregard for the conditions* under which they could be fulfilled. Thus many patients expect to finish their analysis in no time because they are so intelligent. But the progress in analysis has little to do with intelligence. The reasoning power which these people have may, in fact, be used to obstruct progress. What counts are the emotional forces operating in the patients, their capacity to be straight and to assume responsibility for themselves.

This expectation of easy success operates not only in reference to the length of the whole analysis, but equally so in regard to an individual insight gained. For instance, recognizing some of their neurotic claims seems to them the equivalent of having outgrown them altogether. That it requires patient work; that the claims will persist as long as the emotional necessities for having them are not changed—all of this they ignore. They believe that their intelligence should be a supreme moving power. Naturally, then, subsequent disappointment and discouragement are unavoidable. In a similar way, a teacher may expect that, with her long experience in teaching, it should be easy for her to write a paper on a pedagogical subject. If the words do not flow from her pen, she feels utterly disgusted with herself. She has ignored or discarded such relevant questions as: Has she something to say? Have her experiences crystallized to some useful formulations? And even if the answers are affirmative, a paper still means plain work in formulating and expressing thoughts.

The inner dictates, exactly like political tyranny in a police state, operate with a supreme *disregard for the person's own psychic condition*— for what he can feel or do as he is at present. One of the frequent shoulds, for instance, is that one should never feel hurt. As an absolute (which is implied in the "never") anyone would find this extremely hard to achieve. How many people have been, or are, so secure in themselves, so serene, as never to feel hurt? This could at best be an ideal toward which we might strive. To take such a project seriously must mean intense and patient work at our unconscious claims for defense, at our false pride—or, in short, at every factor in our personality that makes us vulnerable. But the person who feels that he should never feel hurt does not have so concrete a program in mind. He simply issues an absolute order to himself, denying or overriding the fact of his existing vulnerability. . . .

Most neurotic disturbances resist even the most strenuous efforts at control. Conscious efforts simply do not avail against a depression, against a deeply ingrained inhibition to work, or against consuming daydreams. One would think that this would be clear to any person who has gained some psychological understanding during analysis. But again the clarity of thinking does not penetrate to the "I should be able to master it." The result is that he suffers more intensely under depressions, etc., because, in addition to its being painful anyhow, it becomes a visible sign of his lack of omnipotence. Sometimes the analyst can catch this process at the beginning and nip it in the bud. Thus a patient who had revealed the extent of her daydreaming, while exposing in detail how subtly it pervaded most of her activities, came to realize its harmfulness—at least to the extent of understanding how it sapped her energies. The next time she was somewhat guilty and apologetic because the daydreams persisted. Knowing her demands on herself, I injected my belief that it would be neither possible nor even wise to stop them artificially, because we could be sure that they fulfilled as yet important functions in her life—which we would have to come to understand gradually. She felt very much relieved and now told me that she had decided to stop the daydreams. But since she hadn't been able to she felt I would be disgusted with her. Her own expectation of herself had been projected to me.

Many reactions of despondence, irritability, or fear occurring during analysis are less a response to the patient's having discovered a disturbing problem in himself (as the analyst tends to assume) than to his feeling impotent to remove it right away. [1950, pp. 64–67, 71–72]

EXERCISES

A Taste of Self-Analysis

Karen Horney was outstanding among psychoanalytic theorists in that she attempted to expand the scope of therapy to include exercises that could be undertaken by interested people without professional help. In *Self-Analysis* (1942) she asks, "If the analyst relies on the patient's unconscious mental activity, if the patient has the faculty to work alone toward the solution to some problem, could this faculty be utilized in some more deliberate fashion? Could the patient scrutinize his self-observations or his associations with his own critical intelligence? . . . Granted it would be a hard job, fraught with hazards and limitations . . . these difficulties should not prevent us from raising the question is it impossible to analyse oneself?" (pp. 16–17).*

In this context you might try the following exercise in self-analysis. In a quiet, private place, with this textbook, writing materials, and a notebook, take a half hour to do the following:

1. Identify one, and only one, problem that is clearly an issue for you. Do not use a problem that you are not quite sure is a problem. After you have made your choice, write it down as succinctly as possible.
2. Now consider your actual behavior in this problem area. With as much of the objectivity of an outside observer as you can muster, write a paragraph or two describing what you do.
3. Reread the section "Neurotic Trends" on moving toward, moving against, and moving away from others. Describe in writing how you see these trends and their compulsive shoulds enter into your problem.
4. Examine the scope of the problem in your life. Is it a relatively minor difficulty that arises only under special conditions? Or is it ever present, ongoing, and entangled with other conflicts? Write down your appraisal of the scope of the problem.
5. With this understanding of the extent of the problem, make a list of the benefits or costs involved, both psychologically and in terms of other real-life losses and gains.
6. Take a moment and sense yourself in the middle of this problem. Have you ever felt that way before? If memories arise, make a note of them, but do not force recall if it doesn't happen spontaneously.
7. Reread what you have written and then let it go. Perhaps the constructive forces in your mind will offer you a dream regarding it, or you will have additional insight at some unexpected time in the near future.
8. If possible, read your notes to another person. Notice what happens when you communicate your self-analysis: how you feel during different parts of the reading, what you censor, and what you feel the need to explain further. Check out your feelings toward the listener. Have they changed, and if so, how?

*In considering this possibility Horney, in her characteristic way, was again following in Freud's footsteps (he analyzed himself), and departing from his fold because for theoretical and technical reasons classical analysts consider it foolhardy, if not down-right impossible, to undertake such a venture alone.

Then switch roles and experience being the listener. This exercise may give you and your classmate a feeling for what the analytic experience is like in self-analysis and in the patient-therapist interaction.

The Relevance of the Idea of the Real Self

One of the cornerstones of Horney's theory of personality development is the concept of basic anxiety that results in the child moving further and further from the real self. Test the applicability of this idea in your own life by using a journal in the following way.

1. Close your eyes, relax, and remember a typical day when you were 13 or 14 years old. Remember it from the time you woke up in the morning, to your experience as you worked and played at school, to the quality of your contact with family and friends in the afternoon and evening. When you are ready, write down a log of that day, including specific thoughts and feelings as well as your general mood.
2. Now do the same for a day when you were 4 or 5 years old. Take a few minutes to remember the experiences with eyes closed and body relaxed. Again write down a log of that day.
3. Compare these days. Is there any difference in the degree to which you maintained your security at the expense of your spontaneity? Did your interests become less or more your own as you grew up? Did your life become constricted by conflicting shoulds, or were you able to keep a genuine sense of what was right for you? Did the quality of love for self and others change in any way?
4. Form a group of six or more, then describe and compare the two days and listen to the accounts of others. Discuss and evaluate Horney's concept of the real self on the basis of the sum total of your individual experiences.

A Matter of Philosophy

In the beginning of *Neurosis and Human Growth* (1950, pp. 14–15), Horney distinguishes three concepts of morality that rest on three views of human nature.

- If the human being is by nature sinful or ridden by primitive impulses, the goal of morality must be to curb them, tame them, overcome them.
- If there is something inherently "good" in human nature and something inherently "bad," the goal of morality must be to ensure the eventual victory of the good by suppressing the bad and directing or reinforcing the good elements, using will, reason, and strength.
- If human nature is seen as inevitably evolving toward self-realization by an intrinsic tendency, not by will, then the goal of morality becomes one of removing obstacles in the way of that evolution in order to provide maximum opportunity for the spontaneous forces of growth to manifest.

1. In a group of at least three students, discuss the three positions and tentatively choose one to support.
2. The third position is, of course, Horney's. Discuss what implications this philosophy had on her attitude toward psychotherapy.
3. Whichever position you have chosen, ask yourself and disclose in the discussion group whether you believe that you yourself will live by this position and in what manner.

ANNOTATED BIBLIOGRAPHY

Most of Horney's books (unlike her articles) were written for the educated layperson.

Horney, K. *The neurotic personality of our time.* New York: Norton, 1937. General review of neurosis as influenced by culture, human relationships, and tendencies toward helplessness, isolation, and hostility.

————. *New ways in psychoanalysis.* New York: Norton, 1939. Evaluation of and expansion of Freudian theory, with particular emphasis on character structure, environmental factors in neurosis, and self-realization as therapeutic goal.

————. *Self-analysis.* New York: Norton, 1942. A description of the possibilities, techniques, and difficulties of self-analysis. Through case description and theoretical discussion Horney describes how the individual can use the techniques of psychoanalysis on his or her own.

————. *Our inner conflicts.* New York: Norton, 1945. Described in detail the three ways of responding to life situations—moving toward, away from, and against other people; also the ways in which those trends can become neurotic and the general definition of neurosis as inner conflict between the "real self" and the "idealized image."

————. *Neurosis and human growth.* New York: Norton, 1950. Includes much of the material from earlier works; the concept of moral evolution as humans' spontaneous nature is explored in more detail than in her other works.

————. *Feminine psychology* (Harold Kelman, Ed.). New York: Norton, 1967. Collected papers and articles that deal mostly with specific Freudian concepts that are related to various aspects of sexuality; explores in detail the problems of the psychology of women in Freudian theory.

REFERENCES

Freud, Sigmund. The infantile genital organization: An interpolation into the theory of sexuality. Standard edition (Vol 19), pp. 41–49. (Originally published, 1923.)

Horney, Karen. The flight from womanhood: The masculinity complex in women as viewed by men and by women.* (Originally published, 1926a.)

————. Inhibited feminity: Psychoanalytical contributions to the problem of frigidity.* (Originally published, 1926b.)

————. Premenstrual tension.* (Originally published, 1931a.)

————. The distrust between the sexes.* (Originally published, 1931b.)

————. The dread of woman: Observations on a specific difference in the dread felt by men and women respectively for the opposite sex.* (Originally published, 1932a.)

————. Problems of marriage.* (Originally published, 1932b.)

*This article is found in Harold Kelman (Ed.), *Feminine Psychology.* New York: Norton, 1967.

_____. Psychogenic factors in functional female disorders.* (Originally published, 1933.)

_____. Personality changes in female adolescents.* (Originally published, 1934.)

_____. The problem of female masochism.* (Originally published, 1935.)

_____. Finding the real self: A letter with a forward by Karen Horney. *American Journal of Psychoanalysis,* 1949, 9:3.

Kelman, Harold. *Helping people: Karen Horney's psychoanalytic approach.* New York: Science House, 1971.

Mead, Margaret. *Male and female.* New York: Morrow, 1949.

Rubins, Jack. *Karen Horney, gentle rebel of psychoanalysis.* New York: Dial Press, 1978.

CHAPTER 5
ERIK ERIKSON
AND THE LIFE CYCLE

Erik Erikson is one of the most widely read and influential neo-Freudian theorists. He has extended the insights of psychoanalysis through cross-cultural studies of child rearing, psychological biographies of great men and women, and interfacing psychological and social dynamics.

Erikson's work is solidly based on psychoanalytic theory; no one else since Freud has done as much to elaborate and apply the principles of psychoanalysis to new fields and to the problems of today's world. In the process Erikson developed an original theory rooted in psychoanalytic understanding, yet significantly different in scope, concepts, and emphasis. Erikson's concepts of identity and identity crisis have had major professional influence throughout the social sciences. They have also become household words.

Erikson is a brilliant, insightful theorist and an elegant writer. At the core of his work is his theory of the human life cycle, a model that integrates human growth and development from birth to old age. Erikson made three major contributions to the study of personality: (1) that along with Freud's psychosexual developmental stages a person simultaneously goes through psychosocial and ego-development stages; (2) that personality development continues throughout life; and (3) that each stage of development can have positive and negative outcomes.

PERSONAL HISTORY

Erikson had varied, even conflicting, roots. He was born on June 15, 1902. His mother left Denmark and her husband for Germany while pregnant, and soon remarried a Jewish physician, Dr. Homburger.

As a young man, Erik took his stepfather's name. Then he began his career as Erik Homburger Erikson, and eventually changed to Erik Erikson. A Dane by parentage and a German by upbringing, he later became an American by choice.

Erikson's formal academic education lasted until he was 18, when he graduated from a classical *gymnasium*. There he had studied Latin, Greek, German literature, and ancient history. He was not a particularly devoted student. After graduation Erik began traveling through Europe. Along with many of his generation, Erik was trying to "find himself." After a year of travel, he returned home and enrolled in art school. He studied art in Munich, then went to live in Florence. The artist's role was good for a young man unready to settle down; it gave him great latitude and time for self-exploration.

Erikson returned home at the age of 25, intending to settle down and teach art. He received a letter from Peter Blos, an old friend who later was to become a well-known child analyst. Blos had been working as a private tutor to the children of a wealthy American couple, who had come to Vienna for psychoanalysis. He was asked to begin a school of his own where he could work with English and American children of other analytic patients. Blos invited Erikson to come to Vienna and teach art, history, and various other subjects. Erikson accepted. He and Blos were given a free hand to create an ideal educational program.

The psychoanalytic community was much less formal in the 1920s. Analysts, patients, and their families and friends attended picnics and other social events together. At these affairs Erikson became acquainted with Anna Freud and other prominent psychoanalysts. Erikson and Blos were screened informally and judged suitable candidates for analytic training. In 1927 Erikson began daily analysis with Anna Freud, in the house she shared with her father.

When he expressed doubts about the possibility of an artist becoming a psychoanalyst, Anna Freud replied that psychoanalysis would need people who help others *see*. Much of Erikson's long and rich career can be viewed as an attempt to do just that: drawing exquisite word pictures of new concepts and perspectives.

> To be surprised belongs to the discipline of a clinician. [Erikson, 1963, p. 100]

Erikson also studied the Montessori system and was one of only two men who graduated from the Montessori Teachers' Association. His interest in play therapy and child analysis came from his ongoing teaching influenced by his Montessori education.

In 1929, at a Mardi Gras masked ball in a Viennese castle, Erikson met a young woman, Joan Serson, and fell in love almost immediately. They were married several months later. Joan's interests were similar to Erikson's. A teacher of modern dance, she had received a B.A. in education and a master's degree in sociology, and had been in psychoanalysis with one of Freud's early followers.

In 1933 Erikson finished his analytic training and was accepted as a full member of the Vienna Psychoanalytic Society. Due to the growth of Fascism in Europe, Erikson, as well as many other psychoanalysts, decided to leave for the United States. The move was made easier by his wife's Canadian-American ancestry. The Eriksons settled in Boston, where Erik became the city's first child analyst. He was offered positions at Harvard Medical School and at the prestigious Massachusetts General Hospital. In addition, he began private practice and became associated with Harvard's Psychological Clinic.

In 1936 Erikson accepted a position at Yale Medical School. While at Yale he took his first anthropological field trip to observe Sioux Indian children in South Dakota. His paper on the Sioux combines the cultural richness of an anthropological field report with the psychologically rich perspective of a highly trained clinician. The Eriksons moved later to California, where they spent 10 years in the San Francisco area. Erikson continued his analytic work with children and worked on research projects at the University of California at Berkeley.

In 1950, Erikson's best-known book, *Childhood and Society,* was first published. This book contains the fundamental formulations of virtually all of Erikson's major contributions: identity, the life cycle, cross-cultural studies, and psychobiography. *Childhood and Society* has been translated into a dozen languages and used as a textbook in psychiatric training centers, psychology courses, and in many other disciplines at the graduate and undergraduate levels.

That same year the Eriksons returned to the east coast to the Austin Riggs Center in Massachusetts, a leading center for psychoanalytic training and research. While at Austin Riggs, Erikson did a psychological study of Martin Luther, entitled *Young Man Luther.* An exciting and innovative combination of psychoanalysis, biography, and history, the book stirred great interest among psychoanalysts, psychologists, historians, and other social scientists.

In 1960 Erikson was appointed a professor at Harvard. His study of Gandhi, published in 1969, won the Pulitzer Prize and the National Book Award. He retired in 1970 and moved back to the San Francisco area, where he continues to write and teach.

INTELLECTUAL ANTECEDENTS

Psychoanalysis

Psychoanalysis is unique. It is *the* treatment situation in which intellectual insight is forced to become emotional insight under very carefully planned circumstances defined by technical rules. But outside of that situation, interpretations cannot do what they can do within a disciplined setting. [Erikson in Evans, 1969]

Throughout his career, Erikson has viewed himself as a psychoanalyst. In his application of psychoanalysis to new areas and his incorporation of recent developments in anthropology, psychology, and other social sciences, Erikson inevitably developed ideas that were significantly different from Freud's basic theories. However, his debt to Freud is evident in Erikson's writings.

Erikson's work on in-depth psychological biographies and on child and adult development are essentially psychoanalytic in nature. In dealing with new material, however, Erikson's psychoanalytic understandings have been reshaped and expanded. "I spoke of 'insight,' rather than knowledge or fact, because it is so difficult to say in the study of human situations what you can really call knowledge" (Evans, 1969).

> When I started to write about twenty-five years ago, I really thought I was merely providing new illustrations for what I had learned from Sigmund and Anna Freud. I realized only gradually that any original observation already implies a change in theory. An observer of a different generation, in a different scientific climate, cannot avoid developing in a field if it is a vital one. Even a great breakthrough like Freud's is characterized by a passionate concern to bring order into data which "haunted him," to use Darwin's phrase, for very complex reasons of his own and of his time. One can follow such a man only by doing likewise, and if one does so, one differs. I say this because some workers want to improve on Freud, as if his theories were opinions, and because they prefer nicer or nobler ones. [Erikson in Evans, 1969, p. 13]

Anthropology

In 1937 Erikson traveled to South Dakota to investigate the cause of apathy among Sioux schoolchildren. He discovered that they were caught between conflicting value systems, the traditional tribal values they learned in early childhood and the white middle-class values taught in school.

Several years later Erikson visited the Yurok Indians living by the Klamath River in Northern California. He was particularly interested in comparing the childhood training and personality styles of these relatively sedentary fishermen with those of the plains hunters he had studied earlier. Erikson found that acquisition of possessions was a continuing preoccupation among the Yuroks. Acquisitiveness was learned early in childhood as Yurok children were taught to be frugal, to value long-term gain over immediate impulses, and to engage in fantasies of catching salmon and accumulating money.

Erikson's work with the Sioux and Yurok Indians had an important influence on his thinking. His field work also reveals his remarkable ability to enter the world views and modes of thinking of cultures far different from his own. On both field trips Erikson was accompanied by anthropologists who had developed long-standing friendships with the older people of the tribes. Their assistance gave him access to informants and information never available before to a psychoanalyst. In the anthropological reports he read on both tribes before going into the field, Erikson found virtually no details on childhood training. A good part of his field research consisted of asking the grandmothers, "Before the white men came, how were your children brought up?" He found they loved to talk about it; they had wondered why no one ever asked.

Erikson's later theoretical developments evolved partly from his cross-cultural observations. He found that Freud's pregenital stages of development were intrinsically related to the technology and world view of Western culture. Erikson's own theoretical focus on healthy personality development was strongly influenced by firsthand knowledge of other cultural possibilities.

MAJOR CONCEPTS

An Epigenetic Model of Human Development

Erikson's model of the stages of human development was the first theory to detail human development from infancy to adulthood and old age. His model is structurally similar to that of embryonic development. The basic principle in any epigenetic theory is that each stage can develop only when the previous stage has laid the foundation for it. Embryonic, or epigenetic, development begins with a single fertilized cell that initiates a process of division and differentiation. A se-

With each passage from one stage of human growth to the next we . . . must shed a protective structure. We are left exposed and

vulnerable—but also
yeasty and embryonic
again, capable of
stretching in ways we
hadn't known before.
[Sheehy, 1977, p. 29]

quence of development from single cell to complex organism follows a clear pattern and sequence.

Each organ system of the body has its own time of special growth and development. It follows a predetermined sequence. For example, specialized sense organs, such as the eyes and ears, could never develop without a developed central nervous system.

Erikson's scheme of human development has two basic underlying assumptions:

> (1) That the human personality in principle develops according to steps predetermined in the growing person's readiness to be driven forward, to be aware of, and to interact with a widening social radius; and (2) that society, in principle, tends to be so constituted as to meet and invite the succession of potentialities for interaction and attempts to safeguard and to encourage the proper rate and the proper sequence of their unfolding. [1963, p. 270]

The strengths and capacities developed at each stage are related to the entire personality and can be affected by developments at any point in one's life. These psychological capacities can be affected most strongly during the stage in which they are developed.

In the development of the embryo, each organ is most vulnerable during its time of development out of undifferentiated cells. However, its functioning can be affected by factors occurring either before or after its development. The eyes, for example, can be strengthened or weakened at any time in one's life by diet, use, or physical injury.

Erikson stresses that each stage is systematically related to all the others and must develop in given sequence.

Table 5.1 is taken from Erikson's first discussion of the eight stages in *Childhood and Society*. The diagram illustrates the progression from one stage to another over time. Also each attribute exists in various forms before and after its critical stage. Trust, for example, takes one form in adolescence and yet another in old age; both are based on a sense of trust developed in infancy.

Crises in Development

In Chinese, the word for
crisis is composed of two
characters, "danger" and
"opportunity."

Each stage has a period of crisis in which the strengths and skills that form essential elements of that stage are developed and tested. By crisis Erikson means a turning point, such as the crisis in a fever. When it is resolved successfully, the fever breaks and the individual begins to recover. Crises are special times in each individual's life, "moments of decision between progress and regression, integration and retardation" (Erikson, 1963, pp. 270–271). Each stage is a crisis in learning—developing new skills and attitudes. The crisis may not seem dramatic or critical; an observer can see only later that it was a major turning point that was reached and passed.

TABLE 5.1 EPIGENETIC CHART: EIGHT STAGES.

		1	2	3	4	5	6	7	8
VIII	Maturity								Ego Integrity vs. Despair
VII	Adulthood							Generativity vs. Stagnation	
VI	Young Adulthood						Intimacy vs. Isolation		
V	Puberty and Adolescence					Identity vs. Role Confusion			
IV	Latency				Industry vs. Inferiority				
III	Locomotor-Genital			Initiative vs. Guilt					
II	Muscular-Anal		Autonomy vs. Shame, Doubt						
I	Oral Sensory	Basic Trust vs. Mistrust							

(From Erikson, 1963, p. 273)

Eight Stages of Human Development

Erikson's stages are essentially an amplification of Freud's work. Freud discussed four major stages: oral, anal, phallic, and genital which are tied to specific organs or specific cultures. Erikson expands these to universal issues of human development.

1. Basic Trust versus Basic Mistrust. Human infants develop a relative sense of trust and mistrust of the world around them. Crucial to this development is the experience with the mother. If she is sensitive and responsive to her child, the infant's sense of security increases, and the frustrations of hunger and discomfort are tolerable. Development of a strong sense of basic trust "implies not only that one has learned to rely on the sameness and continuity of the outer providers, but also that one may trust oneself and the capacities of one's own organs to cope with urges" (Erikson, 1963, p. 248).

Babies control and bring up their parents as much as they're controlled by them. [Erikson, 1963, p. 69]

The relationship between mother and child is tested during the biting stage, which is the beginning of the infant's ability to cause pain. The capacity to express anger, rage, and desire to harm is also connected to the pain of teething, a pain the infant must learn to endure because it cannot be alleviated as simply as hunger. According to Erikson, this inner pain and the growing ability to inflict pain are the child's first experiences of a sense of evil and malevolence.

TABLE 5.2 EIGHT STAGES OF HUMAN DEVELOPMENT

CRISIS	AGE	STAGE	MODE	VIRTUE	SOCIAL INSTITUTION†
1. Basic Trust vs. Basic Mistrust	birth–2	oral-sensory	to get	hope	religion
2. Autonomy vs. Shame and Doubt	2–4	muscular-anal	to let go to hold on	will	law
3. Initiative vs. Guilt	4–6	locomotor-genital	to make	purpose	art, drama
4. Industry vs. Inferiority	6–13	latency	to make things to work	competence	technology
5. Identity vs. Identity Confusion	13–19*	adolescence	to be oneself	fidelity	ideology
6. Intimacy vs. Isolation	19–25*	young adulthood	to lose and find oneself in another	love	community
7. Generativity vs. Stagnation	25–60*	adulthood	to make be to take care of	care	education
8. Ego Integrity vs. Despair	60*–death	maturity, old age	to be to face not being	wisdom	philosophy

*Ages are only approximate—may vary widely.
†There is no one-to-one connection between single virtues or crises and single institutions.

A sense of trust develops not so much from absolute quantities of food or demonstrations of love as from the quality of maternal care. Mothers who trust their ability to care for their babies and trust in the healthy development of their children communicate this, creating the infant's sense of trust in self and in the world.

2. Autonomy versus Shame and Doubt. The next stage develops with muscular maturation and the accompanying ability to hold on or let go. The child interacts with the world in grasping and dropping objects and in toilet training. The child begins to exert control over self and parts of the outside world.

Holding on and letting go have both positive and negative aspects. Holding on can be a destructive or cruel restraint, or it can be a pattern of caring. Letting go can be a release of destructive forces, or it can be a relaxed allowing, a letting be.

A sense of autonomy develops with the sense of free choice, a feeling of being able to choose what to keep and what to reject. The infant's basic faith in existence, a lasting result of the first stage, is tested in sudden and stubborn wishes to choose, to grab demandingly, or to eliminate inappropriately.

Some children turn this urge to control against themselves by developing a precocious and demanding conscience. Rather than mastering the outer environment, they judge and manipulate themselves, which results in a strong sense of shame or self-doubt.

Shame stems from a sense of self-exposure, a feeling that one's deficiencies are exposed to others and that one is "caught with one's pants down." Shame is also associated with the child's first experience of standing upright, small, wobbly, and powerless in an adult world.

Doubt is more closely related to the consciousness of having a front and a back. Our front is the acceptable face that we turn toward the world. The back part of the body cannot be seen by the child. It is unknown and unexplored territory and yet, at the stage of toilet training, one's backside can be dominated by the will of others. Unless the split between front and back is reduced, the child's feelings of autonomy will become tinged with doubt.

3. Initiative versus Guilt. At this stage the child experiences greater mobility and inquisitiveness, an expanding sense of mastery and responsibility. The child is "into everything," finding joy in attack and conquest over the environment. The child is eager to learn and to perform well. Language and imagination develop. The child learns to plan ahead, gaining a sense of direction and purpose.

The sense of mastery is tempered by feelings of guilt. The child's new freedom and assertion of power create anxiety. The child develops a conscience, a parental attitude that supports self-observation, self-guidance, and also self-punishment. At this stage the child can do more than ever before and must learn to set limits.

4. Industry versus Inferiority. This stage marks the beginning of entrance into life outside the family. In our culture, school life begins. In other social systems the child may become an apprentice or a working assistant to father or mother.

This is a stage of systematic instruction, a movement from play to a sense of work. Earlier the child could *play at* activities. No attention was given to the quality of results. Now the child needs to do *well* and develop a sense of work completion and satisfaction in a job well done. Otherwise the child develops a sense of inferiority and inequality.

5. Identity versus Identity Confusion. As childhood ends, adolescents begin to integrate their past experiences into a new whole. They question role models and identifications of the past and try out new roles. A new sense of ego identity develops.

This includes the individual's ability to integrate past identifications with present impulses, aptitudes and developed skills, and with opportunities offered by society and culture. "The sense of ego identity, then, is the accrued confidence that the *inner* sameness and continuity prepared in the past are matched by the sameness and continuity of one's meaning for *others,* as evidenced in the tangible promise of a 'career' " (Erikson, 1963, pp. 261–262, italics mine).

For most of those in the twenties, a fantastic mystery story waits to be written over the next two decades. It races with excitement and jeopardy . . . and leads us down secret passageways in search of our missing personality parts. [Sheehy, 1977, p. 166]

This difficult transition between childhood and adulthood can be strongly affected by social limitations and possibilities. The adolescent is likely to suffer from some confusion of roles. Doubts about one's sexual attractiveness and sexual identity are common. An inability to "take hold" and develop a sense of identification with an individual or cultural role model that gives direction to one's life can lead to a period of floundering and insecurity. Another common reaction at this stage is overidentification (to the point of apparent loss of identity) with youth-culture heroes or clique leaders. The individual often feels isolated, empty, anxious, or indecisive. Under pressure to make important life decisions, the adolescent feels unable, even resistant, to do so.

6. Intimacy versus Isolation.
Only after a relatively firm sense of identity is developed are we capable of committing ourselves to partnership, affiliation, and intimacy with others. A critical commitment that generally occurs at this stage is mutuality with a love partner. This level of intimacy is significantly different from the earlier sexual exploration and intense search for one's sexual identity.

Without a sense of intimacy and commitment, one may become isolated and be unable to sustain intimate relationships. If one's sense of identity is weak and threatened by intimacy, the individual may turn away from or attack whatever encroaches.

The mere fact of having and wanting children does not achieve generativity. [Erikson, 1963, p. 267]

7. Generativity versus Stagnation.
Intimate commitment to others widens to a more general concern for guiding and supporting the next generation. Generativity includes concern for our own children and for the ideas and other products that we have created.

We are teaching as well as learning beings. Creation is important, as is ensuring the ongoing health and maintenance of our creations, ideals, and principles. Unless the sphere of our care and productivity widens, we fall prey to a sense of boredom and stagnation.

8. Ego Integrity versus Despair.
The sense of ego integrity includes the individual's acceptance of a unique life cycle with its triumphs and failures. It brings a sense of order and meaning, personally and in the world around us, as well as a new and different love of parents. A sense of ego integrity includes an awareness of the value of many other life-styles, including those that differ widely from one's own. Those who possess a sense of integrity are ready to defend the dignity of their own life-styles against criticism and threats.

If we have not gained a measure of self-acceptance, we are likely to plunge into despair over the feeling that time is short—too short to start over. Despair may manifest in fear of death or result in contempt and rejection of other values, institutions, and life-styles.

. . . [H]ealthy children will not fear life if their elders have integrity enough not to fear death. [Erikson, 1963, p. 269]

Inner and Outer Attitudes

An individual develops a "sense of trust," never trust itself. The eight stages describe attitudes toward oneself and one's environment, not entities or concrete structures in the psyche. By "sense of" Erikson refers both to conscious and unconscious elements. A sense of autonomy, for example, can be found in an individual's conscious experience and also in unconscious processes, which are accessible by testing and analysis.

Ratio and Balance

At each stage there is a dynamic ratio between two poles. Erikson's terms for them tend to be misleading because, inevitably, one seems positive and the other negative. However, in every case the extremes are unfavorable. This may be seen as follows:

(unhealthy)		(healthy)		(unhealthy)
Extreme trust	Basic trust		Basic mistrust	Extreme mistrust

In the first case, for instance, an individual who develops an unbalanced sense of trust becomes a Pollyanna, as out of touch with reality as the individual paralyzed with extreme mistrust. Healthy ratios vary widely from relative trust to relative suspicion, but in every case elements of both trust and mistrust are present.

Similarly, unbalanced autonomy can become unreasonable stubbornness. Unbalanced initiative is a self-centered preoccupation with one's own goals and concerns. A sense of industry without a sense of limitations leads to an inflated appreciation of one's abilities. An overdeveloped sense of identity is rigid and inflexible and is likely to clash with external reality. The same is true for the other stages.

Modes of Relating to the Environment

Whereas Freud based his description of the stages of human development on specific organ-related experiences, Erikson's stages are based on more general styles of relating to and coping with the environment. Although styles are often initially developed through a particular organ, they refer to broad patterns of behavior. For instance, the mode learned in the first stage, basic trust versus basic mistrust, is *to get*— that is, the ability to receive and to accept what is given. (This stage is comparable to Freud's oral stage.) At this time the mouth is the pri-

The infant may equally absorb the milk of wisdom where he once desired more tangible fluids from more sensuous containers. [Erikson, 1963, p. 62]

mary organ of interchange between the infant and the environment. However, an individual fixated on "getting" may exhibit other forms of *dependency* as an adult, rather than orality.

In the second stage, autonomy versus shame and doubt, the modes are *to let go* and *to hold on.* As with Freud's anal stage, the modes are fundamentally related to retention and elimination of feces; however, the child at this stage also alternates between possessing and rejecting parents, favorite toys, and so on.

The mode of the third stage, initiative versus guilt, Erikson calls *to make.* In one sense the child is "on the make," focused on conquest of the environment. This includes a phallic-intrusive attitude and also a seductive-manipulatory quality. Play is important, from making mud pies to imitating the complex sports and games of older children.

The fourth stage, industry versus inferiority, includes the modes *to do well* and *to work.* There is no single organ system associated with this stage; rather, productive work and accomplishment are central.

Erikson does not discuss in detail the modes involved with the remaining stages. These later stages, less related to Freud's developmental stages, seem less rooted in a particular activity or organ mode.

Identity

Erikson has developed the concept of identity in greater detail than the concepts discussed in the eight stages. He first coined the phrase *identity crisis* to describe the mental state of many of the soldiers he treated at Mt. Zion Veterans Rehabilitation Clinic in San Francisco. These men were easily upset by any sudden or intense stimulus. Their egos seemed to have lost any shock-absorbing capacity. Their sensory systems were in a constant "startled" state, thrown off by external stimuli as well as a variety of bodily sensations, including heat flashes, palpitation, intense headaches, and insomnia. "Above all, the men felt that they 'did not know who they were': There was a distinct loss of ego identity. The sameness and continuity and the belief in one's social role were gone" (Erikson, 1968, p. 67).

The term *identity* brings together the theories of depth psychology with cognitive and ego psychologies; it also provides a meeting place for psychology, sociology, and history. Because of its complexity, Erikson has wisely avoided giving identity a single definition:

> I can attempt to make the subject matter of identity more explicit only by approaching it from a variety of angles. . . . At one time, then, it will appear to refer to a conscious *sense of individual identity*; at another, to an unconscious striving for a *continuity of personal character*; at a third, as a criterion for the silent doings of *ego synthesis*; and, finally, as a maintenance of an *inner solidarity* with a group's ideals and identity. [1980, p. 109]

Erikson spells out these aspects of identity as follows (adapted from Evans, 1967, pp. 218–219):

1. *Individuality*—a conscious sense of one's uniqueness and existence as a separate, distinct entity.
2. *Sameness and continuity*—a sense of inner sameness, a continuity between what one has been in the past and what one promises to be in the future, a feeling that one's life has consistency and meaningful direction.
3. *Wholeness and synthesis*—a sense of inner harmony and wholeness, a synthesis of the self-images and identifications of childhood into a meaningful whole that produces a sense of harmony.
4. *Social solidarity*—a sense of inner solidarity with the ideals and values of society or a subgroup within it, a feeling that one's identity is meaningful to significant others and corresponds to their expectations and perceptions.

Like a trapeze artist, the young person in the middle of vigorous motion must let go of his safehold on childhood and reach out for a firm grasp on adulthood, depending for a breathless interval on a relatedness between the past and the future, and on the reliability of those he must let go of, and those who will "receive" him. Whatever combination of drives and defenses, of sublimations and capacities has emerged from the young individual's childhood must now make sense in view of his concrete opportunities in work and love . . . [and] he must detect some meaningful resemblance between what he has come to see in himself and what his sharpened awareness tells him others judge and expect him to be. [Erikson, 1964, p. 90]

The concept of identity has become particularly popular because it is generally recognized as the major life crisis in the United States today—and perhaps in all of modern society. Our cultural emphasis on extended education as well as the complexity of most modern vocations make the development of a sense of identity particularly difficult in our society. The struggle to gain a healthy, clear sense of identity frequently continues beyond adolescence, erupting later in mid-life crises.

Years ago, most children took on their parents' adult roles. Girls learned to run households and boys followed their fathers' vocations. Children began to learn adult skills, attitudes, and potential adult roles early in life; their parents' vocations were generally integrated with family life. Given our changing values and social roles, not only are children unlikely to take on their parents' roles, but there may not be *any* clear adult role models available to them. The Western adolescent's earlier childhood identifications and experiences are clearly inadequate in the task of anticipating a career and making a major vocational role commitment.

Erikson found that the development of a sense of identity is frequently preceded by a "psychosocial moratorium," a period of time off in which the individual may be occupied with study, travel, or a clearly temporary occupation. This provides time to reflect, to develop a new sense of direction, new values, new purpose. The moratorium may last for months or even years.

Erikson has stressed that the development of a sense of identity has psychological and social aspects:

1. The individual's development of a sense of personal sameness and continuity is based, in part, on a belief in the sameness and continuity of a shared world view.

2. Although many aspects of the search for a sense of identity are conscious, unconscious motivation may also play a major role. At this stage, feelings of acute vulnerability may alternate with great expectations of success.

3. A sense of identity cannot develop without certain physical, mental, and social preconditions (outlined in Erikson's developmental stages). Also it must not be unduly delayed because future stages of development depend on it. Psychological factors may prolong the crisis as the individual seeks to match unique gifts to existing social possibilities. Social factors and historical change may also postpone adult commitment.

4. The growth of a sense of identity is dependent on the past, present, and future. This growth requires the resources of clear identifications made in childhood. It relies on whatever current role and career models are available. It also relies on a sense that one's chosen roles will be viable in the future in spite of inevitable inner and outer changes.

Erikson has pointed out that problems of identity are not new, although they may be more widespread today than ever before. Many creative individuals have wrestled with the problem of identity in carving out careers and social roles that were new personally and also contributed major social innovations, thus offering new role models for others. Freud, for example, began his career as a conventional doctor and neurologist. Only in mid-career did he create a new role for himself (and many others) by becoming the first psychoanalyst.

Psychohistory

Erikson expanded psychoanalysis with the study of major historical personalities by including their psychological growth and development and the psychological impact they had on their generation. In addition to Luther and Gandhi, his psychobiographies have included Maxim Gorky, Hitler, George Bernard Shaw, Freud, and Woodrow Wilson.

Erikson's major psychobiographical subjects were Luther and Gandhi. In the two books he combined clinical insight with historical and social analysis. Erikson illuminated the forces that helped shape these two great men and also the impact they in turn had on their societies.

This interest in combining psychoanalysis and history began when Erikson left Europe for the United States as Hitler came to power. On the boat he wrote of the central reasons that German youths turned toward Hitler. Because of his own background, Erikson was deeply affected by developments in Germany. Although born a Dane, Germany had been his home. But German friends had turned Nazi and were killing other friends and classmates who shared Erikson's Jewish roots. He analyzed what was happening in Germany without writing off the Nazis as "others," as depraved criminals essentially different from the rest of humanity. These notes led to Erikson's first psychohistorical study, which appeared as a chapter on Hitler in *Childhood and Society*.

Erikson made a major contribution to the study of historical figures by applying the same methods used in psychoanalytic case histories for reconstructing the life of a historical figure. Erikson realized that in making the transition from case history to life history the psychoanalyst must broaden his or her concerns and take into account the subject's activities in the outside world with its opportunities and limitations. This appreciation of the interaction of psychological and social currents in turn affected Erikson's theoretical work.

There is one major difference between Erikson's psychological biographies and case histories. In a case history a therapist tries to understand why the patient has fallen apart. In a life history an investigator tries to understand how the person manages to stay whole and function creatively and effectively in spite of conflicts, complexes, and crises.

The Study of "Great Individuals"

In his psychobiographical work Erikson brings the insights of a trained psychoanalyst to the careful study of critical periods in the lives of influential individuals. He is particularly interested in men and women whose identity conflicts mirror the conflicts of their era and whose greatness lies in their finding a personal solution to their own identity crisis, a solution that becomes a model for others. Often they are individuals who had deep personal conflicts. The crisis of the age seems to be intensified in each of them; yet each brings a special urgency and focus to its solution.

Although they all were creative, energetic, and powerful people, they were not without fear, anxiety, and unhappiness. Their lives were often dominated by a sense stemming from childhood that they needed to "settle" or "live down" something. They were generally tied to their fathers in a way that precluded overt rebellion; they also learned a great deal from as well as felt needed and specially chosen by their fathers. These individuals frequently had early sensitive senses of conscience and paid early attention to ultimate values, sometimes convinced they carried special responsibility for part of humankind. These productive men and women might have become simply misfits and cranks except for their ability, energy, concentration, and spiritual devotion.

DYNAMICS

Positive Growth
Psychosocial Strengths or Virtues

Erikson has pointed out that successful resolution of the crisis of each stage of human development promotes a certain psychosocial strength or virtue. Erikson uses *virtue* in its old sense, as in the virtue of a medicine. It refers more to potency than morality. The individual emerges from each crisis with an increased sense of inner unity, clearer judgment, and increased capacity to function effectively.

This focus on positive characteristics developed in each stage distinguishes Erikson's schema from Freud's. Erikson's virtues are not merely resistance to illness or to the negative, nor are they simply attitudes of nobility or morality. These virtues are inherent strengths; they are characterized by a sense of potency and positive development.

1. Hope. The virtue or strength resulting from an achievement of balance between basic trust and mistrust is hope. *"Hope is the enduring belief in the attainability of fervent wishes, in spite of the dark urges and rages which mark the beginning of existence"* (Erikson, 1964, p. 118, italics his). Hope underlies the eventual development of faith.

Hope is established as a basic strength, relatively independent of specific hopes, goals, and desires. As the individual continues to develop, this strength is verified at each stage; rewarding experiences inspire new hopefulness. At the same time, the individual develops a capacity for renunciation and an ability to cope with disappointment, develops imaginable dreams, and focuses expectations realistically.

The strength of hope emerges from three essential sources. First is the mother's relation to her own past childhood—her desire and need to pass on the hope transmitted from her mother and from her culture. Second is the mother-child relationship itself, the mutuality and sensitivity that can develop when it is healthy. Finally, the infant's hope is maintained through social institutions that confirm and restore it through religious ritual, inspired advice, or otherwise. The mature form of an infant's hope is faith. The rituals and practices of religion are designed to support, deepen, and restore faith.

2. Will. The strength acquired at the stage of autonomy versus shame and doubt is will. To will is not to be willful, but to control one's drives with judgment and discrimination. The individual learns to make decisions and act decisively in spite of inevitable frustration. *"Will, therefore, is the unbroken determination to exercise free choice as well as self-restraint, in spite of the unavoidable experience of shame and doubt"* (Erikson, 1964, p. 119, italics his).

An infant's will becomes the adult's ability to control drives and impulses. Ideally, the individual's will joins with others in a way that permits all to retain a sense of power, even when restrained by rules and reason.

Will forms the basis of our acceptance of law and external necessity. It is rooted in an appreciation that parental training is guided and tempered by a spirit of justice. The law is a social institution that gives concrete form to our ego's control of our drives. We surrender our willfulness to the majesty of the law with ambivalence and inevitable small transgressions.

3. Purpose. This virtue is rooted in play and fantasy. Play is to the child what thinking and planning are to the adult. It provides the rudiments of purpose: focus and direction given to concerted activity. *"Purpose, then, is the courage to envisage and pursue valued goals uninhibited by the defeat of infantile fantasies, by guilt and by the foiling fear of punishment"* (Erikson, 1964, p. 122, italics his).

Purpose provides aim and direction, fed by fantasy yet rooted in reality, limited but not inhibited by guilt. The development of fantasy forms the roots of dance, drama, and ritual in adult life.

4. Competence. This virtue is based on a sense of workmanship, the development of practical skills, and general capacities. *"Competence, then, is the free exercise of dexterity and intelligence in the completion of tasks, unimpaired by infantile inferiority"* (Erikson, 1964, p. 124, italics his).

Competence is the psychological basis for technology. At this stage we become joined with our culture as productive members who have mastered the technology developed over centuries of cultural evolution.

5. Fidelity. At the threshold of adulthood each individual faces a need for commitment to a career and a lasting set of values. *"Fidelity is the ability to sustain loyalties freely pledged in spite of the inevitable contradictions of value systems"* (Erikson, 1964, p. 125, italics his). Fidelity is the cornerstone of identity; it requires the validation of acceptable social ideologies and the support of peers who have made similar choices.

At this stage we incorporate over culture's ethical values and belief systems. At the same time, the culture itself is renewed by the affirmation of each generation; it is revitalized as youths selectively offer their loyalties and energies, supporting some traditions and changing others. Those who cannot pledge their loyalties either remain deviant or commit themselves to revolutionary goals and values.

6. Love. This is the greatest virtue and takes many forms. Early in life it is the infant's love for its mother, the child's love for parents, and adolescent infatuation. When real intimacy develops between adults, love includes a shared identity and the validation of each partner in the other. This virtue can manifest in a romantic, sexual relationship, but also in deep ties developed in joint service of ideals, home, or country. The virtue of love manifests in true mutuality and intimacy. *"Love, then, is mutuality of devotion forever subduing the antagonism inherent in divided functions"* (Erikson, 1964, p. 129, italics his).

7. Care. The care and nurturing of children is at the core of this virtue. This includes not only the care of offspring, but also of the children of our minds and hearts—our ideas, ideals, and creations. Unique to our species is the need for care extended over a long childhood and complex education.

As adults we require to be needed, or else we suffer from narcissism and self-absorption. In terms of human psychosocial evolution we are essentially a teaching species. We must teach to fulfill our identity and to keep alive our skills and knowledge. *"Care is the widening concern for what has been generated by love, necessity, or accident; it overcomes the ambivalence adhering to irreversible obligation"* (Erikson, 1964, p. 131, italics his).

8. Wisdom. The strength of wisdom develops out of the encounter of integrity and despair as the individual is confronted with ultimate concerns. Wisdom maintains the integrity of one's accumulated knowledge and experience. Those who have developed wisdom are models of wholeness and completeness. They are inspirational examples to younger generations who have adopted similar values and life-styles. This sense of wholeness and meaning can also alleviate the feelings of helplessness and dependence that mark old age. *"Wisdom, then, is detached concern with life itself, in the face of death itself"* (Erikson, 1964, p. 133, italics his).

Obstacles to Growth
Negative Identity
Our sense of identity always comprises positive and negative elements. These elements include things we want to become and others we do not want to be or know we should not be. Under extremely negative social conditions, it may be impossible for the majority of healthy

young men and women to become committed to anything positive and large-scale. The Nazi era in Germany is an example.

Lack of a healthy sense of identity may be expressed in hostility toward available social goals and values. This hostility can include any role aspect: one's sexuality, nationality, class, or family background. Children of immigrant families may display contempt for their parents' backgrounds, and descendants of established families may reject everything American and overestimate everything foreign.

Many conflict-ridden adolescents would rather be someone bad than a nobody. Thus the choice of a negative identity is based on those roles that have been presented as undesirable or dangerous. If we feel unable to make a commitment to more positive roles, the negative ones become the most real. They may include those of the drunk, the prostitute, the bum, or anything constituting failure in the eyes of society.

STRUCTURE

Body

The role of the bodily organs is especially important in Erikson's early stages. Later in life, development of physical as well as intellectual skills strongly affects the growth of a sense of competence and an ability to choose demanding roles in our complex society.

> Experience is anchored in the groundplan of the body. [Erikson, 1963, p. 108]

As a psychosocial theorist, Erikson is aware of the constant interaction of body, psychological processes, and social forces.

Social Relationships

Social relationships are central in virtually every stage. Interaction with one's parents, family, and with peers is crucial in the first five stages of development. The development of a sense of identity is strongly affected by the presence of affirming peers. The stage of intimacy brings opportunities for new and deeper social relationships. Another qualitative change occurs during the stage of generativity, when each individual learns caring for and nurturing those who are younger, weaker, and less knowledgeable.

Erikson's basic epigenetic principle states that "Personality . . . can be said to develop according to steps predetermined in the human organism's readiness to be driven toward, to be aware of, and to interact with a widening radius of significant individuals and institutions" (1968, pp. 92–93).

> A stage has a new configuration of past and future, a new combination of drive and defense, a new set of capacities fit for a new setting of tasks and opportunities, a new and wider radius of significant encounters. [Erikson, 1964, p. 166]

Will

Erikson details the development of will in his discussion of autonomy versus shame and doubt. The development of a healthy and balanced will (and goodwill) continues throughout life. Crucial to the development of a healthy sense of identity is the sense that "I am what I can will freely."

Traditional psychoanalysis deals primarily with the analysis of an individual's conception of reality, focusing on thoughts, emotions, and essentially private behavior. Erikson emphasises, in addition, the importance of will and action in the world. He feels that one of the goals of psychoanalysis is to restore "a productive interplay between psychological reality and historical actuality" (1964, p. 201), that is, to integrate inner, subjective experiences with the details of external actions and events. Erikson suggests that reality refers to "the world of phenomenal experience, perceived with a minimum of distortion" (1964, p. 165). Although dealing with distortion and misunderstanding is essential, Erikson stresses the need for an understanding of actuality, "the world of participation, shared with other participants . . ." (1964, p. 165). Reanalyzing Freud's classic case study of Anna O., Erikson points out that although Freud did a brilliant job of analyzing Anna's personality dynamics and distortions, he failed to consider her real powerlessness as a young girl in a middle-class Viennese family. Anna was dependent on her father economically, socially, and legally. It was practically and emotionally impossible for her to confront him directly.

Successful action requires both social and historical possibilities and will. To see accurately does not guarantee that one can act effectively.

Emotions

As a psychoanalyst, Erikson stresses the importance of the emotional component of psychological processes. His treatment of the role of the emotions is implicit throughout his theories. As a theorist, his focus has been on adding new cognitive, historical, and social elements to a psychoanalytic framework. Erikson does not discuss explicitly the emotions as a distinct aspect of psychological processes.

Intellect

Similar to emotion, the intellect is seen as an essential element in psychological processes. Erikson does not pay specific attention to the role of intellectual capacities. He does point out, however, that development of intellectual skills is critical in the formation of a sense of competence. Cognitive skills play a major role in mastering the technological skills of one's culture, in forming a sense of identity, and in choosing acceptable social roles and a career.

Self

A sense of identity can be seen as the development and flowering of a sense of self. "The ego, if understood as a central and partially unconscious organizing agency, must at any given stage of life deal with a changing Self which demands to be synthesized with abandoned and anticipated selves. . . . What could consequently be called the *self-identity* emerges from experiences in which temporarily confused selves are successfully reintegrated in an ensemble of roles which also secure social recognition. Identity formation, thus, can be said to have a self-aspect and an ego aspect" (Erikson, 1968, pp. 210–211).

Therapist

Erikson has pointed out that a competent therapist has a strong sense of the patient's potential growth and development. The therapist's job is to foster that growth rather than impose his or her own future or past on the patient. This focus is implicit in the requirement that each psychoanalyst undergoes? training analysis, and in the stress on the role of transference and countertransference in psychoanalysis. In discussing Jung's statement that every patient who came to him took his life in his own hands, Erikson commented, "This is true, but one must add that he came to *me,* and not to somebody else, and after that he will never be the same—and neither will I" (Erikson in Evans, 1969, p. 103).

Every therapist must be prepared to understand and identify with a variety of alternative life-styles. Issues of values and morality are central to therapy. The notion of the impersonality of the classical analyst is, according to Erikson, a misunderstanding of the role of impartial acceptance of the patient's free associations and past history. The therapist is always there as an individual, with the freedom to express whatever he or she wishes, ideally without distortion from irrational countertransference.

Erikson has reformulated the "golden rule" in light of modern psychological understanding. He writes that truly worthwhile, moral acts strengthen the doer even as they strengthen the other, and enhance the relationship between the two. In therapy this version of the rule encourages the therapist to "develop as a practitioner, and as a person, even as the patient is cured as a patient, and as a person. For a real cure transcends the transitory state of patienthood. It is an experience which enables the cured patient to develop and to transmit to home and neighborhood an attitude toward health, which is one of the most essential ingredients of an ethical outlook" (Erikson, 1964, pp. 236–237).

EVALUATION

Erikson has been criticized for his vagueness. He is an artist with words rather than a logician. His beautiful and brilliant formulations can dissolve into sketches of problems rather than into linear, logical analysis.

Erikson has been limited by psychoanalysis. His tools are those

Psychoanalysis is the first systematic and active "consciousness-expansion," and such expansion may be necessary as man concentrates on the conquest of matter and is apt to overidentify with it. [Erikson in Evans, 1969, p. 98]

of a clinician, developed for treatment of unwell patients. Application
of these tools to the development of the healthy personality is not always satisfactory. This is evident in Erikson's studies of great individuals. In his analysis of Gandhi, for example, Erikson applies brilliantly
the tools and insights of the psychoanalyst. He does not, however, address seriously the role of Gandhi's spiritual ideals and spiritual discipline. The dynamics of Gandhi's life and thought are seen more as
those of a patient, rather than as those of someone whose state of consciousness and psychological processes may have been qualitatively different.

Erikson's psychoanalytically rooted tools are not always adequate
for the tasks he takes on. In so doing he has expanded psychoanalysis
and at the same time shown its limitations.

Erikson provides a stimulating, relevant reformulation of psychoanalysis. He successfully brought Freud's brilliant system of thought
into a new era. Erikson's concern for social and cultural determinants
of behavior and his integration of psychology, sociology, and anthropology with the insights of psychoanalysis indicate the future of the psychology of personality.

THE THEORY FIRSTHAND

ROOTS OF IDENTITY

Before we try to understand the meaning of the present-day echo of our
terms, let me take a long look back to our professional and conceptual
ancestors. Today when the term identity refers, more often than not, to
something noisily demonstrative, to a more or less desperate "quest," or
to an almost deliberately confused "search" let me present two formulations which assert strongly what identity feels like when you become
aware of the fact that you do undoubtedly *have* one.

My two witnesses are bearded and patriarchal founding fathers of the
psychologies on which our thinking on identity is based. As a *subjective
sense of an invigorating sameness* and *continuity,* what I would call a
sense of identity seems to me best described by William James in a letter
to his wife:

A man's character is discernible in the mental or moral attitude in
which, when it came upon him, he felt himself most deeply and intensely active and alive. At such moments there is a voice inside which
speaks and says: *"This* is the real me!"

Such experience always includes

. . . an element of active tension, of holding my own, as it were, and
trusting outward things to perform their part so as to make it a full
harmony, but without any *guaranty* that they will. Make it a guaranty
. . . and the attitude immediately becomes to my consciousness stag-
nant and stingless. Take away the guaranty, and I feel (provided I am
ueberhaupt in vigorous condition) a sort of deep enthusiastic bliss, of
bitter willingness to do and suffer anything . . . and which, although
it is a mere mood or emotion to which I can give no form in words, au-

thenticates itself to me as the deepest principle of all active and theoretic determination which I possess . . .

James uses the word "character," but I am taking the liberty of claiming that he describes a sense of identity, and that he does so in a way which can in principle be experienced by any man. To him it is both mental and moral in the sense of those "moral philosophy" days, and he experiences it as something that "comes upon you" as a recognition, almost as a surprise rather than as something strenuously "quested" after. It is an active tension (rather than a paralyzing question)—a tension which, furthermore, must create a challenge "without guaranty" rather than one dissipated in a clamor for certainty. But let us remember in passing that James was in his thirties when he wrote this, that in his youth he had faced and articulated an "identity crisis" of honest and desperate depth, and that he became *the* Psychologist-Philosopher of American Pragmatism only after having experimented with a variety of cultural, philosophic, and national identity elements: the use in the middle of his declaration of the untranslatable German word *"überhaupt"* is probably an echo of his conflictful student days in Europe.

One can study in James's life history a protracted identity crisis as well as the emergence of a "self-made" identity in the new and expansive American civilization. . . . for the sake of further definition, let us now turn to a statement which asserts a unity of *personal and cultural* identity rooted in an ancient people's fate. In an address to the Society of B'nai B'rith in Vienna in 1926, Sigmund Freud said:

> What bound me to Jewry was (I am ashamed to admit) neither faith nor national pride, for I have always been an unbeliever and was brought up without any religion though not without a respect for what are called the "ethical" standards of human civilization. Whenever I felt an inclination to national enthusiasm I strove to suppress it as being harmful and wrong, alarmed by the warning examples of the peoples among whom we Jews live. But plenty of other things remained over to make the attraction of Jewry and Jews irresistible—many obscure emotional forces, which were the more powerful the less they could be expressed in words, as well as a clear consciousness of inner identity, the safe privacy of a common mental construction. And beyond this there was a perception that it was to my Jewish nature alone that I owed two characteristics that had become indispensable to me in the difficult course of my life. Because I was a Jew I found myself free from many prejudices which restricted others in the use of their intellect; and as a Jew I was prepared to join the Opposition, and to do without agreement with the "compact majority."

No translation ever does justice to the distinctive choice of words in Freud's German original. "Obscure emotional forces" are *"dunkle Gefühlsmächte";* the "safe privacy of a common mental construction" is *"die Heimlichkeit der inneren Konstruktion"*—not just "mental," then, and certainly not "private," but a deep communality known only to those who shared in it, and only expressible in words more mythical than conceptual.

These fundamental statements were taken not from theoretical works, but from special communications: a letter to his wife from a man who married late, an address to his "brothers" by an original observer long isolated in his profession. But in all their poetic spontaneity they are the products of trained minds and therefore exemplify the main dimensions of a positive sense of identity almost systematically. Trained minds of genius, of course, have a special identity and special identity problems often leading to a protracted crisis at the onset of their careers. Yet we must rely on them for formulating initially what we can then proceed to observe as universally human.

This is the only time Freud used the term identity in a more than casual way and, in fact, in a most central ethnic sense. And as we would expect of him, he inescapably points to some of those aspects of the matter which I called sinister and yet vital—the more vital, in fact, "the less they could be expressed in words." For Freud's "consciousness of inner identity" includes a sense of bitter pride preserved by his dispersed and often despised people throughout a long history of persecution. It is anchored in a particular (here intellectual) gift which had victoriously emerged from the hostile limitation of opportunities. At the same time, Freud contrasts the *positive identity* of a fearless freedom of thinking with a *negative* trait in "the peoples among whom we Jews live," namely, "prejudices which restrict others in the use of their intellect." It dawns on us, then, that one person's or group's identity may be relative to another's, and that the pride of gaining a strong identity may signify an inner emancipation from a more dominant group identity, such as that of the "compact majority." An exquisite triumph is suggested in the claim that the same historical development which restricted the prejudiced majority in the free use of their intellect made the isolated minority sturdier in intellectual matters. To all this, we must come back when discussing race relations.

And Freud goes farther. He admits in passing that he had to suppress in himself an inclination toward "national enthusiasm" such as was common for "the peoples among whom we Jews live." Again, as in James's case, only a study of Freud's youthful enthusiasms could show how he came to leave behind other aspirations in favor of the ideology of applying the methods of natural science to the study of psychological "forces of dignity." It is in Freud's dreams, incidentally, that we have a superb record of his suppressed (or what James called "abandoned," or even "murdered") selves—for our "negative identity" haunts us at night. [From Erikson, 1980, pp. 19–22]

SON OF A BOMBARDIER

During the last war a neighbor of mine, a boy of five, underwent a change of personality from a "mother's boy" to a violent, stubborn, and disobedient child. The most disquieting symptom was an urge to set fires.

The boy's parents had separated just before the outbreak of war. The mother and the boy had moved in with some women cousins, and when war began the father had joined the air force. The women cousins frequently expressed their disrespect for the father, and cultivated babyish traits in the boy. Thus, to be a mother's boy threatened to be a stronger identity element than to be a father's son.

The father, however, did well in war; in fact, he became a hero. On the occasion of his first furlough the little boy had the experience of seeing the man he had been warned not to emulate become the much-admired center of the neighborhood's attention. The mother announced that she would drop her divorce plans. The father went back to war and was soon lost over Germany.

After the father's departure and death the affectionate and dependent boy developed more and more disquieting symptoms of destructiveness and defiance, culminating in fire setting. He gave the key to the change himself when, protesting against his mother's whipping, he pointed to a pile of wood he had set afire and exclaimed (in more childish words), "If this were a German city, you would have liked me for it." He thus indicated that in setting fires he fantasied being a bombardier like the father, who had told of his exploits.

We can only guess at the nature of the boy's turmoil. But I believe that we see here the identification of a son with his father, resulting from a suddenly increased conflict at the very close of the Oedipus age. The father, at first successfully replaced by the "good" little boy, suddenly becomes both a newly vitalized ideal and a concrete threat, a competitor for the mother's love. He thus devaluates radically the boy's feminine identifications. In order to save himself from both sexual and social disorientation, the boy must, in the shortest possible time, regroup his identifications; but then the great competitor is killed by the enemy—a fact which increases the guilt for the competitive feeling itself and compromises the boy's new masculine initiative which becomes maladaptive.

A child has quite a number of opportunities to identify himself, more or less experimentally, with habits, traits, occupations, and ideas of real or fictitious people of either sex. Certain crises force him to make radical selections. However, the historical era in which he lives offers only a limited number of socially meaningful models for workable combinations of identification fragments. Their usefulness depends on the way in which they simultaneously meet the requirements of the organism's maturational stage and the ego's habits of synthesis.

To my little neighbor the role of the bombardier may have suggested a possible synthesis of the various elements that comprise a budding identity: his temperament (vigorous); his maturational stage (phallic-urethral-locomotor); his social stage (Oedipal) and his social situation; his capacities (muscular, mechanical); his father's temperament (a great soldier rather than a successful civilian); and a current historical prototype (aggressive hero). Where such synthesis succeeds, a most surprising coagulation of constitutional, temperamental, and learned reactions may produce exuberance of growth and unexpected accomplishment. Where it fails, it must lead to severe conflict, often expressed in unexpected naughtiness or delinquency. For should a child feel that the environment tries to deprive him too radically of all the forms of expression which permit him to develop and to integrate the next step in his identity, he will defend it with the astonishing strength encountered in animals who are suddenly forced to defend their lives. And indeed, in the social jungle of human existence, there is no feeling of being alive without a sense of ego identity. Deprivation of identity can lead to murder.

I would not have dared to speculate on the little bombardier's conflicts had I not seen evidence for a solution in line with our interpretation. When the worst of this boy's dangerous initiative had subsided, he was observed swooping down a hill on a bicycle, endangering, scaring, and yet deftly avoiding other children. They shrieked, laughed, and in a way admired him for it. In watching him, and hearing the strange noises he made, I could not help thinking that he again imagined himself to be an airplane on a bombing mission. But at the same time he gained in playful mastery over his locomotion; he exercised circumspection in his attack, and he became an admired virtuoso on a bicycle. . . .

Our little son of a bombardier illustrates a general point. Psychosocial identity develops out of a gradual integration of all identifications. But here, if anywhere, the whole has a different quality from the sum of its parts. Under favorable circumstances children have the nucleus of a separate identity early in life; often they must defend it even against the necessity of overidentifying with one or both of their parents. These processes are difficult to study in patients, because the neurotic self has, by definition, fallen prey to overidentifications which isolate the small individual both from his budding identity and from his milieu.

[From Erikson, 1963, pp. 238–241]

EXERCISES

Identity

1. Relax and think of a time when you felt you had a strong sense of identity. Describe that time. What were the components of that identity (for example, captain of the high school football team, oldest daughter in a large family, good student)?

    List 10 words that describe you then—your sense of self, crucial life issues, and so on.
2. How would you describe your *present* identity? Make a second list.
3. Have there been significant changes? What continuity is in your sense of self over this period of time? What changes?
4. Was the transition from one sense of identity to another smooth and gradual or abrupt?
5. Do you feel your present identity will remain relatively stable or do you foresee major changes? Why might they occur?

Eriksonian Stages

Pick three people who you feel are in different Eriksonian stages. You may wish to include a parent, yourself, and someone much younger. How do Erikson's stages fit each example? What is the central issue that you see in the life of each? What are the major strengths? Major weaknesses? Can you see how the current life of each of your three examples is related to the past? How has each evolved from past strengths and past issues?

Does framing the concerns, strengths, and critical issues for the three examples help you understand them, their differences, possible difficulties in communication, and so on?

ANNOTATED BIBLIOGRAPHY
Erikson, E., *Childhood and society.* 2nd ed. New York: Norton, 1963. Erikson's first and most seminal book. It includes his most detailed description of the eight stages of human development, papers on his work with the Sioux and Yurok, and psychobiographies of Hitler and Maxim Gorky, which provide a look at the psychological implications of German and Russian culture.

_____. *Insight and responsibility*. New York: Norton, 1964. A brilliant set of essays, including a psychobiographical look at Freud, an analysis of the psychosocial strengths, psychological reality, and historical actuality, and the golden rule today.

_____. *Gandhi's truth*. New York: Norton, 1969. An epic psychobiography of Gandhi, which provides a model for looking at a great figure in history through psychological eyes. Also a useful example of the limits of psychoanalysis in its neglect of the spiritual and transpersonal aspect of Gandhi's life.

REFERENCES

Coles, R., *Erik Erikson: The growth of his work*. Boston: Little, Brown, 1970.

Erikson, E. *Young man Luther*. New York: Norton, 1958.

_____. *Childhood and society*. New York: Norton, 1963.

_____. *Insight and responsibility*. New York: Norton, 1964.

_____. *The challenge of youth*. New York: Doubleday Anchor Books, 1965.

_____. *Identity, youth and crisis*. New York: Norton, 1968.

_____. *Gandhi's truth*. New York: Norton, 1969.

_____. *Dimensions of a new identity*. New York: Norton, 1974.

_____. *Life history and the historical moment*. New York: Norton, 1975.

_____. *Adulthood*. New York: Norton, 1978.

_____. *Identity and the life cycle*. New York: Norton, 1980.

Evans, R., *Dialogue with Erik Erikson*. New York: Dutton, 1969.

Sheehy, G. *Passages*. New York: Bantam Books, 1977.

CHAPTER 6
WILHELM REICH
AND
THE PSYCHOLOGY
OF THE BODY

In this chapter we will first discuss the work of Wilhelm Reich, the founder of what might be called body-oriented psychotherapy. Wilhelm Reich was a member of the psychoanalytic inner circle in Vienna and led the technical training seminar for young analysts. In his therapeutic work Reich gradually came to emphasize the importance of dealing with the physical manifestations of an individual's character, especially the patterns of chronic muscle tension that he called body armor. He was also concerned with the role of society in creating instinctual—especially sexual—inhibitions in the individual.

Reich's unique contributions to psychology include (1) his insistence on the unity of mind and body; (2) his inclusion of the body in psychotherapy; (3) his concept of character armor. Reich was also a pioneer in human sexuality education and hygiene, the psychology of politics, social responsibility, and the interfacing of psychology, biology, and physics. Reich was a courageous and stubborn innovator whose ideas were far ahead of his time.

Reich's theories of body-mind interaction are integral to many other body-oriented theories. The second part of this chapter consists of brief summaries of several major body-oriented approaches to therapy and personal growth. This includes three main areas: (1) body-oriented therapies: bioenergetic and dance/movement therapy; (2) systems of improving body structure and function: structural integration, the Alexander technique, the Feldenkrais method, and sensory awareness; and (3) Eastern body-oriented disciplines: hatha-yoga, t'ai chi ch'uan, and aikido.

PERSONAL HISTORY

Wilhelm Reich was born on March 24, 1897, in Galicia, a German-Ukranian part of Austria. He was the son of a middle-class Jewish farmer, a jealous, authoritarian man who dominated his wife and children. The father provided no religious upbringing for his children and insisted that only German be spoken at home. Consequently, Wilhelm was isolated from both the local Ukranian peasant children and from the Yiddish-speaking Jewish children. He had one brother, three years younger, who was both companion and competitor.

Reich idolized his mother. She committed suicide when he was 14, apparently after Reich revealed to his father that she was having an affair with the boys' tutor. Reich's father was devastated by his wife's death. He contracted pneumonia that developed into tuberculosis and died three years later. Reich's brother also died of tuberculosis, at the age of 26. Reich was severely affected by this series of family tragedies.

After his father's death, Reich managed the family farm while continuing his studies. In 1916 the war spread throughout his homeland and destroyed the family property. Reich joined the Austrian army; he became an officer and fought in Italy. In 1918 Reich entered medical school at the University of Vienna. Within a year he became a practicing member of the Vienna Psychoanalytical Society. He received his M.D. degree in 1922, at the age of 25.

Reich was involved in politics as a student, and subsequently sought to reconcile the theories of Freud and Marx. At the university Reich met his first wife, Annie Pink, who was also a medical student and later a psychoanalyst.

In 1922 Freud established a psychoanalytic clinic in Vienna. Reich was Freud's first clinical assistant, later vice-director of the clinic. In 1924 Reich became the director of the Seminar for Psychoanalytic Therapy, the first training institute for psychoanalysts. Many young analysts came to him for personal analysis as well as for training.

Reich underwent personal analysis with several psychoanalysts, but for various reasons these analyses were always broken off. In 1927 Reich sought analysis with Freud, who refused to make an exception to his policy of not treating members of the psychoanalytic inner circle. At this time Reich developed a serious conflict with Freud. It stemmed partly from Freud's refusal to analyze Reich and partly from increasing theoretical differences that resulted from Reich's uncompromising insistence that neurosis was rooted in sexual dissatisfaction. Reich developed tuberculosis at this time and spent several months recovering in a sanatorium in Switzerland.

When he returned to Vienna, Reich assumed his previous duties. He also became extremely active politically and in 1928 joined the Communist party. In 1929 Reich helped found the first sex hygiene clinics for workers, which provided free information on birth control, child rearing, and sex education.

In 1930 Reich moved to Berlin for personal analysis with Rado (a leading psychoanalyst) and also because his political activities had made many Viennese psychoanalysts uncomfortable. In Berlin Reich became more deeply involved with the communist-oriented mental hygiene movement. He traveled throughout Germany, lecturing and helping to establish hygiene centers.

Before long, Reich's political involvement made him unacceptable to other psychoanalysts, and his insistence on radical sexual-education programs made him unacceptable to the communists. In 1933 Reich was expelled from the German Communist party, and in 1934 he was expelled from the International Psychoanalytical Association.

Later in his career, Reich rejected communism and socialism because he felt that both were committed to an ideology at the expense of human considerations. He came to think of himself more as an "individualist" and was deeply suspicious of politics and politicians.

Because of Hitler's rise to power, Reich emigrated to Denmark in 1933. He separated from his wife when they left Berlin because of

[W]here and how is the patient to express his natural sexuality when it has been liberated from repression? Freud neither alluded to nor, as it later turned out, even tolerated this question. And, eventually, because he refused to deal with this central question, Freud himself created enormous difficulties by postulating a biological striving for suffering and death. [Reich, 1973, p. 152]

personal, political, and professional differences. A year earlier Reich had met Elsa Lindenberg, a ballet dancer and a member of his Communist party cell. She joined Reich in Denmark and became his second wife. Because of his controversial theories, Reich was expelled from Denmark and Sweden. He and Elsa moved to Oslo, Norway, in 1934, where he lectured and conducted research in psychology and biology for over five years.

Within a period of six months Reich had been expelled from his two major affiliations—the Communist party and the psychoanalytic movement—and from three different countries. It is not surprising that his subsequent writing is somewhat defensive and polemical. In Reich's case, a certain amount of paranoia represented a fairly realistic assessment of his situation rather than an irrational or unjustified attitude.

After three years of relative quiet in Norway, Reich became the target of a vicious newspaper campaign that attacked his emphasis on the sexual basis of neurosis and his laboratory experiments with bioenergy. He became increasingly isolated and his relations consequently worsened with Elsa, who finally separated from him.

In 1939 Reich was offered the position of associate professor of medical psychology at the New School for Social Research in New York. He packed up his laboratory and moved to the United States. In New York he met Ilse Ollendorf, a German refugee who became his laboratory assistant and later his third wife.

. . . the life process is identical with the sexual process—an experimentally proven fact. . . . In everything living, sexual vegetative energy is at work. [Reich, 1961, p. 55]

Reich founded the Orgone Institute to support research on orgone energy, or life energy. He concluded from his laboratory experimentation that there is a basic life energy present in all living organisms and that this energy is the biological force that underlies Freud's concept of libido. Reich began experimentation with orgone energy accumulators: boxes and other devices that, he claimed, store and concentrate orgone energy. Reich found that various diseases resulting from disturbances of the "automatic apparatus" could be treated with degrees of success by restoring the individual's normal orgone energy flow. This could be accomplished through exposure to high concentrations of orgone energy in the accumulators. The illnesses included cancer, angina pectoris, asthma, hypertension, and epilepsy.

In 1954, on the grounds that Reich's claims of successful treatment of various diseases with the orgone energy accumulators were unfounded, the Food and Drug Administration obtained an injunction against the distribution and further use of the accumulators. They also enjoined the sale of most of Reich's books and journals. Reich violated the injunction by continuing his research, and he insisted that the courts were not competent to judge matters of scientific fact. He eventually was convicted of contempt of court and sentenced to two years' imprisonment. The FDA burned his books and other publications related to the sale or manufacture of orgone accumulators. Reich died in 1957 of heart disease in federal prison.

INTELLECTUAL ANTECEDENTS

Psychoanalysis

Much of Reich's work is clearly rooted in psychoanalytic theory. His early contributions were primarily based on his concepts of character and character armor, which developed out of the psychoanalytic conception of the ego's need to defend itself against instinctual forces. According to Reich, an individual's character includes a consistent, habitual pattern of defenses. Reich came to associate these defenses with specific patterns of muscular armorings. In other words, each pattern of character defenses had a corresponding physical attitude. Reich emphasized the importance of loosening and dissolving muscular armoring in addition to dealing analytically with psychological material. By so doing, the process of psychoanalysis was powerfully assisted because the client released emotions locked into muscular armoring forged in early childhood.

. . . the patient must, through analysis, arrive at a regulated and gratifying genital life—if he is to be cured and permanently so. [Reich, 1976, p. 17, italics his]

Reich's later work with life energy, or orgone energy, is derived in great part from Freud's conception of libido. Later psychoanalytic theorists have tended to deemphasize Freud's libido concept; for Freud, however, especially in his early writings, libido was a real, potentially measurable psychic energy. "[Libido] possesses all the characteristics of quantity (though we have no means of measuring it), which is capable of increase, diminution, displacement, and discharge, and which is spread over the memory traces of ideas somewhat as an electric charge is spread over the surface of a body" (Freud, 1904; in Rycroft, 1971, pp. 14–15).

Reich extended Freud's libido theory to include all basic biological and psychological processes. Reich viewed pleasure as a movement of energy from the core of the organism toward the periphery and the external world; anxiety is represented as a retraction of energy from contact with the external world. Reich eventually came to view therapy as a process of allowing free flow of energy throughout the body by systematically dissolving blocks of muscular armoring. He found that these blocks distort and destroy natural feeling and, in particular, inhibit sexual feelings and prevent complete and fulfilling orgasm.

Neuroses are the result of a stasis (damming-up) of sexual energy. . . . Everyday clinical experience leaves no doubt: *the elimination of sexual stasis through orgastic discharge eliminates every neurotic manifestation.* [Reich, 1961, p. 189, italics his]

Marxism

Reich was seriously concerned with the theories of Freud and Marx; he attempted to reconcile these two systems and wrote several books on this subject (Robinson, 1969). Reich argued that: (1) psychoanalysis is a "materialistic science" in that it deals with real human needs and experiences; (2) psychoanalysis is based on a basically dialectal theme of psychic conflict and resolution; (3) psychoanalysis is a revolutionary science in that it supplements Marx's critique of bourgeois economics with a critique of bourgeois morality based on sexual repression.

In *The Mass Psychology of Fascism* (1970) Reich provides an important analysis of the roots of ideology in the individual character, a topic he felt was insufficiently covered by Marx. Twenty years before the publication of social science research on the authoritarian personality, Reich discussed the relationship between the German predilection for authoritarianism and the character formation of children in the German lower-middle-class family.

Reich's political interests brought on even greater controversy in psychoanalytical circles than did his theoretical innovations. In the tense political climate of Austria and Germany during the 1930s, Reich's membership in the Communist party and his public political activities created tension among his fellow analysts. Reich was asked to discontinue his political activities, and when he refused he was dropped from the German Psychoanalytic Association.

> Every social order produces in the masses of its members that structure which it needs to achieve its aims.
> [Reich, 1970, p. 23]

MAJOR CONCEPTS

Bioenergy

In his work on muscular armoring, Reich discovered that the loosening of chronically rigid muscles often resulted in peculiar physical sensations—feelings of hot and cold, prickling, itching, and emotional arousal. He concluded that these sensations were due to movements of freed biological energy, or bioenergy, which he was later to call orgone energy.

Reich also found that the mobilization and discharge of bioenergy are essential stages in the process of sexual arousal and orgasm. He called this the orgasm formula, a four-part process that he felt was characteristic of all living organisms:

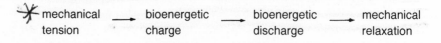

mechanical tension ⟶ bioenergetic charge ⟶ bioenergetic discharge ⟶ mechanical relaxation

After physical contact, energy is built up in both bodies and finally discharged in the orgasm, which is essentially a phenomenon of bioenergy discharge.

1. Sexual organs fill with fluid—mechanical tension.
2. Intense excitation results—bioenergetic charge.

3. Sexual excitation discharged in muscular contractions—bioenergetic discharge.
4. Physical relaxation follows—mechanical relaxation.

Orgone Energy

Reich gradually extended his concern with patients' physical functioning to laboratory research in physiology and biology and eventually to research in physics. He came to believe that the bioenergy in the organism is one aspect of a universal energy present in all things. He coined the term *orgone* energy from organism and orgasm. "Cosmic orgone energy functions in the living organism as specific biological energy. As such, it governs the entire organism; it is expressed in the emotions as well as in the purely biophysical movement of the organs" (Reich, 1976, p. 393).

Orgone energy has the following major properties:

1. Orgone energy is mass free; it has no inertia or weight.
2. It is present everywhere, although in differing concentrations, even in a vacuum.
3. It is the medium for electromagnetic and gravitational activity, the substratum of most basic natural phenomena.
4. Orgone energy is in constant motion.
5. High concentrations of orgone energy attract orgone energy from their less-concentrated surroundings (which "contradicts" the law of entropy).
6. Orgone energy forms units that become centers of creative activity. These include cells, plants and animals, and also clouds, planets, stars, and galaxies. [Kelley, 1962; summarized in Mann, 1973]

In an ultimate sense, in self-awareness and in the striving for the perfection of knowledge and full integration of one's bio-functions, *the cosmic orgone energy becomes aware of itself.* [Reich, 1961, p. 52, italics his]

Reich's extensive research on orgone energy and related topics has been ignored or dismissed by most critics and scientists. His findings contradict a number of established theories in physics and biology, and Reich's work is certainly not without its experimental weaknesses. However, his research has not been disproved or even carefully reviewed and responsibly criticized by reputable scientific critics. One psychologist who worked with Reich has pointed out: "In the twenty-plus years since Reich announced the discovery of orgone energy, no good-faith repetition of *any* critical orgone energy experiment has ever been published refuting Reich's results. . . . The fact is, despite (and partly because of) the ridicule, defamation, and attempts by the orthodox to 'bury' Reich and orgonomy, *there is no counter evidence to his experiments in any scientific publication,* much less a systematic refutation of the volumes of scientific work which support his position" (Kelley, 1962, pp. 72–73).

Human Sexuality

Reich's concern with sexuality formed a major theme that continued throughout his career. As a young medical student, Reich first visited Freud to seek his help in establishing a seminar on sexology in the medical school Reich attended (Higgens & Raphael, 1967). And Reich's major political activity consisted of helping to establish communist-sponsored sex hygiene clinics for the working class in Austria and Germany.

Reich's ideas and his clinics were far ahead of their time. In the 1930s (when Margaret Sanger had been recently imprisoned for advocating planned parenthood for married couples) Reich's program for his clinics included features that are astonishingly modern and still controversial:

1. Free distribution of contraceptives to everyone who wants them; intensive education for birth control.
2. Complete legalization of abortion.
3. Abolition of the legal distinction between the married and unmarried; freedom of divorce.
4. Elimination of venereal disease and avoidance of sexual problems by full sexual education.
5. Training of doctors, teachers, and so forth, in all relevant matters of sexual hygiene.
6. Treatment instead of punishment for sexual offenses.
   [Boadella, 1973]

Reich came to stress the free expression of sexual and emotional feelings within a mature, loving relationship. He emphasized the essentially sexual nature of the energies with which he dealt, and he found that the pelvic area of his patients was the most blocked. Reich came to believe that the goal of therapy must be to free all the blocks in the body and to attain full capacity for sexual orgasm, which he felt was blocked in most people.

Reich's radical views concerning sexuality resulted in misunderstanding and distortion of his work, and they led to vicious (and unfounded) attacks on him, his therapeutic work, and on his research.

Character

The concept of character was first discussed by Freud in 1908. Reich elaborated this concept: he was the first analyst to treat patients by interpreting the nature and function of their character, not their symptoms.

> Orgastic longing, which plays such a gigantic role in the life of animals, appears now [in humans] as an expression of this "striving beyond oneself," as "longing" to reach out beyond the narrow sack of one's own organism. [Reich, 1961, p. 348]

> Every person who has succeeded in preserving a certain amount of naturalness knows this: those who are psychically ill need but one thing—complete and repeated genital gratification. [Reich, 1973, p. 96]

According to Reich, the character is composed of a person's habitual attitudes and pattern of responses to various situations. It includes psychological attitudes and values, style of behavior (shyness, aggressiveness, and so forth), and physical attitudes (posture, habits of holding and moving the body).

Character Armor

Reich felt that the character structure forms as a defense against the child's anxiety over intense sexual feelings and accompanying fear of punishment. The first defense is repression, which temporarily restrains the sexual impulses. As ego defenses become chronically active and automatic, they develop into stable character traits that combine to form the individual's system of character armoring. Character armor includes all repressing defensive forces, which form a coherent pattern within the ego.

Character traits are not neurotic symptoms. The difference, according to Reich, lies in the fact that neurotic symptoms (such as irrational fears or phobias) are experienced as alien to the individual, as foreign elements in the psyche, whereas neurotic character traits (extreme orderliness or anxious shyness, for example) are experienced as integral parts of the personality. One may complain about being shy, but this shyness does not seem to be meaningless or pathological, as do neurotic symptoms. The character defenses are difficult to eradicate because they are well rationalized by the individual and experienced as part of the individual's self-concept.

Reich continually attempted to make his patients more aware of their character traits. He frequently imitated their characteristic gestures and postures, or had patients repeat and exaggerate them, a nervous smile, for example. As patients ceased taking their character makeup for granted, their motivation to change was enhanced.

Genital Character

Freud used the term *genital character* to refer to the final level of psychosexual development. Reich applied it to persons with orgastic potency: "Orgastic potency is the capacity to surrender to the flow of biological energy, free of any inhibitions; the capacity to discharge completely the damned-up sexual excitation through involuntary, pleasurable convulsions of the body" (1973, p. 102). Reich found that as his patients relinquished their armoring and developed orgastic potency, many areas of neurotic functioning changed spontaneously. In the place of rigid neurotic controls, individuals developed a capacity for *self-regulation*. Reich described self-regulating individuals as naturally rather than compulsively moral. They act in terms of their own inner inclinations and feelings rather than following external codes or demands laid down by others.

The "how" . . . the form of the behavior and of the communications, was far more important than what the patient told the analyst. Words can lie. The expression never lies. [Reich, 1973, p. 171]

A conflict which is fought out at a certain age always leaves behind a trace in the person's character . . . revealed as a hardening of the character. [Reich, 1973, p. 145]

The patient's behavior (manner, look, language, countenance, dress, handshake, etc.) not only is vastly underestimated in terms of its analytic importance but is usually completely overlooked. [Reich, 1976, p. 34]

I say on the basis of ample clinical experience that only in a few cases in our civilization is the sexual act based on love. The intervening rage, hatred, sadistic emotions and contempt are part and parcel of the love life of modern man. [Reich, in Rycroft, 1971, p. 81]

After Reichian therapy, many patients who were formerly neurotically promiscuous developed greater tenderness and spontaneously sought more lasting and fulfilling relationships. Also, those in loveless marriages found that they could no longer make love with their spouses merely as a duty.

Genital characters are not imprisoned in their armor and psychological defenses. They are able to shield themselves, if necessary, against a hostile environment. However, this is done fairly consciously and can be dissolved when no longer necessary.

Reich wrote that genital characters have worked through their Oedipal complex, so that the Oedipal material is no longer strongly charged or repressed. The superego has become "sex-affirmative," and thus id and superego are generally in harmony (Reich, 1976). The genital character is able to experience sexual orgasm freely, discharging all excess libido. The climax of sexual activity is characterized by surrender to sexual experience and uninhibited, involuntary movement, as opposed to the forced or even violent movements of the armored individual.

DYNAMICS

Psychological Growth

Reich defined growth as a process of dissolving one's psychological and physical armoring, gradually becoming a more free and open human being, capable of enjoying full and satisfying orgasm.

Reich found that muscular armoring is organized into seven major segments, composed of muscles and organs with related expressive functions. These segments form a series of seven roughly horizontal rings, at right angles to the spine and torso. They are centered in the eyes, mouth, neck, chest, diaphragm, abdomen, and pelvis.[1]

According to Reich, orgone energy naturally flows up and down the body, parallel to the spine. The rings of armor are formed at right angles to this flow and interrupt it. Reich points out that it is not an accident that in Western culture we have learned to say "yes" by moving our heads up and down, in the direction of energy flow in the body, whereas we say "no" by moving the head from side to side, the direction of the armoring.

Armoring restricts the flow of energy and stops free expression

It is solely our *sensation* of the natural process inside and outside ourselves, which holds the keys to the deep riddles of nature. . . . Sensation is the sieve through which all inner and outer stimuli are perceived; sensation is the connecting link between ego and outer world. [Reich, 1961, p. 275]

It is possible to get out of a trap. However, in order to break out of a prison, one first must confess to *being in a prison. The trap is man's emotional structure, his character structure.* There is little use in devising systems of thought about the nature of the trap if the only thing to do in order to get out of the trap is to know the trap and to find the exit. [Reich, 1961, p. 470]

---

[1] Reich's seven armor segments are closely related to the seven chakras of kundalini yoga, although the fit is not a perfect one. It is interesting to note that Reich moves from the top down; the patient is finished once the pelvis, the most important armor segment, is opened and energized. In kundalini yoga the movement is from the base of the spine upward, and the yogi is "finished" once the thousand-petaled lotus of the brain, the most important chakra, is opened and energized.

WILHELM REICH AND THE PSYCHOLOGY OF THE BODY   **181**

of emotion. What begins as a defense against overpowering anxiety becomes a physical and emotional straitjacket.

> In armored human organisms, the orgone energy is bound in the chronic contraction of the muscles. The body orgone does not begin to flow freely as soon as the armor ring has been loosened.... As soon as the first armor blocks have been dissolved, the movement expressive of "surrender" appears more and more, along with the orgonotic currents and sensations. However, its full unfolding is hindered by those armor blocks that have not yet been dissolved. [Reich, 1976, pp. 411–412]

Reichian therapy consists primarily of dissolving the armor in each segment, beginning with the eyes and ending with the pelvis. Each segment is more or less an independent unit and must be dealt with separately.

Loosening the Muscular Armor

Reich found that each character attitude had a corresponding physical attitude expressed in the body as muscular rigidity or muscular armoring. He began to work directly on the muscular armoring in conjunction with his analytic work. He found that loosening the muscular armor freed libidinal energy and aided the process of psychoanalysis. Reich's psychiatric work increasingly dealt with freeing the emotions (pleasure, rage, anxiety) through work with the body. He found that this led to intense experiencing of the psychological material uncovered in analysis.

> The spasm of the musculature is the somatic side of the process of repression, and the basis of its continued preservation. [Reich, 1973, p. 302]

Reich first applied the techniques of character analysis to physical attitudes. He analyzed in detail his patients' posture and physical habits to make them aware of how they suppressed vital feelings in different parts of the body. Reich would have patients intensify particular tensions to become more aware of them and to elicit the emotion that had been bound up in that part of the body. He found that only after the bottled-up emotion was expressed could the chronic tension be fully abandoned. Reich began to work directly on tense muscles with his hands to release the emotions bound up in them.

> In the final analysis, I could not rid myself of the impression that somatic rigidity represents the most essential part in the process of repression. All our patients report that they went through periods in childhood in which, by means of certain practices ... (holding the breath, tensing the abdominal muscular pressure, etc.), they learned to suppress their impulses of hate, anxiety, and love.... It never ceases to be surprising how the loosening of a muscular spasm not only releases the vegetative energy, but, over and above this, reproduces a memory of that situation in infancy in which the repression of the instinct occurred. [Reich, 1973, p. 300]

[The] armor could lie on the "surface" or in the "depth," could be "as soft as a sponge" or "as hard as a rock." Its function in every case was to protect the person against unpleasurable experiences. However, it also entailed a reduction in the organism's capacity for pleasure. [Reich, 1973, p. 145]

Reich found that chronic muscular tension serves to block one of the three basic biological excitations: anxiety, anger, or sexual excitation. He concluded that the physical and psychological armor were essentially the same. "Character armorings were now seen to be functionally identical with muscular [hypertension]. The concept, 'functional identity,' which I had to introduce means nothing more than that muscular attitudes and character attitudes have the same function in the psychic mechanism: they can replace one another and can be influenced by one another. Basically, they cannot be separated. They are identical in their function" (Reich, 1973, pp. 270–271).

Three major tools are used in dissolving the armor: (1) building up energy in the body through deep breathing; (2) directly attacking the chronically tense muscles (through pressure, pinching, and so forth) to loosen them; and (3) maintaining the cooperation of the patient by dealing openly with whatever resistances or emotional restrictions arise.

1. *The eyes.* Armoring of the eyes is expressed by an immobility of the forehead and an "empty" expression of the eyes, which look out from behind a rigid mask. The armor is dissolved by having patients open their eyes wide, as if in fright, in order to mobilize the eyelids and forehead by forcing an emotional expression and by encouraging free movement of the eyes—rolling the eyes and looking from side to side.

2. *The mouth.* The oral segment includes the muscles of the chin, throat, and back of the head. The jaw may be very tight or unnaturally loose. The emotional expressions of crying, angry biting, yelling, sucking, and grimacing are all inhibited by this segment. The armor may be loosened by encouraging the patient to imitate crying, making sounds that mobilize the lips, biting, gagging, and by direct work on the muscles involved.

3. *The neck.* This segment includes the deep neck muscles and also the tongue. The armor functions mainly to hold back anger or crying. Direct pressure on the deep neck muscles is not possible, so screaming, yelling, and gagging are all important means for loosening this segment.

4. *The chest.* The chest segment includes the large chest muscles, the shoulder muscles, the muscles of the shoulder blades, the entire chest cage, and the hands and arms. This segment serves to inhibit laughter, rage, sadness, and longing. Inhibition of breathing, which is an important means of suppressing any emotion, occurs to a great extent in the chest. The armoring may be loosened through work with breathing, especially developing complete expiration. The arms and hands are used to hit, tear, choke, pound, and reach out with longing.

5. *The diaphragm.* This segment includes the diaphragm, stomach, solar plexus, various internal organs, and muscles along the lower thoracic vertebrate. Armoring is expressed by a forward curvature of

the spine so that there is a considerable space between the patient's lower back and the couch. It is much harder to breathe out than to breathe in. The armoring mainly inhibits extreme rage. The first four segments must be relatively free before the diaphragm can be loosened through repeated work with breathing and with the gag reflex. (People with strong blocks in this segment find it virtually impossible to vomit.)

6. *The abdomen.* The abdominal segment includes the large abdominal muscles and the muscles of the back. Tension in the lumbar muscles is related to fear of attack. Armoring in a person's flanks produces ticklishness and is related to inhibition of spite. Dissolution of the armoring in this segment is relatively simple once the higher segments are open.

7. *The pelvis.* This last segment contains all the muscles of the pelvis and lower limbs. The stronger the armoring, the more the pelvis is pulled back and sticks out in the rear. The gluteal muscles are tight and painful; the pelvis is rigid, "dead," and asexual. Pelvic armoring serves to inhibit anxiety and rage as well as pleasure. The anxiety and rage result from inhibitions of sexual pleasure sensations, and it is impossible to experience pleasure freely in this area until the anger has been released from the pelvic muscles. The armoring can be loosened by first mobilizing the pelvis and having the patient repeatedly kick with the feet and also strike the couch with his or her pelvis.

Reich found that as his patients began to develop the capacity for "full genital surrender," their whole being and life-style changed. "The unification of the orgasm reflex also restores the sensations of depth and seriousness. The patients remember the time in their early childhood when the unity of their body sensation was not disturbed. Seized with emotion, they tell of the time as children when they felt at one with nature, with everything that surrounded them, of the time they felt 'alive,' and how finally all this had been shattered and crushed by their education" (Reich, 1973, pp. 357–358).

These individuals began to feel that the rigid norms of society, which previously they had taken for granted, were alien and unnatural. Attitudes toward work also changed noticeably. Many who had done their work as a mechanical necessity quit their jobs to seek new and vital work that fulfilled their inner needs. Often those who were interested in their vocation blossomed with fresh energy and ability.

Obstacles to Growth
Armoring

The armoring is the major obstacle to growth according to Reich. "The armored organism is incapable of breaking down its own armor. But it is equally incapable of expressing its elemental biological emotions. It is familiar with the sensation of tickling but has never experienced orgonotic pleasure. The armored individual cannot express a sigh of

The capacity of the vegetative organism to participate in the tension-charge function in a unified and total way is undoubtedly the basic characteristic of psychic and vegetative health. . . . Disturbances of self-perception do not really disappear until the orgasm reflex has been fully developed into a unified whole. [Reich, 1973, p. 355]

It is a *snake,* thus a symbol of the phallus and simultaneously of the biological original movement, which persuades Eve to tempt Adam. . . . "Whoever eats of the tree of knowledge knows God and life, and that will be punished," we are warned. *The knowledge of the law of love leads to the knowledge of the law of life, and that of the law of life leads to knowledge of God.* [Reich, 1961, p. 273]

pleasure or consciously imitate it. When he tries to do so, the result is a groan, a suppressed, pent-up roar, or even an impulse to vomit. He is incapable of venting anger or of banging his fist in an imitation of anger" (Reich, 1976, p. 402).

I found that people reacted with deep hatred to every disturbance of the neurotic balance of their armor. [Reich, 1973, p. 147]

Reich (1961) felt that the process of armoring has created two distorted intellectual traditions that form the basis of civilization: mystical religion and mechanistic science. Mechanists are so well armored that they have no real sense of their own life processes or inner nature. They have a basic fear of deep emotion, aliveness, and spontaneity. They tend to develop a rigid, mechanical conception of nature and are interested primarily in external objects and in the natural sciences. "A machine has to be *perfect.* Hence the thinking and acts of the physicist must be 'perfect.' *Perfectionism* is an essential characteristic of mechanistic thinking. It tolerates no mistakes; uncertainties, shifting situations are unwelcome. . . . But this principle, when applied to processes in nature, inevitably leads into confusion. *Nature is inexact. Nature operates not mechanically, but functionally"* (Reich, 1961, p. 278).

It was only the mystics who—far removed from scientific insight—always kept in contact with the function of the living. Since, thus, the living became the domain of mysticism, serious natural science shrank from occupying itself with it. [Reich, 1961, pp. 197–198]

According to Reich, religious mystics have not developed their armoring so completely; they remain partly in touch with their own life energy and are capable of great insight because of this partial contact with their innermost nature. However, Reich believed this insight was distorted. Ascetic and antisexual religions lead us to reject our own physical nature and to lose contact with our bodies. They deny the origin of the life-force in the body and locate it in a hypothetical soul that has only a tenuous connection with the body. "In the disruption of the unity of body feeling by sexual suppression, and in the continual longing to re-establish contact with oneself and with the world, lies the root of all sex-negating religions. 'God' is the mysticized idea of the vegetative harmony between self and nature" (Reich, 1973, p. 358).

Sexual Repression

Another obstacle to growth is the social and cultural repression of the natural impulses and sexuality of the individual. Reich felt this repression was the major source of neurosis, and that it occurred during three principal phases of life: early infancy, puberty, and adulthood (Reich, 1973, pp. 197 ff.).

The destructiveness which is bound up in the character is nothing but anger about frustration in general and denial of sexual gratification in particular. [Reich, 1973, p. 219]

Infants and young children are confronted with an authoritarian, sex-suppressing family atmosphere. For this period of life Reich reaffirms Freud's observations concerning the negative effects of parental demands for early toilet training, self-restraint, and "good" behavior.

During puberty, young people are kept from attaining a real sexual life; masturbation is prohibited. Even more important, our society generally makes it impossible for adolescents to attain a meaningful working life. And this unnatural life-style makes it especially difficult for adolescents to outgrow infantile attachments to their parents.

Finally, as adults many become trapped in an unsatisfying marriage for which they are sexually unprepared because of demands for premarital continence. Reich also points out that there are built-in conflicts within marriage in our culture. "Marriages fall to pieces as a result of the ever deepening discrepancy between sexual needs and economic conditions. The sexual needs can be gratified with one and the same partner for a limited time only. On the other hand, the economic tie, moralistic demand, and human habit foster the permanency of the relationship. This results in the wretchedness of marriage" (Reich, 1973, p. 202). The family situation re-creates the same neurotic environment for the next generation of children.

Reich felt that individuals who are brought up in an atmosphere that negates life and sex develop a fear of pleasure, represented in their muscular armoring. "This characterological armoring is the basis of isolation, indigence, craving for authority, fear of responsibility, mystic longing, sexual misery, and neurotically impotent rebelliousness, as well as pathological intolerance" (Reich, 1973, p. 7).

> The life process is inherently "rational." It becomes distorted and grotesque when it is not allowed to develop freely. [Reich, 1973, p. 19]

Reich was not optimistic concerning the possible effects of his discoveries. He believed that most people, because of their strong armoring, would be unable to understand his theories and would distort his ideas.

> A teaching of living Life, taken over and distorted by armored man, will spell final disaster to the whole of mankind and its institutions. . . . By far the most likely result of the principle of "orgastic potency" will be a pernicious philosophy of 4-lettering all over the place everywhere. Like an arrow released from the restraining, tightly tensed spring, the search for quick, easy and deleterious genital pleasure will devastate the human community. [Reich, 1961, pp. 508–509]

The armoring serves to cut us off from our inner nature and from social misery outside. "Nature and culture, instinct and morality, sexuality and achievement become incompatible as a result of the split in the human structure. The unity and congruity of culture and nature, work and love, morality and sexuality, longed for from time immemorial, will remain a dream as long as man continues to condemn the biological demand for natural (orgastic) sexual gratification. Genuine democracy and freedom founded on consciousness and responsibility are also doomed to remain an illusion until this demand is fulfilled" (Reich, 1973, p. 8).

STRUCTURE

Body

Reich viewed mind and body as a unit. As described earlier, he gradually moved from analytic work relying solely on language to analysis of both physical and psychological aspects of character and character armor, to major emphasis on working with muscular armor and developing the free flow of orgone energy.

Social Relationships

Reich believed social relationships are determined by the individual's character. The average individual sees the world through the filter of his or her armoring. Genital characters, having loosened their rigid armoring, are the only ones who are truly able to react openly and honestly to others.

Reich strongly believed in the ideals, enunciated by Marx, of "free organization, in which the free development of each becomes the basis of the free development of all" (Boadella, 1973, p. 212). Reich formulated the concept of work-democracy, a natural form of social organization in which people cooperate harmoniously to further their mutual needs and interests, and he attempted to actualize these principles in the Orgone Institute.

Will

You do not strive to make your heart beat or your legs move, and you do not, by the same token, "strive" for or seek truth. Truth is in you and works in you just as your heart or your eyes work, well or badly, according to the condition of your organism. [Reich, 1961, p. 496]

Reich did not concern himself directly with the will, although he did stress the importance of meaningful and constructive work.

You don't have to do anything special or new. All you have to do is to continue what you are doing: plough your fields, wield your hammer, examine your patients, take your children to the school or to the playground, report on the events of the day, penetrate ever more deeply into the secrets of nature. All these things you do already. But you think all this is unimportant. . . . All you have to do is to continue what you have always done and always want to do: your work, to let your children grow up happily, to love your wife. [Reich, 1945; in Boadella, 1973, p. 236]

Emotions

Reich found that chronic tensions block the energy flow that underlies powerful emotions. The armoring prevents the individual from experiencing strong emotions; it limits and distorts the expression of feeling. Emotions that are blocked in this way are never eliminated because they can never be fully expressed. According to Reich, only by fully experiencing a blocked emotion can an individual become free of it.

Reich also noted that the frustration of pleasure often leads to anger and rage. These negative emotions must be dealt with in Reichian therapy before the positive feelings (which they overlay) can be completely experienced.

Intellect

Reich (1976) opposed any separation of intellect, emotions, and body. He pointed out that the intellect is actually a biological function and that the intellect may have an energetic charge as strong as any of the emotions. He argued that full development of the intellect requires the development of true genitality: "The hegemony of the intellect not only puts an end to irrational sexuality but has as its precondition a regulated libido economy. Genital and intellectual primacy belong together . . . " (1976, p. 203).

Reich believed that the intellect also operates as a defense mechanism. "Human language also often functions as a defense. The spoken word conceals the expressive language of the biological core. In many cases, the function of speech has deteriorated to such a degree that the words express nothing whatever and merely represent a continuous, hollow activity on the part of the musculature of the neck and the organs of speech" (1976, p. 398).

> Intellectual activity can be structured and directed in such a way that it looks like a most cunningly operating apparatus whose purpose is precisely to avoid cognition, i.e., it looks like an activity directing one away from reality. In short, the intellect can operate in the two fundamental directions of the psychic apparatus: toward the world and away from the world. [Reich, 1976, p. 338]

Self

For Reich the self is the healthy, biological core of each individual. Most individuals are not in touch with the self; they are too armored and defended. "What was it that prevented a person from perceiving his own personality? After all, it is what he is. Gradually, I came to understand that it is the entire being that constitutes the compact, tenacious mass which obstructs all analytic efforts. The patient's whole personality, his character, his individuality resisted analysis" (Reich, 1973, p. 148).

According to Reich, the repressed impulses and repressing defensive forces together create a layer of contactlessness. Contactlessness is an expression of the concentrated interplay of the two (Reich, 1973). Contact requires free movement of energy. It only becomes possible as the individual dissolves his or her armor and becomes fully aware of the body and its sensations and needs, coming in contact with the core, the primary drives. Where blocks are present, energy flow and awareness are restricted, and self-perception is greatly diminished or distorted (Baker, 1967).

> In penetrating to the deepest depth and the fullest extent of emotional integration of the Self, we not only experience and feel, we also learn to *understand*, if only dimly, the meaning and working of the cosmic orgone ocean of which we are a tiny part. [Reich, pp. 519–520]

Therapist

In addition to training in therapeutic technique, the therapist must progress in his or her own personal growth. In working both psychologically and physically with an individual, the therapist must have overcome any fears of overtly sexual sounds and of "orgastic streamings"—the free movement of energy in the body.

Baker, one of the leading Reichian therapists in the United States, cautions that "no therapist should attempt to treat patients who have problems he has not been able to handle in himself nor should he expect a patient to do things he cannot do and has not been able to do" (1967, p. 223). Another eminent Reichian has written that "the indispensable prerequisite for whatever methods the therapist uses to release the emotions held in the musculature is that he is in touch with his own sensations and able to empathise fully with the patient and to feel in his own body the effect of particular constrictions on the patient's energies" (Boadella, 1973, p. 120).

Reich himself was considered a brilliant and tough-minded therapist. Even as an orthodox analyst, he was extremely honest, even brutally direct, with his patients. Nic Waal, one of the foremost psychiatrists in Norway, wrote about her experiences in therapy with Reich:

> I could stand being crushed by Reich because I liked truth. And, strangely enough, I was not crushed by it. All through this therapeutic attitude to me he had a loving voice, he sat beside me and made me look at him. He accepted me and crushed only my vanity and falseness. But I understood at that moment that true honesty and love both in a therapist and in parents is sometimes the courage to be seemingly cruel when it is necessary. It demands, however, a great deal of the therapist, his training and his diagnosis of the patient. [In Boadella, 1973, p. 365]

EVALUATION

Reich is the leading pioneer in the psychology of the body and body-oriented therapy. Only a small minority of psychologists have seriously concerned themselves with body psychology. However, appreciation of physical habits and tensions as diagnostic cues is steadily growing. Many therapists have been influenced by the work of Fritz Perls, who was in analysis with Reich and owes much to Reich's theories.

Reich's focus on muscular armoring and emotional release through body work has attracted less interest than it deserves. The encouragement of the expression of suppressed emotions such as rage, fear, and aggression is still a controversial issue in psychology.

Leonard Berkowitz (1973), who has studied violence and aggression experimentally for many years, has attacked what he calls the "ventilationist" approach to therapy, in which the main emphasis is placed on expressing bottled-up emotions. Berkowitz cites a number of experimental studies which show that encouraging the expression of aggression results in increased aggression or hostility. According to behaviorist theory, encouraging the expression of a given emotion serves to reward that behavior, making it more likely that the emotion will be expressed in the future.

This criticism represents a shallow understanding of Reich's work, in which emotional release is never simply encouraged for its own sake. It may be true that the discharge of strong emotions leads to increased occurrence of these emotions. However, Reich's emphasis was always on dissolving the armoring, the blocks to feeling that distort an individual's psychological and physical functioning.

A more cogent criticism of Reich's theories concerns his concept of the genital character as an achievable ideal state. Kelley (1971) has pointed out that Reich developed a system that seems to promise a final cure for all problems. A successful treatment is supposed to leave the individual free of all armor, a "finished product" with no need for further growth or improvement.

The underlying model is a medical disease model in which the patient comes to the doctor in order to be "cured." This model pervades much of therapy, but it is especially strong where there is the assumption that the therapist is fully healthy (unarmored, and so on) and that the patient is ill. Patients stay "one down" to the therapist; they are generally placed in a passive role, relying on the omnipotent, "perfected" therapist for some sort of dramatic or magical cure. This model also places tremendous strains on the therapist, who must always appear superior to patients and is permitted no mistakes or fallibility.

Learning to free oneself from inappropriate blocks to feeling is only one aspect of an individual's total growth. Self-control and goal-directed behavior are also essential, and they require a certain amount of control over one's immediate feelings. "The blocks to feeling that Reich calls 'the armor' . . . are a product of the capacity of man to control his feelings and behavior, and so to direct his life along a path he has chosen. One aspect of this is protection of the self from incapacitating emotions, a second the channeling of behavior towards goals" (Kelley, 1971, p. 9). Thus the individual never can nor should become totally "unarmored." Reich did not consider how to balance self-control and free expression as part of a continual process of growth.

Reich's theories concerning therapy and psychological growth are generally clear and straightforward, as are his therapeutic techniques. He has provided considerable clinical as well as experimental evidence for his work, although to date his ideas have been too controversial to gain widespread acceptance. Interest in Reich and his ideas concerning the body is increasing, and the growth of body-oriented work is one of the more exciting possibilities for future development in psychology.

THE THEORY FIRSTHAND

The following passages are taken from Orson Bean's book *Me and the Orgone*,* an account of the well-known actor's experiences in Reichian therapy with Dr. Elsworth Baker, a prominent Reichian therapist.

> Dr. Baker sat down behind his desk and indicated the chair in front of it for me. . . . "Well," he said, "take off your clothes and let's have a look at you." My eyes went glassy as I stood up and started to undress—"You can leave on your shorts and socks," said Baker, to my relief. I laid my clothes on the chair against the wall in a neat pile, hoping to get a gold star. "Lie down on the bed," said the doctor. . . .
>
> He began pinching the muscles in the soft part of my shoulders. I

wanted to smash him in his sadistic face, put on my clothes and get the hell out of there. Instead I said, "Ow." Then I said, "That hurts."

"It doesn't sound as if it hurts," he said.

"Well, it does," I said, and managed an "Ooo, Ooo."

"Now breathe in and out deeply," he said and he placed the palm of one hand on my chest and pushed down hard on it with the other. The pain was substantial. "What if the bed breaks?" I thought. "What if my spine snaps or I suffocate?"

I breathed in and out for a while and then Baker found my ribs, and began probing and pressing. . . . He began to jab at my stomach, prodding here and there to find a tight little knotted muscle. . . . He moved downward, mercifully passing my jockey shorts, and began to pinch and prod the muscles of my inner thighs. At that point I realized that the shoulders and the ribs and the stomach hadn't hurt at all. The pain was amazing, especially since it was an area I hadn't thought would ever hurt. . . .

"Turn over," said Baker. I did and he started at my neck and worked downwards with an unerring instinct for every tight, sore muscle. . . . "Turn back over again," said Dr. Baker and I did. "All right," he said. "I want you to breathe in and out as deeply as you can and at the same time roll your eyes around without moving your head. Try to look at all four walls, one at a time, and move your eyeballs as far from side to side as possible." I began to roll my eyes, feeling rather foolish but grateful that he was no longer tormenting my body. On and on my eyes rolled. "Keep breathing," said Baker. I began to feel a strange pleasurable feeling in my eyes like the sweet fuzziness that happens when you smoke a good stick of pot. The fuzziness began to spread through my face and head and then down into my body. "All right," said Baker. "Now I want you to continue breathing and do a bicycle kick on the bed with your legs." I began to raise my legs and bring them down rhythmically, striking the bed with my calves. My thighs began to ache and I wondered when he would say that I had done it long enough, but he didn't. On and on I went, until my legs were ready to drop off. Then, gradually, it didn't hurt anymore and that same sweet fuzzy sensation of pleasure began to spread through my whole body, only much stronger. I now felt as if a rhythm had taken over my kicking which had nothing to do with any effort on my part. I felt transported and in the grip of something larger than me. I was breathing more deeply than I ever had before and I felt the sensation of each breath all the way down past my lungs and into my pelvis. Gradually, I felt myself lifted right out of Baker's milk chocolate room and up into the spheres. I was beating to an astral rhythm. Finally, I knew it was time to stop. . . .

The Wednesday morning after my first visit to Baker I woke up, after about five hours sleep, feeling exhilarated. My coffee tasted better than it ever had and even the garbage floating down the East River seemed to me to have a lightness and symmetry to it. The feeling lasted for the rest of the day. It was a sense of well-being and at-peace-with-the-world-ness. My body felt light and little ripples of pleasure rolled up and down my arms, legs, and torso. When I breathed, the sensation of movement continued down into the base of my torso and it felt good. I felt vaguely horny in a tender way and the thought of women in general filled me with love. . . .

I was starting to unwind. The pleasurable ripples were lessening and a sense of anxiety was starting to take over. Brownish marks that would be black and blue by the next day began to appear on my body where Baker had pinched and gouged at me. . . .

I got into bed, realized that I was cold and reached down to the foot of the bed for the extra blanket. Then it occurred to me that I was cold with fear. I tried to examine my feelings as I had learned to do in psychoanalysis. It was a different kind of dread than I had ever experienced before. I thought of a marionette show I had seen as a kid with skeleton puppets who danced to the music of the *Danse macabre* and then began to fly apart, with legs and arms and head coming off and ribs and pelvis coming apart. I felt like I too was starting to come apart. The anxiety was terrific and I was aware that I was involuntarily tightening up on my muscles to hold myself together. The wonderful joyous liberated feeling was going away and in its place was a sense of holding on for dear life. My armoring, if that's what it was, seemed like an old friend now. People say, "I'd rather die in the electric chair than spend my life in prison," but prisoners never say that. A life in chains is better than no life at all, except in theory.

I realized it was going to take all the courage I could muster to de-armor myself. I knew I would fight Dr. Baker every step of the way but I also remembered how I had felt for that thirty-six hours or so after my first treatment and I wanted it more than anything else in the world. . . .

"What kind of week did you have?" asked Baker and I told him.

"Your reaction of clamping down after a period of pleasurable sensations was completely natural and to be expected," he said. "You won't always have those nice feelings but it's important to remember what they were like so you can work towards them again. It will help you tolerate the fear you'll feel as your armor breaks down." . . .

For several weeks on Tuesdays at two, I breathed and kicked. (I have since found out that my chest and breathing were being worked on first to mobilize energy in my body, which would help in the de-armoring process. Energy is built up with the intake of air.) Baker now had me pounding with my fists on the bed as I kicked. I would pound and kick and breathe and the rhythm would take me over and I would be transported. . . .

To start freeing my eye armoring, Dr. Baker held a pencil in front of me and told me to keep looking at it. He then moved it around quickly in random patterns which forced me to look about spontaneously. This would be kept up for what seemed like fifteen or twenty minutes and the results were amazing to me. My eyes felt free in my head and I could sense a direct connection between them and my brain. Then, he would have me roll my eyes about without moving my head, forcing them to focus on each wall in the room as their glance lit upon it. All the time I was doing this I would have to keep breathing deeply and rhythmically.

He would tell me to grimace and make faces (I felt like a fool). He would have me try to make my eyes look suspicious or attempt to get them to express longing. All of these things gradually made my eyes feel like they were being used again for the first time in many many years and it felt wonderful. . . .

On the following Tuesday, instead of a pencil, Dr. Baker pulled out a fountain-pen flashlight. He turned out the lights and shone it in my eyes and moved it around. It was a psychedelic effect. I followed it with my eyes as it made patterns in the dark and the effect was startling. I could actually feel the unlikely sensation of my brains moving in my head. Baker waved the flashlight around in front of me for about fifteen minutes and then he turned on the lights and looked deep into my eyes and said, "They're coming along nicely." Everything about the way he worked with me and the way he passed judgment on how I was responding was not mechanical but was the result of one human being's ability to put himself in touch with the feelings and energy charges of another. . . .

"Make a face at me," said Baker and I turned on him with a stupid leer. "Now accentuate it," he said. I twisted my face into a hideous gargoyle's expression. "What does it make you feel?" he asked.

"I dunno," I lied.

"It must make you feel something."

"Well, I guess . . . contemptuous."

"You guess?" . . .

"All right, dammit, it's a lot of crap . . . lying here rolling my eyes around."

"Stick your finger down your throat," said Baker.

"What?" I said.

"Gag yourself."

"But I'll throw up all over your bed."

"If you want to you can," he said. "Just keep breathing while you do it."

I lay there breathing deeply and stuck my finger down my throat and gagged. Then I did it again.

"Keep breathing," said Baker. My lower lip began to tremble like a little kid's, tears began to run down my face and I began to bawl. I sobbed for five minutes as if my heart would break. Finally, the crying subsided.

"Did anything occur to you?" asked Baker.

"I thought about my mother and how much I loved her and how I felt like I could never reach her and I just felt hopeless and heartbroken," I said. "I felt like I was able to feel these things deeply for the first time since I was little, and it's such a relief to be able to cry and it isn't a lot of crap, I was just scared."

"Yes," he said. "It is frightening. You have a lot of anger to get out, a lot of hate and rage and then a lot of longing and a lot of love. Okay," he said, "I'll see you next time."

And I got up and got dressed and left.

*[New York: St. Martin's Press, 1971]

BODY-ORIENTED
SYSTEMS OF GROWTH

The body-oriented systems covered in this section are by no means all that are available. Dozens of excellent systems work primarily with the body, concerned with improving psychological and physical functioning. The disciplines and techniques mentioned in this chapter are perhaps better known and more available than others. They are also systems that have theoretical significance for body psychology.

BIOENERGETICS

Bioenergetics might be called neo-Reichian therapy. It was founded by one of Reich's students, Alexander Lowen, and focuses on the role of the body in character analysis and in therapy. Lowen has used more easily acceptable terms than Reich—bioenergy for orgone energy, for example—and his work has generally met with less resistance than Reich's. There are many more bioenergetic practitioners than Reichians in this country.

Bioenergetics includes Reichian breathing techniques and many of Reich's emotional release techniques, such as allowing patients to cry, scream, and hit. Lowen also utilizes various stress postures in order to energize parts of the body that have been blocked. In these postures, stress is increased in chronically tense body parts until the tension becomes so great that the individual is eventually forced to relax his or her armoring. These postures include bending down to touch the floor, arching back with the fists at the base of the spine, and bending backward over a padded stool.

Lowen found that Reich's approach to reducing armoring through muscular relaxation could be supplemented with the opposite process: encouraging patients to mobilize the feelings expressed by tense muscles. For example, encouraging a patient's aggression will facilitate the ability to surrender to tender feelings. And if one only works on the attitude of letting go and "giving in," therapy often results in feelings of sadness and anger. Lowen found that these two approaches are best used alternately.

Bioenergetics stresses the need for grounding, or being anchored in one's own physical, emotional, and intellectual processes. Bioenergetic work often concentrates on the legs and pelvis to establish a better, more firmly rooted connection with the ground. This is essentially the opposite of Reich's top-to-down approach. "We begin with the legs and the feet because they are the foundation and support of the ego struc-

Everybody is seeking aliveness, everybody wants to be more alive. What we don't consider is that you have to *learn* to bear being more alive, to assimilate it, to permit an energetic charge to go through your body. [Keleman, 1971, p. 39]

ture. But they have other functions. It is through our legs and our feet that we keep contact with the one invariable reality in our lives, the earth or the ground" (Lowen, 1971, p. 99). Lowen found that his patients lacked a sense of having their feet planted firmly on the floor, which corresponded to their being out of touch with reality.

> Bioenergetics is a therapeutic technique to help a person get back together with his body and to help him enjoy to the fullest degree possible the life of the body. The emphasis on the body includes sexuality, which is one of its basic functions. But it also includes the even more basic functions of breathing, moving, feeling and self-expression. A person who doesn't breathe deeply reduces the life of his body. If he doesn't move freely, he restricts the life of his body. If he doesn't feel fully, he narrows the life of his body. And if his self-expression is constricted, he limits the life of his body. [Lowen, 1975, p. 43]

In the hands of a well-trained practitioner, bioenergetics is an excellent system that provides many of the benefits of orthodox Reichian analysis—opening up blocks to feeling, energizing parts of the body that have been ignored, and so on.

EXERCISE

Stress Postures

It delights me to say that I am my body, with full understanding of what that really means. It allows me to identify with my total aliveness, without any need to split myself. [Keleman, 1971, p. 28]

Stand with legs about shoulder width apart and knees slightly bent; without straining bend over to touch the floor. Let your body stay loose and your head hang down freely. Hold this posture for several minutes. You may find that your legs begin to shake or quiver, or notice other changes in your body. Keep breathing freely and naturally, and don't try to *make* anything happen.

Slowly come up from this position, feeling your spine gradually come to a vertical position, vertebra by vertebra.

Next, try a position that will curve the spine the other way. Stand with feet apart and your knees pointing slightly out. Put your fists in the small of your back and bend backward. Again, keep your neck relaxed and your head hanging back freely, and breathe freely.

These exercises are designed to bring energy to parts of the body that are chronically tense. According to bioenergetic theory, the quivering that accompanies the postures is an indication of the relaxing and energizing of armored parts of the body.

DANCE/MOVEMENT THERAPY

Dance/movement therapy is a joining together of the fields of dance and psychotherapy. Dance therapy developed in the 1940s and 1950s, as dance teachers brought their knowledge of movement into new settings, mental hospitals, and individual work with clients. At the same time, dance teachers found their approaches to movement enriched by their personal analyses.

Reich's stress on the importance of the body in therapy and on character armor has inspired dance/movement therapists to use movement as means of releasing armoring. Jung's use of artistic expression and active imagination in exploring the psyche has been central to one group of dance/movement therapists. Others have developed a system of movement interpretation based on Freud's theories of psychological development.

Dance/movement therapy draws on dance forms found in civilizations throughout the world, including trance dances from Bali and Africa, whirling dervishes from East Africa and the Middle East, Mexican and American Indian rites-of-passage dances, and ritual healing dances found in many cultures. Dance therapy also draws on modern dance's improvisational and creative expression.

Our bodies reveal our inner experience and personality dynamics. Our movement behavior reflects how we experience ourselves in the world, how we express ourselves, and how we repress or restrict feelings. The dance/movement therapist considers the totality of the individual as it is expressed in body movement. Work in movement therapy ranges from free, full-body expressive movement to breath awareness and subtle, almost imperceptible movement.

Dance/movement therapists encourage their clients to explore "authentic" movements. These are natural movements particular to each individual rather than learned, practiced, or intellectualized. Authentic movements are expressions of a person's psychological and emotional state at that moment.

If I could tell you what it meant—there would be no point in dancing it. [Isadora Duncan]

Clients are encouraged to move freely and remain conscious of their movements from an observing position, without interfering with the flow of movement. Clients gain access to their unconscious by expressing it through movement, observing the process. The experience is that of being moved and moving simultaneously.

The following are several major characteristics of dance/movement therapy: (1) It is expressive. Feelings that may be too overwhelming in verbal terms can be expressed and explored in movement. Movement can also uncover weak or suppressed feelings. (2) Beginning at the physical-emotional level, it provides experiences that encourage growth and self-expression. (3) The process is physically, emotionally, and spiritually integrating.

Dance/movement therapy connects inner images to outer expression. Clients are encouraged to bring into expression their psychological images as well as form images of spontaneous movements. In the process there may be considerable verbal interaction to integrate material expressed in movement. Sometimes movement alone is sufficient; there may be little discussion or verbal interaction.

The movement process itself is inherently healing. The usual criteria for elegant dancelike movements are irrelevant. Through

movement the individual can bypass the personality, the patterns of
ego defense, and intellect in order to move deeply into the essence or
core of the psyche.

Mary Whitehouse, a pioneer in Jungian dance/movement therapy, has written:

> The body is the physical aspect of the personality, and movement is the
> personality made visible. The distortions, tensions, and restrictions are
> the distortions, tensions, and restrictions within the personality. They
> are, at any given moment, the condition of the psyche. And the discovery
> of their factual existence, their physical existence, is the beginning of
> what might be called psycho-somatic recognition, for we are psy-
> cho-somatic entities. . . . So there one is, exactly where the movement
> is, exactly as unfree, exactly as conflicted, exactly as frightened. And the
> assimilation of this discovery strengthens and releases consciousness for
> growth which is, I think, the basic meaning of personality. [1963, p. 2]

EXERCISE

Open and Closed

Lie on your back on the floor and choose how you want to begin—"open" or
"closed." Do you prefer to lie with your body fully extended, or to lie tightly curled
up?

If you begin open, expand still further. Become as wide as possible, taking up
more space with your arms and legs, spreading your fingers, feeling the space between your toes and under your back; everything is wide open. When you are as
wide, as big, and as open as you can possibly be right now, begin closing, decreasing
the space between your toes, bringing in your legs, and bringing parts of yourself
together.

If you begin closed, become even smaller and tightly curled. Bring your fingers
together, draw in your legs tightly, hug your arms to your body, tuck your chin
to your chest, and move more and more closely and tightly into your own center.

Next, follow your own rhythm and timing. Move between being open and closed,
drawing yourself as far open and as far closed as you want to be, moment by moment. When you feel fully opened, give yourself permission to begin closing again.
And when you become as tightly closed as you wish, allow yourself to begin the
process of opening.

Listen to your internal rhythms, without judging or criticizing, and without getting stuck in one place. Know that you can be as open or as closed as you like,
without anticipating what might come next. Continue to move from one process
to the other. Once you have explored these ranges of possibilities, choose where
you want to be right now. Let yourself take that position. Then exaggerate it, allowing any words or images to come to mind.

When you feel you have completed this experience, write about it. Think of
movement as a metaphor. Take a look at how this movement experience is relevant right now to your life. [Adapted from Nancy Robinson Zenoff, M.A., D.T.R.]

STRUCTURAL INTEGRATION (ROLFING)

Structural integration is a system of reshaping and realigning body
posture through deep and often painful stretching of the muscle fascia
by direct manipulation. Structural integration is often called rolfing
after its founder, Ida Rolf. Rolf received a Ph.D. in biochemistry and
physiology in 1920 and worked as an assistant in biochemistry at the

Rockefeller Institute for 12 years. For over 40 years she devoted herself to teaching and perfecting her system.

The aim of structural integration is to bring the body into better muscular balance and better alignment with gravity, closer to an optimal posture in which a straight line could be drawn through the ear, shoulder, hip bone, knee, and ankle. This leads to balanced distribution of the weight of the major parts of the body—head, chest, pelvis, and legs—and also more graceful and efficient movement. When the body becomes ideally aligned, the individual is able to function more effectively and with less muscular effort because the body structure is aligned in its gravitational field.

According to Rolf, the basic order inherent in the body is inevitably disturbed in the course of growing up. Physical and emotional traumas, chronic tension, and similar disorders have permanent effects on posture and alignment. These influences create "random bodies." Structural integration treatments are designed to restore the body's ordered and effective patterns.

Rolfing works primarily with the fascial system, connective tissue that supports and connects the muscle and skeletal systems. Rolf (1977) discovered that psychological trauma or even minor physical injury may result in subtle but relatively permanent changes in the body. Bone or muscle tissue becomes displaced; thickening of connective tissues locks these changes into place. Misalignment will occur not only in the immediate area of an injury but also at distant points in the body out of compensation. For example, favoring a sore shoulder over a time may affect the neck, the other shoulder, and the hips.

Rolfing works directly on the tissue to reestablish balance and flexibility. Most structural integration work involves lengthening and stretching tissues that have grown together or unnaturally thickened. "In order to accomplish a permanent change, it is usually necessary that the actual position or distribution of muscular fibres be very slightly altered. This happens spontaneously as individual fibres stretch or as fascial sheaths again slide over each other instead of being glued on some adjacent sheath. Unless such a change is made the body reverts to its original posture and the restrictions to fluid flow and to interpersonal communication are rebuilt" (Rolf, 1962, p. 13).

Structural integration is generally carried out in a series of 10 one-hour sessions, which include the following areas of work:

Session 1.	Includes much of the body, with special focus on muscles of the chest and abdomen that govern breathing, and the hip joint, which controls pelvic mobility.
Session 2.	Concentrates on the feet, reforming the foot and ankle hinges and aligning the legs with the torso.

In any attempt to create an integrated individual an obvious starting place is his physical body, if for no other reason than to examine the old premise that a man can project only that which is within. . . . In some way, as yet poorly defined, the physical body is actually the personality, rather than its expression. [Rolf, 1962, p. 6]

Session 3.	Lengthens the sides, especially the large muscles between the pelvis and rib cage.
Sessions 4–6.	Free the pelvis. Most people hold their pelvis rotated toward the rear. Because of the tremendous importance of the pelvis in posture and in movement, one of the major emphases of rolfing is to make the pelvis more flexible and better aligned with the rest of the body.
Session 7.	Concentrates on the neck and head and also on the muscles of the face.
Sessions 8–10.	Organize and integrate the entire body.

Work on some areas of the body may trigger memories or a deep emotional discharge. However, rolfing is aimed primarily at *physical* integration, and the psychological aspects of the process are not dealt with directly. Many individuals who have combined rolfing with some form of psychological therapy or other growth work have reported that rolfing helped to free their psychological and emotional blocks.

Man is an energy field, as the earth and its outward envelope of forces is an energy field. How well a man can exist and function depends on whether the field which is himself, his psychological and physical personality, is reinforced or disorganised by the field of gravity. [Rolf, 1962, p. 12]

Rolfing is especially useful for those persons whose bodies have become seriously misaligned as a result of physical or psychological trauma, although virtually everyone can benefit from it. Many of the changes from rolfing seem to be relatively permanent, but maximal benefit comes only if the individual remains aware of the changes in body structure and functioning facilitated by the rolfing process. A system called "structural patterning" was developed for this purpose. It consists of a set of exercises involving minor and subtle shifts in body position and balance.

EXERCISE

Posture Observation
Although it is not possible to experience the process of structural integration without a trained practitioner, everyone can learn more about the postural principles central to rolfing. Do this exercise with a partner. Have your partner stand naturally, and observe his or her posture carefully. (Form-fitting clothing or a bathing suit will work best.)

Is one shoulder higher than the other? Is the head balanced on top of the neck, or is it held forward or backward? Is the chest caved in or stuck out? Is one hip higher than the other? Is the pelvis stuck out to the rear? Are the knees held over the feet? Are the feet straight, or the toes pointed either in or out?

Look at your partner from the front, sides, and back. Then have your partner walk slowly and observe from all angles. Finally, you might want to have your partner stand in front of a straight vertical line drawn on the wall (the line formed by a door will serve), to observe alignment more carefully.

Then discuss what you have observed. Also, imitate your partner's posture and walk in order to illustrate your points. When you have finished, switch roles.

Don't approach this exercise as negative criticism of yourself. No one has perfect posture. Make your observations of each other in an objective and positive way, and receive them with the same attitude.

THE ALEXANDER TECHNIQUE

The Alexander technique is designed to improve awareness of one's habits of movement. Alexander students learn how they use their bodies improperly and inefficiently, and how they can prevent this when active or at rest. By use, Alexander refers to our habits of holding and moving our bodies, habits that directly affect the way we function physically, mentally, and emotionally.

He [Alexander] established not only the beginnings of a far-reaching science of the involuntary movements we call reflexes, but a technique of correction and self-control which forms a substantial addition to our very slender resources in personal education. [George Bernard Shaw]

F. Mathias Alexander was an Australian Shakespearean actor who originated this system in the late nineteenth century. He suffered from recurring loss of voice, for which there seemed to be no organic cause. Alexander spent nine years of painstaking self-observation and self-study in a three-way mirror; he discovered that his loss of voice was related to a backward and downward pressing movement of his head. By learning to inhibit this tendency, Alexander found that he no longer developed laryngitis, and, in addition, the inhibition of pressure on the back of his neck had positive effects throughout his body. Out of his work with himself, Alexander developed a technique for teaching integrated movement based on a balanced relationship between the head and the spine.

One teacher describes the Alexander work as follows: "In the lessons, first of all, the student is asked to do nothing. Even if I want the student to sit down on a chair, I don't want him to *do* it. He has to leave himself alone entirely, and let me move him. We are not super-imposing something on top of the habits that he already has; we are stopping him from using the habits he has. He is to be free, open and neutral in order to experience something else. What he is going to experience is the way he used to function once upon a time, before the poor habits took over" (Stransky, 1969, p. 7).

Alexander believed that a prerequisite for free and efficient movement is the lengthening of the spine. He did not mean a forced stretching, but a natural *upward lengthening*. Alexander students work primarily with the following formula: "Let the neck be free to let the head go forward and up, to let the back lengthen and widen." The aim is not to try to engage in muscular activity; it is to allow the body to adjust automatically while the individual concentrates on repeating the formula and, in the lesson, responds to the guiding touch of the teacher. The movements covered in the lesson are taken from common activities, and the student learns gradually to apply the Alexander principles. This balance between head and spine allows for release of physical tensions, improved alignment, and better muscular coordination. On the other hand, interference with this relationship results in tension, malalignment of the body, and poor coordination.

The Alexander teacher is trained to detect ways we block free movement or anticipate moving with preliminary tension. By moving and readjusting the student's body in subtle ways, the teacher gradually gives the student the experience of resting and acting in an integrated, aligned manner. Alexander lessons typically concentrate on sitting, standing, and walking, in addition to "table work," in which the student lies down and experiences, through the teacher's hands, a greater sense of energy flow and length and width in the body. The table work is designed to give the student a sense of freedom and space in all the joints. This experience gradually reeducates the individual in an alternative to chronic tightening and cramping of the joints brought on by habitual tension. The Alexander work has been especially popular with actors, dancers, and other performing artists. It has also been used with great effectiveness with the physically handicapped and those suffering from chronic physical illnesses.

Mr. Alexander has demonstrated a new scientific principle with respect to the control of human behavior, as important as any principle which has ever been discovered in the domain of external nature. [John Dewey]

EXERCISE

Body Awareness

You are sitting or lying down as you read this. Are you aware of how you are holding the book, of the way your fingers and your arm are taking the weight of the book? How are you sitting? Is the weight of your body more on one buttock than the other? How are you holding your arms? Is there excess tension in your chest, shoulders, and forearms, or throughout your body?

Can you shift to a more comfortable position? If so, your habits of using your body are not as efficient or effective as they might be. Because of these habits, we tend to sit and move in ways that are less than optimally comfortable or useful; once we get back in touch with our own bodies, we can recognize this.

This exercise is not, of course, part of the Alexander technique itself, which requires the touch and guidance of a trained Alexander teacher. It is designed to give you a sense of the dynamics of body use that Alexander stresses (adapted from Barlow, 1973).

THE FELDENKRAIS METHOD

The Feldenkrais method is designed to help students recover the natural grace and freedom we all enjoy as children. Feldenkrais works with patterns of muscular movement that help the individual find the most efficient way of moving and eliminating the unnecessary muscular tensions and inefficient patterns we have learned over the years.

Feldenkrais often quotes the Chinese proverb: "I hear and I forget, I see and I remember, I do and I understand." His work focuses on understanding through doing, which is why he calls his exercises "awareness through movement."

Moshe Feldenkrais received a doctorate in physics in France and worked as a physicist until he was 40. He became deeply interested in judo and founded the first judo school in Europe, eventually developing his own judo system. Feldenkrais also worked with F. Mathias Alexander and studied Yoga, Freud, Gurdjieff, and neurology. After World War II he devoted himself to work with the body. Feldenkrais uses a tremendous variety of exercises, which differ from lesson to lesson. They generally begin with very small movements, which are combined in larger patterns. The aim is to develop ease and freedom of movement in every part of the body.

Feldenkrais points out that we need to take responsibility for ourselves to understand how our bodies operate and to learn to live in accordance with our natural constitution and gifts. He contends that the nervous system is primarily concerned with movement. Every action involves muscular activity, including seeing, talking, even hearing (muscles regulate the tension of the eardrum to adjust for sound level). Feldenkrais stresses the need to relax and find one's own rhythm, one's natural pattern of activity, to overcome poor habits. We need to relax, play, and experiment to learn something new. Whenever we are under pressure or tension, or in a hurry, we learn nothing new; we repeat old patterns. Feldenkrais exercises generally break down a seemingly simple activity into sets of related movements in order to unlock old patterns and develop new possibilities of movement.

For Feldenkrais, growth is a gradual acquisition of more effective action patterns. Rather than abandon old habits, the goal is to increase our repertoire; for example, when we begin to type, most of us use just two fingers. Then we learn touch-typing with 10 fingers, but that skill takes time to develop. Touch-typing is easier and faster than the old two-finger method and we come to prefer the new way.

If new habits will be no longer useful or reliable (because of injury or other damage), old habits are available. Feldenkrais recommends gradual and natural change that does not threaten to destroy reliable habitual patterns.

We have one experience at a time. Because we experience with our whole selves, we cannot "do" and "not do" at the same time, or say "yes" and "no" simultaneously. According to Feldenkrais, we learn in every trial. However, old learnings and attitudes impinge on the new, therefore we have to repeat new learning in different ways and different contexts to gain real mastery.

To be aware is to be in the present. It is to be fully focused on what is happening now, without being bored or attached to results, or anticipating what comes next. In the Feldenkrais movement exercises, students pay attention to the whole body, not just to parts that *seem* most involved with movement. Attention broadens naturally and the entire

I read a lot of physiology and psychology and to my great astonishment I found that in regard to using the whole human being for action, there was ignorance, superstition, and absolute idiocy. There wasn't a single book that dealt with *how* we function. [Feldenkrais, 1966, p. 115]

To learn we need time, attention, and discrimination; to discriminate we must sense. This means that in order to learn we must sharpen our powers of sensing, and if we try to do most things by sheer force we shall achieve precisely the opposite of what we need. [Feldenkrais, 1972, p. 58]

body, the entire self, participates. The ideal is to move without trying, as if the thought of moving is all that is necessary.

What is attention? If you suddenly see a tiger, your whole self is naturally attentive. That is the ideal level of attention in "awareness through movement," but most of us do not achieve it easily. At the start, almost no one performs the movements effectively, but later, Feldenkrais students attend to more of themselves, their whole system becoming more effective. Eventually, the movements come easily and naturally for virtually everyone.

Feldenkrais has often said, "If you know what you are doing, you can do what you want." The aim of his exercises is to get you to do what you want, to understand the easiest patterns of movement for you in each new situation.

Feldenkrais works to reestablish connections between the motor cortex and the musculature, connections that have been distorted by habits, tension, or trauma. According to Feldenkrais, increased awareness and flexibility can be achieved through balancing and quieting the motor cortex. The more active the cortex, the less we are aware of subtle changes. One of the fundamental principles of the Feldenkrais work is Weber's Law, which states that our sensitivity to change is proportional to our current level of stimulation. If you are carrying a piano, for example, you cannot feel a matchbook added to the load. But if you are carrying one match, the weight of a matchbook is immediately evident.

For this reason, most people with bad posture are not sensitive enough to improve it. In fact, if it gets worse, they do not notice because they use so much effort just to stand and walk. On the other hand, those with good posture are likely to improve. They sense subtle changes and continue to use themselves more effectively. By balancing the motor cortex and by reducing the level of excitation, Feldenkrais has found that we expand awareness and try new movement combinations that were not possible when the motor cortex and musculature were locked into old patterns.

EXERCISE

Turning the Head

Sit down on the floor or in a chair and slowly turn your head to the right, without straining. Note how far your head will turn, how far to the rear you can see. Turn your head back to the front.

Turn your head to the right again. Leave your head in place, move your eyes to the right. See if your head can move further to the right. Repeat three to four times.

Turn your head to the right. Now move your shoulders to the right and see if you can turn your head further to the rear. Repeat three to four times.

Turn your head to the right. Now move your hips to the right and see if you can turn your head further to the rear. Repeat three to four times.

Finally, turn your head to the right, leave your head in place and move your eyes, shoulders, and hips to the right. How far can you see now?

Turn your head to the *left*. How far can you see? Then repeat each step of the exercise you did on the right side, *mentally only*. Visualize the movement of your head and visualize your eyes to the left. Visualize each step three to four times. Then turn your head to the left and move your eyes, shoulders, and hips to the left. How far can you turn now?

SENSORY AWARENESS

Sensory awareness work emphasizes relaxation and focusing one's attention on immediate experience. It focuses on direct perception, on distinguishing sensations from learned interpretations that overlay our experience. The simple activity of sensing can provide astonishing and rich experience, from which we frequently cut ourselves off by living "in our heads." It requires a sense of inner quiet, an ability to let things happen and remain aware, without forcing or trying to change.

The system of sensory awareness is taught in the United States by Charlotte Selver and Charles Brooks and their students. Their method is based on the work of Elsa Gindler and Heinrich Jacoby, two of Ms. Selver's European teachers. "The study of this work is our whole organismic functioning in the world we perceive, of which we are a part—our personal ecology: how we go about our activities, how we relate to people, to situations, to objects. We aim to discover what is natural in this functioning and what is conditioned: what is our nature, which evolution has designed to keep us in touch with the rest of the world, and what has become our 'second nature,' as Charlotte likes to call it, which tends to keep us apart" (Brooks, 1974, p. 17).

Sensory awareness is a process of getting back in touch with our bodies and our senses, which we were able to do as children. Parents tend to react to children in terms of their own preferences instead of what actually enhances the child's functioning. Children are taught what things and activities are *good* for them, how long to sleep and what to eat, instead of learning to judge for themselves out of their own experience. "Good" children learn to come whenever mother calls, to cut off their natural rhythms and stop activities in midair for the convenience of parents and teachers. After many such interruptions, the child's innate sense of rhythm becomes confused and so does any inner sense of the value of his or her experience.

Another problem is that of *making efforts*. So many parents urge their children to sit, stand, walk, and talk as early as possible, without waiting for natural development. Children learn that the present isn't enough; they learn striving instead of relaxed play. They learn to *overdo*. This begins with the parents' unnatural use of baby talk and artificial gestures and noises in relating with an infant. By their example, parents teach that even communication cannot be peaceful and simple,

The lily is not to be simply watered but must be gilded. [Selver & Brooks, 1966, p. 491]

that something extra is needed, and this attitude is carried out in many other areas as well.

Many exercises in sensory awareness deal with the basic activities of lying, sitting, standing, and walking. These activities offer the easiest opportunity for discovering attitudes to our environment and for developing conscious awareness of what we are doing. Sitting on a stool without padding or a back allows one to sense the support of the chair, the pull of gravity, and the inner life process that occurs in relation to these and other forces. Standing also offers rich possibilities for sensing. Few people learn to stand comfortably as an end in itself; most of us approach standing as the starting point for other activity. Standing allows one to explore *balancing* and moving from familiar postures to new coordination and being.

Another aspect of sensory awareness work involves interaction with others. Many people need to learn how to touch one another and how to receive touch. Various ways of touching can be explored: tapping, slapping, and so forth. The quality of touch can reveal timidity, aggressiveness, impatience, tenderness, and the like.

Most sensory awareness exercises have an inward, meditative orientation. Selver and Brooks have pointed out that as inner quiet develops, unnecessary tension and activity diminish, and receptivity to inner and outer events is heightened; other changes occur simultaneously throughout the whole person. "The closer we come to such a state of greater balance in the head, the quieter we become, the more our head 'clears,' the lighter and more potent we feel. Energy formerly *bound* is now more and more at our disposal. Pressure and hurry change into freedom for speed. We find ourselves being more one with the world where we formerly had to cross barriers. Thoughts and ideas 'come' in lucidity instead of being produced. . . . Experiences can be allowed to be more fully received and to mature in us" (Selver & Brooks, 1966, p. 503).

EXERCISE

Body Awareness, Lying Down

Lie on the floor and relax. Don't try to rush your awareness; experiencing will come in its own time. You may be aware of the floor pressing on part of your body, and you may feel free in some parts and constricted in others. One person may feel light, another heavy. One may become refreshed, another tired. Receive and accept any messages from inside or outside without evaluation or labeling. It isn't wrong to feel constricted or right to feel free. These categories are inappropriate as this is an exercise in *experiencing*.

As tendencies to "expect" diminish, sensations generally become more rich and full. You may become aware of changes that happen by themselves. Tenseness may change to relaxation and the floor may feel more comfortable. You may become conscious of your breath and of changes in breathing.

HATHA-YOGA

Hatha-yoga is the name given to a wide number of practices and disciplines designed to control the body and the *pranas,* or vital energies of the body. It is often thought of as a preliminary discipline to purify the body and overcome physical obstacles with meditation and other spiritual practices of Yoga.

In the West hatha-yoga means the practice of yoga postures. Its main aim is to develop a healthy body. In India, this is known as "physical yoga" rather than hatha-yoga. These two approaches have practices in common; it is the attitudes and goals of practice that are different, as traditional hatha-yoga is essentially a religious discipline.

The most detailed and also the best known aspect of hatha-yoga is the practice of yoga postures—the headstand, lotus posture, and so forth. One aim of posture practice is to enable the individual to sit for long periods of time without physical discomfort, which would interfere with meditation. Certain postures are designed to keep the body limber, exercise the spine, stimulate various nerves and organs, and increase breathing capacity.

The principle behind the practice of yoga postures is first to accustom the body to a given pose and then gradually lengthen the time in that posture. In various postures pressure is taken off some parts of the body and intensified in others, blood flow is increased to certain body parts, and organs are stretched or compressed. Combinations of postures can provide balanced stimulation for the entire body. Many people in India practice routines of 15 to 20 postures daily. A given posture may have several variations, each designed to exercise different muscles or different organs. It is best to study hatha-yoga under a well-qualified teacher, who can correct major mistakes and also provide individualized instruction suited to a person's specific build and other physical characteristics.

One of the aims of hatha-yoga is to purify and strengthen the body as a vehicle for vital energies. There are five major forms of vital energy discussed in the Upanishads; they deal with respiration, digestion, elimination, circulation, and crystalliztion. These and other vital energies flow through subtle channels in the body, known as *nadis.* Many hatha-yoga practices are designed to open and purify the *nadis,* which become clogged as a result of faulty diet and living patterns. Hatha-yoga includes teachings concerning diet and fasting as well as breathing techniques designed to promote energy flow in the body. Prana means breath and vital energy in Sanskrit. The two are seen as closely connected in India (and in many other cultures as well).

There are other methods of purifying the body in hatha-yoga. These include techniques of washing and cleansing the nasal passages

Hatha yoga is a system of health and hygiene involving both body and mind. It aims at the whole man for his full development and self-realization. It takes into account not only the proper growth, strength and tone of the different muscles of the body but also the efficiency and function of the basic factors of constitutional health, namely, the inner organs and the glands. [Majumdar, 1964, p. 99]

and the digestive system and exercises for the muscles of the stomach and internal organs.

EXERCISE

The Corpse Pose

This pose is designed for deep relaxation. It is practiced at the end of a series of postures or when the individual desires to relax. It is best to practice on a thick carpet or pad.

Lie on your back with your arms resting on the floor, palms up. Close your eyes and consciously relax every part of your body, starting from the feet. Feel your body sinking into the floor as you relax. Feel as if you have abandoned your body completely so that it lies perfectly limp, detached from your mind. Observe your body as if you are outside of it. Observe your breath as it flows in and out, without any attempt to control it. After some time, gradually lengthen your breathing and make it rythmical. Practice from 10 to 20 minutes.

There are, in each of us, profound depths of stillness, serenity and wisdom, hidden under restless passions and desires, under our fears, anxieties and illusions—depths we can reach through meditation and by letting go. [Majumdar, 1964, p. 173]

T'AI CHI CH'UAN

It has been said that t'ai chi ch'uan practice leads to the flexibility of a child, the health of a lumberjack, and the peace of mind of a sage. T'ai chi ch'uan literally means "supreme ultimate boxing." As an exercise for health, sport, and self-defense, t'ai chi has long enjoyed great popularity among the Chinese, and is rapidly becoming better known in the West. Chinese of all ages and backgrounds practice this rhythmical, balletlike exercise at dawn and at dusk.

There are a number of theories concerning the origin of t'ai chi ch'uan. The most popular holds that Chang San-feng, a Taoist priest who lived in the thirteenth century, learned it in a dream. Another school dates it back to the T'ang dynasty (618–907). Other historians attribute the development of t'ai chi to the Ch'en family and date it between the fourteenth and eighteenth centuries.

T'ai chi ch'uan is known as an "intrinsic energy" system. One aim of practice is to develop *ch'i,* or vital energy, in the body. The t'ai chi student must learn to relax completely while training, seeking to eliminate all tension in the body so *ch'i* can flow unobstructed. In time the energy of the body becomes integrated and centered in the area of the navel. Eventually, every movement of t'ai chi ch'uan becomes coordinated with the flow of *ch'i*. Besides learning to move in a fully relaxed manner, the student must keep the spine straight and hold the head as if the entire body were suspended by the top of the head from the ceiling. This allows free flow of energy in the spine and neck and enables the body to move as a single unit.

The mind must be calm and concentrated on the movements. Alertness is extremely important; t'ai chi ch'uan has been called moving meditation.

Another important quality in t'ai chi practice is slow, fluid movement. Movements are done slowly. The postures flow evenly from one to the next, without pauses to break the fluid movement and block the flow of *ch'i*. The student learns to move as if swimming in the air, coming to feel the air as heavy and resistant, just like water, and developing a sense of lightness and buoyancy in the body.

The following excerpt from the t'ai chi classics gives a sense of the philosophical and theoretical bases of the art:

> In any action the entire body should be light and agile and all of its parts connected like pearls on a thread.
> The *ch'i* should be cultivated; the spirit of vitality should be retained internally and not exposed externally.
> The entire body is so light that a feather will be felt and so pliable that a fly cannot alight on it without setting it in motion.
> Stand like a balance and move actively like a cart wheel.
> The mind directs the *ch'i,* which sinks deeply and permeates the bones. The *ch'i* circulates freely, mobilizing the body so that it heeds the direction of the mind.
> In resting, be as still as a mountain; in moving, go like the current of a great river.
> When you act, everything moves, and when you stand still, everything is tranquil.
> Walk like a cat and mobilize your energy as if pulling silken threads from a cocoon. [Chen & Smith, 1967, pp. 106–111]

There are a number of different schools of t'ai chi ch'uan. Some styles tend to stress the practical fighting aspects; others, the exercise aspect. The traditional t'ai chi form consists of 128 postures, including many repetitions. A full round takes over 15 minutes when done at the proper speed. However, a number of teachers have developed their own "short form" of approximately 40 to 50 postures, which eliminates many of the repetitions of the longer form. This shorter version can generally be completed in 10 minutes.

Although there are a number of books available on t'ai chi, it is essential to study directly with a teacher. The movements are too subtle and complex to learn correctly without direct supervision.

EXERCISE

In order to develop *ch'i,* or intrinsic energy, t'ai chi students hold one posture for long periods of time. In holding a single pose the student tries to remain as relaxed as possible, sensing that the body is supported by the flow of energy more than by muscle tension.

One basic pose is to stand with feet shoulder width apart and parallel. Keep knees slightly bent and hands held in front as if holding a large bell. The elbows are slightly bent, the palms facing inward, and the fingertips of each hand facing each other several inches apart. The two arms form a large ring of energy.

Hold for 5 minutes at first. Students may work up to 30 minutes or longer.

AIKIDO

Aikido was founded over 50 years ago by Master Morihei Uyeshiba, who studied many of the traditional Japanese martial arts, including judo, jujitsu, sword, spear, and staff arts. He was also deeply involved in the practice of spiritual disciplines in the Buddhist and Shinto traditions. In time Master Uyeshiba changed aikido from a way of becoming strong and defeating others to a way of self-development and personal and spiritual growth.

> Aiki is not a technique to fight with or defeat the enemy. It is the way to reconcile the world and make human beings one family.
>
> The secret of Aikido is to harmonize ourselves with the movement of the universe and bring ourselves into accord with the universe itself. He who has gained the secret of Aikido has the universe in himself and can say, "I am the universe."
>
> Aikido is non-resistance. As it is non-resistant, it is always victorious. Winning means winning over the mind of discord in yourself.
>
> A mind to serve for the peace of all human beings in the world is needed in Aikido, and not the mind of one who wishes to be strong or who practices only to fell an opponent.
>
> True *budo* [martial arts] is a work of love. It is a work of giving life to all beings, and not killing or struggling with each other. Love is the guardian deity of everything. Nothing can exist without it. Aikido is the realization of love. [Uyeshiba, 1963, pp. 177–179]

There is no competition in aikido. The aim of practice is to learn to harmonize with the movements of a partner rather than to see who is stronger. The term *aikido* might be translated as "a way of spiritual harmony." *Ai* means to unite, bring together, or harmonize; *ki* is life energy, will, vital force, or spirit; and *do* means path or way.

One principle of aikido practice is that the mind leads the body. If you can lead your partner's mind, his or her body will follow easily. One aspect of this principle is to learn not to fight force with force, but first to go with the partner's energy and then seek to redirect it. Another important aspect of using mind and body together is using relaxed, fluid, and circular movements, seeking to blend with a partner rather than forcing the partner to move in a certain way. The more tense we are, the more our partners become tense. The more relaxed we become, the more our partners naturally relax.

In order to practice effectively, the aikido student must learn to remain centered. In aikido centering refers to an awareness of the lower abdomen, or *hara* in Japanese. In Japan this is thought of as one's physical and emotional center. The more one can concentrate one's mind on the lower abdomen and move from that center, the more relaxed, fluid, and effective the movement will be. In Japanese psychology, to develop one's *hara* is to become more calm, more mature, and more empathic.

Aikido is different from most martial arts in its lack of competition and in its emphasis on working *with* a partner rather than fighting *against* an opponent. Aikido and t'ai chi ch'uan are very similar in that both emphasize personal development; also both emphasize centering and the use of vital energy.

Aikido can only be practiced with a partner, and blending with a partner's movements is an essential aspect of the art. T'ai chi forms are practiced slowly by oneself to accustom one's body to the proper soft, flowing movements. Other t'ai chi exercises are done with a partner, however. One subtle difference lies in the fact that aikido arts are oriented to throwing, whereas t'ai chi ch'uan is based primarily on kicking and striking movements.

EXERCISE

Have a partner stand 10 to 15 feet away and slowly approach you, pointing his or her finger to poke you (lightly) in the chest. Try the following three responses:

1. Stand in place observing your partner approach. (How does your body feel as he or she comes close?)
2. Step back and try to avoid the finger, as if your partner were actually attacking you.
3. Look on your partner's motion as merely a flow of energy. Instead of trying to step back out of the way, as your partner approaches, turn to face the direction the partner's finger is pointing. The turn should move you slightly out of the way, so that your partner's hand passes by your body. Think of letting the hand and the energy go by you, instead of trying to stop it or get out of its way.

These three ways of dealing with approaching energy generally feel quite different, both to the person approaching and to the person being approached. The first is an example of a clash of energy, the second is a negative drawing back, and the third is an exercise in blending with someone else without being drawn off center.

EVALUATION

The various body-oriented systems we have covered, which have developed independently in widely different parts of the globe, have much in common. They all advocate "nondoing," learning to let the body operate naturally and smoothly. All favor relaxed instead of tense activity and try to teach the individual to reduce habitual tensions in the body. All of these systems treat mind and body as a single whole, an ongoing psychophysiological process in which change at any level will affect all other parts.

There are also some interesting differences among these systems.

Each seems to specialize in a slightly different area of physical functioning. Reichian and bioenergetic therapies deal with emotionally charged blocks in the body, whereas rolfing works to restructure body misalignments that may have been brought about by physical injury or various other causes. The Alexander technique focuses on body use rather than structure. The Feldenkrais method also deals with use; however, Feldenkrais exercises include considerably more complex behavior patterns in order to restore physical effectiveness and efficiency. Sensory awareness focuses on the senses, on touching and being touched, and on becoming more aware of our own bodies and the world around us. Hatha-yoga is a discipline for strengthening and purifying the body. T'ai chi ch'uan and aikido are derived from the martial arts of the Far East; their movements originally evolved as effective fighting techniques, but now they are practiced primarily as centering, balance, and awareness exercises.

All these systems attempt to teach students to be more relaxed and more "natural" both at rest and in activity. They are all concerned with eliminating the unnecessary tensions that we carry around with us, and bringing us back to "nondoing" action in which we learn to allow the body to operate naturally and effectively rather than to strain, push, or overdo. These systems share a conviction that we need not learn something brand new or develop new muscles. The most important thing is to *un*learn the poor habits we have picked up as children and adults, and to return once again to the natural wisdom, coordination, and balance of the body.

ANNOTATED BIBLIOGRAPHY

Wilhelm Reich

Reich, W. *Selected writings.* New York: Farrar, Straus & Giroux (Noonday Press), 1961. An excellent introduction to the full range of Reich's thought. Includes chapters on therapy, orgone theory, and orgone research.
————. *The function of the orgasm.* New York: Touchstone, 1973. Reich's best book, it includes excellent material on character analysis, bioenergy, genital character, and Reichian therapy.
————. *Character analysis.* New York: Pocket Books, 1976. A classic work, Reich's contributions to psychoanalysis; rewritten from the first edition to fit his later theoretical perspectives.
Baker, E. *Man in the trap.* New York: Avon Books, 1967. Detailed discussion of Reichian therapy and theory by an eminent Reichian therapist.
Boadella, D. *Wilhelm Reich: The evolution of his work.* London: Vision, 1973. The best secondary source on Reich; details the historical development of his theories.

Bioenergetics

Keleman, S. *Sexuality, self and survival.* San Francisco: Lodestar Press, 1971. A lively treatment of bioenergetics, including transcripts of work sessions; by a major practitioner.

Lowen, A. *Bioenergetics.* New York: Penguin Books, 1975. The best introduction to Lowen's writings on bioenergetics.

Lowen, A., & Lowen, L. *The way to vibrant health: A manual of bioenergetic exercises.* New York: Harper & Row, 1977. Superb "do-it-yourself" manual of bioenergetic exercises. Fully illustrated, with pictures of Alexander Lowen and his wife.

Dance/Movement Therapy

Bernstein, P. L. *Eight theoretical approaches in dance-movement therapy.* Dubuque, Iowa: Kendall/Hunt, 1979. The major reference on dance/movement therapy, including contributions representing the most important theories and approaches.

Structural Integration (Rolfing)

Rolf, I. *Rolfing: The integration of human structures.* Santa Monica, Calif.: Dennis-Landman, 1977. The major work on structural integration, written by the founder.

Schutz, W., & Turner, E. *Body fantasy.* New York: Harper & Row, 1977. A detailed case study involving the creative integration of Rolfing and psychotherapy.

Alexander Technique

Alexander, F. *The resurrection of the body.* New York: Dell (Delta Books), 1969. A collection of Alexander's writings. Difficult material.

Barlow, W. *The Alexander technique.* New York: Knopf, 1973. A clear discussion of the theory of Alexander work, with various case studies. Written by an eminent practitioner.

Feldenkrais Method

Feldenkrais, M. *Awareness through movement.* New York: Harper & Row, 1972. Theoretical discussion plus a number of fascinating exercises.

————. *The case of Nora: Body awareness as healing therapy.* New York: Harper & Row, 1977. A brilliant case study that provides insight into Feldenkrais's work as therapist.

Sensory Awareness

Brooks, C. *Sensory awareness.* New York: Viking Press, 1974. The only extensive study of this work. Excellent, clearly written with many fine illustrative photos.

Gunther, B. *Sense relaxation.* New York: Collier Books, 1968. Marvelous photos and exercises. An extremely influential book, it was a best-seller for several years.

Schutz, W. *Joy.* New York: Grove Press, 1967. Excellent exercises and discussion by participants of their experiences with each exercise.

Hatha Yoga

Danielou, A. *Yoga: The method of re-integration.* New York: University Books, 1955. Includes summaries and selections from classical Indian texts on hatha yoga.

Iyengar, B. *Light on Yoga.* New York: Schocken Books, 1972. For advanced students. Detailed, technical explanations.

Vishnudevananda. *The complete illustrated book of yoga.* New York: Pocket Books, 1972. One of the best, easily available paperbacks on hatha yoga.

T'ai-chi Ch'uan
Chen, M., & Smith, R. *T'ai-chi.* Rutland, Vt.: Tuttle, 1967. An excellent book
of t'ai-chi theory and practice.
Huang, A. *Embrace tiger, return to mountain—The essence of t'ai chi.* Moab,
Utah: Real People Press, 1973. T'ai-chi practice and principles applied
to calligraphy, movement, and centering exercises.

Aikido
Uyeshiba, K. *Aikido.* New York: Japan Publications, 1963. Excellent material
on the history and the founder of aikido; fine photos.
Westbrook, A., & Ratti, O. *Aikido and the dynamic sphere.* Rutland, Vt.: Tuttle,
1970. Profusely illustrated with marvelous drawings that illuminate
aikido principles and the Japanese martial arts in general.

REFERENCES
Alexander, F. *The resurrection of the body.* New York: Dell (Delta Books), 1969.
Baker, E. *Man in the trap.* New York: Macmillan, 1967.
Barlow, W. *The Alexander technique.* New York: Knopf, 1973.
Bean, O. *Me and the orgone.* New York: St. Martin's Press, 1971.
Berkowitz, L. The case for bottling up rage. *Psychology Today,* 1973, 7(2), 24–31.
Bernstein, P. L. *Eight theoretical approaches in dance-movement therapy.* Du-
buque, Iowa: Kendall/Hunt, 1979.
Boadella, D. *Wilhelm Reich: The evolution of his work.* London: Vision, 1973.
Brooks, C. *Sensory awareness.* New York: Viking Press, 1974.
Chaiklin, S. Dance therapy. *American handbook of psychiatry* (S. Arieti, Ed.)
(2nd ed.) (Vol. 5). New York: Basic Books, 1975, pp. 701–720.
Chen, M., & Smith, R. *T'ai-chi.* Rutland, Vt.: Tuttle, 1967.
Danielon, A. *Yoga: The method of re-integration.* New York: University Books,
1955.
Feldenkrais, M. *Body and mature behavior.* New York: International Universi-
ties Press, 1950.
————. Image, movement, and actor: Restoration of potentiality. *Tulane
Drama Review,* 1966, *3,* 112–126.
————. *Awareness through movement.* New York: Harper & Row, 1972.
————. *The case of Nora: Body awareness as healing therapy.* New York: Har-
per & Row, 1977.
Frey, A. Behavioral biophysics. *Psychological Bulletin,* 1965, *63,* 322–337.
Gunther, B. *Sense relaxation.* New York: Collier Books, 1968.
————. *What to do till the Messiah comes.* New York: Macmillan, 1971.
Higgens, M., & Raphael, C. *Reich speaks of Freud.* New York: Farrar, Straus
& Giroux, 1967.
Huang, A. *Embrace tiger, return to mountain—The essence of t'ai chi.* Moab,
Utah: Real People Press, 1973.
Iyengar, B. *Light on Yoga.* New York: Schocken Books, 1972.
Jones, F. *Body awareness in action.* New York: Schocken Books, 1967.
Keen, S. Sing the body electric. *Psychology Today,* 1970a, (5), 56–58, 88.
————. My new carnality. *Psychology Today,* 1970b, (5), 59–61.
Keleman, S. *Sexuality, self and survival.* San Francisco: Lodestar Press, 1971.
————. *Todtmoos.* San Francisco: Lodestar Press, 1973a.
————. *The human ground.* San Francisco: Lodestar Press, 1973b.
Kelley, C. *What is orgone energy?* Santa Monica: Interscience Workshop, 1962.
————. *Education in feeling and purpose.* Santa Monica, Calif.: Interscience
Workshop, 1970.

————. *Primal scream and genital character: A critique of Janov and Reich.* Santa Monica, Calif.: Interscience Workshop, 1971.

————. *The new education.* Santa Monica, Calif.: Interscience Research Institute, 1972.

Leibowitz, J. For the victims of our culture: The Alexander technique. *Dance Scope,* 1967–1968, *4,* 32–37.

Linklater, K. The body training of Moshe Feldenkrais. *The Drama Review,* 1972, *16,* 23–27.

Lowen, A. *The betrayal of the body.* New York: Macmillan, 1969.

————. *The language of the body.* New York: Macmillan, 1971.

————. *Bioenergetics.* New York: Penguin Books, 1975.

Lowen, A., & Lowen, L. *The way to vibrant health: A manual of bioenergetic exercises.* New York: Harper & Row, 1977.

Macdonald, P. Psycho-physical integrity. *Bulletin of Structural Integration,* 1970, 2, 23–26.

Majumdar, S. *Introduction to Yoga principles and practices.* New Hyde Park, N.Y.: University Books, 1969.

Mann, W. *Orgone, Reich and eros.* New York: Simon & Schuster, 1973.

Reich, Ilse. *William Reich: A personal biography.* New York: St. Martin's Press, 1969.

Reich, W. *Selected writings.* New York: Farrar, Straux & Giroux (Noonday Press), 1961.

————. *The sexual revolution.* New York: Farrar, Straus & Giroux, 1970.

————. *The mass psychology of Fascism.* New York: Farrar, Straus & Giroux, 1970.

————. *The function of the orgasm.* New York: Touchstone, 1973.

————. *Character analysis.* New York: Pocket Books, 1976.

Robinson, P. *The Freudian left.* New York: Harper & Row, 1969.

Rolf, Ida. *Structural integration: Gravity, an unexplored factor in a more human use of human beings.* Boulder, Col.: Guild for Structural Integration, 1962.

————. Exercise. *The Bulletin of Structural Integration Anthology,* nd, *1,* 31–34.

————. *Rolfing: The integration of human structures.* Santa Monica, Calif.: Dennis-Landman, 1977.

Rycroft, C. *Wilhelm Reich.* New York: Viking Press, 1971.

Schutz, W. *Joy.* New York: Grove Press, 1967.

————. *Here comes everybody: Body-mind and encounter culture.* New York: Harper & Row, 1971.

Schutz, W., & Turner, E. *Body fantasy.* New York: Harper & Row, 1977.

Selver, C., & Brooks, C., Report on work in sensory awareness and total functioning. In H. Otto (Ed.), *Explorations in human potentialities.* Springfield, Ill.: Thomas, 1966.

Smallwood, Joan C. Dance therapy and the transcendent function. *American Journal of Dance Therapy,* 1978, *2*(1), 16–23.

Stransky, J. An interview with Judith Stransky. *Bulletin of Structural Integration,* 1969, *2,* 5–11.

Tohei, K. *Aikido in daily life.* New York: Japan Publications, 1966.

Uyeshiba, K. *Aikido.* New York: Japan Publications, 1963.

Vishnudevananda. *The complete illustrated book of yoga.* New York: Pocket Books, 1972.

Westbrook, A., & Ratti, O. *Aikido and the dynamic sphere.* Rutland, Vt.: Tuttle, 1970.

Whitehouse, M. *Physical movement and personality.* Paper presented at the meeting of the Analytical Psychology Club, Los Angeles, 1963.
————. Creative expressions in physical movement is language without words. Unpublished manuscript, nd.
————. The transference and dance therapy. *American Journal of Dance Therapy,* 1977, *1,* 3–7.

CHAPTER 7
FREDERICK S. PERLS
AND
GESTALT THERAPY

Frederick S. Perls, the originator of Gestalt therapy, occupies a somewhat unique position in the framework of this text. Unlike Freud, Jung, Adler, James, and others, his contributions to a psychology of personality are primarily in the area of the practice of psychotherapy rather than in the area of personality theory. In recent years, however, the popularity of Gestalt therapy and its use in a wide variety of contexts other than specifically therapeutic suggest that Perls and the Gestalt view of human beings are worth examining; they represent a current and major trend in the psychology of personality. In fact, the lack of a strictly theoretical emphasis in most of Perls's later work reflects the direction in which he was attempting to move psychology; his conviction was that a genuinely holistic and productive view of people and psychotherapy would require substantial deintellectualization, Western intellect having become, in his words, "the whore of intelligence . . . the poor, pallid substitute for the vivid immediacy of sensing and experiencing" (Perls, 1967, p. 15).

Toward the end of his life, Perls realized that the dangers of overintellectualizing notwithstanding, some theoretical statement of his approach was needed in order to prevent his ideas from being reduced to a set of gimmicks and attempts at instant psychotherapeutic cures. He never completed his last manuscript (*The Gestalt Approach,* 1973), but even in its unfinished form it provides, along with his other less specifically theoretical works, a basis for understanding the Gestalt view of the psychology of personality.

PERSONAL HISTORY

In and out the garbage pail
Put I my creation
Be it lively, be it stale
Sadness or elation.

Joy and Sorrow as I had
Will be re-inspected;
Feeling sane and being mad,
Taken or rejected.

Junk and chaos come to halt
'Stead of wild confusion,
Form a meaningful gestalt
At my life's conclusion.
[Perls, 1969b]

Frederick S. Perls was born in Berlin in 1893, the son of lower-middle-class Jewish parents. In his autobiography, *In and Out of the Garbage Pail* (1969b), Perls describes himself as a black-sheep son, often angry and scornful of his parents, who was expelled from school after twice failing seventh grade and in trouble with authorities throughout his adolescence.

He managed nonetheless to finish his schooling and received an M.D., specializing in psychiatry. While finishing his medical training he joined the German army and served as a medic during World War I. After the war he returned to Berlin and, entering into Berlin Bohemian society, began to formulate some of the philosophical ideas that were to provide a basis for the development of Gestalt therapy. In 1926 Perls worked with Kurt Goldstein at the Institute for Brain-injured Soldiers. Through his work with Goldstein, Perls developed some sense of the importance of viewing the human organism as a whole rather than as a conglomeration of disparately functioning parts.

In 1927 he moved to Vienna and began psychoanalytic training; he was analyzed by Wilhelm Reich and supervised by several other major figures of the early psychoanalytic movement: Karen Horney, Otto Fenichel, and Helene Deutsch among them.

In 1933, with the approach of Hitler, Perls fled to Holland and then to South Africa where he established the South African Institute for Psychoanalysis. He returned to Germany in 1936 to deliver a paper at the Psychoanalytic Congress and to meet Sigmund Freud. The meeting was an immense disappointment to Perls; he recalls that it lasted for perhaps 4 minutes and offered no opportunity for exploring Freud's ideas, which Perls had anticipated for years.

Several years later Perls broke openly with the psychoanalytic movement and in 1946 he emigrated to the United States. He proceeded with the development of Gestalt therapy and established the New York Institute for Gestalt Therapy in 1952. He moved to Los Angeles and then, in the early 1960s, to the Esalen Institute in Big Sur, California, where he offered workshops, taught, and began to become widely known as the exponent of a viable new philosophy and method of psychotherapy. Shortly before his death his interest turned to the establishment of a Gestalt kibbutz. He died in 1970 on Vancouver Island, the site of the first Gestalt therapeutic community (Gaines, 1979; Shepard, 1975).

> My break with the Freudians came a few years later (after my meeting with Freud), but the ghost was never completely laid. . . . I had tried to make psychoanalysis my spiritual home, my religion. . . . Then the enlightenment came . . . I had to take all responsibility for my existence myself. [Perls, 1969b, pp. 59–60, parenthesis added]

INTELLECTUAL ANTECEDENTS

The major intellectual trends that directly influenced Perls were psychoanalysis, Gestalt psychology, and existentialism and phenomenology. Perls also incorporated some of the ideas of J. L. Moreno, a psychiatrist who developed the notion of the importance of role-playing in psychotherapy. Somewhat less explicitly, Perls describes the philosophy and practice of Zen as an important influence, particularly on his later work.

Psychoanalysis
Freud

The first book that Perls wrote, *Ego, Hunger and Aggression,* was not intended to provide a new theory of personality, but instead was to constitute a revision of psychoanalytic theory. In fact, a good part of Perls' work was devoted to developing what he saw to be an extension of Freud's work. Even after his formal break with Freud, Perls continued to view his own ideas as a revision of Freud's work, and, even more, a revision of psychoanalysis as interpreted by many of the psychoanalytic second generation. Perls's disagreements with Freud had primarily to do with Freud's psychotherapeutic treatment methods rather than with Freud's more theoretical expositions of the importance of unconscious motivations, the dynamics of personality, patterns of human relationships, and so on. "Not Freud's discoveries but his philosophy and technique have become obsolete" (Perls, 1969b, p. 14).

> None of us, probably with the exception of Freud himself, realized the prematurity of applying psychoanalysis to treatment. . . . We did not see it for what it actually was: a *research project.* [Perls, 1969b, p. 142]

If the patient is finally to close the book on his past problems, he must close it in the present. For he must realize that if his past problems were really past they would not longer be problems—and they certainly would no longer be present. [Perls, 1973, p. 63]

Perls felt that Freud's work was primarily limited in that it failed to stress a holistic approach to organismic functioning, in which the individual and the environment are viewed as constantly interacting parts of a single field. This holistic approach, in which every element of an organism's expression is intimately connected to the whole, led Perls to lay particular stress, in contrast to Freud, on *obvious* rather than deeply repressed material as being crucial to understanding and working through intrapsychic conflict. Similarly, Perls emphasized the importance of examining one's situation in the present *rather* than investigating past causes, which Freud suggested. Perls believed that the awareness of *how* one behaves, moment to moment, is more relevant to self-understanding and capacity for change than an understanding of *why* one behaves as one does.

Perls's initial departure from Freud's approach concerned Freud's theory of impulses and libido. In Perls's view no impulse (for example, sex or aggression) is "basic"; all needs are direct expressions of organismic impulses. Perls suggested that the psychoanalytic methods of interpretation and free association constituted avoidance of direct experience of the associated and interpreted material and were therefore inefficient and often ineffective methods of self-exploration.

Freud's emphasis on the importance of resistances is slightly shifted in Perls's approach to an emphasis on avoidance of awareness of any kind, particularly stressing the *form* that avoidance takes rather than the specific content of the avoidance. (For example, the relevant question is *how* am I avoiding awareness, not *what* am I avoiding.)

Perls disagreed with Freud's supposition that the important therapeutic task is the freeing of repressions, following which the working through or assimilation of the material occurs naturally. Perls thought that every individual, by nature simply of existing, has plenty of material readily available to him for therapeutic work; the difficult and important task is the assimilation process itself, the chewing and digesting and integrating of previously introjected (swallowed whole) traits, habits, attitudes, and patterns of behavior.

Perhaps most important of all, Perls and the Gestalt approach have increasingly come to represent an alternative world view, a different *Weltanschauung,* to that from which psychoanalytic theory emerges. Yet, given an understanding of this difference in world view (which leads to the utterly different styles and characteristics of psychoanalytic and Gestalt work), a great deal of psychoanalytic theory finds its counterpart in Gestalt work.[1]

[1]Briefly, some of the counterparts may be found in the following general pairs of concepts: Freud's cathexis and Perls's foreground; Freud's libido and Perls's basic excitement; Freud's free association and Perls's continuum of awareness; Freud's "consciousness" and Perls's "awareness"; Freud's focus on resistance and Perls's focus on avoidance

Reich

The other major psychoanalytic influence on Perls was one of his analysts, Wilhelm Reich. Reich developed the notion of "muscular armor"; he also stressed the importance of character (or habitual ways of reacting) in determining how a person functions. He suggested that character develops early in the individual's life and serves as a kind of armoring against internal or external stimuli that the individual finds threatening. This character armor is physiologically rooted (that is, *muscular* armor), and functions as resistance to insight or psychological change. Reich's early work heavily influenced Perls, particularly Perls's view of the body in relation to the psyche.

Gestalt Psychology

Gestalt theory was first put forward in the late 1800s in Germany and Austria. It developed as a protest against the attempt to understand experience by atomistic analysis—analysis in which elements of an experience are reduced to their simplest components, each component is analyzed apart from the others, and the experience is understood simply as the sum of these components. The very notion of a "gestalt" contradicts the validity of this kind of atomistic analysis. Although there is no precise English equivalent for the German word *Gestalt,* the general meaning is a pattern or configuration—a particular organization of parts that makes up a particular whole. The chief principle of the Gestalt approach is to suggest that an analysis of parts can never provide an understanding of the whole because the whole is defined by the interactions and interdependencies of the parts. Parts of a gestalt do not maintain their identity when they are independent of their function and place in the whole.

A gestalt is an irreducible phenomenon. It is an essence that is there and that disappears if the whole is broken up into its components. [Perls, 1969b, p. 63]

Max Wertheimer published in 1912 the paper that is generally considered to be the founding work of the Gestalt school. His paper described an experiment he performed with two colleagues—also central figures in the Gestalt movement—Wolfgang Köhler and Kurt Koffka. Their experiment was designed to explore certain aspects of the perception of motion. They flashed in rapid succession two closely spaced points of light in a dark room, varying the time intervals between the flashes. They found that when the interval between the flashes was less than 3/100 of a second, the flashes appeared simultaneous. When the interval was about 6/100 of a second, the observer reported seeing the flash move from the first point to the second. When the interval was 20/100 of a second or more, the points of light were observed as they

---

of awareness; Freud's repetition compulsion and Perls's unfinished situations; Freud's regression and Perls's withdrawal (from the environment); Freud's therapist who permits/encourages transference and Perls's therapist who is a "skillful frustrator"; Freud's neurotic defense-impulse configuration and Perls's rigid Gestalt formation; Freud's projection transference and Perls's projection . . . and so on.

actually were: two separate flashes of light. The crucial finding of the experiment involved the perception of motion when the flashes were approximately 6/100 of a second apart; the apparent movement was not a function of the isolated stimuli but was dependent upon the relational characteristics of the stimuli and the neural and perceptual organization of the stimuli in a single field.

The results of this experiment led to some major reformulations in the study of perception, and during the 1920s, 1930s, and 1940s, Gestalt theory was applied to the study of learning, problem solving, motivation, social psychology, and, to some degree, personality theory.

A major contribution of the Gestaltists involved, as we have briefly seen, the exploration of how parts constitute and are related to a whole. One aspect of this involves how an organism, in a given field, makes his or her perceptions meaningful, how he or she distinguishes figure and background. Figure 7.1 is an example of how a given stimulus may be interpreted as representing different things depending upon what is perceived as figure and what as ground.

If the white is viewed as figure and the black as background, a white chalice appears; if, on the other hand, the black is viewed as figure and white as background, we see two heads in silhouetted profile. The Gestalt school extended the phenomenon represented by this picture to describe how an organism selects what is of interest to that organism at any particular moment. To a thirsty person, a glass of water placed in the midst of favorite foods emerges as figure against the background of the food; his or her perception adapts, thereby enabling the person to satisfy his or her needs. Once the thirst is satisfied, perception of what is figure and what is ground will probably change in accordance with a shift in dominant need and interest.

Although by 1940 Gestalt theory had been applied in many areas of psychology, it had been for the most part ignored in examining the dynamics of personality structure and personal growth. And there was as yet no formulation of Gestalt principles specifically as psychotherapy.

Every organ, the senses, movements, thoughts, subordinate themselves to this emerging need and are quick to change loyalty and function as soon as that need is satisfied and then retreat into the background. . . . All the parts of the organism *identify* themselves temporarily with the emergent *gestalt*. [Perls, 1969b, p. 115]

Figure 7.1 An Example of the Figure-Ground Phenomenon

Existentialism and Phenomenology

Perls described Gestalt therapy as an existential therapy, based in existential philosophy and utilizing principles generally considered to be both existentialist and phenomenological. Below are some of the primary similarities between Perls's work and major trends in existentialism and phenomenology.

Most generally, Perls objected strenuously to the notion that the study of human beings could be encompassed by an entirely rational, mechanistic, natural-scientific approach. Following from this, Perls aligned himself with most existentialists in insisting that the experiential world of an individual can only be understood through that individual's direct description of his or her own unique situation.

The idea that mind and body constitute two different and wholly separable aspects of existence was a notion that Perls, in company with most existentialists, found insupportable. Rather than viewing each human being as encountering a world which that person experiences as entirely separate from himself or herself, Perls believed that people create and constitute their own worlds; the world exists, for a given individual, as his or her own disclosure of the world.

Two major themes in most existentialist thinking are the experience of nothingness and concern with death and dread. As we shall see in examining Perls's view of the structure of neurosis, these also constitute important elements in his theory of psychological functioning.

The phenomenological method of understanding through description is basic to Perls's thought; all actions imply choice, all criteria in making choices are themselves chosen, and causal explanations are not sufficient to explain one's actions or choices. And the phenomenological reliance on intuition in the knowing of essences resembles Perls's reliance on what he calls the intelligence or wisdom of the organism.

Perls's style is imaginative and personal; his attempt is existential in that it is an attempt to suggest a theory of psychological development that is inextricable from Perls's own involvement with his own development.

I feel rather desperate about this manuscript. I've got a view looking at a tapestry, nearly completely woven, yet unable to bring across the total picture, the total gestalt. Explanations don't help much towards understanding. I can't give it to you; you may take what I offer, but do I know your appetites? . . . I am still stuck and determined to get through this impass. I am too easily inclined to give up and let go. . . . I would not be a phenomenologist if I could not see the obvious, namely the experience of being bogged down. I would not be a Gestaltist if I could not enter the experience of being bogged down with confidence that some figure will emerge from the chaotic background. . . . [Perls, 1969b]

MAJOR CONCEPTS

The Organism as a Whole

Perls insisted that human beings are unified organisms, that there is no difference in kind between mental and physical activity. Perls defined mental activity simply as activity of the whole person that is carried on at a lower energy level than physical activity.

Perls suggested that any aspect of an individual's behavior may be viewed as a manifestation of the whole—the person's being. Thus in therapy, what the patient *does*—how he or she moves, speaks, and so on—provides as much information about the patient as what he or she thinks and says.

Perls stressed the importance of viewing the individual as being perpetually part of a wider field, which includes both the organism and the organism's environment. Just as Perls protested against the notion of a mind-body split, he protested against an inner-outer split; he viewed the question of whether people are ruled by internal or external forces as essentially meaningless. There is however a *contact boundary* between the individual and his or her environment; it is this boundary that defines the relationship between them. In a healthy individual this boundary is fluid, perpetually permitting contact with, then withdrawal from, the environment. Contacting constitutes the forming of a gestalt; withdrawing represents its closure. In a neurotic individual the contact and withdrawal functions are disturbed, and the individual finds himself or herself faced by a conglomerate of gestalten that are in some sense unfinished—not fully formed or not fully closed.

Perls suggested that the cues for this rhythm of contact and withdrawal are dictated by a *hierarchy of needs*. Dominant needs emerge as foreground or figure against the background of the total personality; effective action is directed toward the satisfaction of a dominant need. Neurotics are often unable either to sense which of their needs are dominant or to define their relationship to the environment in such a way that their dominant needs are satisfied.

Here and Now Emphasis

The holistic view led Perls to lay particular stress on the importance of an individual's present, immediate self-perception of his or her environment. Neurotics are unable to live in the present because they chronically carry with them unfinished situations from the past. Their attention is at least partially absorbed by these unfinished situations, and they thus have neither the awareness nor the energy to deal fully with the present. Since the destructive nature of these unfinished situations appears in the present, neurotic individuals experience themselves as unable to live successfully in the present. So the Gestalt approach is not to investigate the past for memories of trauma or unfinished situations, but to ask the patient simply to focus on becoming aware of his or her *present* experience, assuming that the bits and pieces of unfinished situations and unsolved problems from the past will inevitably emerge as part of that present experience. As these unfinished situations appear, the patient is asked to reenact them, to reexperience them in order to finish and assimilate them in the present.[2]

The organism acts with and reacts to its enviroment with greater or lesser intensity; as the intensity diminishes, physical behavior turns to mental behavior. As the intensity increases, mental behavior turns into physical behavior. [Perls, 1973, p. 13]

Nothing is ever really repressed. All relevant gestalten are emerging, they are on the surface, they are obvious like the emperor's nakedness. Your eyes and ears are aware of them, provided your computer-analyzing thinking has not blinded you. [Perls, 1969b, p. 272]

---

[2]Although this focus on the present is particularly emphasized in Gestalt work, it derives from the psychoanalytic notion that one's past is neurotically *transferred* into the present. Thus in both psychoanalytic work and Gestalt work one attempts to "finish" in the present unfinished situations from the past.

Perls defined anxiety as the gap, the tension between the "now" and the "then." The inability of people to tolerate this tension, Perls suggested, causes them to fill the gap with planning, rehearsing, and attempts to make the future secure. This not only absorbs energy and attention away from the present (thereby perpetually creating unfinished situations), it also prevents the kind of openness to the future that growth and spontaneity imply.

In addition to the strictly therapeutic nature of this focus on present awareness, an underlying current to Perls's work is that living with attention to the present, rather than the past or future, is in itself something good, something leading to psychological growth.[3]

Importance of How Over Why

A natural outcome of Perls's orientation is his stress on the importance of understanding experience in a descriptive fashion. Structure and function are identical; if an individual understands *how* he or she does something, that person is in a position to understand the action itself. The causal determination—the why—of the action is, according to Perls, irrelevant to any full understanding of it. Every action is multiply caused, and every cause is multiply caused, and explanations of such causes lead one further and further from understanding the action itself.

Awareness

The three major concepts in Perls's approach that we have examined thus far—the organism as a whole, the here and now emphasis, and the importance of how over why—constitute a foundation for examin-

> Anxiety is nothing but the tension from the *now* to the *then* . . . for instance, if I were to ask, "Who wants to come up here to work?" you probably would quickly start to rehearse "What shall I do there?" and so on. And of course probably you will get stage fright because you leave the secure reality of the now and jump into the future. [Perls, 1969a]

[3]As Claudio Naranjo has pointed out in his article "Present-Centeredness: Technique, Prescription and Ideal" (in Fagan & Shepherd, *Gestalt Therapy Now,* 1970), present-centeredness is an attitude leading to psychological development that is central to many Eastern psychologies. In a passage of the *Pali Canon* Buddha suggests:

> Do not hark back to things that passed,
> And for the future cherish no fond hopes;
> The past was left behind by thee,
> The future state has not yet come.

> But who with vision clear can see
> The present which is here and now
> Such wise one should aspire to win
> What never can be lost or shaken.

[in Fagan & Shepherd, *Gestalt Therapy Now,* 1970, p. 67]

And in the Sufi tradition, Omar Khayyam suggests:

> Never anticipate tomorrow's sorrow
> live always in this paradisal Now— . . .

> Rise up, why mourn this transient world of men?
> Pass your whole life in gratitude and joy.

[*The Rubáiyát of Omar Khayyám,* translated by Robert Graves and Omar Ali-Shah, 1968, p. 54]

ing *awareness,* the focal point of his therapeutic approach. The process of growth is, in Perls's terms, a process of expanding areas of self-awareness; the major factor inhibiting psychological growth is avoidance of awareness.

Perls believed strongly in what he called the wisdom of the organism. He saw the healthy, mature individual as a self-supporting, self-regulating individual. And he saw the cultivation of self-awareness to be directed toward recognizing this self-regulating nature of the human organism. Following Gestalt theory, Perls suggested that the hierarchy-of-needs principle is always operating in the human individual. In other words, the most urgent need, the most important unfinished situation will always emerge if one is simply *aware* of one's experience of oneself, moment to moment.

To be aware is to pay attention to the perpetually emerging foreground of one's own perception. To avoid awareness is to rigidify the naturally free-flowing delineation of foreground and background.

Perls suggested that for every individual there are three zones of awareness: awareness of self, awareness of the world, and awareness of what lies between—a kind of intermediate fantasy zone. Perls saw the exploration of this last zone (which prevents awareness of the other two) as Freud's great contribution. He suggested, however, that Freud focused so completely on understanding this intermediate zone that he ignored the importance of working to develop the capacity to be aware in the other two zones of the self and the world. By contrast, much of Perls's approach includes a very deliberate attempt to gain awareness of and direct contact with oneself and the world.

DYNAMICS

Psychological Growth

Perls defined psychological health and maturity as the capacity to emerge from environmental support and environmental regulation to self-support and self-regulation. The crucial element in both self-support and self-regulation is balance. One of the basic propositions of Gestalt theory is that every organism possesses the capacity to achieve an optimum balance within itself and with its environment. The conditions for achieving this balance involve an unimpeded awareness of the hierarchy of needs.

A full appreciation of this hierarchy of needs can only be achieved through the awareness that involves the whole organism because needs are experienced by every part of the organism and their hierarchy is established through their coordination.

Perls views the rhythm of contact with and withdrawal from the environment as the major component of organismic balance. Immaturity and neurosis imply either an inappropriate perception of what this rhythm constitutes or an incapacity to regulate its balance.

I believe that this is a great thing to understand: *that awareness per se—by and of itself—can be curative.* [Perls, 1969a, p. 16]

Any disturbance of the organismic balance constitutes an incomplete gestalt, an unfinished situation forcing the organism to become creative, to find means and ways to restore that balance. . . . And the figure/background foundation which is the strongest will temporarily take over the control of the total organism. Such is the basic law of organismic self-regulation. [Perls, 1969b, pp. 79, 92]

Self-regulating, self-supporting individuals are characterized by freely flowing and clearly delineated figure-ground formations (definitions of meaning) in expression of their needs for contact and withdrawal. They recognize their own capacity to choose the means of fulfilling needs as such needs emerge. They are aware of the boundaries between themselves and others and are particularly aware of the distinction between their fantasies of others and what they experience through direct contact.

In stressing the *self*-supporting, *self*-regulating nature of psychological well-being, Perls does not suggest that an individual can exist in any sense separate from his or her environment. In fact, organismic balance presumes a constant interaction with the environment. The crucial thing for Perls is that we can choose *how* we relate to the environment; we are self-supporting and self-regulating in that we recognize our own capacity to determine how we support and regulate ourselves within a field that includes much more than ourselves.

Perls describes several ways in which psychological growth is achieved. The first involves the finishing of unfinished situations. He also suggests that neurosis may be loosely viewed as a kind of five-layered structure, and that growth (and eventually freedom from the neurosis) occurs in the passage through these five layers.

Perls calls the first layer the *cliché layer,* or the layer of token existence. It includes all the tokens of contact: "good morning," "hello," "nice weather, isn't it?" The second layer is the *role layer,* or *game-playing layer.* This is the "as-if" layer where people pretend to be the person they would like to be: the always competent businessman, the perpetually nice little girl, the very important person.

Having reorganized these two layers, Perls suggests that we reach the *impasse layer,* also called the *anti-existence layer* or *phobic avoidance layer.* Here we experience emptiness, nothingness; this is the point at which, out of avoiding the nothingness, we generally cut off our awareness and retreat back to the role-playing layer. If, however, we are able to maintain awareness of ourselves in this emptiness, we reach the death or *implosive layer.* This layer appears as death or as fear of death because it consists of a paralysis of opposing forces; in experiencing this layer we contract and compress ourselves—we implode.

But if we can stay in contact with this deadness, we reach the last layer, the *explosive layer.* Perls suggests that becoming aware of this level constitutes emergence into the authentic person, the true self, the person capable of experiencing and expressing his or her emotions. And he warns:

Now, don't be frightened by the word *explosion.* Many of you drive a motor car. There are hundreds of explosions per minute in the cylinder. This is different from the violent explosion of the catatonic—that would be like an explosion in a gas tank. Also, a single explosion doesn't mean a thing. The so-called breakthroughs of the Reichian therapy, and all that, are as little useful as the insight in psychoanalysis. *Things still have to work through.* [Perls, 1969a, p. 56, emphasis added]

There are four basic kinds of explosions that an individual may experience when emerging from the death layer. There is the explosion of *grief* that involves the working through of a loss or death that was previously unassimilated. There is the explosion into *orgasm* in people who are sexually blocked. There is the explosion into *anger* when the expression of anger has been repressed. And, finally, there is the explosion into what Perls calls *joie de vivre*—joy and laughter, the joy of life.

There are a couple of points absolutely crucial to Gestalt. One is that you already know everything you need to know to lead a fully satisfying, happy, effective life. [Enright, 1980, p. 17]

The structure of our role-playing is cohesive because it is designed to absorb and control the energy of these explosions. The basic misconception that this energy *needs* to be controlled derives from our fear of emptiness and nothingness (the third layer). Perls suggests that Eastern philosophies, particularly Zen, have a good deal to teach us about the life-giving, positive experience of nothingness and about the importance of permitting the experience of nothingness without interrupting it.

Throughout his descriptions of how an individual develops, Perls maintains the notion that change cannot be forced and that psychological growth is a natural, spontaneous process.

Obstacles to Growth

Perls views avoidance of awareness and the resultant rigidities in perception and behavior as the major obstacles to psychological growth. Neurotics (those who interrupt their own growth) cannot see their own needs clearly, nor can they make appropriate distinctions between themselves and the rest of the world. Consequently, they are unable to find and maintain the proper balance between themselves and the rest of the world. Neurosis consists of defensive maneuvers designed to protect oneself against and balance oneself in this impinging world.

Perls suggests that there are four basic neurotic mechanisms—boundary disturbances—that impede growth: *introjection, projection, confluence,* and *retroflection.*

Introjection

[These concepts] are the chief actors in the endless self-nagging and inner argument between ideal and real self in which so many people fritter away their lives. [Enright, 1975, p.20]

Introjection, or "swallowing whole," is the mechanism by which individuals incorporate standards, attitudes, and ways of acting and thinking that are not their own and that they do not assimilate or digest sufficiently to make their own. One of the ill effects of introjection is that introjecting individuals find it very difficult to distinguish between what they really feel and what others want them to feel—or simply what others feel. Introjection can also constitute a disintegrating force in the personality because when the concepts or attitudes that are swallowed are incompatible with each other, the introjecting individuals will find themselves torn.

Projection

Another neurotic mechanism is *projection;* it is, in a sense, the opposite of introjection. Projection is the tendency to make others responsible for what originates in the self. It involves a disowning of one's impulses, desires, and behaviors, placing what belongs to the self outside.

Confluence

The third neurotic mechanism is (pathological) *confluence.*[4] In confluence, individuals experience no boundary between themselves and the environment. Confluence makes a healthy rhythm of contact and withdrawal impossible because both contact and withdrawal presuppose an *other.*

Retroflection

The fourth neurotic mechanism is *retroflection*. Retroflection means, literally, "turning back sharply against"; retroflecting individuals turn against themselves, and instead of directing their energies toward changing and manipulating their environment, they direct those energies toward themselves. They split themselves and become both subject and object of all of their actions; they are the target of all of their behavior.

Perls points out that these mechanisms rarely operate in isolation from each other, although people balance their neurotic tendencies among the four mechanisms in varying proportion. The crucial function that all of these mechanisms fill is the confusion of boundary discrimination. Given this confusion of boundaries, an individual's well-being—defined as the capacity to be self-supporting and self-regulating—is severely circumscribed.

Perls's view of these four mechanisms is basic to much of his psychotherapeutic approach. For example, Perls saw introjection as being central to what he called the top dog-underdog struggle. The top dog consists of a bundle of introjected standards and attitudes; Perls suggests that as long as the top dog (or, according to Freud, superego) remains introjected and unassimilated, the demands expressed by the top dog will continue to feel unreasonable and imposed from outside. Projection, Perls suggested, is crucial in the formation and understanding of dreams. In his view all parts of a dream are projected, disowned fragments of ourselves. Every dream contains at least one unfinished situation that involves these projected parts. To

> The introjector does as others would like him to do, the projector does unto others what he accuses them of doing to him, the man in pathological confluence doesn't know who is doing what to whom, and the retroflector does to himself what he would like to do to others. . . . As introjection displays itself in the use of the pronoun "I" when the real meaning is "they"; as projection displays itself in the use of the pronouns "it" and "they," when the real meaning is "I"; as confluence displays itself in the use of the pronoun "we" when the real meaning is in question; so retroflection displays itself in the use of the reflective [sic], "myself." [Perls, 1973, pp. 40–41]

> I especially prefer to work with dreams. I believe that in a dream we have a clear existential message of what's missing in our lives, what we avoid doing and living, and we have plenty of material to reassimilate and re-own the alienated parts of ourselves. [Perls, 1969a, p. 76]

---

[4]Perls notes that the experience of confluence is not always pathological; he is talking here, however, of *neurotic* confluence.

work on the dream is to reown these projected parts and thereby to close the unfinished gestalt.

STRUCTURE

Body

Perls views the mind-body split of most psychologies as both arbitrary and misleading. Mental activity is simply activity that is carried on at a less intense level than physical activity. Thus our bodies are direct manifestations of who we are. Perls suggests that by simply observing our most apparent physical behaviors—posture, breathing, movements—we can learn an immense amount about ourselves.

Social Relationships

Perls views the individual as participating in a field from which the individual is differentiated but inseparable. Contact and withdrawal functions are crucial in determining an individual's existence; one aspect of contact and withdrawal from the environment includes relationships with other people. In fact, the sense of relatedness to a group is, Perls suggests, our primary psychological survival impulse. Neurosis results from rigidities in defining the contact boundary with regard to other people and an inability to find and maintain proper balance with them.

Will

Perls lays a good deal of stress on the importance of being aware of one's preferences and being able to act on them. Knowing one's own preferences entails knowing one's needs; emergence of the dominant need is experienced as preference for what will satisfy the need. Perls's discussion of preference is very close to what is generally called will. In choosing to use the term *preference,* Perls is emphasizing the organismic, natural quality of healthy willing. Willing is simply one of various mental activities; it entails the limiting of awareness to certain specific areas in order to carry through a set of actions directed toward satisfying certain specific needs.

Emotions

Emotions are the very life of us . . . emotions are the very language of the organism; they modify the basic excitement according to the situation which has to be met. [Perls, 1973, p. 23]

Perls views emotion as the force that energizes all action. Emotions are the expression of our basic excitement, the ways and means of expressing our choices as well as satisfying our needs. Emotion is differentiated according to varying situations—for example, by the adrenal glands into anger and fear or by the sex glands into libido. The emotional excitement mobilizes the muscular system. If muscular expression of emotion is prevented, we build up anxiety, which is the bottling up of excitement. Once we are anxious, we try to desensitize our sensory systems in order to reduce the built-up excitement; it is at this point that symptoms such as frigidity and not listening—what Perls calls the "holes in our personalities"—develop. This emotional desensitizing is at the root of the avoidance of awareness that Perls finds basic to neurosis.

Intellect

Perls believed that intellect in our society has been overvalued and overused, particularly in attempts to understand human nature. He believed strongly in what he called the wisdom of the organism, but he saw this wisdom to be a kind of intuition based more in emotion than in intellect, and more in nature than in conceptual systems.

The intellect, Perls frequently asserted, has been reduced to a computerlike mechanism used for playing a series of fitting games. Preoccupation with asking *why* things happen prevents people from experiencing *how* they happen; thus genuine emotional awareness is blocked in the interest of providing explanations. Explaining, according to Perls, is the property of the intellect and constitutes something much less than understanding.

Perls felt that verbiage production, one expression of intellect, is particularly overvalued in our culture. He suggests that there are three levels of such production: chickenshit (social chitchat), bullshit (excuses, rationalization), and elephantshit (theorizing, particularly of a philosophical/psychological sort).

Self

Perls had no interest in glorifying the concept of self to include anything beyond the everyday, obvious manifestations of who we are. We are who we are; maturity and psychological health involve being able to claim that statement, rather than being caught by feeling that we are who we should be or we are who we would like to be. Our self-boundaries are constantly shifting in interaction with our environments. We can, given some level of awareness, rely on our organismic wisdom to define those boundaries and to direct the rhythm of contact with and withdrawal from the environment.

The notion of "self" or "I" is for Perls not a static, objectifiable notion. The "I" is identified with whatever the emerging foreground-figure experience happens to be; all aspects of the healthy organism (sensory, motor, psychological, etc.) identify themselves temporarily with the emergent gestalt, and the experience of "I" is this totality of identifications.

THERAPY

Therapist

Perls suggests that the therapist is basically a projection screen on which the patient sees his or her own missing potential; the task of

With full awareness you become aware of this organismic self-regulation, you can let the organism take over without interfering, without interrupting; we can rely on the wisdom of the organism. And the contrast to this is the whole pathology of self-manipulation, environmental control, and so on, that interferes with this subtle organismic self-control. [Perls, 1969a]

In Gestalt Therapy we write the "self" with lower case "s" not capital S. Capital S is a relic from the time when we had a soul, or an ego, or something extra special; "self" means just yourself—for better, for worse, in sickness, in health and nothing else. [Perls, 1969a, p. 76]

therapy is the patient's reowning of this potential. The therapist is, above all, a skillful frustrator. While offering the patient satisfaction through offering attention and acceptance, the therapist frustrates the patient by refusing to give the patient the support that he or she lacks within. The therapist acts as a catalyst in helping the patient break through avoidance and impasse points; the therapist's primary catalytic tool is helping the patient to see *how* he or she consistently interrupts himself or herself, avoids awareness, plays roles, and so forth.

Finally, the therapist is human, and the therapist's encounter with a patient involves the meeting of two individuals, which includes but also extends beyond the role-defined therapist-patient encounter.

Perls believed that individual therapy was obsolete, both inefficient and often ineffective. He suggested that work in groups had a good deal more to offer, whether the work explicitly involved the entire group or took the form of interaction between the therapist and one individual within the group. He suggested that the group can be enormously valuable in providing a microcosmic world situation in which people can explore their attitudes and behavior toward each other. Group support in the "safe emergency" of the therapeutic situation also can be extremely useful to an individual, as can identification with other members' conflicts and their working out of those conflicts.

Work with Dreams

Perls suggests that dreams are messages that can help us to understand the unfinished situations we are carrying around with us, what we are missing in our lives, what we are avoiding doing, and how we are avoiding and disowning parts of ourselves. He describes the opportunities for growth through work with dreams as follows:

> In Gestalt Therapy we don't interpret dreams. We do something more interesting with them. Instead of analyzing and further cutting up the dream, we want to bring it back to life. And the way to bring it back to life is to re-live the dream as if it were happening now. Instead of telling the dream as if it were a story in the past, act it out in the present, so that it becomes a part of yourself, so that you are really involved.
>
> If you understand what you can do with dreams, you can do a tremendous lot for yourself on your own. Just take any old dream or dream fragment, it doesn't matter. As long as a dream is remembered, it is still alive and available, and it still contains an unfinished, unassimilated situation. When we are working on dreams, we usually take only a small bit from the dream, because you can get so much from even a little bit.
>
> So if you want to work on your own, I suggest you write the dream down and make a list of *all* the details in the dream. Get every person, every thing, every mood, and then work on these to *become* each one of them. Ham it up, and really transform yourself into each of the different items. Really *become* that thing—whatever it is in a dream—*become* it. Use your magic. Turn into that ugly frog or whatever is there—the dead

When I work I am not Fritz Perls. I become nothing—no thing, a catalyst, and I enjoy my work. I forget myself and surrender to your plight. And once we have closure I come back to the audience, a prima donna demanding appreciation. I can work with anybody. I cannot work successfully with everybody. [Perls, 1969b, pp. 228–229]

thing, the live thing, the demon—and stop thinking. Lose your mind and come to your senses. Every little bit is a piece of the jigsaw puzzle, which together will make up a much larger whole—a much stronger, happier, more completely *real* personality.

Next, take each one of these different items, characters, and parts, and let them have encounters between them. Write a script. By "write a script," I mean have a dialogue between the two opposing parts and you will find—especially if you get the correct opposites—that they always start out fighting each other. All the different parts—any part in the dream is yourself, is a projection of yourself, and if there are inconsistent sides, and you use them to fight each other, you have the eternal conflict game, the self-torture game. As the process of encounter goes on, there is a mutual learning until we come to a oneness and integration of the two opposing forces. Then the civil war is finished, and your energies are ready for your struggles with the world. . . .

We find all we need in the dream, or in the perimeter of the dream, the environment of the dream. The existential difficulty, the missing part of the personality, they are all there. It's a kind of central attack right into the midst of your non-existence.

The dream is an excellent opportunity to find the holes in the personality. So if you work on dreams it is better if you do it with someone else who can point out where you avoid. Understanding the dream means realizing when you are avoiding the obvious. The only danger is that this other person might come too quickly to the rescue and tell you what is going on in you, instead of giving yourself the chance of discovering yourself.

And if you understand the meaning of each time you identify with some bit of a dream, each time you translate an *it* into an *I,* you increase in vitality and in your potential. [Perls, 1969a, pp. 68–70]

Dreamwork Sample

LINDA: *I dreamed that I watch . . . a lake . . . drying up, and there is a small island in the middle of the lake, and a circle of . . . porpoises—they're like porpoises except that they can stand up, so they're like porpoises that are like people, and they're in a circle, sort of like a religious ceremony, and it's very sad—I feel very sad because they can breathe, they are sort of dancing around the circle, but the water, their element, is drying up. So it's like a dying—like watching a race of people, or a race of creatures, dying. And they are mostly females, but a few of them have a small male organ, so there are a few males there, but they won't live long enough to reproduce, and their element is drying up. And there is one that is sitting over here near me and I'm talking to this porpoise and he has prickles on his tummy, sort of like a porcupine, and they don't seem to be a part of him. And I think that there's one good point about the water drying up, I think—well, at least at the bottom, when all the water dries up, there will probably be some* sort of treasure there, because at the bottom of the lake there should be things that have fallen in, like coins or something, but I look carefully and all that I can find is an old license plate. . . . That's the dream.

FRITZ: *Will you please play the license plate.*

LINDA: *I am an old license plate, thrown in the bottom of a lake. I have no use because I'm no value—although I'm not rusted—I'm outdated, so I can't be used as a license plate . . . and I'm just thrown on the rubbish heap. That's what I did with a license plate, I threw it on a rubbish heap.*

FRITZ: *Well, how do you feel about this?*

LINDA: *(quietly) I don't like it. I don't like being a license plate—useless.*

FRITZ: *Could |you| talk |about |this. | That |was| such |a |long |dream until you come to find the license plate, I'm sure this must be of great importance.*

LINDA: *(sighs) Useless. Outdated. . . . The use of a license plate is to allow—give a car permission to go . . . and I can't give any more permission to do anything because I'm outdated. . . . In California, they just paste a little—you buy a sticker—and stick it on the car, on the old license plate. (faint attempt at humor) So maybe someone could put me on their car and stick this sticker on me, I don't know . . .*

FRITZ: *OK, now play the lake.*

LINDA: *I'm a lake . . . I'm drying up, and disappearing, soaking into the earth . . . (with a touch of surprise) dying. . . . But when I soak into the earth, I become part of the earth—so maybe I water the surrounding area, so . . . even in the lake, even in my bed, flowers can grow (sighs). . . . New life can grow . . . from me (cries). . . .*

FRITZ: *You get the existential message?*

LINDA: *Yes. (sadly, but with conviction) I can paint—I can create—I can create beauty. I can no longer reproduce, I'm like the porpoise. . . . but I . . . I'm . . . I . . . keep wanting to say I'm food . . . I . . . as water becomes . . . I water the earth, and give life—growing things, the water—they need both the earth and water, and the . . . and the air and the sun, but as the water from the lake, I can play a part in something, and producing—feeding.*

FRITZ: *You see the contrast: On the surface, you find something, some artifact—the license plate, the artificial you—but then when you go deeper, you find the apparent death of the lake is actually fertility . . .*

LINDA: *And I don't need a license plate, or a permission, a license in order to . . .*

FRITZ: *(gently) Nature doesn't need a license plate to grow. You*

> *don't have to be useless, if you are organismically creative, which means if you are involved.*
> LINDA: *And I don't need permission to be creative. . . . Thank you.* [Perls, 1969a, pp. 81–82]

EVALUATION

Gestalt therapy is, above all, a synthesis of approaches to understanding human psychology and behavior. This does not take away from either its uniqueness or its usefulness; in appropriately Gestalt fashion, uniqueness and usefulness lie in the nature of the whole rather than in the derivation of parts.

As such a synthesis, Gestalt therapy has usefully incorporated a great deal from psychoanalytic and existential psychology, as well as bits and pieces from behaviorism (the emphasis on behavior and the obvious), psychodrama (the enacting of conflicts), group psychotherapy (work in groups), and Zen Buddhism (minimum intellectualization and focus on present awareness). The spirit of Gestalt therapy is a humanistic, growth-oriented one which, in addition to Perls's associations with the Esalen Institute, has made Gestalt therapy a major force in the human-potential movement. The commonsensical, conversational nature of the literature of Gestalt therapy, as well as the attitudes of many Gestalt therapists, is beginning to contribute to a demystification of psychotherapy that many people are finding welcome.

Perls's work was more explicitly focused around the practice of psychotherapy than around a theory of personality. Not surprisingly, this leaves certain holes in any attempt to extrapolate a cohesive theory out of his work. Yet this is in itself consistent with his view of the usefulness of theory as theory. If the attitude and the experience that are the Gestalt approach fit in some basic way with our own attitudes and experience, the Gestalt approach offers us a great deal in the realm of extending our own awareness.

Gestalt therapy developed in reaction to what Perls saw to be an increasing tendency toward rigidity and dogmatism in psychology, particularly psychoanalytic psychology. Perls has made a significant contribution to a holistic psychology of the human organism and to the psychology of human awareness.

> Most people take explaining as being identical with understanding. There is a great difference. Like now, I can explain a lot to you. I can give you a lot of sentences that help you build an intellectual model of how we function. Maybe some of you feel the coincidence of these sentences and explanations with your real life, and this would mean understanding.
>
> Right now I can only hypnotize you, persuade you, make you believe I'm right. You don't know. I'm just preaching something. You wouldn't learn from my words. Learning is discovery. . . . And I hope I can assist you in learning, in discovering something about yourself. [Perls, 1969a, p. 25]

THE THEORY FIRSTHAND

This is the introduction to *Gestalt Therapy Verbatim.* It is a compressed and direct example of the way Fritz Perls presented his point of view.

I want to talk about the present development of humanistic psychology. It took us a long time to debunk the whole Freudian crap, and now we

are entering a new and more dangerous phase. We are entering the phase
of the turner-onners: turn on to instant cure, instant joy, instant sensory-awareness. We are entering the phase of the quacks and the con-men,
who think if you get some breakthrough, you are cured—disregarding
any growth requirements, disregarding any of the real potential, the inborn genius in all of you. If this is becoming a faddism, it is as dangerous
to psychology as the year-decade-century-long lying on the couch. At
least the damage we suffered under psychoanalysis does little to the patient except for making him deader and deader. This is not as obnoxious
as this quick-quick-quick thing. The psychoanalysts at least bring good
will with them. I must say I am *very* concerned with what's going on right
now.

One of the objections I have against anyone calling himself a Gestalt
Therapist is that he uses technique. A technique is a gimmick. A gimmick should be used only in the extreme case. We've got enough people
running around collecting gimmicks, more gimmicks, and abusing
them. These techniques, these tools, are quite useful in some seminar
on sensory awareness or joy, just to give you some idea that you are
still alive, that the myth that the American is a corpse is not true, that
he *can* be alive. But the sad fact is that this jazzing-up more often becomes a dangerous substitute activity, another phony therapy that *prevents* growth. . . .

In Gestalt Therapy, we are working for something else. We are here
to promote the growth process and develop the human potential. We do
not talk of instant joy, instant sensory awareness, instant cure. The
growth process is a process that takes time. We can't just snap our fingers and say, "Come on, let's be gay! Let's do this!" You can turn on if
you want to with LSD, and jazz it up, but that has nothing to do with
the sincere work of that approach to psychiatry which I call Gestalt
Therapy. In therapy, we have not only to get through the role-playing.
We also have to fill in the holes in the personality to make the person
whole and complete again. And again, as before, this can't be done by
the turner-oners. In Gestalt Therapy we have a better way, but it is no
magic shortcut. You don't have to be on a couch or in a Zendo for
twenty or thirty years, but you have to invest yourself, and it takes
time to grow.

The conditioners also start out with a false assumption. Their basic
premise that behavior is "law" is a lot of crap. That is: we learn to
breathe, to eat, we learn to walk. "Life is nothing but whatever conditions
into which it has been born." *If,* in the behaviorist reorganization of our
behavior, we get a modification towards better self-support, and throw
away all the artificial social roles we have learned, then I am on the side
of the behaviorists. The stopping block seems to be anxiety. Always anxiety. Of course you are anxious if you have to learn a new way of behavior,
and the psychiatrists usually are afraid of anxiety. They don't know what
anxiety *is*. Anxiety is the excitement, the *élan vital* which we carry with
us, and which becomes stagnated if we are unsure about the role we have
to play. If we don't know if we will get applause or tomatoes, we hesitate,
so the heart begins to race and all the excitement can't flow into activity,
and we have stage fright. So the formula of anxiety is very simple: anxiety is the gap between the *now* and the *then*. If you are in the now, you
can't be anxious, because the excitement flows immediately into ongoing
spontaneous activity. If you are in the now, you are creative, you are in-

ventive. If you have your senses ready, if you have your eyes and ears open, like every small child, you find a solution.

A release to spontaneity, to the support of our total personality—yes, yes, yes. The pseudo-spontaneity of the turner-oners as they become hedonistic—just, let's do something, let's take LSD, let's have instant joy, instant sensory-awareness—*No*. So between the Scylla of conditioning, and the Charybdis of turning on, there is something—a person that is real, a person who takes a stand.

As you know, there is a rebellion on in the United States. We discover that producing things, and living for things, and the exchange of things, is not the ultimate meaning of life, We discover that the meaning of life is that it is to be lived, and it is not to be traded and conceptualized and squeezed into a pattern of systems. We realize that manipulation and control are not the ultimate joy of life.

But we must also realize that so far we only have a rebellion. We don't have a revolution yet. There is still much of substance missing. . . . It is protest, it's a rebelliousness, which is fine as such, but it's not an end. I've got plenty of contact with the youngsters of our generation who are in despair. . . . To be able to do this, there is only one way through: to become real, to learn to take a stand, to develop one's center, to understand the basis of existentialism: a rose is a rose is a rose. I am what I am, and at this moment I cannot possibly be different from what I am. That is what this book is about. I give you the Gestalt prayer, maybe as a direction. The prayer in Gestalt Therapy is:

I do my thing, and you do your thing.
I am not in this world to live up to your expectations
And you are not in this world to live up to mine.
You are you and I am I,
And if by chance we find each other, it's beautiful.
If not, it can't be helped.

[PERLS, 1969A, PP. 1–4]

Exercises
Continuum of Awareness
In discussing Perls's concept of awareness, we mentioned his use of a *continuum of awareness* as a means of encouraging self-awareness. Paradoxically, the continuum of awareness is an exercise that requires immense discipline in its practice, although it has as a goal the development of one's capacity for spontaneity.

The instructions are simple: Just be aware, from second to second, of what you are experiencing—*how* you experience your existence *now*. Observe the progress of your awareness. When do you interrupt yourself with planning, rehearsing, fantasizing, remembering? Do you evaluate rather than permit pure awareness? What does the discipline of awareness feel like? *Pay particular attention to the ways in which you sabotage your own attempts at sustained awareness.* Are these ways in which you habitually prevent yourself from fully contacting the world and your own experience? You might also try to prolong and stay in contact with the moment at which you want to avoid continued awareness. Can you get a sense of what you are avoiding? Does a situation emerge that you feel is unfinished?

The attempt in this exercise is to enhance your capacity for experiencing by developing the capacity to fully experience what *is*. The assumption is that by *paying attention* to our experience, moment to moment, we can avail ourselves of what we need to live fulfilled and meaningful lives.

ANNOTATED BIBLIOGRAPHY

Perls, Frederick S. *Ego, hunger, and aggression.* New York: Random House, 1947. Perls' most intellectually oriented work, it explains in detail the theory of Gestalt therapy in its development from psychoanalysis and Gestalt psychology.

———. *The Gestalt approach; Eyewitness to therapy.* Ben Lomond, Calif.: Science and Behavior Books, 1973. Perls' last manuscripts, published together and posthumously. *The Gestalt Approach* offers an excellent, readable, and theoretical exposition of Gestalt therapy, while *Eyewitness to Therapy* includes the transcripts from a series of films of therapy sessions, which Perls planned to use as teaching material.

———. *Gestalt therapy verbatim.* Lafayette, Calif.: The Real People Press, 1969a. Another (in addition to *The Gestalt Approach* above) really excellent discussion of the basics of Gestalt therapy, including transcripts of therapy sessions.

———. *In and out of the garbage pail.* Lafayette, Calif.: The Real People Press, 1969b. Perls' autobiography, full of anecdotes and written in a casual, humorous style; an experience in Gestalt writing which describes the origins and development of Gestalt therapy.

Fagan, Joen, and Shepherd, Irma (Eds.) *Gestalt therapy now.* Palo Alto, Calif.: Science and Behavior Books, 1970. Includes papers by a number of Gestalt therapists in addition to several of Fritz Perls' lectures. It offers an interesting selection of viewpoints concerning the theory, techniques, and applications of Gestalt therapy.

REFERENCES

Enright, John. An introduction to Gestalt therapy. In *Gestalt therapy primer.* F. D. Stephenson (Ed.) Springfield, Ill.: Charles C. Thomas, 1975.

———. *Enlightening Gestalt: waking up from the nightmare.* Mill Valley, California: Pro Telos, 1980.

Fagan, Joen, and Irma Shepherd (Eds.) *Gestalt therapy now.* Palo Alto, Calif.: Science and Behavior Books, 1970.

Gaines, Jack. *Fritz Perls: here and now.* Millbrae, Calif.: Celestial Arts, 1979.

Khayaám, Omar. *The original Rubáiyát of Omar Khayaám.* Translated by Robert Graves and Omar Ali-Shah. New York: Doubleday, 1968.

Naranjo, Claudio. *The techniques of Gestalt therapy.* Berkeley, Calif.: SAT Press, 1973.

Perls, Frederick S. *Ego, hunger and aggression.* New York: Random House, 1947.

———. Workshop vs. individual therapy. *Journal of Long Island Consultation Center* 15(2), 13–17, 1967.

———. *Gestalt therapy verbatim,* Lafayette, Calif.: The Real People Press, 1969a.

———. *In and out of the garbage pail.* Lafayette, Calif.: The Real People Press, 1969b.

———. 1973. *The Gestalt approach; Eyewitness to therapy.* Ben Lomond, Calif.: Science and Behavior Books, New York: Bantam, 1976.

Perls, F. S.; Hefferline, R. F.; and Goodman, Paul. *Gestalt therapy*. New York: Dell, 1951.

Shepard, Martin. *Fritz: an intimate portrait of Fritz Perls and gestalt therapy*. New York: (Saturday Review Press) Dutton. 1975.

CHAPTER 8
WILLIAM JAMES AND THE PSYCHOLOGY OF CONSCIOUSNESS

The philosophy of William James (1842–1910) is emerging from a period of relative obscurity. Only recently have his major works been reprinted and his theories reevaluated. His interest in inner experiences passed out of fashion as psychology became more involved in the discoveries of psychoanalysis and behaviorism. In addition, the increasing fixation on objective data left little room for the brilliant and incisive speculations of James's philosophy.

Now we are in the midst of a new wave of research into the nature of consciousness. Researchers concerned with the implications of altered states of consciousness, paranormal phenomenon, and intuitive and mystical states are once again turning to James.

James's works are free of the arguments that currently divide psychological theorists. He acknowledged that different models were necessary to understand different kinds of data and was concerned more with clarifying the issues than with developing a unified approach. James's philosophies prefaced the development of the field of psychology; he anticipated Skinner's behaviorism, existential psychology, Gestalt theory, and the Rogerian self-concept.

James was a self-confessed "moral" psychologist, a term that has almost vanished from our modern vocabulary. He was fully aware that no researcher can be truly objective. He tried to remind other teachers that their actions always had ethical and moral implications: If your students believe what you are teaching them and act on these beliefs, your teaching has real consequences. James himself took full responsibility for his actions and worked passionately for the side he advocated. "I can't bring myself, as so many men seem able to, to blink the evil out of sight, and gloss it over. It's as real as the good, and if it is denied, good must be denied too. It must be accepted and hated, and resisted while there's breath in our bodies" (James, 1926, I, p. 158).

His major works, *The Principles of Psychology, The Varieties of Religious Experience,* and *Pragmatism,* continued to be read. The questions that he posed are still largely unanswered but are more and more in the center of current controversies within psychology and philosophy.

PERSONAL HISTORY

William James was born into a well-to-do New England family on January 11, 1842. In his early years he traveled with his parents to Newport, New York, Paris, London, Geneva, Boulogne, and Bonn. He studied painting for a year, then he became interested in science. He entered Harvard, unsure of what area to pursue. Initially, he studied chemistry, then comparative anatomy. In 1863 he transferred to the medical school. In 1865 he took a leave of absence to accompany the naturalist Louis Agassiz on an expedition to the Amazon Basin. The hazards and discomforts of the trip convinced James that he was better suited to thinking and writing about science than engaging in active scientific exploration.

William James is a towering figure in the history of American thought—without doubt the foremost psychologist this country has produced. His depiction of mental life is faithful, vital, subtle. In verve he has no equal. [Allport, 1961, p. xiii]

James was neither a phenomenologist nor an existentialist . . . to speak of him as a pragmatist is also inadequate. He was a genius of his own kind, who gave . . . a perspective and a context wholly novel in implication. [McDermott, 1977, p. xi]

He returned to Harvard for another year, left again to study in Germany, returned, and finally received his medical degree in 1869. After his graduation, he entered into a long, pronounced depression. He experienced himself as worthless; several times he considered suicide. One incident occurred during this period that had lasting and profound effects on his life.

My coming was a mistake . . . I am convinced now, for good, that I am cut out for a speculative rather than an active life. . . . I had misgivings to this effect before starting: but I was so filled with enthusiasm, and the romance of the thing seemed so great, that I stifled them. Here on the ground the romance vanishes and the misgivings float up. [James, 1926, I, pp. 61–63]

Whilst in this state of philosophic pessimism and general depression of spirits about my prospects, I went one evening into a dressing-room in the twilight to procure some article that was there; when suddenly there fell upon me without any warning, just as if it came out of the darkness, a horrible fear of my own existence. Simultaneously there arose in my mind the image of an epileptic patient whom I had seen in the asylum, a black-haired youth with greenish skin, entirely idiotic, who used to sit all day on one of the benches, or rather shelves against the wall, with his knees drawn up against his chin, and the coarse gray undershirt, which was his only garment, drawn over them inclosing his entire figure. He sat there like a sort of sculptured Egyptian cat or Peruvian mummy, moving nothing but his black eyes and looking absolutely non-human. This image and my fear entered into a species of combination with each other. *That shape am I,* I felt, potentially. Nothing that I possess can defend me against that fate, if the hour for it should strike for me as it struck for him. There was such a horror of him . . . it was as if something hitherto solid within my breast gave way entirely, and I became a mass of quivering fear. After this the universe was changed for me altogether. I awoke morning after morning with a horrible dread at the pit of my stomach, and with a sense of the insecurity of life that I never knew before, and that I have never felt since. . . . It gradually faded, but for months I was unable to go out into the dark alone.

In general I dreaded to be left alone. I remember wondering how other people could live, how I myself had ever lived, so unconscious of that pit of insecurity beneath the surface of life. My mother in particular, a very cheerful person, seemed to me a perfect paradox in her unconsciousness of danger, which you may well believe I was very careful not to disturb by revelations of my own state of mind. [James, 1958, pp. 135–136]*

His diary and letters recorded the steps in his recovery:

February 1, 1870: Today I about touched bottom, and perceive plainly that I must face the choice with open eyes: shall I *frankly* throw the moral business overboard, as one unsuited to my innate aptitudes, or shall I follow it, and it alone, making everything else merely stuff for it? I will give the latter alternative a fair trial. [In Perry, 1935, I, p. 322]

The depression continued, however, until April 30, 1870, when James made a conscious and a purposeful end to it. He chose to believe

---

*In this passage James does not state that he is describing himself; however, he is quoting from his own journal of that period [H. James, 1926, I, pp. 145-148.]

in free will. "My first act of free will shall be to believe in free will. For the remainder of the year, I will . . . voluntarily cultivate the feeling of moral freedom. . . ." (James, 1926, I, p. 147).

After his recovery James took a teaching position at Harvard. He taught first in the department of anatomy and physiology; several years later, he taught the first courses in psychology.

In 1878 he married and began to work on his textbook, *The Principles of Psychology,* published in 1890. His colorful prose as well as his concern with moral and practical issues made him a popular lecturer. Two collections of talks, *The Will to Believe and Other Popular Essays* (1896) and *Talks to Teachers* (1899a), promoted his growing national reputation. In 1902 he published a lecture series entitled *Varieties of Religious Experience.* In the last decade of his life he wrote and lectured on pragmatism, a philosophic movement founded by James, which proposed that meaning could be evaluated by its utility and that truth might be tested by the practical consequences of belief.

After teaching a semester at Stanford University (interrupted by the great earthquake of 1906) he returned to the East, retired from Harvard, and continued to write and lecture until his death in 1910.

He was the third president of the American Psychological Association (1894–1895) and was active in establishing psychology as a discipline independent of neurology and philosophy. James's definition of psychology, "the description and explanation of states of consciousness as such" (1892, p. 1) is exciting a new generation of students and researchers.

> Inborn rationalists and inborn pragmatists will never convert each other. We shall always look on them as spectral and they on us as trashy—irredeemably both! . . . why not simply express ourselves positively, and trust that the truer view quietly will displace the other.
> [James, 1926, II, p. 272]

INTELLECTUAL ANTECEDENTS

James grew up as a member of a remarkable and gifted family. His father was one of the most controversial writers on politics and religion in the nineteenth century. Their home was a hothouse of new ideas. James became a passionate and skilled speaker in a family that rewarded and demanded such skills. His brother, Henry James, more introspective than William, became one of the great masters of fiction. The brothers were in constant communication and remained devoted fans and thorough critics of each other's works (Matthiessen, 1980).

James was familiar with most of the leading philosophers, researchers, writers, and educators of the day and corresponded with a number of them. He frequently acknowledged his debt to this or that thinker but did not seem to be a disciple of any. A single exception may be the French philosopher Renouvier, whose work sparked James's early decision to believe in free will. Renouvier's approach to other thorny metaphysical problems influenced James's own brand of pragmatism. In psychology he was impressed with the work of Wundt, Helmholtz, and Hobart in Germany; the research of Binet and Charcot in France; the writings of Bain and Myers in England; and the Canadian contributions of Maurice Bucke. James read extensively and peppers his work with long quotes from literally hundreds of other writers.

MAJOR CONCEPTS

James was interested in the full range of human psychology, from brain-stem functioning to religious ecstacy, from the perception of space to ESP research. He often argued both sides of a controversy with equal brilliance. "There was no limit to James's curiosity and there was no theory, however unpopular, with which he was not willing to play" (MacLeod, 1969, p. v). He pursued most vigorously the task of understanding and explaining the basic units of thought. Fundamental concepts including the nature of thought, attention, habit, will, and emotion held his interest.

For James personality arises from the continual interplay of instincts, habits, and personal choices. He viewed personal differences, developmental stages, psychopathology, and the rest of personality as arrangements and rearrangements of the basic building blocks supplied by nature and slowly refined by evolution.

Reading James carefully reveals some contradictions. He was aware of this, understanding that what holds in one case may not hold in other cases. Instead of attempting to create a grand and unified scheme, he indulged in what he called "pluralistic thinking," that is, holding more than one theory at a time. James acknowledged that psychology was an immature science with not enough information to formulate consistent laws of sensation, perception, or even the nature of consciousness. Thus he was at ease with a multitude of theories, even with those that contradicted his own. In an introduction to a book attacking his theories of personality he wrote: "I am not convinced of all of Dr. Sidis' positions, but I can cordially recommend this volume to all classes of readers as a treatise both interesting and instructive, and original in a high degree . . ." (in Sidis, 1898, p. vi).

In the conclusion to the briefer edition of his textbook (1892) he admits to the limits of psychology, limits that are still present today.

> It seems to me that psychology is like physics before Galileo's time—not a single elementary law yet caught a glimpse of. [James, 1890,]

When, then, we talk of "psychology as a natural science," we must not assume that that means a sort of psychology that stands at last on solid ground. It means just the reverse; it means a psychology particularly fragile, and into which the waters of metaphysical criticism leak at every joint. . . . A string of raw facts; a little gossip and wrangle about opinions; a little classification and generalization on the mere descriptive level; a strong prejudice that we *have* states of mind, and that our brain conditions them . . . This is no science, it is only the hope of a science. [1961, pp. 334–335]

Characteristics of Thought
Personal Consciousness

"Every thought tends to be part of a personal consciousness" (James, 1890, I, p. 225). Therefore, says James, there is no such thing as individual consciousness independent of an owner. There is only the process of thought as experienced or perceived by an individual. Consciousness always exists in relation to a person; it is not a special kind of stuff.

Changes in Consciousness

The only thing which psychology has a right to postulate at the outset is the fact of thinking itself. . . . [James, 1890, I, p. 224]

"Within each personal consciousness thought is always changing" (James, 1890, I, p. 225). We can never have the same exact thought twice. We may see the same object, hear the same tone, taste the same food, but our consciousness of those perceptions changes each time. What seems upon cursory inspection to be repetitious thought is actually a changing series, each unique, each partially determined by previous modifications of the original thought.

> Often we are ourselves struck at the strange differences in our successive views of the same thing. We wonder how we ever could have opined as we did last month about a certain matter. We have outgrown the possibility of that state of mind, we know not how. From one year to another we see things in new light. What was unreal has grown real, and what was exciting is insipid. The friends we used to care the world for are shrunken to shadows; the women, once so divine, the stars, the woods, and the waters, how now so dull and common; the young girls that brought an aura of infinity, at present hardly distinguishable existences; the pictures so empty; and as for the books, what *was* there to find so mysteriously significant in Goethe, or in John Mill so full of weight? [James, 1890, I, p. 233]

Continuous Thought

"Within each personal consciousness, thought is sensibly continuous" (James, 1890, I, p. 237). Whereas some theorists shy away from the seeming paradox of personality as something continuous and undergoing continual change, James suggested a resolution: "The passing thought, according to Professor James, is the thinker. Each passing wave of consciousness, each passing thought is aware of all that has preceded in consciousness; each pulse of thought as it dies away transmits its title of ownership of its mental content to the succeeding thought" (Sidis, 1898, p. 190). What is present at the moment, conscious or not, is the personality.[1]

Each emerging thought takes part of its force, focus, content, and direction from preceding thoughts. "Consciousness, then, does not ap-

[1]See the sections on "Self" in Rogers, Perls, Skinner, and Zen Buddhism for different conclusions derived from this assumption.

pear to itself chopped up in bits. Such words as 'chain' or 'train' do not describe it fitly. . . . It is nothing jointed: it flows. A 'river' or a 'stream' are the metaphors by which it is most naturally described. *In talking of it hereafter, let us call it the stream of thought, of consciousness, or of subjective life"* (James, 1890, I, p. 239).[2]

This stream is continuous. James (as did Freud) based many of his ideas about mental functions on the assumption of continuous thought. There are gaps in feelings; there are gaps in awareness; but even when there are perceived gaps in consciousness, there is no accompanying feeling of discontinuity. For example, when you awaken in the morning, you never wonder who it is who is waking up. You feel no need to rush to a mirror to verify, to see, if it is *you*. You need no convincing that the consciousness you awoke with is the same as the one that went to sleep.

The traditional psychology talks like one who should say a river consists of nothing but pailsful, spoonsful, quartpotsful, barrelsful, and other moulded forms of water. Even were the pails and the pots all actually standing in the stream, still between them the free water would continue to flow. It is just this free water of consciousness that psychologists resolutely overlook. [James, 1890, I, p. 255]

Consciousness Chooses

Consciousness is selective: "It is always interested more in one part of its object than in another, and welcomes and rejects, or chooses, all the while it thinks" (James, 1890, I, p. 284). What an individual chooses and what determines the choice is the subject matter of most of psychology. James draws attention to the major variables: attention and habit.

Attention

Philosophers before James (Locke, Hume, Harley, Spencer and others) assumed that the mind is passive and experience simply rains upon it. The personality then develops in direct proportion to the amounts of various experiences received. James considered this idea naive and the conclusions patently false. Before experience can be *experienced*, it must be attended to. *"My experience is what I agree to attend to.* Only those items which I *notice* shape my mind—without selective interest, experience is an utter chaos. Interest alone gives accent and emphasis, light and shade, background and foreground—intelligible perspective, in a word" (James, 1890, I, p. 402). Although the capacity to make choices is restricted by conditioned habits, it is still possible, and for James essential, to make real and meaningful decisions from moment to moment.

The mind is at every stage a theatre of simultaneous possibilities. Consciousness consists in the comparison of these with each other, the selection of some, and the suppression of the rest. . . . [James, 1890, I, p. 288]

Habit

Habits are actions or thoughts that are seemingly automatic responses to a given experience. They differ from instincts in that a habit can be

---

[2]*Stream of consciousness*, a form of writing that attempts to mimic the flow and jumble of thought, arose in part from James's teaching. Gertrude Stein, a major exponent of this genre, was a student of James at Harvard.

created, modified, or eliminated by conscious direction. Habits are valuable and necessary. "Habit simplifies the movements required to achieve a given result, makes them more accurate and diminishes fatigue" (James, 1890, I, p. 112). In this sense habits are one facet of the acquisition of skills. On the other hand, "habit diminishes the conscious attention with which our acts are performed" (James, 1890, I, p. 114). Whether this is advantageous or not depends on the situation. Withdrawing attention from an action makes that action easier to perform but also makes it resistant to change. "The fact is that our virtues are habits as much as our vices. All our life, so far as it has definite form, is but a mass of habits—practical, emotional, and intellectual—systematically organized for our weal or woe, and bearing us irresistibly toward our destiny, whatever the latter may be" (James, 1899a, p. 33).

James was struck by the complexity of acquired habits as well as by their resistance to extinction. The following is one of his examples:

> With a view of cultivating the rapidity of visual and tactile perception, and the precision of respondent movements, which are necessary for success in every kind of prestidigitation, Houdin* early practised the art of juggling with balls in the air; and having, after a month's practice, become thorough master of the art of keeping up four balls at once, he placed a book before him, and, while the balls were in the air, accustomed himself to read without hesitation. "This," he says, "will probably seem to my readers very extraordinary; but I shall surprise them still more when I say that I have just amused myself with repeating this curious experiment. Though thirty years have elasped since the time I was writing, and though I have scarcely once touched the balls during that period, I can still manage to read with ease while keeping three balls up." (1890, I, p. 117)

> *[A stage magician who was the namesake of the famous Houdini.]

As an educator of students and teachers James was concerned with the formation of proper habits, habits that develop the capacity of attention. He suggested that systematic training of habits was far more important in education than the rote learning still so popular. "Continuity of training is the great means of making the nervous system act infallibly right" (James, 1899a, p. 35). Although much of our life is determined by habit, we still have the choice of which habits to cultivate.

A new habit is formed in three stages. First there must be need or desire, for example, the desire to exercise regularly or to understand French. Then one needs information: methods of learning how to maintain the habit. One might read books, attend classes, and consciously explore ways how others have developed the desired habit. The last state is simple repetition; consciously doing exercise or actually reading and speaking French until the acts become usual and *habitual*.

Habit is thus the enormous fly-wheel of society, its most precious conservative agent. . . . It is well for the world that in most of us, by the age of thirty, the character has set like plaster, and will never soften again. . . . [James, 1890, I, pp. 121–122]

The only things which we commonly see are those which we preperceive. [James, 1890, I, p. 444]

Fortunately, we can solve the problem of education without discovering or inventing additional reinforcers. We merely need to make better use of those we have. [Skinner, 1972, p. 173]

Will

Will is the pivotal point from which meaningful action can occur. "Acts of will are such acts only as cannot be inattentively performed. A distinct idea of what they are, and a deliberate *fiat* on the mind's part, must precede their execution" (James, 1899a, p. 83). James defined will as the combination of attention (focusing consciousness) and effort (overcoming inhibitions, laziness, or distractions). According to James, an idea inevitably produces an action unless another idea conflicts with it. Will is that process which holds one choice among the alternatives long enough to allow the actions to occur. "The essential achievement of the will, in short, when it is most 'voluntary', is to ATTEND to a difficult object and hold it fast before the mind" (James, 1890, II, p. 561).

> Suppose, for instance, that you are climbing a mountain, and have worked yourself into a position from which the only escape is by a terrible leap. Have faith that you can successfully make it, and your feet are nerved to its accomplishment. But mistrust yourself, and think of all the sweet things you have heard the scientists say of *maybes,* and you will hesitate so long that, at last, all unstrung and trembling, and launching yourself in a moment of despair, you roll in the abyss. In such a case (and it belongs to an enormous class), the part of wisdom as well as of courage is to *believe what is in the line of your needs,* for only by such belief is the need fulfilled. Refuse to believe, and you shall indeed be right, for you shall irretrievably perish. But believe, and again you shall be right, for you shall save yourself. You make one or the other of two possible universes true by your trust or mistrust. . . ." [James, 1896, p. 59]

Strengthening the Will

Being able to do what one wishes to do is not easy. Developing a strong enough will was a major concern to James in his writings. He suggested that one easy and available method was to accomplish a *useless* exercise every day. "Be systematically heroic in little unnecessary points, do something every day for no other reason than its difficulty, so that, when the hour of dire need draws nigh, it may find you not unnerved and untrained to stand the test. . . . The man who has daily inured himself to habits of concentrated attention, energetic volition, and self denial in unnecessary things will stand like a tower when everything rocks around him, and his softer fellow-mortals are winnowed like chaff in the blast" (James, 1899a, p. 38). The act itself is unimportant, being able to do it, *in spite of its being unimportant,* is the critical element.

Surrender of the Will

There are rare times when rather than strengthen his or her will, a person must surrender it, must allow it to be overwhelmed by inner experiences. In his studies of spiritual states, James found that at these moments other aspects of consciousness appeared to assume control.

Will is necessary to bring "one close to the complete unification aspired after, [however] it seems that the very last step must be left to other forces and performed without the help of its activity" (James, 1958, p. 170). By complete unification James means a state in which all the facets of the personality seem to be in harmony with one another and the person perceives the inner world and the external world as unified. Transcendence of limitations, mystical union, cosmic or unitive consciousness are some of the terms used to describe this transformation. It reorganizes the personality to include more than the will and more than personal identity. It is as if one finds oneself to be part of a larger system rather than a single, time-bound consciousness.

The Sentiment of Rationality

A man who thought he was dead was talking to a friend. Unable to convince him otherwise the friend finally asked, "Do dead men bleed?" "Of course not." The man took a needle and jabbed it into his friend's thumb. It began to bleed. The man looked at his thumb and then turned to his friend. "Hey, dead men do bleed!"

Why do you accept one rational idea or theory and reject another? James suggested that it is partly an emotional decision; we accept the one because it enables us to understand the facts in a more emotionally satisfying way. James describes this emotional satisfaction as "a strong feeling of ease, peace, rest. . . . This absence of all need to explain it, account for it, or justify it—is what I call the sentiment of rationality" (1948, pp. 3–4). Before a person will accept a theory (for example, any of the theories expounded in this book) two separate sets of needs must be satisfied. First, the theory must be intellectually palatable, consistent, logical, and so on. Second, it must be emotionally palatable; it must encourage us to think or act in ways that we find personally satisfying and acceptable.

An example can be seen in the way we seek advice. If, for instance, you wanted to get information about the effects of smoking marijuana, who would you go to for such information? Could you predict the kind of information and suggestions that would be offered by your parents, friends who don't smoke marijuana, friends who do, someone who sells marijuana, a police officer, a psychiatrist, a priest or minister, or a person working in a college counseling center? It is likely that you can predict in advance the kind and quality of information that each might offer as well as your willingness to accept the information once you hear it.

This aspect of decision making is often denied. We like to believe that we can make decisions based on purely rational grounds; yet there is this other critical variable, the desire to find facts that please us, that will make us most comfortable. James's sentiment of rationality is a first cousin to the defense mechanism that Freud calls rationalization. Rationalization involves the process of desiring and acquiring reasons to justify an act *already committed* for other, often irrational, reasons. The sentiment of rationality is the emotional loading brought to bear on an idea *before* we move toward accepting or not accepting it.

DYNAMICS

Psychological Growth

James rejected absolutes, such as "God" or "truth" or "idealism," in favor of personal experience and the discovery of what works for a person's self-improvement. A recurrent theme in his writings is that personal evolution is possible and that everyone has an inherent capacity to modify or change his or her attitudes and behaviors. He concludes that there is an underlying drive in human beings toward increasing their own well-being.

Nonattachment to Feelings

It was James's contention that a balance between detachment and the expression of feelings serves the organism best. He quotes Hannah Smith: "Let your emotions come or let them go . . . and make no account of them either way. . . . They really have nothing to do with the matter. They are not the indicators of your spiritual state, but are merely the indicators of your temperament or of your present physical condition" (in James, 1899a, p. 100).

Emotional Excitement

Although detachment is a desirable state, there are also advantages to being overwhelmed by one's feelings. Emotional upset is one means by which long-standing habits can be disrupted; it frees people to try new behaviors or to explore new areas of awareness. James himself experienced and researched psychological states arising from mystical experiences, hypnosis, faith healing, mediumship, psychedelic drugs, alcohol, and personal crisis. He concluded that the precipitating event was not the critical factor, it was the response the individual made to the arousal that formed the basis for change.

Healthy-Mindedness

Healthy-mindedness is James's term for acting as if things could go well, acting on ideals. Idealism was more than a philosophic concept to James; it was an active force. His own return to mental health began with his decision to hold fast to the ideal of free will. James argued that a positive attitude was more than useful; it was necessary. "I do not believe it to be healthy-minded to nurse the notion that ideals are self-sufficient and require no actualization to make us content. . . . Ideals ought to aim at the *transformation of reality*—no less!" (1926, II, p. 270).

Pragmatism

Pragmatism, originally a method of looking at experiences, became a school of philosophy in its own right. James developed it to clarify or

> I have no doubt whatever that most people live, whether physically, intellectually or morally, in a very restricted circle of their potential being. They make use of a very small portion of their possible consciousness . . . much like a man who, out of his whole bodily organism, should get into a habit of using and moving only his little finger. . . . We all have reservoirs of life to draw upon, of which we do not dream. [James, 1896]

eliminate unnecessary considerations about issues in one's life or one's thought. "Grant an idea or belief to be true, . . . what concrete difference will its being true make in any one's actual life?" (1909, p. v). If no practical differences exist whether an idea is true or false, then, James suggests, further discussion is pointless. From this he proposes a pragmatic or useful definition of truth. "True ideas are those we can assimilate, validate, corroborate, and verify. False ideas are those that we cannot" (1907, p. 199). He understands that there are truths that cannot be assimilated, and so on, but he points out that this second class of truths (which he sees as useless) may be put aside when one is faced with a personal choice or a real decision. Although this point of view may appear obvious to some, it was roundly attacked and criticized at its inception. James writes: "I fully expect the pragmatist's view of truth to run through the classic stages of a theory's career. First, you know, a new theory is attacked as absurd; then it is admitted to be true, but obvious and insignificant; finally it is seen to be so important that its adversaries claim that they themselves discovered it" (1948, p. 159).

Obstacles to Growth
Bad Habits

Pessimism is essentially a religious disease. [James, 1896]

Most obvious and most prevalent among the obstacles to growth in our daily lives are our own bad habits. They are, by definition, those forces that retard our development and limit our happiness. James suggested that we even have the bad habit of overlooking or ignoring our other bad habits. Examples might include fat people who "don't notice" the size of the portions they serve themselves and poor students who remain steadfastly unaware of when papers are due and when exams are to be given.

Most of our activities are habitual actions that we do with a minimum of awareness; habit patterns preclude new learning. James's concern is that many of our daily routines actually harm our overall well-being. The resistance to changing a habit becomes critical in that it prevents new possibilities from becoming part of our lives.

Unexpressed Emotions

Long before the rise of modern psychotherapy or the more evocative encounter movement, James saw that it was imperative to do something with emotional energy. To block it or to bottle it could lead to mental and physical illnesses. He felt it was unnecessary to express the exact emotion, especially if it might hurt oneself or others. But it was important to find some outlet for the arousal. He felt it was as necessary to express "noble" feelings as to express hostile ones. If one was feeling brave or charitable or compassionate, those feelings should be translated into actions rather than be allowed to subside.

Errors of Excess

It is common practice to call some personal characteristics beneficial and others detrimental. We say that being loving is a virtue, being stingy is a vice. James was convinced that this simple dichotomy is valid only for moderate displays of feelings. An excess of love becomes possessiveness, an excess of loyalty becomes fanaticism, an excess of concern becomes sentimentality; each virtue can diminish a person if allowed to assume its extreme form.

Personal Blindness

In an essay that was a favorite of his, James describes a "certain blindness," the inability to understand another person. Our failure to be aware of our blindness is a major source of our unhappiness with one another. Whenever we presume we can decide for others what is good for them or what they should be taught or what their needs are, we fall into error.

The blindness we have in relation to one another is only a symptom of a more pervasive blindness, a blindness to an inner vision of reality. For James this vision was not at all mysterious; it was tangible in the immediacy of experience itself. Our blindness prevents us from being aware of the intensity and the perfection of the present moment. Like Whitman and Tolstoy before him, James advocated grasping nature directly, without the filters of habit, manners, or taste. "Wherever it is found, there is the zest, the tingle, the excitement of reality; and there *is* 'importance' in the only real and positive sense in which importance ever anywhere can be" (James, 1899a, p. 115). "Life is always worth living, if one has such responsive responsibilities. We are trained to seek the choice, the rare, the exquisite exclusively, and to overlook the common. We are stuffed with abstract conceptions and glib with verbalities and verbosities ... the peculiar sources of joy connected with our simpler functions often dry up, and we grow stone-blind and insensible to life's more elementary and general goods and joys" (James, 1899a, p. 126).

Other symptoms of this blindness are the inability to express our feelings, the lack of awareness that leads to errors of excess, and the willing acceptance of our bad habits that restrict consciousness and prevent their removal.

> Hands off: neither the whole of truth nor the whole of good is revealed to any single observer, although each observer gains a partial superiority of insight from the peculiar position in which he stands! [James, 1977, p. 645]

STRUCTURE

Body

James's own bouts with illness caused him continually to reexamine the relationship between the body and consciousness. He concluded that even the most spiritual person must be concerned with and aware of physical needs because the body is the initial source of sensation.

> My experience is only what I agree to attend to. [James, in Rieber, 1980, p. 203]

However, consciousness can transcend any level of physical excitement for a limited period of time. The body, necessary for the origin and maintenance of personality, is subservient to the activities of the mind. For example, intellectual concentration can be so tightly focused "as not only to banish ordinary sensations, but even the severest pain" (James, 1890, I, p. 49). There are numerous reports of soldiers who suffer severe wounds but do not notice them until the intensity of the fighting abates. Common also are cases of athletes who break a wrist, a rib, or a collarbone, but who are unaware of the break until the end of a playing period. Examining this evidence, James concludes that it is the focus of attention that determines whether or not external physical sensations will affect conscious activity. The body is an expressive tool of the indwelling consciousness rather than the source of stimulation itself.

Although James wrote that the body is not more than the place where consciousness dwells, he never lost sight of the importance of the body. Good physical health, rare in James's own life, had its own inner logic "that wells up from every part of the body of a muscularly well-trained human being, and soaks the indwelling soul of him with satisfaction. . . . [It is] an element of spiritual hygiene of supreme significance" (James, 1899a, p. 103).

Social Relationships

Relationships are initially instinctual and shaped to fit different cultural requirements. Much of what we call a relationship is a reciprocal habit pattern. Two instincts predominate. The first is the urge to be with other people. "To be alone is one of the greatest of evils for [a person]. Solitary confinement is by many regarded as a mode of torture too cruel and unnatural for civilized countries to adopt" (James, 1890, II, p. 430). The other instinct is the drive to be noticed, to be singled out, to be preceived as unique or special. James called this an instinct, that is, *the kind of behavior that seems to occur without training and repeatedly without the need of reward or in spite of punishment.*

Some of the evidence James quotes to bolster this position are accounts of criminals who ask, immediately after their arrest, if their names are sure to appear in the newspapers. He notes also that political assassins crave personal notoriety. The society pages of daily papers are little more than lists of names of people who wish to be noticed. "The noteworthy thing about the desire to be 'recognized' by others is that its strength has so little to do with the worth of the recognition computed in sensational or rational terms" (James, 1890, I, p. 308).

James called the personal habit patterns that form the mainstay of our relationships the "social self." He viewed it as a shifting, malleable, surface personality, often little more than a set of masks, changed to suit different audiences. He argued that social habits are necessary;

they make life orderly. Habit is a cushion; it renders relationships safe and predictable. James believed the constant interplay between cultural conformity and individual expression to be beneficial to both. "The community stagnates without the impulse of the individual. The impulse dies away without the sympathy of the community" (James, 1896, p. 232).

Emotions

The James-Lange theory of emotion[3] states that an emotion depends on feedback from one's own body. It is a biological theory of emotion that includes a psychological component. James says that we perceive a situation, then an instinctual physical reaction occurs, and then we are aware of an emotion (sadness, joy, surprise). The emotion is based on a recognition of the physical feelings, not of the initial situation. "Were this bodily commotion suppressed, we should not so much *feel* fear as call the situation fearful; we should not feel surprise, but coldly recognize that the object was indeed astonishing. One enthusiast [James himself] has even gone so far as to say that when we feel sorry it is because we weep, when we feel afraid it is because we run away, and not conversely" (James, 1899a, p. 99).

This seems contrary to popular conceptions. Most of us assume that we see a situation, begin to have feelings about it, and then have physical responses—we laugh, cry, grit our teeth, or run away. If James is correct, we should expect different emotions to arise from different physical reactions. Evidence that sensory feedback contributes to the awareness of emotions continues to be verified experimentally (Hohman, 1966; Laird, 1974) and clinically (Bandler & Grinder, 1979).

Critics of the theory have pointed out that there is no clear-cut pattern between emotional states and patterns of physiological arousal (Cannon, 1927). However, James suggests that "the emotions of different individuals may vary indefinitely" and quotes Lange: "We have all seen men dumb instead of talkative, with joy . . . we have seen grief run restlessly about lamenting, instead of sitting bowed down and mute; etc., etc . . ." (1890, II, p. 454). Thus what current researchers are finding is that emotion does not exist without arousal (Schacter, 1971) and that the pattern of arousal is individual, repeatable, and predictable (Shields & Stern, 1979).

Work by Schacter and Singer (1962) has demonstrated that when subjects do not understand the real cause for their emotional arousal, they will label their feelings to fit the external cures. They will decide by not relying on their internal perception; instead, they can be swayed by social and environmental influences, which may actually conflict

In short, there is considerable theoretical agreement with, and empirical support for, the assumption that the experience of emotion is basically an interpretation of behavior. [Averill, 1980, p. 161]

---

[3]So called because the Danish psychologist Carl Lange published a similar theory about the same time.

with their own visceral feelings. If they are aware of why they are aroused (informed that their feelings are due to side effects of a drug, for example), they are less likely to label their own feelings inappropriately. The event *plus* the individual *plus* the setting will determine the experienced emotion. Our reactions are based on our physical reactions plus our perception of the situation, not on our physical sensations alone. James's general position also seems to be partially borne out by the continuing developments in psychopharmacology. It is more and more possible to evoke specific emotional states by inhibiting or stimulating physiological processes through the ingestion of specific drugs. Groups of drugs are commonly labeled by the changes in moods they produce or suppress. The emotional difficulties that are often experienced by mental hospital patients can be controlled or even eliminated through daily doses of these drugs.

Intellect

Mind engenders truth upon reality. . . . Our minds are not here simply to copy a reality that is already complete. They are here to complete it, to add to its importance by their own remodeling of it, to decant its contents over, so to speak, into a more significant shape. In point of fact, the use of most of our thinking is to help us to change the world. [James in Perry, 1935, II, p. 479]

There are two levels of knowing: knowing through direct experience and knowing through abstract reasoning. James calls the first level "knowledge of acquaintance." It is sensory, intuitive, poetic, and emotional. "I know the color blue when I see it, and the flavor of a pear when I taste it; I know an inch when I move my finger through it: a second of time when I feel it pass . . .but *about* the inner nature of these facts or what makes them what they are, I can say nothing at all . . ." (James, 1890, I, p. 221).

The higher level of knowledge James calls "knowledge-about." It is intellectual, focused, relational; it can develop abstractions; it is objective and unemotional. "When we know about it, we can do more than merely have it; we seem, as we think over its relations, to subject it to a form of *treatment* and *operate* upon it with our thought. . . . Through feelings we become acquainted with things but only with our thoughts do we know about them" (James, 1890, I, p. 222).

Who can decide offhand which is better, to live or understand life. [James, 1911]

Although James's work is rich in metaphors and is still valued as much for its poetry and style as for its content, he is clear in his opinion that the more rational, objective knowledge is the more highly evolved form. "Though it would be absurd in an absolute way to say that a given analytic mind was superior to any intuitional one, yet it is none the less true that the former *represents* the higher state" (James, 1890, II, p. 353).[4]

Self

The self is that personal continuity that each one of us recognizes each time we awaken. James described several layers of the self.

---

[4]See the sections on "Intellect" in Freud, Jung, and Sufism for contrary points of view.

The Material Self

The material layer of the self includes those things that we identify with ourselves. The material self includes not only our bodies but also our homes, possessions, friends, and family. To the extent that a person identifies with an external person or object, it is part of his or her identity.

> *In its widest possible sense, however, a man's Self is the sum total of all that he CAN call his,* not only his body and his psychic powers, but his clothes and his house, his wife and children, his ancestors and friends, his reputation and works, his lands and horses, and yacht and bank-account. All these things give him the same emotions. If they wax and prosper, he feels triumphant; if they dwindle and die away, he feels cast down,—not necessarily in the same degree for each thing, but in much the same way for all. [James, 1890, I, pp. 291–292]

Test this proposition yourself. Imagine that someone is ridiculing some person, idea, or thing that matters to you. Are you objective in evaluating the merits of the attack, or do you react as if you yourself were under attack? If someone insults your brother, your parents, your hairstyle, your country, your jacket, your religion, can you be aware of the investment that you have in each? Some of the confusion between ownership and identification can be clarified by understanding this expanded concept of the self.

The Social Self

"A man's social self is the recognition which he gets from his mates" (James, 1890, I, p. 293). It is any and all roles that we willingly or unwillingly accept. A person may have many or few social selves, consistent or inconsistent, but whatever they are, one identifies with each in the proper setting. James suggests that the proper course of action is to pick one to stake your life on. "All other selves thereupon become unreal, but the fortunes of this self are real. Its failures are real failures, its triumphs real triumphs . . ." (James, 1890, I, p. 310).

The Spiritual Self

The spiritual self is one's inner and subjective being. It is the active element in all consciousness. "It is the home of interest—not the pleasant or the painful, not even pleasure or pain, as such, but that within us to which pleasure and pain, the pleasant and the painful, speak. It is the source of effort and attention, and the place from which appear to emanate the fiats of the will" (James, 1890, I, p. 298). One expression of this self is exemplified in religious experiences, which "have no proper *intellectual* deliverance of their own, but belong to a region deeper and more vital and practical, than that which the intellect inhabits" (H. James, 1926, II, p. 149).

To give up pretensions is as blessed a relief as to get them gratified. . . . How pleasant is the day when we give up striving to be young—or slender! Thank God! we say, *those* illusions are gone. Everything added to the self is a burden. [James, 1890, I, pp. 310–311]

James remained undecided on the question of the personal soul; however, he did feel that there was something beyond individual identity. "Out of my experience . . . one fixed conclusion dogmatically emerges . . . there is a continuum of cosmic consciousness, against which our individuality builds but accidental fences, and into which our several minds plunge as into a mother-sea or reservoir" (James in Murphy & Ballou, 1960, p. 324).

The Role of the Teacher

A professor has two functions: (1) to be learned and distribute bibliographical information; (2) to communicate truth. The 1st function is the essential one, officially considered. The 2nd is the only one I care for. [James, 1926, II, p. 268]

James was first and foremost a teacher. As such, he understood the problems and was acutely concerned with improving the quality of teaching at the primary levels as much as at the college level. His most widely read books were about education and he was in constant demand as a lecturer to teachers. In *Talks to Teachers* (1899a) James applied general psychological principles to the art and practice of instruction. He proposed that children were innately interested in and capable of learning. The task of the teacher was to establish a climate that would encourage the natural process of learning. Teaching, therefore, was less a matter of content and more a matter of intent. Teachers should teach behaviors that could become the foundation for additional effective learning. "My main desire has been to make them conceive, and if possible, reproduce sympathetically in their imagination, the mental life of the pupil . . ." (James, 1899a, p. v).

Voluntary attention cannot be continuously sustained, it comes in beats. [James, 1899a, p. 51]

The cardinal responsibility of the teacher is to encourage the student to increase his or her capacity for sustained attention. Sustained attention to a single subject or idea is not a natural state for children or adults. Normal consciousness is a series of patterned interruptions; thoughts shift rapidly from one object to another. Training is necessary to alter this tendency until longer and longer periods of focused attention can be maintained. The teacher should recognize and inhibit the involuntary lapses of attention for the child's own development. "This reflex and passive character of the attention . . . which makes the child seem to belong less to himself than to every object which happens to catch his notice, is the first thing which the teacher must overcome" (James, 1890, I, p. 417).

Experience has taught me that teachers have less freedom of intellect than any class of people I know. . . . A teacher wrings his very soul out to understand you, and if he does ever understand anything you say, he lies down on it with his whole weight like a cow on a doorstep so that you can neither get out or in with him. He never forgets it or can reconcile anything else you say with it, and carries it to the grave like a scar." [James, in Perry, 1935, II, p. 131]

To aid teachers, James offered some suggestions. First, the content of education must be made relevant to the needs of the students or made to appear so. Students should be aware of connections between what they are learning and their own needs, however remote those connections actually are. This draws the child's initial interest, fitful though it may be. Second, the subject matter may need to be enriched in order to encourage the return of students' drifting attention because "from an unchanging subject the attention inevitably wanders away" (James, 1899a, p. 52).

James rejected punishment as a way of teaching, as Skinner did

50 years later. Instead of punishing students for being bored, James suggests they be given work that will reengage their interest. He suggests that more class time be devoted to active projects than to passive study. The goal, however, is not just to accomplish tasks but to improve the students' underlying capacity to control and direct their attention. The aim of teaching is to train students in basic learning skills and habits so they might have the capacity and the motivation to learn whatever they choose to learn.

Training the Will

Improving voluntary attention includes training the will. A developed will allows consciousness to attend to ideas, perceptions, and sensations that are not immediately pleasant or inviting and, in fact, may be difficult or even distasteful. Try, for example, to imagine yourself eating your favorite food. Keep the images and sensations uppermost in your mind for 20 seconds. You will probably find that this is not too difficult. Now for 20 seconds imagine that you are cutting the surface of your thumb with a razor blade. Notice how your attention scoots off in every direction as soon as you are aware of the subjective sensation of pain, the color and wetness of your own blood, and the mixture of fear, fascination, and revulsion. Only an act of will can constrain your initial and instinctual attempt to move away from the experience.

To one who proposed that, in the Medical School, lectures be replaced by the "case system," he said: "I think you're entirely right, but your learned professor would rebel. He much prefers sitting and hearing his own beautiful voice to guiding the stumbling minds of the students. [Perry, quoting James, 1935, I, p. 444]

Unless a person develops the capacity to learn, the content of the teaching is of little importance. "The great thing in all education is to *make our nervous system our ally instead of our enemy*. It is to fund and capitalize our acquisitions, and live at ease upon the interest of the fund. *For this we must make automatic and habitual, as early as possible, as many useful actions as we can,* and as carefully guard against the growing into ways that are likely to be disadvantageous" (James, 1899a, p. 34).

EVALUATION

For James psychology was bounded by biology on one side and metaphysics on the other; it included any area of *human* existence and experience. James introduced psychology to the United States. He taught the first course and established the first laboratory in the United States. The span of his interests and his writing has been unequaled in psychology. He was as concerned about the experiences of saints as about the biological substrata of behavior. After James, psychology was divided up into specialties, like the lands of a great kingdom divided up by the sons of the king into smaller, less ambiguous portions.

James' *Principles* is without question the most literate, the most provocative, and at the same time the most intelligible book on psychology that has ever appeared in English or any other language. [Bray et al., 1969, p. iii]

There are lamentably few psychology books one can recommend simply for the pleasure of reading them. James's *The Varieties of Religious Experience* is one; *Talks to Teachers* is another. Although many

portions of his mammoth textbook are dated, his own remarks, speculations, and colorful examples still are read, quoted, and remembered.
His writing is stunning.

James's completed *Principles of Psychology* included numerous
theories in various areas of psychology, each supported by some data.
Now psychology texts still include a variety of theories (as does this
volume) and each one is supported by much more data. Inasmuch as
the present theories have more research to substantiate their respective merits, we are still not much closer now to resolving theoretical
differences than we were in 1890 (see Wolman & Knapp, 1981, for example).

I spent two delightful
evenings with William
James alone and I was
tremendously impressed
by the clearness of his
mind and the complete
absence of intellectual
prejudices. [Jung in
Adler & Jaffe, 1978]

James advocated an active, involved, psychology-in-the-market-
place role for the science he helped to establish. It mattered to him
what people did with their lives, and he felt that psychology could and
should be helpful to them. In many ways we are still in his debt and
in his shadow. The broad scope of phenomena he laid out for psychology
to investigate is wider than most psychologists have been able to maintain. James was what we would call today a humanistic psychologist,
keenly aware of the moral responsibilities inherent in teaching and
counseling others. He was not only a behaviorist, convinced that behavior was the primary and fundamental source of information; he was
also a transpersonal psychologist, sensitive to the reality of higher
states of consciousness and intrigued with the effects those states had
upon those who experienced them.

His insistence that there was much to be learned from the examination of mental healers, psychics, and visionaries has been validated
by contemporary research on altered states of consciousness.

No one could be more
disgusted than I at the
sight of the book
[*Principles*]. *No* subject
is worth being treated of
in 1000 pages! Had I ten
years more, I could
rewrite it in 500; but as
it stands it is this or
nothing—a loathsome,
distended, tumefied,
bloated, dropsical mass
testifying to nothing but
two facts: 1st, that there
is no such thing as a
science of psychology,
and 2nd, that WJ is an
incapable. [James, to his
publisher, 1890]

James has had lasting effects on education (through his student
Dewey and Dewey's followers) and philosophy. His work in these areas
has been absorbed into the mainstreams of the disciplines. James's
ideas have come in and out of fashion in academic psychology. His
moral and ethical concerns have been regarded as pivotal and also have
been dismissed as metaphysical meanderings. His concern with religious and spiritual states has been spoken of as mental hogwash or profound insights into human functioning. However, no one (including his
most severe critics) ever suggested that the way he portrayed his findings and ideas was anything less than inspiring. Psychology, as we
know it, rests on the foundation established by William James.

THE THEORY FIRSTHAND

Because of the wide range of James's work, we have included two excerpts. The first is part of a lecture he gave to teachers. It is James at
his most moral and most pragmatic. The second part is an excerpt from

The Varieties of Religious Experience, and illustrates some of James's transpersonal concerns.

It is very important that teachers should realize the importance of habit, and psychology helps us greatly at this point. We speak, it is true, of good habits and of bad habits; but, when people use the word "habit," in the majority of instances it is a bad habit which they have in mind. They talk of the smoking-habit and the swearing-habit and the drinking-habit, but not of the abstention-habit or the moderation-habit or the courage-habit. But the fact is that our virtues are habits as much as our vices. All our life, so far as it has definite form, is but a mass of habits—practical, emotional, and intellectual—systematically organized for our weal or woe, and bearing us irresistibly toward our destiny, whatever the latter may be.

Since pupils can understand this at a comparatively early age, and since to understand it contributes in no small measure to their feeling of responsibility, it would be well if the teacher were able to talk to them of the philosophy of habit in some such abstract terms as I am now about to talk of it to you.

I believe that we are subject to the law of habit in consequence of the fact that we have bodies. The plasticity of the living matter of our nervous system, in short, is the reason why we do a thing with difficulty the first time, but soon do it more and more easily, and finally, with sufficient practice, do it semi-mechanically, or with hardly any consciousness at all. Our nervous systems have (in Dr. Carpenter's words) *grown* to the way in which they have been exercised, just as a sheet of paper or a coat, once creased or folded, tends to fall forever afterward into the same identical folds.

Habit is thus a second nature, or rather, as the Duke of Wellington said, it is "ten times nature,"—at any rate as regards its importance in adult life; for the acquired habits of our training have by that time inhibited or strangled most of the natural impulsive tendencies which were originally there. Ninety-nine hundredths or, possibly, nine hundred and ninety-nine thousandths of our activity is purely automatic and habitual, from our rising in the morning to our lying down each night. Our dressing and undressing, our eating and drinking, our greetings and partings, our hat-raisings and giving way for ladies to precede, nay, even most of the forms of our common speech, are things of a type so fixed by repetition as almost to be classed as reflex actions. To each sort of impression we have an automatic, ready-made response. My very words to you now are an example of what I mean; for having already lectured upon habit and printed a chapter about it in a book, and read the latter when in print, I find my tongue inevitably falling into its old phrases and repeating almost literally what I said before.

So far as we are thus mere bundles of habit, we are stereotyped creatures, imitators and copiers of our past selves. And since this, under any circumstances, is what we always tend to become, it follows first of all that the teacher's prime concern should be to ingrain into the pupil that assortment of habits that shall be most useful to him throughout life. Education is for behavior, and habits are the stuff of which behavior consists. . . .

There is no more miserable human being than one in whom nothing is habitual but indecision, and for whom the lighting of every cigar, the drinking of every cup, the time of rising and going to bed every day, and the beginning of every bit of work are subjects of express volitional deliberation. Full half the time of such a man goes to the deciding or regretting of matters which ought to be so ingrained in him as practically not to exist for his consciousness at all. If there be such daily duties not yet ingrained in any one of my hearers, let him begin this very hour to set the matter right.

In Professor Bain's chapter on "The Moral Habits" there are some admirable practical remarks laid down. Two great maxims emerge from the treatment. The first is that in the acquisition of a new habit, or the leaving off of an old one, we must take care to *launch ourselves with as strong and decided an initiative as possible.* Accumulate all the possible circumstances which shall reinforce the right motives; put yourself assiduously in conditions that encourage the new way; make engagements incompatible with the old; take a public pledge, if the case allows; in short, envelope your resolution with every aid you know. This will give your new beginning such a momentum that the temptation to break down will not occur as soon as it otherwise might; and every day during which a breakdown is postponed adds to the chances of it not occurring at all.

I remember long ago reading in an Austrian paper the advertisement of a certain Rudolph Somebody, who promised fifty gulden reward to any one who after that date should find him at the wineshop of Ambrosius So-and-so. "This I do," the advertisement continued, "in consequence of a promise which I have made my wife." With such a wife, and such an understanding of the way in which to start new habits, it would be safe to stake one's money on Rudolph's ultimate success. . . .

A maxim may be added to the preceding: *Seize the very first possible opportunity to act on every resolution you make, and on every emotional prompting you may experience in the direction of the habits you aspire to gain.* It is not in the moment of their forming, but in the moment of their producing motor effects, that resolves and aspirations communicate the new "set" to the brain.

No matter how full a reservoir of maxims one may possess, and no matter how good one's sentiments may be, if one has not taken advantage of every concrete opportunity to act, one's character may remain entirely unaffected for the better. With good intentions, hell proverbially is paved. This is an obvious consequence of the principles I have laid down. A "character," as J. S. Mill says, "is a completely fashioned will"; and a will, in the sense in which he means it, is an aggregate of tendencies to act in a firm and prompt and definite way upon all the principal emergencies of life. A tendency to act only becomes effectively ingrained in us in proportion to the uninterrupted frequency with which the actions actually occur, and the brain "grows" to their use. When a resolve or a fine glow of feeling is allowed to evaporate without bearing practical fruit, it is worse than a chance lost: it works so as positively to hinder future resolutions and emotions from taking the normal path of discharge. There is no more contemptible type of human character than that of the nerveless sentimentalist and dreamer, who spends his life in a weltering sea of sensibility, but never does a concrete manly deed. [1899a, pp. 33–36]

The following selection includes portions of the final lecture James gave on religious experiences. He has given literally hundreds of examples of different kinds of experiences, their effects, and his analysis of them. Now he attempts to come to some conclusions:

> Summing up in the broadest possible way the characteristics of the religious life, as we have found them, it includes the following beliefs:—
>
> 1. That the visible world is part of a more spiritual universe from which it draws its chief significance;
> 2. That union or harmonious relation with that higher universe is our true end;
> 3. That prayer or inner communion with the spirit thereof—be that spirit "God" or "law"—is a process wherein work is really done, and spiritual energy flows in and produces effects, psychological or material, within the phenomenal world.
>
> Religion includes also the following psychological characteristics:—
>
> 4. A new zest which adds itself like a gift to life, and takes the form either of lyrical enchantment or of appeal to earnestness and heroism.
> 5. An assurance of safety and a temper of peace, and, in relation to others, a preponderance of loving affections.
>
> In illustrating these characteristics by documents, we have been literally bathed in sentiment. In re-reading my manuscript, I am almost appalled at the amount of emotionality which I find in it. After so much of this, we can afford to be dryer and less sympathetic in the rest of the work that lies before us.
>
> The sentimentality of many of my documents is a consequence of the fact that I sought them among the extravagances of the subject. If any of you are enemies of what our ancestors used to brand as enthusiasm, and are, nevertheless, still listening to me now, you have probably felt my selection to have been sometimes almost perverse, and have wished I might have stuck to soberer examples. I reply that I took these extremer examples as yielding the profounder information. To learn the secrets of any science, we go to expert specialists, even though they may be eccentric persons, and not to commonplace pupils. We combine what they tell us with the rest of our wisdom, and form our final judgment independently. Even so with religion. We who have pursued such radical expressions of it may now be sure that we know its secrets as authentically as any one can know them who learns them from another; and we have next to answer, each of us for himself, the practical question: what are the dangers in this element of life? and in what proportion may it need to be restrained by other elements, to give the proper balance?
>
> But this question suggests another one which I will answer immediately and get it out of the way, for it has more than once already vexed us. Ought it to be assumed that in all men the mixture of religion with other elements should be identical? Ought it, indeed, to be assumed that the lives of all men should show identical religious elements? In other words, is the existence of so many religious types and sects and creeds regrettable?
>
> To these questions I answer "No" emphatically. And my reason is that I do not see how it is possible that creatures in such different positions and with such different powers as human individuals are, should have

exactly the same functions and the same duties. No two of us have identical difficulties, nor should we be expected to work out identical solutions. Each, from his peculiar angle of observation, takes in a certain sphere of fact and trouble, which each must deal with in a unique manner. One of us must soften himself, another must harden himself; one must yield a point, another must stand firm,—in order the better to defend the position assigned him. If an Emerson were forced to be a Wesley, or a Moody forced to be a Whitman, the total human consciousness of the divine would suffer. The divine can mean no single quality, it must mean a group of qualities, by being champions of which in alternation, different men may all find worthy missions. Each attitude being a syllable in human nature's total message, it takes the whole of us to spell the meaning out completely. So a "god of battles" must be allowed to be the god for one kind of person, a god of peace and heaven and home, the god for another. We must frankly recognize the fact that we live in partial systems, and that parts are not interchangeable in the spiritual life. If we are peevish and jealous, destruction of the self must be an element of our religion; why need it be one if we are good and sympathetic from the outset? If we are sick souls, we require a religion of deliverance; but why think so much of deliverance, if we are healthy-minded? Unquestionably, some men have the completer experience and the higher vocation, here just as in the social world; but for each man to stay in his own experience, whate'er it be, and for others to tolerate him there, is surely best. . . .

We must next pass beyond the point of view of merely subjective utility, and make inquiry into the intellectual content itself.

First, is there, under all the discrepancies of the creeds, a common nucleus to which they bear their testimony unanimously?

And second, ought we to consider the testimony true?

I will take up the first question first, and answer it immediately in the affirmative. The warring gods and formulas of the various religions do indeed cancel each other, but there is a certain uniform deliverance in which religions all appear to meet. It consists of two parts:—

1. An uneasiness; and
2. Its solution.
1. The uneasiness, reduced to its simplest terms, is a sense that there is *something wrong about us* as we naturally stand.
2. The solution is a sense that *we are saved from the wrongness* by making proper connection with the higher powers.

In those more developed minds which alone we are studying, the wrongness takes a moral character, and the salvation takes a mystical tinge. I think we shall keep well within the limits of what is common to all such minds if we formulate the essence of their religious experience in terms like these:

The individual, so far as he suffers from his wrongness and criticizes it, is to that extent consciously beyond it, and in at least possible touch with something higher, if anything higher exists. Along with the wrong part there is thus a better part of him, even though it may be but a most helpless germ. With which part he should identify his real being is by no means obvious at this stage; but when stage 2 (the stage of solution or salvation) arrives, the man identifies his real being with the germinal higher part of himself; and does so in the following way. *He becomes con-*

scious that this higher part is conterminous and continuous with a MORE of the same quality, which is operative in the universe outside of him, and which he can keep in working touch with, and in a fashion get on board and save himself when all his lower being has gone to pieces in the wreck.

It seems to me that all the phenomena are accurately describable in these very simple general terms. They allow for the divided self and the struggle; they involve the change of personal centre and the surrender of the lower self; they express the appearance of exteriority of the helping power and yet account for our sense of union with it; and they fully justify our feelings of security and joy. There is probably no autobiographic document, among all those which I have quoted, to which the description will not well apply. One need only add such specific details as will adapt it to various theologies and various personal temperaments, and one will then have the various experiences reconstructed in their individual forms.

So far, however, as this analysis goes, the experiences are only psychological phenomena. They possess, it is true, enormous biological worth. Spiritual strength really increases in the subject when he has them, a new life opens for him, and they seem to him a place of conflux where the forces of two universes meet; and yet this may be nothing but his subjective way of feeling things, a mood of his own fancy, in spite of the effects produced. I now turn to my second question: What is the objective "truth" of their content?

The part of the content concerning which the question of truth most pertinently arises is that "MORE of the same quality" with which our own higher self appears in the experience to come into harmonious working relation. Is such a "more" merely our own notion, or does it really exist? If so, in what shape does it exist? Does it act, as well as exist? And in what form should we conceive of that "union" with it of which religious geniuses are so convinced?

It is in answering these questions that the various theologies perform their theoretic work, and that their divergencies most come to light. They all agree that the "more" really exists; though some of them hold it to exist in the shape of a personal god or gods, while others are satisfied to conceive it as a stream of ideal tendency embedded in the eternal structure of the world. They all agree, moreover, that it acts as well as exists, and that something really is effected for the better when you throw your life into its hands. It is when they treat of the experience of "union" with it that their speculative differences appear most clearly. Over this point pantheism and theism, nature and second birth, works and grace and karma, immortality and reincarnation, rationalism and mysticism, carry on inveterate disputes. [1958, pp. 367–369, 383–385]

THE PSYCHOLOGY OF CONSCIOUSNESS

The whole drift of my education goes to persuade me that the world of our present consciousness is only one of many worlds of consciousness that exist, and that those other worlds must contain experiences which have a meaning for our life also; and that although in the main their experiences and those of this world keep discrete, yet the two become continuous at certain points and higher energies filter in. [James, 1958, p. 391]

James studied a wide range of states of consciousness and drew no lines between abnormal and normal experience; however, portions of his work on altered states, religious states, hypnosis, and paranormal states were ignored. As psychology has evolved new methods of investigation, these areas are once again of growing concern. "The study of consciousness as yet has no sure perch anywhere in psychology. Rather it is emerging as a field of study because of the ardent interest of people scattered throughout the many arms of psychology and well beyond . . ." (Goleman & Davidson, 1979, p. xvii). In recent years the pendulum has swung back and the study of consciousness is flourishing. Professional associations such as the Biofeedback Research Society and the Association for Transpersonal Psychology have emerged, publishing journals and supporting new lines of research. There has been a corresponding wave of popular interest, with articles and best-selling books about consciousness appearing regularly.

A few areas have particular implications for personality theory. The research with psychedelic drugs, biofeedback, hypnosis, meditation, and extrasensory perception has produced findings that question basic assumptions about consciousness and the nature of reality as we experience it. We are utilizing new methods, new instruments, and a renewed willingness to research subjective phenomena in an effort to put a scientific foundation under James's philosophical speculations.

We cannot yet answer the basic question—the question of what consciousness is—because it may not be answerable; but we are learning more about the contents of consciousness and the forms that it takes. Ornstein (1972) argues that consciousness can never be understood using an objective approach alone. "There is no way to simply write down the answer, as we might give a textbook definition. The answers must come personally, experientially" (p. ix).

Altered states of consciousness can be triggered by hypnosis, meditation, psychedelic drugs, deep prayer, sensory deprivation, and the onset of acute psychosis. Sleep deprivation or fasting can induce them. Epileptics and migraine sufferers often experience an altered awareness in the aura that precedes attacks. Hypnotic monotony, as in solo high-altitude jet flight, may bring on an altered state. Electronic stimulation of the brain (ESB), alpha or theta brain-wave training, clairvoyant or telepathic insights, muscle-relaxation training, isolation (as in Antarctica), and photic stimulation (light flicker at certain speeds) may bring on a sharp change in consciousness. [Ferguson, 1973, p. 59]

PSYCHEDELIC RESEARCH

Most cultures, primitive or civilized, have used herbs, seeds, or plants to alter body chemistry, emotional outlook, and levels of awareness. James experimented with nitrous oxide (laughing gas) and was impressed by his experiences.

> With me, as with every other person of whom I have heard, the keynote of the experience is the tremendously exciting sense of an intense metaphysical illumination. Truth lies open to the view in depth beneath depth of almost blinding evidence. The mind sees all the logical relations of being with an apparent subtlety and instantaneity to which its normal consciousness offers no parallel; only as sobriety returns, the feeling of insights fades, and one is left staring vacantly at a few disjointed words and phrases, as one stares at a cadaverous-looking snow-peak from which the sunset glow has just fled, or at the black cinder left by an extinguished brand. [1969, pp. 359–360]

Although other reports of the unusual effects of drugs appeared from time to time, more intensive studies did not begin until the synthesis of lysergic acid diethylamide-25 (LSD-25) in 1943 by the Swiss chemist Albert Hoffman. The ready availability of a measurable synthetic material opened up a broad international research effort. Results of initial studies received widespread publicity and aroused public interest. One lasting effect has been the pervasive introduction of psychedelic drugs into American life. Millions of people who have experimented with such drugs have come to agree with James that "our normal waking consciousness . . . is but one special type of consciousness, whilst all about it, parted from it by the filmiest of screens, there lie potential forms of consciousness entirely different" (James, 1958, p. 298).

Implications of Psychedelic Research for Personality Theory

1. Most theories of personality are based on normal, waking consciousness. One characteristic of normal consciousness is that you know who you are; your sense of identity and individuality is stable and explicit. Studies of body image and ego boundaries have concluded that if your impression of yourself is different from what an objective observer would report, that is clear evidence of psychopathology (Schilder, 1935; Fisher & Cleveland, 1958). This idea, accepted in psychiatry, is in contrast to some of the reports from psychedelic researchers. Grof, for example, reports the following range of experiences correlated with a decline in pathology and a restoration of psychological health.

> In the "normal," or usual, state of consciousness the individual experiences himself as existing within the boundaries of his physical body (the

The future may teach us how to exercise a direct influence, by means of particular chemical substances, upon the amounts of energy and their distribution in the apparatus of mind. [Freud, 1940]

body image). His perception of the environment is restricted; both his internal perception and his perception of the environment are confined within the usual space-time boundaries. In psychedelic transpersonal experiences, one or several of these limitations appear to be transcended. In some cases, the subject experiences loosening of his usual ego boundaries, and his consciousness and self-awareness seem to expand to include and encompass other individuals and elements of the external world. In other cases, he continues experiencing his own identity but at a different time, in a different place, or in a different context. In yet other cases, the subject experiences a complete loss of his own ego identity and a complete identification with the consciousness of another entity. Finally, in a rather large category of these psychedelic transpersonal experiences (archetypal experiences, encounters with blissful and wrathful deities, union with God, etc.), the subject's consciousness appears to encompass elements that do not have any continuity with his usual ego identity and cannot be considered simple derivatives of his experiences in the three-dimensional world. [1971, p. 49]

It appears that some of the distinctions we maintain between ourselves and the outer world are arbitrary and are alterable. Our usual perceptions may be partially due to the state of consciousness we are in. As we view the world with its many colors, these colors are only a small part of the spectrum that exists. The finding that a person may lose what he or she calls "personal" identity without feeling a loss of identity (now hard to define) leads us back to James. He describes the self not as a stable, fixed structure but as a constantly fluctuating field. This description fits the data better than the more conservative descriptions found in current psychological literature.

2. When James wrote *The Varieties of Religious Experience* in 1902, he observed that experiencing so-called "mystical consciousness" was a rare and unpredictable event. The widespread use of psychedelics (especially marijuana) has made such states, or at least the subjective impression of having experienced such states, more available. A number of psychedelic researchers report that their subjects have what they call religious, spiritual, or transpersonal experiences. It has become important to determine the value as well as the validity of these experiences now that they appear to be more common (Grof, 1975).

This question is of concern to the religious community as well. Religious conversion, experiences in prayer, visions, and talking in tongues, all occur during altered states of consciousness. The validity of these experiences is the foundation of a number of diverse religious doctrines. The discovery and examination of substances used in religious rituals, which have proved to be active psychedelic agents, has revived interest among theologians in the origin and meaning of chemically induced religious experience.

3. Consciousness, time, and space appear to be affected by each

other. Modern physicists and ancient mystics are sounding more and more alike in their attempts to describe the known universe (LeShan, 1969). Results from psychedelic experiences suggest that the nature and genesis of consciousness may be more realistically described by mystics and modern physics than by contemporary psychology (Capra, 1975; Zukav, 1979).

4. The mushrooming literature and research into various states of consciousness (Valle & von Eckartsberg, 1981) suggests that any theory of personality that does not take into account altered states of consciousness is an incomplete description of fundamental human experiences. Consciousness may best be described as a spectrum (Wilber, 1975) in which our normal awareness is only a small segment. Normal consciousness seems to be a special case (Bentov, 1977; Tart, 1975) with its own rules and limitations. Although this is an underlying assumption of the older psychologies described in Part II of this book, it is still a radical idea in conventional personality theory.

BIOFEEDBACK RESEARCH

James's theory that emotion depends on feedback from one's body has been extended in a variety of ways through biofeedback research. Biofeedback is an application of the engineering concept of feedback—the mechanical principle that controls most automatic machinery. A furnace and its thermostat, for instance, form a self-contained feedback system. Biofeedback is the means of monitoring a physical process that is going on in your own body. For example, when you use your fingers to feel your pulse, you are getting feedback on your heart rate.

Through new methods of providing accurate and immediate feedback, researchers found that subjects could control a wide range of physical parameters that included heart rate, blood pressure, skin temperature, and brain-wave frequency (*Biofeedback and Self-Control,* 1971–1978). It is safe to say that almost any bodily process that can be monitored can be consciously modified and controlled. The fact that people are not aware of how they are doing it does not limit this capacity to control. People and animals can literally "think" their temperatures up and down, retard or accelerate their heart rates, or shift from one brain-wave frequency to another.

The research now has widespread practical uses and has spawned a host of clinical applications for conditions that include the following: tension headaches, migraine headaches, Raynaud's disease (cold hands and feet), asthma, epilepsy, Parkinson's disease, ulcers, bedwetting, hypertension, and cardiac abnormalities including fibrillation (Olton & Noonberg, 1980).

A monkey has learned to fire a single nerve cell to obtain a reward. At Queen's University in Kingston, Ontario, John Basmajian trained human subjects to discharge a single motor nerve cell, selected from the brain's ten billion cells. Miller's rats [Neal Miller of Rockefeller University] learned to form urine at greater or lesser rates, to redden one ear and blanch the other, and increase or decrease the blood in their intestinal lining. [Ferguson, 1973, pp. 32–33]

Implications of Biofeedback Research for
Personality Theory

1. The capacities of the nervous system have been redefined. We used to believe that there was a voluntary nervous system, capable of being under conscious control, and an autonomic or involuntary nervous system that was not capable of being consciously controlled; however, this distinction has all but vanished. Now it is more realistic to speak of the gross nervous system—open to conscious control with little or no training—and the subtle nervous system—open to conscious control with specialized training. These changed definitions bring our own view of physiology much closer to those Eastern systems whose ideas about personality are based on exactly these and related physical distinctions.

All the "wonders of the mysterious East"—yogis resting on a bed of nails, saints being buried alive, devotees able to walk slowly over hot coals—were feats used by adepts to demonstrate more of the range of human possibilities. As we are now able to replicate some of these kinds of feats in our own laboratories, it behooves us to look again at the implications of these exhibitions (Brown, 1974; Karlins & Andrews, 1972; Rama et al., 1976).

We may need to redefine what it means to be *in control.* Physical control may be closely linked or may lead to emotional control. If so, there could be advantages to teaching children or disturbed adults basic biofeedback to increase their awareness and their abilities to control their own reactions. Initial reviews (Kamiya & Kamiya, 1981; Peper & Williams, 1981) indicate positive and lasting results from this training.

2. James defined will as the combination of attention and volition (wishing). Kimble and Perlmuter have found that the role of the will is critical to understanding how biofeedback training actually occurs. They note that the role of attention is critical in the willing process. They present a trivial example of what can occur if you wish to do something but do not pay close attention.

> **ARE YOU PAYING ATTENTION?**
> QUESTION: *What do you call the tree that grows from acorns?*
> ANSWER: *Oak.*
> QUESTION: *What do we call a funny story?*
> ANSWER: *Joke.*
> QUESTION: *The sound made by a frog?*
> ANSWER: *Croak.*
> QUESTION: *What do we call the white of an egg?*
> ANSWER: ...
>
> *[From Kimble & Perlmuter, 1970, p. 373]*

Only if you pay close attention will you escape the habit pattern established in the series, which tends to elicit the incorrect answer "yolk." (If you wish to further verify this, try reading these questions to a friend and asking him or her to respond.) You may wish to give the correct answer, but it is the combination of your wish (volition) plus your attention that makes it possible to do what you will.

3. Passive volition is defined as the willingness to let things happen. It refers to the particular state of consciousness that subjects learn to use in successful biofeedback training. It is attention without effort. An example of a task in biofeedback research might be to learn to lower the temperature in your right hand. At first subjects will "try"; the temperature in the right hand will rise. Then many subjects will "try not to." This usually results in the temperature rising. Eventually, over the course of training, the subject learns to stop trying and to "allow" the temperature to fall. Passive volition is not part of our cultural training. We are brought up to be assertive, to succeed, to resist those forces that prevent us from doing what we wish. James's distinctions between passive and active willing have become an important variable in effective biofeedback training.

4. Most theories of personality specify the genesis and necessary conditions of various kinds of mental illness. Biofeedback research has shown alternate ways of inducing or eliminating a number of "psychological" symptoms without considering the psychological reasons for the symptom. As Green and Green (1972) have suggested, because we can become physically ill in responding to psychological stress, perhaps we can eliminate the illness by learning to control the physiological response.

Perhaps some aspects of our personalities can be modified by biofeedback, a form of external, mechanistic, nonpsychological training. Areas usually associated with psychotherapy now being researched for biofeedback use include alcoholism, chronic anxiety, drug abuse, learning disabilities, insomnia, obsessive phobic-depressive syndrome, and writer's cramp (O'Regan, 1979). James did the initial research into what was then called "mind cure" (Meyer, 1980); one might conclude that biofeedback training is but the scientific application of this area of James's pioneering investigations.

MEDITATION

Meditation can be defined as the directing, stilling, quieting, or focusing of one's attention in a systematic manner. It may be practiced either in silence or in the presence of noise, with eyes open or shut, while sitting or standing, and even while walking. There are literally hundreds of techniques, practices, and systems of meditation. Research is beginning to uncover how physiological behaviors are affected by meditation (Shapiro & Walsh, 1981). Most of the early laboratory work was done on one meditation system, Transcendental Meditation (Kanelakos & Lukas, 1974). Apparently the data obtained are also valid for other systems (Benson, 1975).

With the widespread acceptance and proliferation of groups and teachers who offer training in meditation, large cities and most college campuses house several organizations offering such training. A continuing interest in the practical application of meditation practice in psychotherapy (Carrington, 1978) and evidence of its utility in the treatment of cancer (Simonton et al., 1978) and drug abuse (Benson & Wallace, 1972) ensures its continual use as a therapy technique and subject of further research.

Implications of Meditation Research for Personality Theory

1. What are the contents of consciousness? James proposed that we might consider consciousness like a stream or a river. Research reports indicate that for a more complete description it may be necessary to consider consciousness as having many tracks or streams, all flowing simultaneously. Awareness may move from track to track like a searchlight playing over different tracks in a train depot.

What is there in consciousness besides discrete thoughts? Reports from meditators suggest something more than the varied thought forms that float to the surface of the mind. As one explores consciousness, there are changes in the contents and in the structure and form of thought itself.

Of all the hard facts of science, I know of none more solid and fundamental than the fact that if you inhibit thought (and persevere) you come at length to a region of consciousness below or behind thought . . . and a realization of an altogether vaster self than that to which we are accustomed. [Edward Carpenter, 1844–1929]

Tart (1972) has encouraged researchers to consider that specialized training may be necessary in order to enter and observe these specific states. Just as a dentist must have special training to be able to detect tiny irregularities in X rays of the teeth, or astronauts need special training to be able to work in null-gravity situations, so scientists working in "state-specific science" should have appropriate training. James's complaint that the insights available under nitrous oxide "fade out" may reflect his own lack of training, not just the effect of the gas.

2. What effects does meditation have on personal values, life-style, and motivation? Ram Dass (1974) comments that his previous beliefs, developed while teaching Western motivational psychology, were severely threatened by his experiences in meditation. Some of the mediational systems he worked with did not even assume that the so-called basic drives for affiliation, power, or achievement—or even the biologically rooted drives for food, water, or survival—were necessary for personal well-being. The writings of Ram Dass (1978), Sayadaw (1954), and others makes it evident that there are models of personality based on considerations beyond those we have considered here thus far.

HYPNOSIS

Although hypnosis has been an area of research for over a hundred years, it is not a well-defined phenomenon. Some of its applications include psychotherapy, aids to athletic training, techniques for modulating pain, and nightclub entertainment. Well-trained subjects have demonstrated unusual physical, emotional, perceptual, and even psychic capacities while in a hypnotically induced state. Because hypnotic inductions lead into so many altered states, we shall consider hypnosis a tool for exploring consciousness rather than a means of inducing a single specific altered state.

Subjective reality and the responses of the subject to external stimuli are markedly changed in hypnosis. Tart (1970) describes some of the range of effects.

> One of the standard tests we use, for instance, is to tell someone they can't smell and then you hold a bottle of ammonia under their nose and say, "take a good deep breath." They sit there with a blank face if they're a good subject. (It horrifies me every time I see it done, but it works beautifully.) You can induce total analgesia for pain for surgical operations, for instance. You can have people hallucinate. If you tell them there's a polar bear in the corner, they'll see a polar bear in the corner. You can tamper with their memory in certain ways. . . . You can take them back in time so they feel as if they were a child at a certain age level and so forth. [pp. 27–28]

Implications of Hypnosis Research for Personality Theory

1. Who is in control of your consciousness? In stage hypnosis it appears that the hypnotist is in full control, forcing the subject to do foolish and embarrassing things. Laboratory research indicates that the relationship is more cooperative than it often appears to be. The subject trusts the hypnotist and will therefore go along with many kinds of suggestions. If you do what you are told, are you responsible for your act? Are you conscious of the source of the suggestion? To some extent we are all hypnotized by advertising and television (Harman, 1967). How does this kind of conditioning compare to hypnotic induction?

2. In dental hypnosis the patient is taught to move the pain out of the teeth or to "turn the pain off." How is this done? We don't know, but we do know it is successful. If pain is subjective, that is, subject to voluntary control, what does it mean to say I am in pain or even I am tired or I am angry? All these sensations can be turned on and off by a good hypnotic subject. Arnold (1950) asked subjects to tense their muscles in various patterns. The subjects reported emotions that correlated with the kinds of muscle tensions requested. For James, Arnold's work would be additional evidence that it is the physical sensation plus

Within the province of the mind, what I believe to be true is true or becomes true, within the limits to be found experientially and experimentally. These limits are further beliefs to be transcended. [John Lilly, 1973]

attention to it that determines the effect on consciousness. The evidence from hypnosis suggests that consciousness *can* be highly selective in what it admits into awareness.

A different approach to pain control, one that you can try for yourself, makes use of the mind's natural tendency to wander. The next time you are in pain—from a burn, insect sting, or a sprained ankle—close your eyes and consciously try to intensify the pain. Concentrate fully on only the pain and the affected part of your body. Experience it as completely as you can. Try and maintain this total absorption for at least 30 seconds. When you relax, the pain will be greatly diminished or gone (adapted from Ferguson, 1973).

To what extent is our acceptance of external stimulation simply a result of not understanding alternative ways of dealing with sensations?

3. In what is labeled "deep hypnosis" (Tart, 1970; Sherman, 1972), personality appears to undergo a series of radical transformations. One by one, aspects of identity seem to be put aside. The sense of time passing, awareness of one's own body, awareness of the room, and awareness of personal identity itself fades away. Although there still is communication between subject and experimenter, even that awareness thins out until the experimenter is just a distant voice.

> I asked him about his sense of identity at various points. "Who are you?" "What's your identity?" That sort of thing. He starts out as himself, ego, and then his sense of identity tends to become less distributed through his body and more just his head; just sort of a thinking part. And that becomes a little more so and then that begins a kind of dropping out until his ordinary identity—let's call him John Smith—steadily decreases and as he goes deeper into hypnosis John Smith no longer exists. But there is a change taking place in who he is. He becomes more and more identified with a new identity, and that identity is *potential*. He's not anybody in particular; he's potential. He could be this, he could be that. He's aware of identifying with this flux of potentiality that could evolve into many sorts of things. [Tart, 1970, p. 35]

4. What effect does perception have on personality? Most theorists assume that we all see approximately the same world, see the same colors, have the same sense of time, and so forth. Aaronson (1968, 1979) has conducted a number of studies which question that assumption. He has found that hypnotically induced changes in perception (altering the way time, form, or space is perceived) can cause psychoticlike, euphoric, or other short-term changes in personality. Changing perceptual parameters results in emotional and behavioral changes that parallel descriptions of catatonia, paranoia, and other mental disorders. Here is one example of Aaronson's work with a normal, well-adjusted subject.

Subject 5 reacted [to the hypnotic instruction that there is no dimension of depth] with marked primitivization of behavior. He displayed shallow, inappropriate humor and could not conceive what lay over the brow of a hill or around a corner. He crossed himself repeatedly, although nothing in his background suggested this type of religious symbolism. His affect seemed shallow and blunted, his sense impressions seemed dulled, and his behavior was not unlike that of a chronic schizophrenic. [1979, pp. 227–228]

It may be as fruitful to investigate how others perceive the universe as to investigate their childhood experiences in order to understand their present-day behavior. Do you know anyone who always seems to be hurrying, who can't slow down? Do you know people who seem unnaturally gloomy or perpetually cheerful? It is possible that some of the differences we ascribe to "personality variables" may be due to "perceptual variables" instead.

The Hidden Observer

In hypnosis it appears that one part of a person may be aware of some of what is going on while another part of the personality is absolutely unaware of it. The early controversial work in this area by James (1899b) languished. He reported on a hypnotic subject whose right hand commented in writing about pinpricks it had been given. When questioned about it, the subject was unaware of the physical sensations and upon reading the writings of his own hand dismissed them.

It must be admitted, therefore, that in certain persons . . . the total possible consciousness may be split into parts which coexist but mutually ignore each other. . . . [James, 1890, I, p. 206]

Hilgard (1977, 1978) did a series of similar experiments and reported that there seemed to be divided awareness, meaning that both parts of the personality were equally capable and intelligent, but not aware of each other.

The hidden observer was rediscovered by accident:

. . . we first found the phenomenon in a young man—a blind subject who had achieved hypnotic deafness. He had been unperturbed by noises and by the remarks the students were yelling at him. At one point one of the students said, "How do we know he isn't hearing anything?" So I asked him to raise his finger if he could hear what was being said. The finger went up. Then the subject said, "Would you mind bringing me out so you can tell me what just happened—what caused my finger to lift?"
I then told him that when I placed my hand on his head, I wanted to be in touch with the part of him that had lifted the finger. As soon as I placed my hand on his head, I was able to get from him descriptions of what had been said, how many times I had clapped the wooden blocks together and so on. When I lifted my hand, he reverted to the earlier hypnotic state and said, "The last thing I remember, you told me I would talk to you when you placed your hand on my head. Did I say anything?" [Hilgard, 1977, p. 186]

Is it plausible that there is a part of you aware, observing, and yet unknown to you? There is growing evidence that the answer is yes. If this is so, then what are the characteristics of that part? What does it know, and how does it affect your behavior?

ESP—PARANORMAL RESEARCH

We are so far from knowing all the forces of nature and the various modes of their action that it is not worthy of a philosopher to deny phenomena only because they are inexplicable in the present state of our knowledge. [Pierre Laplace, French mathematician]

Although James attracted students who carried on his pragmatic approach to education and philosophy, his paranormal concerns were not continued after his death. Psychology until recently has tried to ignore work in this area. The reason for the collective distaste is summarized well by Tart (1966): "One of the difficulties for many scientists in accepting the existence of extrasensory perception (ESP) is that it does not make sense in terms of what we know about the physical universe. We do not have any comprehensive theories, any good models, or any sort of generally accepted explanation of the phenomena" (p. 448). James was more interested in investigating the instances available to him than in developing theoretical models. He was also aware, as are parapsychologists today, that there is often fraud mixed in with genuine phenomena.

The rising tide of research on altered states has included the growth of parapsychological investigations. Books such as *Psychic Discoveries Behind the Iron Curtain* (by Sheila Ostrander and Lynn Schroeder, 1970) and *Psychic Exploration* (by Edgar Mitchell, the astronaut, 1974) revived popular, professional, and government interest.

Present-day researchers tend to be concerned with training, measuring, and controlling specific paranormal abilities, rather than worrying over more and more elaborate proofs for their existence.

I will not say it is possible. I will only say that it is true. [Charles Richet, parapsychologist and Nobel Prize winner]

Have I given you the impression that I am secretly inclined to support the reality of telepathy in the occult sense? If so, I should very much regret that it is so difficult to avoid giving such an impression. In reality, however, I was anxious to be strictly impartial. I have every reason to be so, for I have no opinion. I know nothing about it. [Freud, 1922]

It is worth noting the logical distinction that exists between proving something and disproving it. For example, I have inserted between this page and the one immediately following (in each and every copy of this book) a feather from the wing of an invisible being. For those of you who have not perceived such a feather, turn the page now and notice if there is a nonmaterial, invisible object there. (Some of you who lack the training or the natural capacity may not see it at first.) You may scoff at this, but you will find it is extremely difficult to *disprove* my statement. I may not be able to prove it to your satisfaction, but it is most unlikely that you will be able to disprove it to mine. This kind of stand-off between researchers and skeptics in the past has made it impossible to sustain meaningful dialogue about the validity or plausibility of various kinds of paranormal experiences.

The current thrust is away from this kind of confrontation and toward more accurate measurements and closer identification of critical variables. Research includes training paranormal abilities in people who have not demonstrated these capacities before.

Most parapsychological researchers accept the following phenomena:

1. Telepathy: communication from one mind to another.
2. Clairvoyance: obtaining information not available to the physical senses, such as information from a closed book in another room.
3. Precognition: obtaining information that does not yet exist; for example, dreaming of an event that occurs some days later.
4. Psychokinesis: influencing physical objects or processes without any physical contact.

There are other paranormal capacities under investigation, but these four illustrate the scope of the field (Wohlman, 1977; Bowles & Hynds, 1978).

Implications of Paranormal Research for Personality Theory

1. To what extent is the link between mother and child telepathic? The biological point of view supposes that the link between mother and child is severed at birth. Evidence indicates that this bond, partly physical, partly telepathic, is still active after birth. This is especially evident when either the child or the mother undergoes intense emotional arousal.

2. A more general question is the problem of determining whether any of our capacities to empathize with others are due to subtle telepathic cues. Researchers are finding that the links between relatives or even between pets and their owners are continuous and not limited by conscious awareness of each other.

3. If it is possible to obtain information from another's mind, from a sealed room, or even from a future time, how then can we define the limits of the personality? Is identity restricted to the body, as we usually assume, or is it loosely localized there with possible extensions? As in the psychedelic literature, the published results raise questions about space and time. If, as Einstein said, "the distinction between past, present, and future is only an illusion, even if a stubborn one," then we cannot feel secure in our present models of psychological causality.

Work on "remote viewing" (gathering information from a location far away from the observer's physical body), which appeared in hard-nosed engineering journals and was sponsored by military funding agencies (Targ & Puthoff, 1974, 1977), suggests that the personality is located inside the body *almost* all of the time. The few exceptional circumstances (Monroe, 1971) continue to disturb but have not yet dislodged conventional theories (Wilber, 1981).

4. The data on reincarnation raise sticky questions for all personality theories. Reincarnation is the belief that upon death the personality does not disappear but may, in some sense, be reestablished in a new-

Esser, director of the hospital's Psychiatric Foundation, found that identical twins isolated from each other displayed simultaneous plethsmographic [measurement of blood flow, sensitive to emotional changes] changes even when the agent twin reacted to statements of only mild emotional impact. Esser and Douglas Dean found that a dog in isolation would show a strong physiological reaction when researchers threw ice water on his master in another room. [Ferguson, 1973, p. 324]

born child or other living form. Contemporary cases of reported reincarnation have been researched; the stories are consistent and have been verified in many cases (Stevenson, 1966; David-Neel, 1971; Govinda, 1970; Gunaratna, 1971). Although other parts of the world subscribe to the reality of reincarnation, it plays no part in Western thinking.[5]

It is not everyone who is able to recall spontaneously the memory of a past existence. Such a recall is possible only in exceptional cases . . . in nearly all the cases of spontaneous recall the previous lives were cut off in early childhood by some form of violent death such as an accident or serious illness. [Gunaratna, 1971, p. 65]

If one can accept the phenomena, then the possible source of personality and physical characteristics may include events or experiences from former incarnations. All that can definitely be said is that there is evidence which cannot be easily argued away.

All of these areas include data that do not fit into the existing paradigms of conventional personal theory. Either the data must be disproved or invalidated or personality theory must enlarge its scope to take in these troublesome findings.

EXERCISES

Regeneration

James wrote about consciousness throughout his career, modifying and developing his ideas (Taylor, 1981). Few of his propositions are easily testable. One of the exceptions is the following from his introductory textbook:

> The way to success is by surrender to passivity, not activity. Relaxation, not intentness should be now the rule. Give up the feeling of responsibility, let go your hold. . . . It is but giving your private convulsive self a rest and finding that a greater self is there. . . .
>
>   The regenerative phenomena which ensue on the abandonment of effort remain firm facts of human nature. [1890I,]

Choose a time when you are engaged in long difficult activity, either intellectual or physical. If you are a coffee drinker or a candy muncher, pick a time when you really want such a stimulant. Instead of getting it, lie flat on the floor for 5 minutes, breathe slowly and fully. Do not try to do anything, simply allow your muscles to relax, your thoughts to wander, your breathing to slow down. Don't do this on a bed; you may have the habit of falling asleep on beds. Use the floor or a tabletop.

After 5 minutes get up and check yourself. Are you refreshed? How does this inactivity compare with pacing around or getting something to eat? Can you now better determine what James calls regenerative phenomena?

Stream of Consciousness

1. Take 5 minutes to sit quietly and let your thoughts wander. Afterward write down as many of the *different thoughts* as you can recall.

---

[5]This has not always been the case; reincarnation was a part of Christian doctrine until its formal repudiation in A.D. 553, at the Second Council of Constantinople.

2. Take 1 minute, still allowing your thoughts to wander. When the minute is over, try and recall what thoughts you had during that minute. Write down, if possible, the *series of thoughts*. An example might be the following: "The exercise . . . pencil to write it down . . . my desk has pencils . . . bills on my desk . . . do I still want to buy fluoridated spring water . . . Yosemite last year . . . lakes frozen at the edge in the morning . . . my sleeping bag stuck at night, freezing cold."
3. Again take 1 minute. This time control your thoughts, keeping them on a single track. Write down the *series of linked thoughts*.

Looking over your own records of your thinking, does it seem realistic to consider your consciousness as a stream? When you controlled your thoughts, did they seem actually under your control or did they continue to "flow," moving from one idea or image to another? This exercise is more useful if you are able to share and discuss your findings with others in your class.

The James-Lange Theory of Emotions

James says his theory is easiest to observe with "grosser" emotions, which include love, anger, and fear. This exercise provides you with an opportunity to experience the interplay between physical sensations and the accompanying feelings.

I

1. Allow yourself to become angry. It may be easier if you visualize a person, situation, or political figure you have been angry with. Let the emotion build, allowing your posture to change, your hands to tighten into fists, your teeth to clench, your jaw to move forward slightly and up. Try to be aware of these or other physical changes. If possible, work in pairs. Have your partner make notes on the posture and muscle changes you assume while becoming angry.
2. Relax, move around, shake yourself, take a few deep breaths. Let go of the emotion and look around you.
3. Then allow yourself to become lonely, withdrawn, isolated. This is probably easier to do on the floor. Let your body curl up; your knees may be drawn in close to your body, your head close to your chest. Notice what your hands do. As before, your partner should pay close attention and make notes.
4. Relax as before.
5. Change roles and allow your partner to go through the same two sequences: anger and relaxation, loneliness and relaxation. You observe and note the physical changes.

II

1. Assume the physical postures, mimicking your former physical state and coached by your partner.
2. Observe your own feelings. Did the postures alone cue off the emotions?

Strengthening the Will I

"Useless Exercise"

James writes that it is possible to train the will, to strengthen its capacity. One of his suggestions was to perform an exercise for a few minutes each day. Here is one to experiment with.

1. Obtain a small box of matches, paper clips, pushpins, or candies.
2. Place the box on the desk in front of you.
3. Open the box.
4. Take out the items inside one by one.
5. Close the box.
6. Open the box.
7. Put the items back in the box one by one.
8. Close the box.
9. Go through instructions 3–8 until time is called (5 minutes).

After the exercise is completed, write down the feelings you had while doing this exercise. Pay special attention to all the reasons you thought of for not doing this kind of useless exercise.

If you repeat this for several days, changes will occur. Each day you will discover a host of new reasons why you should stop. The first few days you may find this exercise extremely difficult. Should you continue, however, it will be followed by a period when it will not only be easy to complete the 5 minutes, but you also will feel a sense of personal power and self-control after the exercise.

The reasons you come up with for *not* doing this exercise are a partial list of the elements in your own personality that inhibit your will. You have only your will to counter these many (and excellent) reasons. There is no "good reason" to continue the exercise, only your decision to do so.

After you have done the exercise for five days, you may wish to reconsider the role of will in your life.

Strengthening the Will II*

Daily Exercise

1. Decide to exercise for one week, 15–20 minutes each day.
2. Decide what kind of exercise you will do: running, swimming, riding a bike, and so on.
3. Do it.
4. Observe what interferes with easily carrying out your intentions.
5. Observe how you feel each time you complete the exercise you have set out for yourself.
6. Observe the interaction between your body and your will.

*Suggested by Lolly Font.

ANNOTATED BIBLIOGRAPHY

Books by William James

James, William. *Psychology: The briefer course.* New York: Harper & Row, 1961. An edited version of the *Principles of Psychology,* his basic textbook. Easy to read and sensible, it contains most of the sections of James that are still of interest to students today.

———. *The varieties of religious experience.* New York: New American Library (Mentor Books), 1958. James' lectures on the psychology of religion and religious experience. A full introduction to the more general psychology of altered states of consciousness although almost all the many examples come from specifically religious literature.

———. *Talks to teachers and other essays.* New York: Dover, 1962. A popular exposition of James' ideas in relation to education. Full of sensible advice about the way to cultivate and train young minds.

———. *The Writings of William James* (John J. McDermott, Ed.). Chicago: University of Chicago Press, 1977. The best single-volume collection of James' writings. A good introduction with ample selections from his psychological and philosophical writings.

Biography of William James

Perry, Ralph Barton. *The thought and character of William James* (2 vols.). Boston: Little, Brown, 1935. Cambridge, Mass.: Harvard University Press (abridged), 1948. A masterpiece of exposition that is primarily composed of letters to and from James. Mainly James but with enough Perry to make it flow easily.

Books on Altered States

Brown, Barbara. *New mind, new body.* New York: Harper & Row, 1974. A thorough, but not overly technical, look at the whole field of biofeedback. Some implications of the research as they affect health care, psychology, philosophy, and the biological sciences are spelled out.

Goleman, Daniel, & Davidson, Richard. *Consciousness: Brain, states of awareness, and mysticism.* New York: Harper & Row, 1979. A collection of highly readable accurate articles on many facets of altered states research. An excellent starting place.

Wohlman, Benjamin. *Handbook of Parapsychology.* New York: Van Nostrand Reinhold, 1977. A solid and heavily referenced state-of-the-science volume. Try Mitchell (1974) for an easier but still substantial overview.

REFERENCES

Aaronson, Bernard S. Hypnotic alterations of space and time. *International Journal of Parapsychology,* 1968, *10,* 5–36.

———. Hypnotic alterations of space and time: Their relationship to psychopathology. In James Fadiman & Donald Kewman (Eds.), *Exploring madness: Experience, theory, and research.* Monterey, Calif.: Brooks/Cole, 1979, pp. 223–236.

Adler, Gebard, & Jaffe, Amelia. *Letters of C. G. Jung* (Vol. I). Princeton, N.J.: Princeton University Press, 1978.

Allport, Gordon. *William James: Psychology, the briefer course* (Gordon Allport Ed.). New York: Harper & Row, 1961, Introduction.

Arnold, M. B. An excitatory theory of emotion. In M. L. Reymett (Ed.), *Feelings and emotions: the mooseheart symposium.* New York: McGraw-Hill, 1950, pp. 11–33.

Averill J. R. Autonomic response patterns during sadness and mirth *Psychophysiology,* 1980, 99–214.

Bandler, Richard, & Grinder, John. *Frogs into princes: Neurolinguistic programming.* Moab, Utah: Real People Press, 1979.

Benson, H. *The relaxation response.* New York: Morrow, 1975.

Benson, H., & Wallace, R. K. Decreased drug abuse with transcendental meditation: A study of 1862 subjects. In *Proceedings of drug abuse, international symposium for physicians.* Philadelphia: Lea & Ferbinger, 1972, pp. 369–376.

Bentov, Itzhak. *Stalking the wild pendulum.* New York: Dutton, 1977.

Biofeedback and self-control: An Aldine annual (T. X. Barber, Leo Dicara, Joe Kamiya, David Shapiro, & Johann Stoyva, Eds.). Chicago: Aldine, 1971, 1972, 1973, 1974, 1975–1976, 1976–1977, 1977–1978.

Bowles, Norma, & Hynds, Fran. *Psi search.* San Francisco: Harper & Row, 1978.

Bray, C. W., Boring, E. G., Macleod, R. B. & Solomon, R. L. *William James: Unfinished business* (Robert Macleod, Ed.). Washington, D.C.: American Psychological Association, 1969, Preface, pp. iii–iv.

Brown, Barbara. *New mind, new body.* New York: Harper & Row, 1974. Also excerpted in *Psychology Today,* 1974, *8*(3), 48–56, 74–107.

Cannon, Walter B. The James-Lange theory of emotions: A critical examination and an alternative theory. *American Journal of Psychology,* 1927, *39,* 106–124.

Capra, Fritjof. *The tao of physics.* New York: Bantam Books, 1975.

Carrington, Patricia. The uses of meditation in psychotherapy. In A. Sugarman & R. Tarter (Eds.), *Expanding dimensions of consciousness.* New York: Springer-Verlag, 1978.

Ferguson, Marilyn. *The brain revolution.* New York: Taplinger, 1973.

Fisher, Roland, & Cleveland, Sidney. *Body image and personality.* Princeton, N.J.: Van Nostrand, 1958.

Freud, Sigmund. Dreams and telepathy. Standard edition (Vol. 18), pp. 196–200. (Originally published, 1922.)

———. *Outline of Psychoanalysis.* Standard edition (Vol. 23), pp. 141–205. (Originally published, 1940.)

Coleman, Daniel, & Davidson, Richard. *Consciousness: Brain, states of awareness, and mysticism.* New York: Harper & Row, 1979.

Govinda, Lama Anagarika. *The way of the white clouds: A Buddhist pilgrim in Tibet.* Berkeley, Calif.: Shambala, 1970.

Green, E., & Green, A., *How to make use of the field of mind theory.* In *The dimensions of healing.* Los Altos, Calif.: Academy of Parapsychology and Medicine, 1972.

Grof, Stanislav. Varieties of transpersonal experience: Observations from LSD psychotherapy. *Journal of Transpersonal Psychology,* 1971, *4,* 45–80.

———. *Realms of the Human Unconscious.* New York: Viking Press, 1975.

Gunaratna, V. F. *Rebirth explained.* The Wheel Publication No. 167/168/169. Kandy, Ceylon: Buddhist Publication Society, 1971.

Harman, Willis W. Old wine in new wineskins—The reasons for the limited world view. In James Bugenthal (Ed.), *Challenges of humanistic psychology.* New York: McGraw-Hill, 1967, pp. 321–335. Also in James Fadiman (Ed.), *The proper study of man* New York: Macmillan, 1971, pp. 132–145.

Hilgard, Ernest. *Divided consciousness.* New York: Wiley, 1977.

————. New approaches to hypnosis. *Brain Mind Bulletin,* 1978, *3*(7), 3.

Hohman, G. W., Some effects of spinal cord lessions on experienced emotional feelings. *Psychophysiology,* 1966, *3,* 143–156.

James, Henry (Ed.). *The letters of William James (2 vols.).* Boston: Little, Brown, 1926.

James, William. *Grundzuge der physiologischen psychologie* (W. Wundt, Reviewer). Originally published in the *North American Review,* 1875, *121,* 195–201. In Rieber, R. W. (Ed.), *Wilhelm Wundt and the making of a scientific psychology.* New York: Plenum Press, 1980, pp. 199–206.

————. *The principles of psychology* (2 vols.). New York: Holt, Rinehart and Winston, 1890. Unaltered republication, New York: Dover, 1950.

————. *Psychology: The briefer course.* New York: Holt, Rinehart and Winston, 1892; New edition, New York: Harper & Row, 1961.

————. *The will to believe and other essays in popular philosophy.* New York and London: McKay, 1896.

————. *Talks to teachers on psychology and to students on some of life's ideals.* New York: Holt, Rinehart and Winston, 1899. Unaltered republication, New York: Dover, 1962.

————. Automatic writing. *Proceedings of the American Society for Psychical Research,* 1899, *199,* 548–564.

————. *Pragmatism: A new name for some old ways of thinking.* New York and London: McKay, 1907.

————. *The meaning of truth.* New York: McKay, 1909.

————. *Some problems in philosophy.* New York: McKay, 1911.

————. *Essays in pragmatism* (Alburey Castell, Ed.). New York: Hafner Press, 1948.

————. The tigers in India. In R. B. Perry (Ed.), *Pragmatism and four essays from the meaning of truth.* Harcourt Brace Jovanovich, 1955, pp. 225–228.

————. *The varieties of religious experience.* New York: New American Library, 1958.

————. Subjective effects of nitrous oxide. In C. Tart, (Ed.), *Altered states of consciousness,* New York: Wiley, 1969, pp. 359–362.

Kamiya, Joe, & Kamiya, Joanne. Biofeedback. In A. Hastings, J. Fadiman, & J. Gordon (Eds.), *Health for the whole person.* New York: Pocket Books, 1981, pp. 115–130.

Kanelakos, Demetri, & Lukas, Jerome. *The psychobiology of transcendental meditation: A literature review.* Menlo Park, Calif.: Benjamin, 1974.

Karlins, Marvin, & Andrews, Lewis. *Biofeedback: Turning on the power of your mind.* Philadelphia: Lippincott, 1972.

Kimble, Gregory A., & Perlmuter, Lawrence C. The problem of volition. *Psychological Record,* 1970, *77,* 361–384.

Laird, J. D., Self-attribution of emotion: The effects of expressive behavior on the quality of emotional experience. *Journal of Personality and Social Psychology,* 1974, *29,* 475–486.

LeShan, Lawrence. Physicists and mystics: Similarities in world view. *Journal of Transpersonal Psychology,* 1969 *1,* 1–20.

Lilly, John C. *The center of the cyclone.* New York: Bantam Books, 1973.

Matthiessen, T. H. *The James family.* New York: Random House, 1980.

McDermott, John J. (Ed.). *The writings of William James: A comprehensive edition.* Chicago: University of Chicago Press, 1977.

MacLeod, Robert B. (Ed.). *William James: Unfinished business.* Washington, D.C.: American Psychological Association, 1969.

Meyer, Donald. *The positive thinkers.* New York: Pantheon Press, 1980.

Mitchell, Edgar. *Psychic exploration* (John White, Ed.). New York: Putnam, 1974.

Monroe, Robert A. *Journeys out of the body.* New York: Doubleday, 1971.

Murphy, Gardner, & Ballou, Robert (Eds.). *William James on psychical research.* New York: Viking Press, 1960.

Olton, David S., & Noonberg, Aaron R. *Biofeedback: Clinical applications in behavioral medicine.* Englewood Cliffs, N.J.: Prentice-Hall, 1980.

O'Regan, Brendan. Biofeedback: The growth of a technique. *Institute of Noetic Sciences Newsletter,* 1979, 7(1), 10.

Ornstein, Robert. *The psychology of consciousness.* San Francisco: Freeman; New York: Viking Press, 1972.

Ostrander, Sheila, & Schroeder, Lynn. *Psychic discoveries behind the iron curtain.* Englewood Cliffs, N.J.: Prentice-Hall, 1970.

Peper, Eric, & Williams, Elizabeth Ann. Autogenic Therapy. In A. Hastings, J. Fadiman, & J. Gordon (Eds.), *Health for the whole person.* New York: Pocket Books, 1981, pp. 131–138.

Perry, Ralph Baton. *The thought and character of William James* (2 vols.). Boston: Little, Brown, 1935.

Plutchik, Robert. *The emotions: Facts, theories, and a new model.* New York: Random House, 1962.

Ram Dass. *The only dance there is.* New York: Doubleday, 1974.

———. *Journey of awakening, a mediator's guidebook.* New York: Doubleday, 1978.

Rama, Swami; Ballentine, Rudolph; & Weinstock, Allan. *Yoga and psychotherapy.* Glenview, Ill.: Himalayan Institute, 1976.

Sayadaw, Mahasi. *Satipatthana Vipassana meditation.* Original edition in Burmese. English edition, nd. San Francisco: Unity Press, 1954.

Schacter, Stanley. Pain, fear, and anger in hypertensives and normotensives; a psychophysiologic study. *Psychosomatic Medicine,* 1957, *19,* 17–29.

———. *Emotion, obesity, and crime.* New York: Academic Press, 1971.

Schacter, Stanley, & Singer, Jerome. Cognitive, social and physiological determinants of emotional states. *Psychological Review,* 1962, *69,* 379–399.

Schilder, Paul. *The image and appearance of the human body.* London: Routledge & Kegan Paul, 1935.

Shapiro, Dean, & Walsh, Roger (Eds). *The science of meditation: Research, theory, and experience.* New York: Aldine, 1981.

Sherman, Spencer E. Brief report: Continuing research on "very deep hypnosis." *Journal of Transpersonal Psychology,* 1972, *4,* 87–92.

Shields, Stephanie, & Stern, Robert. Emotion: The perception of bodily change. In P. Pliner, K. Blankstein, & I. Spigel (Eds.), *Perception of emotion in self and others.* New York: Plenum Press, 1979, pp. 85–106.

Sidis, Boris. *The psychology of suggestion.* William James. New York: Appleton-Century-Crofts, 1898, Introduction.

Simonton, Carl; Mathews-Simonton, Stephanie, & Creighton, James. *Getting well again.* Los Angeles: Tarcher, 1978.

Skinner, B. F. *Cumulative record: A selection of papers* (3rd ed.). New York: Appleton-Century-Crofts, 1972.

Stevenson, Ian. *Twenty cases suggestive of reincarnation.* Proceedings of the American Society for Psychical Research (Vol. 26). New York, 1966.

Targ, Russel, & Puthoff, Hal. Information transmission under conditions of sensory shielding. *Nature,* 1974, *251,* 602–607.

———. *Mind-reach.* New York: Dell (Delacorte Press), 1977.

Tart, Charles T. Models for the explanation of extrasensory perception. *International Journal of Neuropsychiatry,* 1966, *2,* 488–504.

———. Transpersonal potentialities of deep hypnosis. *Journal of Transpersonal Psychology,* 1970, *2,* 27–40.

———. Scientific foundations for the study of altered states of consciousness. *Journal of Transpersonal Psychology,* 1971, *3,* 93–124. Shorter version in *Science,* 1972, *176,* 1203–1210.

———. *States of consciousness.* New York: Dutton, 1975.

Taylor, Eugene. The evolution of William James' definition of consciousness. *Revision,* 1981, *4*(2), 40–47.

Valle, Ronald, & von Eckartsberg, Rolf. *The metaphors of consciousness.* New York: Plenum Press, 1981.

Wilber, Ken. *Up from Eden.* New York: Doubleday, 1981.

———. *The spectrum of consciousness.* Wheaton, Ill.: Theosophical Publishing Co., 1977.

Wolman, Benjamin B., & Knapp, Susan. *Contemporary theories and systems in psychology.* New York: Plenum Press, 1981.

———. *Handbook of parapsychology.* New York: Van Nostrand Reinhold, 1977.

Zukav, G. *The dancing Wu Li masters.* New York: Morrow, 1979.

CHAPTER 9
B. F. SKINNER AND RADICAL BEHAVIORISM

B. F. Skinner is perhaps the most famous psychologist in the United States. His works are studied and have had effects far beyond the confines of professional psychology. He bases his ideas on the observable behavior of people and animals. His distaste for and distrust of mental, subjective, intervening, or "fictional" explanations led him to formulate distinct ways of observing, measuring, predicting, and understanding behavior and society.

No theorist since Freud has been so lauded, quoted, misquoted, attacked, and supported. Skinner, in turn, has delighted in meeting his critics and debated with major thinkers who oppose his position (Wann, 1964; Skinner, 1972d, 1977b). The widespread applications of his seminal ideas, coupled with his personal charm, his willingness to speculate on all the implications of his position and an absolute, unshakable faith in his fundamental assumptions, have made him a pivotal figure in contemporary psychology.

Freud wrote that his detractors displayed, in the emotional nature of their criticisms, those very facets of psychoanalytic theory whose existence they so vigorously denied. Similarly, Skinner's critics appear to him to display the nonscientific and inaccurate ways of thinking that his work attempts to overcome. Both men have been vigorously criticized and acclaimed; both have been responsible for developing alternative visions of human nature.

In a survey of department chairmen at American universities . . . Skinner was chosen overwhelmingly as the most influential figure in modern psychology. [*New York Times* Magazine]

PERSONAL HISTORY

B. F. Skinner was born in 1904 and raised in Susquehanna, Pennsylvania, a small town in the northeastern part of the state. His father practiced law. Skinner recalls that his home was "warm and stable. I lived in the house I was born in until I went to college" (Skinner, 1967a, p. 387).

His boyhood fascination with mechanical inventions foreshadowed his later concern with modifying observable behavior.

Some of the things I built had a bearing on human behavior. I was not allowed to smoke, so I made a gadget incorporating an atomizer bulb through which I could "smoke" cigarettes and blow smoke rings hygienically. (There might be a demand for it today.) At one time my mother started a campaign to teach me to hang up my pajamas. Every morning while I was eating breakfast, she would go up to my room, discover that my pajamas were not hung up, and call to me to come up immediately. She continued this for weeks. When the aversive stimulation grew unbearable, I constructed a mechanical device that solved my problem. A special hook in the closet of my room was connected by a string-and-pulley system to a sign hanging above the door to the room. When my pajamas were in place on the hook, the sign was held high above the door out of the way. When the pajamas were off the hook, the sign hung squarely in the middle of the door frame. It read: "Hang up your pajamas"! [Skinner, 1967a, p. 396]

After completing his work at Hamilton College, which sustained and enriched his interest in literature and the arts, he returned home and attempted to become a writer. "I built a small study in the attic and set to work. The results were disastrous. I fretted away my time. I read aimlessly, built model ships, played the piano, listened to the newly-invented radio, contributed to the humorous column of a local paper but wrote almost nothing else, and thought about seeing a psychiatrist" (Skinner, 1967a, p. 394). He finally terminated this experiment and went to New York for six months; he spent the summer in Europe and on his return entered Harvard graduate school in psychology. His personal failure as a writer led to a generalized distrust of the literary method of observation. "I had failed as a writer because I had nothing important to say, but I could not accept that explanation. It was literature which must be at fault. . . . A writer might portray human behavior accurately, but he did not therefore understand it. I was to remain interested in human behavior, but the literary method had failed me; I would turn to the scientific" (Skinner, 1967a, p. 395).

During graduate school he worked diligently but not as hard as he liked to recall. In an early autobiographical essay (1967a) he wrote: "I would rise at six, study until breakfast, go to classes, laboratories, and libraries with no more than fifteen minutes unscheduled during the day, study until exactly nine o'clock at night and go to bed. I saw no movies or plays, seldom went to concerts, had scarcely any dates and read nothing but psychology and physiology." Much later he amended his description of his graduate years, recalling a normal blend of classes, activities, friends, dull papers, incompleted work, and dating (Skinner, 1979a).

I'm taking it easy my first semester . . . After January I expect to settle down and solve the riddle of the universe. Harvard is fine. [Skinner, 1979a]

After receiving his Ph.D., he worked for five years at the Harvard Medical School doing research on the nervous system of animals. In 1936 Skinner accepted a teaching position at the University of Minnesota where he taught introductory and experimental psychology. He notes with pride that a number of his students went on to graduate school and are important behaviorists today.

In 1938 he published *The Behavior of Organisms,* which established Skinner as an important learning theorist and laid the foundations for his subsequent publications. Skinner's work can be seen as an expansion, elaboration, and clarification of the seminal ideas in his first major book.

After nine years at Minnesota he accepted the chairmanship of the psychology department at the University of Indiana. Three years later he moved to a post at Harvard where he has remained until and after his retirement.

While pursuing his animal research studies, he had time and the creative capacity to apply his ingenuity in other directions. One device, which catapulted him into national prominence, was the invention of an "air crib" in 1945. This is a glassed-in, temperature-controlled crib with a bottom of absorbent cloth. In it, a child may move freely without cumbersome diapers, pants, and other clothes. The absorbent bottom is easily replaced as the child soils it. There was a popular rush of interest when the crib first appeared. However, the fact that the child is glassed in, instead of being behind bars (as in the conventional crib), ran counter to many closely held beliefs about child rearing. Although Skinner used it successfully for one of his own children, the crib never became popular. Skinner still regrets that its utility was not better understood (Skinner, 1979a).

My experience with American industry has been very sad. Nobody ever took up the air crib properly. [Skinner, in Goodell, 1977]

Ever the scientist, he reflects on his concerns that led to the invention. "I must confess also to an ulterior motive. If, as many people have claimed, the first year is extraordinarily important in the determination of character and personality, then by all means let us control the conditions of that year as far as possible in order to discover the important variables" (Skinner, 1979a, p. 290).

I really wrote *Walden Two* for the sake of feminine liberation but very few women liked it. [Skinner, in Goodell, 1977]

In 1948 Skinner published a novel, *Walden Two*, which he had written several years earlier. It was a description of a utopian community based on behaviorist learning principles. It was Skinner's initial effort to generalize his laboratory findings to human situations. From its initial release the book has been controversial and has sold over 1.5 million copies. Writing it was for Skinner a remarkable experience. "In general I write very slowly and in longhand. It took me two minutes to write each word of my thesis and that still is about my rate. From three or four hours each day I eventually salvage about one hundred publishable words" (Skinner, 1967a, p. 403). This was in sharp contrast to his writing of the novel, "I wrote my utopia in seven weeks. I would dash off a fair version of a short chapter in a single morning. I wrote directly on the typewriter . . . and I revised sparingly . . . I wrote some parts with an emotional intensity that I have never experienced at any other time" (Skinner, 1979a, pp. 297–298). "It was pretty obviously a venture in self-therapy, in which I was struggling to reconcile two aspects of my own behavior represented by Burris and Frazier [the two major characters]" (Skinner, 1967a, p. 403).[1]

Skinner has written a series of books that have successively defined his ideological stance and moved his work further and further from its experimental beginnings. These include: *Science and Human Behavior* (1953), *Cumulative Record* (1959, 1961, 1972a), *The Technology of Teaching* (1968), *Beyond Freedom and Dignity* (1971), *About Behaviorism* (1974), and *Reflections on Behaviorism and Society* (1978a). His more personal books include *Particulars of My Life* (1976c), *The Shaping of a Behaviorist* (1979a), and *Notebooks* (1980).

[1]Skinner's first name is Burrhus, his middle name is Frederic.

His willingness to appear in the media (Skinner, 1977a, 1978b, 1979b) has kept his ideas before the general public. He continues to write, taking on any challengers of his ideas (1977b) while working on recording the details of his life.

INTELLECTUAL ANTECEDENTS

B. F. Skinner says, like Francis Bacon before him, "I have 'studied nature not books,' asking questions of the organism rather than of those who have studied the organism. . . . I have studied Bacon in organizing my data . . . I classify not for the sake of classification but to reveal properties" (Skinner, 1967a, p. 409). This stance led Skinner to begin his work with careful laboratory experimentation and the accumulation of measurable behavioral data.

When we consider the possible richness of human personality, this may seem austere; yet it is the foundation upon which all of Skinner's propositions firmly rest.

Darwinism

The idea that working with animal studies is relevant to understanding human behavior is an indirect result of Darwin's research and the subsequent development of evolutionary theories. Many psychologists, including Skinner, now assume that humans are not essentially different from other animals.

The first researchers of animal behaviors were interested in discovering the reasoning capacities of animals. In effect, they tried to raise the status of animals to thinking beings. This idea—that animals have complex personalities—has always been part of our folklore. Walt Disney's creations personify the idea that animals have human characteristics. Charles Schultz's Snoopy carries this theme further, with Snoopy's possession of a van Gogh and a pool table in his doghouse.

We prefer to imagine that animals are like ourselves, rather than the reverse. The behaviorists, however, take the approach that we are more similar to animals than we have been willing to observe or admit. The initial thrust in examining higher thought processes in animals was deterred by the suggestions of Lloyd Morgan and the research of Edward Thorndike. Morgan proposed a "canon of parsimony": given two explanations, a scientist should always accept the simpler one. Thorndike conducted research which demonstrated that although animals seemed to display reasoning, their behaviors could be more parsimoniously explained as the result of noncognitive processes (Skinner, 1964). Consequently, the emphasis shifted. Researchers began to speculate freely that human behavior could also be understood without taking into account the little-understood complexities of consciousness.

Behaviorism is a formulation which makes possible an effective experimental approach to human behavior. . . . It may need to be clarified, but it does not need to be argued. I have no doubt of the eventual triumph of the position—not that it will eventually be proved right, but that it will provide the most direct route to a successful science of man. [Skinner, 1967a, pp. 409–410]

After the horror of atheism, there is nothing that leads weak minds further astray from the paths of virtue than the idea that the minds of other animals resemble our own, and that, therefore, we have no greater right to future life than have gnats and ants. [René Descartes, "A Treatise on the Passions of the Soul," 1649]

Watson

The time seems to have come when psychology must discard all references to consciousness. [Watson, 1913, p. 163]

John B. Watson, the first avowed psychological behaviorist, defined behaviorism as follows: "Psychology as the behaviorist views it is a purely objective branch of natural science. Its theoretical goal is the prediction and control of behavior. Introspection forms no essential part of its methods. . . . The behaviorist, in his efforts to get a unitary scheme of animal response, recognizes no dividing line between man and brute" (1913, p. 158). Watson argued that there was no such thing as consciousness, that all learning was dependent upon the external environment, and that all human activity is conditioned and conditionable in spite of variation in genetic makeup. Watson was a popular and persuasive writer. Skinner was attracted to the broad philosophical outlines of his works but not to some of his more extreme suggestions (Watson, 1928a). For example, one of Watson's most widely read books on child rearing contains the following advice: "Never hug and kiss them [children], never let them sit on your lap. If you must, kiss them once on the forehead when they say good-night. Shake hands with them in the morning" (1928b, pp. 81–82).

Watson's emphasis was viewed as extreme even at the time. Skinner criticizes Watson for his denial of genetic characteristics, as well as for his tendency to generalize, unsupported by actual data. "His new science was also, so to speak, born prematurely. Very few scientific facts about behavior—particularly human behavior—were available. A shortage of facts is always a problem in a new science, but in Watson's aggressive program in a field as vast as human behavior it was especially damaging. He needed more factual support than he could find, and it is not surprising that much of what he said seemed oversimplified and naive" (Skinner, 1974, p. 6).

Pavlov

Ivan Pavlov did the first important modern work on conditioning behavior (1927). His research demonstrated that autonomic functions, such as salivation at the approach of food, could be conditioned so that salivation could be evoked by a stimulus other than food, such as a flashing light. He was able to do more than merely predict statistically the behavior of an animal. Pavlov was not merely observing and predicting the behaviors he was studying; he could produce them on command.

A prediction of what the *average* individual will do is often of little or no value in dealing with a particular individual. [Skinner, 1953, p. 19]

Whereas other animal experimenters might be content with statistical analysis to predict the likelihood that a behavior would occur, Skinner was fascinated with the step beyond prediction—control. Pavlov's work pointed Skinner toward laboratory experiments using animals in settings where the circumstances were tightly controlled. He found that by restricting an animal's environment under limited conditions, he could achieve almost perfectly replicable results. Individual differences could be effectively controlled, and laws of behavior valid for any member of a species might be discovered. Skinner's contention was that, in this way, psychological research could eventually be elevated from a probabilistic science to an exact one.

Philosophy of Science

Skinner was impressed with the ideas of philosophers of science, including Percy Bridgman, Ernst Mach, and Jules Henri Poincaré. They created new models of explanatory thinking that did not depend on any metaphysical substructures. To Skinner, behaviorism is a special case of the philosophy of science; it "is not the science of human behavior; it is the philosophy of that science" (Skinner, 1974, p. 3). Behaviorism allows questions to be clearly formulated for which answers can be found. For example, only when biology left metaphysics behind, dismissing its concern with "vital fluids" and other unmeasurable, unprovable, and unpredictable notions, could it become an experimental science.

I often say that when you can measure what you are speaking about, and express it in numbers, you know something about it; but when you cannot express it in numbers, your knowledge is of a meager and unsatisfactory kind; it may be the beginning of knowledge, but you have scarcely, in your thoughts, advanced to the stage of Science. . . . [Lord Kelvin, 1824–1907]

Skinner has contended that his position is essentially nontheoretical (1950, 1956) and that he works from observable data alone. However, his impact on psychology and society has come from the extrapolations of his data into theories reaching far beyond the confines of his animal research.

MAJOR CONCEPTS

Scientific Analysis of Behavior

"Science is a disposition to deal with the facts rather than what someone has said about them. . . . It is a search for order, for uniformities, for lawful relations among the events in nature. It begins, as we all begin, by observing single episodes, but it quickly passes on the general rule, to scientific law" (Skinner, 1953, pp. 12–13). Past events are assumed to be sufficient data to begin to predict similar future events.

A scientific analysis of behavior must, I believe, assume that a person's behavior is controlled by his genetic and environmental histories rather than by the person himself as an initiating, creative agent. [Skinner, 1974, p. 189]

Behavior, although very complex, can be investigated, like any other observable phenomena. "Since it is a process, rather than a thing, it can not easily be held still for observation. It is changing, fluid, and evanescent, and for this reason it makes great technical demands upon the ingenuity and energy of the scientist. But there is nothing essentially insoluble about the problems which arise from this fact" (Skinner, 1953, p. 15). "Behavior is that which an organism can be observed doing. It is more to the point to say that behavior is that part of the functioning of an organism which is engaged in acting upon or having commerce with the outside world" (Skinner, 1938, p. 6). The goal is to be able to look at a behavior and its *contingencies* (from a Latin word, meaning "to touch on all sides"). For Skinner this includes the antecedents of the behavior, the response to it, and the consequences or results of the response. A complete analysis would also take into consideration the genetic endowment of the individual and the previous history of behaviors related to the behavior being studied.

The scientific analysis of behavior begins by isolating single parts of a complex event so that the single part can be better understood. Skinner's experimental research followed this analytic procedure, restricting itself to situations that are amenable to rigorous scientific analysis. The results of his experiments can be verified independently, and his conclusions can be checked against the recorded data.

Although Freud and the psychodynamic theorists have been equally interested in the developmental history of the individual as the basis for action, Skinner advocates a more extreme position, stating that it is behavior, and behavior alone, that can be studied. Behavior can be fully described, that is, it is measurable, observable, and perceivable with measuring instruments.

Personality

Skinner argues that if you base your definition of the self on observable behavior, it is not necessary to discuss the self or the personality at all.

Personality, therefore, in the sense of a separate self has no place in a scientific analysis of behavior. Personality as defined by Skinner is a *collection of behavior patterns*. Different situations evoke different response patterns. Each individual response is based solely on previous experiences and genetic history.

Buddhism also concludes that there is no individual self. Buddha did not believe that there was an entity called "personality"; there are only overlapping behaviors and sensations, all of which are impermanent. Skinner and the Buddhists develop their ideas based on the assumption that there is no ego, no self, no personality, except as characterized by a collection of behaviors. Both theories go on to stress that a proper understanding of the causes of behavior eliminates confusion and misunderstanding. The theories, however, diverge widely in their explanation of the causes.[2]

Explanatory Fictions

Explanatory fictions are those terms that nonbehaviorists use to describe behavior. Skinner describes them as concepts that people make use of when they do not understand the behavior involved or are unaware of the pattern of reinforcements that preceded or followed the behavior. Some examples of explanatory fictions are *freedom, autonomous man, dignity,* and *creativity.* Using any of these terms, as if they explained anything, is a disservice to everyone concerned. "Skinner believes it is a most harmful type of explanation simply because it has

[2]See the section on "Selflessness" in Zen Buddhism.

the misleading appearance of being satisfactory and therefore tends to retard the investigation of those objective variables that might yield genuine behavioral control" (Hall and Lindzey, 1978, pp. 646–647).

Freedom

Freedom is a label that we attach to behavior when we are unaware of the causes for the behavior. Although the full argument cannot be presented here, one example may clarify Skinner's meaning. A series of studies conducted by Milton Erickson (1939) demonstrated that through hypnosis, subjects could produce various kinds of psychopathological symptoms. While a subject was in a trance, Erickson would make posthypnotic suggestions. In most cases, the subjects carried out the suggestion and developed the symptom. In no case did the subject recall, when asked, that a suggestion had been given under hypnosis. Whenever subjects were asked what the reasons were for their unusual behavior, they would invent (and apparently believe) a host of explanations. In every case, if one simply listened to the subject's explanation, one would conclude that he or she was acting of his or her own free will. The subjects were convinced that their behaviors were due to their own decisions. The observers, knowing that the subjects had no recall of the preceding events, were equally convinced that "free will" was not the full explanation.

> When I can do what I want to do, there is my liberty for me, but I can't help wanting what I do want. [Voltaire, 1694–1778]

Skinner suggests that the "feeling of freedom" is not freedom; furthermore, he believes that the most repressive forms of control are those that reinforce the "feeling of freedom" but in fact restrict and control action in subtle ways not easily discovered by the people being controlled. "The hypothesis that man is not free is essential to the application of scientific method to the study of human behavior. The free inner man who is held responsible for the behavior of the external biological organism is only a pre-scientific substitute for the kind of causes which are discovered in the course of a scientific analysis. *All* of these *causes* lie outside the individual. . . . Science insists that action is initiated by forces impinging upon the individual, and that freedom is only another name for behavior for which we have not yet found a cause" (Skinner, 1953).

> There is no subjugation so perfect as that which keeps the appearance of freedom . . . [Jean Jacques Rousseau, 1712–1778]

Autonomous Man

This explanatory fiction is described by Skinner as an "indwelling agent," an inner person, who is moved by vague inner forces independent of the behavioral contingencies. To be autonomous is to initiate behavior that is "uncaused," that does not arise from prior behaviors, and that is not attributable to external events. Because Skinner finds no evidence that such a being exists, he is distressed that so many people believe in it.

> The objection to inner states is not that they do not exist, but that they are not relevant in a functional analysis. [Skinner, 1953, p. 35]

Intelligent people no longer believe that men are possessed by demons, . . . but human behavior is still commonly attributed to indwelling agents. [Skinner, 1971, p. 5]

As soon as one puts aside the indwelling agent, one can freely examine the similarities between the learning patterns of humans and animals. Skinner's research has demonstrated that if one plots certain kinds of learning experiences, the shape of the resulting curve (and the rate of the learning) is the same for pigeons, rats, monkeys, cats, dogs, and human children (Skinner, 1956). This parallelism between animal and human learning underlies Skinner's analysis of human behavior. Ever since his first book, *The Behavior of Organisms* (1938), he has performed and has been interested in experiments that postulate no major differentiation between humans and other species. In that book he states: "I may say that the only differences I expect to see revealed between the behavior of rat and man (aside from enormous differences of complexity) lie in the field of verbal behavior" (p. 442).

Dignity

Dignity (or credit or praise) is as much an explanatory fiction as is freedom. "The amount of credit a person receives is related in a curious way to the visibility of the causes of his behavior. We withhold credit when the causes are conspicuous . . . we do not give credit for coughing, sneezing, or vomiting even though the result may be valuable. For the same reason, we do not give much credit for behavior which is under conspicuous aversive control even though it may be useful" (Skinner, 1971, p. 42).

Rights and duties, like a moral or ethical sense, are examples of hypothetical internalized environmental sanctions. [Skinner, 1975, p. 48]

In other words, we give praise when we see an act *and* we do not know the circumstances or the additional contingencies that pushed the individual into that behavior. We do not praise acts of charity if we know they are done only to lower income taxes. We do not praise a confession of a crime if the confession has come out under extreme pressure. We do not censure a person whose acts inadvertently cause others damage. Skinner suggests that we should admit our ignorance and withhold both praise and censure.

Creativity

I have never been able to understand why he [the poet I. A. Richards] feels that Coleridge made an important contribution to our understanding of human behavior, and he has never been able to understand why I feel the same way about pigeons. [Skinner, 1972c, p. 34]

With a certain amount of puckish delight, Skinner dismisses the last stronghold of the indwelling agent, the poetic or creative act. It is for Skinner still another example of using a metaphysical label to avoid the fact that we do not know the specific causes of a given behavior.

Skinner derides the opinions of creative artists who maintain their works are spontaneous or that they arise from sources beyond the life experience of the artist. The evidence from hypnosis, the evidence from the vast body of literature on the effectiveness of propaganda and advertising, and the findings of psychotherapy concur that an individual may be unaware of what lies behind his or her own behavior. It is unlikely that poets, or anyone else, are aware of all of their own prehistory. Skinner asks the question, "Does the poet create, originate, initiate the thing called a poem, or is his behavior merely the product of his genetic and environmental histories?" (Skinner, 1972c, p. 34). His conclusion is that creative activity is no different from other behaviors except that the behavioral elements preceding it and determining it are more obscure. He sides with Samuel Butler, who wrote that "a poet writes a poem as a hen lays an egg, and both of them feel better afterwards."

Skinner is convinced that if we would look afresh at this behavior, we would help, not hinder, the production of new artistic expressions. "To accept a wrong explanation because it flatters us is to run the risk of missing a right one—one that in the long run may offer more by way of 'satisfaction' " (Skinner, 1972c, p. 35).

Conditioning and Reinforcement
Respondent Conditioning

Respondent behavior is reflexive behavior. The organism responds automatically to a stimulus. Your knee jerks when the patellar tendon is struck; your body begins to perspire as the outside temperature increases; the pupil in your eye contracts or expands depending upon the amount of light hitting its surface. Pavlov's discovery was that respondent behavior can be conditioned. His classic experiment paired a neutral stimulus, a bell, with the arrival of a dog's food. The dog normally salivates when food is presented. Pavlov demonstrated that after a few exposures to food plus the sound of the bell, the dog would salivate to the sound of the bell without food being presented. The dog had been conditioned so that it now responded to a stimulus that previously had evoked no response. Like Pavlov's dog, we may be conditioned to salivate when we enter a restaurant or hear a dinner bell. Respondent conditioning is readily learned and exhibited.

Operant Conditioning

Skinner has always been more interested in operant behavior than in respondent behavior. "Operant behavior is strengthened or weakened by the events that *follow* the response. Whereas respondent behavior is controlled by its antecedents, operant behavior is controlled by its consequences" (Reese, 1966, p. 3). The conditioning that takes place depends on what occurs after the behavior has been completed.

The following example illustrates some facets of operant conditioning: I am attempting to teach my daughter to swim. She enjoys the water but is unwilling or afraid to get her head or face wet or to blow bubbles under water. This has hindered the process considerably. I have agreed to give her a piece of candy if she wets her face. Once she can freely wet her face, I will give her a piece of candy only if she ducks her whole head. After she is able to do that, she will get a piece of candy only for blowing bubbles under water. At present, we are still in the

Operant conditioning is not pulling strings to make a person dance; it is arranging a world in which a person does things that affect that world, which in turn affects him. [Skinner, 1972b, p. 69]

initial stages of this arrangement. At times she wishes to earn candy and puts her face in the water. At other times she does not and refuses to carry out the behavior of wetting her face.[3]

Operant conditioning is the process of shaping and maintaining a particular behavior by its consequences. Therefore it takes into account not only what is presented before there is a response but what happens after the response. With my daughter, I am trying to condition her behavior by giving her a piece of candy *after* she performs certain acts. The candy is used to reinforce certain of her behaviors in the water. "When a bit of behavior is followed by a certain kind of consequence, it is more likely to occur again, and a consequence having this effect is called a reinforcer" (Skinner, 1971, p. 25).

Reinforcement

A reinforcer is any stimulus that follows the occurrence of a response and increases or maintains the probability of that response. In the example above candy was the reinforcer. It was offered after a specific behavior was correctly or successfully exhibited.

Reinforcers may be either positive or negative. "*A positive reinforcer* strengthens any behavior that *produces* it: a glass of water is positively reinforcing when we are thirsty, and if we then draw and drink a glass of water, we are more likely to do so again on similar occasions. *A negative reinforcer* strengthens any behavior that *reduces* or *terminates* it: when we take off a shoe that is pinching, the reduction in pressure is negatively reinforcing, and we are more likely to do so again when a shoe pinches" (Skinner, 1974, p. 46). Negative reinforcers are aversive in the sense that they are stimuli that a person or an animal turns away from or tries to avoid.

Positive and negative consequences regulate or control behaviors. This is the core of Skinner's position; he proposes that all behavior can be understood to be conditioned by a combination of positive and negative reinforcers. Moreover, it is possible to explain the occurrence of any behavior if one has sufficient knowledge of the prior reinforcers.

Skinner's original research was done on animals; the reinforcers he used included food, water, and electric shocks. The connection between the reinforcers and the animals' needs was straightforward. A hungry animal learned to do a task, such as open a hatch or push a lever, and was rewarded. The reinforcements are more difficult to perceive when one investigates more complex or abstract situations. What are the reinforcers that lead to overeating? What reinforces a person

When I was a Freudian somebody would say, "I've been thinking about my mother's vagina," and I'd write down "mother's vagina" you know and pretty soon I've got the patient reinforced so that every time I pick up my pencil he gets a flash . . . he's winning my attention and love . . . pretty soon he's talking about his mother's vagina 15 minutes of the hour. And then I think, "Ah, we're getting some place." [Ram Dass, 1970, p. 114]

[3]My daughter is a better behaviorist than I am. I had assumed that getting one's face wet meant to put one's face in the water. But my daughter was more accurate in defining "getting my face wet"; she demanded a reward for scooping her hands into the water and wetting her face. I accepted her correction as an additional step in the training sequence.

who volunteers for a job that is likely to cause his or her death? What keeps students studying courses when they have no interest in the content?

Primary reinforcers are events or stimuli that are innately reinforcing. They are unlearned, present at birth, and are related to physical needs and survival. Examples are air, water, food, shelter. *Secondary* reinforcers are neutral stimuli that become associated with primary reinforcers so that they in turn function as reinforcers. Money is one example of a secondary reinforcer; it has no intrinsic value but we have learned to associate it with many primary reinforcers. Money or the eventual promise of money is one of the most widely used and effective reinforcers in our culture.

The effectiveness of money as a secondary reinforcer is not limited to humans. Chimpanzees have learned to work for tokens they were allowed to "spend" in vending machines that dispense bananas and other rewards. When they were denied access to the machine for a while, they would continue to work, hoarding their tokens until the machine was once more available.

Schedules of Reinforcement

How often or how regularly a behavior is reinforced affects how quickly a new behavior is learned and how long or how often it will be repeated (Ferster & Skinner, 1957). *Continuous* reinforcement will increase the speed at which a new behavior is learned. *Intermittent* or *partial* reinforcement will produce more stable behavior, that is, behavior that will continue to be produced even after the reinforcement stops or appears very rarely. Thus in changing or maintaining behaviors, researchers have found that this scheduling is as important as the reinforcement itself (Kimble, 1961).

Behavioral Control

Many psychologists are concerned with predicting behavior; Skinner is interested in the control of behavior. If one can make changes in the environment, one can begin to control behavior.

> We are all controlled by the world in which we live, and part of that world has been and will be constructed by men. The question is this: Are we to be controlled by accident, by tyrants, or by ourselves in effective cultural design?
>
> The danger of the misuse of power is possibly greater than ever. It is not allayed by disguising the facts. We cannot make wise decisions if we continue to pretend that human behavior is not controlled, or if we refuse to engage in control when valuable results might be forthcoming. Such measures weaken only ourselves, leaving the strength of science to others. The first step in a defense against tyranny is the fullest possible exposure of controlling techniques. . . .
>
> It is not time for self-deception, emotional indulgence, or the assump-

tion of attitudes which are no longer useful. Man is facing a difficult test. He must keep his head now, or he must start again—a long way back. [Skinner, 1955, pp. 56–57]

DYNAMICS

Psychological Growth
Growth, in Skinner's terms, is minimizing adverse conditions and increasing the beneficial control of our environment. By clarifying our thinking, we can make better use of the available tools to predict, maintain, and control our own behavior.

Functional Analysis
Functional analysis is an examination of cause-and-effect relationships. It treats every aspect of behavior as a "function" of a condition that can be described in physical terms. Thus the behavior and its cause can be defined without explanatory fictions.

> When we see a man moving about a room, opening drawers, looking under magazines, and so on, we may describe his behavior in fully objective terms. "Now he is in a certain part of the room; he has grasped a book between the thumb and forefinger of his right hand; he is lifting the book and bending his head so that any object under the book can be seen." We may also interpret his behavior or "read a meaning into it" by saying "he is looking for something" or, more specifically, that "he is looking for his glasses." What we have added is not a further description of his behavior but an inference about some of the variables responsible for it. This is so even if we ask what he is doing and he says, "I am looking for my glasses." This is not a further description of his behavior but of the variables of which his behavior is a function; it is equivalent to "I have lost my glasses," "I shall stop what I am doing when I find my glassess," or "When I have done this in the past, I have found my glasses." [Skinner, in Fabun, 1968, p. 18]

Precise descriptions of behavior help make accurate predictions of future behaviors and improve the analysis of the prior reinforcements that led to the behavior. To understand ourselves, we must recognize that our behavior is neither random nor arbitrary but is an ongoing, lawful process that can be described by considering the environment in which the behavior is embedded.

Skinner is not negating the use of terms such as *will, imagination, intelligence,* or *freedom;* he is saying that explanations that depend on these terms are not functional. They don't truly describe what is occurring; they obscure rather than clarify the causes of behavior.

Reward (Reinforcement)
Reinforcing a correct response improves learning. It is more effective than aversive control (punishment) because reinforcement selectively

directs behavior toward a predetermined goal. The use of reinforcement is a highly focused and effective strategy to shape and control desired behaviors.

Obstacles to Growth
Punishment

Skinner's position is that punishment neither meets the demands of the person doing the punishing nor benefits the person being punished. Punishment does not offer information on how to do things correctly; it only sets up a situation in which the wrong behavior is punished. What people would like to know is not how wrong their act was but what can they do to make it better next time. Perhaps you can recall getting a paper back in which your wrong answers were marked off, but you were not told what the correct answers were. The frustration that people experience in such settings is part of the problem of punishment.

Punished behaviors usually do not go away. Unless new learning is available, the punished responses will return, often disguised or coupled with new behaviors. The new behaviors may be ways to avoid further punishment, or they may be forms of retaliation against the person who administered the original punishment. It is the teacher who uses punishment the most who has the most discipline problems. Prisons appear to illustrate the ineffectiveness of punishment. Prison life rarely teaches inmates more socially acceptable ways to satisfy their needs; rather, it punishes them for their prior behaviors. If a prisoner has not learned behaviors to replace those that landed him or her in prison, it is reasonable to expect that once released—exposed to the same environment and still subject to the same temptations—a convict will repeat the same behaviors. The high proportion of criminals returning to prison for the same crimes supports these observations.

A related problem with punishment is that it selectively reinforces and encourages the person who is punishing.

> Thus, a slave driver induces a slave to work by whipping him when he stops; by resuming work the slave escapes from the whipping (and incidentally reinforces the slave driver's behavior in using the whip). A parent nags a child until the child performs a task; by performing the task the child escapes nagging (and reinforces the parent's behavior). The blackmailer threatens exposure unless the victim pays; by paying the victim escapes from the threat (and reinforces the practice). A teacher threatens corporal punishment or failure until his students pay attention; by paying attention the students escape from the threat of punishment (and reinforce the teacher for threatening it). In one form or another intentional aversive control is the pattern of most social coordination—in ethics, religion, government, economics, education, psychotherapy, and family life. [Skinner, 1971, p. 26]

Skinner concludes that although punishment may be used briefly to suppress a very undesirable behavior, what is useful is to establish a situation in which a new competing behavior can be learned and reinforced.

Ignorance

Skinner defines ignorance as not knowing what causes a given behavior. The first step in overcoming ignorance is to acknowledge it; the second is to change the behaviors that have maintained the ignorance. One change that Skinner suggests is to stop describing events with words that are not descriptions of behavior but are nondescriptive, mental terms. Skinner offers an example of how an individual's description of an event prevents that person from seeing the causes of the behavior being observed.

> The practice is widespread. In a demonstration experiment, a hungry pigeon was conditioned to turn around in a clockwise direction. A final, smoothly executed pattern of behavior was shaped by reinforcing successive approximations with food. Students who had watched the demonstration were asked to write an account of what they had seen. Their responses included the following: (1) The organism was conditioned to *expect* reinforcement for the right kind of behavior. (2) The pigeon walked around, *hoping* that something would bring the food back again. (3) The pigeon *observed* that a certain behavior seemed to produce a particular result. (4) The pigeon *felt* that food would be given it because of its action; and (5) the bird came to *associate* his action with the click of the food-dispenser. The observed facts could be stated respectively as follows: (1) The organism was reinforced *when* it emitted a given kind of behavior. (2) The pigeon walked around *until* the food container again appeared. (3) A certain behavior *produced* a particular result. (4) Food was given to the pigeon when it acted in a given way; and (5) the click of the food-dispenser *was temporarily related* to the bird's action. These statements describe the contingencies of reinforcement. The expressions "expect," "hope," "observe," "feel," and "associate" go beyond them to identify effects on the pigeon. The effect actually observed was clear enough; the pigeon turned more skillfully and more frequently; but that was not the effect reported by the students. (If pressed, they would doubtless have said that the pigeon turned more skillfully and more frequently *because* it expected, hoped, and felt that if it did so food would appear.) [Skinner, in Wann, 1964, pp. 90–91]

STRUCTURE

Body

The body is that which behaves. Skinner treats a person as an unopened, but certainly not empty, box. Behaviorists emphasize the inputs and outputs, because those are all that are observable. "Rather than hypothesize the needs that may propel a particular activity, they try to discover the events that strengthen its future likelihood, and that maintain or change it. Thus they search for the conditions that regulate behavior rather than hypothesize need states inside the person" (Mischel, 1976, p. 62).

Extensive research on the variables that affect operant conditioning have led to the following conclusions.

1. *Conditioning can and does take place without awareness.* Numerous demonstrations illustrate that what we perceive depends, in large measure, on our past perceptions, which in turn have been partially conditioned. For example, the optical illusions used by Ames (1951) were thought to be a function of the physiology of vision (see Figure 9.1). However, when the same illusions are shown to people in cultures where the dwellings and windows are not made with right angles, they do not see the illusion. It is a culturally conditioned response. A summary of research concludes that conditioning can take place "in human beings . . . in the state of sleep, and in the waking state while the subject is entirely unaware of the fact that he is learning to respond to a conditioned stimulus" (Berelson & Steiner, 1964, p. 138).

2. *Conditioning is maintained in spite of awareness.* It is disconcerting to realize that you can be conditioned in spite of being aware of what is going on and consciously deciding not to remain conditioned. One experimenter trained subjects to lift a finger at the sound of a tone paired with a shock. The subjects continued to raise their fingers even after they had been told that the shock had been turned off. They continued to raise their fingers even when asked by the experimenter not to do so. Only after the electrodes had been removed from their fingers could they control their own recently conditioned responses (Lindley & Moyer, 1961).

3. *Conditioning is most effective when the subject is aware and cooperative* (Goldfried & Merbaum, 1973). Efficient conditioning is a collaboration. There is an inherent instability in conditioning when it is not undertaken with full cooperation. The following story exemplifies the problem:

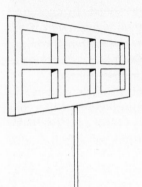

FIGURE 9.1 "AMES" ILLUSION
This is not a rectangle at an angle. It is a trapezoid looked at straight on. Seeing a rectangle is a conditioned, not an innate response.

A half dozen old and tattered alcoholics in a Midwestern Veterans Administration hospital a few years ago were given an alcohol treatment.* The men were thoroughly conditioned, and just the thought of drinking made them shake.

One afternoon, the old men started talking about their new lives and each discovered that the others hated it. They decided they would rather be in danger of being drunkards again than be terrified of the bottle.

So they plotted an evening to escape. They sneaked out to a bar, crowded together on their barstools, and through their sweating, shaking and vomiting, they bolstered and chided one another to down drink after drink. They downed enough so their fears left them. [Hilts, 1973]

*[The treatment paired drinking with a drug that caused vomiting. The men were conditioned until drinking alone brought on the vomiting behavior.]

The role of the body in a system based solely on observable data is of primary importance. However, it is not necessary to know the neuroanatomy or the physiological processes that occur concurrent with behavior in order to predict how people behave as they do.

Social Relationships

Skinner's interest is in the forces that shape and control individuals from outside themselves. Although there is interest in social interaction, the theory does not view relationships as a distinct kind of activity. There is "no special significance to social behavior as distinct from other behavior. Social behavior is characterized only by the fact that it involves an interaction between two or more people" (Hall & Lindzey, 1978, p. 660).

Skinner devotes considerable attention to verbal behavior (1957) and to the importance of the *verbal community's* role in shaping behavior, especially early language development and other behavior in children. For Skinner, verbal includes speaking, reading, writing; anything that uses words. The verbal community is defined as the people (including yourself) who respond to the verbal behavior of others in the same community. For example, a child responds to parents, siblings, other children, teachers, and so forth. He or she responds by changing or maintaining various behaviors. This is common sense, even if expressed in behavioral terms; but Skinner goes on to say that there are *no other relevant variables* beyond a person's past history, genetic endowment, and external events in the immediate environment.

The reinforcements you receive in a social situation depend partly on your behavior, partly on how others react to your behavior. In a conversation you say something and then you receive feedback. The feedback you receive, however, is based not only on what you said, but also on how the other person behaved after hearing it. For example, you say something as a joke. The other person takes it seriously and becomes upset. You modify your behavior and add, "I was only kidding." The person you are speaking to appears to relax. Thus we modify our behaviors in interpersonal relationships as much on the basis of others' reactions as on our own perceptions. This is the verbal community in action.

Although Skinner as psychologist does not write about social relationships, Skinner as novelist has his characters in *Walden Two* discuss them at length. Frazier, the designer of the utopian community, describes the place of the conventional family.

> The significant history of our times is the story of the growing weakness of the family.... A community must solve the problem of the family by revising certain established practices. That's absolutely inevitable. The family is an ancient form of community, and the customs and habits which have been set up to perpetuate it are out of place in a society which isn't based on blood ties. Walden Two replaces the family, not only as an economic unit, but to some extent as a social and psychological unit as well. What survives is an experimental question. [Skinner, 1948, p. 138]

The Psychology of Women

Skinner, in keeping with his general theoretical outlook, has not described a psychology of women per se. According to Skinner, "a self is a repertoire of behavior appropriate to a given set of contingencies. ... The identity conferred upon a self arises from the contingencies responsible for the behavior" (Skinner, 1971, pp. 189–190). Thus, woman's identity is unique and different from man's identity only insofar as the contingencies responsible for women's and men's behaviors differ. To the extent, then, that a society indeed offers different contingencies to men and to women (in terms, say, of roles and behaviors reinforced as culturally appropriate), the "psychologies" of men and women will differ. In the society Skinner has envisioned in *Walden Two,* (1976), for example, the contingencies determining behavior are in fact quite different from those prevalent in contemporary Western society, and conceptions of femininity and masculinity differ accordingly.

Will

Skinner considers the notion of *will* a confusing and unrealistic way of viewing behavior. He defines will, free will, and willpower as unobservable explanatory fictions. These terms imply an inner sense that is important in determining actions; Skinner prefers to assume that no action is free. "When we recognize this, we are likely to drop the notion of responsibility altogether and with it the doctrine of free will as an inner causal agent" (Skinner, 1953, p. 116).

To say that the "central pathology of our day is a failure of will, which brought psychoanalysis into being," seems more profound than to say that in the world of our day very little behavior is positively reinforced and much is punished and that psychoanalysis came into being to arrange better contingencies. [Skinner, 1974, p. 163]

Other psychologists, however, point to experimental evidence that a person who believes external forces condition behavior behaves differently than one who feels personally responsible. Davison and Valins found that "if a person realizes that his behavior change is totally dependent upon an external reward or punishment, there is no reason for the new behavior to persist once the environmental contingencies change" (1969 p. 33).

Lefcourt reviewed studies in which subjects were tested when they operated under the belief that they could control outcomes, and when they operated under the belief that they couldn't. The results suggest that depriving animals or people of the "illusion" of freedom has measurable behavioral effects. "The sense of control, the illusion that one can exercise personal choice, has a definite and positive role in sustaining life. The illusion of freedom is not to be easily dismissed without anticipating undesirable consequences" (Lefcourt, 1973, pp. 425–426).

If one could measure which parts of Skinner's work have drawn the most criticism, his ideas on will would be near the top. Considerable research literature has emerged investigating what is now called the *locus of control,* or "Who do I think is in charge—me or my environment?" The data continue to strongly favor the position that one's belief in the possibility of directing one's behavior matters (Lefcourt, 1980). Even prominent behaviorists such as Mahoney and Thoresen (1974) talk about self-control and a sense of freedom as the core of successful behavioral manipulation.

Emotions

The "emotions" are excellent examples of the fictional causes to which we commonly attribute behavior. [Skinner, 1953, p. 160]

Instead of treating emotions as vague inner states, Skinner suggests the more pragmatic approach of observing associated behaviors. "We define an emotion—insofar as we wish to do so—as a particular state of strength or weakness in one or more responses induced by any one of a class of operations" (Skinner, 1953, p. 166). Skinner advocates an essentially descriptive approach to emotions. He points out also that a well-defined emotion like anger will include different behaviors on different occasions, even with the same individual.

> When the man in the street says that someone is afraid or angry or in love, he is generally talking about predispositions to act in certain ways. The "angry" man shows an increased probability of striking, insulting, or otherwise inflicting injury and a lowered probability of aiding, favoring, comforting, or making love. The man "in love" shows an increased tendency to aid, favor, be with, and caress and a lowered tendency to injure in any way. "In fear" a man tends to reduce or avoid contact with specific stimuli—as by running away, hiding, or covering his eyes and ears; at the same time he is less likely to advance toward such stimuli or into unfamiliar territory. These are useful facts, and something like

the layman's mode of classification has a place in a scientific analysis. [Skinner, 1953, p. 162]

Skinner feels that the current difficulties in understanding, predicting, and controlling emotional behaviors could be reduced by observing behavioral patterns; he doubts that they can be reduced by references to unknown internal states.

. . . James and others were on the right track. . . . We both strike *and* feel angry for a common reason, and that reason lies in the environment. [Skinner, 1975, p. 43]

Intellect

The function of the intellect is to think about what one knows and to use one's knowledge. For Skinner the preceding sentence is useless; it does not describe anything observable, nor does it allow any prediction of any behavior. His own definitions are more detailed and exact.

"Thinking" often means "behaving weakly," where the weakness may be due, for example, to defective stimulus control. Shown an object with which we are not very familiar, we may say, "I think it is a kind of wrench," where "I think" is clearly opposed to "I know." We report a low probability for a different reason when we say, "I think I shall go," rather than "I shall go" or "I know I shall go."

There are more important uses of the term. Watching a chess game, we may wonder "what a player is thinking of" when he makes a move. We may mean that we wonder what he will do next. In other words, we wonder about his incipient or inchoate behavior. To say, "He was thinking of moving his rook," is perhaps to say, "He was on the point of moving it." Usually, however, the term refers to completed behavior which occurs on a scale so small that it cannot be detected by others. [Skinner, 1974, p. 103]

Skinner defines knowledge as a repertoire of behavior. "A man 'knows his table of integrals' in the sense that under suitable circumstances he will recite it, make corresponding substitutions in the course of a calculation, and so on. He 'knows his history' in the sense of possessing another highly complex repertoire" (1953, pp. 408–409).

Knowledge is the behavior displayed when a particular stimulus is applied. Other theorists tend to consider behaviors such as naming the major character in *Hamlet* or explaining the influence of German silver-mine production on medieval European history as "signs" or evidence of knowledge; Skinner regards those behaviors as knowledge itself. Another way he defines knowledge is the probability of skilled behavior. If a person "knows how to read," Skinner would interpret that as when an occasion occurs where reading is reinforced, the person produces the behavioral repertoire called reading. Skinner feels that the conventional ways of teaching suffer by not understanding or using the tools of behavioristic analysis. His concern moved him to devise learning situations and devices that accelerate the pace and enlarge the scope of established learning.

But if a behavioristic interpretation of thinking is not all we should like to have, it must be remembered that mental or cognitive explanations are not explanations at all. [Skinner, 1974, p. 103]

Self and Self-Knowledge

As you will probably anticipate, Skinner considers the term *self* an explanatory fiction. "If we cannot show what is responsible for a man's behavior, we say that he himself is responsible for it. The precursors of physical science once followed the same practice, but the wind is no longer blown by Aeolus, nor is the rain cast down by Jupiter Pluvius. . . . The practice resolves our anxiety with respect to unexplained phenomena and is perpetuated because it does so. . . . A concept of self is not essential in an analysis of behavior . . ." (Skinner, 1953, pp. 283, 285).

> There is no place in the scientific position for a self as a true originator or initiator of action. [Skinner, 1974, p. 225]

　　　Although Skinner does explore the repertoire of behavior labeled self-knowledge, he also describes a number of cases where self-knowledge is lacking. "A man may not know that *he has done something* . . . may not know that *he is doing something* . . . may not know that *he tends to,* or *is going to, do something* . . . may not recognize *the variables of which his behavior is a function*" (Skinner, 1958, pp. 288–289). These cases are of intense interest to nonbehaviorists because they are said to be manifestations of various internal states (for example, complexes, habit patterns, repressions, phobias). Skinner labels these incidents simply as behaviors for which there has been no positive reinforcement for noticing or remembering them. "The crucial thing is not whether the behavior which a man fails to report is actually observable by him, but whether he has ever been given any reason to observe it" (Skinner, 1953, p. 289).

Therapist

Skinner describes therapy as a controlling agency of almost unlimited power. In the relationship the therapist is designated as a highly likely source of some relief; any promise of relief becomes positively reinforcing, thus increasing the therapist's influence.

　　　One conclusion that arises from Skinner's theory of "no self" is that the goal of therapy cannot be to make a person feel better, be better adjusted, or achieve insight or self-understanding. From the behaviorist's position the goal of therapy must be to modify the shape or order of behaviors—that is, to prevent undesirable behaviors from recurring and to have desirable behaviors occur more often. Seen in this light, behavior therapy has successfully treated problems that are not easily helped by psychodynamic therapies.

　　　A massive review of behavior therapies (Rachman & Wilson, 1980) lists the following areas where there was a sufficient number of well-designed studies with generally favorable results:

　　　Sexual dysfunction
　　　Sexual deviance
　　　Marital conflict

Addictive disorders
    Alcoholism
    Smoking
    Obesity
Psychotic disorders

Although there are a number of different approaches to the practice of behavior therapy, it is generally accepted that a behavior therapist is primarily interested in actual behaviors, not in inner states or historical antecedents. According to behaviorists, *the symptom is the disease,* not a manifestation of an underlying illness. The "symptom"—such as a facial tic, premature ejaculation, chronic drinking, fear of crowds, or a peptic ulcer—is dealt with directly. Symptoms are not used as an opening wedge to investigate past memories or the patients' existential perspectives.

The therapist offers the patient a nonthreatening audience, as is true of the psychodynamic therapies. The client is therefore free to express previously unexpressed behaviors such as weeping, hostile feelings, or sexual fantasies. However, the therapist is not interested in reinforcing these expressions. The therapist is interested in teaching, training, and rewarding behaviors that can effectively compete with and eliminate behaviors that are uncomfortable or disabling. For example, progressive relaxation may be taught to counteract specific anxiety reactions, or assertiveness training may be used to overcome timid behaviors.

The following statements describe the special nature of behavior therapy as well as its commonality with other therapy forms.

1. Behavior therapy tries to help people become able to respond to life situations the way they would like to respond. This includes increasing the frequency and/or range of a person's desired behaviors, thoughts, and feelings; and decreasing or eliminating unwanted behaviors, thoughts, and feelings.
2. Behavior therapy does not try to modify an emotional core of attitudes or feelings within the personality.
3. Behavior therapy takes the posture that a positive therapeutic relationship is a necessary, but not sufficient, condition for effective psychotherapy.
4. In behavior therapy the complaints of the client are accepted as valid material for psychotherapy to be focused upon—not as symptoms for some underlying problem.
5. In behavior therapy the client and the therapist come to an explicit understanding of the problem presented, in terms of the actual behavior of the client (e.g. actions, thoughts, feelings). They decide mutually on specific therapy goals, stated

in such a way that both client and therapist know when these goals have been attained. [Jacks, 1973]

Applications of Behaviorism

The strict or radical behaviorism of B. F. Skinner is at the core of behavior therapies; however, there have been significant liberalizations of his positions that have allowed behavior therapies to become the fastest growing and most eclectic group of therapies in the English-speaking world.

Cognitive Therapy

In spite of Skinner's pronouncements, most people, including behaviorists, persist in their belief that thinking, although not easily measured, exists nonetheless. The task of the "cognitive" behavior therapist is to modify behaviors and emotional expressions, but *to do it through modifying the patient's thoughts.* "The fundamental assumption on which all cognitive behavior therapy methods are based is that emotional disorders are a function of maladaptive thought patterns . . ." (Rachman & Wilson, 1980). Thoughts are treated as *covert* behaviors, that is, behaviors hidden from view. Given this way of redefining thinking, cognitive therapists can apply the methods derived from behaviorism proper to do their work.

The theory says that any thought that leads to maladaptive behavior can be modified, thus there is no limit to the areas open to cognitive behavioral manipulation and support. For example, the range of studies appearing in a single issue of a leading journal in the field included test anxiety, activity levels of elderly patients, acting-out behavior in third graders, and slumps and "hot" periods in basketball playing (Mahoney, 1981).

The extension of therapeutic goals into normal areas of thinking, feeling, and acting relaxes some of the limitations that have been traditionally associated with psychotherapy. In the psychodynamic models it is implied, if not stated, that one must be ill, defective, unbalanced, and in some way abnormal to ask for or be given therapy. The behaviorist position has no such moral implications. If everything is behavior, then the only question is, is the behavior functioning optimally for the individual or not? If it can be improved, the behaviorist is willing to try to enhance it in whatever direction the person involved deems appropriate.

Applied Behavior Analysis

Rather than blame and punish people when they exhibit deviant behavior, it may be more realistic to modify contingencies in their environment. If behavior is due to selective reinforcement, then deviant behavior is a function of the environment. This line of thinking has led to the development of applied behavioral analysis where attention is paid to the total environment rather than the psychodynamics of the deviant's behavior.

Skinner did some of the first work in modifying the behavior of persons in institutions. He was demonstrating his thesis that if one could control the outer environment, one could then control behavior (Lindsley et al., 1953).

If the reinforcers are changed so that the deviant behavior will no longer be reinforced, it should pass out of the behavioral repertoire. Furthermore, the environment can be adjusted to reinforce whatever new behaviors are deemed to be more desirable (Goodall, 1972a, 1972b). The focus is on extinguishing behaviors that are in themselves deviant or lead to deviant or criminal activities. These ideas are being applied in educational and custodial institutions that include hospitals, prisons, juvenile probation departments, and schools.

The critics have argued that the amount of control necessary to eliminate the undesirable behaviors is excessive. The advocates counter by pointing out that their approach is simply a more comprehensive and formal extension of what their institutions were originally set up to do. The university is set up to educate students, but it operates inefficiently. The prison is mandated to deter and to reform persons who display criminal behavior, but in this it often fails. The mental hospital exists to help return people to adequate functioning, but it frequently does not succeed. The long-standing ineffectiveness of our traditional institutions makes it easier to suggest implementing behavioral models that impose tighter controls over more of the environment. If, for example, a back ward catatonic can be reinforced into speaking, feeding and dressing himself or herself, and taking care of personal needs, it is clearly an improvement for the patient as well as a relief to the staff responsible for his or her care.

Programmed Learning

Skinner's most important research, outside of his animal experiments, has been in the development of programmed learning. It has become an accepted, established alternative way of teaching. In its basic form a student sits before a "teaching machine." A single frame or statement (drawing, problem) is presented to the student. The student *actively* responds (writes, presses a button, etc.). After completing a response, the student is then shown the correct one and is invited to check if his or her response is correct. This feedback occurs *before* the next statement is presented. In every case the student is shown the correct response. In a simple program students move from statement to statement, having opportunities from time to time to redo or review their errors (Skinner, 1958). Skinner's research showed that people learn more easily and quickly when they are

given instant and accurate feedback on their progress. The basic hypotheses are:

1. *Learning is accelerated if discrete units of material are presented.* In programmed learning simpler units are presented first. Each
unit of content is given as a distinct entity while embedded in a larger
and more complex learning program. Thus, although $4 \times 7 = 28$ is
a single unit, it is part of the 4 multiplication table and the 7 multiplication table. These tables are, in turn, part of a group of methods used
in performing mathematical calculations. "Lectures, textbooks, and
their mechanized equivalents, on the other hand, proceed without making sure that the student understands and can easily leave him behind"
(Skinner, 1958, p. 971).

2. *The learner must make a response.* Content is most likely to be
retained if the learner actively participates in the learning process. In
programmed instruction the student chooses an answer, writes a response, presses a button, opens a slide, or makes some other response.
If the student is not interested enough to respond to the item in the
program, then the program waits until the student decides to continue.
In the preface to their programmed-learning text, Holland and Skinner
(1961) sum up the arguments that favor programmed learning.

> Machine programs share with the individual tutor many advantages
> over other techniques of teaching: (1) Each student advances at his own
> rate, the fast learner moving ahead rapidly while the slower learner
> moves at a speed convenient for him. (2) The student moves on to ad-
> vanced material only after he has thoroughly mastered earlier stages.
> (3) Because of this gradual progression and with the help of certain tech-
> niques of hinting and prompting, the student is almost always right. (4)
> The student is continuously active and receives immediate confirmation
> of his success. (5) Items are so constructed that the student must compre-
> hend the critical point in order to supply the answer. (6) "Concept" is rep-
> resented in the program by many examples and syntactical arrange-
> ments, in an effort to maximize generalization to other situations. (7) A
> record of students' responses furnishes the programmer with valuable
> information for future revisions. [The present program has been thor-
> oughly revised twice, and minor changes have been made from time to
> time. The number of errors made by students was halved (reduced to
> about 10 percent) as a result of the first revision.] [pp. v–vi]

3. *Punishment does not lead to learning.* Skinner once remarked
that he had observed that drugstores were less likely to be vandalized
than schools because drugstores did not engage in punishment. Programmed learning allows students to reinforce their own learning behavior and to reinforce it at their own pace. "Programmed instruction is perhaps most successful in attacking punitive methods by
allowing the student to move at his own pace. The slow student is released from the punishment which inevitably follows when he is
forced to move on to material for which he is not ready, and the fast

If the bell is sounded many times when nothing brushes the eye, the conditioned eye-blink reflex will be _____. (TT) 5-6	extinguished 5-6
After a sufficient number of pairings of tone and food, the tone becomes a(n) (1) _____ _____ which will (2) _____ _____ salvation. 5-15	(1) conditioned stimulus (2) elicit 5-15
Conditions which give rise to the so-called emotions of fear, anger, and anxiety produce a(n) _____ in the electrical resistance of the skin. 5-24	drop (decrease) (acceptable change) 5-24
If the dentist's behavior continues to provide unconditioned stimuli for fear reflexes, the child's conditioned fear of the dentist's office will not become _____. (TT) 5-33	extinguished 5-33
A favorable predisposition to a political candidate might be conditioned by serving a free lunch at a political really. The food is a(n) _____ _____ used to condition many "favorable" reflex responses. 5-42	unconditioned stimulus 5-42
A stimulus which has acquired the ability to evoke a reflex response is the (1) _____ _____; the response it evokes is the (2) _____ _____. 5-51	(1) conditioned stimulus (2) conditioned response 5-51

Sample page of programmed learning textbook (Holland & Skinner, 1961)

student escapes the boredom of being forced to go too slow" (Skinner, 1978a, p. 146).

There are, of course, objections to programmed learning. First of all, it is socially isolating; students are encapsulated in their own private world while learning. The benefits of group experience and the utilization of group energy and enthusiasm are missing (as are the negative effects of group pressures and competition). In addition, learning based on a carefully designed hierarchy of linked concepts is progressively less useful in areas that cannot be so clearly defined. Also, students have no opportunity to disagree with the program writer's bias.

In the light of our present knowledge a school system must be called a failure if it cannot induce students to learn except by threatening them for not learning. [Skinner, 1958, p. 977]

Augmented Learning

The development of interactive computer learning is a step beyond simple programmed learning. The learner still works with discrete units, still must respond, and still gets immediate feedback; but the computer feedback is much more detailed, individual, and complex than with the teaching machine. The learning experience becomes a dialogue between student and computer. The students are not simply informed whether their response is right or wrong. They may receive encouragement, pictures, suggestions, alternative approaches, reminders of previous successes with similar items, or displays of the question in another form. While some programmed texts and teaching machines have failed to maintain student interest, this has not been a problem in computer-augmented situations (see Figure 9.2).

The computer's flexibility has other implications as well.

> As a result of more imaginative application, we are beginning to recognize still another aspect of machine teaching that in time will become the most important of all. The child, in intimate dialog with the machine, finds himself in a unique psychological situation. The computer becomes a nonjudgmental reflector of his thoughts. He is encouraged to open up his imagination, to try some of the unlikely possibilities, and to follow his curiosity and see what happens. A wrong answer is as valuable as the right one when the alternatives can be explored and he is shown *why* it is wrong. [Brown & El-Ghannam, 1971, p. 2]

This kind of learning is not limited to factual material; it can encourage creative expression as well. Here is part of a teaching situation using a computer. The computer is using a program first developed for freshman writing courses at Stanford University. The student, in this case, describes herself as "someone who doesn't ever write poetry."

COMPUTER: Hi! What shall I call you today?
STUDENT: Gail.
COMPUTER: O.K. Gail, this time we're going to talk about what you can

Figure 9.2
What appears to be a revolution in education, beginning only six years ago, is now under way as scholars prepare programs in areas ranging from beginning arithmetic to calculus, from modern behaviorism to the Old Testament, from spelling and English grammar to many modern languages, from biology and physics to medical-school courses, and in hundreds of fields of industrial education. (Holland and Skinner, 1961, p.v.)

and can't see, hear, touch, taste and feel. You just touched
the computer terminal. How does it feel?

STUDENT: Like plastic and steel, gray and growling.

COMPUTER: Fine. Now say it in a different way. It feels like . . .

STUDENT: strings of steel licking at my finger bottoms.

COMPUTER: Good. Even more far out? It feels as if . . .

STUDENT: a noise from nowhere beating into an empty room.

COMPUTER: Believe it or not, you've just written a poem. Here
it is:

TERMINAL
Like plastic and steel, gray and growling.
Like strings of steel licking at my finger bottoms.
Just as if a noise from nowhere beating into empty rooms.

COMPUTER: Do you want to change the poem to make it better?

STUDENT: Yes.

COMPUTER: Good. Use the next three lines to type in your changes.

STUDENT: Gray and growling, the terminal licks at my fingers.
Strings of steel, gloved in gray.
Noises from nowhere sing into empty rooms.

COMPUTER: That's the way! Now, Gail, would you like to take an imaginary walk in the woods?

STUDENT: Sure I would this is neat.

COMPUTER: Good. It's autumn, and as you're walking through the woods,
what colors do you see?

STUDENT: Yellow, brown, dashes of rose and red, blue sky

COMPUTER: What do yellow, brown, dashes of rose and red, blue sky remind you of?

STUDENT: A paintpot drawn by a chariot of the sun.

COMPUTER: Walking in the woods can lead to thoughts of abstract ideas
such as death, change, beauty or cycles. Can you think of
more? Type them in.

STUDENT: Renewal, quiet, wonder, silence.

COMPUTER: How do you feel when you think about renewal, quiet, wonder, silence?

STUDENT: In awe of the perfect beauty of the unknown.

COMPUTER: Would you like to write a short poem, Gail?

STUDENT: Sure.

COMPUTER: O.K., a suggestion is to type three lines using the colors yellow, brown, dashes of rose and red, blue sky which you mentioned, renewal, quiet, wonder, silence, your abstract ideas,
and the feelings you have about renewal, quiet, wonder, silence . . .

GAIL'S POEM

STUDENT: *Yellow like wheat dying to be renewed in bread.*
Brown of the earth alive even in silence and in death.
Silence only for moments broken by the whir of falling red
leaves.

COMPUTER: *Nice, Gail.*

[Nold, 1974, used with permission]

*Elementary, My Dear
Apple,* is a collection of
four programs designed
to help youngsters learn
to spell, understand
arithmetic concepts, and
sharpen problem-solving
skills. . . . The first
program is *Lemonade,* a
business simulation
game for one or two
players. The remaining
three, each designed for
a single player, are
Darts, Supermath, and
Don't Fall. Respectively,
they help students
understand fractions,
solve basic arithmetic
problems, and improve
word recognition and
spelling. [Software for
the Apple, 1981]

Skinner did not envision the next step in computer-based learning, the presentation of material in game form. The home television screen has become a potential teaching machine. Only the ingenuity of programmers seems to limit the kinds of content that can be made more reinforcing through adaptation to a game format. One example is a game developed by a computer company that teaches typing skills. The student types words that become missiles to repel enemy space attackers. As the student types more quickly and more accurately, the missiles that will work must be longer and longer words typed in the same amount of time. Not only does this next generation of programmed teaching devices minimize punishment, but it also appears to be so positively reinforcing that an entire industry has emerged simply to create games that are partially derived from Skinner's early rat and pigeon research.

EVALUATION

Skinner's ideas have launched a major school of psychology. Behaviorism has been utilized and applied to form new modes of therapy and instruction. The impact of his ideas has lead to modifications of programs in universities, jails, mental hospitals, clinics, and primary schools. Several experimental communities have been formed attempting to bring the visions of *Walden Two* into reality (Roberts, 1971; Kinkade, 1973).

I think the main
objection to behaviorism
is that people are in love
with the mental
apparatus. If you say
that doesn't really exist,
that it's a fiction and
let's get back to the
facts, then they have to
give up their first love.
[Skinner, 1967b, p. 69]

As Skinner has extended his interests into the workplace, the family, and the schoolroom, he has attracted a horde of admirers and critics. His disdain for the ideas of freedom, creativity, and the self, and his unswerving belief in a world dominated by external forces are chilling and compelling.

No person striving to understand the human predicament can ignore the challenge posed by Skinner to older established notions. Whereas Freud's suggestion that we are immoral and subject to lust and greed scandalized a generation of Victorians, Skinner's suggestion that we are amoral and being pushed and turned by whatever is the most potent force around us has disturbed a generation brought up to admire and value self-generated choices and independence.

In light of his writings, which have moved well beyond the laboratory studies, it is realistic to say that Skinner's work has become steadily more theoretical. Still, he must be seen as a philosopher and a researcher who insists that differences should be resolved on the basis of actual evidence, not abstract speculations. With his background in science and philosophy, Skinner has forged a systematic approach to understanding human behavior, an approach that is having a considerable effect on current cultural practices and beliefs.

In his urge to render life more understandable, Skinner has proposed a view of human nature that is inherently appealing in its compactness, its directness, and its dismissal of all metaphysical speculation. It is firmly rooted in the methodology of modern science, and it offers the hope of understanding ourselves without recourse to intuition or divine intervention.

I am a radical behaviorist simply in the sense that I find no place in the formulation for anything which is mental. [Skinner, 1964, p. 106]

Although we have considered Skinner to be a psychologist whose basic ideas originated from laboratory findings with rats and pigeons, he has shed that role and its limitations long ago. With the writing of *Walden Two* he made a "critical transition, from laboratory scientist . . . to outspoken public advocate for a behavioristic science of *human* behavior" (Elms, 1981, p. 478). Skinner's own thrust for the past 30 years is best stated in his words: "I am proceeding on the assumption that nothing less than a vast improvement in our understanding of human behavior will prevent the destruction of our way of life or of mankind" (1975, p. 42). His research has been important for parts of academic psychology; however, it is his social theorizing that continues to make him important and to make behaviorism an active current force.

THE THEORY FIRSTHAND

HUMANISM AND BEHAVIORISM BY B. F. SKINNER*

There seem to be two ways of knowing, or knowing about, another person. One is associated with existentialism, phenomenology, and structuralism. It is a matter of knowing what a person is, or what he is like, or what he is coming to be or becoming. We try to know another person in this sense as we know ourselves. We share his feelings through sympathy or empathy. Through intuition we discover his attitudes, intentions, and other states of mind. We communicate with him in the etymological sense of making ideas and feelings common to both of us. We do so more effectively if we have established good *interpersonal* relations. This is a passive, contemplative kind of knowing: If we want to predict what a person does or is likely to do, we assume that he, like us, will behave according to what he is; his behavior, like ours, will be an expression of his feelings, state of mind, intentions, attitudes, and so on.

The other way of knowing is a matter of what a person *does*. We can usually observe this as directly as any other phenomenon in the world; no special kind of knowing is needed. We explain why a person behaves as he does by turning to the environment rather than to inner states or activities. The environment was effective during the evolution of the species, and we call the result the human genetic endowment. A member of the species is exposed to another part of that environment during his lifetime, and from it he acquires a repertoire of behavior which converts

*From *The Humanist,* July/August, 1972. Reprinted by permission.

an organism with a genetic endowment into a person. By analyzing these effects of the environment, we move toward the prediction and control of behavior.

But can this formulation of what a person *does* neglect any available information about what he *is*? There are gaps in time and space between behavior and the environmental events to which it is attributed, and it is natural to try to fill them with an account of the intervening state of the organism. We do this when we summarize a long evolutionary history by speaking of genetic endowment. Should we not do the same for a personal history? An omniscient physiologist should be able to tell us, for example, how a person is changed when a bit of his behavior is reinforced, and what he thus becomes should explain why he subsequently behaves in a different way. We argue in such a manner, for example, with respect to immunization. We begin with the fact that vaccination makes it less likely that a person will contract a disease at a later date. We say that he becomes immune, and we speak of a state of immunity, which we then proceed to examine. An omniscient physiologist should be able to do the same for comparable states in the field of behavior. He should also be able to change behavior by changing the organism directly rather than by changing the environment. Is the existentialist, phenomenologist, or structuralist not directing his attention precisely to such a mediating state?

A thoroughgoing dualist would say no, because for him what a person observes through introspection and what a physiologist observes with his special techniques are in different universes. But it is a reasonable view that what we feel when we have feelings are states of our own bodies, and that the states of mind we perceive through introspection are other varieties of the same kinds of things. Can we not, therefore, anticipate the appearance of an omniscient physiologist and explore the gap between environment and behavior by becoming more keenly aware of what we are?

It is at this point that a behavioristic analysis of self-knowledge becomes most important and, unfortunately, is most likely to be misunderstood. Each of us possesses a small part of the universe within his own skin. It is not for that reason different from the rest of the universe, but it is a private possession: We have ways of knowing about it that are denied to others. It is a mistake, however, to conclude that the intimacy we thus enjoy means a special kind of understanding. We are, of course, stimulated directly by our own bodies. The so-called interoceptive nervous system responds to conditions important in deprivation and emotion. The proprioceptive system is involved in posture and movement, and without it we would scarcely behave in a coordinated way. These two systems, together with the exteroceptive nervous system, are essential to effective behavior. But knowing is more than responding to stimuli. A child responds to the colors of things before he "knows his colors." Knowing requires special contingencies of reinforcement that must be arranged by other people, and the contingencies involving private events are never very precise because other people are not effectively in contact with them. In spite of the intimacy of our own bodies, we know them less accurately than we know the world around us. And there are, of course, other reasons why we know the private world of others even less precisely.

The important issues, however, are not precision but subject matter.

Just what can be known when we "know ourselves"? The three nervous systems just mentioned have evolved under practical contingencies of survival, most of them nonsocial. (Social contingencies important for survival must have arisen in such fields as sexual and maternal behavior.) They were presumably the only systems available when people began to "know themselves" as the result of answering questions about their behavior. In answering such questions as "Do you see that?" or "Did you hear that?" or "What is that?" a person learns to observe his own responses to stimuli. In answering such questions as "Are you hungry?" or "Are you afraid?" he learns to observe states of his body related to deprivation and emotional arousal. In answering such questions as "Are you going to go?" or "Do you intend to go?" or "Do you feel like going?" or "Are you inclined to go?" he learns to observe the strength or probability of his behavior. The verbal community asks such questions because the answers are important to it, and in a sense it thus makes the answers important to the person himself. The important fact is that such contingencies, social or nonsocial, involve nothing more than stimuli or responses; *they do not involve mediating processes*. We cannot fill the gap between behavior and the environment of which it is a function through introspection because, to put the matter in crude physiological terms, we do not have nerves going to the right places. We cannot observe the states and events to which an omniscient physiologist would have access. What we feel when we have feelings and what we observe through introspection are nothing more than a rather miscellaneous set of collateral products or by-products of the environmental conditions to which behavior is related. (We do not act because we feel like acting, for example; we act *and* feel like acting for a common reason to be sought in our environmental history.) Do I mean to say that Plato never discovered the mind? Or that Aquinas, Descartes, Locke, and Kant were preoccupied with incidental, often irrelevant by-products of human behavior? Or that the mental laws of physiological psychologists like Wundt, or the stream of consciousness of William James, or the mental apparatus of Sigmund Freud have no useful place in the understanding of human behavior? Yes, I do. And I put the matter strongly because, if we are to solve the problems that face us in the world today, this concern for mental life must no longer divert our attention from the environmental conditions of which human behavior is a function. . . .

Since the only selves we know are human selves, it is often said that man is distinguished from other species precisely because he is aware of himself and participates in the determination of his future. What distinguishes the human species, however, is the development of a culture, a social environment that contains the contingencies generating self-knowledge and self-control. It is this environment that has been so long neglected by those who have been concerned with the inner determination of conduct. The neglect has meant that better practices for building self-knowledge and self-management have been missed.

It is often said that a behavioristic analysis "dehumanizes man." But it merely dispenses with a harmful explanatory fiction. In doing so it moves much more directly toward the goals that fiction was designed, erroneously, to serve. People understand themselves and manage themselves much more effectively when they understand the relevant contingencies.

Important processes in self-management lie in the fields of ethics and morals, where conflicts between immediate and deferred consequences are considered. One of the great achievements of a culture has been to bring remote consequences to bear upon the behavior of the individual. We may design a culture in which the same results will be achieved much more efficiently by shifting our attention from ethical problem-solving or moral struggle to the external contingencies. . . .

The values affecting those who are in charge of other people supply good examples of the importance of turning from supposed attributes of an inner man to the contingencies affecting behavior. There are five classical types of human beings who have been mistreated: the young, the elderly, prisoners, psychotics, and retardates. Are they mistreated because those who are in charge of them lack sympathy, compassion, or benevolence, or have no conscience? No, the important fact is that they are unable to retaliate. It is easy to mistreat any one of these five kinds of people without being mistreated in turn.

Better forms of government are not to be found in better rulers, better educational practices in better teachers, better economic systems in more enlightened management, or better therapy in more compassionate therapists. Neither are they to be found in better citizens, students, workers, or patients. The age-old mistake is to look for salvation in the character of autonomous men and women rather than in the social environments that have appeared in the evolution of cultures and that can now be explicitly designed. . . . [1972]

EXERCISES

General note: Observing behavior and recording what you observe is the cornerstone of behavior modification. In all the exercises that follow, they are most effective and instructive when you keep good records; use tally sheets, graph paper, counters—whatever will help you recall and record your observations.

Modify Your Own Behavior

Keep a record of the time you spend working on different subjects. A simple bar graph, marked off in hours, with different bars for each subject would be appropriate. Keep records for a week to establish a base line. Then pick a subject you believe you should spend more time on.

For the next week, each time you work on that subject, give yourself a positive reinforcement; a chapter of a novel, some candy, time with a friend, and so forth. Make sure the reinforcement is something that you really enjoy. Keep a record of the reinforcements and when you gave them to yourself.

Do you find the amount of time you are spending on this activity increasing? What are the possible causes for this increase (if there is any)?

Modify Someone Else's Behavior

It has been established by many experiments that you can condition verbal behavior by selectively rewarding parts of speech or kinds of speech (Berelson & Steiner, 1964). The reward that you can use is simply nodding your head or saying "mmm-hmmm" or "yeah."

In conversation, nod or express agreement every time a particular behavior is expressed (for example, the use of long, complex words; swear words; or emotional statements). Notice if the number of such expressions begins to increase as you continue to reinforce them.

Modify Your Professor's Behavior

This is a popular stunt designed by behaviorist students. Choose as your subject a professor who ambles about as he lectures. The experimenters are as many of the class members as will agree to participate. As the professor walks and talks, experimenters reinforce walking toward one side of the room. As the professor turns or moves to the right, let us say, experimenters lean forward, write notes diligently, and pay close attention to what he is saying. If the professor turns to the left, experimenters relax, look distracted, and do not appear to be paying much attention. Most classes have found that they can keep their professor in a corner for most of the class, after several lectures. It might be well to restrict this exercise to professors in psychology, so that when it is explained to them, they will not punish your industriousness, but with behavioristic goodwill reinforce you.

Effects of Reinforcement and Punishment

Punishment

Write down a behavior of your own that you wish to modify. You might choose coming to class late, writing letters during class, eating too much, going to sleep late, or being rude to strangers. If you are married, if you live with someone, or if you have a roommate, you can each pick a habit and help each other.

Once you have decided on a target behavior, punish yourself or have your coexperimenter punish you each time the offending behavior occurs. The punishment might be an insult ("Hey, piggy, you're overeating again"), denying yourself some treat, or some other deprivation. One easy punishment is to fine yourself a given amount of money each time the behavior occurs. The accumulated fines are then given to a charity. (A variation of this is to give the fines to your coexperimenter so that he or she is rewarded every time you are punished. For relationships that stand the strain, this will make your coexperimenter very involved in the exercise.)

After a week, review your progress. Are you doing it more or less often? How do you feel about the behavior? How do you feel about the exercise?

Positive Reinforcement

Stop the punishment procedure. Choose a behavior that you prefer to the one you have been working with aversively, a behavior you would like to perform more often.

For example, if you bite your nails, would it be preferable for you to clean and clip them? Would a glass of juice be better for you than another dessert? If you come early instead of late, does this relax you and give you time to prepare for things?

Decide on the behavior you wish to occur instead of the one you have been punishing. Now begin to reinforce yourself every time you perform the preferred behavior. Give yourself, or have your coexperimenter give you, small gifts, praise, gold stars, or some other reward. Being noticed is among the most effective rewards, so be sure that both you and your coexperimenter notice your desired behavior when it occurs.

After a week, review your behavior pattern. Have there been any changes? How do you feel about this way of modifying your behavior? Consider the different effects punishment and reward have had in your life.

Desensitization

One of the procedures used by behavior therapists is called desensitization. *This exercise is not intended to show you how a therapist would actually work.* It is a way for you to experience some of the dynamics that occur if you focus on a single item of behavior.

This is a difficult exercise. If you are going to try it, do it carefully.

Identifying a Problem

Think of a fear you have had for some time, perhaps a phobia (because phobias are the easiest to work with); fears of snakes, worms, blood, or heights are good examples of phobias. Should you not be able to think of, or not be willing to consider a phobia, think of an emotional reaction you have to a given situation. For example, you may become anxious every time a police car drives behind you, or you may get defensive whenever someone mentions your religion. What you are looking for is a response you have that seems stereotyped and disturbing.

Relaxation

Sit in a comfortable chair or lie down. Let your whole body relax. Concentrate on each part of your body, telling it to relax and noticing the relaxation. Let your toes relax, your feet, your ankles, knees, legs, and so forth. This will take a few minutes. Practice this progressive relaxation a few times until you are sure of your ability to relax. If you cannot tell whether or not a part of your body has relaxed, tense the muscles in that area and then relax them. You will soon learn to feel the difference.

First Steps in Desensitization

Now that you are relaxed and awake, think of something that has a very distant relationship to the phobia or habit you are working with. If it is a fear of snakes, think of reading about a small harmless snake that is only found in another country. If you have a fear of a policeman, think about a clown dressed like a policeman giving away balloons at a circus.

What you are trying to do is maintain an image in your mind that is related to the anxiety-provoking stimulus while you are physically relaxed. If you start getting tense (for example, "Yuck, a snake . . ."), stop concentrating on the image and renew your relaxation, going back over your body until it is once again relaxed. Go over this procedure until you can hold the image in your mind while fully relaxed.

Further Desensitization

The next step and all following steps are to think of an image or situation that is more vivid, more like the real object or situation. Visualize or imagine it and maintain your relaxation. For the snake phobia, for example, other steps might include actually reading about snakes, pictures of snakes, a snake in a cage across the room from you, the cage next to you, and eventually holding the snake in your hand.

Make up a set of 3×5 cards with one image on each to refer to while you are working. Do not go to a later image or situation until you can be relaxed in all the earlier ones (don't skip steps).

As you continue your practice, continue to spend time before each session working on improving your relaxation.

Cognitive Behavior Therapy (Thoughts Are Covert Behaviors)

1. Recall a situation in which you have felt anxious in the past, or one in which you anticipate feeling anxious in the future. Let yourself experience the feelings that occur.
2. Keeping the image in your mind, focus on your breathing, giving yourself instructions, "Let go. Relax."
3. Keeping the image in your mind, imagine yourself acting in that situation as you would like to act. It's your mind—you can have it imagine anything you want.
4. Repeat this exercise until you can control the situation in your mind, imagining yourself acting without anxiety.
5. If possible, find an opportunity to actually confront the real situation. Evaluate your capacity to cope before and after working in this way. [Shapiro, 1978, pp. 107–108; slightly modified by the authors]

ANNOTATED BIBLIOGRAPHY

Skinner, B. F. *Walden two.* New York: Macmillan, 1948, 1976. A novel about a full-blown utopian community that is designed and managed by a behaviorist. No plot to speak of, but all facets of the culture are fully described and discussed, from raising children to work schedules to planned leisure.

———. *Science and human behavior.* New York: Macmillan, 1953. The most complete exposition of Skinner's basic ideas.

———. *Beyond freedom and dignity.* New York: Knopf, 1971. An examination of contemporary culture, especially its failure to apply behavioral analysis to personal understanding. A powerful, popular book on the folly of thinking the way most of us still do.

———. *Cumulative record.* New York: Appleton-Century-Crofts, 1972. Skinner's choices of what he considers to be his most important papers; covers a number of areas that are not included in this chapter.

———. *About behaviorism.* New York: Knopf, 1974. A direct answer to Skinner's critics. It explores the popular misconceptions that people have about behaviorism. It is a scaled-down version of *Science and Human Behavior,* written for the general public.

Books on Behavior Therapy

Behavior Change. (Various Eds.) Chicago: Aldine, 1974–present. A yearly collection of best articles from the journals. Earlier volumes were called *Psychotherapy and Behavior Change* but the behaviorists dominate now. An easy way to get up to date.

Franks, Cyril M., & Wilson, G. Terrence. *Annual review of behavior therapy, theory and practice, 1980.* 1979, Another collection with a wider range of topics. Solid critical evaluation of the field, introduces the topical papers.

Krumboltz, John, & Krumboltz, Helen. *Changing children's behavior.* Englewood Cliffs, N.J.: Prentice-Hall, 1972. A sensible, well-written collection of ideas. The how, when, where, and why of changing specific behavior patterns in children. Cartoons, dialogues, and examples make this book more interesting than texts usually are.

Mahoney, Michael. *Cognition and behavior modification.* Cambridge, Mass.: Ballinger, 1974. A thoughtful, solid examination of the behaviorist position and its development from laboratory to field studies to clinical applications.

REFERENCES

Ames, A., Jr. Visual perception and the rotating trapezoidal window. *Psychological Monographs,* 1951, *65,* 324.

Berelson, Bernard, & Steiner, Gary A. *Human behaviour: An inventory of scientific finding.* New York: Harcourt Brace Jovanovich, 1964.

Brown, Dean, & El-Ghannam, Mohammed, A. *Computers for teaching,* 1971. Transcript of a series of talks presented at the Second Specialized Course on New Technologies in Education at the Regional Center of Planning and Administration of Education for the Arab Countries, Beirut, Lebanon.

Davison, G., & Valins, S. Maintenance of self-attributed and drug-attributed behavior change. *Journal of Personality and Social Psychology,* 1969, *11,* 25–33.

Elms, Alan. Skinner's dark year and *Walden Two. American Psychologist,* 1981, *36*(5), 470–479.

Erickson, Milton H. Experimental demonstrations of the psychopathology of everyday life. *The Psychoanalytic Quarterly,* 1939, *8,* 338–353.

Fabun, Don. On motivation., *Kaiser Aluminum News,* 1968, *26*(2).

Ferster, C. B., & Skinner, B. F. *Schedules of reinforcement.* New York: Appleton-Century-Crofts, 1957.

Goldfried, Marvin R., & Merbaum, Michael (Eds.). *Behavior change through self control.* New York: Holt, Rinehart and Winston, 1973.

Goodall, Kenneth. Field report: Shapers at work. *Psychology Today,* 1972a, *6* (6), 53–63, 132–138.

———. Margaret, age ten, and Martha, age eight: A simple case of behavioral engineering. *Psychology Today,* 1972, *6*(6), 132–133.

Goodell, Rae, B. F. Skinner: High risk, high gain. In *The visible scientists.* Boston: Little, Brown, 1977, pp. 106–119.

Hall, Calvin, & Lindzey, Gardner. *Theories of personality* (3rd ed.). New York: Wiley, 1978.

Hilts, Philip J. Pros and cons of behaviorism. *San Francisco Chronicle,* May 3, 1973. (Originally printed in the *Washington Post*).

Holland, James G., & Skinner, B. F. *The analysis of behavior: A program for self-instruction.* New York: McGraw-Hill, 1961.

Jacks, Richard N. What therapies work with today's college students: Behavior therapy. Paper presented at the annual meeting of the American Psychiatric Association, Honolulu, Hawaii, 1973.

Kimble, Gregory, A. *Hilgard and Marquis' conditioning and learning.* New York: Appleton-Century-Crofts, 1961.

Kinkade, Kathleen. *A walden two experiment: The first five years of Twin Oaks Community.* New York: Morrow, 1973. Excerpts published in 1973. *Psychology Today,* 1973, *6*(8), 35–41, 90–93; *6*(9), 71–82.

Lefcourt, Herbert M. The function of the illusions of control and freedom. *American Psychologist,* 1973, *28,* 417–425.

———. Locus of control and coping with life's events. In Ervin Staub (Ed.), *Personality: Basic aspects and current research.* Englewood Cliffs, N.J.: Prentice-Hall, 1980, pp. 201–235.

Lindley, Richard II., & Moyer, K. E. Effects of instructions on the extinction of conditioned finger-withdrawal response. *Journal of Experimental Psychology,* 1961, *61,* 82–88.

Lindsley, O. R., Skinner, B. F., & Solomon, H. C. *Studies in behavior therapy.* Status Report 1, Waltham, Mass.: Metropolitan State Hospital, 1953.

Mahoney, Michael. *Cognitive therapy and research, 5*(1). 1981.

Mahoney, Michael, & Thoresen, C. E. *Self control: Power to the person.* Monterey, Calif.: Brooks/Cole, 1974.

Mischel, Walter. *Introduction to personality.* New York: Holt, Rinehart and Winston, 1976.

Palo Alto, Calif.: Stanford University Library of Creative Writing Programs. 1974. [By Ellen Nold]

Pavlov, I. P. *Conditioned reflexes.* London: Oxford University Press, 1927.

Rachman, S. J., & Wilson, G. T. *The effects of psychological therapy,* (2nd. ed.). Elmford, N.Y.: Pergamon Press, 1980.

Ram Dass, Baba. Baba Ram Dass lecture at the Menninger Clinic. *Journal of Transpersonal Psychology,* 1970, *2,* 91–140.

Reese, Ellen P. The analysis of human operant behavior. In Jack Vernon (Ed.), *General psychology: A self-selection textbook.* Dubuque, Iowa: Brown, 1966.

Roberts, Ron E. *The new communes: Coming together in America.* Englewood Cliffs, N.J.: Prentice-Hall, 1971.

Shapiro, Deane. *Precision Nirvana.* Englewood Cliffs, N.J.: Prentice-Hall, 1978.

Skinner, B. F. *The behavior of organisms: An experimental analysis.* New York: Appleton-Century-Crofts, 1938.

———. Baby in a box. *Ladies Home Journal,* October 1945. Also in Skinner, B. F., cumulative record 1972, pp. 567–573.

———. *Walden two.* New York: Macmillan, 1948.

———. Are theories of learning necessary? *Psychological Review,* 1950, *57,* 193–216.

———. *Science and human behavior.* New York: Macmillan, 1953.

———. Freedom and the control of men. *The American Scholar,* 1955, *25,* 47–65.

———. A case history in scientific method. *The American Psychologist,* 1956, *11,* 211–233.

———. *Verbal behavior.* New York: Appleton-Century-Crofts, 1957.

———. Teaching machines. *Science,* 1958, *128,* 969–977.

———. *Cumulative record.* New York: Appleton-Century-Crofts, 1959.

———. *Cumulative record.* (Enlarged ed.). New York: Appleton-Century-Crofts, 1961.

———. Behaviorism at fifty. In W. T. Wann (Ed.), *Behaviorism and phenomenology: Contrasting bases or modern psychology.* Chicago: University of Chicago Press, 1964, pp. 79–108.

———. Autobiography. In E. G. Boring & G. Lindzey (Eds.), *History of psychology in autobiography,* Vol. 5. New York: Appleton-Century-Crofts, 1967a. pp. 387–413.

———. An interview with Mr. Behaviorist: B. F. Skinner. *Psychology Today,* 1967b, *1*(5), 20–25, 68–71.

———. *The technology of teaching.* New York: Appleton-Century-Crofts, 1968.

———. *Contingencies of reinforcement: A theoretical analysis.* New York: Appleton-Century-Crofts, 1969.

———. *Beyond freedom and dignity.* New York: Bantam Books, 1971.

———. *Cumulative record: A selection of papers* (3rd ed.). New York: Appleton-Century-Crofts, 1972a.

———. Interview with E. Hall. *Psychology Today,* 1972b, *6*(6), 65–72, 130.

———. On "having" a poem. *Saturday Review,* July 15, 1972c, pp. 32–35; Also in *Cumulative record: A selection of papers.* (3rd ed.). New York: Appleton-Century-Crofts, 1972.

———. "I have been misunderstood . . . ," an interview with B. F. Skinner. *The Center Magazine,* 1972d, *5*(2), 63–65.

———. *About behaviorism.* New York: Knopf, 1974.

———. The steep and thorny way to a science of behavior. *American Psychologist,* 1975, *30,* 42–49.

———. Walden Two revisited. *Walden Two.* New York: Macmillan, Preface, 1976b.

———. *Particulars Of my life.* New York: Knopf, 1976c.

———. A conversation with B. F. Skinner. *Harvard Magazine,* 1977a, *79*(8), 53–58.

———. Hernstein and the evolution of behaviorism. *American Psychologist,* 1977b, *32,* 1006–1016.

———. *Reflections on behaviorism and society.* Englewood Cliffs, N.J.: Prentice-Hall, 1978a.

———. Why don't we use the behavioral sciences? *Human Nature,* 1978b, *1*(3), 86–92.

———. *The shaping of a behaviorist.* New York: Knopf, 1979a.

———. Interview. *Omni,* 1979b. *1*(12), 76–80.

———. *Notebooks* (Robert Epstein, Ed.). Englewood Cliffs, N.J.: Prentice-Hall, 1980.

Wann, T. W. (Ed.). *Behaviorism and phenomenology: Contrasting bases for modern psychology.* Chicago: University of Chicago Press, 1964.

Watson, John B. Psychology as the behaviorist views it. *Psychological Review,* 1913, *20,* 158–177.

———. *The ways of behaviorism.* New York: Harper & Row, 1928a.

———. *Psychological care of infant and child.* New York: Norton, 1928b.

CHAPTER 10
CARL ROGERS AND THE PERSON-CENTERED PERSPECTIVE

Carl Rogers has had an indelible influence on psychology, education, and psychotherapy. He created and fostered "client-centered therapy," pioneered the encounter-group movement, and was one of the founders of humanistic psychology.

Although over the past 50 years his interests have expanded from individual psychotherapy to groups and to educational and social systems, his philosophical viewpoint has remained consistently optimistic and humanitarian.

I have little sympathy with the rather prevalent concept that man is basically irrational, and thus his impulses, if not controlled, would lead to destruction of others and self. Man's behavior is exquisitely rational, moving with subtle and ordered complexity toward the goals his organism is endeavoring to achieve. The tragedy for most of us is that our defenses keep us from being aware of this rationality, so that consciously we are moving in one direction, while organismically we are moving in another.

[Rogers, 1969, p. 29]

It will have been evident that one implication of the view I have been presenting is that the basic nature of the human being, when functioning freely, is constructive and trustworthy. [Rogers, 1969, p. 290]

Unwilling to be limited by the popularity and acceptance of his earlier works, Rogers has continued to modify his ideas and change his approach. He encourages others to test his assertions, but discourages the formation of a "Rogerian school" that would only mimic or repeat his own discoveries. Outside of formal psychology his work "has been one of the factors in changing concepts of industrial (even military) leadership, of social work practice, of nursing practice, and of religious work. . . . It has even influenced students of theology and philosophy" (Rogers, 1974, p. 115).

What started for me in the 30's as a changing but supposedly well-accepted way of working therapeutically with individuals, was clumsily articulated as my own view in the early 1940's. . . . One might say that a "technique" of counseling became a practice of psychotherapy. This in turn brought into being a theory of therapy and of personality. The theory supplied the hypotheses which opened a whole new field of research. Out of this grew an approach to all interpersonal relationships. Now it reaches into education as a way of facilitating learning at all levels. It is a way of conducting intensive group experiences, and has influenced the theory of group dynamics.

[Rogers, 1970]

Through the 1970s and early 1980s Rogers shifted his interests away from therapy with clients to an international involvement in team building and large-scale community development. His determination to extend his ideas and his support of others' capacities to help themselves continue to influence counselors and psychologists worldwide.

PERSONAL HISTORY

Carl Rogers, the fourth of six children, was born on January 8, 1902, in Oak Park, Illinois, into a prosperous and narrowly fundamentalist home. His childhood was restricted by the beliefs and attitudes of his parents and by his own incorporation of their ideas.

> I think the attitudes toward persons outside our large family can be summed up schematically in this way: Other persons behave in dubious ways which we do not approve in our family. Many of them play cards, go to movies, smoke, dance, drink, and engage in other activities—some unmentionable. So the best thing to do is be tolerant of them, since they may not know better, and to keep away from any close communication with them and live your life with the family. [Rogers, 1973a, p. 3]

Neither aggressive nor athletic, Rogers was a gifted student whose love for books contributed to an introspective and lonely childhood. "Anything I would today regard as a close and communicative interpersonal relationship was completely lacking during that period" (1973a, p. 4). To further protect their children from the "corrupting influences of the city and suburbs" (Kirschenbaum, 1980, p. 10), Rogers's parents moved to a farm near Glen Ellyn, Illinois, during his high school years. He became an excellent student with avid scientific interests. "I realized by now that I was peculiar, a loner, with very little place or opportunity for a place in the world of persons. I was socially incompetent in any but superficial contacts. My fantasies during this period were definitely bizarre, and probably would be classed as schizoid by a diagnostician, but fortunately I never came in contact with a psychologist" (Rogers, 1973a, p. 4).

> Something of the gently suppressive family atmosphere is perhaps indicated by the fact that three of six children developed ulcers at some period in their lives. [Rogers, 1967, p. 352]

His college experiences at the University of Wisconsin were meaningful and rewarding. "For the first time in my life outside of my family I found real closeness and intimacy" (Rogers, 1967, p. 349). In his sophomore year he began to study for the ministry. The following year, 1922, he went to China to attend a World Student Christian Federation conference in Peking; subsequently he went on a speaking tour through west China and the Orient. The trip liberalized his fundamentalist religious attitudes and gave him his first opportunity to develop psychological independence. "From the date of this trip, my goals, values, aims, and philosophy have been my own and very divergent from the views which my parents held and which I had held up to this point" (1967, p. 351).

In 1924 he married Helen Elliott whom he had known since grammar school. Although both families opposed the idea of additional schooling after marriage instead of getting a job, Rogers asserted himself, made his own decision, and the couple moved to New York City.

He began graduate studies in theology at Union Theological Seminary but chose to finish his work in psychology at Teachers College, Columbia University. This shift was prompted in part by a student-directed seminar that gave him the opportunity to examine his rising doubts about his religious commitment. Later, in a psychology course, he was pleasantly surprised to discover that a person could earn a living *outside* the church working closely with individuals who needed help.

His first job was in Rochester, New York, in a child guidance center working with children who had been referred by various social agencies. "I wasn't connected with a university, no one was looking over my shoulder from any particular treatment orientation . . . [the agencies] didn't give a damn how you proceeded but hoped you could be of some assistance" (Rogers, 1970, p. 514–515). During the years in Rochester (1928–1939), Rogers's understanding of the process of psychotherapy moved from a formal, directive approach toward what he would later call client-centered therapy.

It began to occur to me that unless I had a need to demonstrate my own cleverness and learning, I would be better to rely upon the client for the direction of movement in the process. [Rogers, 1967, p. 359]

While in Rochester, Rogers wrote *The Clinical Treatment of the Problem Child* (1939). The book was well received and led to an offer of a full professorship at Ohio State University. Rogers has said that by starting at the top he escaped the pressures and tensions that exist on the lower rungs of the academic ladder—pressures that stifle innovation and creativity. His teaching and the stimulation he received from graduate students prompted Rogers to write a more formal examination of the nature of the therapeutic relationship in *Counseling and Psychotherapy* (1942).

In 1945 the University of Chicago offered him the chance to establish a new counseling center based on his ideas. He served as its director until 1957. Rogers's growing emphasis on trust was reflected in the democratic decision-making policies of the center. If patients could be trusted to direct their own therapy, certainly staff could be trusted to administer their own working environment.

In 1951 Rogers published *Client-Centered Therapy;* it contained his first formal theory of therapy, his theory of personality, and some of the research that reinforced his conclusions. In it he suggests that the major directing force in the therapy relationship should be the client, not the therapist. This reversal of the usual relationship was revolutionary and attracted considerable criticism. It struck directly at the expertise of the therapist and the supposed lack of awareness of the patient—assumptions unchallenged for the most part by other theorists. The general implications of this position, beyond therapy, were spelled out in *On Becoming a Person* (1961).

Although the time in Chicago was exciting and satisfying, there was also a period of personal difficulties. While working closely with an extremely disturbed client, Rogers became enmeshed in her pathology. Close to a breakdown himself, he literally fled the center, took a three-month vacation, and returned to enter therapy with one of his colleagues. After the therapy, Rogers's own interactions with clients became increasingly free and spontaneous.

In 1957 Rogers went to the University of Wisconsin at Madison with a joint appointment in psychiatry and psychology. It was a difficult time professionally; Rogers found himself in growing conflict with the psychology department. He felt that his freedom to teach and his students' freedom to learn were being restricted. "I'm pretty good at living and letting live, but when they wouldn't let my *students* live, that became a dissatisfying experience" (Rogers, 1970, p. 528).

Rogers's rising indignation is captured in the paper, "Current Assumptions in Graduate Education: A Passionate Statement" (1969). Although rejected by *The American Psychologist* for publication, it enjoyed a wide distribution through the graduate student underground before it was eventually printed. "The theme of my statement is that we are doing an unintelligent, ineffectual and wasteful job of preparing psychologists, to the detriment of our discipline and society" (Rogers, 1969, p. 170). Some of the implicit assumptions that Rogers attacked were: "The student cannot be trusted to pursue his own scientific and professional learning." "Evaluation is education; education is evaluation." "Presentation equals learning: What is presented in the lecture is what the student learns." "The truths of psychology are known." "Creative scientists develop from passive learners" (1969, pp. 169–187).

Not surprisingly, Rogers left his tenured professorship in 1963 and moved to the newly founded Western Behavioral Science Institute in La Jolla, California. A few years later he helped establish the Center for the Studies of the Person, a loosely structured collection of people in the helping professions.

His growing effect on education had become so evident that he wrote a book to clarify the kinds of educational settings he was advocating and was actively engaged in establishing. *Freedom to Learn* (1969) contains his clearest statement on the nature of human beings.

His work with encounter groups stems from his years in California where he has been free to experiment, invent, and test his ideas without the binding influences of social institutions or academic respectability. His encounter research is summed up in *Carl Rogers on Encounter Groups* (1970).

One of his moves away from psychotherapy was his exploration of changing trends and values in normal marriages. His naturalistic study, *Becoming Partners: Marriage and Its Alternatives* (1972) is an examination of the advantages and disadvantages of different patterns of relationship.

After splitting his interests for several years, Rogers finally combined his group work and his efforts in educational innovation. Along with some members of the Center for the Studies of the Person, he ran ongoing intensive groups for the faculty and students of a Jesuit training college and a Catholic school system (elementary through college.)

I have often been grateful that by the time I was in dire need of personal help, I had trained therapists who were persons in their own right, not dependent upon me, yet able to offer me the kind of help I needed. [Rogers, 1967, p. 367]

What do I mean by a person-centered approach? It expresses the primary theme of my whole professional life, as that theme has become clarified through experience, interaction with others, and research. I smile as I think of the various labels I have given to this theme during the course of my career—nondirective counseling, client-centered therapy, student-centered teaching, group-centered leadership. [Rogers, 1980a, p. 114]

He also did extensive consultations for the Louisville, Kentucky, school system (Rogers, 1975a, b).

Emboldened by the highly disruptive and yet successful results, Rogers moved away from client-centered relationships that had been his focus over most of his career. He looked instead to "person-centered" situations with their revolutionary implications for every sort of political and social system. His own internal revolution and resulting conclusions are described in *Carl Rogers on Personal Power* (1978).

He is now based full time at the Center for the Studies of the Person. He writes, lectures, and works in his garden. He has time to answer mail, talk with younger colleagues, and to be with his family.

He has become interested in altered states of consciousness, "inner space—the realm of the psychological powers and the psychic capabilities of the human person" (Rogers, 1980b, p. 12). (Also Kirschenbaum, 1980, p. 398) He has also become more open and expressive in his relationships. He says of these shifts, "I am no longer simply talking about psychotherapy, but about a point of view, a philosophy, an approach to life, a way of being in which *growth*—of a person, a group, or a community—is part of the goal" (1980a, p. ix).

He summarizes his own position by quoting Lao-Tse:

If I keep from meddling with people, they take care of themselves,
If I keep from commanding people, they behave themselves,
If I keep from preaching at people, they improve themselves,
If I keep from imposing on people, they become themselves.

[Rogers, 1973a, p. 13]

INTELLECTUAL ANTECEDENTS

Rogers' theory of personality developed primarily from his own clinical experiences. He feels that he has retained his objectivity by avoiding close identification with any particular school or tradition. "I have never really *belonged* to *any* professional group. I have been educated by or had close working relationships with psychologists, psychoanalysts, psychiatrists, psychiatric social workers, social caseworkers, educators, and religious workers, yet I have never felt that I really belonged, in any total or committed sense, to any one of these groups. . . . Lest one think I have been a complete nomad professionally I should add that the only groups to which I have ever *really* belonged have been close-knit, congenial task forces which I have organized or helped organize" (Rogers, 1967, p. 375).

His students at the University of Chicago suggested that he would find that the ideas of Martin Buber and Sören Kierkegaard echoed his own emerging position. Indeed, these writers were a source of support

I garden. Those mornings when I cannot find time . . . I feel cheated. My garden supplies the same intriguing question I have been trying to meet in all my professional life: What are the effective conditions for growth? But in my garden, though the frustrations are just as immediate, the results, whether success or failure, are more quickly evident. [Rogers, 1974, pp. 122–123]

There has never been any one outstanding person in my learning . . . so as I went on there was no one I had to rebel against or leave behind. [Rogers, 1970, p. 502]

and confirmation for his brand of existential philosophy. More recently, Rogers has discovered parallels to his own work in Eastern sources, notably Zen Buddhism and the works of Lao-Tse. Whereas Rogers's work has undoubtedly been affected by his understanding of the works of others, his is distinctly a homegrown contribution to our understanding of human nature.

MAJOR CONCEPTS

Fundamental to all of Rogers's work is the assumption that people define themselves through observing and evaluating their own experiences. His underlying assumption is that peoples' realities are private affairs and can be known only by the individuals themselves. In his major theoretical work (1959) Rogers defines the concepts that are at the core of his theory of personality, therapy, and personal relationships. These primary constructs establish a framework upon which people build and modify their images of themselves.

The Field of Experience

There is a field of experience unique to each individual; this field contains "all that is going on within the envelope of the organism at any given moment which is potentially available to awareness" (Rogers, 1959, p. 197). It includes events, perceptions, sensations, and impacts of which a person is not aware but could be if he or she focused on these inputs. It is a private, personal world that may or may not correspond to observed, objective reality.

This field of experience is selective, subjective, and incomplete (Van Belle, 1980), yet is bounded by psychological limitations (what we are willing to be aware of) and biological limitations (what we are able to be aware of). Our attention, while theoretically open to any experience, is focused on immediate concerns excluding almost everything else. When we are very hungry, our field of experience is filled with thoughts of food and how to get food. When we are lonely, the field is focused toward the presence or absence of others.

> Words and symbols bear to the world of reality the same relationship as a map to the territory which it represents. . . . We live by a perceptual "map" which is never reality itself. [Rogers, 1951, p. 485]

The Self

Within the field of experience is the self. The self is not a stable, unchanging entity. Observed at any moment, however, it *appears* to be firm and predictable. This is because we freeze a section of experience in order to observe it. Rogers concluded that "we were not dealing with an entity of slow accretion, of step by step learning . . . the product was clearly a gestalt, a configuration in which the alteration of one minor aspect could completely alter the whole pattern" (1959, p. 201). The self is an organized, consistent gestalt, constantly in the process of forming and reforming as situations change.

As a photograph is a "still" of something that is changing, so the self is not any of the stills we take of it but the underlying, fluid process.

Whereas others use the word *self* to point to that part of our personal identity which is stable and unchanging, Rogers's meaning of the word is almost the opposite. Rogers's self is a *process,* a system that by definition is changing. It is this difference, this emphasis on change and flexibility, that underlies his theory. This leads to his belief that people are not only capable of growth, change, and personal development, but that such positive change is also a natural and expected progression. The self or self-concept is a person's understanding of himself or herself, based on past experience, present inputs, and future expectancies (Evans, 1975).

The Ideal Self

The ideal self is "the self-concept which the individual would most like to possess, upon which he places the highest value for himself" (Rogers, 1959, p. 200). Like the self, it is a shifting, changing structure, constantly undergoing redefinition. If one's ideal self is very different from the actual self, the person may be uncomfortable, dissatisfied, and experience neurotic difficulties. To be able to see oneself accurately and be comfortable with oneself is one sign of mental health. One's ideal self is a model toward which a person can strive. Conversely, to the extent that it is grossly different from one's actual behavior and values, the ideal self may inhibit one's capacity to develop.

An excerpt from a case history may clarify this. A student was planning to drop out of college. He had been the best student in his junior high school and the top student in his high school, and he had been doing extremely well in college. He was leaving, he explained, because he had received a *C* in a course. His image of always being the best was endangered. The only course of action he could envision was to escape, to leave the academic world, to deny the discrepancy between his actual performance and his ideal vision of himself. He said that he would work toward being the "best" in some other way.

To protect his ideal self-image he was willing to foreclose his academic career. He left school, went around the world, and held a host of odd jobs for several years. When he was seen again, he was able to discuss the possibility that it *might* not be necessary to be the best from the beginning, but he still had great difficulties in exploring any activity where he might experience failure.

Self-Actualizing Tendency

There is a basic aspect to human nature that inclines a person toward greater congruence and realistic functioning. Moreover, this urge is not limited to human beings; it is part of the process of all living things. "It is the urge which is evident in all organic and human life—to expand, extend, become autonomous, develop, mature—the tendency to express and activate all the capacities of the organism, to the extent that such activation enhances the organism or the self" (Rogers, 1961, p. 35). Rogers suggests that in each of us there is an inherent drive toward being as competent and capable as we are biologically able to be. As a plant attempts to become a healthy plant, as a seed contains within it the drive to become a tree, so a person is impelled to become a whole, complete, and self-actualized person.[1]

The drive toward health is not an overwhelming force that sweeps aside obstacles; rather, it is easily blunted, distorted, twisted, and repressed. Rogers sees it as the dominant motive force in a person who is "functioning freely," not crippled by past events or current beliefs that maintain incongruence. Maslow came to similar conclusions; he called this tendency a small weak internal voice, one that is easily muffled. The assumption that growth is possible, and central to the purpose of the organism is crucial to the rest of Rogers's thought.

For Rogers, the tendency toward self-actualization is not simply another motive among many. "It should be noted that this basic actualizing tendency is *the only motive* which is postulated in this theoretical system. . . . The self, for example, is an important construct in our theory, but the self does not 'do' anything. It is only one expression of the general tendency of the organism to behave in those ways which maintain and enhance itself" (Rogers, 1959, p. 196).

The Self in Society: Personal Power

As Rogers has turned his attention away from strictly therapeutic situations, his thinking has shifted to consider the problems of individuals in political and social contexts. The person-centered approach in society he calls *personal power*. It is concerned with *"the locus of decision-making power:* who makes the decisions which, consciously or unconsciously, regulate or control the thoughts, feelings, or behavior of others or oneself. . . . In sum it is the process of gaining, using, sharing or relinquishing power, control, decision making" (Rogers, 1978, pp. 4–5). Rogers assumes that each of us has an enormous capacity to use our personal power correctly and beneficially if giventhe opportunity. "The individual has within himself vast resources for self-understanding, for altering his self-concept, his attitudes, and his self-directed behavior . . ." (1978, p. 7). This drive toward self-development is impeded by placing people under others' control. This domination, when overt, as in a dictatorship, is often resisted.

What concerns Rogers are the more subtle and accepted kinds of

---

[1]Although Rogers did not include any religious or spiritual dimensions in his earlier formulations, others have extended his theories to include transcendental experiences (Campbell & McMahon, 1974). Rogers has also become interested in this extension (Rogers, 1980a, pp. 96–108).

domination. In particular he singles out therapists who control and manipulate patients, teachers who control and manipulate students, government bodies that control and manipulate various segments of the population, and businesses that control and manipulate their employees. He predicts that, without these agreed-upon restrictions of personal power, individuals and groups would collaborate and come up with solutions to their problems—solutions that do not demand the inhibition of the many by the few. This development in his work, from the intimacy of the therapeutic situation to the rough-and-tumble of political, social, and community organization, he describes as radical and revolutionary. He is not suggesting a change in the kinds of control (one government for another) but supports a gradual restructuring of organizations to fully take into account the personal power of the members.

Congruence and Incongruence

Rogers does not label people as adjusted or maladjusted, sick or well, normal or abnormal; instead, he writes about their capacity to perceive the reality of their situation. The term *congruence* he defines as the degree of accuracy between experience, communication, and awareness. A high degree of congruence means that communication (what you are expressing), experience (what is occurring), and awareness (what you are noticing) are all very similar. Your observations and those of an external observer would be consistent.

Small children exhibit high congruence. They express their feelings as soon as possible with their whole beings. When a child is hungry, he or she is all hungry, right now! When children are loving or angry, they express these emotions fully and completely. This may account for the rapidity with which children flow from one emotional state to another. Full expression of their feelings allows them to finish a situation quickly instead of carrying the unexpressed emotional baggage of previous experiences into each new encounter. Congruence is accurately described by a Zen Buddhist saying: "When I am hungry, I eat; when I am tired, I sit; when I am sleepy, I sleep."

Incongruence occurs when there are differences between awareness, experience, and communication. People who appear to be angry (fists clenched, voices raised, cursing) but (if asked) reply that they are not at all angry, or people who say that they are having a wonderful time yet act bored, lonely, or ill at ease, exhibit incongruence. Incongruence is the inability to perceive accurately, the inability or an unwillingness to communicate accurately, or both.

When the incongruence is between awareness and experience, it is called *repression* or *denial*. The person is simply not aware of what he or she is doing. Most psychotherapy works on this symptom of incon-

The more the therapist is able to listen acceptantly to what is going on within himself, and the more he is able to be the complexity of his feelings, without fear, the higher the degree of his congruence. [Rogers, 1961, p. 61]

gruence, helping people to become more aware of their actions, thoughts, and attitudes as they affect themselves and others.

When incongruence is a discrepancy between awareness and communication, a person does not express what he or she is actually feeling, thinking, or experiencing. This kind of incongruence is perceived by others as *deceitful, inauthentic,* or *dishonest.* Often these behaviors become the focus of discussions in group therapy or encounter settings. Whereas such behaviors appear malicious, trainers and therapists report that the lack of social congruence—the apparent unwillingness to communicate—is usually a lack of self-control and a lack of personal awareness. The person is not able to express real emotions and perceptions because of fears or old habits of concealment that are difficult to overcome. Another possibility is that the person has difficulty understanding what others want, or it may be that a person cannot express his or her perceptions in such a way that others understand (Bandler & Grinder, 1975).

Incongruence may be experienced as tension, anxiety, or, in more extreme circumstances, disorientation and confusion. A mental hospital patient who doesn't know where he is, doesn't understand he is in a hospital, or what time of day it is, or even who he is, is exhibiting high incongruency. The discrepancy between his external reality and subjective experience has become so great that the patient is no longer able to function without protection.

Most of the symptoms described in the psychopathology literature can be understood as various forms of incongruence. The important issue for Rogers is that incongruence demands resolution; the type of incongruence a person exhibits is less relevant. Incongruence is not that you have conflicting feelings, ideas, or concerns; that is normal and healthy. Incongruence is when you are not aware of these conflicts, do not understand them, and therefore cannot begin to resolve or balance them.

Our incongruence can be observed in remarks such as, "I'm not able to come to any decisions," "I don't know what I want," and "I never seem to be able to stick to anything." When you are not able to sort out the different inputs you are exposed to, you become confused. Consider the case of a client who reports, "My mother tells me I have to take care of her; it's the least I can do. My girl friend tells me to stand up for myself, not to be pushed around. I think I'm pretty good to Mother, a lot better than she deserves. Sometimes I hate her, sometimes I love her. Sometimes she's good to be with, at other times she belittles me."

This client is beset with different inputs. Each one is partially valid and leads to congruent action *some of the time.* Sorting out the inputs that the client truly agrees with from those that the client would like to agree with but does not is difficult. Recognizing that we have different, even opposed, feelings is healthy and challenging. We behave differently at different times. Such ambivalence is neither unusual nor unhealthy; not being able to recognize, cope, or admit to it can cause anxiety.

DYNAMICS

Psychological Growth

The positive forces toward health and growth are natural and inherent in the organism. Based on his own clinical experience, Rogers concludes that individuals have the capacity to experience and to become aware of their own maladjustments. That is, you can experience the incongruences between your self-concept and your actual experiences. This indwelling capacity is coupled with an underlying tendency to modification of the self-concept so that it is, in fact, in line with reality. Thus Rogers postulates a natural movement away from conflict and toward resolution. He sees adjustment not as a static state but as a process in which new learning and new experiences are accurately assimilated.

Rogers is convinced that these tendencies toward health are facilitated by any interpersonal relationship in which one member is free enough from incongruence to be in touch with his or her own self-correcting center. The major task in therapy is to establish such a genuine relationship. Acceptance of one's self is a prerequisite to an easier and more genuine acceptance of others. In turn, being accepted by another leads to a greater willingness to accept one's self. This self-correcting and self-enhancing cycle is the major way one overcomes obstacles and facilitates psychological growth.

Obstacles to Growth

Obstacles arise in childhood and are inherent in the normal stages of development. Lessons that are beneficial at one age can become detrimental at a later stage. Freud described situations where childhood lessons were carried on into adult life as neurotic fixations. Rogers does not dwell on specific details but sees an overall pattern of potential restrictions occurring as a child grows.

Conditions of Worth

As the infant begins to have an awareness of self, he or she develops a need for love or positive regard. "This need is universal in human beings, and in the individual is pervasive and persistent. Whether it is an inherent or learned need is irrelevant to the theory" (Rogers, 1959, p. 223). Because children do not separate their actions from their total beings, they often react to approval for an *action* as if it were approval for *themselves*. Similarly, they react to being punished for an action as if they were being disapproved of in general.

So important is love to an infant that "he comes to be guided in his behavior not by the degree to which an experience maintains or enhances the organism, but by the likelihood of receiving maternal love" (Rogers, 1959, p. 225). The child begins to act in ways that gain love or approval whether or not the behaviors are healthy. Children may act against their own self-interest, coming to view themselves in terms originally designed to please or placate others. Theoretically, this situation might not develop if the child always felt accepted, if feelings were accepted even if some behaviors were inhibited. In such an ideal setting the child would never be pressured to disown or deny unattractive but genuine parts of his or her personality. "This, as we see it, is the basic estrangement in man. He has not been true to himself, to his natural organismic valuing of experience, but for the sake of preserving the positive regard of others has now come to falsify some of the values he experiences and to perceiving them in terms based only on their value to others. Yet this has not been a conscious choice, but a natural—and tragic—development in infancy" (Rogers, 1959, p. 226).

Behaviors or attitudes that deny some aspect of one's self are called *conditions of worth,* meaning conditions thought to be necessary to be worthy and get love. Conditions of worth inhibit not only behavior but also maturation and awareness; they lead to incongruence and eventual rigidity of personality.

These conditions are the basic obstacles to accurate perception and realistic thinking. They are selective blinders and filters, used by a child to hopefully insure a supply of love from parents and others. As children we learn certain attitudes and actions to which we adhere to in order to retain love, to be worth loving. We learn certain conditions, attitudes, or actions that we feel we must fulfill to remain worthy of love. To the extent that these attitudes and actions are contrived, they are areas of personal incongruence. In the extreme, conditions of worth are characterized by the belief that "I must be loved or respected by everyone I come in contact with." Conditions of worth create a discrepancy between the self and the self-concept.

For example if you have been told, "You must love your new baby sister or mommy won't love you," the message is that you must deny or repress any genuine negative feelings toward her. Only if you manage to hide your ill will, your desire to hurt her, and your normal jealousy, will your mother continue to love you. If you admit such feelings, you risk the loss of your parents' love. A solution (which creates a condition of worth) is to deny such feelings whenever they occur, blocking them from your awareness. You may now respond in ways such as, "I really do love my little sister; I hug her until she screams," or "My foot slipped under hers, that's why she tripped," or the more universal, "She started it!"

This author can still recall the enormous joy that my older brother exhibited when he was given an opportunity to hit me for something I had done. My mother, my brother, and I were all stunned by his violence. In recalling the incident my brother remembers that he was not especially angry at me, but he understood that this was a rare occasion and wanted to unload as much accumulated ill will as possible while he had permission. Admitting such feelings and allowing some continuing expression of them as they occur is healthier, says Rogers, than denying or disowning them.

As the child matures the problem may persist. Growth is impeded to the extent that a person is denying inputs that differ from the artificially "nice" self-concept. To support the false self-image a person continues to distort experiences—the more distortion, the greater the chance for mistakes and the creation of additional problems. The behaviors, mistakes, and confusion that result are manifestations of the fundamental initial distortions.

The situation feeds back on itself. Each experience of incongruence between the self and reality leads to increased imbalance, which in turn leads to increased defensiveness, shutting off experiences and creating new occasions for incongruence.

Sometimes the defensive maneuvers don't work. The person becomes aware of the obvious discrepancies between behaviors and beliefs. The results may be panic, chronic anxiety, withdrawal, or even psychosis. Rogers has observed that psychotic behavior often seems to be the acting out of a previously denied aspect of one's experience. Perry (1974) corroborates this, presenting evidence that the psychotic episode is a desperate attempt of the personality to rebalance itself and allow realization of frustrated internal needs. Client-centered therapy strives to establish an atmosphere in which detrimental conditions of worth can be set aside, thus allowing the healthy forces in a person to regain their original dominance.

The Ideal Self

The ideal self (described earlier) can be an obstacle to growth if it is very different from the real self. If there is a deep-seated need to act as the ideal self would act and one cannot act that way, the result is a constriction in the normal process of health and growth. An inability to admit to what is actually occurring is seen by others as bizarre behavior and not seen clearly by oneself. For example, some parents say they will "do anything" for their children, but are actually resentful and do not wish to do the things they say. The result is a confused child and parents unwilling to see reality.

STRUCTURE

Body

Although Rogers defines personality and identity as an ongoing gestalt, he does not give special attention to the role of the body. Even in his own encounter work he does not promote or facilitate physical contact or work directly with physical gestures. As he points out, "My background is not such as to make me particularly free in this respect" (1970, p. 58). His theory is based on awareness of *experience;* it does not single out the physical as different in kind or in value from emotional, cognitive, or intuitive experiences.

Social Relationships

The fundamental importance of relationships is an ongoing concern in Rogers's work. Early relationships can be congruent and supportive, or they can create conditions of worth and personality constriction. Later relationships can restore congruence or degrade it. Interactions with others are the critical incidents in developing awareness and the capacity to be congruent to oneself.

Rogers believes that interaction with another enables an individual to directly discover, uncover, experience, or encounter his or her actual self. *Our personalities become visible to us through relating to others.* In therapy, in encounter situations, and in daily interactions, the feedback from others offers us opportunities to experience ourselves.

If we think of people who do not have relationships, we can envision two contrasting extremes. The first is the unwilling recluse, unskilled in dealing with others. The other is the contemplative who has withdrawn from the world to pursue other goals.

Neither figure appeals to Rogers. For him relationships offer the best opportunity to be "fully functioning," to be in harmony with oneself, others, and the environment. Through relationships, the basic organismic needs of the individual can be fulfilled. The desire for fulfillment motivates people to invest incredible amounts of energy in relationships, even in those that may not appear to be healthy or fulfilling.

I would like to propose . . . that the major barrier to mutual interpersonal communication is our very natural tendency to judge, to evaluate, to approve or disapprove, the statement of the other person, or the other group. [Rogers, 1952a]

Marriage

Marriage is an unusual relationship; it is potentially long-term, it is intensive, and it carries within it the possibility of sustained growth and development. Rogers believes that marriage follows the same general laws that hold true for encounter groups, therapy, and other relationships. Better marriages occur between partners who are congruent themselves, have few impeding conditions of worth, and are capable of genuine acceptance of others. When marriage is used to sustain incongruence or to reinforce existing defensive tendencies, it is less fulfilling and less likely to maintain itself.

Rogers's conclusions about any long-term intimate relationship, such as marriage, are focused on four basic elements: ongoing commitment, expression of feelings, not accepting specific roles, and the capacity to share one's inner life. He summarizes each element as a pledge, an agreed-upon ideal for a continuing, beneficial, and meaningful relationship.

1. **Dedication of commitment.** Each member of a marriage should view "a partnership as a continuing process, not a contract. The work that is done is for *personal* as well as mutual satisfaction" (1972, p. 201). A relationship is work; it is work for separate as well as common goals. Rogers suggests that this commitment be expressed as follows: "We each commit ourselves to working together on the changing process of our present relationship, because that relationship is currently enriching our love and our life and we wish it to grow" (1972, p. 201).

2. **Communication—the expression of feelings.** Rogers insists on full and open communication. "I will risk myself by endeavoring to communicate any persistent feeling, positive or negative, to my partner—to the full depth that I understand it in myself—as a living part of *me*. Then I will risk further by trying to understand, with all the empathy I can bring to bear, his or her response, whether it is accusatory and critical or sharing and self-revealing" (1972, p. 204). Communication has two equally important phases; the first is to express the emotion, the second is to remain open and experience the other's response.

Rogers is not simply advocating the acting out of feelings. He is suggesting that one must be as committed to the effect your feelings have on your partner as to the original expression of the feelings themselves. This is far more difficult than simply "letting off steam" or being "open and honest." It is the willingness to accept the real risks involved: rejection, misunderstandings, hurt feelings, and retribution.

3. **Nonacceptance of roles.** Numerous problems develop from trying to fulfill the expectations of others instead of determining our own. "We will live by our own choices, the deepest organismic sensings of which we are capable, but we will

All our troubles, says somebody wise, come upon us because we cannot be alone. And that is all very well. We must all be able to be alone. Otherwise we are just victims. But when we are able to be alone, then we realize that the only thing to do is to start a new relationship with another—or even the same—human being. That people should all be stuck up apart, like so many telegraph poles, is nonsense. [D. H. Lawrence, 1960, pp. 114–115]

Is not marriage an open question when it is alleged, from the beginning of the world, that such as are in the institution wish to get out, and such as are out wish to get in? [Ralph Waldo Emerson, 1803–1882]

not be shaped by the wishes, the rules, the roles which others are all too eager to thrust upon us" (1972, p. 260). Rogers reports that many couples suffer severe strain attempting to live out their partial and ambivalent acceptance of the images that their parents and society have thrust upon them. A marriage laced with too many unrealistic expectations and images is inherently unstable and potentially unrewarding.

4. **Becoming a separate self.** This commitment is a profound attempt to discover and accept one's total nature. It is the most challenging of the commitments, a dedication to removing masks as soon and as often as they form. "Perhaps I can discover and come closer to more of what I really am deep inside—feeling sometimes angry or terrified, sometimes loving and caring, occasionally beautiful and strong or wild and awful—without hiding these feelings from myself. Perhaps I can come to prize myself as the richly varied person I am. Perhaps I can openly be more of this person. If so, I can live by my own experienced values, even though I am aware of all of society's codes. Then I can let myself be all this complexity of feelings and meaning and values with my partner—be free enough to give of love and anger and tenderness as they exist in me. Possibly then I can be a real member of a partnership, because I am on the road to being a real person. And I am hopeful that I can encourage my partner to follow his or her own road to a unique personhood, which I would love to share" (1972, p. 209).

Wen you're a married man, Samivel, you'll understand a good many things as you don't understand now; but vether it's worth while goin' through so much to learn so little, as the charity boy said ven he got to the end of the alphabet, is a mater o' taste. [Charles Dickens, 1812–1870, *Pickwick Papers*]

Emotions

The healthy individual is aware of his or her emotional feelings, whether or not they are expressed. Feelings denied to awareness distort perception of and reactions to the experience that triggered them.

An example is feeling anxiety without being aware of the cause. Anxiety appears when an experience has occurred that, *if admitted to awareness,* could threaten one's self-image. The unconscious reaction (McCleary & Lazarus, 1949) alerts the organism to possible danger and causes psychophysiological changes. These defensive reactions are one way the organism maintains incongruent beliefs and behaviors. A person can act on these but be unaware of why he or she is acting. For example, a man might become uncomfortable at seeing overt homosexuals. His own self-report would include the discomfort but would not mention the cause. He cannot admit his own concern, his unresolved sexual identity, or perhaps the hopes and fears he has concerning his own sexuality. Distorting his perceptions, he may in

Yet, if we are truly aware, we can hear the "silent screams" of denied feelings echoing off of every classroom wall and university corridor. And if we are sensitive enough, we can hear the creative thoughts and ideas that often emerge during and from the open expression of our feelings. [Rogers, 1973b, p. 385.]

turn react with open hostility to homosexuals, treating them as an external threat instead of admitting his internal conflict.

Intellect

Rogers does not segregate the intellect from other functions; he values it as one tool that may be used effectively in integrating one's experience. He is skeptical of educational systems that overemphasize intellectual skills and undervalue the emotional and intuitive aspects of full human functioning.

In particular, Rogers finds graduate training in many fields demanding, demeaning, and depressing. The pressure to produce limited and unoriginal work, coupled with the passive and dependent roles pressed on graduate students, effectively stifles or retards their creative and productive capabilities. He quotes a student's complaint: "This coercion had such a deterring effect (upon me) that, after I had passed the final examination, I found the consideration of any problem distasteful for me for an entire year" (1969, p. 177).[2]

If intellect, like other freely operating functions, tends to direct the organism toward more congruent awareness, then forcing the intellect into specified channels may not be beneficial. Rogers's contention is that people are better off deciding what to do for themselves, with support from others, than doing what others decide for them.

Knowing

Rogers describes three ways of knowing, of determining what is real, that are used by a psychologically mature person. They are subjective knowing, objective knowing, and interpersonal knowing.

Most important is *subjective knowing*—the knowledge of whether one loves, hates, is disdainful of, or enjoys a person, an experience, or an event. One improves the quality of subjective knowing by getting more in touch with one's inner emotional processes. By paying attention to "gut" feelings, to inner indications, a person perceives that one course of action feels better than another. It is the capacity to know enough in order to act without verifiable evidence. In science, for example, it is following one's hunches toward specific problems. Research on creative problem solvers indicates that a person "knows" that he or she is on the right track long before he or she knows what the solution will include (Gordon, 1961).

Objective knowing is a way of testing hypotheses, speculations, and conjectures against external frames of reference. In psychology, reference points may include observations of behavior, test results, questionnaires, or the judgments of other psychologists. The use of col-

We all know the effects on children of compulsory spinach and compulsory rhubarb. It's the same with compulsory learning. They say, "It's spinach and the hell with it." [Rogers, 1969]

Who can bring into being this whole person? From my experience I would say the least likely are university faculty members. Their traditionalism and smugness approach the incredible. [Rogers, 1973b, p. 385]

---

[2]The student quoted was Albert Einstein.

leagues rests on the idea that people who are trained in a given discipline can be relied upon to apply the same methods of judgment to a given event. Expert opinion may be objective, but it may also be a collective misperception. Any group of experts can exhibit rigidity and defensiveness when asked to consider data that contradict axiomatic aspects of their own training. Rogers notes that theologians, communist dialecticians, and psychoanalysts exemplify this tendency in his experience.

Rogers is hardly alone in questioning the validity of so-called objective knowledge, especially in attempting to understand someone else's experience. Polanyi (1958), a philosopher of science, has clarified the different uses and limitations of personal or subjective knowledge and public or objective knowledge. Each type of knowledge is useful for describing and understanding different kinds of experiences. Tart (1971, 1975) describes the necessity of different kinds of training to even perceive, let alone evaluate, different kinds of subjective experiences.

It has been considered slightly obscene to admit that psychologists feel, have hunches, or passionately pursue unformulated directions. [Rogers, 1964]

The third form of knowledge is *interpersonal knowing* or *phenomenological knowing*. It is at the core of Rogerian psychotherapy. It is the practice of empathic understanding: penetrating the private, unique, subjective world of the other to check on our understanding of the other's views. The goal is not merely to be objectively correct, not just to see if it agrees or disagrees with our point of view, but to be able to comprehend the other person's experience as *he* or *she* experiences it. This empathic knowing is tested by asking the other person if he or she has been understood. One might say, for example: "You seem depressed this morning, are you?" "It seems to me that you are telling the group that you need their help." "I wonder if you are too tired to finish this right now." This capacity to truly know another's reality is the foundation for forming genuine relationships.

Do not judge another man's road until you have walked a mile in his moccasins. [Saying of the Pueblo Indians]

Self

Textbook writers generally class Rogers as a "self" theorist (Krasner & Ullman, 1973; Hall & Lindzey, 1978). In fact, although Rogers regards the self as the focus of experience, he is more concerned with perception, awareness, and experience than with the hypothetical construct, the "self." As we have already described Rogers's definition of the self, we can now turn to a description of the *fully functioning person:* a person who is most fully aware of his or her ongoing self.

" 'The fully functioning person' is synonymous with optimal psychological adjustment, optimal psychological maturity, complete congruence, complete openness to experience. . . . Since some of these terms sound somewhat static, as though such a person 'had arrived,' it should be pointed out that all the characteristics of such a person are *process* characteristics. The fully functioning person would be a person-in-process, a person continually changing" (Rogers, 1959, p. 235).

The fully functioning person has several distinct characteristics, the first of which is an *openness to experience*. There is little or no use of the early warning signals that restrict awareness. The person is continually moving away from defensiveness and toward direct experience. "He is more open to his feelings of fear and discouragement and pain. He is also more open to his feelings of courage, and tenderness, and awe.... He is more able fully to live the experience of his organism rather than shutting them out of awareness" (Rogers 1961, p. 188).

A second characteristic is *living in the present*—fully realizing each moment. This ongoing, direct engagement with reality allows "the self and personality [to] emerge *from* experience, rather than experience being translated or twisted to fit preconceived self-structure" (Rogers, 1961, pp. 188–189). A person is capable of restructuring his or her responses as experience allows or suggests new possibilities.

A final characteristic is *trusting in one's inner urgings and intuitive judgments,* an ever increasing trust in one's capacity to make decisions. As a person is better able to take in and utilize data, he or she is more likely to value his or her capacity to summarize that data and respond. This is not only an intellectual activity but also a function of the whole person. Rogers suggests that in the fully functioning person the mistakes that are made will be due to incorrect information, not incorrect processing.

The good life is a *process,* not a state of being. It is a direction, not a destination. [Rogers, 1961, p. 186]

This trust is similar to the behavior of a cat dropped to the ground from a height. The cat does not consider wind velocity, angular momentum, or the rate of descent; yet all these are taken into account by its total response. The cat does not reflect on who pushed it off, what the motives might have been, or what is likely to occur in the future. The cat deals with the immediate situation, the most pressing problem. It turns in midair and lands upright, instantly adjusting its posture to cope with the next event.

The fully functioning person is free to respond and free to experience his or her response to situations. This is the essence of what Rogers calls living the good life. Such a person "would be continually in a process of further self-actualization" (Rogers, 1959, p. 235).

Client-Centered Therapy

Rogers has been a practicing therapist through most of his professional career. His theory of personality arises from and is integral to his methods and ideas about therapy. Rogers's theory of therapy has gone through a number of developmental phases and shifts in emphasis, yet there are a few foundation stones that have remained in place. Rogers quotes from a 1940 speech where he first described his new ideas about therapy:

1. "This newer approach relies much more heavily on the individual drive towards growth, health, and adjustment. [Therapy] is a matter of freeing [the client] for normal growth and development."
2. "This therapy places greater stress upon the feeling aspects of the situation than upon the intellectual aspects."
3. "This newer therapy places greater stress upon the immediate situation than upon the individual's past."
4. "This approach lays stress upon the therapeutic relationship itself as a growth experience." [1970, p. 12]

Rogers uses the word *client* rather than the traditional term *patient*. A patient is usually someone who is ill, needs help, and goes to be helped by trained professionals. A client is someone who desires a service and does not think that he or she can perform that service alone. The client, although he or she may have problems, is still viewed as a person who is inherently capable of understanding his or her own situation. There is an equality implied in the client model that is not present in the doctor-patient relationship.

The therapy assists a person in unlocking his or her own dilemma with a minimum of intrusion from the therapist. Rogers defines psychotherapy as "the releasing of an already existing capacity in a potentially competent individual, not the expert manipulation of a more or less passive personality" (1959, p. 221). The therapy is called client-directed or client-centered because it is the client who does whatever directing is necessary. Rogers feels strongly that "expert interventions" of any sort are ultimately detrimental to a person's growth.

The Client-Centered Therapist

The client holds the keys to recovery, but the therapist should have certain personal qualities that aid the client in learning how to use those keys. "These powers [within the client] will become effective if the therapist can establish with the client a relationship sufficiently warm, accepting and understanding" (Rogers, 1952b, p. 66). Before the therapist can be anything to a client, he or she must be authentic, genuine, and not playing any role—especially that of a therapist—when he or she is with the client. This "involves the willingness to be and to express in my words and my behavior, the various feelings and attitudes which exist in me. This means that I need to be aware of my own feelings, in so far as possible, rather than presenting an outward facade of one attitude, while actually holding another" (Rogers, 1961, p. 33).

The individual has within him the capacity, at least latent, to understand the factors in his life that cause him unhappiness and pain, and to reorganize himself in such a way as to overcome those factors. [Rogers, 1952b]

Therapists in training often ask, "How do you behave if you don't like the patient or if you are bored or angry? Won't this genuine feeling be just what he gets from everyone else whom he offends?"

The client-centered response to these questions involves several levels of understanding. At one level the therapist serves as a model of a genuine person. The therapist offers the client a relationship in which the client can test his or her own reality. If the client is confident of getting an honest response, the client can discover if his or her anticipation or defensiveness is justified. The client can learn to expect real—not distorted or diluted—feedback from his or her inner searching. This reality testing is crucial if the client is to let go of distortions and to experience himself or herself directly.

When the therapy relationship is equalitarian, when each takes responsibility for himself in the relationship, independent (and mutual) growth is much more rapid. [Rogers, 1978, p. 287]

At another level the client-centered therapist is helpful to the extent that he or she is accepting and able to maintain "unconditional positive regard." Rogers defines this as "caring which is not possessive, which demands no personal gratification. It is an atmosphere which simply demonstrates, 'I care,' not 'I care for you *if* you behave thus and so'" (1961, p. 283). *It is not a positive evaluation,* because any evaluation is a form of moral judgment. Evaluation tends to restrict behavior by rewarding some things and punishing others; unconditional positive regard allows the person to be what he or she actually is, no matter what it may be.

It is close to what Maslow calls "Taoistic love," a love that does not prejudge, does not restrict, does not define. It is the promise to accept someone simply as he or she turns out to be.[3] To do this, a client-centered therapist must constantly be able to see the self-actualizing core of the client, not the destructive, damaging, or offensive behaviors. If one can retain an awareness of an individual's positive essence, one can be authentic with that person and not be bored, irritated, or angry at particular expressions of his or her personality. The client-centered therapist maintains a certainty that the inner, and perhaps undeveloped, personality of the client is capable of understanding itself. Rogerian therapists admit that they often are unable to maintain this quality of understanding as they work.

Acceptance cannot be merely tolerance, a nonjudgmental stance that may or may not include real understanding. This is inadequate; unconditional positive regard must also include "empathic understanding . . . to sense the client's private world as if it were your own, but without ever losing the 'as if' quality" (Rogers, 1961, p. 284). This added dimension allows the client more freedom to explore inner feelings. The client is assured that the therapist will do more than accept them, that he or she will actively engage in attempting to feel the same situations within himself or herself.

The final criterion for a good therapist is that he or she must have the ability to convey this understanding to the client. The client needs

[3]This also resembles the Christian love described by the Greek word *agape*. See 1 Cor. 13, and 1 John 4:7–12, 18–21.

to know that the therapist is authentic, does care, does listen, and does understand. It is necessary that the therapist be visible in spite of the selective distortions of the client, the defensive reactions, and the crippling effects of misplaced self-regard. Once this bridge between client and therapist is established, the client can begin to work in earnest.

The foregoing description may sound static, as if the therapist reaches a plateau and then does therapy; it is nonetheless an ongoing dynamic process in a state of continual renewal. The therapist, like the client, is always in the process of becoming more congruent.

In an early book, *Counseling and Psychotherapy* (1942, pp. 30–44), Rogers outlined characteristic steps in the helping process as follows:

The client comes for help.
The situation is defined.
The encouragement of free expression.
The counselor accepts and clarifies.
The gradual expression of positive feelings.
The recognition of positive impulses.
The development of insight.
The clarification of choices.
Positive actions.
Increasing insight.
Increased independence.
The decreasing need for help.

This suggested series of events displays Rogers's concern that the client determine his or her own path with the therapist's encouraging and supporting efforts.

Whereas some aspects of Rogerian therapy can be learned easily and in fact are used by many therapists, the personal characteristics that the effective therapist is asked to maintain are extremely difficult to understand, to experience, and to practice. The capacity to be truly present for another human being—empathic to that person's pain, confident of that person's growth, and able to convey all this—is a difficult personal demand.

In spite of a considerable body of research that seems to support these basic assumptions, some of it under Rogers's direction (Rogers et al., 1967; Traux & Mitchell, 1971; Mitchell et al., 1977), the experimental results are still inconclusive. A volume reviewing many major schools of psychotherapy (written with a strong behavioristic bias) suggests that the research is limited by an inability to define and measure the relevant therapist variables. This leads to their conclusion that "the development of Rogerian therapy turned into a story of unfilled promise" (Rachman & Wilson, 1980).

While the debate continues among researchers, Rogers's insist-

ence on certain fundamental qualities as prerequisites for being a therapist have been absorbed into the mainstream of most counseling training programs, which include lay persons working on hot lines or in
local crisis centers, ministers, social workers, marriage, child, and family counselors, and psychologists of many different persuasions. Rogers
stresses that therapy is not a science, perhaps not even an art; instead,
it is a relationship that depends partially on the mental health of the
therapist to evoke the thwarted mental health of the client (Rogers,
1977).

Encounter Groups

Rogers's assertion that people, not experts, were inherently therapeutic made it almost inevitable that he would eventually become involved
in encounter groups. When he moved to California, he devoted time
to participating in, establishing, and evaluating this form of group experience.

Apart from group therapy, encounter groups have a history that
predates their resurgence in the 1950s and 1960s. Within the American
Protestant tradition and, to a lesser extent, within Hassidic Judaism,
there have been group experiences engineered to alter people's attitudes toward themselves and to change their behaviors with others.
Techniques have included working within small peer groups, insisting
on honesty and disclosure, focusing on the here and now, and maintaining a warm, supportive atmosphere (Ogden, 1972).

Modern encounter groups originated in Connecticut in 1946 with
a training program for community leaders. This program included evening meetings of the trainers and observers to evaluate the day's
events. Participants came to listen and eventually to take part in these
extra sessions. The trainers realized that giving feedback to participants enhanced everyone's experience.

Some of the trainers of the Connecticut groups joined with others
to establish National Training Laboratories (NTL) in 1947. NTL helped
to extend and develop the T-group (training group) as a tool in government and industry. Participation in these groups gave people experience in observing their own functioning and in learning how to respond
to direct feedback about themselves.

What was striking in the T-group experiences was that a few
weeks of working with peers in a relatively accepting setting could
lead to major personality changes previously associated only with severe trauma or long-term psychotherapy. In a review of 106 studies,
Gibb (1971) concluded that "the evidence is strong that intensive
group training experiences have therapeutic effects" (in Rogers, 1970,
p. 118).

Whereas NTL was forming and developing primarily on the East
Coast, Esalen Institute in California was exploring more intensive, less

structured group processes. Dedicated to understanding new trends that emphasize the potentialities and values of human existence, Esalen hosted a series of workshops in the 1960s that came to be called encounter or basic encounter groups. Rogers's group work, developed independently, resembles the basic encounter form developed by Esalen. His groups are not as uninhibited, however, and reflect some of the structural components (including the unobtrusive role of the leader) from the NTL format.

Common characteristics of all encounterlike groups include a climate of psychological safety, encouragement of the expression of immediate feelings, and subsequent feedback from group members. The leader, whatever his or her orientation, is responsible for setting and maintaining the tone and focus of a group. This can range from a functional business atmosphere to encouraging emotional or sexual excitement to promoting fear, anger, or even violence. There are reports of groups of all descriptions (Howard, 1970; Maliver, 1973).

Rogers's contribution to and his ongoing work with encounter groups are applications of his theory. In *Carl Rogers on Encounter Groups* (1970) he describes the major phenomena that occur in groups extending over several days. Although there are many periods of dissatisfaction, uncertainty, and anxiety in the description of encounters that follow, each of these gives way to a more open, less defended, more exposed, more trusting climate. The emotional intensity and the capacity to tolerate intensity appear to increase as a group continues.

The Process of Encounter

A group begins with *milling around,* waiting to be told how to behave, what to expect, how to deal with the expectations about the group. There is growing frustration as the group realizes that the members themselves will determine the way the group will function.[4]

There is *initial resistance* to personal expression or exploration. "It is the public self that members tend to show each other, and only gradually, fearfully, and ambivalently do they take steps to reveal something of the private self" (Rogers, 1970, p. 16). This resistance is visible in most group situations—cocktail parties, dances, or picnics—where there usually is some activity other than self-exploration available to participants. An encounter group discourages seeking any other outlet.

As people continue to interact, they share *past feelings* associated with people who are not present in the group. Whereas these may be important experiences for the individual, they are still a form of initial resistance; past experiences are safer, less likely to be affected by criti-

[4]The following descriptions apply to groups Rogers has run or observed. Other styles of group leadership lead to other kinds of effects. See Schutz (1971, 1973); Egan (1970); and Lieberman, et al. (1973) for alternative ways of describing the group process.

cism or support. People may or may not respond to the telling of a past event, but it is still a past event.

When people begin to express their present feelings, most often the *first expressions are negative.* "I don't feel comfortable with you." "You have a bitchy way of talking." "I don't believe you really mean what you said about your wife."

"Deeply positive feelings are much more difficult and dangerous to express than negative ones. If I say I love you, I am vulnerable and open to the most awful rejection. If I say I hate you, I am at best liable to attack, against which I can defend" (Rogers, 1970, p. 19). Not understanding this apparent paradox has led to a number of encounter programs whose failures were predictable. For example, the Air Force developed race-relations programs including black-white encounter sessions conducted by trained leaders. The end result of these encounters, however, often seemed to be an intensification of hostile racial feelings on both sides. Because of the complications in scheduling people within the military, these meetings lasted no more than three hours—just enough time for the negative expressions to be expressed and not long enough for the rest of the process to unfold.

As the negative feelings are expressed and the group does not crumble, or split apart, *personally meaningful material* begins to emerge. It may or may not be acceptable to members of the group, but the "climate of trust" is beginning to form and people start to take real risks.

As meaningful material emerges, people begin to *express immediate feelings* to one another, both positive and negative. "I like that you could share that with the group." "Every time I say something you look as if you'd like to strangle me." "Funny, I thought I'd dislike you. Now I'm sure of it."

As more and more emotional expressions surface and are reacted to by the group, Rogers notes the *development of a healing capacity.* People begin to do things that seem to be helpful, that help others become aware of their own experience in nonthreatening ways. What the well-trained therapist has been taught to do through years of supervision and practice begins to emerge spontaneously from the group itself. "This kind of ability shows up so commonly in groups that it has led me to feel that the ability to be healing or therapeutic is far more common in human life than we suppose. Often it needs only the permission granted—or freedom made possible—by the climate of a free-flowing group experience to become evident" (Rogers, 1970, p. 22).

One of the effects of the group's feedback and acceptance is that *people can accept themselves.* "I guess I really do try to keep people from getting close to me." "I am strong, even ruthless at times." "I want so much to be liked that I'll pretend half a dozen different things." Paradoxically, this acceptance of one's self, even one's faults, leads to the beginning of change. Rogers notes that the closer one is to congruence, the easier it is for one to become healthy. If a person can admit to being a certain way, then he or she can consider possible alternative ways to behave. "Acceptance, in the realm of psychological attitudes, often brings about a change in the thing accepted. Ironic, but true" (Nelson, unpublished article, 1973).

As the group continues, there is an increasing *impatience with defenses.* The group seems to demand the right to help, to heal, to open up people who appear constricted and defensive. Gently at times, almost savagely at others, the group *demands* that individuals be themselves, that is, that they do not hide their current feelings. "The expression of self by some members of the group has made it very clear that a deeper and more basic encounter is *possible,* and the group appears to strive intuitively and unconsciously toward this goal" (Rogers, 1970, p. 27).

It's all right to be me with all my strengths and weaknesses. My wife told me that I seem more authentic, more real, and more genuine. [In Rogers, 1970, p. 27]

Within every exchange or encounter there is *feedback.* The leader is continually being told of his or her effectiveness or lack of it. Each member who reacts to another may, in turn, get feedback about his or her reaction. This feedback may be difficult for a person to accept, but a person in a group cannot easily avoid coming to grips with the group opinion.

Rogers calls the extreme form of feedback *confrontation:* "There are times when the term feedback is far too mild to describe the interactions that take place—when it is better said that one individual *confronts* another, directly 'leveling' with him. Such confrontations can be positive, but frequently they are decidedly negative" (1970, p. 31). Confrontation builds feelings to such a pitch that some kind of resolution is demanded. This is a disturbing and difficult moment for a group and, potentially, far more disturbing to the individuals involved.

Most of us consist of two separated parts, trying desperately to bring themselves together into an integrated soma, where the distinctions between mind and body, feelings and intellect, would be obliterated. [Rogers, 1973b, p. 385]

For each surge of negative feelings, for each eruption of a fear, there also seems to be a following expression of support, of positive feelings, and closeness. Rogers, quoting a group member: "The incredible fact experienced over and over by members of the group was that when a negative feeling was fully expressed to another, the relationship grew and the negative feeling was replaced by a deep acceptance for the other . . ." (1970, p. 34). It would appear that each time the group successfully demonstrates that it can accept and tolerate negative feelings without rejecting the person expressing them, the group members grow more trusting and open to each other. Many people report their experiences in groups as the most positive, empathic, and accepting experiences of their lives. The popularity of group experiences lies as much in the emotional warmth they generate as in their capacity to facilitate personal growth.

Are there dangers in the encounter experience? As with any intense form of interaction, there can be and have been unfortunate results. There have been psychotic breaks, suicides, and depressions, perhaps precipitated by participation in an encounter group. In most cases the encounter experience seems to foster the underlying mechanisms that allow one human being to help another. That this does not inevitably occur should come as no surprise. What can be said is that due to the work of Rogers and others, small group experiences are now understood as one way of developing personal skills, of counseling, exciting, and helping people, and of allowing people an opportunity for an unusually intense personal experience.

EVALUATION

In a conversation in 1966 Rogers described his status: "I don't have very much standing in psychology itself, and I couldn't care less. But in education and industry and group dynamics and social work and the philosophy of science and pastoral psychology and theology and other fields my ideas have penetrated and influenced in ways I never would have dreamt" (1970, p. 507).

Critics focus on his view of the human condition, seeing it as less universal than Rogers suggests. To base therapy and learning on the innate capacity of a person for self-actualization is spoken of as hopelessly naive by a number of writers (Thorne, 1957; Ellis, 1959). They argue that Rogers does not take into account the ingrained habit patterns of psychopathology that can and do prevent any possibility of improvement. Another level of criticism is that his theory cannot be tested rigorously. "Whether human nature, unspoiled by society, is as satisfactory as this viewpoint leads us to believe is certainly questionable. And it will be difficult either to confirm or to infirm this proposition, on empirical grounds. . . . The emphasis on self-actualization . . . suffers, in our opinion, from the vagueness of its concepts, the looseness of its language, and the inadequacy of the evidence related to its major contentions" (Coffer & Appley, 1964, pp. 691–692).

Others suggest that self-actualization is neither innate nor fundamental in human development but derives from a more primary drive, the need for stimulation (Butler & Rice, 1963).

Reading the emotional and the sensible critics of Rogers, one comes away concluding that either they have seen different kinds of patients or they simply do not accept the Rogerian ideas of trusting others to find their own way (Rogers & Skinner, 1956). Karl Menninger feels that Rogers's insistence on the indwelling thrust toward health is uttering at best a half truth. "Many patients whom we see seem to have committed themselves, consciously or unconsciously, to stagnation or slow spiritual death" (Menninger, 1963, p. 398).

The image of humanity described by Rogers seems to make so little sense to his critics that it is doubtful whether any continuation of favorable research findings would have any effect. For Rogers, the test of the validity of his position is not dependent on theoretical elegance but on general utility. Rogers's works are constantly gaining in importance, and are more widely read each year; and his popularity within clinical psychology continues to increase (Lipsey, 1974).

Although it is clearly a simplification, it is true that just as Freud's ideas met a growing need to understand some aspects of human nature, so Rogers's ideas meet a different need, a need that can be seen as especially American. Rogers's philosophy "fits snugly into the American democratic tradition. The client is treated as an equal who has within him the power to 'cure' himself with no need to lean heavily on the wisdom of an authority or expert" (Harper, 1959, p. 83). Roger's close alignment to the American zeitgeist (world view) has helped facilitate the widespread acceptance of his ideas, his ways of doing therapy, his concern with affirming the capacity and the desire of the individual to be whole.

His intense focus on the person is well expressed in a series of statements Rogers calls "significant learnings." They are the summation of "the thousands of hours I have spent working intimately with people in personal distress" (1961, p. 16). The following are some of his conclusions:

> This new world will be more human and humane. It will explore and develop the richness and capacities of the human mind and spirit. It will produce individuals who are more integrated and whole. It will be a world that prizes the individual person—the greatest of our resources. [Rogers, 1980a, p. 356]

1. In my relationships with persons, I have found that it does not help in the long run to act as though I am something that I am not.
2. I find that I am more effective when I can listen acceptantly to myself, and can be myself.
3. I have found it of enormous value when I can permit myself to understand another person.
4. I have found it enriching to open channels whereby others can communicate their feelings, the private perceptual world to me.
5. I have found it highly rewarding when I can accept another person.
6. The more I am open to the realities in me and in the other person the less do I find myself wishing to rush in to "fix things."
7. I can trust my experience. [pp. 16–22]

THE THEORY FIRSTHAND

The two excerpts included here illustrate different aspects of Rogers's work. The first comes from a chapter on client-centered therapy; the second (not previously published) describes an event that occurred during an extended group experience.

ILLUSTRATION OF THE THEORY OF THERAPY[1]

The theoretical concepts that have been defined and the brief, formal statements of the process and outcomes of client-centered psychotherapy are astonishingly well illustrated in a letter written to the author by a

---

[1]Copyright © 1975, Williams and Wilkins Co., Baltimore.

young woman named Susan who has been in therapy with an individual who has obviously created the conditions for a therapeutic climate. The letter appears below, followed by an explanation of the way the theoretical statements have operated in her case.

Dear Dr. Rogers: I have just read your book, *On Becoming a Person,* and it left a great impression on me. I just happened to find it one day and started reading. It's kind of a coincidence because right now I need something to help me find *me.* Let me explain . . . [She tells of her present educational situation and some of her tentative plans for preparing herself for a helping vocation] . . . I do not feel that I can do much for others until I find me. . . .

I think that I began to lose me when I was in high school. I always wanted to go into work that would be of help to people but my family resisted, and I thought they must be right. Things went along smoothly for everyone else for four or five years until about two years ago, I met a guy who I thought was ideal. Then nearly a year ago I took a good look at us, and realized I was everything that *he* wanted me to be and nothing that *I* was. I have always been emotional and I have had many feelings. I could never sort them out and identify them. My fiancé would tell me that I was just mad or just happy and I would say okay and leave it at that. Then when I took this good look at us I realized that I was angry because I wasn't following my true emotions.

I backed out of the relationship gracefully and tried to find out where all the pieces were that I had lost. After a few months of searching had gone by I found that there were many more pieces than I knew what to do with and I couldn't seem to separate them. I began seeing a psychologist and am presently seeing him. He has helped me to find parts of me that I was not aware of. Some parts are bad by our society's standards but I have found them to be very good for me. I have felt more threatened and confused since going to him but I have also felt more relief and more sure of myself.

I remember one night in particular. I had been in for my regular appointment with the psychologist that day and I had come home feeling angry. I was angry because I wanted to talk about something but I couldn't identify what it was. By 8 o'clock that night I was so upset I was frightened. I called him and he told me to come to his office as soon as I could. I got there and cried for at least an hour and then the words came. I still don't know all of what I was saying. All I know is that *so much hurt* and *anger* came out of me that I *never really knew existed.* I went home and it seemed that an *alien* had taken over and I was hallucinating like some of the patients I have seen in a state hospital. I continued to feel this way until one night I was sitting and thinking and I realized that this alien was the *me* that I had been trying to find.

I have noticed since that night that people no longer seem so strange to me. Now it is beginning to seem that life is just starting for me. I am alone right now but I am not frightened and I don't have to be doing something. I like meeting me and making friends with my thoughts and feelings. Because of this I have learned to enjoy other people. One older man in particular—who is very ill—makes me feel very much alive. He accepts everyone. He told me the other day that I have changed very much. According to him, I have begun to open up and love. I think that I have always loved people and I told him so. He said, "Were they aware of it?"

I don't suppose I have expressed my love any more than I did my anger and hurt.

Among other things, I am finding out that I never had too much self-respect. And now that I am learning to really like me I am finally finding peace within myself. Thanks for your part in this.

THE LINKAGE TO THEORY

By summarizing some of the key portions of Susan's letter, the relationship between her statements and the theoretical ones will be evident.

"I was losing me. I needed something to help find *me.*" As she looks back, she realizes that she felt a vague discrepancy between the life she was experiencing and the person she believed herself to be. This kind of vague awareness of discrepancy or incongruence is a real resource for the person who becomes aware of it and attends to it. She also gives clues as to some of the reasons for her loss of contact with her own experiencing.

"My inner reactions meant to me that I wanted to do a certain type of work, but my family showed me that that was not their meaning." This certainly suggests the way in which her false self-concept has been built. Undoubtedly, the process began in childhood or she would not have accepted the family's judgment now. A child experiences something in his organism—a feeling of fear, or anger, or jealousy, or love, or, as in this case, a sense of choice, only to be told by parents that this is not what he is experiencing. Out of this grows the construct "Parents are wiser than I and know me better than I know myself." Also, there grows an increasing distrust in one's own experiencing and a growing incongruence between self and experiencing. In this case, Susan distrusts her inward feeling that she knows the work she wants to do and accepts the judgment of her family as right and sound. Only the vague sense of discrepancy gives any clue to the extent to which she has introjected many perceptions of herself from her parents and undoubtedly others as well.

"Things went along smoothly for everyone else." This is a marvelously revealing statement. She has become a very satisfactory person for those whom she is trying to please. This false concept of self that they have unwittingly built up is just what they want. It is unlikely that the behavior of her parents grew out of any malice but, nevertheless, they have thwarted the development of her real or congruent self. Then, because of the lack of confidence engendered by this experience with her parents, she permits herself to be molded by another person.

"I left me behind and tried to be the person my boyfriend wanted." Once more, she has denied to her awareness (not consciously) the experiencing of her own organism, and is simply trying to be the self desired by her lover. It is the same process all over. The extent to which she has sacrificed her organismic experiencing is indicated by the fact that she even turns to her boyfriend to find out what she is feeling and accepts his answer.

"Finally, something in me rebelled and I tried to find me again. But I couldn't, without help." Why did she at last rebel against the manner in which she had given herself away? This rebelling indicates the strength of the tendency toward actualization. Although suppressed and distorted for so long, it has reasserted itself. No doubt some particular experience or experiences triggered this, but her organism recognized in some dim way that her present path could lead only to disaster. Thus, she took a square look at herself; but to profit from this was difficult since she had distrusted her own experiencing for so long and the self by which she was living was so sharply different from the experiencing going on within her. When this discrepancy is great, the individual frequently has to turn to therapeutic help. She was fortunate in finding a counselor who evidently created a real and personal relationship, fulfilling the conditions of therapy.

"Now I am discovering *my* experiences—some of them bad, according to society, parents and boyfriend—but all constructive as far as I am concerned." She is now reclaiming as her own the right to evaluate her own experiences. The "locus of evaluation" now resides in herself, not in others. It is through exploring her own experiencing that she determines the meaning of the evidence being provided within her. When she says, "some parts are bad by society's standards but I have found them good for me," she might be referring to any of several feelings—her rebellion against her parents, against her boyfriend, her sexual feelings, her anger and bitterness, or other aspects of herself. At least as she trusts her own valuing of her experience, she finds that it is of worth and significance to her.

"An important turning point came when I was frightened and upset by unknown feelings within me." When aspects of experiencing have been denied to awareness, they may, in a therapeutic climate, come close to the surface of awareness with resulting strong anxiety or fright. Client-centered theory would explain this by the fact that the emergence of any feelings that change the self-concept is always threatening. Susan does not consciously know that what is stirring underneath will change very sharply her self-concept, but she senses it. The term "subception" has been coined to describe this sensing without awareness. The whole organism can be aware of threat even when the conscious mind is not.

"I cried for at least an hour." Without yet knowing what she is experiencing, she is somehow preparing herself to come in contact with these feelings and meanings which are so foreign to her concept of self.

"When the denied experiences broke through the dam, they turned out to be deep hurts and anger of which I had been *absolutely* unaware." Individuals are able completely to deny experiencings that are highly threatening to the concept of self. Yet, in a safe and nonthreatening relationship, they may be released. Here, for the first time in her life, Susan is *experiencing* all the pent-up feelings of pain and rage that have been boiling under the facade of her false self. To experience something *fully* is not an intellectual process; in fact, Susan cannot even remember clearly what she said, but she did feel, in the immediate moment, emotions that for years had been denied to her awareness.

"I thought I was insane and that some foreign person had taken over in me." To find that "I am a person full of hurt, anger and rebellion," when formerly she had thought, "I am a person who always pleases others, who doesn't even know what her feelings are," is a very drastic shift in the concept of self. Small wonder that she felt this was an alien, a frightening someone she had never known. Perhaps it was even proof of insanity.

"Only gradually did I recognize that this alien was the real *me.*" What she has discovered is that the submissive, malleable self by which she had been living, the self that tried to please others and was guided by their evaluations, attitudes, and expectations is no longer her self. This new self is a hurt, angry self, feeling good about parts of herself which others disapprove, experiencing many things, from wild hallucinatory thoughts to loving feelings. She will now be able to explore her experiencing further. It is likely that she will find out that some of her anger is directed against her parents and her boyfriend. Probably, some of the feelings and experiences that society regards as bad but that she finds good and satisfying are experiences that have to do with the whole sexual area. In any event, her self is becoming much more firmly rooted in her own organismic processes. Her concept of herself is beginning to be rooted in the spontaneously felt meanings of her experiencing. She is becoming a more congruent, a more integrated, person.

"I like meeting me and making friends with my thoughts and feelings." Here is the dawning self-respect, self-acceptance, and self-confidence of which she has been deprived for so long. She is even feeling some affection for herself. Now that she is much more acceptant of herself, she will be able to give herself more freely to others and to be more genuinely interested in others.

"I have begun to open up and love." She will find that as she is more expressive of her love she can also be more expressive of her anger and hurt, her likes and dislikes, her "wild" thoughts and feelings, which later may well turn out to be creative impulses. She is in the process of changing from a person with a false facade, a false self-concept, to a more healthy personality with a self that is much more congruent with experiencing, a self that can change as her experience changes.

"I am finally finding peace within myself." She has discovered a peaceful harmony in being a whole and congruent person—but she will be mistaken if she thinks this is a permanent reaction. Instead, if she is really open to her experience, she will find other hidden aspects of herself that she has denied to awareness, and each such discovery will give her uneasy and anxious moments or days until they are assimilated into a revised and changing picture of herself. She will discover that moving toward a congruence between her experiencing organism and her concept of herself is an exciting, sometimes disturbing, but never-ending adventure.

This case illustration pictures well the process and some of the outcomes of client-centered therapy. (Rogers, in Freedman et al., 1975)

LINDA MOURNS

by A Participant[2]

I want to write down, while it is fresh in my feelings, an incident which occurred in a large workshop. It was a 17-day workshop consisting of 70 very diverse people, focused on cognitive and experiential learning. All had been in encounter groups for 6 sessions in the first 6 days. There had been special interest topical groups, and almost daily meetings of all 70 people. These community meetings had become deeper and more trusting. This episode occurred on the 8th day in a morning community meeting.

The group had been discussing, with great sensitivity, listening to all points of view, the issue raised by the fact that some people had brought visitors to the community sessions. Linda had been one of these, bringing her husband to the previous meeting, but she was not present this morning. A consensus was finally reached that in the future (without criticizing any person up to this point), anyone thinking of bringing a visitor should first raise the question with the community. The group passed on to another issue.

At this point Linda arrived, very late. Stephen, trying to be helpful, quickly described to her the conclusion we had reached. None of us gave Linda opportunity to respond though she evidently tried to. The group went on in its discussion. After a few moments someone sitting close to her called attention to the fact that Linda was shaking and crying, and the community immediately gave her space for her feelings. At first it seemed that she felt criticized, but Susan gave her a more complete description of what had gone on, and she seemed to accept that she was not being blamed or criticized. But still she was physically trembling, and very upset because she felt she had been cut off. It was not the first time, she said. She had felt cut off before. Encouraged to say more she turned to Natalie, Carl's daughter, and said, "I've felt you as very cold, and you've cut me off twice. I keep calling you Ellen—I don't know why and when I came to you to tell you how sorry I felt about that, you just said that was my problem, and turned away."

Natalie replied that her perception was very different. "I realized you were quite upset because you called me by the wrong name, but I said that though I could see it troubled *you*, it didn't bother me at all. I realize I haven't reached out to you, and I think you do want contact with me, but I don't feel I have rebuffed you."

It seemed that Linda felt more and more strongly about all this, and that she had not heard, or certainly had not accepted, Natalie's response. She said that she had observed the close relationship Natalie had with Lola, a Chicana, and that perhaps it was only with minority persons that Natalie could relate, rather than to her—tall, blonde, and middle class. This led to an angry outburst from Lola about being stereotyped, and about five minutes was spent in rebuilding the relationship between Linda and Lola. The group brought Linda back to the issue between her and Natalie. It seemed quite obvious that her feelings were so strong that they could not come simply from the incident she mentioned. Robert said he had noticed that he, Linda, and Natalie were all similar—tall, slim, blonde—and that perhaps Linda was feeling that Natalie should at least relate to someone so like her, rather than to Lola, who was short and dark. Linda considered this, wondered if there might be something to it, but clearly was not deeply touched by the idea.

At least two other possible bases for her strong feelings were caringly and tentatively suggested to her. To the first she said, "I'm trying on that hat, but it doesn't seem to fit." To the second she said, "That doesn't seem to fit either."

I sat there feeling completely mystified. I wanted to understand just what it was she was troubled about, but I couldn't get any clue to follow. I believe many others were feeling the same way. Here she was with tears in her eyes, feeling something far beyond some possible imaginary rebuff, but what was it?

Then Annette said, "This may be inappropriate, but I'm going to say it anyway. When you arrived, Linda, I thought you *were* Natalie, you looked so much alike. I feel envious when I watch the beautiful open relationship between Natalie and her father. I had that kind of relationship with my father. I wonder if there is any connection between you and your father and Carl?" "That's it!" Linda sobbed, acting as though she had been struck by a bolt of lightning. She collapsed into herself, weeping her heart out. Between sobs she said, "I didn't really cry at all at my father's death. . . . He really died for me long before his death. . . . What can I do?" People responded that he was still part of her, and she could still mourn for him. Annette, who was near her, embraced and comforted her. After quite a time she quieted down, and then in an almost inaudible voice, asked Carl if she could hold his hand. He reached out and she came across the circle and fell into his arms and her whole body shook with sobs as he held her close. Slowly she felt better and sat between Carl and Natalie, saying to Carl, "And you look like him too, but I never realized *that* was what I was feeling."

As the three sat there with their arms around each other, someone remarked on how much alike Linda and Natalie looked. They could be sisters. Carl said, "Here we are, sitting for a family portrait." Linda said, "But they'll ask, 'Why is that girl in the middle sitting there with such a big smile on her face?,' " and the incident was rounded off as the whole group joined in her sparkling laughter of release and relief.

CARL ROGERS' COMMENTS, LATER

I was very much involved personally and emotionally in this incident, which has, I believe, been quite accurately described. I have also thought about it much since. It is temptingly easy to diagnose the causes of it: Linda, repressing her pain at losing her father, and seeing a good daughter-father relationship, projects her pain onto Natalie, first by distorting an incident so she could be angry at Natalie, then distortedly expressing her pain through anger at Natalie's close relationship with another woman—etc., etc. To me such "explanations" are irrelevant. But as I try to view it with some perspective it exemplifies many aspects of the existential dynamics of change in personality and behavior.

1. It shows clearly the depth to which feelings can be buried, so that they are totally unknown to the owner. Here it is particularly interesting because it was obvious to Linda and to the group that she was feeling *something* very deeply. Yet she was clearly labelling it in ways which were not truly significant. The organism closes itself to the pain of recognizing a feeling clearly, if that would involve reorganizing the concept of self in some significant way.

2. It is a splendid example of how the flow of experiencing (Gendlin's concept) is used as a referent for discovering the felt meaning. Linda tried on the various descriptions and labels which were given to her and they didn't "fit." Didn't fit what? Clearly it is something organismic against which she is checking. But when Annette pointed—by telling of her own feelings—at another possibility, Linda realized *immediately* and with complete certainty that *this* was what she was experiencing. It *matched* what was going on in her. As is so often true when a person is understood, she was able to follow her experiencing further, and to realize that in addition to the envy, she felt much pain, and that she had never mourned for her father, because he had died for her years before his death.

3. To me this is a very precise example of a moment of irreversible change, the minute unit of change which taken with other such units constitutes the whole basis for alteration of personality and behavior. I have defined these moments of change in this way. When a previously denied feeling is experienced in a full and complete way, in expression and in awareness, and is experienced acceptantly, not as something wrong or bad, a fundamental change occurs which is almost irreversible. What I mean by this last term is that Linda might, under certain circumstances, later deny the validity of this moment, and believe that she was not envious, or not in mourning. But her whole organism has *experienced* those feelings completely and at most she could only temporarily deny them in her awareness.

4. We see here an instance of a change in the way she perceives herself. She has been, in her own eyes, a person with no close relationship to her father, unmoved by his death, a person who did not care. Quite possibly she had also believed she was guilty because of those elements. Now that

facet of her concept of self is clearly changed. She can now see herself as a person wanting very much a close relationship, and mourning the lack of that as well as his death. The almost inevitable result of this alteration in her self-concept will be a change in some of her behaviors. What those changes will be can only be speculation at this point—possibly a change in behavior toward older men, possibly more open sorrow over other tragedies. We cannot yet know.

5. It is an example of the kind of therapeutic climate in which change can occur. It is a caring group, a group which respects her worth enough to listen to her intently, even when such listening breaks into the "task" on which the group was working. They are trying very hard to convey as much understanding as they can. Annette's realness in exposing her own feelings is an example of the openness and "transparency" of the group members. So all the ingredients for growth and change are there, and Linda makes use of them.

6. It is exciting evidence that this growth-promoting climate can evolve, even in such a large group. Sixty-nine people can be therapists, perhaps even more effectively than one, if the group is trustworthy, and if the individual can come to realize that, and to trust their caring, understanding and genuineness.

To me it is a small gem—personally meaningful in my experience, but also rich in theoretical implications.

EXERCISES

The Concept of the Real and the Ideal Self

The list of adjectives below was picked from a long list and is simply a sample of a number of personality characteristics. In the first column, Real Self, check those that apply to you. These characteristics reflect what you know yourself to be, whether or not anyone else may characterize you as such. Move to the second column, How Others See Me, and do the same, this time checking only those qualities that you think others who know you would check for you. In the last column check off those attributes that describe you at your best. Remember this last column is *your* ideal self, not some plaster saint with whom you couldn't possibly identify.

It is assumed that none of us is any of these adjectives all the time, so don't worry if you are not always cheerful but still wish to mark it.

Now, if you wish, circle the adjectives where there is some inconsistency between the columns. These represent possible areas of incongruence in your own life. Whether you circle many or only a few is not of great importance. Few people doing such an exercise find that they are completely congruent.

From this point on, the exercise is up to you. You can work in small groups to discuss your internal discrepancies or you can write about them if you keep a journal. For further class work you can role-play column 3 and see how it feels to act like the ideal self you described.

The purpose of this exercise is to help you to become aware of the nature of the self as Rogers has described it. Although Rogers does not specifically include the self as it is seen by others, we have included it to further clarify the ideas of congruence in one's daily experience.

Listening and Understanding

This exercise is from Rogers (1952a). He suggests it as a way to assess the quality of your understanding of others.

ADJECTIVE	1 REAL SELF	2 HOW OTHERS SEE ME	3 IDEAL SELF
cheerful			
persistent			
noisy			
responsible			
absent-minded			
restless			
demanding			
snobbish			
frank			
honest			
excitable			
immature			
courageous			
self-pitying			
ambitious			
calm			
individualistic			
serious			
friendly			
mature			
artistic			
intelligent			
humorous			
idealistic			
understanding			
warm			
relaxed			
sensitive			
sexy			
active			
lovable			
selfish			
shrewd			
affectionate			
opinionated			

The next time you get into an argument with your wife, or your friend, or with a small group of friends, just stop the discussion for a moment and for an experiment, institute this rule. "Each person can speak up for himself only *after* he has first restated the ideas and feelings of the previous speaker accurately, and to that speaker's satisfaction." You see what this would mean. It would . . . mean that before presenting your own point of view, it would be necessary for you to really achieve the other speaker's frame of reference—to understand his thoughts and feelings so well that you could summarize them for him. Sounds simple, doesn't it? But if you try it you will discover it one of the most difficult things you have ever tried to do. However, once you have been able to see the other's point of view, your own comments may have to be drastically revised. You will also find the emotion going out of the discussion, the differences being reduced, and those differences which remain will be more rational and understandable.

Self Versus Ideal Self

Write down a list of your faults, drawbacks, limitations. Use full sentences. For example:

1. "I'm 10 pounds overweight."
2. "I'm selfish, especially with my books."
3. "I will never understand mathematical concepts."

Rewrite the statements as discrepancies between your self and your ideal self. For example:

1. "My ideal self weighs 10 pounds less than I do."
2. "My ideal self is generous, lending or even giving books to friends who ask for them."
3. "My ideal self is a good mathematician, not a professional but able to learn easily and to remember what I learn."

Evaluate your ideal self. Does it seem that some of your aspirations are unrealistic? Is there any reason to think that you could modify some of the goals that are assumed by your ideal self-description? Have you any reason to do so?

The Client-Centered Therapist

Choose a partner to work with. One of you is to be the therapist, the other is the client. You will switch roles so that you both experience both positions. The client tells the therapist an incident from his or her own life that was embarrassing and that might be hard to relate. (For example, there might have been times when you lied or cheated; you were accused of being unjust or unkind.)

As the therapist, you make every effort to understand what you are being told, listening so that you can repeat what you have been hearing. Rephrase what you're hearing so that you are sure you are understanding what is said. You, as a therapist, are not to take a stand on the rightness or wrongness, not to offer advice, not to console or criticize. You are to continue to appreciate the client as another human being, no matter what he or she is telling you.

This is a difficult exercise. Try to notice the times when you want to comment, when you are judging, feeling sorry for, or disturbed by your client. You may begin to notice the difficulties in simultaneously being aware of your own experience, remaining empathic, and maintaining positive regard. You may find it is easy to play as if you were behaving this way, but try to be aware of your actual feelings.

Reverse roles and let the therapist be a client. As the client, you can become aware of what the effect of being listened to has on what you choose to speak about.

This is a challenging exercise which is not easy for either client or therapist. It is not intended to give you an idea of what client-centered therapy is like but to give you an inkling of the demands which Rogers suggests are vital for effective counseling or therapy.

ANNOTATED BIBLIOGRAPHY

Rogers, C. R. *Client-centered therapy: Its current practice, implications and theory.* Boston: Houghton Mifflin, 1951. The core volume for what is called Rogerian therapy. Rogers himself sees some of the material here as too rigid. Still a useful and important book.

————. A theory of therapy, personality, and interpersonal relationships, as developed in the client-centered framework. In S. Koch (Ed.), *Formulations of the person and the social context* (Vol. 3). Psychology, the study of a science. New York: McGraw-Hill, 1959, pp. 184–225. The only time Rogers laid out his work as a formal, detailed, and organized theory. He succeeds, but it remains one of his least read works. The obscurity is undeserved. If you stick with Rogers, eventually you will want to read this.

————. *On becoming a person: A therapist's view of psychotherapy.* Boston: Houghton Mifflin, 1961. A personal, practical, and extensive consideration of the major themes in Rogers' work. A book that is lucid and useful to people in the people-helping professions.

————. *Freedom to learn.* Columbus, Ohio: Merrill, 1969. A set of challenges to educators. Rogers sees that most teaching is set up to discourage learning and encourage anxiety and maladjustment. More strident than his gentler, therapy-oriented volumes.

————. *Carl Rogers on encounter groups.* New York: Harper & Row, 1970. A sensible discussion of the ups and downs of the encounter group. Most of the discussion is drawn from groups that Rogers has run or observed so it is both representative and explicit. Probably the best introduction to this form of interpersonal gathering in print. Not sensational and not critical.

————. *Becoming partners: Marriage and its alternatives.* New York: Harper & Row, 1972. Rogers interviews a number of couples who have taken varying approaches to marriage. He points out the strengths and weaknesses of the relationships. Mainly reporting, he calls attention to those forces that lead toward successful and unsuccessful long-term relationships. Useful.

————. *Carl Rogers on personal power.* New York: Dell, 1978. The first book in which Rogers considers the wide social implications in his work. It is subtitled accurately: "Inner strength and its revolutionary impact. The extension of ideas developed in therapy to educational, and political systems."

————. *A way of being.* Boston: Houghton Mifflin, 1980. A collection of essays and speeches that serves as a small autobiography and illustrate Rogers' growing realization of the social impact of his work beyond psychology. Moving and optimistic, this is his most intimate and gentle book.

Rogers, C. R., Stevens, Barry et al. *Person to person.* Walnut Creek: Real Peoples Press, 1967. New York: Pocket Books, 1971. A delightful exchange between articles, most by Rogers and commentaries by Barry Stevens. The articles come to life under Stevens' probing commentaries.

REFERENCES

Bandler, Richard, & Grinder, John. *The structure of magic* (Vols. 1–2). Palo Alto, Calif.: Science and Behavior, 1975.

Butler, J. M., & Rice, L. N. Adience, self-actualization, and drive theory. In J. M. Wepman & R. W. Heine (Eds.), *Concepts of personality*. Chicago: Aldine, 1963, pp. 79–110.

Campbell, Peter, & McMahon, Edwin. Religious type experiences in the context of humanistic and transpersonal psychology. *Journal of Transpersonal Psychology,* 1974, 6, 11–17.

Coffer, Charles N., & Appley, Mortimer. *Motivation: Theory and research.* New York: Wiley, 1964.

Egan, Gerard. *Encounter: Group processes for interpersonal growth.* Monterey, Calif.: Brooks/Cole, 1970.

Ellis, A. Requisite conditions for basic personality change. *Journal of Consulting Psychology,* 1959, *23,* 538–540.

Evans, Richard I. *Carl Rogers: The man and his ideas.* New York: Dutton, 1975.

Freedman, Alfred M.; Kaplan, Harold I., & Sadock, Benjamin J. *Comprehensive textbook of psychiatry.* Baltimore: William & Wilkins, 1975.

Gibb, Jack R. The effects of human relations training. In Allan E. Bergin & Sol. L. Garfield (Eds.), *Handbook of psychotherapy and behavior change.* New York: Wiley, 1971, pp. 2114–2176.

Gordon, William, *Synectics.* New York: Harper & Row, 1961.

Hall, Calvin & Lindzey, Gardner. *Theories of personality* (3rd ed.). New York: Wiley, 1978.

Harper, R. A. *Psychoanalysis and psychotherapy.* Englewood Cliffs, N.J.: Prentice-Hall, 1959.

Holden, Constance. Carl Rogers: Giving people permission to be themselves. *Science,* 1977, *198,* 31–34.

Howard, Jane. *Please touch: A guided tour of the human potential movement.* New York: McGraw-Hill, 1970.

Kirschenbaum, Howard. *On becoming Carl Rogers.* New York: Dell (Delacorte Press), 1980.

Krasner, Leonard, & Ullman, Leonard. *Behavior influence and personality: The social matrix of human action.* New York: Holt, Rinehart and Winston, 1973.

Lawrence, D. H. *The ladybird; and The captain's doll.* London: Harborough, 1960.

Lieberman, Morton A., Miles, Matthew B., & Yalom, Irvin D. *Encounter groups: First facts.* New York: Basic Books, 1973.

Lipsey, Mark W. Research and relevance: A survey of graduate students and faculty in psychology. *The American Psychologist,* 1974, *29,* 541–554.

Maliver, Bruce L. *The encounter game.* New York: Stein and Day, 1973.

McCleary, R. A., & Lazarus, R. S. Autonomic discrimination without awareness. *Journal of Personality,* 1949, *19,* 171–179.

Menninger, Karl. *The vital balance: The life process in mental health and illness.* New York: Viking Press, 1963.

Mitchell, K.; Bozarth, J.; & Krauft, C. A reappraisal of the therapeutic effectiveness of accurate empathy, nonpossessive warmth and genuineness. In A. Gurman & A. Razin (Eds.), *Effective Psychotherapy.* Oxford: Pergamon Press, 1977.

Nitya, Swami. Excerpts from a discussion. *Journal of Transpersonal Pychology* 1973, *5,* 200–204.

Odgen, Thomas. The new pietism. *Journal of Humanistic Psychology,* 1972, *12,* 24–41. Also appears in Ogden, Thomas, *The intensive group experience; The new pietism.* Philadelphia: Westminster Press, 1972.

Perry, John W. *The far side of madness.* Englewood Cliffs, N.J.: Prentice-Hall, 1974.

Polanyi, M. *Personal knowledge.* Chicago: University of Chicago Press, 1958.
———. *The study of man.* Chicago: University of Chicago Press, 1959.

Rachman, S. J., & Wilson, G. T. The effects of psychological therapy (2nd ed.). Oxford: Pergamon Press, 1980.

Rogers, C. R. *The clinical treatment of the problem child.* Boston: Houghton Mifflin, 1939.
———. *Counseling and psychotherapy.* Boston: Houghton Mifflin, 1942.
———. *Client-centered therapy.* Boston: Houghton Mifflin, 1951.
———. Communication: Its blocking and its facilitation. *Northwestern University Information,* 1952a, *20*(25).
———. Client-centered psychotherapy. *Scientific American,* 1952b, *187*(5), 66–74.
———. A theory of therapy, personality, and interpersonal relationships, as developed in the client-centered framework. In S. Koch (Ed.), *Formulations of the person and the social context* (Vol. 3). Psychology; the study of a science. New York: McGraw-Hill, 1959, pp. 184–256.
———. *On becoming a person: A therapist's view of psychotherapy.* Boston: Houghton Mifflin, 1961.
———. Towards a science of the person. In T. W. Wann (Ed.), *Behaviorism and phenomenology: Contrasting bases for modern psychology.* Chicago: University of Chicago Press, 1964, pp. 109–133.
———. Carl Rogers. In E. Boring & G. Lindzey (Eds.), *History of psychology in autobiography.* (Vol. 5). New York: Appleton-Century-Crofts, 1967.
———. *Freedom to learn.* Columbus, Ohio: Merrill, 1969.
———. *Carl Rogers on encounter groups.* New York: Harper & Row, 1970.
———. *Becoming partners: Marriage and its alternatives.* New York: Dell (Delacorte Press), 1972.
———. My philosophy of interpersonal relationships and how it grew. *Journal of Humanistic Psychology,* 1973a, *13,* 3–16.
———. Some new challenges. *The American Psychologist,* 1973b, *28,* 379–387.
———. In retrospect: Forty-six years. *The American Psychologist,* 1974, *29,* 115–123.
———. Empathic: An unappreciated way of being. *The Counseling Psychologist: Carl Rogers on Empathy* (special topic), 1975a, *5*(2), 2–10.
———. The emerging person: A new revolution. In Richard I. Evans (Ed.), *Carl Rogers: The man and his ideas.* New York: Dutton, 1975b.
———. A therapist's view of personal goals. Pendle Hill Pamphlet 108. Wallingford, Pa.: Pendle Hill, 1977.
———. *Carl Rogers on personal power.* New York: Dell, 1978.
———. *A way of being.* Boston, Mass.: Houghton Mifflin, 1980a.
———. Growing old—Or older and growing. *Journal of Humanistic Psychology,* 1980b, *20*(4), 5–16.

Rogers, C. R., Gendlin, E. T., Kiesler, D. J., & Truax, C. G. *The therapeutic relationship and its impact: A study of psychotherapy with schizophrenics.* Madison: University of Wisconsin Press, 1967.

Rogers, C. R. with Hart, Joseph. Looking back and ahead: A conversation with

Carl Rogers. In J. T. Hart & T. M. Tomlinson (Eds.), *New directions in client-centered therapy*. Boston: Houghton Mifflin, 1970a, pp. 502–534.

Rogers, Carl, & Skinner, B. F. Some issues concerning the control of human behavior. *Science,* 1956, *124,* 1057–1066.

Schutz, William C. *Here comes everybody.* New York: Harper & Row, 1971.

————. *Elements of encounter.* Big Sur, Calif.: Joy Press, 1973.

Tart, Charles T. Scientific foundations for the study of altered states of consciousness. *Journal of Transpersonal Psychology,* 1971, *3,* 93–124.

————. Some assumptions of orthodox, Western psychology. In Charles T. Tart (Ed.), *Transpersonal Psychologies.* New York: Harper & Row, 1975, pp. 59–112.

Thorne, F. C. Critique of recent developments in personality counseling therapy. *Journal of Clinical Psychology,* 1957, *13,* 234–244.

Traux, C., & Mitchell, K. Research on certain therapist interpersonal skills. In Allan Bergin & Sol Garfield (Eds.), *Handbook of psychotherapy and behavior change.* New York: Wiley, 1971, p. 299.

Van Belle, Harry A. *Basic intent and therapeutic approach of Carl Rogers.* Toronto, Can.: Wedge Foundation, 1980.

CHAPTER 11
ABRAHAM MASLOW
AND
SELF-ACTUALIZATION
PSYCHOLOGY

Maslow believed that an accurate and viable theory of personality must include not only the depths but also the heights that each individual is capable of attaining. He is one of the founders of humanistic psychology and transpersonal psychology, two major new fields that were founded as alternatives to behaviorism and psycho-analysis.

Before Maslow, Western psychology can be said to have been divided into two great camps: the experimentally oriented laboratory study of human and animal behaviors on the one hand, and the clinically oriented therapeutic approaches to human behavior, rooted in psychoanalysis, on the other. Both of these camps have tended to ignore or to explain away the great cultural, social, and individual achievements of humanity, including creativity, love, altruism, and mysticism. These were the areas of Maslow's greatest interest.

Maslow was a pioneer. He was most interested in exploring new issues and new fields. His work is rather a collection of thoughts, opinions, and hypotheses than a fully developed theoretical system. More an armchair philosopher than a scientist, Maslow rarely came up with final answers. His great genius was in formulating significant questions—questions that are considered critical by many social scientists today.

Maslow's approach to psychology can be summed up in the opening sentence of his most influential book, *Toward a Psychology of Being:* "There is now emerging over the horizon a new conception of human sickness and of human health, a psychology that I find so thrilling and so full of wonderful possibilities that I yield to the temptation to present it publicly even before it is checked and confirmed, and before it can be called reliable scientific knowledge" (1968, p. 3).

PERSONAL HISTORY

Abraham Maslow was born in Brooklyn, New York, in 1908, of Russian-Jewish immigrant parents. His father was a barrel maker by trade who moved to the United States from Russia as a young man and later brought out his future wife. In his youth Abe was extraordinarily shy and very neurotic, "during all my first twenty years—depressed, terribly unhappy, lonely, isolated, self-rejecting . . ." (Maslow, in International Study Project, 1972).

Maslow was an extremely bright high school student. He entered New York City College at the age of 18. His father wanted Abe to become a lawyer, but Abe could not stand law school. When his father asked what he wanted to do instead, Abe said he wanted to go on studying; his father asked him what, and Abe replied, "Everything."

He fell in love with his first cousin as a teen-ager and found excuses to spend time with her family, looking hopelessly at her without daring to touch her. He finally kissed her when he was 19, the first time he had ever kissed a girl. This Maslow later described as one of the peak experiences of his life. Her acceptance of him, instead of the rejection he so feared, was a tremendous boost to his shaky self-esteem. They were married a year later. Marriage and his immersion in psychology began a whole new life for Abe.

In his first year in college, Maslow discovered music and drama. He fell in love with both, a love that remained with him throughout his life. Maslow transferred to the University of Wisconsin, where his interest focused on psychology. He was captured by J. B. Watson's vision of behaviorism as a powerful tool for affecting human life. Maslow trained in experimental method at Wisconsin and worked in the psychology laboratory there, conducting research on rats and other animals. He received his bachelor's degree in 1930, and his Ph.D. in 1934, at the age of 26.

After graduation Maslow returned to New York to work with Edward Thorndike, a brilliant and eminent Columbia University psychologist. Thorndike was particularly impressed with Maslow's performance on the intelligence test Thorndike developed. Maslow achieved the second highest IQ score recorded on that test, an IQ of 195. Eighteen months later Maslow found a teaching job at Brooklyn College, where he remained for 14 years. New York at this time was a tremendously stimulating intellectual center, housing many of the finest scholars who had fled Nazi persecution. Maslow studied with various psychotherapists, including Alfred Adler, Erich Fromm, and Karen Horney. He was most strongly influenced by Max Wertheimer, one of the founders of Gestalt psychology, and by Ruth Benedict, a brilliant cultural anthropologist.

Maslow's interest in the practical applications of psychology dates back to the beginning of his career. Even as a behaviorist graduate student, Maslow was convinced that Freud was right in his emphasis on the importance of sexuality. Maslow chose for his dissertation research the relationship between dominance and sexual behavior among primates. After leaving Wisconsin he began an extensive investigation of human sexual behavior. Maslow believed that any improvement in our understanding of sexual functioning would improve human adjustment tremendously.

During World War II, when he realized how little psychology had contributed to major world problems, Maslow's interests shifted from experimental psychology to social and personality psychology. He wanted to devote himself to "discovering a psychology for the peace table" (Hall, 1968, p. 54).

In addition to his professional work, Maslow became involved with family business affairs during a prolonged illness. His interest in business and in practical applications of psychology eventually resulted in *Eupsychian Management* (1965), a compilation of thoughts and articles related to management and industrial psychology written during a summer Maslow spent as Visiting Fellow at a small plant in California.

In 1951 Maslow moved to Brandeis University, which had just been established, and remained until 1968. He was chairman of the first psychology department and pioneered in the development of Brandeis. Throughout his career, Maslow's pioneering work was generally ignored as unscientific and out of the mainstream of psychology. He was personally liked by his colleagues and his ideas gradually became better appreciated. Much to his own surprise, Maslow was elected president of the American Psychological Association in 1967–1968.

Maslow left Brandeis to accept a fellowship that allowed him full time for writing. He died at the age of 62 of a heart attack in June 1970.

Although Maslow is considered to be one of the founders of humanistic psychology, he disliked the limitations of labels. "We shouldn't have to say 'humanistic psychology.' The adjective should be unnecessary. Don't think of me as being antibehavioristic. I'm antidoctrinaire . . . I'm against anything that closes doors and cuts off possibilities" (Hall, 1968, p. 57).

> Human nature is not nearly as bad as it has been thought to be. [Maslow, 1968, p. 4]

INTELLECTUAL ANTECEDENTS

Psychoanalysis

Psychoanalytic theory significantly influenced Maslow's life and thought. Freud's sophisticated description of the neurotic and maladaptive aspects of human behavior inspired Maslow to develop a scientifically grounded psychology relevant to the full range of human behavior. Maslow's own personal analysis profoundly affected him and demonstrated the tremendous difference between intellectual knowledge and actual gut-level experience.

> To oversimplify the matter somewhat, it is as if Freud supplied to us the sick half of psychology and we must now fill it out with the healthy half. [Maslow, 1968, p. 5]

Maslow believed that psychoanalysis provided the best system for analyzing psychopathology and also provided the best psychotherapy available. (This was in 1955.) However, he found the psychoanalytic system quite unsatisfactory as a general psychology for all of human thought and behavior. "The picture of man it presents is a lopsided, distorted puffing up of his weaknesses and shortcomings that purports then to describe him fully. . . . Practically all the activities that man prides himself on, and that give meaning, richness, and value to his life, are either omitted or pathologized by Freud" (Maslow, in Krippner, 1972, p. 71).

Social Anthropology

As a student at Wisconsin, Maslow was seriously interested in the work of social anthropologists, such as Malinowski, Mead, Benedict, and Linton. In New York he was able to study with leading figures in the field of culture and personality, which is concerned with the application of psychoanalytic theories to the analysis of behavior in other cultures. In addition, Maslow was fascinated by William Sumner's book, *Folkways* (1940), and Sumner's analysis of the ways in which much of human behavior is determined by cultural patterns and prescriptions. Maslow was so deeply inspired by Sumner that he vowed to devote himself to the same areas of study.

Gestalt Psychology

Maslow was also a serious student of Gestalt psychology, which stresses the importance of studying perception, cognition, and other sophisticated human activities in terms of complex whole systems. He sincerely admired Max Wertheimer, whose work on productive thinking is closely related to Maslow's writings on cognition and to his work on creativity. For Maslow, as for Gestalt psychologists, an essential element in creative thinking and effective problem solving is the ability to perceive and think in terms of wholes or patterns rather than isolated parts.

Another extremely important influence on Maslow's thinking was the work of Kurt Goldstein, a neurophysiologist who emphasized that the organism is a unified whole, that what happens in any part affects the entire organism. Maslow's work on self-actualization was inspired in part by Goldstein, who was the first to use the term.

Maslow dedicated *Toward a Psychology of Being* to Goldstein. In the preface he stated: "If I had to express in a single sentence what Humanistic Psychology has meant for me, I would say that it is an integration of Goldstein (and Gestalt Psychology) with Freud (and the various psychodynamic psychologies), the whole joined with the scientific spirit that I was taught by my teachers at the University of Wisconsin" (1968, p. v).

Kurt Goldstein

A neurophysiologist whose main work dealt with brain-damaged patients, Goldstein viewed self-actualization as a fundamental process in every organism, a process that may have negative as well as positive effects on the individual. Goldstein wrote that every organism has one primary drive, that "an organism is governed by the tendency to actualize, as much as possible, its individual capacities, its 'nature,' in the world" (1939, p. 196).

Goldstein argued that tension release is a strong drive only in sick organisms. For a healthy organism, the primary goal is "the *formation* of a certain level of tension, namely, that which makes possible further ordered activity" (Goldstein, 1939, pp. 195–196). A drive such as hunger is a special case of self-actualization, in which tension reduction is sought to return the organism to optimal condition for further expression of its capacities. However, only in an extreme situation does such a drive become demanding. Goldstein asserts that a normal organism can temporarily put off eating, sex, sleep, and so forth if other motives, such as curiosity or playfulness, are present.

Capacities clamor to be used, and cease their clamor only when they *are* used sufficiently. [Maslow, 1968, p. 152]

According to Goldstein, successful coping with the environment often involves a certain amount of uncertainty and shock. The healthy self-actualizing organism actually invites such shock by venturing into new situations in order to utilize its capacities. For Goldstein (and for Maslow also), self-actualization does not mean the end of problems and difficulties; on the contrary, growth may often bring a certain amount of pain and suffering. Goldstein wrote that an organism's capacities determine its needs. The possession of a digestive system makes eating a necessity; muscles require movement. A bird *needs* to fly and an artist needs to create, even if the act of creation requires painful struggle and great effort.

MAJOR CONCEPTS

Self-Actualization

Maslow loosely defined self-actualization as "the full use and exploitation of talents, capacities, potentialities, etc." (1970, p. 150). Self-actualization is not a static state. It is an ongoing process of using one's capacities fully, creatively, and joyfully. "I think of the self-actualizing man not as an ordinary man with something added, but rather as the ordinary man with nothing taken away. The average man is a full human being with dampened and inhibited powers and capacities" (Maslow in Lowry, 1973b, p. 91).

Most commonly, self-actualizing people see life clearly. They are less emotional and more objective, less likely to allow hopes, fears, or ego defenses to distort their observations. Without exception, Maslow found that self-actualizing people are dedicated to a vocation or cause. Two requirements for growth seem to be commitment to something greater than oneself and to doing well at one's chosen tasks. Creativity, spontaneity, courage, and hard work are all major characteristics of self-actualizing people.

Maslow consciously decided to study only those who were relatively free from neurosis and emotional disturbance. He found that his psychologically healthy subjects were low in self-conflict, independent, self-accepting, and able to enjoy both play and work. They personally preferred "better" values, what is usually considered right, reasonable, and healthy. Only one of Maslow's subjects was an orthodox religious believer, yet virtually all believed in a meaningful universe and in a life that could be called spiritual.

Maslow found that his self-actualizing people enjoy and appreciate life more. Despite pain, sorrow, and disappointments, they get more out of life. They have more interests and less fear, anxiety, boredom, or purposelessness. They are more aware of beauty and more able to appreciate the sunrise, nature, their marriage—again and again. Whereas most other people enjoy only occasional moments of joy, triumph, or peak experience, self-actualizing individuals seem to love life in general and to enjoy practically all its aspects.

Research on Self-Actualization

Maslow's investigations of self-actualization were first stimulated by his desire to understand more completely his two most inspiring teachers, Ruth Benedict and Max Wertheimer. Although Benedict and Wertheimer were dissimilar personalities and were concerned with different fields of study, Maslow felt they shared a common level of personal fulfillment in their professional and private lives that he had rarely sensed in others. Maslow saw in Benedict and Wertheimer not merely brilliant and eminent scientists, but deeply fulfilled, creative human beings. He began his own private research project to try to discover what made them so special, and he kept a notebook filled with all the data he could accumulate about their personal lives, attitudes, values, and so forth. Maslow's comparison of Benedict and Wertheimer was the first step in his lifelong study of self-actualization.

Maslow argued that it was more accurate to generalize about human nature from studying the best examples he could find, than from cataloging the problems and faults of average or neurotic individuals. "Certainly a visitor from Mars descending upon a colony of birth-injured cripples, dwarfs, hunchbacks, etc., could not deduce what they *should* have been. But then let us study not cripples, but the closest approach we can get to whole, healthy men. In them we find qualitative differences, a different system of motivation, emotion, value, thinking, and perceiving. In a certain sense, only the saints *are* mankind" (Maslow, in Lowry, 1973a, p. 90).

By studying the best and healthiest men and women, it is possible to explore the limits of human potential. In order to study how fast human beings can run, for example, one should work with the finest athletes and track performers available. It would make no sense to test an "average sample" from the general population. Similarly, Maslow argued, to study psychological health and maturity, one should investigate the most mature, creative, and well-integrated people.

Maslow had two criteria for including people in his initial study. First, all subjects were relatively free of neurosis or other major personal problems. Second, all those studied made the best possible use of their talents, capabilities, and other strengths.

This group consisted of 18 individuals: 9 contemporaries and 9 historical figures, including Abraham Lincoln, Thomas Jefferson, Albert Einstein, Eleanor Roosevelt, Jane Adams, William James, Albert Schweitzer, Aldous Huxley, and Baruch Spinoza. It is interesting to

Self-actualizing people are, without one single exception, involved in a cause outside their own skin, in something outside of themselves. [Maslow, 1971, p. 43]

note that Maslow's list includes intellectual giants and great social re-formers, but no great spiritual teachers or mystics. His interest in transpersonal psychology only developed later in his career. Obviously, Maslow's bias toward active, successful, and intellectual people as the "best" people has strongly affected his writing on self-actualization. Another psychologist, who valued introverted, emotionally developed, and spiritual qualities in people, would have developed a very different theory.

Maslow lists the following characteristics of self-actualizers (1970, pp. 153–172):

1. "more efficient perception of reality and more comfortable relations with it"
2. "acceptance (self, others, nature)"
3. "spontaneity; simplicity; naturalness"
4. "problem centering," as opposed to being ego-centered
5. "the quality of detachment; the need for privacy"
6. "autonomy; independence of culture and environment"
7. "continued freshness of appreciation"
8. mystic and peak experiences
9. *"Gemeinschaftsgefühl"* (the feeling of kinship with others)
10. "deeper and more profound interpersonal relations"
11. "the democratic character structure"
12. "discrimination between means and ends, between good and evil"
13. "philosophical, unhostile sense of humor"
14. "self-actualizing creativeness"
15. "resistance to enculturation; the transcendence of any particular culture"

[Self-actualization] is not an absence of problems but a moving from transitional or unreal problems to real problems. [Maslow, 1968, p. 115]

Maslow pointed out that the self-actualizers he studied were not perfect or even free of major faults. Their strong commitment to their chosen work and values may even lead self-actualizers to be quite ruth-less at times in pursuing their own goals; their work may take prece-dence over others' feelings or needs. In addition, self-actualizers can carry their independence to the point of shocking more conventional acquaintances. Self-actualizers also share many of the problems of av-erage people: guilt, anxiety, sadness, conflict, and so forth.

I very soon had to come to the conclusion that great talent was not only more or less independent of goodness or health of character but also that we know little about it. [Maslow, 1968, p. 135]

> *There are no perfect human beings!* Persons can be found who are good, very good indeed, in fact, great. There do in fact exist creators, seers, sages, saints, shakers and movers. This can certainly give us hope for the future of the species even if they *are* uncommon and do *not* come by the dozen. And yet these very same people can at times be boring, irritating, petulant, selfish, angry, or depressed. To avoid disillusionment with human nature, we must first give up our illusions about it. [Maslow, 1970, p. 176]

Self-Actualization Theory

In his last book, *The Farther Reaches of Human Nature* (1971), Maslow describes eight ways in which individuals self-actualize, eight behaviors leading to self-actualization. It is not a neat and clean, logically tight listing, but it represents the culmination of Maslow's thinking on self-actualization.

1. Concentration. "First, self-actualization means experiencing fully, vividly, selflessly, with full concentration and total absorption" (Maslow, 1971, p. 45). We are usually relatively unaware of what is going on within or around us. (Most witnesses will recount different versions of the same occurrence, for example.) However, we have all had moments of heightened awareness and intense interest, moments that Maslow would call self-actualizing.

2. Growth Choices. If we think of life as a process of choices, then self-actualization means to make each decision a choice for growth. We often have to choose between growth and safety, between progressing and regressing. Each choice has its positive and its negative aspects. To choose safety is to choose to remain with the known and the familiar, but to risk becoming stultified and stale. To choose growth is to open oneself to new and challenging experiences, but to risk the new and the unknown.

> One cannot choose wisely for a life unless he dares to listen to himself, *his own self,* at each moment in life. . . . [Maslow, 1971, p. 47]

3. Self-Awareness. Self-actualizing is becoming more aware of one's own inner nature and acting in accord with it. This means to decide for yourself if *you* like certain films, books, or ideas, regardless of others' opinions.

4. Honesty. Honesty and taking responsibility for one's actions are essential elements in self-actualizing. Rather than posing and giving answers that are calculated to please another or to make ourselves look good, Maslow advocates looking within for the answers. Each time we do this, we get in touch with our inner selves.

5. Judgment. The first four steps help us develop the capacity for "better life choices." We learn to trust our own judgment and our own instincts, and to act in terms of them. Maslow believes that this leads to better choices about what is constitutionally right for each individual—choices in art, music, and food, as well as major life choices, such as a husband or wife and a career.

6. Self-development. Self-actualization is also a continual process of *developing* one's potentialities. It means using one's abilities and intelligence and "working to do well the thing that one wants to do" (Maslow, 1971, p. 48). Great talent or intelligence are not the same as self-actualization; many gifted people fail to use their abilities fully, and others, with perhaps only average talents, accomplish a tremendous amount.

Self-actualization is not a "thing" that someone either has or does not have. It is a never-ending process of making real one's potentials. It refers to a way of continually living, working, and relating to the world rather than to a single accomplishment.

7. Peak Experiences. "Peak experiences are transient moments of self-actualization" (Maslow, 1971, p. 48). We are more whole, more integrated, more aware of ourselves and of the world during peak moments. At such times we think, act, and feel most clearly and accurately. We are more loving and accepting of others, more free of inner conflict and anxiety, and more able to put our energies to constructive use.

8. Lack of Ego Defenses. A further step in self-actualization is recognizing one's ego defenses and becoming able to drop them when appropriate. A first step is to become more aware of the ways in which we distort our images of ourselves and of the external world—through repression, projection, and other defenses.

Peak Experiences

Peak experiences are especially joyous and exciting moments in the life of every individual. Maslow notes that peak experiences are often inspired by intense feelings of love, exposure to great art or music, or experiencing the overwhelming beauty of nature. "All peak experiences may be fruitfully understood as completions-of-the-act . . . or as the Gestalt psychologists' closure, or on the paradigm of the Reichian type of complete orgasm, or as total discharge, catharsis, culmination, climax, consummation, emptying or finishing" (Maslow, 1968, p. 111).

The term peak experiences is a generalization for the best moments of the human being, for the happiest moments of life, for experiences of ecstasy, rapture, bliss, of the greatest joy. [Maslow, 1971, p. 105]

Virtually everyone has had a number of peak experiences, although we often take them for granted. One's reactions while watching a beautiful sunset or listening to an especially moving piece of music are examples of peak experiences. According to Maslow, peak experiences tend to be triggered by intense, inspiring occurrences: "It looks as if any experience of real excellence, of real perfection . . . tends to produce a peak experience" (1971, p. 175). These experiences may also be triggered by tragic events. Recovering from depression, a serious illness, or confronting death can initiate extreme moments of love and joy. The lives of most people are filled with long periods of relative inattentiveness, lack of involvement, or even boredom. In contrast, in their broadest sense, peak experiences are those moments when we become deeply involved, excited by and absorbed in the world.

The most powerful peak experiences are relatively rare. They have been portrayed by poets as moments of ecstasy; by the religious, as deep mystical experiences. For Maslow the highest peaks include "feelings of limitless horizons opening up to the vision, the feeling of being simultaneously more powerful and also more helpless than one ever was before, the feeling of great ecstasy and wonder and awe, the loss of placing in time and space . . ." (1970, p. 164).

Plateau Experiences

A peak experience is a "high" that may last a few minutes or several hours, but rarely longer. Maslow also discusses a more stable and long-lasting experience that he refers to as a "plateau experience." The plateau experience represents a new and more profound way of viewing and experiencing the world. It involves a fundamental change in attitude, a change that affects one's entire point of view and creates a new appreciation and intensified awareness of the world. Maslow experienced this himself late in life, after his first heart attack. His intensified consciousness of life and of the imminent possibility of death brought about a whole new way of perceiving the world. (For a more complete description in Maslow's own words, see "The Theory Firsthand.")

Transcendence and Self-Actualization

Maslow found that some self-actualizing individuals tend to have many peak experiences, whereas others have them rarely if ever. He came to distinguish between self-actualizers who were psychologically healthy, productive human beings, with little or no experience of transcendence, and others for whom transcendent experiencing was important or even central.

Maslow wrote that transcending self-actualizers are more often aware of the sacredness of all things, the transcendent dimension of life, in the midst of daily activities. Their peak or mystical experiences tend to be valued as the most important aspects of their lives. They tend to think more holistically than "merely healthy" self-actualizers; they are better able to transcend the categories of past, present, and future, and good and evil, and to perceive a unity behind the apparent complexity and contradictions of life. They are more likely to be innovators and original thinkers than systematizers of the ideas of others. As their knowledge develops, so does their sense of humility and ignorance, and they are likely to regard the universe with increasing awe.

> At the highest levels of development of humanness, knowledge is positively rather than negatively correlated with a sense of mystery, awe, humility, ultimate ignorance, reverence, and a sense of oblation. [Maslow, 1971, p. 290]

Transcenders are more likely to regard themselves as the carriers of their talents and abilities, hence they are less ego-involved in their work. They are honestly able to say, "I am the best person for this job, and therefore I should have it"; or, on the other hand, to admit, "You are the best one for this job, and you should take it from me."

Not everyone who has had a mystical experience is a transcending self-actualizer. Many who have had such experiences have not developed the psychological health and the productiveness Maslow considered an essential aspect of self-actualization. Maslow also pointed out that he found as many transcenders among businessmen, managers, teachers, and politicians as he found among those who are socially labeled as such—poets, musicians, ministers, and the like.

Hierarchy of Needs

Maslow defined neurosis and psychological maladjustment as "deficiency diseases," that is, they are caused by deprivation of certain basic needs, just as the absence of certain vitamins causes illness. The best examples of basic needs are physiological needs, such as hunger, thirst, and sleep. Deprivation clearly leads to eventual illness, and the satisfaction of these needs is the only cure for the illness. Basic needs are found in all individuals. The amount and kind of satisfaction will vary in different societies, but basic needs (like hunger) can never be completely ignored.

Certain psychological needs must also be satisfied in order to remain healthy. Maslow includes the following as basic needs: the need for safety, security, and stability; the need for love and a sense of belonging; and the need for self-respect and esteem. In addition, every individual has growth needs: a need to develop one's potentials and capabilities and a need for self-actualization.

Living at the higher need level means greater biological efficiency, greater longevity, less disease, better sleep, appetite, etc. [Maslow, "Higher and Lower Needs," *Journal of Psychology*, 1948]

MASLOW'S BASIC NEED HIERARCHY

physiological needs	(hunger, sleep, sex, etc.)
safety needs	(stability, order)
belonging and love needs	(family, friendship)
esteem needs	(self-respect, recognition)
self-actualization needs	(development of capacities)

Man's higher nature rests upon man's lower nature, needing it as a foundation and collapsing without this foundation. That is, for the mass of mankind, man's higher nature is inconceivable without a satisfied lower nature as a base. [Maslow, 1968, p. 173]

According to Maslow, the earlier needs must be fulfilled before needs listed later are met. For example, both physiological and love needs are essential to the individual; however, when one is truly starving, the need for love (or any other higher need) is not a major factor in behavior. On the other hand, Maslow argues, even when frustrated in love we still need to eat (romantic novels to the contrary).

One of Maslow's main points is that we are always desiring something and rarely reach a state of complete satisfaction without any goals or desires. His need hierarchy is an attempt to predict what kinds of new desires will arise once the old ones are sufficiently satisfied so that they no longer dominate behavior. There are many exceptions in individual cases, especially in our culture where most basic needs are partially satisfied and still serve to motivate without dominating the person. Maslow developed his hierarchy as part of a general theory of motivation, not as a precise predictor of individual behavior. "It is quite true that man lives by bread alone—when there is no bread. But what happens to man's desires when there *is* plenty of bread and when his belly is chronically filled? *At once other (and higher) needs emerge,* and these, rather than physiological hungers, dominate their organism. And when these in turn are satisfied, again new (and still higher) needs emerge, and so on" (Maslow, 1970, p. 38, italics his).

Metamotivation

Metamotivation refers to behavior inspired by growth needs and values. According to Maslow, this kind of motivation is most common among self-actualizing people, who are by definition already gratified in their lower needs. Metamotivation often takes the form of devotion to ideals or goals, to something "outside oneself." Maslow points out that metaneeds are also on a continuum with basic needs, and that frustration of these needs brings about "metapathologies." Metapathology refers to a lack of values, meaningfulness, or fulfillment in life. Maslow argues that a sense of identity, a worthwhile career, and commitment to a value system are as essential to one's psychological well-being as security, love, and self-esteem.

> Growth is theoretically possible *only* because the "higher" tastes are better than the "lower" and because the "lower" satisfaction becomes boring. [Maslow, 1971, p. 147]

Grumbles and Metagrumbles

Maslow suggests there are different levels of complaints that correspond with the levels of frustrated needs. In a factory situation, for example, low-level grumbles might deal with unsafe working conditions, arbitrary and authoritarian foremen, and a lack of job security from one day to the next. These are complaints that deal with deprivations of the most basic needs for physical safety and security. A higher level of complaint might deal with lack of adequate recognition for accomplishments, threats to one's prestige, or lack of group solidarity, that is, complaints based on threats to belonging needs or esteem needs.

Metagrumbles deal with frustration of metaneeds such as perfection, justice, beauty, and truth. This level of grumbling is a good indication that everything else is actually going fairly smoothly. When people complain about the unaesthetic nature of their surroundings, it means that they are relatively satisfied as far as more basic needs are concerned.

Maslow assumes that we should never expect an end to complaints; we should only hope to move to higher levels of complaint. Grumblers about the imperfection of the world, the lack of perfect justice, and so forth, are healthy indications that in spite of a high degree of basic satisfaction, people are striving for still greater improvement and growth. In fact, Maslow suggests that one good measure of the degree of enlightenment of a community is the height of the grumblers of its members.

> To have committees . . . heatedly coming in and complaining that rose gardens in the parks are not sufficiently cared for . . . is in itself a wonderful thing because it indicates the height of life at which the complainers are living. [Maslow, 1965, p. 240]

Deficiency and Being Motivation

Maslow has pointed out that most psychologies deal only with deficiency motivation, that is, they concentrate on behavior oriented to fulfill a need that has been deprived or frustrated. Hunger, pain, and fear are prime examples of deficiency motivations.

However, a close look at human or animal behavior reveals another kind of motivation. When an organism is not hungry, in pain, or fearful, new motivations emerge, such as curiosity and playfulness. Under these conditions activities can be enjoyed as ends in themselves, not always pursued solely as a means to need gratification. "Being motivation" refers primarily to enjoyment and satisfaction in the present or to the desire to seek a positively valued goal (growth motivation or metamotivation). On the other hand, "deficiency motivation" includes a need to change the present state of affairs because it is felt to be unsatisfactory or frustrating.

Peak experiences are generally related to the being realm, and being psychology also tends to be most applicable to self-actualizers. Maslow distinguishes between B- and D- (being and deficiency) cognition, B- and D-values, and B- and D-love.

Deficiency and Being Cognition

In D-cognition, objects are seen solely as need fulfillers, as means to other ends. This is especially true when needs are strong. Maslow (1970) points out that strong needs tend to channel thinking and perception, therefore the individual is only aware of those aspects of the environment related to need satisfaction. A hungry person tends to see only food, a miser only money.

B-cognition is more accurate and effective because the perceiver is less likely to distort his or her perceptions to accord with needs or desires. B-cognition is nonjudgmental, without comparison or evaluation. The fundamental attitude is one of appreciation of what is. Stimuli are exclusively and fully attended to, and perception seems richer, fuller, and more complete.

A section of cancer seen through a microscope, if only we can forget that it is a cancer, can be seen as a beautiful and intricate and awe-inspiring organization. [Maslow, 1968, p. 76]

The perceiver remains somewhat independent of what is perceived. External objects are valued in and of themselves rather than for their relevance to personal concerns. In fact, in a state of B-cognition the individual tends to remain absorbed in contemplation or appreciation, and active intervention is seen as irrelevant or inappropriate. One advantage to D-cognition is that the individual may feel impelled to act and try to alter existing conditions.

Deficiency and Being Values

Maslow does not explicitly deal with D-values, although he discusses B-values in detail. B-values are intrinsic to every individual. "The highest values [exist] within human nature itself, to be discovered there. This is in sharp contradiction to the older and more customary beliefs that the highest values can come only from a supernatural God, or from some other source outside human nature itself" (Maslow, 1968, p. 170).

Maslow has listed the following as B-values: truth, goodness, beauty, wholeness, dichotomy transcendence, aliveness, uniqueness, perfection, necessity, completion, justice, order, simplicity, richness, effortlessness, playfulness, and self-sufficiency.

Deficiency and Being Love

Deficiency love is love of others because they fulfill a need. The more one is gratified, the more this kind of love is reinforced. It is love out of a need for self-esteem or sex, out of fear of loneliness, and so forth.

Being love is love for the essence, the "being" of the other. It is nonpossessive and concerned more with the good of the other than with selfish satisfaction. Maslow often wrote of B-love as demonstrating the Taoist attitude of noninterference or letting things be, appreciating what *is* without trying to change and "improve" matters. B-love of nature tends to express appreciation for the beauty of flowers by watching them grow and leaving them, whereas D-love is more likely to involve picking the flowers and making an arrangement of them. B-love is also the ideal unconditional love of a parent for a child, which even includes loving and valuing the child's small imperfections.

Maslow argues that B-love is richer, more satisfying, and longer lasting than D-love. It stays fresh, whereas D-love tends to grow stale with time. Being love can be a trigger for peak experiences and is often described in the same exalted terms used for describing deeply religious experiences.

Eupsychia

Maslow coined the term *eupsychia* (yu-psi-ki-a) to refer to ideal, human-oriented societies and communities. He preferred it to *utopia,* which Maslow felt was overused and also had a strong sense of impracticality and ungrounded idealism. He believed that an ideal society could be developed by a community of psychologically healthy, self-actualizing individuals. All members of the community would be engaged in seeking personal development and fulfillment in their work and in their personal lives.

But even an ideal society will not *produce* self-actualizing individuals. "A teacher or a culture doesn't create a human being. It doesn't implant within him the ability to love, or to be curious, or to philosophize, or to symbolize, or to be creative. Rather it permits, or fosters, or encourages, or helps what exists in embryo to become real and actual" (Maslow, 1968, p. 161).

Maslow also discussed eupsychian, or enlightened, management practices as opposed to authoritarian business management. Authoritarian managers assume that workers and management have basically different, mutually incompatible goals—that workers want to earn as

There is a kind of a feedback between the Good Society and the Good Person. They need each other. . . . [Maslow, 1971 p. 19]

much as possible with minimal effort and therefore must be closely watched.

Enlightened managers assume that employees *want* to be creative and productive and that they need to be supported and encouraged rather than restricted and controlled by management. Maslow points out that the enlightened approach works best with stable, psychologically healthy employees. Some hostile, suspicious people work more effectively in an authoritarian structure and would take unfair advantage of more freedom. Eupsychian management only works with people who enjoy and can handle responsibility and self-direction, which is why Maslow suggested that eupsychian communities be composed of self-actualizing people.

Synergy

The term *synergy* was originally used by Maslow's teacher, Ruth Benedict, to refer to the degree of interpersonal cooperation and harmony within a society. Synergy means cooperation. The original Greek word literally means "work together." Synergy also refers to a combined action of elements resulting in a total effect that is greater than all the elements taken independently.

As an anthropologist, Benedict was aware of the dangers of making value judgments in comparing societies and of measuring another civilization by how closely it conforms to our own cultural standards. However, in her study of other civilizations, Benedict clearly saw that people in some societies were happier, healthier, and more efficient than in others. Some groups had beliefs and customs that were basically harmonious and satisfying to their members, whereas the practices of other groups promoted suspicion, fear, and anxiety.

Under conditions of low social synergy, the success of one member brings about a loss or failure for another. For example, if each hunter shares his catch only with his immediate family, hunting is likely to become strongly competitive. A man who improves his hunting techniques or discovers a new source of game may try to hide his achievements from his fellows. Whenever one hunter is highly successful, there is that much less food available for other hunters and their families.

Under high social synergy, cooperation is maximized. One example would be a similar hunting group with a single important difference—the communal sharing of the catch. Under these conditions, every hunter benefits from the success of the others. Under high social synergy, the cultural belief system reinforces cooperation and positive feelings between individuals and helps minimize conflict and discord.

Maslow also writes of synergy in individuals. Identification with others tends to promote high individual synergy. If the success of another is a source of genuine satisfaction to the individual, then help is freely and generously offered. In a sense, both selfish and altruistic motives are merged. In aiding another, the individual is also seeking his or her own satisfaction.

Synergy can also be found *within* the individual as unity between thought and action. To force oneself to act indicates some conflict of motives. Ideally, individuals do what they *should* do because they *want* to do it. The best medicine is taken not only because it is effective, but also because it tastes good.

Transpersonal Psychology

Maslow added transpersonal psychology to the first three forces in Western psychology—behaviorism, psychoanalysis, and humanistic psychology. For Maslow, behaviorism and psychoanalysis were too limited in scope to form the basis for a complete psychology of human nature. Psychoanalysis has been derived largely from studies of psychopathology. Behaviorism has attempted to reduce the complexities of human nature to simpler principles and has ignored issues such as values, consciousness, and love.

In the early 1960s humanistic psychology emerged out of the work of Maslow and other theorists concerned with psychological health and effective functioning. Many humanistic psychologists have used Maslow's theories, especially his work on self-actualization, as the basic framework for their writing and research.

In 1968 Maslow called attention to the limitations of the humanistic model. He found that in exploring the farther reaches of human nature, there were possibilities beyond self-actualization.

Transpersonal psychology adds to the traditional concerns and contents of psychology an acknowledgment of the importance of the spiritual aspect of human experience. This level of experience has been described primarily in religious literature, in unscientific and often theologically biased language. One of the major tasks of transpersonal psychology is to bring this material into psychological language and a scientific framework.

> The human being needs a framework of values, a philosophy of life . . . to live by and understand by, in about the same sense that he needs sunlight, calcium or love. [Maslow, 1968, p. 206]

> I should say also that I consider Humanistic, Third Force Psychology to be transitional, a preparation for a still "higher" Fourth Psychology, transpersonal, transhuman, centered in the cosmos rather than in human needs and interest, going beyond humanness, identity, self-actualization and the like. . . . We need something "bigger than we are" to be awed by and to commit ourselves to in a new, naturalistic, empirical, non-churchly sense, perhaps as Thoreau and Whitman, William James and John Dewey did. [Maslow, 1968, pp. iii–iv]

Webster's Third New International Dictionary defines *transpersonal* as "extending or going beyond the personal or individual." The term *transpersonal* refers to an extension of identity beyond both individuality and personality. The underlying model of human nature in transpersonal psychology has been found throughout human cultures and throughout history. It has been called the "perennial philosophy" (Huxley, 1944), the "perennial religion" (Smith, 1976), or the "perennial psychology" (Wilber, 1977).

Major contributors to the field of transpersonal psychology differ in their approach and interest, including the following:

> Without the transcendent and the transpersonal, we get sick, violent and nihilistic, or else hopeless and apathetic. [Maslow, 1968, p. iv]

Anthony Sutich, the founder and first editor of the *Journal of Transpersonal Psychology,* defined transpersonal psychology as the investigation of "ultimate human capacities and potentialities," capacities that have no systematic place in other approaches to psychology. (1969, p. 15)

This field is the study of transpersonal experiences, which involve an expansion of consciousness beyond the usual ego boundaries and limitations of time and space. [Grof, 1975, p. 154]

Transpersonal psychology is bringing together the insights of the individualistic psychologies of the West with the spiritual psychologies of the East and Middle East. The realization that our own training has been limited and that Western ideas are not the center of the psychological universe is disturbing at first. The feeling passes when one becomes aware of the amazing amount of work that has already been accomplished, but which awaits validation with the scientific and experimental tools of Western psychology, to be fully realized. [Fadiman, 1980, p. 181]

The term *transpersonal* was adopted after considerable deliberation to reflect the reports of people practicing various consciousness disciplines who spoke of experiences of an extension of identity beyond both individuality and personality. Thus transpersonal psychology cannot strictly be called a model of personality, because personalities consider only one aspect of our psychological nature; rather it is an inquiry into the essential nature of being. [Walsh & Vaughan, 1980, p. 16]

In various spiritual traditions, authorities point out that our usual state of consciousness is not only limited, it is also dreamlike and illusory. From this perspective, psychotherapies that deal only with personality dynamics are superficial palliatives, such as visiting someone in the hospital and cheering him or her up with candy. The person may feel better, but the underlying causes of his or her problems are not addressed.

These realms of human experience were formerly the exclusive domain of the guru or spiritual teacher, but it now has become increasingly evident that psychologists also need to learn to deal with these realms. In dealing with human problems involving values, meaning, and purpose, psychological growth inevitably raises issues of a spiritual, transpersonal nature.

DYNAMICS

Psychological Growth

The pursuit of self-actualization cannot begin until the individual is free of the domination of the lower needs, such as needs for security and esteem. According to Maslow, early frustration of a need may fixate the individual at that level of functioning. For instance, someone who was not very popular as a child may continue to be deeply concerned with self-esteem needs throughout life.

The pursuit of higher needs is in itself one index of psychological health. Maslow argues that fulfillment of higher needs is intrinsically more satisfying and that metamotivation is an indication that the individual has progressed beyond a deficiency level of functioning.

Self-actualization represents a long-term commitment to growth and the development of capabilities to their fullest. Self-actualizing work involves the choice of worthwhile, creative problems. Maslow writes that self-actualizing individuals are attracted to the most challenging and intriguing problems, to questions that demand their best and most creative efforts. They are willing to cope with uncertainty and ambiguity, and prefer challenge to easy solutions.

> As the person becomes integrated, so does his world. As he feels good, so does the world look good. [Maslow, 1971, p. 165]

Obstacles to Growth

Maslow pointed out that growth motivation is relatively weak compared to physiological needs and needs for security, esteem, and so forth. The process of self-actualization can be limited by (1) negative influences from past experience and resulting habits that keep us locked into unproductive behaviors; (2) social influence and group pressure that often operate against our own taste and judgment; and (3) inner defenses that keep us out of touch with ourselves.

Poor habits often inhibit growth. For Maslow these include addiction to drugs or drinking, poor diet, and other habits that adversely affect health and efficiency. Maslow points out that a destructive environment or rigid authoritarian education can easily lead to unproductive habit patterns based on a deficiency orientation. Also, any strong habit generally tends to interfere with psychological growth because it diminishes the flexibility and openness necessary to operate most efficiently and effectively in a variety of situations.

> There are two sets of forces pulling at the individual, not just one. In addition to the pressures forward toward health, there are also fearful-regressive pressures backward, toward sickness and weakness. [Maslow, 1968, p. 164]

Group pressure and social propaganda also tend to limit the individual. They act to diminish autonomy and stifle independent judgment as the individual is pressured to substitute external, societal standards for his or her own taste or judgment. A society may also inculcate a biased view of human nature—for example, the Western view that most human instincts are essentially sinful and must continually be controlled or subjugated. Maslow argued that this negative attitude tends to frustrate growth and that the opposite is in fact correct; our instincts are essentially good and impulses toward growth are the major source of human motivation.

Ego defenses are seen by Maslow as internal obstacles to growth. The first step in dealing with ego defenses is to become aware of them and to see clearly how they operate. Then each individual should attempt to minimize the distortions created by these defenses. Maslow adds two new defense mechanisms—*desacralizing* and the *Jonah complex*—to the traditional psychoanalytic listing of projection, repression, denial, and the like.

Desacralizing refers to impoverishing one's life by the refusal to treat anything with deep seriousness and concern. Today, few cultural or religious symbols are given the care and respect they once enjoyed; consequently, they have lost their power to thrill, inspire, or even motivate us. Maslow often referred to modern values concerning sex as an example of desacralization. Although a more casual attitude toward sex may lead to less frustration and trauma, it is also true that sexual experience has lost the power it once had to inspire artists, writers, and lovers.

The Jonah complex refers to a refusal to try to realize one's full capabilities. Just as Jonah attempted to avoid the responsibilities of becoming a prophet, so too many people are actually afraid of using their capacities to the fullest. They prefer the security of average and undemanding achievements, as opposed to truly ambitious goals that would require them to extend themselves fully. This attitude is not uncommon among many students who "get by" utilizing only a fraction of their talents and abilities. In the past this has been true of many women who were taught that a successful career was somehow incongruent with femininity or that intellectual achievement might make them less attractive to men. (See, for example, Horner, 1972.)

Though, in principle, self-actualization is easy, in practice it rarely happens (by my criteria, certainly in less than 1% of the adult population). [Maslow, 1968, p. 204]

This "fear of greatness" may be the greatest barrier to self-actualization. Living fully is more than many of us feel we can bear. At times of deepest joy and ecstacy, people often say, "It's too much," or, "I can't stand it." The root of the Jonah complex is a fear of letting go of a limited but manageable existence and risk losing control, being torn apart, or disintegrating.

STRUCTURE

Body

Maslow does not discuss in detail the role of the body in the process of self-actualization. He assumes that once physiological needs are met, the individual is free to deal with needs that are higher in the need hierarchy. However, he writes that it is important that the body be given its due. "Asceticism, self-denial, deliberate rejection of the demands of the organism, at least in the West, tend to produce a diminished, stunted, or crippled organism, and even in the East, bring self-actualization to only a very few, exceptionally strong individuals" (1968, p. 199).

Maslow mentions the importance of intense stimulation of the physical senses in peak experiences, which are often triggered by natural beauty, art, music, or sexual experience. He also indicated that training in dance, art, and other physical media of expression could provide an important supplement to traditional, cognitively oriented education and that physical and sense-oriented systems of instruction require the kind of active participatory learning that should be included in all forms of education.

Social Relationships

According to Maslow, love and esteem are basic needs essential to everyone and take precedence over self-actualization in the need hierarchy. Maslow often deplored the failure of most textbooks in psychology even to mention the word *love,* as if psychologists considered love unreal, something that must be reduced to concepts like libido projection or sexual reinforcement.

The fact is that people are good, if only their fundamental wishes [for affection and security] are satisfied. . . . Give people affection and security, and they will give affection and be secure in their feelings and behavior. [Maslow, in Lowry, 1973b, p. 18]

Will

Will is a vital ingredient in the long-term process of self-actualization. Maslow found that self-actualizing individuals work long and hard to attain their chosen goals. "Self-actualization means working to do well the thing that one wants to do. To become a second-rate physician is not a good path to self-actualization. One wants to be first-rate or as good as he can be" (Maslow, 1971, p. 48). Because of his faith in the essential health and goodness of human nature, Maslow was little concerned with the need for willpower to overcome unacceptable instincts or impulses. For Maslow, healthy individuals are relatively free from internal conflict, except perhaps the need to overcome poor habits. They need to employ will to develop their abilities still further and to attain ambitious, long-range goals.

If you deliberately plan to be less than you are capable of being, then I warn you that you'll be deeply unhappy for the rest of your life. [Maslow, 1971, p. 36]

Emotions

Maslow emphasized the importance of the positive emotions in self-actualization. He encouraged other psychologists to begin serious research on happiness, calmness, joy, and to investigate fun, games, and play. He believed that negative emotions, tension, and conflict drain energy and inhibit effective functioning.

For Maslow, maturity includes "being able to give oneself over completely to an emotion, not only of love but also of anger, fascination . . ." (1966, p. 38). Maslow goes on to point out that it is our fear of deep emotions that leads us to desacralize much of life or to use intellectualization as a defense against feeling. He felt that orthodox science has mistakenly taken "cool" perceiving and mental thinking as best for discovering scientific truth. This limited approach has tended to banish from scientific study experiences of wonder, awe, ecstacy, and other forms of transcendence.

Intellect

Maslow emphasized the need for holistic thinking, dealing with systems of relationships and wholes rather than with individual parts. He found that peak experiences often contain striking examples of thinking that has broken through the usual dichotomies with which we view reality. Individuals have often reported seeing past, present, and future as one, viewing life and death as part of a single process, or seeing good and evil within the same whole.

Holistic thinking is also found in creative thinkers who are able to break with the past and look beyond conventional categories in investigating possible new relationships. This requires freedom, openness, and an ability to deal with inconsistency and uncertainty. Although such ambiguity can be threatening to some, it is part of the essential joy of creative problem solving for self-actualizers.

Maslow (1970) has written that creative people are "problem-centered" rather than "means-centered." Problem-centered activities are determined primarily by the demands and requirements of the desired goals. Means-centered individuals, on the other hand, often become so concerned with means, technique, or methodology that they tend to carry out precise work on trivial topics. "Problem-centering" is also in contrast with "ego-centering" (an example of D-cognition), which tends to bias one's vision to see things as one might like them to be rather than as they are.

Self

Maslow defines the self as an individual's inner core or inherent nature—one's own tastes, values, and goals. Understanding one's inner nature and acting in accord with it is essential to actualizing the self.

Maslow approaches understanding the self through studying those individuals who are most in tune with their own natures, those who provide the best examples of self-expression or self-actualization. However, he did not explicitly discuss the self as a specific structure within the personality.

Self-actualizing people, those who have come to a high level of maturation, health, and self-fulfillment, have so much to teach us that sometimes they seem almost like a different breed of human beings. [Maslow, 1968, p. 71]

Therapist

For Maslow, psychotherapy is effective primarily because it involves an intimate and trusting relationship with another human being. Along with Adler, Maslow felt that a good therapist is like an older brother or sister, someone who treats another in a caring and loving way. Maslow proposed the model of the "Taoist helper," someone who is able to help without interfering. A good coach does this when he or she works with the natural style of an athlete in order to strengthen that individual's style and improve it. A coach does not try to force all athletes into the same mold.

Maslow rarely discusses psychotherapy in his writings. Although he underwent psychoanalysis for several years and received informal training in psychotherapy, his interests always centered on research and writing rather than therapy.

Maslow viewed therapy as a way of satisfying the basic needs for love and esteem that are frustrated in virtually everyone who seeks psychological help. He argued (1970) that warm human relationships can provide much of the same support found in therapy.

Good therapists should love and care for the being or essence of the people they work with. Maslow (1971) wrote that those who seek to change or manipulate others lack this essential attitude. For example, he believed that a true dog lover would never crop a dog's ears or tail, and one who really loves flowers would not cut or twist them to make fancy flower arrangements.

> It has been pointed out that a therapist can repeat the same mistakes for 40 years and then call it "rich clinical experience." [Maslow, 1968, p. 87]

EVALUATION

Maslow's great strength lies in his concern for the areas of human functioning that most other theorists have almost completely ignored. He is one of the few psychologists who has seriously investigated the positive dimensions of human experience.

Maslow's experimental work was mostly inconclusive; *exploratory* might be a better term, and he was the first to acknowledge this:

> It's just that I haven't got the time to do careful experiments myself. They take too long, in view of the years that I have left and the extent of what I want to do.
>
> So I myself do only "quick-and-dirty" little pilot explorations, mostly with a few subjects only, inadequate to publish but enough to convince myself that they are probably true and will be confirmed one day. Quick little commando raids, guerrilla attacks. [Maslow in Krippner, 1972, pp. 66–67]

> I am a new breed—a theoretical psychologist parallel to . . . theoretical biologists. . . . I think of myself as a scientist rather than an essayist or philosopher. I feel myself very bound to and by the facts that I am trying to *perceive*, not to create. [Maslow, in International Study Project, 1972, p. 63]

There are, of course, some serious disadvantages to this procedure; data from Maslow's small and biased samples are statistically unreliable, for example. However, Maslow never sought to experimentally "prove" or verify his ideas. His research was more a way of clarifying and adding detail to his theories.

Even so, Maslow sometimes seems very much like an armchair philosopher who remains somewhat aloof from the possible contradictions of new facts or experiences. He was generally fairly clear on what he wanted to demonstrate in his research, and he rarely seemed to find any new data to alter his preconceived ideas. For example, Maslow always stressed the importance of positive "triggers" for peak experiences: experiences of love, beauty, great music, and so forth. Negative triggers tend to be ignored in his writings, although many people report that their most intense peak experiences are preceded by negative emotions (fear, depression) that are then transcended and become strongly positive states. (See, for example, William James's *Varieties of Religious Experience,* 1943.) For some reason, Maslow's investigations seldom seemed to uncover this kind of new information.

Maslow's greatest strength is as a psychological thinker who has continually stressed the positive dimensions of human experience, the potential that men and women are capable of reaching. Maslow has been an inspiration for virtually all humanistic psychologists. He has been called "the greatest American psychologist since William James" (*Journal of Transpersonal Psychology* 2 (1970): iv). Although many might consider this praise somewhat extravagant, no humanistically oriented psychologist would deny Maslow's central importance as an original thinker and a pioneer in human potential psychology.

THE THEORY FIRSTHAND

The following quotation is taken from the *Journal of Transpersonal Psychology.* These are excerpts from a discussion between Maslow and several other psychologists.

> I found that as I got older, my peak experiences became less intense and also became less frequent. In discussing this matter with other people who are getting older, I received this same sort of reaction. My impression is that this may have to do with the aging process. It makes sense because to some extent, I've learned that I've become somewhat afraid of peak experiences because I wonder if my body can stand them. A peak experience can produce great turmoil in the autonomic nervous system; it may be that a decrease in peak experiences is nature's way of protecting the body. . . .
>
> As these poignant and emotional discharges died down in me, something else happened which has come into my consciousness which is a very precious thing. A sort of precipitation occurred of what might be called the sedimentation or the fallout from illuminations, insights, and other life experiences that were very important—tragic experiences included. The result has been a kind of unitive consciousness which has certain advantages and certain disadvantages over the peak experiences. I can define this unitive consciousness very simply for me as the simultaneous perception of the sacred and the ordinary, or the miraculous and the rather constant or easy-without-effort sort of thing.
>
> I now perceive under the aspect of eternity and become mythic, poetic, and symbolic about ordinary things. This is the Zen experience, you know. There is nothing excepted and nothing special, but one lives in a world of miracles all the time. There is a paradox because it is miraculous and yet it doesn't produce an autonomic burst.

This type of consciousness has certain elements in common with peak experience—awe, mystery, surprise, and esthetic shock. These elements are present, but are constant rather than climactic. It certainly is a temptation to use as kind of a model, a paradigm for the peaking experience, the sexual orgasm, which is a mounting up to a peak and a climax, and then a drop in the completion and its ending. Well, this other type of experience must have another model. The words that I would use to describe this kind of experience would be "a high plateau." It is to live at a constantly high level in the sense of illumination or awakening or in Zen, in the easy or miraculous, in the nothing special. It is to take rather casually the poignancy and the preciousness and the beauty of things, but not to make a big deal out of it because it's happening every hour, you know, all the time.

This type of experience has the advantage, in the first place, that it's more voluntary than peak experience. For example, to enter deeply into this type of consciousness, I can go to an art museum or a meadow rather than into a subway. In the plateau experiences, you're not as surprised because they are more volitional than peak experiences. Further, I think you can teach plateau experiences; you could hold classes in miraculousness.

Another aspect I have noticed is that it's possible to sit and look at something miraculous for an hour and enjoy every second of it. On the other hand, you can't have an hour-long orgasm. In this sense, the plateau type of experience is better. It has a great advantage, so to speak, over the climactic, the orgasm, the peak. The descending into a valley, and living on the high plateau doesn't imply this. It is much more casual.

There are some other aspects of this experience. There tends to be more serenity rather than an emotionality. Our tendency is to regard the emotional person as an explosive type. However, calmness must also be brought into one's psychology. We need the serene as well as the poignantly emotional.

My guess is that the plateau experience one day will be observed on psychophysiological instruments. I believe that peak experiences have something to do with automatic discharge, which we should be able to catch easily enough if the instrumentation is available. Brain wave measurement techniques and biofeedback sound very much like a possibility for measuring, detecting, and teaching serenity and calmness and peacefulness. If so, we should be able to work with it, which means that we may be able to teach serenity to our children and pass it on. . . .

The important point that emerges from these plateau experiences is that they're essentially cognitive. As a matter of fact, almost by definition, they represent a witnessing of the world. The plateau experience is a witnessing of reality. It involves seeing the symbolic, or the mythic, the poetic, the transcendent, the miraculous, the unbelievable, all of which I think are part of the real world instead of existing only in the eyes of the beholder.

There is a sense of certainty about plateau experience. It feels very, very good to be able to see the world as miraculous and not merely in the concrete, not reduced only to the behavioral, not limited only to the here and now. You know, if you get stuck in the here and now, that's a reduction.

Well, it's very easy to get sloppy with your words and you can go on about the beauty of the world, but the fact is that these plateau experiences are described quite well in many literatures. This is not the standard description of the acute mystical experience, but the way in which the world looks if the mystic experience really takes. If your mystical experience changes your life, you go about your business as the great mystics did. For example, the great saints could have mystical revelations, but also could run a monastery. You can run a grocery store and pay the bills, but still carry on this sense of witnessing the world in the way you did in the great moments of mystic perception. [Maslow, in Krippner, 1972, pp. 112–115]

EXERCISES

An Exercise in B-Love
For Maslow, being love is selfless; it demands nothing in return. The very act of loving, appreciating the essence and beauty of the object of love, is its own reward. In our daily experience we usually feel a mixture of being and deficiency love. We generally expect and receive something in return for our feelings of love.

This exercise is derived from an old Christian practice designed to develop feelings of pure love. Sit in a darkened room in front of a lit candle. Relax and gradually get in touch with your body and your surroundings. Allow your mind and body to slow down, to become calm and peaceful.

Gaze at the candle flame. Extend feelings of love from your heart to the flame. Your feelings of love for the flame are unrelated to any thought of the worthiness of the flame itself. You love for the sake of loving. (It may seem strange at first to try to love an inanimate object, a mere flame, but that is just the point—to experience the feeling of loving in a situation in which there is no return, no reward aside from the feeling of love itself.) Expand your feelings of love to include the entire room and everything in it.

Analyzing Peak Experiences
Try to recall clearly one peak experience in your own life—a joyous, happy, blissful moment that stands out in your memory. Take a moment to relive the experience.

1. What brought about this experience? Was anything unique about the situation that triggered it?
2. How did you feel at the time? Was this feeling different from your usual experience—emotionally, physically, or intellectually?
3. Did you seem different to yourself? Did the world about you appear different?
4. How long did the experience last? How did you feel afterward?
5. Did the experience have any lasting effects (on your outlook or your relations with others, for example)?
6. How does your own experience compare with Maslow's theories concerning peak experiences and human nature?

To get a clearer sense of peak experiences, compare your experiences with others. Look for differences as well as similarities. Are the differences the result of different situations or perhaps of variations in personality or background? What do the similarities imply about Maslow's ideas or about human potential in general?

Self-Actualization

List several examples of self-actualizing people. What do these people have in common? Are they different from your own personal heroes and heroines, or the same people? In what ways do these concrete examples bear out Maslow's theories? How do they differ from his model of self-actualization?

ANNOTATED BIBLIOGRAPHY

Maslow, A. H. *The farther reaches of human nature.* New York: Viking Press, 1971. In many ways Maslow's best book. A collection of articles on psychological health, creativeness, values, education, society, metamotivation, and transcendence; also, a complete bibliography of Maslow's writings.

———. *Toward a psychology of being.* New York: Van Nostrand, 1968. Maslow's most popular and widely available book. It includes material on deficiency versus being, growth psychology, creativity, and values.

———. *Motivation and personality.* New York: Harper & Row, 1970. A psychology textbook that provides a more technical treatment of Maslow's work. Chapters dealing with motivation theory, the need hierarchy, and self-actualization.

REFERENCES

Benedict, R. Synergy: Patterns of the good culture. *American Anthropologist,* 1970, *72,* 320–333.

Fadiman, J. The transpersonal stance. In Walsh & Vaughan (Eds.), *Beyond ego.* Los Angeles: Tarcher, 1980.

Goble, F. *The third force: The psychology of Abraham Maslow.* New York: Pocket Books, 1971.

Goldstein, K. *The organism.* New York: American Book, 1939.

———. *Human nature in the light of psychopathology.* New York: Schocken Books, 1940.

Grof, S. *Realms of the human unconscious.* New York: Viking Press, 1975.

Hall, M. A conversation with Abraham Maslow. *Psychology Today,* 1968, *2*(2), 34–37, 54–57.

Horner, M. The motive to avoid success and changing aspirations of college women. In J. Bardwick (Ed.), *Readings on the psychology of women.* New York: Harper & Row, 1972, pp. 62–67.

Huxley, A. *The perennial philosophy.* New York: Harper & Row, 1944.

———. *Island.* New York: Bantam Books, 1963.

International Study Project. *Abraham H. Maslow: A memorial volume.* Monterey, Calif.: Brooks/Cole, 1972.

James, W. *The varieties of religious experience.* New York: Random House (Modern Library), 1943.

Journal of Transpersonal Psychology Editorial Staff. An appreciation. *Journal of Transpersonal Psychology,* 1970, *2* (2), iv.

Krippner, S. (Ed.). The plateau experience: A. H. Maslow and others. *Journal of Transpersonal Psychology,* 1972, *4,* 107–120.

Lowry, R. (Ed.). *Dominance, self-esteem, self-actualization: Germinal papers of A. H. Maslow.* Monterey, Calif.: Brooks/Cole, 1973a.

———. *A. H. Maslow: An intellectual portrait.* Monterey, Calif.: Brooks/Cole, 1973b.

Maslow, A. *Higher and Lower Needs. Journal of Psychology,* 1948, *25,* 433-436.

———. *Religions, values and peak experiences.* Columbus: Ohio State University Press, 1964.

————. *Eupsychian management: A journal.* Homewood, Ill.: Irwin, 1965.

————. *The psychology of science: A reconnaisance.* New York: Harper & Row, 1966.

————. *Toward a psychology of being* (2nd ed.). New York: Van Nostrand, .

————. *Motivation and personality* (Rev. ed.). New York: Harper & Row, 1970.

————. *The farther reaches of human nature.* New York: Viking Press, 1971.

Maslow, A. H. with Chiang H. *The healthy personality: Readings.* New York: Van Nostrand, 1969.

Ornstein, R. *The psychology of consciousness.* New York: Viking Press, 1972.

————. *The nature of human consciousness.* New York: Viking Press, 1973.

Smith, H. *Forgotten truth.* New York: Harper & Row, 1976.

Sumner, W. *Folkways.* New York: New American Library, 1940.

Sutich, A. Some considerations regarding transpersonal psychology. *Journal of Transpersonal Psychology,* 1969, *1,* 11–20.

Tart, C. *Altered states of consciousness.* New York: Wiley, 1969.

————. (Ed.). *Transpersonal psychologies.* New York: Harper & Row, 1975.

Timmons, B., & Kamiya, J. The psychology and physiology of meditation and related phenomena: A bibliography. *Journal of Transpersonal Psychology,* 1970, *2,* 41–59.

Timmons, B., & Kanellakos, D. The psychology and physiology of meditation and related phenomena: Bibliography II. *Journal of Transpersonal Psychology,* 1974, *6,* 32–38.

Walsh, R. & Vaughan, F. *Beyond ego: Transpersonal dimensions in psychology.* Los Angeles: Tarcher, 1980.

Wilber, K. *The spectrum of consciousness.* Wheaton, Ill.: Theosophical Publishing, 1977.

————. *The Atman project.* Wheaton, Ill.: Quest, 1980.

PART TWO
INTRODUCTION TO EASTERN THEORIES OF PERSONALITY

The final three chapters of this book are devoted to the theories of personality developed in three Eastern disciplines: Yoga, Zen Buddhism, and Sufism. Thus, Part II represents a broadening of the traditional limits of "personality theory." Because this is the first textbook to treat these disciplines in the context of personality theory, we feel that it is appropriate to discuss their relationship to Western theories and to the orientation of this volume.

CONTEMPORARY CONCERN WITH EASTERN SYSTEMS

There is growing interest in Eastern thought throughout the United States. In a time of continuous questioning of the established views of organized religion, science, and political systems, there is a corresponding search for alternative models of human behavior, models that are based on different observations and lead to alternative conclusions.

The proliferation of teachers, books, and organizations based on various Eastern models is one indication of this concern. A growing number of our own students, friends, and colleagues have devoted themselves to intensive study or practice of an Eastern discipline in search of new values and personal and spiritual growth. Psychology is becoming more of an international field of study, less tied to American and Western European intellectual and philosophical assumptions.

These chapters are included to provide you with the opportunity to consider, evaluate, and, to some extent, experience these additional perspectives on personality in the context of a critical and comparative course within psychology. We have ample evidence of the interest and time that students are already devoting to these questions. Yet the degree of fundamental knowledge of the Eastern traditions is often very low in comparison to the amount of interest or even the amount of time many people are spending in these pursuits.

MORALITY AND VALUES IN EASTERN DISCIPLINES

Yoga, Zen, and Sufism originated from a common need to understand the relationship between religious practice and everyday life. They differ from most Western personality theories in their greater concern with values and moral considerations, and in their stress on the advisability of living in accord with certain spiritual standards. However, all three view morals and values in a practical, even an iconoclastic way. They argue that we should live within a moral code because such a way of life has definite, recognizable, and beneficial effects on our consciousness and overall well-being, not because of any artificial, external considerations about "goodness" or virtue. Each of these traditions stresses the futility and foolishness of valuing external form over inner function.

A Zen story tells of a wandering monk, warming himself in front of a fire he made from a wooden statue of the Buddha. When the local priest comes in, he is horrified at the sacrilege.

"What are you doing?"

"I'm burning this image to extract the *sarira*" (a holy relic found in the ashes of a Buddhist saint).

"How could you possibly get a relic from a statue?"

"Then," replied the monk, "it's just a piece of wood and I'm burning it to keep warm."

These systems, like their Western counterparts in psychology, were derived from careful observations of human experience. They are built on centuries of empirical observations of the psychological and spiritual effects of a variety of ideas, attitudes, behaviors, and exercises.

The central, ethical core of each tradition is based on the personal experiences and insights of their founders. The vitality and importance of these traditions rest on the continual testing, reworking, and modifying of their initial insights to fit new settings, different cultural conditions, and new interpersonal situations. Hinduism, Buddhism, and Islam represent the perspectives of millions of people today in over 100 different countries. They are living realities for their adherents, not academic, scholarly, or impractical abstractions.

TRANSPERSONAL EXPERIENCE

Each of these disciplines is focused on transpersonal growth, or growth beyond the ego and personality. Western psychologists generally discuss growth in terms of strengthening the ego: increased autonomy, self-determination, self-actualization, freedom from neurotic process, and healthy-mindedness.

Angyal describes each of these viewpoints. One centers on personal growth and full development of the personality; the other deals with transpersonal growth, or the tendency to expand the boundaries of the self.

Viewed from one of these vantage points [the full development of the personality] the human being seems to be striving basically to assert and to expand his self-determination. He is an autonomous being, a self-growing entity that asserts itself actively instead of reacting passively like a physical body to the impacts of the surrounding world. This fundamental tendency expresses itself in a striving of the person to consolidate and increase his self-government, in other words, to exercise his freedom and to organize the relevant items of his world out of the autonomous center of government that is his self. This tendency—which I have termed "the trend toward increased autonomy"—expresses itself in spontaneity, self-assertiveness, striving for freedom and for mastery. [Angyal, 1956, pp. 44–45]

Seen from another vantage point, human life reveals a very different basic pattern from the one described above. From this point of view the person appears to seek a place for himself in a larger unit of which he strives to become a part. In the first tendency we see him struggling for centrality in his world, trying to mold, to organize, the objects and events of his world, to bring them under his own jurisdiction and government. In the second tendency he seems rather to surrender himself willingly to seek a home for himself in and to become an organic part of something that he conceives as greater than himself. The super-individual unit of which one feels oneself a part, or wishes to become a part, may be variously formulated according to one's cultural background and personal understanding. [Angyal, 1956, pp. 45–46]

This second tendency would seem to be more applicable to those who have already achieved a certain degree of self-possession, maturity, and self-actualization. The development of a strong autonomous personality and sense of self seems to be a prerequisite for this second type of growth.

Many psychologists and other scientists have been strongly influenced by preconceived ideas and prejudices regarding transpersonal growth and transcendent or religious experiences. The connotations associated with these issues have led some to believe that such topics are more suitable for theologians than psychologists. This bias is strengthened by the fact that virtually the only concepts available to describe transpersonal phenomena come from religious terminology.

As a matter of fact, this identity is so profoundly built into the English language that it is almost impossible to speak of the "spiritual life" (a distasteful phrase to a scientist, and especially to a psychologist) without using the vocabulary of traditional religion. There just isn't any other satisfactory language yet. A trip to the thesaurus will demonstrate this very quickly. This makes an almost insoluble problem for the writer who is intent on demonstrating that the common base for all religions is human, natural, empirical, and that so-called spiritual values are also naturally derivable. But I have available only a theistic language for this "scientific" job. [Maslow, 1964, p. 4n]

Transpersonal experiences have been important, even central, elements of human life throughout history. Most cultures and societies have been profoundly religious; their value systems have supported such experiences and given them worth. However, modern Western society has been somewhat less open to transpersonal phenomena for the past few decades, actually an extremely short span of time in Western history. We should remember that the transpersonal dimension has been of central importance in most societies throughout history.

As a student of personality, it would be as foolish to neglect this sector of consciousness as it would be to ignore psychopathology. It is a reflection on the youth of psychology, not its sophistication, that it has devoted more effort to understanding human illness than human transcendence. The Eastern theories have slowly acquired the tools and concepts necessary to investigate this more elusive and more subjective side of human experience.

The following three chapters present comprehensive and practical theories of personality described in psychologically relevant terms. Each system is deeply concerned with questions of ultimate values, with transpersonal experience, and with the relationship of the individual self to a greater whole. Each theory has received considerable attention in the West and many aspects of these systems are already being applied in different facets of psychology.

The test of these Eastern systems is no different than the evaluations you have made of the Western theories presented thus far. You do not have to become a Buddhist to appreciate or to utilize some of the concepts or perspectives found in Zen; you do not have to become a yogi to practice breathing or relaxation exercises. We hope that you will appreciate the Eastern systems of thought as expansions of your own Western psychological background and take from them whatever tools and insights you find of value.

REFERENCES

Angyal, A. A theoretical model for personality studies. In C. Moustakas (ed.), *The self.* New York: Harper & Row, 1956.

Campbell, Peter, and McMahon, Edwin. Religious type experience in the context of humanistic and transpersonal psychology. *Journal of Transpersonal Psychology* 1974, *6,* 11–17.

Goleman, Daniel. Perspective on psychology, reality, and the study of consciousness. *Journal of Transpersonal Psychology* 1974, *6,* 73–85.

Maslow, Abraham. *Religions, values and peak experiences.* Columbus: Ohio State University Press, 1964.

CHAPTER 12
YOGA AND THE HINDU TRADITION

Yoga has two aspects. First, it encompasses virtually all the religious and ascetic practices of India, including meditation, physical discipline, and devotional chanting. Second, Yoga is a specific school of Indian philosophy systematized by Patanjali and first mentioned in India's ancient Vedas, the world's oldest recorded literature. The roots of Yoga practice undoubtedly go even farther back to Indian prehistory.

Yoga is a Sanskrit word meaning "to join" or "to unite." The goal of Yoga practice is Self-realization, which occurs when consciousness is turned within and united with its source, the Self. Yoga also means method. It embraces the goal of union and the techniques meant to accomplish this end.

In its broadest sense Yoga embraces all systematic disciplines designed to promote self-realization through calming the mind and focusing consciousness on the Self, the immortal, unchanging essence in all people.

HISTORY

The Vedic Period

The Vedas were originally an oral transmission, handed down from teacher to disciple for many centuries. The earliest Vedas date back to 2500 B.C. There are four major sections of the Vedas. The oldest section consists of the Vedic hymns, which include the most sophisticated philosophy. The second section deals with rituals and sacrifices; perfect performance of long and complex rituals was believed essential to ensure good fortune. The third section, on contemplation and inner truth, comprises the forest treatises, written for forest-dwelling ascetics. The last section contains the *Upanishads,* or the *Vedanta,* literally "the end of the Vedas," which discuss the goal of knowing the Self. The Vedas form the basis of all subsequent Indian thought and philosophy.

Lead me from the unreal to the real. From darkness lead me to light. From death lead me to immortality. [*Brihadaranyaka Upanishad,* I, iii, 28]

In the Vedic period Yoga was closely related to shamanism (Eliade, 1969). Early yogis placed great value on ecstatic trance and the development of supernatural powers through the practice of severe austerities. They believed that individuals could literally compel the Hindu gods to fulfill their requests through superhuman self-discipline and self-mortification. The exercise of austerities and self-control has remained a major part of Yoga practice to this day.

The Bhagavad-Gita

The *Bhagavad-Gita* is the first and perhaps the finest treatise on Yoga. The *Gita* is a part of the great Indian epic *Mahabharata,* which is the story of the five Pandava brothers, their upbringing, education, and many adventures. The *Gita* can be read as a single great metaphor for an individual's spiritual quest. The characters in the *Gita* represent various psychological and physical qualities. The five brothers are the five senses and the battlefield is the body and the consciousness of the individual.

The *Bhagavad-Gita* is a dialogue between Arjuna (the ego) and Krishna (the Self). Arjuna is a warrior, and Krishna, his charioteer, is an incarnation of God and a great spiritual teacher. Krishna discusses duty and the Yoga of action. He teaches Arjuna the importance of devotion, self-control, meditation, and other yogic practices to serve as an example for others. As charioteer, Krishna symbolizes the *guru*, or spiritual teacher, who can bring students face to face with the problems they must solve, the conflicts they must face in spiritual development. However, the guru, like the charioteer, cannot fight the students' battles for them.

> He who works not for an earthly reward, but does the work to be done . . . he is a Yogi.
> [*Bhagavad-Gita*, VI, 1][1]

MAJOR CONCEPTS

Spirit

In Yoga philosophy Spirit *(Purusha)* is pure consciousness. Spirit knows no limitations or qualifications. Spirit includes consciousness within and beyond the universe; the manifestation of Spirit in the individual is the Self. The Self is changeless, unaffected by physical or mental activity; however, the mind distorts our *awareness* of the Self.

Self is Spirit in essence. The Self is like a wave, a form that the ocean takes on for a time. The Vedas teach that only Spirit exists, that we *are* the Self and we *have* a mind and a body. However, most of us believe just the reverse—that we *are* a mind and a body, and that we might have a soul or Self. Through the discipline of Yoga the individual can correct this delusion.

> The whole universe is filled by the Purusha (Spirit), to whom there is nothing superior, from whom there is nothing different, than whom there is nothing either smaller or greater; who stands alone, motionless as a tree, established in His own glory.
> [*Svetasvatara Upanishad*, III, 9]

The classic treatise on Yoga, the *Yoga Sutras* of Patanjali, describes Spirit as consciousness. Other scriptures add two fundamental characteristics: eternal existence and endless bliss; that is, Spirit is the most enjoyable state of consciousness imaginable—eternal, ever new bliss. The Self shares these characteristics, although we are fated to remain unaware of them until we attain self-realization.

The ideal of Yoga is to seek joy from its source—the Self within. One Indian parable concerns the musk deer, whose musk glands become active when the mature deer enters the mating season. The deer is often so taken with this entrancing scent that it begins to run through the forest, seeking the source of the odor. The frenzied deer may lose all sense of direction and become entangled in underbrush or even plunge off a cliff. Frantically seeking the musk without, the deer will never discover the source of the odor—within itself.

> Everyone is the Self and, indeed, is infinite. Yet each person mistakes his body for his Self.
> [Ramana Maharshi, in Osbourne, 1962, p. 23]

[1]Quotes from the *Bhagavad-Gita* are taken from Mascaro (1962), and Prabhavananda Isherwood (1951).

To the seer, all things have verily become the Self: what delusion, what sorrow, can there be for him who beholds that oneness? [*Isa Upanishad,* 7]

One authority writes that Spirit is not limited either by form or formlessness. "God, though without form, is with form too; He has the power to take any form according to the wish of the devotee. The yogi who wants to meditate on a form, may choose any form he likes, concentrate on it, and solve his problem" (Purohit, 1938, pp. 37–38). In other words, the individual can concentrate on Spirit represented by a certain form and certain qualities, such as beauty, love, strength, or wisdom.

Those who are devotional often choose to worship God with form, a God they can visualize and represent with images and concrete symbols. Others prefer to believe in formless Spirit, to conceive of Spirit more abstractly, as pure light or love or cosmic consciousness. The great Indian yogi Ramakrishna counseled a disciple: "It is enough to have faith in either aspect. You believe in God without form; that is quite all right. But never for a moment think that this alone is true and all else false. Remember that God with form is just as true as God without form. But hold fast to your own conviction" (Nikhilananda, 1948, pp. 61–62).

Three Principles of Creation

Nature is created by, and always consists of, three principles, the three *gunas: tamas* (inertia), *rajas* (activity), and *sattva* (clarity or light). These three principles form the basic aspects of creation, which function today to generate all activity. All conceivable manifestations of nature (matter, thought, and so forth) are composed of the three *gunas.*

In the process of creating a statue, for example, *tamas* can be seen in the untouched, inert stone. *Rajas* is the act of carving, and *sattva* is the image in the sculptor's imagination. All three are essential. Pure *tamas* alone is inert, dead matter. Pure *rajas* is energy without direction or goal. Pure *sattva* is a plan that remains unrealized.

Every individual exhibits some balance among these three qualities, although most are dominated by one of them. *Sattva* is considered the most spiritual. Virtually everything can be classified in terms of the *gunas.* Rich or heavy foods are tamasic because they are difficult to digest and cause laziness or sleepiness. Spicy, hot foods are rajasic as they lead to activity, strong emotions, or nervousness. Fresh fruit and vegetables are sattvic and promote calmness. Certain places, such as mountains and the ocean shore, are sattvic and thus suitable for spiritual practice.

Consciousness

In Yoga terminology, Mind *(chitta)* embraces all thought processes. For Patanjali, Yoga is control of the mind or thought waves. This stops the incessant "chatter" of mental activity and brings about a state of deep calm and inner peace. The individual's mind, when calm, clearly reflects the Self. When mental processes or waves of consciousness are active, the Self is obscured, like a bright light suspended in churning water.

All Yoga practices work toward one end: to quiet the waves and calm the mind. Some schools of Yoga focus on control of the body and others on breathing techniques; still others teach meditation practices. In a sense all of the Yoga techniques and practices are only preliminary exercises designed to still the mind. Once mind and body are calm and disciplined, awareness of the Self is possible.

> The mind is like a miraculous rubber band that can be expanded to infinity without breaking. [Yogananda, 1968a]

Karma

Karma means action and also its results. Every activity brings with it certain consequences, and every individual's life is influenced by past actions. This influence occurs in part through the creation of subconscious tendencies in the following sequence:

subconscious tendencies → waves of consciousness → actions → subconscious tendencies

> Before you act, you have freedom, but after you act, the effect of that action will follow you whether you want it to or not. That is the law of *karma*. You are a free agent, but when you perform a certain act, you will reap the results of that act. [Yogananda, 1968b]

In order to avoid the formation of new subconscious tendencies or the strengthening of old ones, the yogi refrains from "acting out." In other words, anger tendencies are strengthened by angry thoughts and feelings and reinforced further by angry speech and actions. The yogic ideal is not supression of unacceptable tendencies, but transmutation of negative action and thought into positive action and thought. One effective way of dealing with strong emotions is to look calmly and deeply at their roots. Inner awareness can transform subsequent thoughts and feelings. Through self-discipline, right action, and Yoga practice, the individual gradually changes his or her consciousness, transmuting old habits and thought patterns.

Subconscious Tendencies

Control of the waves of consciousness is only possible when the subconscious tendencies are diminished. Such tendencies *(samskaras)* shape mental activity. These subconscious habit patterns are created by past actions and experiences, from this life and from past lives. Tendencies are built up by the continued action of thought waves or waves of consciousness. For example, anger waves of consciousness gradually create anger tendencies, which predispose the individual to angry reactions.

> You cannot achieve emancipation unless you have burned the seeds of past actions in the fires of wisdom and meditation. [Yogananda, 1968a, p. 110]

The discipline of Yoga must include a *complete* reformation of consciousness. Otherwise the subconscious tendencies eventually will seek to actualize themselves, sprouting suddenly like dormant seeds. Through meditation, self-analysis, and other powerful inner disciplines, it is possible to "roast" such seeds, to destroy their potential for further activity; that is, through fundamental inner change we can grow free of the influence of the past.

Schools of Yoga

Several major schools of Yoga developed in India. These suit different personalities. *Karma-yoga,* the yoga of action, especially suits those with a strong will or those who need to develop their will as their next stage of growth. It is also chosen by those who hold service to others as a central ideal. *Jnana-yoga,* the yoga of knowledge, suits those with keen minds and provides an essential discipline for those who need to develop discrimination. *Bhakti-yoga,* the yoga of devotion, is ideal for those with a strong emotional nature. *Hatha-yoga* is for those with strong self-discipline and interest in developing physical mastery. *Kundalini-yoga* generally involves meditative techniques most suited to those with potential for subtle awareness of inner processes. *Raja-yoga* fits those with potential for deep concentration and mental control.

A sophisticated teacher may prescribe a particular form of yoga practice that builds on a disciple's strengths or assign a specific practice that calls forth underdeveloped attributes. Less sophisticated teachers simply will assign their own practices, without considering individual differences.

> My own temperament is principally devotional. It was disconcerting at first to find that my guru, saturated with *jnana* but seemingly dry of *bhakti,* expressed himself chiefly in terms of cold spiritual mathematics. But, as I attuned myself to his nature, I discovered no diminution but rather an increase in my devotional approach to God. A Self-realized master is fully able to guide his various disciples along the natural lines of their essential bias. [Yogananda, 1972, p. 145]

Karma-Yoga, the Yoga of Action

Everything we do, physical or mental, is karma, and it leaves its marks on us. [Vivekananda, 1978b, pp. 3–4]

Karma-yoga teaches us to act selflessly, without attachment to gain or loss, success or failure. The karma-yogi seeks to serve others as well as high ideals. This is a tremendous discipline to learn to overcome our selfishness, laziness, and pride.

Swami Vivekananda writes:

> This is the one central idea in the *Gita:* Work incessantly, but be not attached to it. . . . God is unattached because He loves; that real love makes us unattached. . . . To attain this nonattachment is almost a life work. But as soon as we have reached this point we have attained the goal of love and become free. [Vivekananda, 1978b, pp. 38, 45–46]

Offer all thy works to God, throw off selfish bonds, and do thy work. No sin can then stain thee, even as waters do not stain the leaf of the lotus. [*Bhagavad-Gita,* V, 10]

Karma-yoga can be an important discipline for everyone—for those who live in secluded caves in the Himalayas as well as for those who have jobs and families. As long as we are alive we must act. We all can learn to act well.

> Karma in its effect on character is the most tremendous power that man has to deal with. Man is as it were a centre, and is attracting all the powers of the universe towards himself, and in this center is fusing them all and again sending them off in a big current. [Vivekananda, 1978b, p. 5]

The practitioner of karma-yoga need not believe in a particular religious doctrine, or even in God or Spirit. The karma-yogi is transformed by developing selflessness through service rather than through ostensibly religious discipline.

Jnana-Yoga, the Yoga of Knowledge

The yoga of knowledge is a discipline of rigorous Self-analysis, a path for those endowed with a clear, refined intellect. It is basically a path of discrimination. The jnana-yogi seeks to understand the forces of delusion and bondage, and to counter or avoid the influences of passion, sense attachment, and identification with the body.

This yogi is a true philosopher, a deep spiritual thinker who wants to go beyond the visible, beyond the little things of this world. "Not even the teaching of thousands of books will satisfy him. Not even all the sciences will satisfy him; at the best, they only bring this little world before him. . . . His very soul wants to go beyond all that into the very heart of Being, by seeing Reality as It is; by realizing It, by being It, by becoming one with that Universal Being" (Vivekananda, 1976, p. 395).

The individual seeks the Self by discarding, through intelligent discrimination, all that is not the Self, all that is limiting, perishable, or illusory.

Ramana Maharshi is regarded by many as India's greatest modern sage and exemplar of jnana-yoga. He taught his followers a technique called "Self-Inquiry" for regaining identification with the Self. It is a method of continuously inquiring "Who am I?" and looking beyond the body, the thoughts, and emotions for the source of consciousness. Some of the flavor of this approach can be seen in Maharshi's responses to questions.

> Self-scrutiny, relentless observance of one's thoughts, is a stark and shattering experience. It pulverizes the stoutest ego. But, true self-analysis mathematically operates to produce seers. [Yogananda, 1972, p. 51]

> *"How is one to realize the Self?"*
> *"Whose Self? Find out."*
> *"Mine; but, who am I?"*
> *"It is you who must find out."*
> *"I don't know."*
> *"Just think over the question, Who is it that says: 'I don't know?' Who is the 'I' in your statement? What is not known?"*

> *"Why was I born?"*
> *"Who was born? The answer is the same to all your questions."*

> *"However much I may try, I do not seem to catch the 'I.' It is not even clearly discernible."*
> *"Who is it that says that the 'I' is not discernible? Are there two*

'I's' in you, that one is not discernible to the other?" [Osbourne, 1962, pp. 121–122]

Ramana Maharshi stressed self-realization as a task of removing delusive understanding, not a matter of acquiring something new. "Once the false notion 'I am the body' or 'I am not realized' has been removed, Supreme Consciousness or the Self alone remains and in people's present state of knowledge they call this 'Realization.' But the truth is that Realization is eternal and already exists, here and now" (Osbourne, 1962, p. 23).

The first and foremost of all the thoughts that arise in the mind is the primal "I"-thought. It is only after the rise of origin of the "I"-thought that innumerable other thoughts arise. . . . Since every other thought can occur only after the rise of the "I"-thought and since the mind is nothing but a bundle of thoughts, it is only through the enquiry "Who am I?" that the mind subsides. . . . Even when extraneous thoughts sprout up during

Figure 12.1 A jnana yoga model of the Self and consciousness. (Adapted from Osbourne, 1969, pp. 23–24)

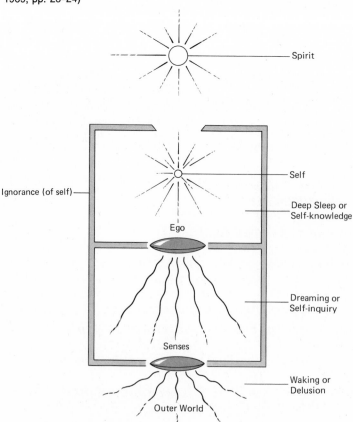

such enquiry, do not seek to complete the rising thought, but instead, deeply enquire within, "To whom has this thought occurred?" No matter how many thoughts thus occur to you, if you would with acute vigilance enquire immediately as and when each individual thought arises to whom it has occurred, you would find it is to "me." If then you enquire "Who am I?" the mind gets introverted [focused within] and the rising thought also subsides. In this manner as you persevere more and more in the practice of Self-enquiry, the mind acquires increasing strength and power to abide in its Source. [Osbourne, 1969, p. 41]

> By steady and continuous investigation into the nature of the mind, the mind is transformed into that to which "I" refers; and that is in fact the Self. [Ramana Maharshi in Osbourne, 1962, p. 113]

Bhakti-Yoga, the Yoga of Devotion

In contrast to self-discipline, will, or discrimination, bhakti-yoga is a way of reforming one's personality through the development of love and devotion. Its proponents argue that this simple path is most suitable to the modern era, when few people have time and discipline to pursue fully the other traditional paths of yoga.

Followers of bhakti-yoga use intense devotion to concentrate the mind and transform the personality. It is easier for most people to love God personified in human form than to love abstract spirit or consciousness. The practice of devotional yoga is closer to traditional religions than any other form of yoga. It includes ritual worship, chanting, and the worship of God. The great incarnations of God, such as Rama and Krishna, are a common focus of devotion in some parts of India, and Kali, or the Divine Mother, in others.

> If you must be mad, be it not for the things of the world. Be mad with the love of God. [Ramakrishna, 1965, p. 187]

Long sessions of spiritual chanting typically form an important part of traditional Indian religious practice as well as a basic bhakti-yoga practice. Chants are often simple and repetitive, inspiring concentration on one aspect of the Divine. Chanting practices can also help channel emotions, develop single-pointed concentration, and energize mind and body. A spiritual chant is "a song born out of the depths of true devotion to God and continuously chanted, audibly or mentally, until response is consciously received from Him in the form of boundless joy" (Yogananda, 1963, p. xiii).

> He is the nearest of the near, the dearest of the dear. Love Him as a miser loves money, as an ardent man loves his sweetheart, as a drowning person loves breath. When you yearn for God with intensity, He will come to you. [Yogananda, 1968a, p. 1]

Hatha-Yoga, the Yoga of the Body

The practices of hatha-yoga are designed to purify and strengthen the body for advanced meditation and higher states of consciousness. The body is seen as a vehicle for vital energies, or *pranas*. Hatha-yoga disciplines strengthen these energies and bring control of them, enhancing physical, mental, and spiritual functioning. According to yoga physiology, all functions require vital energy. The more energy that is available, the healthier and more effective is the individual.

Practice of yoga postures is only part of hatha-yoga. In fact, most hatha-yoga taught in the United States is more a form of gymnastics for physical health than a complete system of Yoga. In addition to postures, classical hatha-yoga includes the practice of strict celibacy, vege-

> When the flower develops into fruit, the petals drop off of themselves. So, when the divinity in you increases, the weakness of human nature in you will vanish of its own accord. [Ramakrishna, 1965, p. 139]

tarian diet, breathing and concentration exercises, and techniques for washing and cleansing the nasal passages and the entire alimentary canal from the throat to the intestines.

The discipline of hatha-yoga includes physical, psychological, and spiritual aspects. Through hatha-yoga practice it is possible to develop great mental and physical abilities. However, without mental and spiritual discipline, these abilities can be used to feed the ego. One authority commented that the followers of hatha-yoga he had met "had great powers, strong healthy bodies and immense vanity . . . some more worldly than average worldly men" (Purohit, 1938, p. 30). One of the authors met a yogi of this type in India. The yogi had been a subject of considerable physiological research, demonstrating extraordinary control over his brain waves, heartbeat, and other bodily functions. However, at a major conference on yoga, the man insisted on challenging all the other yogis present to demonstrate "scientifically" their mastery of yoga and to determine who was the "greatest yogi."

Kundalini-Yoga

According to yoga physiology, a subtle energy known as kundalini lies coiled at the base of the spine. All energies of mind and body are manifestations of kundalini energy, which can be consciously controlled by an accomplished yogi.

This energy is generally latent. It begins to flow freely as a result of the disciplines of kundalini-yoga. They include meditation, visualization, breathing exercises, and the purification techniques of hatha-yoga. Once fully active, kundalini energy rises through all the levels of consciousness, leading to major physical, psychological, and spiritual changes in the individual.

When a person's mind and body are sufficiently strengthened and purified, kundalini is said to travel up the spine through six consciousness centers (chakras), reaching the seventh, the center of the brain. As it reaches the higher centers, this spiritual energy produces various degrees of illumination. Each center is associated with different physical and spiritual attributes; some are related to various senses and elements, and some to other qualities, such as form or color.

1. The *muladhara chakra* is located at the base of the spinal column. It is associated with the element earth, inertia, the birth of sound, and the sense of smell.[2]
2. The *svadisthana chakra* is situated several inches above the first center. It is associated with the element water, the color white, and the sense of taste.
3. The *manipura chakra* is located at the level of the navel. It

[2]The descriptions of the *chakras* are taken from Eliade (1969).

is related to the element fire, the sun, and the sense of sight.

4. The *anahata chakra* is located at the level of the heart. It is associated with the color red, the element air, and the sense of touch.

5. The *vishuddha chakra* is located in the region of the throat. It is associated with the element ether, the color white, and sound.

6. The *ajna chakra* is situated between the eyebrows. It is the seat of cognitive faculties and the subtle senses.

7. The *sahasrara chakra* is located at the top of the head. It is known as the chakra of the thousand-petaled lotus.

The seventh center includes the brain. When the brain is stimulated and energized by kundalini, the individual experiences a tremendous change in consciousness, an experience of deep illumination, or *samadhi,* "the blossoming of the thousand-petaled lotus."

Raja-Yoga

Raja-yoga ("royal" yoga) emphasizes the development of mental control as the most effective and efficient discipline. It has been called "psychological yoga." Some consider it a combination of all the schools of Yoga. Others see raja-yoga as but one of the major Yoga schools.

Figure 12.2 The centers of consciousness in the body. (From Danielou, 1955, p. ii)

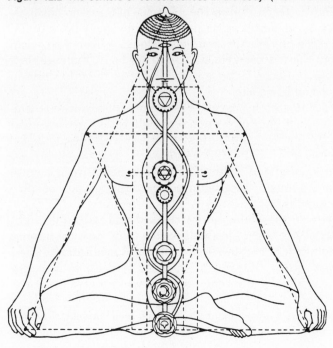

The classic Yoga discipline outlined in the *Yoga Sutras* of Patanjali is designed to transform and purify the body and to direct systematically the energy flow within it. This path is systematized by Patanjali in eight limbs of yoga: (1) abstentions, (2) observances, (3) postures, (4) vital energy control, (5) interiorization, (6) concentration, (7) meditation, (8) illumination.

They can be thought of as successive levels of achievement, each limb building upon the one that precedes it. However, the eight limbs are closely interrelated branches of a single discipline, and improvement in one branch tends to benefit the others.

The *abstentions* and *observances* are the moral code that serves as the foundation for yoga practice. Abstentions include nonviolence, truthfulness, nonstealing, chastity, and nongreed. The observances are purity, austerity, contentment, study, and devotion. They are the yogic equivalent of the Ten Commandments, the principles of right action found in all religions. The abstentions and observances are not an arbitrary system of morality. They are followed for practical reasons to strengthen the effectiveness of the rest of yoga practice. Without a calm and disciplined daily life, the concentration and peace gained from yoga practice is soon dissipated, like water carried in a pail full of holes.

It is impossible to progress without developing abstentions and observances. However, we cannot expect to master them at first. Nonviolence and truthfulness, for example, are profound disciplines.

The *Yoga Sutras* teach that in the presence of one who has mastered nonviolence, no violence can occur. This is obviously not a beginning level. The seeds of violence in us—arrogance, anger, rage—can be removed so that there is not a violent cell in our body. Violence then cannot arise in our presence because the violence in the other person doesn't find a hook to hang on.

There is depth to abstentions and observances. They are not simple early stages and not like conventional morality; they are practical principles in harmony with a life that is consistent with the consciousness that yoga aims at.

Purification of mind and body also prepares the entire system to handle the higher "voltage," the greater power of the full flow of spiritual energy in samadhi.

Posture refers to the ability to sit relaxed and with a straight spine for long periods of time. Patanjali writes that "posture implies steadiness and comfort. It requires relaxation and meditation on the Immovable" (*Yoga Sutras,* II, 46–47).[3] In India students of Yoga attempt to increase gradually the time they can sit in a given posture.

It is not your passing inspirations or brilliant ideas so much as your everyday mental habits that control your life. [Yogananda, 1968b]

A master bestows the divine experience of cosmic consciousness when his disciple, by meditation, has strengthened his mind to a degree where the vast vistas would not overwhelm him. Mere intellectual willingness or open-mindedness is not enough. Only adequate enlargement of consciousness by yoga practice and devotional *bhakti* can prepare one to absorb the liberating shock of omnipresence. [Yogananda, 1973, pp. 169–170]

---

[3]Quotes from the *Yoga Sutras* of Patanjali are taken from Purohit (1938).

The student masters a posture upon being able to hold that pose for three hours without stirring.

Control of vital energy is the most unique and most fundamental aspect of yoga. The original Sanskrit term *pranayama* is often mistranslated as breath control. Breathing exercises can slow the metabolism and free vital energy; however, this is only an indirect means of controlling vital energy.

The goal is complete mastery over vital energy. It can be attained through various yoga practices. Accomplished yogis have demonstrated this mastery by stopping their heartbeat or their breathing at will, and in the past some yogis have buried themselves alive for days or weeks (see, for example, Yogananda, 1972). Modern physiological studies have confirmed the ability of practicing yogis to control their heartbeat and to achieve breathlessness. (For a detailed bibliography of research on Yoga and various forms of meditation, see Timmons & Kamiya, 1970; Timmons & Kanellakos, 1974.)

Interiorization refers to the shutting off of the senses. Vital energy is withdrawn from the sense organs and the yogi is no longer distracted by ceaseless bombardment of outer stimuli. This has been verified by Indian scientists who found that brain waves of meditating yogis are unaffected by outside stimuli (Anand et al., 1969). Patanjali defines interiorization as "the Restoration of sense to the original purity of mind, by renouncing its objects" (*Yoga Sutras,* II, 54).

When we sit still, the outward rush of consciousness begins to slow. We learn then to slow down our breathing and to quiet our minds. Interiorization means that consciousness stops flowing out through our senses into the world. We begin to become aware of the source within as the energy flow turns back to the spine and brain.

Concentration is "attention fixed upon an object" (*Yoga Sutras,* III, 1). There are two aspects of concentration: the *withdrawal* of the attention from objects of distraction and the *focusing* of attention upon one thing at a time. Concentration is a relaxed state, not a struggle or forcing of attention. Some development of interiorization must precede the practice of concentration. When all five senses are active, it is like trying to concentrate with five telephones constantly ringing. External sensations bring thoughts that in turn lead to endless trains of memories and speculations. The sound of a car leads us to think, "Oh, there is a car going by." Then we think about cars we once owned, cars we would like to buy, and so forth.

Meditation is a term used loosely in the West. In yogic terminology meditation is a highly advanced practice in which only a single thought, the object of meditation alone, remains in the consciousness of the meditator. The mind is fully concentrated, completely one-pointed. (See Figure 12.3.)

It is thought which is the propelling force in us. Fill the mind with the highest thoughts, hear them day after day, think them month after month. . . .
[Vivekananda, 1976, pp. 141–142]

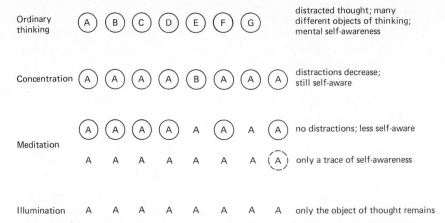

Figure 12.3 Thought processes in yoga practice. The circles indicate self-awareness. (Adapted from Taimni, 1967, p. 284)

Illumination (samadhi) is, in a sense, the essence of Yoga practice. It is the state that defines Yoga, and only those who have attained illumination can be regarded as true yogis. All others are students of Yoga. According to Patanjali, illumination is a state where "union as union disappears, only the meaning of the object on which the attention is fixed being present" (*Yoga Sutras,* III, 3).

Realization of the Self occurs once the mind is totally calm and concentrated, reflecting the qualities of the Self within. As the Self is infinite, illumination is not a final or static state. It includes innumerable levels of awareness of the Self and of Spirit. Patanjali distinguishes two major types of illumination: illumination with and without contents in the field of consciousness. The contents in the field of consciousness become more and more subtle as meditation deepens. They progress from consciousness of a thought form, such as the image of a deity, to consciousness of abstract ideas, such as love. Eventually, there exists only consciousness of deep joy or peace, and finally, all that remains is consciousness of the Self.

Illumination without content defies description, as there is nothing in the field of consciousness to which words refer. Those who have reached this stage are said to have become totally free of the influences of karma and of their subconscious tendencies.

DYNAMICS

Psychological Growth
Four Stages of Life
The yogic way of life best known in the West is that of ascetic renunciation, including celibacy, poverty, and "giving up" the world to devote oneself completely to the disciplines of Yoga. In India there is another

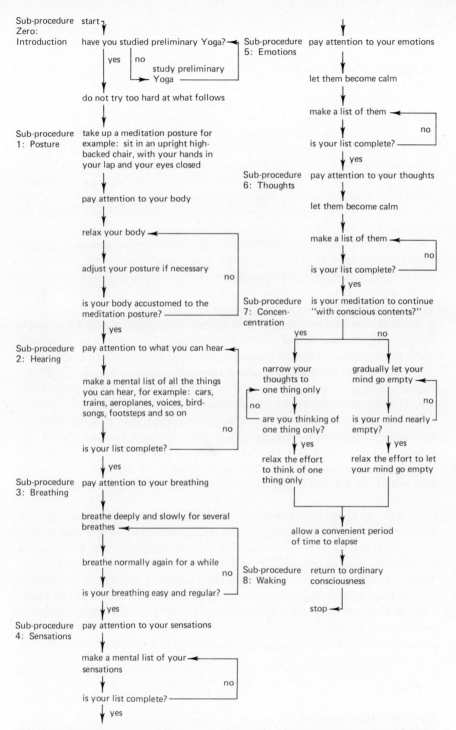

Figure 12.4 The Flow of Meditation. Instructions in the "Yoga Aphorisms of Patanjali" formalized by Dr. John H. Clark of Manchester University in a flow diagram of the type prepared for computers. (Adapted from Dr. Clark's article in *New Society* magazine [23 July 1970])

ideal path of spiritual growth, that of a balanced life of worldly service and responsibilities plus the practice of spiritual discipline.[4]

There are four stages in this idealized Indian life cycle: student, householder, forest dweller, and renunciant (Smith, 1958). According to traditional Indian conceptions, each stage should last 25 years, as the normal life-span was said to be 100 years in the more highly developed past ages.

In many classic Indian works, it is emphasized that an individual must pass through all four stages to achieve self-realization. Each stage has its own duties, and each provides certain essential lessons and experiences.

During the first stage, the student traditionally serves as an apprentice, living with a teacher and the teacher's family. In addition to the acquisition of occupational skills, the traditional Indian education is devoted to character building through emotional and spiritual discipline. The goal is to become a mature individual, fully equipped to live a harmonious and productive life, rather than remain a slave to one's moods, habits, and drives.

At the completion of this stage, the apprentice returns home and, after marrying, enters the stage of the householder. The duties of the householder include carrying on the family business and raising a family. The householder seeks satisfaction in family pleasures, in achieving vocational success, and in serving the community as an active, responsible citizen. The householder is able to live a self-controlled life because of the character training received during the first stage. He or she is not compulsively motivated by desires for sex, fame, or wealth but is able to enjoy the pleasures and duties of the householder in a moderate way.

> If you run after the world the world will run from you. If you run from the world, it will run after you. [Hari Dass]

The third stage is literally that of the forest dweller. It refers to gradual retirement from family and occupational affairs. When a man and his wife are over 50 years of age, their children have become old enough to assume the family responsibilities. The older couple might retire to a small, secluded cottage in the forest or remain in the family house after withdrawing from all duties and affairs. They remain available to the rest of the family, consulting with and advising their children when needed.

The individual's last quarter century is to be devoted to the fourth

---

[4]The Vedas describe various types of ascetics who practiced austerities and other yogic disciplines and were most likely the forerunners of the wandering yogic ascetics of modern India. The ancient *rishis,* or sages, on the other hand, emphasized the importance of sacrifices and hymns and were more a part of the Indian social order. (For a fuller discussion, see Feuerstein & Miller, 1972).

stage, renunciation. Entrance into this stage is marked by a ritual closely resembling funeral rites. The individual is now officially dead to all social obligations and personal ties, and free to pursue self-realization without external demands or restrictions.

Self-Realization

The details of spiritual growth and development vary with different branches of Yoga. For the karma-yogi, growth involves the development of self-discipline, willpower, and selfless service. For the bhakti-yogi, growth is most closely related to an increase in devotion to an aspect of God. For the jnana-yogi, growth is a matter of development of discrimination and self-analysis. In various other schools of Yoga, growth is viewed in terms of development of the ability to meditate, to withdraw one's attention from the world and the senses, and to concentrate more and more deeply on some aspect of Self or Spirit.

All of the diverse branches of Yoga share certain fundamental principles. The path of yoga is basically a process of turning the consciousness away from the activities of the external world back to the source of consciousness—the Self. The karma-yogi seeks to act with self-awareness without becoming overinvolved in the action itself or in the possible results of action. The bhakti-yogi endeavors to keep the mind devotionally focused on a person or representation that symbolizes an aspect of Spirit or Self. The jnana-yogi seeks the Self by bringing the mind back to the roots of thought and rejecting all that is not Self.

Ramakrishna, the great devotional yogi, wrote: "The secret is that the union with God (Yoga) can never happen unless the mind is rendered absolutely calm, whatever be the 'path' you follow for God-realization. The mind is always under the control of the Yogi, and not the Yogi under the control of his mind" (Ramakrishna, 1965, p. 186).

As we mentioned, yoga literally means "union," union with the Self, or illumination. One classic commentary by Vyasa on Patanjali's *Yoga Sutras* states that yoga *is* illumination. All the various paths and disciplines included in Yoga share this fundamental goal of illumination and self-realization.

> The wise man beholds all beings in the Self, and the Self in all beings. [Isa Upanishad, 6]

Obstacles to Growth

Patanjali lists five major afflictions or causes of suffering: ignorance, egoism, desire, aversion, and fear (*Yoga Sutras*, II, p. 3).

The afflictions are gradually weakened by Yoga disciplines, especially austerity and self-control, scriptural study, and devotion. The yogi gradually strengthens subconscious tendencies that oppose the afflictions, weakening their influence. Afflictions have two aspects: gross and subtle. In their gross forms the afflictions are actual thought waves (of fear, desires, and so forth). In their finer aspects the afflictions are subconscious tendencies (toward fear, desires, and so forth) that remain until the attainment of illumination.

Ignorance

Ignorance is the major obstacle to growth. "Ignorance is the cause, the others are the effects. . . . Ignorance thinks of the perishable as imperishable, of the pure as impure, of the painful as pleasurable, of the non-Self as Self" (*Yoga Sutras,* II, pp. 4–5). Consciousness is projected outward from the Self with such great force that it is extremely difficult to direct the mind back to its source. Concern with the external world and with continually active senses has replaced self-awareness. Ignorance is mistaking the effect for the cause; that is, attributing the qualities of the Self to the world by treating the world as the source of experience and remaining unaware of the Self as the ultimate cause.

Egoism

Egoism results from the identification of the Self with the body and the thoughts. "Egoism is the identification of the Seer with the limitations of the eye" (*Yoga Sutras,* II, p. 6). Identification with the body leads to fear, desire, and a sense of limitation, and identification with the thoughts leads to restlessness and emotionality.

Desire and Aversion

Satisfying the sensory desires cannot satisfy you, because you are not the senses. They are only your servants, not your Self. [Yogananda, 1968a, p. 60]

Desire and aversion are defined by Patanjali simply and elegantly: "Desire is longing for pleasure. Aversion is recoiling from pain" (*Yoga Sutras,* II, pp. 7–8). These afflictions tie the individual to the constant change and fluctuation of the external world, and they make deep calmness or peace impossible. One major aim of Yoga discipline is to overcome our tremendous sensitivity to pain, pleasure, success, failure, and other changes in the outer world. The yogi seeks freedom from the domination of the world, learning to be in control of physical, mental, and emotional reactions rather than being controlled by them.

Desire and aversion bring about *attachment* to whatever brings pleasure or avoids pain. Attachment arises from the feeling that we must have something for our own pleasure or fulfillment. Overcoming attachments does not mean, however, that yoga is a negative, joyless self-discipline. The idea of nonattachment means to enjoy whatever one receives, ready to give it up without a sense of loss or sorrow.

Ramakrishna often explained nonattachment through the example of a maidservant who leaves her village to work for a wealthy family in a big city. She may grow to love the children of the family and call them "my little boy" or "my little girl" and say "this is our house." But all the while she knows that they are not her own children, that the house is not her own, and that her real home is far away in a distant village. "I tell those who come to me, to lead a life unattached like the maid-servant. I tell them to live unattached to this world—to be in the world, but not of the world . . ." (Ramakrishna, 1965, p. 104).

A young disciple studying nonattachment was shocked to find his guru relishing a meal of exotic fruits and nuts. His teacher seemed to be deeply attached to the food he was eating, rather than properly unconcerned with what he ate. His master explained that nonattachment does not mean dry, joyless experience of good food or other pleasures; rather, it means to enjoy fully what one has, and not to miss any pleasures when they are no longer available. One who has mastered nonattachment enjoys the present without trying to change it by wishing for more pleasure or less pain.

Fear

Fear is the fifth affliction. "Fear is that constant natural terror of death, that is rooted even in the minds of the learned" (*Yoga Sutras,* II, p. 9). Fear is the result of identification with the perishable body instead of the imperishable Self. In his commentary on the *Yoga Sutras,* Purohit writes: "Fear of death is constant in the mind, and as desire and aversion are the result of some experience in the past, so is the fear of death the result of dying in the past" (1938, p. 48).

> The knowing Self is not born; It does not die. It has not sprung from anything; nothing has sprung from it. Birthless, eternal, everlasting, and ancient, It is not killed when the body is killed. [*Katha Upanishad,* I, ii, 18]

STRUCTURE

Body

Schools of Yoga regard the body in different ways. These attitudes range from outright rejection of the body as the source of desires and attachments to an appreciation of the body as the main vehicle for spiritual growth.

Most Yoga disciplines advocate a moderate approach to the body, neither indulgent nor unduly ascetic. The *Bhagavad-Gita* counsels that "Yoga is a harmony. Not for him who eats too much, or for him who eats too little; not for him who sleeps too little, or for him who sleeps too much" (VI, p. 16).

Social Relationships

Traditionally, yoga has been associated with isolation from the world, involving meditation in the depths of the forests and in caves on remote mountain peaks. However, the *Bhagavad-Gita* teaches that each individual has his or her own duty in this world; and this duty must be carried out fully whether it involves renunciation or service to others within society. "And do thy duty, even if it be humble, rather than another's, even if it be great. To die in one's duty is life: to live in another's is death" (*Bhagavad-Gita,* III, p. 35).

Religious devotion can also be learned through social relationships. In the West we have tended to view God solely as a cosmic father

> Learn to see God in all persons, of whatever race or creed. You will know what divine love is when you begin to feel your oneness with every human being, not before. [Yogananda, 1968b]

figure, but in India the Divine has many faces: parent, child, friend, guru, or beloved. By practicing love and devotion in one's relations with family and friends, the individual learns to expand and spiritualize these feelings, to love others as brothers and sisters.

Will

The earliest forms of yoga involved severe asceticism and tremendous will. The concept of *tapas,* ascetic discipline or austerity, still remains central in much of yoga practice today. Austerity refers to disciplining mind and body, going beyond comfortable limits and overcoming tendencies of self-indulgence and restlessness. Fasting and holding the body motionless in asana and meditation practice are among the most popular austerities in yoga today. Exercise of will also provides yoga students with direct experience of laziness, resistance to discipline, and similar personality traits. One yoga master summarized this attitude of disciplined will: "Daily renewed sense yearnings sap your inner peace. . . . Roam in the world as a lion of self-control; don't let the frogs of sense weakness kick you around!" (Sri Yukteswar, in Yogananda, 1972, p. 149).

> True freedom consists in performing all actions . . . in accordance with right judgments and choice of will, not in being compelled by habits. [Yogananda, 1968b]

Emotions

Patanjali distinguishes between painful and nonpainful waves of consciousness (*Yoga Sutras,* I, p. 5). Painful waves are thoughts and emotions that increase ignorance, confusion, or attachment. They do not always seem unpleasant (pride, for example). Nonpainful waves lead to greater freedom and knowledge. The greatest obstacles to peace are painful waves of consciousness such as anger, desire, and fear. These can be countered by nonpainful waves such as love, generosity, and courage. Cultivation of nonpainful waves creates positive subconscious tendencies that counteract the negative tendencies. However, the goal of yoga is to eventually transcend even the positive emotions (Prabhavananda & Isherwood, 1953). It may seem unnatural to transcend feelings of love and joy, but even the most positive experiences tend to bind us to the world of the senses. We must go beyond that to see the Self.

> The man who sees Brahman [God] abides in Brahman; his reason is steady, gone is his delusion. When pleasure comes he is not shaken, and when pain comes he trembles not. [*Bhagavad Gita,* V, 20]

Another approach to the emotions is to direct their energy to spiritual growth:

> So long as these passions [of anger, lust, and so forth] are directed towards the world and its objects, they behave like enemies. But when they are directed towards God, they become the best friends of man, for then they lead him into God. The lust for the things of the world must be changed into the hankering for God, the anger that man feels in relation to his fellow man should be turned towards God for not revealing Himself to him. One should deal with all the passions in the same manner. These passions cannot be eradicated but can be educated. [Ramakrishna, 1965, p. 138]

Intellect

Intellectual development in yoga is not a matter of acquiring new information but of attaining understanding through experience. In ancient India students studied sacred texts by carefully digesting one stanza at a time.

> Dabru Ballav [a renowned teacher] had gathered his disciples around him in the sylvan solitudes. The holy *Bhagavad-Gita* was open before them. Steadfastly they looked at one passage for half an hour, then closed their eyes. Another half hour slipped away. The master gave a brief comment. Motionless, they meditated again for an hour. Finally the guru spoke.
> "Do you now understand the stanza?"
> "Yes, sir." One in the group ventured this assertion.
> "No, not fully. Seek the spiritual vitality that has given these words the power to rejuvenate India century after century." Another hour passed in silence. [Yogananda, 1972, p. 136]

Through yoga practice the individual develops self-awareness and increased understanding of the world, gradually overcoming restlessness, lack of concentration, and the mental distortion of desires. Scholars who study scriptures without attempting to put them into practice remain trapped in sterile intellectualism. "They consider philosophy to be a gentle setting-up exercise. Their elevated thoughts are carefully unrelated either to the crudity of outward action or to any scourging inner discipline" (Yogananda, 1972, p. 152).

Teacher

The word *guru* comes from the Sanskrit root "to uplift." Many teachers in India are called gurus; the name connotes a spiritual teacher, one who can raise the student's consciousness. (In India, teachers of music, dance, and other traditional skills do more than instruct students in technique; they are considered masters of disciplines that affect one's whole life and character.) A guru is considered essential in Yoga for several reasons. The techniques taught are complex and subtle and easily misunderstood if learned from a book. Also, many techniques have to be adapted by the teacher to the specific physical and mental makeup of the students.

The guru is also a disciplinarian, who pushes the student beyond self-imposed limitations. As one who has been through the discipline already, the guru knows through experience the extent of human capacity. Thus the guru is able to demand that students exert themselves to the limits of their capabilities. In addition, students are inspired by their teacher's living example to realize their highest potential.

There is a beautiful example of the role of the guru found in the *Bhagavad-Gita.* In the great battle Krishna, the guru, is Arjuna's charioteer. Krishna does not fight but leads Arjuna from battle to battle,

Do not confuse understanding with a larger vocabulary. . . . Sacred writings are beneficial in stimulating desire for inward realization, if one stanza at a time is slowly assimilated. Otherwise, continual intellectual study may result in vanity, false satisfaction, and undigested knowledge. [Yogananda, 1972]

Religion, which is the highest knowledge and the highest wisdom, cannot be bought, nor can it be acquired from books. . . . You will not find it anywhere until your heart is ready for receiving it and your teacher has come. [Vivekananda, 1978a, pp. 35–36]

testing and strengthening his disciple. At one point a great enemy warrior throws a magic spear that is enchanted to pass through all obstacles. Knowing that Arjuna cannot cope with this weapon, Krishna causes the wheels of the chariot to sink deep into the ground, and the dreaded missile passes overhead. Similarly, the guru brings the disciple from spiritual trial to spiritual trial, only intervening when the test is too great for the disciple's capabilities.

"Gurus can be had by hundreds and thousands, but Chelas (disciples) there is not one" is an ancient saying. It means that many are the persons who can give good advice, but those who follow it are few. [Ramakrishna, 1965, p. 328]

The guru also fosters the student's emotional and psychological development. The teacher is like a mirror, exposing faults and limitations of the student, but always remaining conscious of the essential purity and perfection of the Self behind such limitations. This kind of discipline can be administered only by someone who is relatively free of ego and strong personal biases or blind spots, which would distort the guru's reactions to a student.

> The question is often asked, "Why should we look into the character and personality of a teacher? We have only to judge what he says and take that up." This is not right. If a man wants to teach me something of dynamics, or of chemistry, or any other physical science, he may be anything he likes, because what the physical sciences require is merely an intellectual equipment; but in the spiritual sciences it is impossible from first to last that there can be any spiritual light in the soul that is impure. . . . Hence with the teacher of religion we must see first what he *is,* and then what he says. He must be perfectly pure, and then alone comes the value of his words, because he is only then the true "transmitter." What can he transmit, if he has not spiritual power in himself? . . . The function of the teacher is indeed an affair of the transference of something, and not one of mere stimulation of the existing intellectual or other faculties in the taught. Something real and appreciable as an influence comes from the teacher and goes to the taught. Therefore the teacher must be pure.
> . . .
> The teacher must not teach with any ulterior selfish motive—for money, name, or fame; his work must be simply out of love, out of pure love for mankind at large. The only medium through which spiritual force can be transmitted is love. . . . God is love, and only he who has known God as love, can be a teacher of godliness and God to man. [Vivekananda, 1978a, pp. 32–33]

In India the guru's most important attribute is spiritual consciousness. A teacher who has realized the Self transmits a sense of inner peace and bliss. Yogananda describes this kind of inspiration he received in his guru's presence. "If I entered the hermitage in a worried or indifferent frame of mind, my attitude imperceptibly changed. A healing calm descended at the mere sight of my guru. Each day with him was a new experience in joy, peace, and wisdom" (Yogananda, 1972, pp. 137–138).

I can cook for you, but I can't eat for you. [Hari Dass, 1973]

A guru is not a magician who transforms students without any effort on their part. Gurus are teachers of subtle truths and practices; as in any learning situation, students' achievements are in proportion to their effort, ability, and receptivity.

> The conditions for the taught are purity, a real thirst after knowledge, and perseverance. . . . Purity in thought, speech, and act is absolutely necessary for anyone to be religious. As to the thirst after knowledge, it is an old law that we all get whatever we want. None of us can get anything other than what we fix our hearts on. . . . The success may sometimes come immediately, but we must be ready to wait patiently even for what may look like an infinite length of time. The student who sets out with such a spirit of perseverance will surely find success in realization at last. [Vivekananda, 1978a, pp. 28–29]

EVALUATION

The essence of yoga is reformation of the psyche through a system of concrete, practical exercises designed to transform our consciousness. Yoga treats in depth the relationship of consciousness to vital energy, or prana, which links the physical world and consciousness. Yoga exercises work with subtle energy flow in a uniquely direct way; no other system works as directly and effectively on consciousness.

As the energy and consciousness of the Self flow outward, they become distorted by a series of lenses, our subconscious tendencies, habits, personality, and so on. Subconscious tendencies bias our thoughts, which then affect our action. Action patterns become habits, and habits in turn reinforce these lenses. Then the Self, which is pure joy, pure love and bliss, cannot manifest within our consciousness or in the world.

The aim of yoga practice is to reduce the distortion and direct the flow of consciousness to its source, the Self. To reduce distortion, we can cleanse our bodies and our personality tendencies. In hatha-yoga this cleansing is accomplished primarily through physical disciplines and concentration exercises. In karma-yoga right action gradually purifies. Bhakti-yoga works through devotion; by embracing the highest ideals psyches are refined. The self-analysis of jnana-yoga can transform personality, much like the process of psychotherapy.

Yoga practice slows the flow of consciousness from the Self to the environment and begins drawing it back inward. This process is most clearly found in raja- and kundalini-yoga. By turning our consciousness back to its source, the Self, we begin to get in touch with the Self, with joy, bliss, and purity. This in itself cleanses personality.

Most schools of Yoga focus on inner experience at the expense of outward interests, which may not appeal to everyone. Worldly sensory experiences are seen as distractions from the Self within. This attitude can lead to a retreat from life's problems and a certain kind of passivity. Also, the doctrine of karma is frequently misunderstood to mean passive acceptance of one's lot in life. Although yoga does include the discipline of action, most branches tend to emphasize inner peace at the expense of outward activity.

Yoga as practiced in the West often seems more a system for health and mental concentration than a complete spiritual discipline. Without mental and emotional discipline, or without practice of the moral precepts of Yoga, the practice of postures, breathing, or concentration techniques can result in unbalanced development. These practices alone may not affect the yoga student's personality and may even reinforce pride and egotism.

The major emphasis in yoga lies in the practical effectiveness of the techniques. Experience, rather than theoretical knowledge, is the heart of yoga. The various disciplines can suit virtually any individual, whether active, intellectual, or emotional in disposition. No other practice contains so many different methods for developing self-discipline, gaining a sense of inner peace, and attaining self-realization.

> Success is immediate where effort is intense. [Yoga Sutras, I, 21]

THE THEORY FIRSTHAND

The following passage describes the first experience of illumination of Ramakrishna, the great devotional saint of modern India.

> Sri Ramakrishna began to spend the whole night in meditation, returning to his room only in the morning with eyes swollen as though from much weeping. While meditating he would lay aside his cloth and his brāhminical thread. Explaining this strange conduct, he once said to Hriday: "Don't you know that when one thinks of God one should be freed from all ties? From our very birth we have the eight fetters of hatred, shame, lineage, pride of good conduct, fear, secretiveness, caste, and grief. The sacred thread reminds me that I am a brāhmin and therefore superior to all. When calling on the Mother one has to set aside all such ideas." Hriday thought his uncle was becoming insane.

> As his love for God deepened, he began either to forget or to drop the formalities of worship. Sitting before the image, he would spend hours singing the devotional songs of great devotees of the Mother, like Kamalākānta and Rāmprasād. Those rhapsodical songs, describing the direct vision of God, only intensified Sri Ramakrishna's longing. He felt the pangs of a child separated from its mother. Sometimes, in agony, he would rub his face against the ground and weep so bitterly that people, thinking he had lost his earthly mother, would sympathize with him in his grief. Sometimes, in moments of skepticism, he would cry: "Art Thou true, Mother, or is it all fiction—mere poetry without any reality? If Thou dost exist, why do I not see Thee? Is religion a mere fantasy and art Thou only a figment of man's imagination?" Sometimes he would sit on the prayer carpet for two hours like an inert object. He began to behave in an abnormal manner, most of the time unconscious of the world. He almost gave up food; and sleep left him altogether.

> But he did not have to wait very long. He has thus described his first vision of the Mother: "I felt as if my heart were being squeezed like a

> The ideal of man is to see God in everything. But if you cannot see Him in everything, see Him in one thing, in that thing which you like best, and then see Him in another. [Vivekananda, 1976, p. 142]

wet towel. I was overpowered with a great restlessness and a fear that it might not be my lot to realize Her in this life. I could not bear the separation from Her any longer. Life seemed to be not worth living. Suddenly my glance fell on the sword that was kept in the Mother's temple. I determined to put an end to my life. When I jumped up like a madman and seized it, suddenly the blessed Mother revealed Herself. The buildings with their different parts, the temple, and everything else vanished from my sight, leaving no trace whatsoever, and in their stead I saw a limitless, infinite, effulgent Ocean of Consciousness. As far as the eye could see, the shining billows were madly rushing at me from all sides with a terrific noise, to swallow me up! I was panting for breath. I was caught in the rush and collapsed, unconscious. What was happening in the outside world I did not know; but within me there was a steady flow of undiluted bliss, altogether new, and I felt the presence of the Divine Mother." On his lips when he regained consciousness of the world was the word "Mother." [Nikhilananda, 1948, pp. 9–10]

The next passage is a description of the spiritual illumination of Ramana Maharshi, India's great twentieth-century sage.

It was about six weeks before I left Madura for good that the great change in my life took place. It was quite sudden. I was sitting alone in a room on the first floor of my uncle's house. I seldom had any sickness, and on that day there was nothing wrong with my health, but a sudden violent fear of death overtook me. There was nothing in my state of health to account for it, and I did not try to account for it or to find out whether there was any reason for the fear. I just felt "I am going to die" and began thinking what to do about it. It did not occur to me to consult a doctor or my elders or friends; I felt that I had to solve the problem myself, there and then. The shock of the fear of death drove my mind inwards and I said to myself mentally, without actually framing the words: "Now death has come; what does it mean? What is it that is dying? This body dies." And I at once dramatized the occurrence of death. I lay with my limbs stretched out stiff as though *rigor mortis* had set in and imitated a corpse so as to give greater reality to the enquiry. I held my breath and kept my lips tightly closed so that no sound could escape, so that neither the word "I" nor any other word could be uttered. "Well then," I said to myself, "this body is dead. It will be carried stiff to the burning ground and there burnt and reduced to ashes. But with the death of this body am I dead? Is the body I? It is silent and inert but I feel the full force of my personality and even the voice of the 'I' within me, apart from it. So I am Spirit transcending the body. The body dies but the Spirit that transcends it cannot be touched by death. That means I am the deathless Spirit." All this was not dull thought; it flashed through me vividly as living truth which I perceived directly, almost without thought-process. "I" was something very real, the only real thing about my present state, and all the conscious activity connected with my body was centered on that "I." From that moment onwards the "I" or Self focused attention on itself by a powerful fascination. Fear of death had vanished once and for all. Absorption in the Self continued unbroken from that time on. [Osbourne, 1970, pp. 18–19]

EXERCISES

Breathing Exercises

Observing the Breath

Sit on a chair or on the floor, with your back straight and your body relaxed. Close your eyes. Exhale and then inhale calmly and deeply for as long as comfortable without straining. Observe your breath flowing in and out, as if you were on the seashore observing the ocean waves. With each in-breath, feel that you are breathing in fresh energy and vitality with the oxygen. With each out-breath, feel that you are breathing out tiredness, fatigue, and negativity as you expel carbon dioxide. Feel the fresh, vitalizing energy permeating your mind and body as you continue the exercise.

Then sit quietly with your mind peaceful and calm.

Austerities

General Principles

The simplest, most direct, and most difficult practice of austerity is to give up satisfying one's desires—that is, if you are preoccupied with food, fast. If you love to sleep, make yourself do with less. Giving up small pleasures and comforts can be an important self-discipline. If you usually get up at 8 A.M., try getting up at 4 every morning. If you like sleeping on a comfortable bed, start sleeping on a thin mat on the floor.

There are some important cautions in this kind of practice. Austerities can enhance or strengthen the ego. Pride in one's accomplishments, pride in suffering, or masochistic enjoyment of austerities for their own sake are all indications of ego involvement. Another thing to watch for is excessive austerity. This is another demonstration of ego and may actually cause mental or physical harm to the individual.

Fasting

Short periods of fasting are an excellent practice of austerity. You can begin simply by deliberately missing one or two meals. A one-day fast is not too difficult for anyone in good health. Drink plenty of water, and drink orange juice if you feel the need for additional nourishment. Fasting for one day a week is an excellent practice. Fasting directly confronts the individual with the need to overcome temptation and to set one's will against the desire for food.

Silence

Silence is another beneficial practice. Try remaining silent for a few hours at home or around friends who understand your intention. Or spend a day by yourself in silence. Carry paper and pencil with you to communicate in writing if necessary. Observe yourself and others, your reactions to conversations. Try to overcome your need to communicate actively. Learn to just *be*, in silence.

Meditation Exercises

Heartbeat

Sit with spine erect and body relaxed. Close your eyes and drop your mind into the depths of your heart. Become aware of your heart bubbling with life-giving blood, and keep your attention on the heart until you feel its rhythmic beat. With every heartbeat feel the pulse of infinite life throbbing through you. Picture that same all-pervading life flowing through all other human beings and in billions of other creatures. Open your heart, body, mind, and feelings to receive more fully that universal life.

Expanding Love
Sit erect with eyes closed. Expand your realm of love, long limited by your love for the body and identification with your body. With the love you have given to the body, love all those who love you. With the expanded love of all those who love you, love all those who are close to you. With the love for yourself and for your own, love those who are strangers. Extend your love to those who do not love you as well as those who do love you. Bathe all beings in your unselfish love. See your family, friends, all people, all beings in the sea of your love.

Peace
Sit erect with eyes closed. Look inwardly between the eyebrows at a shoreless lake of peace. Observe the waves of peace expanding, spreading from the eyebrows to the forehead, from the forehead to the heart, and on to every cell in your body. As you watch, the lake of peace deepens and overflows your body, inundating the vast territory of your mind. The flood of peace flows over the boundaries of your mind and moves on in infinite directions. (These three exercises are adapted from Yogananda, 1967.)

ANNOTATED BIBLIOGRAPHY

Eliade, M. *Yoga: Immortality and freedom.* Princeton, N.J.: Princeton University Press, 1969. Scholarly treatment of the many diverse Yoga traditions.

Mascaro, J. *The Bhagavad Gita.* Baltimore: Penguin Books, 1962. A good, available translation.

Prabhavananda, Swami, & Isherwood, C. (Trans.). *The Song of God: Bhagavad Gita.* New York: New American Library (Mentor Books), 1951. Readable and easily available.

Prabhavananda, Swami, & Isherwood, C. *How to know God: The Yoga aphorisms of Patanjali.* New York: New American Library, 1953. Very good, easily available, but a somewhat Westernized translation of the Yoga Sutras.

Purohit, Swami. *Aphorisms of Yoga by Bhagwan Shree Patanjali.* London: Faber, 1938. Best translation and commentary in English.

Radha, S. *Kundalini: Yoga for the West.* Spokane, Wa.: Timeless Books, 1978. By far, the most detailed and psychologically sophisticated treatment of kundalini yoga, the chakras, and the images and symbols of yoga.

Ram Dass, Baba. *Be here now.* San Cristobal, N.M.: Lama Foundation, 1970. A modern, hip interpretation of Yoga, including sections on meditation techniques and other disciplines, the transformation of Richard Alpert into Baba Ram Dass, a spiritual reading list, and an inspiring interpretation of Indian philosophy and Yoga through integrated text and pictures.

Taimni, I. K. *The science of Yoga.* Wheaton, Ill.: Quest, 1961. Solid and scholarly translation of the Yoga Sutras. Extensive commentary.

Vishnudevananda. *The complete illustrated book of Yoga.* New York: Pocket Books, 1960. Very good practical hatha yoga paperback.

Yogananda, Paramahansa. *The Autobiography of a yogi.* Los Angeles:

Self-Realization Fellowship, 1972. A classic account of yogis and Yoga training in India. Excellent introduction to the Indian tradition.

REFERENCES

Anand, B., Chhina, G., & Singh, B. Some aspects of electroencephalographic studies in yogis. *Electroencephalography and Clinical Neurology,* 1961, *13,* 452–456.

Danielou, A. *Yoga: The method of re-integration.* New Hyde Park, N.Y.: University Books, 1955.

Dass, Hari. *The yellow book.* San Cristobal, N.M.: Lama Foundation, 1973.

Digambari, S., and Sahai, M. *Yogakoʹsa. vol. 1* Poona, India: Calvalyadhama, 1972.

Eliade, M. *Yoga: Immortality and freedom.* Princeton, N.J.: Princeton University Press, 1969.

Feuerstein, G., & Miller, Jeanine. *Yoga and beyond.* New York: Schocken Books 1972.

Majumdar, S. *Introduction to Yoga principles and practices.* New Hyde Park, N.Y.: University Books, 1964.

Mascaro, J. (Trans.). *The Bhagavad Gita.* Baltimore: Penguin Books, 1962.

Nikhilananda, Swami. *Ramakrishna: Prophet of new India.* New York: Harper & Row, 1948.

————. *The Upanishads.* New York: Harper & Row, 1964.

Osbourne, A. *The teachings of Ramana Maharshi.* London: Rider, 1962.

————. *Ramana Maharshi and the path of self-knowledge.* New York: Weiser, 1970.

————. (Ed.). *The collected works of Ramana Maharshi.* London: Rider, 1969.

Prabhavananda, Swami, & Isherwood, C. (Trans.). *The Song of God: Bhagavad Gita.* New American Library, 1951.

————. *How to know God: The Yoga aphorisms of Patanjali.* New York: New American Library, 1953.

Purohit, Swami (Trans.). *Aphorisms of Yoga.* London: Faber, 1938.

Purohit, Swami, & Yeats, W. B. (Trans.). *The ten principal Upanishads.* London: Faber, 1970.

————. (Trans.). *The Geeta: The gospel of Lord Shri Krishna.* London: Faber, 1965.

Radha, S. *Kundalini: Yoga for the West.* Spokane, Wa.: Timeless Books, 1978.

Ramakrishna. *Sayings of Sri Ramakrishna.* Madras, India: Sri Ramakrishna Math, 1965.

Smith, H. *The religions of man.* New York: Harper & Row, 1958.

Taimni, I. K. *The science of Yoga.* Wheaton, Ill.: Quest, 1961.

Timmons, Beverly, & Kamiya, J. The psychology and physiology of meditation and related phenomena: A bibliography. *Journal of Transpersonal Psychology,* 1970, *2,* 41–59.

Timmons, Beverly, & Kanellakos, D. The psychology and physiology of meditation and related phenomena: Bibliography II. *Journal of Transpersonal Psychology,* 1974, *4,* 32–38.

Vishnudevananda, Swami. *The complete illustrated book of Yoga.* New York: Pocket Books, 1960.

————. *Jnana-yoga.* Calcutta: Advaita Ashrama, 1976.

————. *Bhakti-yoga.* Calcutta: Advaita Ashrama, 1978a.

————. *Karma-yoga.* Calcutta: Advaita Ashrama, 1978b.

Wood, E. *Yoga dictionary.* New York: Philosophical Library, 1956.

Yogananda, Paramahansa. *Cosmic chants*. Los Angeles: Self-Realization Fellowship, 1963.

———. *Metaphysical meditations*. Los Angeles: Self-Realization Fellowship, 1967.

———. *Sayings of Yogananda*. Los Angeles: Self-Realization Fellowship, 1968a.

———. *Spiritual diary*. Los Angeles: Self-Realization Fellowship, 1968b.

———. *The autobiography of a yogi*. Los Angeles: Self-Realization Fellowship, 1972.

GLOSSARY

The terms used in this chapter have detailed and precise technical definitions within Yoga philosophy. They have been used somewhat more loosely in the text to facilitate the reader's understanding of the psychological principles and implications involved. This glossary is intended to give students seriously interested in Yoga psychology an introduction to the more precise meanings of central yogic terms. The source for this glossary is a compilation of original sources by Swami Digambari and M. Sahai (1972).

Bhakti-yoga—In the *Gheranda Samhita* (VII, 6, 14), bhakti-yoga is described as devotion to God, the means of bringing about one of the five aspects of raja-yoga. Through bhakti-yoga the individual can acquire an ever-living consciousness of God in his or her heart, becoming filled with bliss, leading to samadhi.

Chakra—I translated *chakra* in the text as "center of consciousness." In *Goraksa Śatakam* (15,60,62,63,78,80), the locations of the chakras in the body are described, although the word is not defined. Only four chakras are mentioned by *Goraksa Śatakam*. Presumably the chakras are nerve centers situated at the side of or in the spinal cord. In *Gheranda Samhita* (III, 38), the term *chakra* is not defined, although the yogi is instructed to meditate on the sixth chakra. In *Trisikhibrahmanopanisad* (60), chakra is described as a wheellike structure with 12 spokes. The spokes are supposed to bear the images of various gods. The chakra is compared to the web of a spider and the individual is said to wander through its spokes, which may be the beginnings of the nadis. The nadis are "the subtle nerves" that conduct vital energy through the body. Only 10 nadis are mentioned in TSM, although according to *Goraksa,* the subtle energy operates through thousands of nadis.

Citta—According to Patanjali, citta includes all cognitive functions: perceiving, thinking, remembering, and imagining. In *Yogakundalinyupanisad, Yogasikhopanisad,* and *Hathapradipika,* citta includes every kind of mental activity, cognitive, affective, and conative.

Guna—According to *Vyasa Bhasyam,* the gunas in action consist of movements or vibrations at different frequencies. These are relative terms, sattva corresponding to the highest frequency of vibrations, followed by rajas, with tamas the comparatively lowest.

Guru—According to *Hathapradipika,* a guru is a teacher who imparts traditional knowledge. Only knowledge learned from a guru is effective. According to *Advayatarakopanisad,* a true guru must be devoted to his or her own guru. One is a guru because of one's ability to remove the darkness of ignorance from people's minds.

Hatha-yoga—This is one of the four kinds of yoga mentioned in the *Upanishads,* the other three being mantra-, laya-, and raja-yoga. According to *Yogasikhopanisad,* hatha-yoga includes Patanjali's 8 limbs of yoga and 12 additional practices. These four systems are said to make up one yoga. According to *Hathapradipika,* hatha-yoga forms a ladder for ascending the heights of raja-yoga. In this text the two yogas are described as two aspects of the same discipline.

Jnana-yoga—According to *Trisikhibrahmanopanisad* (23,27), jnana-yoga and karma-yoga represent the two ways in which the mind can be focused on the spiritual and withdrawn from distractions. Jnana-yoga is defined as unswerving fixation of the mind on the highest good. This text stresses the importance of practice of karma-yoga and jnana-yoga together.

Karma—According to *Goraksa S atakam*, karma is action that creates fruits. Our past karmas are said to be the cause of our present lot, including our bodies. The cycle of life and death is also governed by one's karmas.

Kundalini—In *Hathapradipika*, kundalini is described as a special ability, which when evoked begins a series of tactile sensations in the back, traveling up to the brain. According to *Upanisadbrahmyogi*, the soul is liberated only when kundalini rises from its seat; if kundalini does not rise, the person is forced to return to this earth in another incarnation after death. According to *Yogakundalinyupanisad*, kundalini is imagined as a snake that holds its tail in its mouth; the kundalini blocks the opening of the passage along the susumna, the nadi that runs along the center of the spinal cord. *Gheranda Samhitā* considers kundalini to be a power inherent in everyone, but only used by the yogis. It is imagined as a serpent-shaped goddess who sleeps in the first chakra, coiling itself three and a half times. If this power is not aroused, thousands of yogic practices will not produce liberation. This closed door is to be opened by hatha-yoga as if by a key. Kundalini is described by those who have experienced it as a uniquely full and rich experience. It is said to bring about full illumination.

Prana—According to *Goraksa S atakam*, prana is respiration, one of the principal functions of the body; other functions are inspiration, expiration, digestion, movement, and illumination. Prana includes all the nervous currents and motor impulses, the reflex and instinctive actions of the body. All the impulses of the autonomic nervous system function together, as if there were a living being residing in the autonomic nervous system. According to *Hathapradipika*, prana includes all the autonomic reflexes that preserve life. When these cease to function, life ceases; therefore prana is life. Patanjali refers to prana only as breath.

Pranayama—According to Patanjali the essence of pranayama is a pause in breathing, which may occur either during inspiration or expiration; the lungs may be (1) completely empty or (2) full to capacity or (3) in a state of balance between these two extremes. In *Gheranda Samhitā*, dhyana (meditation) is an essential part of pranayama. This text mentions two types of respiratory pranayama: in one inhalation is done with the left nostril and exhalation with the right nostril; in the other one the nostrils are reversed.

Samadhi—According to *Hathapradipika*, this is a state of concentration in which the self is completely forgotten. It is brought about by the merging of the subject of consciousness and the object of consciousness—that is, consciousness is transformed from its ordinary state and there is no subject-object relationship left. Patanjali calls samadhi a meditative state. In another passage Patanjali defines samadhi as a state of living perfectly, uninfluenced by subconscious tendencies or other personality aspects.

Samskara—According to Patanjali it is the potentiality of behavior or consciousness. It may be innate or acquired. Dispositions that are innate are believed to have been acquired in past lives.

Yoga—According to *Hathapradipika*, it is a whole discipline, consisting of many components. An essential element is belief in reincarnation. Yoga is the science and art of (1) accelerating progress toward liberation; (2) all the various ways and means adopted by Indian yogis to achieve this end. According to *Yogasikhopanisad*, yoga is union of (1) prana (inspiration) and apana (expiration); (2) the energies in the spine, resulting in the awakening of kundalini; and (3) the individual consciousness and divine consciousness.

CHAPTER 13
ZEN BUDDHISM

Zen Buddhism is primarily concerned with leading others to a direct, personal understanding of Truth. The Buddha's teachings emphasize experience over theology or abstract philosophy. Zen is a school of Buddhism, a particular branch that emphasizes meditation and spiritual practice. In a broader sense, Zen provides an approach to spirituality applicable to all religions and limited to none. As the great Zen philosopher D. T. Suzuki has written, "The basic idea of Zen is to come in touch with the inner workings of our being, and to do this in the most direct way possible, without resorting to anything external or super-added" (Suzuki, 1964, p. 44). When asked how one should evaluate religious teachings and spiritual teachers, the Buddha replied: "You who follow me, consider this carefully. Keep an eye open, seekers of truth. Weigh rumor, custom, and hearsay. Don't let anyone's excellence in the Scriptures mislead you. Logic and argument, supply of elaborate reasons, approval of considered opinion, plausibility of ideas, respect for the leader who guides you—beware of too much trust in them. Only when you *know,* and are sure that you know—this is not good, this is erroneous, this is censured by the intelligent, this will lead to loss and grief—only when you know, should you reject or accept it" (*Dhammapada,* 1967, p. 17).[1]

Remember thou must go alone; The Buddhas do but point the way. [Shakyamuni Buddha]

HISTORY

Buddhism is based on the teachings of Siddhartha Gautama, the Buddha. The term *Buddha* is a title, not a proper name. It means "one who knows," or one who exemplifies a certain level of understanding, one who has attained full humanness. There were many other Buddhas before Gautama, and there are still Buddhas to come, according to Buddhist doctrine. The Buddha never claimed to be more than a man whose realization, attainments, and achievements were the result of his purely human capacities. He developed himself into a completely mature human being, which is such a rare achievement that we tend to look on it as somehow superhuman or divinely inspired. The central attitude in Buddhism is that every individual possesses this Buddha nature, the capacity for developing into a complete human being, becoming a Buddha.

The life of Gautama has been recorded as Buddhist religious history; there is little reliable evidence of specific dates and activities. However, his official life story can be read as an illuminating parable of Buddhist ideals and principles.

Gautama was born a prince in a tiny kingdom in North India in the sixth century B.C. He was married at 16 to a beautiful princess and lived in his palace surrounded by comfort and luxury. When Gautama

[1]All quotes from the major Buddhist scripture, the *Dhammapada,* are taken from the translation by P. Lal (1967).

slipped out of his palatial prison, he was suddenly confronted with the reality of life and the suffering of human kind. First, Gautama encountered an old man, worn by a life of toil and hardship. On his second trip he saw a man who was suffering from a serious illness. On his third trip Gautama watched a corpse being carried in a sorrowful funeral procession. Finally, Gautama met a religious ascetic engaged in the traditional Indian path of spiritual discipline. Gautama realized that sickness, old age, and death are unavoidable endings to the happiest and most prosperous life. The inevitability of human suffering became the fundamental problem at the heart of Gautama's spiritual search. He saw that his present way of life could not possibly provide an answer to the problem of suffering and he decided to leave his family and palace to seek a solution through religious discipline.

At the age of 29, soon after the birth of his only son, Gautama left his kingdom and studied for six years with two different teachers, engaging in severe self-discipline. Eventually, he sat beneath a Bodhi tree and resolved that he would not eat or leave his seat until he reached enlightenment, even if he died in the attempt. Finally, weakened by his long fast, Gautama realized that mortification of the body would never bring about enlightenment, and he accepted some food to give him strength to go on with his spiritual efforts. This was the first example of the Buddhist conception of the Middle Way: seeking a healthy and useful discipline without either extreme of complete indulgence of the senses or self-torture. After deep and prolonged meditation, Gautama experienced a profound inner transformation that altered his entire perspective on life. His approach to the questions of sickness, old age, and death changed because *he* changed. He became the Buddha.

> Planners make canals, archers shoot arrows, craftsmen fashion woodwork, the wise man molds himself.
> [*Dhammapada*]

The Buddha decided to spread his understanding to others, and he taught for 44 years, walking from town to town in India with an ever growing band of followers. He died in 483 B.C. at the age of 80.

For many centuries Buddhism flourished in India and spread gradually throughout Asia. Between A.D. 1000 and 1200, Buddhism died out in India, due to a combination of the growing weakness of Indian Buddhism, the revival of Hinduism, and Islamic persecution.

There are two major schools within Buddhism today. The Theravada or Hinayana tradition is found primarily in Southeast Asia, in Sri Lanka, Burma, and Thailand. The Mahayana school has flourished mainly in Tibet, China, Korea, and Japan. The Mahayana school began as a liberal movement within Hinayana Buddhism. This school is less strict in interpreting the traditional monastic disciplinary rules, less exclusive with regard to householders, and more willing to adopt later additions to the Buddhist scriptures. The Mahayanists have also tended to stress the importance of compassion as opposed to a Hinayana emphasis on self-discipline. Originally, these two great traditions were seen as alternative personal interpretations within Buddhism. Adherents of both Mahayana and Hinayana approaches lived together in the same monasteries under the same basic monastic rules.

Zen is one of the major sects of the Mahayana tradition. Zen is said to have been founded in China in the sixth century by Bodhidharma, an Indian Buddhist monk, who stressed the importance of contemplation and personal discipline over religious ritual. Under the influence of a series of great Chinese masters, Zen gradually developed as an independent school of Buddhism, with its own monasteries, monastic rules, and organization. By A.D. 1000, Zen had become the second most popular school of Buddhism in China.

In the thirteenth century two Japanese monks, Eisai and Dogen, traveled to China to study Buddhism. When they returned to Japan, these monks founded temples, taught prominent disciples, and founded the two great sects of Japanese Zen Buddhism, Soto and Rinzai. Master Eisai (1141–1215), who introduced Rinzai Zen in Japan, stressed the achievement of enlightenment through the use of "Zen riddles," or *koan*. Master Dogen (1200–1253), the founder of Japanese Soto Zen, stressed two major points: (1) that there is no gap between daily practice and enlightenment, and (2) that our right daily behavior is Buddhism itself.

Although this chapter deals explicitly with Zen Buddhism only, it can be read as a treatment of basic Buddhist principles from a Zen perspective. Basically, there is only one Buddhism. Different teachers and different schools have interpreted the basic truths of Buddhism to fit the cultures and societies in which they lived and taught.

MAJOR CONCEPTS

The Three Characteristics of Existence

There are three major characteristics of existence according to Buddhist thought: *impermanence, selflessness,* and *dissatisfaction.*

Impermanence

O Buddha, going, going, going on beyond, and always going on beyond,
Always becoming Buddha.
[The Scripture of Great Wisdom]

Everything is constantly changing; nothing is permanent. Certainly nothing physical lasts forever. Trees, buildings, the sun, moon, stars—all have a finite existence; furthermore, all are in flux at any given moment.

Impermanence also applies to thoughts and ideas. The concept of impermanence implies that there can be no such thing as a final authority or permanent truth. There is only a level of understanding suitable for a certain time and place. Because conditions change, what seems to be true at one time inevitably becomes false or inappropriate at others. Therefore, Buddhism cannot be said to have a fixed doctrine. To truly accept the concept of impermanence is to realize that nothing ever fully becomes Buddha, that even Buddha is subject to change and can still progress, that Buddha *is* change.

Selflessness

Other religions have taught that the Self, or soul, is unchanging and imperishable. The Buddhist notion of impermanence, however, is applied to our innermost self as well.

The concept of selflessness holds that there is no immortal soul or eternal Self existing in each individual. The individual is seen as an aggregate of attributes—intellect, emotions, body—all of which are impermanent and constantly changing.

The Buddhist sage Nagasena attempted to explain this principle to King Milinda, using the example of the king's chariot:

> *"Pray, great king, is the pole the 'chariot'?"—"No indeed, Reverend Sir."*
>
> *"Is the axle the 'chariot'?"—"No indeed, Reverend Sir."*
>
> *"Are the wheels the 'chariot'?"—"No indeed, Reverend Sir."*
>
> *"Is the chariot-body the 'chariot'?"—"No, indeed, Reverend Sir."*
>
> *"Is the flagstaff of the chariot the 'chariot'?"—"No indeed, Reverend Sir."*
>
> *"Is the yoke the 'chariot'?"—"No indeed, Reverend Sir."*
>
> *"Are the reins the 'chariot'?"—"No indeed, Reverend Sir."*
>
> *"Is the goad-stick the 'chariot'?"—"No indeed, Reverend Sir."*
>
> *"Well, great king! Is the sum total of pole, axle, wheels, chariot-body, flagstaff, yoke, reins, and goad—is this the 'chariot'?"—"No indeed, Reverend Sir."*
>
> *"Well, great king! Is something other than the sum total of pole, axle, wheels, chariot-body, flagstaff, yoke, reins, and goad—is this the 'chariot'?"—"No indeed, Reverend Sir."*
>
> *"Great king, I have asked you every question I can think of, but I cannot discover the 'chariot'! Apparently the 'chariot' is nothing but a sound."*
>
> *[The king replied] "Because of the pole, and because of the axle, and because of the wheels, and because of the chariot-body, and because of the flagstaff, the epithet, designation, appellation, style, name—'chariot'—comes into use."*
>
> *[Nagasena replied that the same is true of the individual as well. Because of the various organs of the body, because of sensation, perception, and consciousness,] "because of all these, there comes into use the epithet, designation, appellation, style, name—but name only—'Nagasena.' In the highest sense of the word, however, no 'individual' is thereby assumed to exist." [Burlingame, 1922, pp. 202–204]*

The forms of man or animal are merely the temporary manifestations of the life force that is common to all. [Kennett, 1976, p. 8]

In other words, our bodies and our personalities are composed of mortal, constantly changing components. The individual is not something other than these component parts. When the parts perish, so does the individual. No part of ourself goes on forever.

Dissatisfaction

Time flies quicker than an arrow and life passes with greater transience than dew. However skillful you may be, how can you ever recall a single day of the past? [Dogen Zenji]

Dissatisfaction, or suffering, is the third characteristic of existence. It embraces birth, death, decay, sorrow, pain, grief, despair, and existence itself. Suffering comes not from the world around us but from ourselves. It lies in the limited ego—the relative consciousness—of each individual. Buddhist teachings are designed to help us change or transcend our sense of selfishness and limitation and thus achieve a sense of relative satisfaction with ourselves and with the world.

To interpret the principle of dissatisfaction to mean only that suffering is an inescapable part of existence is incorrect. The Buddha taught that the source of suffering lies within the individual and optimistically concluded that something can be done about this basic dissatisfaction.

The Four Noble Truths

We are what we think, having become what we thought. [Dhammapada]

Gautama searched for a way to overcome the suffering and limitation he saw as an inevitable part of human life. He outlined the essential characteristics of human existence in terms of the Four Noble Truths.

The first Truth is the existence of dissatisfaction. Given the psychological state of the average individual, dissatisfaction, or suffering, is inescapable.

The second Truth is that dissatisfaction is the result of craving or desire. Most people are unable to accept the world as it is. They are caught up in attachment for the positive and pleasurable and aversion for the negative and painful. Craving creates an unstable frame of mind in which the present is never satisfactory. If our desires are unsatisfied, we are driven by a need to change the present. If satisfied, we come to fear change, which would bring about a renewal of frustration and dissatisfaction. Because all things pass, the enjoyment of fulfilled desires is always tempered by the realization that our enjoyment is only temporary. The stronger the craving, the more intense is our dissatisfaction knowing that fulfillment will not last.

Like the spider woven in its own web is the man gripped by his craving. [Dhammapada]

The third Truth is that the elimination of craving brings the extinction of suffering. According to Buddhist doctrine, it is possible to learn to accept the world as it is without feeling dissatisfaction because of its limitations. Eliminating craving does not mean extinguishing all desires. When you believe that your happiness depends on fulfilling a desire, or you become controlled by your desires, then they become unhealthy cravings. Desires are normal and necessary because we must eat and sleep to stay alive. Desires also help keep us awake. If all wants are immediately cared for, it is easy to slip into a passive, unthinking state of complacency. Acceptance refers to an even-minded attitude of enjoying fulfilled desires without becoming seriously disturbed over the inevitable periods of nonfulfillment.

The fourth Truth is that there is a way to eliminate craving and dissatisfaction; this is the Noble Eightfold Path, or the Middle Way. Most people seek the highest possible degree of sense gratification. Others, who realize the limitations of this approach, tend to the other extreme of self-mortification. The Buddhist ideal is moderation.

> Avoid these two extremes, monks. Which two? On the one hand, low, vulgar, ignoble, and useless indulgence in passion and luxury; on the other, painful, ignoble, and useless practice of self-torture and mortification. Take the Middle Path advised by the Buddha, for it leads to insight and peace, wisdom and enlightenment. . . . [*Dhammapada*, 1967, p. 22]

The Eightfold Path consists of right speech, right action, right livelihood, right effort, right mindfulness, right concentration, right thought, and right understanding. The basic principle is that certain ways of thinking, acting, and so forth, tend to harm others and to injure or limit oneself.

Do not sell the wine of delusion. But there is nothing to be deluded about. If we realize this there is enlightenment itself. [Diamond Sutra]

There are three essentials in Buddhist training and discipline: ethical conduct, mental discipline, and wisdom. The divisions of the Eightfold Path fall under these three categories.

Ethical conduct is built on the fundamental Buddhist teachings of universal love and compassion for all living beings. Under ethical conduct are included right speech, right action, and right livelihood.

Right speech means abstention (1) from telling lies, (2) from gossip, slander, or any talk that might bring about disunity and disharmony, (3) from harsh, rude or abusive language, and (4) from useless and foolish chatter and gossip. On the positive side, we should speak the truth and use words that are friendly, pleasant, gentle, and useful. We should not speak carelessly, but consider what is appropriate for the right time and place. If we cannot say something useful, the ideal is to keep "noble silence."

Right action means moral, honorable, and peaceful conduct. This includes to abstain (1) from destroying life, (2) from stealing, (3) from dishonest actions, (4) from illegitimate sexual intercourse, and also to help others lead a peaceful and honorable life.

Right livelihood means to abstain from making one's living through any profession that brings harm to others, such as dealing in weapons, intoxicating drinks, poisons, killing animals, or cheating. The ideal is to live by a profession that is honorable, blameless, and innocent of harm to others.

Under the category of mental discipline are included right effort, right mindfulness, and right concentration.

Right effort refers to the active will, used (1) to prevent unwholesome states of mind from arising, (2) to get rid of such states once they have arisen, (3) to facilitate and produce good and wholesome states of mind, and (4) to develop and bring to perfection those good, wholesome states already present.

Right mindfulness is to be aware, mindful, and attentive to (1) the activities of the body, (2) sensations or feelings, (3) the activities of the mind, (4) specific ideas, thoughts, and conceptions. Various schools of meditation—including concentration on breathing, on sensations, and on mental activities—have been developed in different schools of Buddhism in order to develop right mindfulness.

Buddhist psychology distinguishes between generalized activities of the mind and its specific contents. Concerning the activities of the mind, one is to become aware whether one's mind is given to hatred or not, deluded or not, lustful or not, distracted or concentrated, and so on. In focusing on specific ideas and concepts, one learns how they appear and disappear, how they were developed, how suppressed, and so on.

Right concentration leads to four levels of meditation. In the first stage, we discard passionate desires and unwholesome thoughts such as ill will, worry, restlessness. Feelings of joy and happiness develop. In the second stage, all intellectual activities are dropped. Tranquility and "one-pointedness of mind" are developed, and feelings of joy and happiness developed in the first stage are retained. In the third stage, the feelings of joy, an active sensation, also disappear. Mindful equanimity and happiness remain. In the fourth stage, all sensations disappear, including happiness. Only pure equanimity and awareness remain.

Wisdom is made up of right thought and right understanding. Right thought includes selfless detachment, love, and nonviolence. Right understanding is the understanding of things as they are, namely, the Four Noble Truths. In Buddhist psychology there are two levels of understanding. The first is knowledge, accumulated memory, and intellectual grasping of the subject. Deep understanding is seeing a thing in its true nature, undistorted by name and label. This is possible only when the mind becomes free from impurities and fully developed through meditation.

For a Zen monk the primary prerequisite for improvement is the practice of concentrated *zazen*. Without arguing about who is clever and who inept, who is wise and who foolish, just do *zazen*. You will then naturally improve. [Dogen]

Zen Meditation

Zen comes from the Sanskrit word for meditation, *dyhāna* (which evolved to *ch'an* in Chinese and *zen* in Japanese). Meditation is a central discipline in Zen. There are two major practices in Zen meditation, or *zazen* (literally "seated zen"). One can focus on a *koan*, or else simply sit with concentrated awareness and no external focus.

A koan is traditionally contained in a dialogue between a Zen student and Zen master. Some koans are based on questions that were asked by serious Zen students in ancient China. Others are taken from questions posed by a Zen master to stimulate or awaken the student's understanding. The koans vividly and immediately illustrate some aspect of the Zen master's deep understanding of Buddhism. They tend to be paradoxical and beyond logic, and force the questioner to go beyond the inherent limitations of the categories with which he or she had viewed experience up to that point. Meditation on classical koans is still practiced by present-day Zen students of the Rinzai school of Zen.

One of the most famous koans is known as "Mu":

A monk in all seriousness asked Joshu: "Has a dog Buddha-nature or not?" Joshu retorted, "Mu!"

The monk was deeply concerned with the Buddhist teaching that all sentient beings have Buddha-nature. (In China at that time, the dog was considered unclean, the lowest of the animals, and the monk was questioning seriously if such a low creature could be said to have the Buddha-nature.)

Joshu's answer might be translated as "nothing!" or read as an exclamation. It is not a simple yes-or-no answer. Joshu does not fall into the trap of accepting his questioner's assumption that there is a particular thing called Buddha-nature that can be possessed. "Mu" is a vigorous denial of dualistic thinking, a window through which the student can first glimpse Joshu's nondualistic perspective. Another Zen teacher comments, "It is clear, then, that Mu has nothing to do with the existence or nonexistence of Buddha-nature but is itself Buddha-nature" (Kapleau, 1965, p. 76)

In meditating on this koan the individual should not indulge in intellectual speculation on the question and answer or the implications of each. The aim of the koan is to lead Zen students to see their own ignorance, to entice them to go beyond abstract conceptualizing, and to search for truth within themselves. One Zen master gave the following instructions to students working on this koan:

> Let all of you become one mass of doubt and questioning. Concentrate on and penetrate fully into Mu. To penetrate into Mu means to achieve absolute unity with it. How can you achieve this unity? By holding to Mu tenaciously day and night! . . . Focus your mind on it constantly. "Do not construe Mu as nothingness and do not conceive it in terms of existence or nonexistence." You must not, in other words, think of Mu as a problem involving the existence or nonexistence of Buddha-nature. Then what do you do? You stop speculating and concentrate wholly on Mu--just Mu! [Kapleau, 1965, p. 79]

In the Soto school of Zen, students are taught that the most important aspect of Zen training concerns their daily lives, and that they

All you have to do is cease from erudition, withdraw within and reflect upon yourself. Should you be able to cast off body and mind naturally, the Buddha Mind will immediately manifest itself. [Evening Service]

must learn to deal with their own personal koan, the problem of daily life, as it manifests itself for each individual.

A personal koan has no final solution. The problem can be handled only by changing oneself, by altering one's point of view, which results from changing one's personality. The problem is not different, but one's attitude toward it and the way one copes with it alter. The individual never fully finishes with a koan, but learns to deal with the problem at a higher level. For instance, Gautama began his religious quest in hopes of solving the koan of sickness, old age, and death. Even after he became the Buddha, these problems remained unchanged. The Buddha did not become immortal or ageless; however, his new level of understanding transcended his previous personal concern with these problems.

As a smith removes flaws in silver, a wise man removes flaws in himself, slowly, one by one, carefully. [Dhammapada]

For some people, their personal koan involves a sense of inadequacy, a feeling of not being enough, not knowing enough, not able to achieve enough. For others, the central koan is dealing with a sense of complacency, a feeling that one has it made and need not really take a hard look at oneself and try to change.

The Soto approach to meditation can be thought of as "just sitting," without a koan or other exercise to occupy the mind. The meditator strives to maintain a state of concentrated awareness, neither tense nor relaxed but totally alert. The attitude is like that of someone seated by the roadside watching traffic. The meditator is to observe the thoughts going by, without getting caught up in them and forgetting to remain an aware observer. This approach is also found in the Sufi literature. A man visiting a dervish's house found the dervish meditating. The visitor was impressed with the depth and quality of the meditator's concentration and asked the dervish where he learned to meditate like that. The dervish explained that he learned it watching a cat waiting to pounce on a mouse. (See the exercises at the end of this chapter for a full description of this practice.)

Visions and similar experiences should not result from properly performed Zen meditation. Generally, they are the result of tensions that accumulate from sitting improperly in meditation, or from daydreamlike states that arise at a certain point in one's meditation. These makyo, or illusions, are considered valueless in one's spiritual growth. They are at best distractions and at worst a source of pride, egotism, and delusion. One Zen teacher has pointed out that "to see a beautiful vision of a Bodhisattva does not mean that you are any nearer becoming one yourself, any more than a dream of being a millionaire means that you are any richer when you awake" (Kapleau, 1965, pp. 40–41).

Meditation is an important discipline for developing an inner peace and calm and for learning to stay concentrated and balanced. One first learns to become peaceful and focused in meditation and then to extend that sense of calm awareness to activity. Eventually, nothing can pull an experienced meditator off center. He or she learns to cope with problems and pleasures from that calm base, with a certain amount of detached perspective. "Zazen practice is the direct expression of our true nature. Strictly speaking, for a human being, there is no other practice than this practice, there is no other way of life than this way of life" (Suzuki, 1970, p. 23).

Enlightenment

The term *enlightenment* tends to be misleading because it seems to refer to some state that one can attain permanently; this would, of course, violate the Buddhist concept of impermanence.

One Japanese word that has been frequently used in Zen is *satori*, which literally means "intuitive understanding." Another term is *kensho*, which means "to see into one's own nature." Both terms refer to the individual's firsthand experience of the truth of Buddhist teachings. The experience is not static; it is a progressive and ever changing, dynamic state of being, very much like Maslow's concept of self-actualization.

Enlightenment is not experienced in stages, nor are there types of enlightenment, it is an ongoing flow—[Kennett, 1977, p. 1]

First Kensho

This first level of enlightenment experience has been described as the "great flash of deep understanding" (Kennett, 1977). This kensho is realization with one's entire being of the timeless spiritual truths of Buddhism. One truly knows one's unity with what is greater than oneself, with the "immaculacy of nothingness" (Kennett, 1977). This kensho grows deeper as one continues meditation and training.

Second Kensho

This is known as the "ongoing kensho." It is not as dramatic an event as the first kensho (the one usually featured in the stories of Zen monks and their masters). It is a long stage of imperceptible growth rather than a single dramatic event. This can be a very difficult period in which, to progress further, one's Zen training becomes more and more demanding. The individual must act in terms of more subtle and sophisticated understandings of right thought and right activity. To do wrong now violates one's own inner understanding of the truth rather than merely contradicting precepts one has heard or read. This in fact violates one's own sense of self, a much more serious consequence than earlier mistakes.

Be a lamp unto yourself, be like an island. [*Dhammapada*]

When D. T. Suzuki was asked about his own enlightenment experience, he admitted that he had experienced the first kensho, and then later discussed the second level of kensho: "Once or twice I have had the great experience but a million times the little moments that make one dance" (in Kennett, 1977). These "little moments that make one dance" make up this ongoing kensho. They are reminders of that first dramatic kensho experience.

Third Kensho

The third level of kensho is rarely reported in the Zen literature. Often this deep kensho includes real visions and other mystical experiences. Zen students are told at the beginning of their training that any experience in meditation is *makyo,* illusion brought on by the overactive mind and generally by improper sitting habits. In this stage of kensho the visions are far different from the *makyo* of the early stages. Nevertheless, Zen teaches us not to cling to any experience, however valid.

The third kensho may often be experienced during a final illness, shortly before death. However, a Zen master or any serious spiritual seeker can experience the third kensho without dying by plunging deeply into meditation and training, without worrying about the results. In her book *How to Grow a Lotus Blossom* (1977), Kennett describes in detail 43 stages of this kensho. It is a detailed version of the same basic stages that are described in the 10 Ox-herding pictures later in this chapter.

Enlightenment is not some good feeling, or some particular state of mind. The state of mind that exists when you sit in the right posture is, in itself, enlightenment. [Suzuki, 1970, p. 28]

In the third Kensho personal realization truly becomes the core of one's life, and there is a sense of swelling for a time within this core of being. Eventually, the Zen master will move beyond this, back into activity in the world, without clinging to this experience, no matter how edifying or inspiring.

Kennett makes a major distinction between enlightenment and kensho. "Kensho experience, even the second type through its tiny moments, can be fixed in time; enlightenment is an ongoing process, ever flowing like a river. You cannot hold a river within your hand, but you can trail your hand in the river. By grasping you lose all; by letting the flow continue you possess all whilst possessing nothing" (Kennett, 1977, p. 5).

Arhat and Bodhisattva

The Theravada and Mahayana traditions contain different conceptions of the nature of the ideal human being. The Theravada ideal is the Arhat, one who has completely cut off all the limitations of attachment to family, possessions, and comfort to become perfectly free of this world. The Arhat is basically an unworldly ascetic. Arhat literally means one who has slain the enemy, or one who has slain all passions in the process of intensive spiritual discipline.

One Buddhist text, the *Avadana Sataka,* describes the Arhat: "He exerted himself, he strove and struggled, and thus he realized that this circle of 'Birth-and-Death' . . . is in constant flux. He rejected all the conditions of existence which are brought about by a compound of conditions, since it is their nature to decay and crumble away, to change and to be destroyed. He abandoned all the 'defilements' and won Arhat-ship. . . . Gold and a clod of earth were the same to him. The sky and the palm of his hand to his mind the same" (in Conze, 1959a, p. 94).

The Mahayana ideal is the Bodhisattva, literally "enlighten-ment-being." The Bodhisattva is a deeply compassionate being who has vowed to remain in the world until all others have been delivered from suffering.

Let others gain Enlightenment; I shall not enter Nirvana until the last blade of grass has entered Buddhahood. [Bodhisattva vow]

In truly understanding the principle of selflessness, the Bodhi-sattva realizes that he or she is part of all other sentient beings and that until all beings are freed of suffering, he or she can never attain complete satisfaction. The Bodhisattva vows not to enter Nirvana until every sentient being, every blade of grass is enlightened.

> As many beings as there are in the universe of beings . . . egg-born, born from a womb, moisture-born, or miraculously born; with or without form; with perception, without perception, or with neither perception nor no-perception—as far as any conceivable form of beings is conceived; all these I must lead to Nirvana. . . . [Diamond Sutra, in Conze, 1959b, p. 164]

Compassion is the great virtue of the Bodhisattva, the result of truly feeling the sufferings of all others as one's own. From the Maha-yana point of view, this attitude *is* enlightenment. In the experience of enlightenment the world is not transcended, but the selfish ego is.

> When one studies Buddhism one studies oneself; when one studies oneself one forgets oneself; when one forgets oneself one is enlightened by every-thing, and this very enlightenment breaks the bonds of clinging to both body and mind, not only for oneself but for all beings as well. [Dogen, in Kennett, 1972a, pp. 142–143]

The Bodhisattva path includes abandoning the world, but not the beings in it. The path of the Arhat emphasizes the quest for spiritual perfection and abandonment of the world, without the emphasis on ser-vice. The attitude of the Arhat is that those who desire to help others must first work on themselves. Someone who is lost in delusion is not effective in helping or teaching others, therefore self-development must naturally come first.

These two ideals can be seen as complementary rather than con-tradictory. The Arhat model focuses on self-discipline and work on one-self, whereas the Bodhisattva ideal stresses dedicated service to others; both are essential ingredients in spiritual development.

DYNAMICS

Psychological Growth

The path of spiritual growth has been illustrated in the Zen tradition by a series of 10 Ox-herding pictures. The Ox is a symbol of the Buddha-nature, and the process of finding the Ox refers to the internal search and spiritual development of the Zen student.

Zen masters have often discussed their students' development in terms of the Ox-herding pictures, which provide clear and graphic illustrations of Zen thinking. One teacher outlined the major points of this series in counseling an advanced Zen student:

> If you continue with zazen, you will reach the point of grasping the Ox, i.e., the fourth stage. Right now you do not, so to speak "own" your realization. Beyond the stage of grasping the Ox is the stage of taming it, followed by riding it, which is a state of awareness in which enlightenment and ego are seen as one and the same. Next, the seventh stage, is that of forgetting the Ox; the eighth, that of forgetting the Ox as well as oneself; the ninth, the grade of grand enlightenment, which penetrates to the very bottom and where one no longer differentiates enlightenment from non-enlightenment. The last, the tenth, is the stage in which . . . one moves, as himself, among ordinary people, helping them wherever possible, free from all attachment to enlightenment. [Taji-roshi, in Kapleau, 1965, p. 231]

Obstacles to Growth
Greed, Hate, and Delusion

Three major sources of suffering, the "Three Fires" of Buddhism, are greed, hate, and delusion. Some individuals are dominated by greed, others by hate, and others by delusion. Virtually everyone is a mixture of all three qualities, with one predominating, although the balance may also change, depending on the circumstances. Certain situations will awaken an individual's greed, others will stimulate tendencies toward anger or delusion.

Greed is the major problem for most people. Most of us always want more—more money, more food, more pleasure. Children are generally the most obviously greedy, and it is often virtually impossible to satisfy a child's greed. One piece of candy only stimulates the desire for another one; no matter how many presents I bring home, my daughter always wants one more. The Buddhist scriptures have described greed types as characterized by vanity, discontent, craftiness, and by love of rich, sweet food and fine clothes (Visuddhimagga, in Conze, 1959b).

Those dominated by hate have sharp tempers and are quick to anger. For them life is a continual round of fighting with enemies, getting back at others for real and imagined injuries, and defending themselves against possible attack. Hate types tend to hold grudges, belittle others, and suffer from arrogance, envy, and stinginess (Conze, 1959b).

Delusion refers to a general state of confusion, lack of awareness, and vacillation. Those for whom delusion is strongest find it difficult to make up their minds or to go deeply into anything. Their reactions and opinions depend on imitating others rather than forming their own

Better than a thousand vacuous speeches is one sane word leading to peace. [Dhammapada]

One man on the battlefield conquers an army of a thousand men. Another conquers himself—and he is greater. [Dhammapada]

FIGURE 13.1 "SEEKING THE OX"

This picture represents the beginning of the spiritual quest. The man is now aware of spiritual possibilities and potentials. Having become a spiritual seeker, he has become focused on spiritual attainment. The search itself creates a new obstacle, that of seeking outside oneself for what is within. Those who are searching must eventually come to believe that they can "find" the Buddha-nature within themselves. Kakuan, the Zen master who first drew this series, added commentaries to each picture.

"The Ox has never really gone astray, so why search for it? Having turned his back on his True-nature, the man cannot see it. Because of his defilements he has lost sight of the Ox. Suddenly he finds himself confronted by a maze of crisscrossing roads. Greed for worldly gain and dread of loss spring up like searing flames, ideas of right and wrong dart out like daggers" (Kakuan in Kapleau, 1965, p. 302).

FIGURE 13.2 "FINDING THE TRACKS"

The seeker has begun to study Buddhism seriously. Study of various scriptures and accounts of the lives of Buddhist sages brings an intellectual understanding of basic Buddhist truths, although the student has not yet experienced these truths firsthand.

"He is unable to distinguish good from evil, truth from falsity. He has not actually entered the gate, but sees in a tentative way the tracks of the Ox" (Kakuan in Kapleau, 1965, p. 303).

FIGURE 13.3 "FIRST GLIMPSE OF THE OX"

The sight of the Ox is the first direct experience of the seeker's own Buddha-nature. The encounter with the Ox is not a result of study or abstract contemplation, but through direct experience. This first glimpse is for but a moment, realization which comes and goes. Further discipline is required to expand and stabilize this experience.

"If he will but listen intently to everyday sounds, he will come to realization and at that instant see the very Source. The . . . senses are no different from this true Source. In every activity the Source is manifestly present. It is analogous to the salt in water or the binder in paint" (Kakuan in Kapleau, 1965, p. 304).

FIGURE 13.4 "CATCHING THE OX"

The mind is restless. To control it is good. A disciplined mind is the road to Nirvana. [*Dhammapada*]

Now the Zen student must make certain that Buddhist self-discipline permeates the whole of daily life. The goal is to extend the awareness of one's Buddha-nature to all activities and to manifest that awareness in all circumstances.

The Ox here illustrates the raw energy and power of Enlightenment. Due to the overwhelming pressures of the outside world, the Ox is hard to keep under control. If disciplined practice is abandoned now, this power and energy may dissipate.

"Today he encountered the Ox, which had long been cavorting in the wild fields, and actually grasped it. For so long a time has it reveled in these surroundings that breaking it of its old habits is not easy. It continues to yearn for sweet-scented grasses, it is still stubborn and unbridled. If he would tame it completely, the man must use his whip" (Kakuan in Kapleau, 1965, p. 305).

FIGURE 13.5 "TAMING THE OX"

An effortless intimacy or friendship with the Ox is now established. The sense of struggle is gone. This is the stage of precise and perfect training. Every act, every thought, begins to reflect the True Self. The individual ceaselessly works to manifest Buddhism at all times, without a single interruption. Only because some traces of illusion still remain is there still a distinction between the seeker and the Ox.

"He must hold the nose-rope tight and not allow the Ox to roam, lest off to muddy haunts it should stray. Properly tended, it becomes clean and gentle. Untethered, it willingly follows its master" (Kakuan in Kapleau, 1965, p. 306).

FIGURE 13.6 "RIDING THE OX HOME"

The struggle is over. The student has now become the sage. Although the Ox is still seen as separate, the relation between man and Ox is so intimate that he can ride it effortlessly without needing to pay the slightest attention to where it is going. Life has become simple, natural, and spontaneous. Formal external training is no longer essential once one has become firmly anchored in awareness of the Buddha-nature. The discipline that was once seen as a burden is now embraced as a source of real freedom and satisfaction.

" 'Gain' and 'loss' no longer affect him. He hums the rustic tune of the woodsman and plays the simple songs of the village children. Astride the Ox's back, he gazes serenely at the clouds above. His head does not turn [toward temptation]. Try though one may to upset him, he remains undisturbed" (Kakuan in Kapleau, 1965, p. 307).

FIGURE 13.7 "OX FORGOTTEN, SELF ALONE"

The seeker has returned home and the Ox is forgotten. The distinction between religious and worldly categories disappears, as everything is seen to possess the Buddha-nature. Training and discipline have become indistinguishable from daily life. The state of meditation is as normal now as walking or breathing and is no longer associated with any sense of motivation or of separation from the goal. Everything is sacred, and there is no distinction between enlightenment and ignorance.

"In the Dharma [Teaching] there is no two-ness. The Ox is his Primal-nature: this he has now recognized. A trap is no longer needed when a rabbit has been caught, a net becomes useless when a fish has been snared. Like gold which has been separated from dross, like the moon which has broken through the clouds, one ray of luminous Light shines eternally" (Kakuan in Kapleau, 1965, p. 308).

FIGURE 13.8 "BOTH OX AND SELF FORGOTTEN"

This refers to the experience of void, the essential nothingness of all creation. The individual nature and the Buddha-nature were transcended in the previous stage, and now it is enlightenment itself that is transcended. The perfect circle, made by the single brushstroke of the Zen master, is left open. Because the circle is not closed, further growth is possible. The process of enlightenment is able to go on without becoming frozen or static.

"All delusive feelings have perished and ideas of holiness too have vanished. He lingers not in 'Buddha,' and he passes quickly on through 'not Buddha.' Even the thousand eyes [of the Buddhas and Patriarchs] can discern in him no specific quality. If hundreds of birds were now to strew flowers about his room, he could not but feel ashamed of himself"* (Kakuan in Kapleau, 1965, p. 309).

*There is a legend of a Chinese Zen master who was so holy that the birds came to offer him flowers as he sat meditating in his mountain retreat. After he became fully enlightened, the birds ceased their offerings, because he no longer gave off any aura, even of devotion and holiness.

FIGURE 13.9 "RETURNING TO THE SOURCE"

If the eighth stage is thought of as the static aspect of absolute Truth, the ninth stage may be said to bring a new dynamic appreciation of the world. Nature is not merely void or sacred, it *is.* If seen clearly, any aspect of the world can serve as a perfect mirror to show us ourselves. There is still a subtle duality here between the manifestation of Truth in nature and its manifestation in deluded, suffering humankind. This level must eventually deepen to include our return to human civilization.

"He observes the waxing and waning of life in the world while abiding unassertively in a state of unshakable serenity. This [waxing and waning] is no phantom or illusion [it comes from the Source]. Why then is there need to strive for anything? The waters are blue, the mountains are green. Alone with himself, he observes things endlessly changing" (Kakuan in Kapleau, 1965, p. 310).

FIGURE 13.10 "ENTERING THE CITY WITH BLISS-BESTOWING HANDS"

Cease from evil, do only good, do good for others. [The three Pure Precepts]

This is the final stage, the stage of the Bodhisattva who is free to associate with and help all other beings without limitations. The city refers to the secular world, in contrast to the secluded Zen temple or contemplation retreat. The Bodhisattva is shown with a big belly and a gourd of wine slung over his shoulder. He is willing to share all the amusements and activities of the world, not because of personal desires or attachments, but in order to teach others.

"The gate of his cottage is closed and even the wisest cannot find him. His mental panorama [concepts, opinions, and so forth] has finally disappeared. He goes his own way, making no attempt to follow the steps of earlier sages. Carrying a [wine] gourd, he strolls into the market; leaning on his staff, he returns home. He leads innkeepers and fishmongers in the Way of the Buddha" (Kakuan in Kapleau, 1965, p. 311).

The Zen master, who realizes that everything is Buddha, can now return to the activities of the early stages, with a different perspective.

opinions. Delusion types tend to do everything inattentively and sloppily. They are characterized by laziness, obstinacy, confusion, worry, and excitability (Conze, 1959b).

At their worst, these tendencies can blossom into what Westerners term neurosis or psychosis. However, according to Buddhist thinking, even a psychosis is but a temporary intensification of one of these tendencies. It is viewed as a transient state, as are all mental and physical states.

By working on oneself, all three obstacles can be transcended. Greed can be turned into compassion, hate into love, and delusion into wisdom. Self-discipline and the discipline of following the Buddha's precepts offer the opportunity for the individual to confront and control his or her greed. The Buddhist teachings, with their emphasis on love and respect for others, provide a way to overcome hate. And the realization that everything is the Buddha controls delusion; as even the smallest thing contains the Buddha-nature, everything merits our deepest care and attention.

Pride

Pride can be another major obstacle to growth. Pride can lead to a lack of respect for one's teacher and create distortions of the teachings. A Zen teacher will attempt to lead students to see and acknowledge their own pride and egotism. One of the Zen patriarchs points out, "Should the teaching you hear from a Zen master go against your own opinion, he is probably a good Zen master; if there is no clash of opinions in the beginning, it is a bad sign" (Dogen in Kennett, 1972a, p. 111).

> To see the self is not to be pleased with the self; not to be pleased with the self is to want to do something about the self; and to want to do something about the self is to study Buddhism. [Dogen]

Pride can enter at virtually any point in training, even after a first-stage kensho. Normally, the direct kensho experience confirms the student's understanding of Buddhism, and the student's convictions about the validity of Buddhist teachings become truly unshakable. However, at this stage many students tend to believe they have learned everything, that they understand Buddhism fully and no longer need a teacher.

A good teacher will insist that the student continue with regular duties and training at this point in order to ensure that pride and ambition do not distort the initial deep understanding of Buddhism. Delusion is extremely difficult to break if it develops at this point because the student's convictions are now firmly rooted in actual experience. If training is continued, one can overcome the inevitable pride and sense of holiness, or what some Zen masters have called the "smell of enlightenment." The student must be reminded of the doctrine of impermanence and the fact that training in Buddhism is endless.

STRUCTURE

Body

The Buddhist concept of the Middle Way is of central importance in one's attitudes toward the body. It involves neither full indulgence of all one's desires nor extreme asceticism or self-mortification. The body is a vehicle for service to others and for one's pursuit of truth. It should be cared for in this light.

Both your life and your body deserve love and respect, for it is by their agency that Truth is practiced and the Buddha's power exhibited. [Dogen]

The mealtime ceremonial recited in Zen temples affirms:

The first bite is to discard all evil;
The second bite is so that we may train in perfection;
The third bite is to help all beings;
We pray that all may be enlightened.
We must think deeply of the ways and means by which this food has come.
We must consider our merit when accepting it.
We must protect ourselves from error by excluding greed from our minds.
We will eat lest we become lean and die.
We accept this food so that we may become enlightened.

[Mealtime Ceremonial, in Kennett, 1972a, pp. 236–237]

Hyakujo, who was the founder of Zen monastic life, always worked with his monks at manual labor, even when he was in his eighties. Although his students tried to restrain him from working as hard as they did, he insisted, saying, "I have accumulated no merit to deserve service from others; if I do not work, I have no right to take my meals" (Ogata, 1959, p. 43).

Social Relationships

A liar with a shaven head does not make a monk. [*Dhammapada*]

A common misconception found within all meditative disciplines is quietism, or withdrawing from the world for fear of disturbing one's meditative peace. Buddhist teaching stresses responsibility, the opposite of withdrawal. Meditation is never an end in itself. One may devote periods of time to meditative practice, with the understanding of the need to work and eventually to help others. Everyone has the Buddha-nature. We should ideally look on all other human beings as the Buddha and ask ourselves, "Here comes the Buddha. How can I help it?" The Buddha is not beyond this world of suffering, not beyond the need for help and compassion. Also, being Buddha is not a permanent state (because nothing is seen as permanent in Buddhism).

Someone who is inebriated can be treated as a drunken Buddha, not allowed to disturb others, but not treated disrespectfully either. Similarly, one who is acting badly, wrongly, or evilly can be seen as a "baby Buddha," who needs to be taught, but is never to be punished for the sake of revenge or thrown out as evil or worthless. Throwing that person out throws out the Buddha as well. In these ways, social interactions offer crucial opportunities to practice Buddhist ideals and principles and to put into practice the calm awareness developed in meditation.

Will

Dogen has written, "It is by means of the will that we understand the will" (in Kennett, 1976, p. 170). Will develops through the exercise of the will. To grasp the will is to make a real commitment to one's training and to take responsibility for one's own actions, realizing that no one else can do your training for you. "It is not easy for anyone, however, to cast away the chain of ignorance and discrimination all at once. A very strong will is required, and one has to search single-heartedly for his True Self, within himself. Here hard training is needed in Zen, and it never resorts to an easygoing, instant means" (Shibayama, 1970, p. 31).

One basic Buddhist principle is that daily life and activity should be brought into harmony with ideals and values. Training oneself is not merely a means to an end, but training is an end in itself. Dogen wrote "It is heretical to believe that training and enlightenment are separable, for in Buddhism the two are one and the same . . . as this is so, the teacher tells his disciples never to search for enlightenment outside of training since the latter mirrors enlightenment. Since training is already enlightenment, enlightenment is unending; since enlightenment is already training, there can be no beginning whatsoever to training" (in Kennett, 1972a, p. 121).

> There is only one thing, to train hard, for this is true enlightenment. [Evening Service]

Training is a continual process because there is no end to the realization of Buddhist principles. Someone who stops and remains satisfied with an initial enlightening experience will soon be left with nothing but a beautiful memory.

A contemporary Zen teacher cautioned one of his disciples: "Your enlightenment is such that you can easily lose sight of it if you become lazy and forego further practice. Furthermore, though you have attained enlightenment you remain the same old you—nothing has been added, you have become no grander" (Taji-roshi in Kapleau, 1965, p. 231).

> O Buddha, going, going, going on beyond, and always going on beyond, always becoming Buddha. [The Scripture of Great Wisdom in Kennett, 1972a, p. 224]

Emotions

An important goal of Buddhist training is to learn to be in control of one's emotions rather than be controlled by them. There is nothing wrong with most emotions; however, few people experience their emotions properly or appropriately. They become angry or outraged at trivia and then carry that emotion over into other, inappropriate situations. Through training, the Zen student gradually develops a state of meditative awareness in all daily activities. By becoming more fully aware of emotional reactions to various situations, these emotions tend to lose their hold. One Zen teacher commented that if one does get angry, it should be like a small explosion or a thunderclap; the anger is then fully experienced and can be dropped completely afterward (Suzuki-roshi, n.d.). "The precept 'do not be angry' means that when anger arises don't *become* anger. Remain still inside and watch the anger arise and depart. See its cause. Anger is always a symptom of something deeper. It is the outward sign that something needs changing." (Sacco, n.d.)

The ideal Buddhist emotional state is compassion. Compassion can be thought of as transcended emotion, a feeling of unity with all other beings.

Intellect

The study of Buddhist scriptures and intellectual understanding of Buddhist teachings are important first steps in Buddhist training, as mentioned in the commentaries to the Ox-herding pictures. However, reliance on the intellect alone can become a great hindrance to true understanding. Ananda, the most clever and most learned of Buddha's disciples, took almost five times longer than the others to reach enlightenment. After the Buddha's passing, the other disciples went to Ananda, whose memory was so prodigious that he was able to recite word for word all of the talks of the Buddha. But his love of argument and his pride in his learning stood in the way of real understanding.

Although erudition alone is not particularly helpful, intellectual understanding plus the actual practice of that understanding are essential. Ideally, intellectual understanding deepens and becomes clarified through meditation and training in daily life in accordance with Buddhist principles. One who reads about the concept of compassion without actually serving others understands compassion only as a shallow abstraction. Buddhist teachings are meant to be living truths, actively expressed in people's lives.

Pure intellect and abstract reasoning alone are seen as useful but limited in their ability to fully comprehend ourselves and the world around us. The intellect is essentially powerless to satisfy our deepest spiritual needs. "It is not the object of Zen to look illogical for its own sake, but to make people know that logical consistency is not final, and that there is a certain transcendental statement that cannot be obtained by mere intellectual cleverness" (D. T. Suzuki, 1964, p. 67).

Self

In Buddhist thought there is a distinction made between the lesser self and the greater self. The lesser self is the ego, the consciousness of one's mind and body. The lesser self remains focused on the limitations of the individual, the consciousness of separateness between the individual and the rest of the world. This level of consciousness must be transcended in order to develop a real sense of unity with other beings and with nature.

In one sense, the lesser self is created by one's sense of inadequacy. The size of the personal ego directly corresponds with the amount of inadequacy that the individual feels. As we become whole, integrated individuals, our lesser selves naturally diminish in strength. We never lose our egos; however, the mature person is in control of the ego, not run by it.

It is possible to identify oneself with one's greater self, which is as large as the entire universe, embracing all beings and all creation. This level of understanding is an essential element in the experience of enlightenment.

> Earth penetrates heaven whenever Zazen is truly done. [Kennett]

Identification with the greater self does not mean that the lesser self must be done away with. Training brings about a transcending of the lesser self so that one is no longer dominated by it. Nirvana is not annihilation of the ego, or smaller self, but transcendence of ego orientation. In Buddhist art the Bodhisattva Monju is depicted sitting on a ferocious beast. Monju is sitting in serene meditation, although the beast is awake with its fierce eyes open wide. The beast represents the ego, a useful tool that is not to be killed, although it must be watched and firmly sat upon.

Teacher

A true Buddhist teacher is one who not only believes in Buddhist principles, but who also is seen by all to live those teachings completely. If he or she fails to live up to this ideal, the teacher must be ready to acknowledge the fault. The pupils approach their teacher as the ideal example to follow, as the living Buddha. However, genuine Zen teachers realize their actual limitations and try never to cut themselves off from their pupils by placing themselves on a pedestal. Disciples must see their teacher's humanness and limitations, yet recognize Buddha in the teacher in spite of the teacher's faults.

> When you meet a Zen master who teaches the Truth, do not consider his caste, his appearance, shortcomings or behavior. Bow before him out of respect for his great wisdom and do nothing whatsoever to worry him. [Dogen]

A teacher is primarily involved in his or her own training. Others who recognize certain exceptional qualities in a teacher choose to model themselves after the teacher's example. The teacher does not try to be good for others, or worry about whether or not pupils choose to follow. By example, and by great patience, love, and forebearance, a good teacher can serve as an inspiration so that others will exert their best efforts in their own training. A teacher who tries too hard to teach inevitably creates in pupils a sense of guilt for not living up to various external standards. The teacher can serve best as a standard against which disciples freely choose to measure their own attitudes and training.

> To follow a Zen master is not to follow in old ways nor to create new ones; it is simply to receive the teaching. [Dogen]

Dogen stressed the necessity of a teacher.

If a true teacher is not to be found, it is best not to study Buddhism at all. They who are called good teachers, however, are not necessarily either young or old but simple people who can make clear the true teaching and receive the seal of a genuine master. Neither learning nor knowledge is of much importance, for what characterises such teachers is their extraordinary influence over others and their own will power. They neither rely on their own selfish opinions nor cling to any obsession, for training and understanding are perfectly harmonised within them. These are the characteristics of a true teacher. [in Kennett, 1972a, p. 109]

Students often decide to judge their teacher to decide whether the teacher is a "Zen master" or not. Some discrimination is necessary because there are those who call themselves teachers who may be unprepared and unqualified. But for a pupil to worry about the degree of realization of a qualified Zen teacher is nothing but egotism. The student is really asking "Is this teacher worthy of teaching *me*?" "Does he or she conform to *my* standards?" Buddhist teachings hold that anything and everything can teach, if only the individual has an open mind.

If you wonder "Can I trust?" you are really wondering, "Can I develop a strong enough opinion to please me?" [Bahaudin, a Sufi master]

Originally, there were no statues of the Buddha in Buddhist temples; there were only the footprints of the Buddha. This was a reminder to the student of the principle, "Thou must go alone, the Buddhas only point the way." Also, when there is a concrete image, students begin to believe that a teacher should look like a Buddha and that only those who superficially resemble that image are teachers.

EVALUATION

One exciting and intriguing aspect of Buddhism is a sense of a vital dialectic, the simultaneous appreciation of the real and the ideal and the recognition of the tension between the two. Along with the ideals of Buddhism, the limitations of actuality are acknowledged. The individual must realize that "I am Buddha, and I am not Buddha, and I am Buddha" (Kennett-roshi, personal communication). This dialectic approach manifests itself in virtually all aspects of Buddhist life and thought. It provides a creative tension, at once a way to cope with present limitations, and also an attraction to move toward the ideal.

Lo! with the ideal comes the actual, like a box with its lid . . . like two arrows in mid-air that meet. [Sandokai]

To say flatly that "such and such is true" is to ignore the principle of impermanence. Such a statement is misleading at best. However, the opposite statement is as misleading. It is better to say "It is so, and it is not so, *and* it is so." Virtually every statement and every situation can be better understood by applying this dialectic.

There is great depth in the Zen notion that training *is* enlightenment. The trainee who maintains this attitude does not get caught in the trap of working for an unattainable ideal. To work continually for a future goal or reward may mean you are never fully involved in the present. If the path is not in harmony with the goal, how can one ever reach the goal?

This issue is made clear in a well-known Zen story about Baso, a monk who was making great efforts in meditation. Nangaku, his teacher, asked: "Worthy one, what are you trying to attain by sitting?"

> Baso replied: "I am trying to become a Buddha."
> Then Nangaku picked up a piece of roof tile and began grinding it on a rock in front of him.
> "What are you doing, Master?" asked Baso.
> "I am polishing it to make a mirror," said Nangaku.
> "How could polishing a tile make a mirror?"
> "How could sitting in zazen [meditation] make a Buddha?"
> Baso asked: "What should I do, then?"
> Nangaku replied: "If you were driving a cart and it didn't move, would you whip the cart or whip the ox?"
> Baso made no reply.
> Nangaku continued: "Are you training yourself in zazen? Are you striving to become a sitting Buddha? If you are training yourself in zazen, [let me tell you that] zazen is neither sitting nor lying. If you are training yourself to become a sitting Buddha, Buddha has no one form. The Dharma [Teaching], which has no fixed abode, allows of no distinctions. If you try to become a sitting Buddha, this is no less than killing the Buddha. If you cling to the sitting form you will not attain the essential truth."
> [In Kapleau, 1965, p. 21]

Dogen has pointed out that "since Buddhist trainees do almost nothing for themselves, how is it possible that they should do anything for the sake of fame and gain? Only for the sake of Buddhism must one train in Buddhism" (in Kennett, 1972a, p. 107).

The Buddhist dialectic also applies to the role of the teacher. As mentioned earlier, the ideal Buddhist teacher recognizes his or her own limitations and acknowledges these limitations to the students. This is a major point of contrast to the Indian Yoga tradition, in which the guru tends to be venerated as the embodiment of all divine virtues and characteristics.

However much any human being might *theoretically* come to approximate these divine ideals, the vast majority of religious teachers are only too human, and they still retain their own foibles and imperfections. To try to maintain a role of holy perfection before one's disciples inevitably leads to a certain amount of posing and hypocrisy. Unless teachers acknowledge their real limitations, they are likely to become egotistical and defensive about their slightest faults or mistakes.

A seemingly perfect teacher tends to lead disciples to avoid accepting responsibility for their own development because they can make no real connection between their own imperfections and the assumed perfection of the master. Rather than continue the hard work of training and self-discipline, students can convince themselves that their teacher is a "master" who can accomplish all kinds of things which they cannot, so they need not even make the effort.

To live by Zen is the same as to live by an ordinary daily life. [Evening service]

In Zen, religion and daily life are not separated, they are seen as one and the same. Practical, unspectacular experience is stressed and the esoteric and miraculous aspects of religion are played down. A Zen master once said, "*My* miracle is that when I feel hungry I eat, and when I feel thirsty I drink" (Reps, n.d., p. 68). Life is to be lived with full awareness by accepting and fulfilling the requirements of daily life. The Zen master Jyoshu was once asked for instruction by a new monk.

> JYOSHU: *"Have you breakfasted yet?"*
> MONK: *"I have had my breakfast."*
> JYOSHU: *"Then wash out your bowl."*

The monk suddenly understood the true nature of Zen.

There is no final doctrine or dogma because there can be no absolute truths, or even an absolute Buddha, in the face of impermanence. Buddhist teachings are oriented to human realities. They are aimed at eliminating the sense of dissatisfaction and inadequacy caused by a limited, selfish ego. In the passage quoted at the beginning of this chapter, the Buddha is reported to have told his followers not to follow any teachings because of a teacher's reputation or skill with words, but to rely on their own judgment and experience. The final criterion for Zen is experience. If teaching and discipline aid people in becoming more mature, more responsible, and more complete human beings, that is considered to be good Buddhism.

THE THEORY FIRSTHAND

The following excerpts are taken from the diary (*The Wild White Goose,* ms.) of Jiyu Kennett, a British woman who studied for many years at a major Zen training temple in Japan. She is now teaching in the United States at her own Zen temple, Shasta Abbey, in Mt. Shasta, California.

11th January.
   Reverend Hajime called me into his room early this evening so that we could get on with the translation for as long a time as possible before the bell went for bed.
   "Shakyamuni* Buddha and I are one, as are all Buddhists with both him and me, and not merely all Buddhists but all people and all things both animate and inanimate. And none of us have anything to do with

Shakyamuni Buddha." I paused for a moment so that he could thoroughly digest what I had written, then I continued. "Shakyamuni Buddha is of no importance at all at the present time and Shakyamuni Buddha lives for ever in me."*

He was silent, simply looking deeply into my eyes; then he spoke softly.

"You should ask Zenji Sama for the Transmission," he said.

"If Transmission is what I think it is, I do not understand you. As I know of it. Transmission is received when all training is finished and the master wishes to give his seal of approval to a disciple before he goes out to teach. I am anything but ready for that."

"That is a popular misconception. Admittedly it is the giving of the seals of the master to someone whom he knows has understood his own nature but they are only given when the master is certain that the disciple concerned regards his training as just beginning every minute of his life and not when he thinks of it as being over. In other words, not when he thinks of himself as being enlightened and having nothing more to do. Understand the 'gyate, gyate' of the Hannyashingyo as 'going, going,' not 'gone, gone.' "

"Doesn't one have to have had some great kenshō [enlightenment] before such a thing takes place? All that happened to me in October was that I realized that there was nothing more I could do but train myself constantly every day of my life and that I was the worst trainee in existence."

"In so short a time after the event, that is all you are going to understand of it," he said smiling softly. "But as you continue to train constantly many things will become deeper and clearer to you as a result of that kenshō. The peace within you will become more profound. Look back on yourself to last summer and what do you see? Read over this conversation on Shakyamuni Buddha; you did not know that you could make it and you know that it did not come out of your intellect, and I have not told it to you. Therefore, who did tell it to you?"

16th January.

"You have understood the Lord of the House. You have understood that you are indestructible. You have understood eternal meditation, but you have not yet understood the 'with' within the *Denkoroku;*† for the 'with' is everything else around you and you must regard all that as Buddha as well."*

I was enlightened simultaneously with the universe. [Denkoroku]

"What you are telling me is that I have to regard the Queen of England, the President of the United States and the Emperor of Japan as symbols of the Buddha Nature just as are you and I, and, my God, do you realize that we'd have to include Hitler in this as well?" . . .

"It is not 'we would have to include Hitler,' we do include Hitler. If you cannot see that he, too, possesses the Buddha Nature, however misguided he may have been, you are never going to understand Buddhism completely. You are always going to chop off a part of the Buddha Nature and say, 'That little bit isn't clean; that little bit isn't nice.' You cannot do that."

Even as he spoke I understood completely what he meant. There is no part of me that can ever be chopped off. There is no emotion, no feeling, no thought, no word, no deed that does not come out of the Buddha Mind. I said this to him, and went on. "Then the sex act is part of the Buddha Nature and expresses the Buddha Nature at every turn, for it is, of itself, clean. What we have done is made it dirty with our own guilts and misuse."

"You are correct."

"Eating and going to the toilet and washing clothes and scrubbing the floor are all part of the 'with' for they are all expressions of the Buddha Nature." I stopped, amazed at myself.

"Go on," he said.

". . . and the sun and the moon and the stars and the earth; and the digging of the earth and the flowing water; these too are all expressions of the Buddha Nature, and the tongue I use to speak these words, and the food I eat, and the differences in the tastes; 'by comparing them you can'—Yes! that's what the scripture means. 'By comparing them you can distinguish one from other,'—and yet they're all the same thing; they're all expressions of the Buddha Nature, and there is no way in which they can be separated off from it; and there is no way in which one can separate off any person or being or any living thing . . ."

"Going back to the business with regard to Hitler, what we've just been talking about means that what we couldn't stand in him, what gave us such awful horror was the realization that we could do identically the same things as he did; we all had the potential of cruelty in us and that shocked us so horribly that we had to kill it in him. We realized that it was within us, good and evil both being part of the Buddha Nature; he allowed evil to be in the ascendency and we knew he was wrong. Our mistake was that we could not *accept,* and so transcend, the evil side of ourselves. I am not saying we should have allowed Hitler to run the world; obviously he could not be allowed to get away with evil; we had to go to war. But we wished to turn our eyes away from the fact that we *could* do the same things that Hitler did. We decided that he alone was evil instead of saying 'I could be evil too, Hitler is a mighty example of what I must *not* become. Looked at this way Hitler becomes an important teacher for me and I must be grateful to him for showing me what I could become.' This is the reason why it is so difficult to keep the Precepts and why the Truth can't be given to us until we have kept them and learned to make them our blood and bones. We don't want to *know* that we can be evil, so where is there any need for Precepts? Thus, no-one can enter into the Truths of Buddhism until he has made the commitment of becoming a priest, otherwise he could use the knowledge of his own indestructibility for all sorts of evil purposes. They would know their own true freedom and they wouldn't care two hoots what they got up to with other people."

"That is completely right. You have understood the 'with' at last. You see, from now on you can carry on from there and there will be no difficulty in understanding, and you will know that you must hold everyone and everything as the 'with' aspect of the Buddha Mind and recognize that, whatever aspect of the Buddha Mind it shows, the Precepts must always hold it within itself."

"Then making the Precepts part of my blood and bones means that the Precepts will eventually fall away."

"Haven't you realized that, in your case, the early moral form of them already has? You have gone on beyond morality."

"I thought they had, but . . . oh dear, there goes the bell. We'd better go to service. Can we continue this later?"

"Tomorrow. I have to go out this evening."

We bowed to each other, the first time he had bowed to me fully, and I left the room.

*In Sanskrit, Shakyamuni means "wise man of the Shakyas." It is one of the terms frequently used to refer to the Buddha, Siddhaitha Gautama, a prince of the Shakya clan.

†The *Denkoroku* is a collection of the sayings attributed to the great Buddhist patriarchs. It was compiled in China in 1004.

EXERCISES

Zen Meditation

First, it is essential that your sitting posture be correct. You should be able to sit comfortably with a straight back, without becoming tense. By straight back, Zen teachers mean with the spine curved naturally just below the middle back. (Trying to sit with a literally straight back will only distort the natural curve of the spine and cause discomfort and tension.)

If you wish, there is nothing wrong with sitting in a chair because the chief requirement of a correct back can be maintained just as easily. Use a chair that is as flat as possible. A small, flat cushion is optional. Sit forward on the front third of the chair, with your feet flat on the floor. The lower legs should be more or less at right angles to the floor and to the upper legs.

If you are going to sit on the floor, use a small, firm cushion to raise the buttocks. (Meditation cushions are often available at local Zen centers.) It is better to sit on a rug or blanket than on the bare floor. You sit on the edge of the cushion only, with just the tip of the bottom of the spine resting on the cushion. This way nothing presses on your thighs to restrict the blood circulation. You can place your legs in full lotus (with each foot over the opposite thigh) or in half lotus (with only the left foot over the right thigh). For most long-legged Westerners, it is more comfortable to sit Burmese style, your left foot tucked into the juncture of the right thigh and pelvis and your right leg placed immediately in front of your left leg and parallel to it. Both legs are flat on the ground.

The head should be straight, neither bent forward or backward. Your head should feel comfortable and almost weightless when it is positioned properly. Place your left hand over your right in your lap, with the thumbs lightly touching, and the palms up.

Sit facing a wall far enough away that you can focus comfortably (approximately 6 to 9 feet away). Keep your eyes lowered to a comfortable place on the wall. Do not close them completely.

Sway gently from side to side, backward and forward, to find the most comfortable erect posture. Lift up your rib cage slightly to take the pressure off your lower back and to allow your spine to curve naturally. Take two or three slow, deep breaths before you begin to concentrate.

Now comes the part that is easiest to describe and hardest to do. Just sit. Don't try to do anything. But don't try *not* to do anything, either. Just sit, with a positive mental attitude.

More explicit instructions regarding mental activity during meditation have been given by Kennett-roshi:

Now don't deliberately try to think and don't deliberately try not to think; in other words, thoughts are going to come into your head; you can either play with them or you can just sit there and look at them as they pass straight through your head and out the other side. That is what you need to do—just continue to sit; don't bother with the thoughts, don't be highjacked by them and don't try to push them away—both are wrong. . . .

While you are doing zazen neither despise nor cherish the thoughts that arise; only search your own mind [or heart] the very source of these thoughts. [Bassui]

I have often given the likeness of sitting under a bridge watching the traffic go by. You do have to watch the thoughts that travel back and forth, but not be bothered by them in any way. If you do get caught by a thought—and in the beginning it is quite likely—then OK. Right. So you got caught by a thought. Come back to the beginning again and start your meditation over. It's no good sitting there and saying, "Oh, now there, I got caught by another thought," because you will get caught over the annoyance about the other thought, and so it builds up and you never get back to the quiet within. If you get caught in that way, just come back and start again. [Kennett, 1974, pp. 16–17]

Meditation and Activity

Meditation can be seen primarily as a way of developing calmness and a sense of centered awareness by learning not to get caught up in your thoughts and emotions. Once you begin to understand this meditative attitude while sitting quietly, you can begin to extend this feeling to your outward activities as well.

Begin with an hour of daily meditative activity. First sit quietly for 5 minutes, then tell yourself that you are going to remain self-aware, an observer of your thoughts, emotions, and activity for the next hour. If something does pull you off center, stop what you are doing and try and regain that sense of calmness and awareness.

It is easiest to begin with an hour of quiet physical work—cleaning, cooking, and so forth. Intellectual activity is more difficult and conversation still more so. As you extend this practice to more of your daily life, you can begin to see where you are the most sensitive and easily disturbed. Make a list of these situations and see what the list tells you.

ANNOTATED BIBLIOGRAPHY

Conze, Edward. *Buddhism: Its essence and development.* New York: Harper & Row, 1959a. An excellent survey of the major Buddhist traditions.

———— (Trans.). *Buddhist scriptures.* Baltimore: Penguin Books, 1959b. Good collection of various Buddhist texts.

Kapleau, P. (Ed.). *The three pillars of Zen.* Boston: Beacon Press, 1965. Includes lectures on training and meditation by a contemporary Zen master and first-person accounts of Zen training experiences.

Kennett, J. *Zen is eternal life.* Berkeley: Dharma Publishing, 1976. Written by a fully trained Western Zen master. Includes an excellent introduction to Zen Buddhist thought: two newly translated classic Zen works; and the major Zen scriptures and ceremonials. For the serious Zen student.

————. *How to grow a lotus blossom, or how a Zen Buddhist prepares for death.* Mount Shasta, Calif.: Shasta Abbey Publishing, 1977. A detailed account of a third-order kensho, the mystical experiences of a Zen master, including past life experiences and the deep transformation of mind and body in meditation.

Lal, P. (Trans.). *The dhammapada.* New York: Farrar, Straus & Giroux, 1967. Fine translation of a major Buddhist scripture.

Reps, Paul (Ed.). *Zen flesh Zen bones.* New York: Doubleday (Anchor Books), nd. A marvelous collection of Zen stories and koans.

REFERENCES

Burlingame, E. *Buddhist parables.* New Haven, Conn.: Yale University Press, 1922.

Conze, E. *Buddhism: Its essence and development.* New York: Harper & Row, 1959a.

————. (Trans.). *Buddhist scriptures.* Baltimore: Penguin Books, 1959b.

Dhammadudhi, S. *Insight meditation.* London: Committee for the Advancement of Buddhism, 1968.

Evans-Wentz, W. *Tibet's great yogi.* Milarcpa. New York: Oxford University Press, 1951.

————. *The Tibetan book of the great liberation.* New York: Oxford University Press, 1954.

————. *Tibetan yoga.* New York: Oxford University Press, 1958.

————. *The Tibetan book of the dead.* New York: Oxford University Press, 1960.

Glozer, G. Sitting on a chair or mediation bench. *Journal of the Zen Mission Society,* 1974, *5*(3), 18–20.

Kapleau, P. (Ed.). *The three pillars of Zen.* Boston: Beacon Press, 1965.

Kennett, J. The five aspects of self. *Journal of the Zen Mission Society,* 1972a, *3*(2), 2–5.

————. The disease of second mind. *Journal of the Zen Mission Society,* 1972b, *3*(10), 13–17.

————. How to sit. *Journal of the Zen Mission Society,* 1974, *5*(1), 12–21.

————. *Zen is eternal life.* Berkeley: Dharma Publishing, 1976.

————. *The wild white goose* (Vol. 1). Mount Shasta, Calif.: Shasta Abbey Publishing, 1977a.

————. *How to grow a lotus blossom.* Mount Shasta, Calif.: Shasta Abbey Publishing, 1977b.

————. *The wild white goose* (Vol. 2). Mount Shasta, Calif.: Shasta Abbey Publishing, 1978.

Lal, P. (Trans.). *The dhammapada.* New York: Farrar, Straus & Giroux, 1967.

Leggett, T. *A first Zen reader.* London: Rider, 1960.

————. *The tiger's cave.* London: Routledge & Kegan Paul, 1977.

————. *Zen and the ways.* Boulder, Col.: Shambhala, 1978.

Masnnaga, R. (Trans.). *A primer of Soto Zen.* Honolulu: East-West Center Press,

Olcott, H. *The Buddhist catechism.* Wheaten, Ill.: Quest, 1970.

Ogata, S. *Zen for the West.* London: Rider, 1959.

Rahula, W. *What the Buddha taught.* New York: Grove Press, 1959.

Sacco, I. Personal communication, nd.

Sangharakahita. *The three jewels.* New York: Doubleday (Anchor Books), 1970.

Shibayama, Z. *A flower does not talk.* Tokyo: Tuttle, 1970.

Stryl, L., & Ikemoto, T. (Eds. and trans.). *Zen: Poems, sermons, anecdotes, interviews.* New York: Doubleday (Anchor Books), 1963.

Suzuki, D. T. *Zen Buddhism.* New York: Doubleday (Anchor Books), 1956.

————. *Zen and Japanese culture.* New York: Pantheon Books, 1959.

————. *Manual of Zen Buddhism.* New York: Grove Press, 1960.

————. *An introduction to Zen Buddhism.* New York: Grove Press, 1964.

Suzuki, S. *Zen mind, beginner's mind.* New York: Weatherhill, 1970.

————. *Teachings and disciplines of Zen.* Lecture, San Rafael, Calif.: Big Sur Recordings, nd.

Woodward, F. I. *Some sayings of the Buddha.* New York: Oxford University Press, 1973.

Yampolsky, P. *The Zen master Hakuin: Selected writings.* New York: Columbia University Press, 1971.

CHAPTER 14
SUFISM

"Bismillah ir Rahman ir Rahim"
("In the Name of God, the Compassionate, the Merciful")

Know, O beloved, that man was not created in jest or at random, but marvellously made and for some great end.

[Al-Ghazzali, 1964a, p. 17]

For thousands of years, Sufism has offered a path on which one can progress toward this "great end" of self-realization. It is a collection of teachings, manifested in many forms, that have a common goal: a transcendence of ordinary personal and perceptual limitations. It is not a set of theories or propositions, but has been variously described as a way of love, a way of devotion, and a way of knowledge. Through its many manifestations, it is an approach that reaches beyond the intellectual and emotional obstacles that inhibit spiritual progress.

It is both fashionable and realistic in psychology to admit how little we know and how much more research is necessary before we can begin to understand human behavior. Sufism, on the other hand, is explicit in what it says it does know. Sufis state that there are teachers who know what is important—that is, they know how to teach their students to reawaken themselves to their natural, alert state. The task of the Sufis is not to understand all of behavior; they need only know how to transmit what al-Ghazzali called useful knowledge. This is the knowledge that can help us unravel our personal and cultural predicaments more easily and more surely.

Sufi teachings are not systematized; many cannot be communicated in words. The teachings are found in various forms that include rituals, exercises, readings and study, special buildings, shrines, special language forms, stories, dance movements, and prayer.

Sufism is often taught as a "path." The metaphor suggests both an origin and a destination. Along the path one can acquire knowledge of reality. "Real self-knowledge consists in knowing the following things: What are you in yourself and where did you come from? Where are you going and for what purpose are you tarrying here awhile? In what does your real happiness and misery consist?" (al-Ghazzali, 1964a, pp. 19–20). Yet, there are many pitfalls that render us unable, uninterested, or even unwilling to seek this other knowledge. What we have included here is a representative selection of Sufi teachings that have been used to foster inner development.[1]

---

[1]The following presentation of Sufism is centered on a single figure whose psychological orientation is consonant with the general approach of this text. No one teacher, no one approach, no one set of beliefs can be said to "represent" Sufism. There is a growing availability of Sufi writings and Sufi teachings that present a variety of other ways, aside from the one presented here. These works include the historical approach of Nicholson (1964a) and Arberry (1970); the philosophical approach of Burckhardt (1959); the personal contemporary approaches of Gurdjieff (1950, 1968), Ouspensky (1949), Meher Baba (1967, 1972), Pir Vilayat Khan (1974), and Siraj-Ed-Din (1970); the more eclectic works by Farzan (1973, 1974) and Perry (1971); and the more devotional presentations of Nurbakhsh (1978, 1979, 1981) and Ozak (1981).

HISTORY

Historians usually describe Sufism as the mystical core of Islam and date its appearance to about the same time that Islam emerged as a major religious force.

Sufism is more prominent in the Middle East and in countries that embrace Islam, but its ideas, practices, and teachers are to be found in India, Europe, and the Americas as well (Shah, 1964). "Sufis always were, and are, scattered among all nations of the world" (Dabistran, 1943, p 27). Because Sufism is defined more by its effect than by its form, its teachers often worked within locally understood traditions to protect its members from harassment during times of religious fanaticism. This was often the case in parts of the Islamic world. "Sufis responded to this oppressive environment by cloaking their teachings and their activities in the outward garb of religion. . . . They also culti-vated cultural pursuits . . . as a means of maintaining communication with the people at all levels of society. . . . Almost every Persian classic, valued for its beauty and originality, is a Sufic textbook as well as a work of art" (el-Qadiri, 1974, p. 8).

. . . Sufis were before the Prophet. Sufism always was; it is the Ancient Wisdom. [In Tweedie, 1979, p. 148]

Sufis hold that the teaching arises from human experience, thus it cannot be placed within any single historical tradition. It emerges in different cultures under different guises. The many different visible aspects of Sufi teachings are not studied for their academic interest, nor are they studied for emotional stimulation; they are studied be-cause these teachings can be of current use. The following exchange may clarify this:

QUESTION: *For how long has Sufism existed?*

ANSWER: *Sufism has always existed. It has been practiced in a very wide variety of ways; the outer shells of these being differ-ent . . .*

QUESTION: *Is Sufism restricted to a certain language, a certain com-munity, a certain historical period?*

ANSWER: *The obvious face of Sufism at any given time, place or community may often vary because Sufism must present itself in a form which will be perceptible to any people. [Tchaq-maqzade in Shah, 1970a, pp. 286–287]*

One working definition of Sufism is that it is "a means of concen-trating a certain teaching and passing it on, through a human vehicle, through climates prepared for its reception" (Shah, 1964, p. 285). The core of Sufism, therefore, is the teaching activity that is currently under way. Thus any historical codification must be concerned with practices that were used earlier and may or may not be useful now.

The emphasis is not upon the richness of a past tradition; the emphasis is on what is practical from the past and of immediate value for today.

ABU HAMID AL-GHAZZALI

Look not at my exterior form, but take what is in my hand. [Rumi in Shah, 1970a, p. 31]

The writings of Abu Hamid al-Ghazzali (1058–1111) are among the most widely read Sufi teachings. It is because of his influence that many Islamic theologians finally accepted Sufism within formal Islam. He is called "The Proof of Islam" and "The Restorer of Islam," and he is one of the most important figures in Islamic theology. Western authorities agree that al-Ghazzali was among the few Muslim thinkers who exercised profound effects upon later Christian thought. "With the time came the man. He was al-Ghazzali . . . certainly the most sympathetic figure in the history of Islam, and the only teacher of the after generations ever put by a Muslim on a level of the four great Imams [founders of the four major schools of law in Islam]" (MacDonald, 1903, p. 215).

His work redefined the public view of Sufism from that of a suspect, even heretical teaching, to a valued and essential part of Islam. "The accepted position of Sufism, whereby it is acknowledged by many Moslem divines as the inner meaning of Islam, is a direct result of Ghazzali's work" (Shah, 1964, p. 148). Although Sufism is accepted by Sufis and others as having existed before Islam and therefore has been practiced in various forms beyond the Arab world, it has flourished and developed mainly within the Islamic world since the time of al-Ghazzali.

Al-Ghazzali was born in the small town of Tus in Iran. His father died when al-Ghazzali was young, and he and his brother were raised by a Sufi who also provided for their early education. Al-Ghazzali was an excellent student; when he was old enough, he went to a larger town to study theology and canon law. He was attracted to those areas, he later wrote, because they were the most direct paths to possible fame and wealth. However, his studies offered him additional, more personal lessons. For example, once when he was returning to Tus, he was set upon by a band of thieves who took all his belongings, including his lecture notes. Unable to bear the loss of the notes, he ran after the thieves pleading for their return. The leader asked him why pieces of paper should be so important. Al-Ghazzali replied that there was learning in them. "I travelled for the sake of hearing them and writing them down and knowing the science in them" (in MacDonald, 1899, p. 76). The robber laughed at al-Ghazzali and told him that knowledge that can be stolen is not knowledge at all. He returned the notes, but al-Ghazzali took the incident as a message from God; he spent the next few years learning and memorizing his scholarly notes.

After studying under a number of distinguished teachers, he was offered a position at the Nizamiya Academy at Baghdad, the most important seat of Islamic learning. He gained an international reputation as a teacher, and he also gained the respect of politicians and religious leaders. By the age of 34, he had reached the absolute pinnacle of the Islamic intellectual world (Qayyum, 1976).

In the midst of his growing fame, however, al-Ghazzali became severely depressed; he lost confidence in his teaching, his own training, and his own capacities. Eventually, he grew to doubt even the experiences of his senses. Finally, he suffered a partial paralysis of his vocal cords, which prevented him from teaching. The doctors who examined him could find no physical cause for the symptoms. After two months he withdrew from the university and let it be known that he was making a pilgrimage to Mecca. Actually, he put all his property in trust, left his family, and became a dervish: a religious wanderer and seeker of truth.

"Do you not see," I reflected, "that while asleep you assume your dreams to be indisputably real? Once awake, you recognize them for what they are—baseless chimeras. Who can assure you, then, of the reliability of notions which, when awake, you derive from the senses and from reason?" [Al-Ghazzali, 1968a, p. 18]

He had studied the systems of formal philosophy and theology, but they seemed no longer fruitful; he had read the Sufi mystics, but knew he could not understand them. "I saw that in order to understand it [Sufism] thoroughly one must combine theory with practice" (al-Ghazzali, 1968a, p. 46). A desire to understand Sufi teachings led to a transformation of his own psychological structure. He was determined to become an initiate: one who has seen and experienced.

> He proceeded straightway, hiding himself from public view into the wilderness adjoining Damascus and Jerusalem. There in solitude he sought the saints of various creeds, from whom he learnt practices of mysticism on recollection, contemplation and remembrance of the Name of the Lord, and wooed solitude and meekness, practiced the hardest austerities. This led to the development of intuition and unfoldment of hidden faculties within him. [Behari, 1972, p. xxii]

During the next 10 years al-Ghazzali wrote his most important work, *The Revival of Religious Sciences,* (1972), which aligned Sufi experiences with Islamic beliefs and practices. He established a framework in which pathological, normal, and mystical behaviors are linked in a single, unified field of human experience. He reinstated the elements of personal development and transpersonal experiences into an Islam that was rapidly becoming rigid and restrictive. He wrote *Deliverance from Error,* a semiautobiographical work, to answer those who asked how he had arrived at his own world view. In addition to other scattered writings, he wrote a popular abridged version of *The Revival of Religious Sciences* titled *The Alchemy of Happiness* (1964a), which describes how one can overcome his or her lower nature and find happiness through correct knowledge of the self, God, this world, and the next world.

After 11 years of wandering, he accepted, under pressure from the sultan, a teaching position at Naysabur. Several years later he returned to his birthplace and, in the company of his disciples, lived a religious life until his death at age 55.

Al-Ghazzali attempted to teach others to replace dogma with practice, piety with self-examination, and belief with a relentless examination of the actual situations of daily life. His books are still widely read throughout the Middle East. His ideas extended to the West where they influenced St. Thomas Aquinas and St. Francis of Assisi (Shah, 1964).

MAJOR CONCEPTS

Drawing on al-Ghazzali's model and the work of other teachers, Sufis continue to use orthodox Islamic practices in their own teaching. It is helpful to know the basic structure of Islam.

Orthodox Islam

The pious are always saying "I take refuge in God." Satan laughs at such pious ejaculations. Those who utter them are like a man who should meet a lion in a desert, while there is a fort at no great distance, and, when he sees the evil beast, should stand exclaiming, "I take refuge in that fortress," without moving a step towards it. [Al-Ghazzali, 1964a, p. 11]

Islam, the Arabic word for "peace" or "surrender," is the religious system associated with its prophet, Muhammad. It is described in the Koran as the original monotheistic religion revealed to successive teachers (including Abraham, Moses, and Jesus) in a constant succession. Muhammad had his initial revelation in the year 610. The Muslim era dates from 622, the year Muhammad fled from Mecca to the city of Medina. Islam is a religion that sees humanity as having the necessary intellect to make choices and the will to make correct choices even in the face of conflicting desires.

The Koran

It is the Merciful who has taught you the Koran. He created man and taught him articulate speech. The sun and the moon pursue their ordered course. The plants and the trees bow down in adoration. He raised the heaven on high and set the balance of all things, that you might not transgress it. Give just weight and full measure. [Koran, Chapter 55, verse 1]

The Koran, or Quran, the holy book of Islam, was revealed to Muhammad so that mankind could know what is true. It contains essentially three levels of instruction. The first is a set of doctrines that describes one view of reality and humanity's special role in it. The second level is a commentary on the opportunities and pitfalls that occur in life. The third level is a tangible manifestation of divinity; the words of the Koran are the direct words of God channeled through the messenger Muhammad.

The Koran discusses religious and secular matters. It includes laws of inheritances, rules for marriage and divorce, and questions of property rights, as well as ethical and religious proscriptions. The central premise of Islam is that there can be no division of church and state; every act, every object, every relationship is part of the divine nature. The possibility of realizing the divine nature at every moment is interwoven into the daily practice of Islam. It is what the Prophet preached and how he lived.

Muhammad

Muhammad (or Mohammed, 570–632 A.D.) transmitted the message of the Koran to humanity. He was not divine, but he was inspired. He is looked upon as the man who comes as close as one can to living the ideal life set forth in the Koran. As a civic leader, he was very much involved with worldly issues; he settled civic disputes, led armies, married and raised children, in addition to instructing his followers in the understanding of the Koran. He instituted and practiced the "five pillars."

When a person is reading the Koran two angels are kissing his forehead. [Al-Ghazzali, 1972, p. 17]

Pillars

The five pillars are ritual practices instituted to help Muslims remember their divine inner nature and to support them in fulfilling the message of the Koran.

The Confession of Faith

A practicing Muslim must daily restate two articles of faith. He or she must say and believe that:

1. There is no God but God.
2. Muhammad is the Prophet.

Daily Prayer

Five times a day there is a call to prayer. The prayers deliberately interrupt the daily activities to reorient members of the community to their moral and religious concerns. The times of prayer are visible manifestations of the doctrine that all are equal in the eyes of God, irrespective of class, social, and economic distinctions. "Is anything more precious than prayer that any frivolous thought overtakes you at that hour? . . . Prayer is like unto eternity, so when you have entered it how can the uneternal (worldly) thought linger in your mind at the time?" (al-Ghazzali, 1972, p. 15).

Fasting

Each year all Muslims who are able fast from dawn to sunset for a month. One is also supposed to abstain from sex and from impure thoughts and deeds during this time. It is a difficult practice, intended to help one remain aware of the conflicting forces between the lower and the higher natures.

> The fasting of the general public involves refraining from satisfying the appetite of the stomach and the appetite of the sex, as has already been discussed.
> The fasting of the select few is to keep the ears, the eyes, the tongue, the hands, and the feet as well as the other senses free from sin.
> The fasting of the elite among the select few is the fast of the heart

from mean thoughts and worldly worries and its complete unconcern with anything other than God and the last day, as well as by concern over this world. [Al-Ghazzali, 1968b, p. 20]

Charity

Each year every household is asked to give a predetermined percentage of its wealth to the poor. It is said that all things originate from God; having goods and money is seen as a custodianship in that one retains the right to possessions by returning some of them to the larger Muslim community from which they came. "If God had wished he could make all creation rich, but for your trial he has created the poor that you might make gifts to them" (al-Ghazzali, 1972, p. 16).

Pilgrimage to Mecca

The city of Mecca in Saudi Arabia is the holy city of Islam. Every Muslim is enjoined to try to visit it once in his or her lifetime. This annual influx of pilgrims has kept the different Muslim peoples aware of their common bond through the centuries. The pilgrimage is a time in adult life when all social or commercial interests are put aside and pilgrims devote themselves to spiritual questions.

Sufi Teaching and Orthodox Islam

Al-Ghazzali wrote in a time that stressed formal observance of a practice, rather than the capacity of any practice to transform a person's inner being. His stories and illustrative examples serve to remind readers that formal practice, by itself, might be fruitless. One such story tells of an encounter between a Sufi teacher and a conventionally pious man:

> One day a man came to the teacher Bayazid and said: "I have fasted and prayed for thirty years and have found none of the spiritual joy of which you speak."
> "If you had fasted and prayed for three hundred years, you would never find it," answered the sage.
> "How is that?" asked the man.
> "Your selfishness is acting as a veil between you and God."
> "Tell me the cure."
> "It is a cure you cannot carry out," said Bayazid.
> Those around him pressed him to reveal it. After a time he spoke. "Go to the nearest barbershop and have your head shaved; strip yourself of your clothes except for a loincloth. Take a nosebag full of walnuts, hang it around your neck. Go into the market place and cry out—'Anybody who gives me a slap on the neck shall have a walnut.' Then proceed to the law courts and do the same thing."
> "I can't do that," said the man, "suggest some other remedy."
> "This is the indispensable preliminary to a cure," answered Bayazid, "but as I told you, you are incurable." [Adapted and condensed from al-Ghazzali, 1964a, pp. 128–130]

Women in Sufism and in Islam

It is often difficult to distinguish cultural, religious, and psychological ideas concerning the special status of women; nevertheless, the attempt is necessary in examining the role of women in Sufi thought.

From the early rise of Islam as a world religion, there has been a succession of women regarded as saints in Sufi circles and within Orthodox Islam. From Rabia (717–801 A.D.) to the current period, these saints have been venerated and their work studied in similar fashion to their male counterparts (M. Smith, 1977). An early Sufi teacher made it clear that in the spiritual life there could be neither male nor female. (Shabistari in M. Smith, 1977). In contemporary Sufi teachings and groupings women are present. The course of training is based on the capacities of the individual, not on the sex.[2]

Also, the rise of Islam changed the status of women, affording them "legal protections in the area of marriage, divorce and inheritance that are considered to mark a vast improvement over the situation of women in pre-Islamic society" (J. Smith, 1980, p. 517).

In spite of this equality in spiritual possibilities and the improved status through Islam, the position of women in most Islamic cultures is far less than equal. As in Europe and the Americas, women have been denied equal access to education, property rights, and freedom to travel and to develop themselves. There is a growing literature in the West that is beginning to distinguish between the repressive attitudes still current in many Muslim countries and the lack of religious and spiritual doctrines to support this repression (Smith & Haddad, 1975).

In Sufi teaching the numerous assertions about the status, special skills, and limitations of women within Islam have been secondary to the issues of personal development for men and women alike. Equally important within Sufism are concepts relating to forms of knowing, states of consciousness, and the nature of love.[3]

Knowledge

The first volume of al-Ghazzali's major work, *The Revival of Religious Sciences,* is *The Book of Knowledge* (1966). In it he divides knowledge into detrimental and useful branches. Detrimental knowledge is

---

[2]Irina Tweedie (1979) has written a vivid and detailed personal account of her own training and liberation with a contemporary Sufi teacher.

[3]In actual practice a Sufi teacher may or may not avail himself or herself of any of the terms defined here. Certainly, a Sufi teaching outside of Islam would not lean heavily on religious concepts foreign to the majority of the students. The special terms, ideas, and exercises are only tools a teacher may choose to employ. Superseding any terminology is the degree to which the student can benefit from the teaching; contrary to more conventional disciplines, the truth or falsity of an idea is secondary to its effectiveness in properly influencing the progress of a student. As the Sufi proverb says, "There are as many ways as there are souls of men." [S. Shah, 1933, p. 124]

knowledge that distracts from or retards understanding of our inner selves. Sufism has traditionally viewed scholarly training as antithetical to true understanding, and al-Ghazzali's own legal and scholarly background made him especially sensitive to its limits. He describes three limiting forms. *Logic* is limited, especially in evaluating spiritual questions, because logic does not generally allow the inclusion of novel or apparently contradictory information. *Philosophy* does not consider realistic situations and is self-limiting by not validating its conclusions through actual experience. *Academic knowledge* is vain posturing; it is detrimental when it parades itself as the exclusive path to learning.

A donkey with a load of books is still a donkey. [Sufi saying]

Because someone has made up the word "wave," do I have to distinguish it from water? [Kabir, 1977, p. 29]

Useful knowledge furthers a person's growth. The most important form is *direct knowledge;* it cannot be described but it can be experienced. It cannot be taught but it can be received. Ibn 'Arabi called it knowledge of reality. With it, "man can perceive what is right, what is true, beyond the boundaries of thought and sense" (in Shah, 1970a, p. 78). Sufi writings and teaching practices are the records of the ways in which generations of teachers have helped their students to have the experience of direct knowledge coupled with intuitive understanding. Intuition is developed to go beyond the limits of reason; therefore, it can perceive and integrate what reason alone could not accept.

Almost all systems of intuition and direct knowledge describe visionary events, moments of complete clarity. One goal of Sufi training is to hold onto this higher state, to become attuned to that level of reality so that it is not simply a memory. With proper teaching it can become ongoing awareness, as readily accessible as normal waking consciousness. The goal is not simply to glimpse or even experience these states but to come to rest in them, to be at home with this other world view.[4]

States of Consciousness

Beyond learning, beyond conventional knowledge, is the clear perception of reality. It can be understood during unusual states of consciousness. The states described here are not separate and distinct from each other but are different ways of understanding a common set of experiences.

Certainty

Certainty is having continuous access to direct knowledge. Certainty is immediate; it is knowledge that your whole being knows (Siraj-Ed-Din, 1970). For example, imagine that you wish to know about peaches. One way would be to see slides of different peaches, to study their biology; to learn about the methods of cultivation, where they are grown, how much they cost, what pests they attract, and so on. This would be academic knowledge and useful in its own fashion. However,

I laugh when I hear that the fish in the water is thirsty. [Kabir, 1977, p. 9]

[4]This closely resembles Maslow's description of "plateau experiences."

until you have touched, smelled, tasted, and eaten peaches you do not have direct knowledge of them. Experiencing a peach is comparable to certainty.

Conscious or Awake Existence

Being conscious means to respond to every situation as it is—not as it appears to be, not as one wishes it to be, not as if it were another, similar situation. When one is awake there is little concern with personal identity. It has two aspects. The first is a state of union or annihilation *(fana)* in which individual identity seems merged with the whole of reality. In this state a person erects no barriers between the self and God because it is clear that no barriers exist. If a drop of water were aware of being part of the ocean, if a column of air were conscious of the wind, that would be similar to the consciousness of those who are awake.

> What the eye sees is knowledge. What the heart knows is certainty. [Dhun'nun, in Shah, 1971a, p. 195]

The second is a state of return or persistence *(baqa')* in which one is part of the world but not concerned about one's position or rewards in it. The awareness of the divine element in things is so great that personal issues become secondary to being of service to others (ibn-'Arabi, 1981, Arberry, 1966, pp. 131–145).

Love

The end point of knowledge in the Sufism of al-Ghazzali is also called love. Similarly, the end point of love leads to the state of certainty. For the Sufi teacher the two are the same, only the approaches are different. Each path has been taken by different Sufi teachers. The way of knowledge has been most clearly defined by al-Ghazzali; the path of love, by the Persian poet Rumi (1207–1273).

> "The Sufi is he whose thought keeps pace with his foot," i.e., he is entirely present: his soul is where his body is, and his body where his soul is, and his soul is where his foot is, and his foot where his soul is. This is the sign of presence without absence. [Hujwîrî, 1959, p. 39]

For Rumi, love was the only force that could transcend the bounds of reason, the distinctions of knowledge, and the isolation of normal consciousness. The love he experienced was not sensual pleasure. It might be more aptly described as love for all things, for creation itself. Love is a continually expanding capacity that culminates in certainty, in the recognition that there is nothing in the world or in the spirit that is not both loved and loving.

> *Thou didst contrive this "I" and "we" in order that*
> *Thou mightest play the game of worship with Thyself,*
> *That all "I's" and "thou's" should become one soul and*
> *at last should be submerged in the Beloved.*
>
> [Rumi, Mathnavi I, in Arasteh, 1972, p. 146]

The perception of God as the Beloved, common to both Christian and Sufi writings, comes from direct experience. As you channel your energy into loving God, there appears to be a response, as if you are being loved in return; just as in a personal relationship, the act of loving brings forth or awakens love in another. The reach toward the divine is met with a grasp from that which is called the divine.

Within Sufism it is described as follows: When a person comes to a certain distance along the path of love, God reaches out and begins to assist the aspirant by drawing him or her toward his presence. As this occurs, the individual stops striving and begins to allow himself or herself to let go, be helped, be accepted, and be taken in.

> *Never, in sooth, does the lover seek without being sought by his beloved.*
> *When love of God waxes in thy heart, beyond any doubt God hath love for thee.*
> *No sound of clapping comes from one hand without the other hand.*
>
> [Rumi, Mathnavi III, in Nicholson, 1964b, p. 122]

DYNAMICS

Psychological Growth
Stages of Personal Development

Many Sufi teachers have described different stages in the course of personal development. Each stage trains or exposes different facets of the aspirant's character and perception.

We will describe each stage separately in order to facilitate an understanding of al-Ghazzali and others. This does not mean that any single linear pattern is typical or would be the actual experience of a Sufi student. Although other writers describe the stages differently (Arberry, 1970; Rice, 1964; Shah, 1964; Trimingham, 1971), they all acknowledge their debts to al-Ghazzali's earlier descriptions.

Initial Awakening. This stage begins when a person concludes that the external world is not fulfilling and it becomes necessary to reevaluate one's life. Such a realization is often preceded by a personal crisis, often coupled with bewilderment about the meaning of existence. It is the beginning of a fundamental reorientation of personal values. What one has strived for may appear to be worthless; what one casts aside as absurd may become filled with meaning. In al-Ghazzali's own case, he gave up his promising and successful career and became a dervish. This was only the beginning of the process of transformation, although it was the most dramatic change in his life. Rumi, too, left his academic teaching position to work with a Sufi teacher.

Patience and Gratitude. One soon comes to the realization that patience is required for progress and that it takes time to overcome personal limitaitons. Patience is not merely a passive acceptance of one's faults; it is the willingness to accept the fact that psychological change takes time and that one's efforts are not immediately rewarded. A person begins to reshape his or her personality gradually, the way a tree is shaped, nourished, and pruned, again and again. The growth of patience is accompanied by a sense of gratitude that one is given the time to make progress at all.

Fear and Hope. In this stage a person becomes more aware of the implications of daily actions. The rightness or wrongness of a behavior can no longer be based on the conventional morality. For example, giving food to the needy is commonly considered to be a moral act. However, if the food gives people enough strength to kill themselves or the energy to commit a crime, is the act truly beneficial? The intent of the action does not excuse its unintended effects.

It is impossible to know the full effects of your own actions. You hope that what you do is beneficial, but this hope is linked to the fear that your action may be detrimental. The hope of success is balanced by the fear of failure; the hope for security is coupled with the fear of stagnation. The task becomes the "avoidance of whatever has the least semblance or suspicion of wrong. . . ." (Hāfi, in Rice, 1964, pp. 40–41).

Self-Denial and Poverty. It should be evident that it is almost impossible to be secure in the stage of hopes and fears. It is always possible to construe one's actions as having some unfortunate results. One possible solution lies in detaching yourself from the world and doing as little as possible that might cause harm. Whereas poverty may be practiced in a literal sense—one may have no or few possessions—what is important is to be free of attachment. "When the heart is cleared (of all except God) poverty is not better than wealth nor is wealth better than poverty" (Hujwîrî, 1959, p. 24). What is important is the loss of desire, not the loss of property. "The vacant heart [is] more important than the vacant hand" (Rice, 1964, p. 42).

> Higher than the state of asceticism is the state wherein on the approach and departure of wealth the person remains unaffected equally. If it comes he is not glad and if it leaves him he is not sorry. [Al-Ghazzali, 1972, p. 206]

Our normal understanding of these matters is satirized in a traditional story about a rich man who asks a poor man what is the cause of the poor man's suffering. The poor man replies, "Half my wages go for food." "I see the cause of your trouble," says the rich one. "You spend your money foolishly. Less than one tenth of my money goes for food."

Trust in God (Belief in the Oneness of God). In this stage a person seeks neither support nor consolation from the external world. If one is sincere in one's personal quest, the earnestness of the effort begins to supplement the other forces that are helping the aspirant toward the goal.

> Some fools consider trust in God consists in sitting idle, hand on hand, doing nothing. [Al-Ghazzali, 1972, p. 254]

This is a period of activity, not a time of indolence, passivity, or dependency. The balance between acting for oneself and trusting in the divine is captured in the saying of Muhammad: "Trust in God but tie your camel first." Trust arises from assuming that your efforts are part of a larger system, the details of which you are unaware.

Love, Yearning, Intimacy, and Satisfaction.

In this stage the developing personality has only one desire, which is to love God; to love anything other than God is "veiled heresy." It becomes clear that this single desire is the only desire—the only desire that ever truly existed. The earlier stages of giving up attachments, overcoming greed, and the awareness of personal sin fade away under the all-encompassing power of this later realization.

> If you cannot discover and understand the secret of which I speak, it is not because it does not exist but because you do not seek rightly. If you make a distinction between the things which come from God you are not a man on the path of the spirit. If you consider yourself honoured by the diamond and humiliated by the stone, God is not with you. [Attar, 1961, p. 99]

Intent, Sincerity, and Truthfulness.

This stage is dominated by a concern for the intent, not the forms, of action. If one's intentions are correct, then the actual practice is less important. There is less interest in observable behaviors and an ever increasing awareness of the inner meaning of an action.

Al-Ghazzali tells the following story about the power of sincerity and the slackening of that personal power when sincerity is diminished:

> Amongst the Israelites was a pious man, reputed for his austerities. He heard that some people worshiped a tree. He took an axe and went to cut it. The Devil met him in the way and said, "Why worry with the worship others carry on? Let them do what they like. Who are you to interfere with it?" He replied, "This act of mine is also worship." The Devil said, "I shall not let you cut it." They both fought and the Devil lost. He prayed to the man to leave him telling him that he shall reveal a secret to him. The Devil then on release told the pious man that the Lord has created no obligation on him to cut the tree, besides if another person sins in his worship, its consequences will fall on him. Besides, there are many prophets of the Lord in the world and he could direct any one of them to go to the owners of the tree and order them to cut the tree. It did not behove him to perform an act which was not a duty cast on him.
>
> But the man insisted on cutting it. The Devil resisted and in the duel he again lost against the pious man. Again he persuaded the man to release him telling him he shall reveal a more valuable secret to him. The Devil began, on obtaining his release, "I have heard that you are very poor, living on the charity of others. Such is your good nature that you ever wish that if you had money you would distribute it amongst the needy and the poor, but you do not want to beg for that purpose. I have

Perhaps the wisdom of the sages was that, in fact, . . . the world was a divine conspiracy to liberate us and re-create us. [Dallas, 1973, p. 56]

I'm a kind of paranoiac in reverse. I suspect people of plotting to make me happy. [Salinger, 1965, p. 76]

Love came and like blood filled my veins and tissues, Emptied me of myself and filled me with the Friend. The Friend has taken possession of every atom of my being. [Rumi in Rice, 1964, p. 61]

But if you look at things with the eye of ordinary reason you will never understand how necessary it is to love. [Attar, 1961, p. 102]

Learning is the seed, practice is the field and intent is the water. With the help of the three does the crop of spirituality flourish. [Al-Ghazzali, 1972, p. 323]

therefore decided to leave every morning under your pillow some coins with which you shall easily feed your family and also play the samaritan. The charities will prove more beneficial to you than cutting down the tree. Even if you cut down the tree they can plant another at the spot. Your effort will then be useless and your family shall not gain anything thereby." Hearing this the man of piety thought that the Devil was right, inasmuch as he was no Prophet with commission from God to cut the tree, nor is it an obligatory duty on him to do so nor is there any reason for God to be angry with him if he did not cut it down. So he returned back home. In the morning when he got up from sleep he found coins under his pillow. He spent them on himself and on charity. That continued for some days. Then the Devil stopped his gift, so in resentment the man got up and went his way to cut the tree. On the way the Devil in the attire of an old man met him, and on learning that he was going to cut the tree told him that he had not the strength to do that now, and he was a liar if he boasted that he could cut down the tree. This irritated the man of piety and both began to fight. This time the Devil (in the form of the old man) defeated him and wanted to cut his throat when the man begged for life. The Devil excused him on the condition that he promise in the future never to cut the tree. He then asked the Devil, "How could you overcome me this time after losing twice?" The Devil replied that formerly he was fighting for God, and his intent was to reap a benefit in eternity, but now he was a slave of his carnal self and for the sake of world (money) he wanted to cut the tree. So he lost. [1972, pp. 321–322]

Contemplation and Self-Examination. Al-Ghazzali describes and considers the distractions that might prevent one from being calm and thus render one unable to perceive inner reality. His concerns are similar to those voiced in Yoga and Buddhism with regard to clearing the mind. He describes various ways of meditation and quotes incidents from the lives of teachers who were well versed in meditation. In one story al-Ghazzali tells of the saint Shibli who went to Abul Hasan Nuri. Nuri "was seated quiet in the corner of his room, steadfast in concentration and was not moving any limb. He asked him where had he learnt that secret practice? He replied, 'from a cat which was waiting to pounce on a rat' " (al-Ghazzali, 1972, p. 335).

The Recollection of Death. Contemplating death can be a powerful tool in releasing an individual from undesirable habits and attitudes. Thinking about one's own death is an exercise in becoming more aware of one's present experiences. It is one way of beginning the process of personal growth. In some sense, what al-Ghazzali described is a cycle beginning with conversion and repentance and ending with reflection on death. It can easily begin the other way, reflection on death leading to the psychological state that precedes conversion. Until recently Western psychology has avoided death. We are a death-fearing culture. Al-Ghazzali suggests the following exercise to engrave the awareness of death into your consciousness:

Remember your contemporaries who have passed away, and were of your age.

Remember the honours and fame they earned, the high posts they held and the beautiful bodies they possessed, and today all of them are turned to dust.

How they have left orphans and widows behind them and how their wealth is being wasted after them and their houses turned into ruins.

No sign of them is left today, and they lie in the dark holes underneath the earth.

Picture their faces before your mind's eye and ponder.

Do not fix hopes on your wealth and do not laugh away life. Remember how they walked and now all their joints lie separated and the tongue with which they talked lightly is eaten away by the worms and their teeth are corroded. They were foolishly providing for twenty years when even a day of their lives was not left. They never expected that death shall come to them thus at an unexpected hour. . . .[Al-Ghazzali, 1972, pp. 378–379]

Obstacles to Growth
Heedlessness (Forgetfulness)

The inability to pay attention and to remember what we know are the cardinal problems of humanity. It is the foundation that supports all other human weaknesses and psychopathology. It is inherent in our constitution that we lose sight of our divine origin; it is habitual that even as we remember we begin to forget. The thrust of Sufi teaching is to encourage people to pay attention long enough to *develop* their capacities to remain awake.

Man, like a sleepwalker who suddenly "comes to" on some lonely road, has in general no correct idea as to his origins or his destiny. [Shah, 1972f, p. 133]

Although many systems of morality describe the right way to live, they often fail to show how their principles can be put into practice. A first step in overcoming heedlessness is to learn to recognize it in your own life. It is as mundane as misplacing your glasses or as extreme as the story told about Norbert Weiner, the famous cybernetic researcher: One day he was walking along a path at the Massachusetts Institute of Technology when he met a colleague. They talked for a few minutes and as they parted, Weiner asked his friend to tell him in which direction he had been walking when they met. Weiner could not recall if he had been on his way to lunch or if he had just finished it.

Man is asleep, must he die before he wakes? [Saying of Muhammad]

Some of those who have been influenced by Sufi teachings indicate that the initial task is to wake up enough to be aware of one's predicament. Orage writes:

Our present waking state is not really being awake at all. . . . It is, the tradition says, a special form of sleep comparable to a hypnotic trance. . . . From the moment of birth and before, we are under the suggestion that we are not fully awake; and it is universally suggested to our consciousness that we must dream the dream of this world—as our parents and friends dream it. . . . Just as in night-dreams the first symptom of waking is to suspect that one is dreaming, the first symptom of waking from the waking state—the second awakening of religion—is the suspicion that our present waking state is dreaming likewise. To be aware that we are asleep is to be on the point of waking; and to be aware that we are only partially awake is the first conditioning of becoming and making ourselves more fully awake. [1965, p. 89]

As Harman concludes, "We are all hypnotized from infancy. . . . The apparent corollary is that we do not perceive ourselves and the world about us as they are but as we have been persuaded to perceive them" (1967, p. 323).

Incapacity

Sufi teachers point out that at any given moment not everyone is capable of assimilating Sufi teaching. If the student lacks the capacity to use the teachings, it is like pouring water into sand. There is a saying: "When the student is ready the teacher appears." This does not mean when the student thinks that he or she is ready; it means instead that when the teacher decides the student is ready for learning, the teacher will attract the student. The student's opinion has little to do with the actual level of readiness and nothing to do with the teacher's decision to accept or refuse the student.

Nafs

The *nafs* are impulses, or drives, to satisfy desires. They dominate reason or judgment and are defined as the forces in one's nature that must be brought under control. They prevent us from activating our totality.

All nafs are products of the self-centered consciousness—the ego, the "I"—and eventually can be controlled. The ideal of controlling the nafs is that *all impulses,* no matter what their effects are, can and should be subdued. This is true even if the effects are socially desired and rewarded; they still are an indication of a lack of inner capacity. The goal is to achieve a balance between impulsive excesses and arid detachment. The following descriptions are derived from a number of sources (Arasteh, 1973; al-Ghazzali, 1963; Trimingham, 1971; Shafii, 1974; Ozak, 1981).

The Commanding Nafs. Descriptions of these nafs are similar to descriptions of the id in psychoanalytic theory; they are closely linked to lust and aggression. Al-Ghazzali calls them the swine and the dogs of the soul—the sensual nafs behave like swine, the ferocious ones like dogs or wolves. Wrath, greed, sensual appetites, passion, and envy are examples of these nafs. A person dominated by these impulses is unlikely to grow beyond them. These impulses are not to be denied; however, they are to be properly redirected.

The Accusatory Nafs. These nafs parallel aspects of the psychoanalytic superego. They are evident in excessive self-accusation,
self-belittlement, or defensiveness, which appears in the form of excessive vanity. Typical manifestations include an insatiable need for
praise, hunger for recognition, or a need to control others. "In this stage
it is possible for one's motives to become so distorted that it is difficult
to distinguish between fantasy and reality" (Beg, 1973). You become
increasingly dependent on others' evaluations of yourself, and you are
unable to accept criticism if you are dominated by these nafs.

The Inspired Nafs. These nafs and those still higher in development
do not arise from the animal level; they arise from higher levels of personal consciousness. The problem is not their detrimental effects on
others, but their limiting effects on self-development. Behaviors common to the inspired nafs include gentleness, compassion, creative acts,
and moral action. Overall, a person who is impelled by the inspired nafs
seems to be an emotionally mature, respectable, and respected person.[5]
For many this is a high state to achieve. The Sufis teach that there is
far more potentially available to the aspiring soul.

The Tranquil Nafs. These nafs predispose one to be liberal, grateful,
trusting, and adoring. If you accept difficulties with the same overall
sense of security that you accept benefits, it may be said that you are
dominated by the tranquil nafs. Developmentally, these nafs mark a
period of transition. The soul can now begin to "disintegrate" and let
go of all previous concern with self-boundaries; it can begin to "reintegrate" as an aspect of the universal self (Arasteh, 1973). In this stage
actions are not performed for conventionally pious reasons but because
one is becoming aware of the divine will; one's actions are in accord
with the inner natural law. "The Sufi reaches a stage where one transcends the duality of good and bad and perceives all of the manifest
dualities as part of a unitary continuum of existence. Categorizing observations or experiences into good-bad, beautiful-ugly, rich-poor, plea-
sure-pain disappears" (Shafii, 1974, p. 6).

> The radical division into
> good and bad can be *the*
> sickness of the Mind.
> [Erikson, 1964]

The Fulfilled, the Fulfilling, and the Perfected Nafs. These final
levels are not easily distinguished or described. They are the obstacles
that plague spiritual leaders. These nafs can include the sight of the
teachers' own good deeds (which can rearouse vanity) and the sight of
their effectiveness with their students (which can rearouse feelings of
power or pride).

   The nafs are parallel to the stages of development described earlier. Each stage of growth has within it nafs, or impulses, that are contrary to the values of that stage. The conflict leads to growth when the
nafs are subdued or to regression if the nafs predominate.

---

[5]This is similar to the māna personality described by Jung.

STRUCTURE

Body

Al-Ghazzali says that one should consider the body as the carrier and the soul as the rider. "The soul should take care of the body, just as a pilgrim on his way to Mecca takes care of his camel; but if the pilgrim spends his whole time in feeding and adorning his camel, the caravan will leave him behind, and he will perish in the desert" (al-Ghazzali, 1964a, p. 49). Good health is encouraged to the extent that it allows the inner work to proceed without impediment.

Some Sufi schools employ exercises that entail a "fine tuning" of the body and mind. The so-called "dervish dancing," a combination of music and movement, is the most widely known. "The objective is to produce a state of ritual ecstasy and to accelerate the contact of the Sufi's mind with the world-mind of which he considers himself to be a part" (Burke, 1966, p. 10). An exercise may be movement, movement with music, or music alone. Sufi teachers maintain that although music may be effective in bringing on certain states for limited purposes and periods, the adept neither needs any stimulus nor experiences any ecstasy at all. In fact, it might be taken as axiomatic that the purpose of ecstasy is to go beyond it.

> The Body too is a great and necessary principle, and without it the task fails and the purpose is not attained. [Rumi, 1972, p. 31]

The use of dance to bring about this state of ecstasy is described by Burke (1966): "A dance is defined as bodily movements linked to a thought and a sound or a series of sounds. The movements develop the body, the thought focuses the mind, and the sound fuses the two and orientates them towards a consciousness of divine contact . . ." (1975, p. 49). This ecstatic state is a physical condition that allows certain inner experiences to be felt and understood; it is not simply a joyful, hyperaroused state. The body is not the source of experience; it is the channel through which experience passes.

Social Relationships

Whereas Western theorists as different as James and Skinner describe much of personality in terms of social roles, there is far less emphasis on roles in Sufism. Many authors simply suggest that one behaves within the cultural values of the culture one lives in. Al-Ghazzali wrote pragmatic letters to government officials (1976) and even set out suggestions for rulers (1964b) that were a mixture of strict adherence to Islamic law and compassionate intuition in specific situations.

He did, however, discuss two special situations: the relationship of teachers to students and the relationship between close companions.

The crucial elements in a teaching relationship are to be determined by the teacher, not by the students. The establishment and organization of a group is an important element in Sufi studies. What kind of group a student is in is a decision of critical importance. Some groups may perform exercises, others will do none. A group may be "rested" from exercises—that is, they are told to refrain from the practices they have been working with. Random or self-selected groups are prohibited; some people may be put into a group for a short time or not at all. The purpose of working in a group is to further the development of the individuals and to maximize the effectiveness of the lessons that the teacher is offering. The effect on each individual is a combination of the lessons and the degree of awareness of the student.

> The kernel of the human development called "Sufism" is the basic human unit: the members who meet together and carry on the studies prescribed for them by a contemporary teacher. . . .
> This is necessary to the realization which comes from being a Sufi. It may be called community, communion, meeting. . . . It is often called the *Jam*—coming together. . . . No higher attainment is possible to man unless the circumstances of the coming-together are correct; unless it is a communion including the right people, at the right time, in the right place. [Foster, 1968, p. 14]

It is the special nature of a Sufi group (an association of people selected to complement each other) to be able to work correctly toward a certain goal that produces the right alignment and reduces the likelihood of undesirable developments. What Carl Rogers calls "the innate healing capacity of the group" has been well understood by Sufi teachers.

A teaching story by Sa'di (c. 1200–1291) catches the matter-of-fact way in which teachers deal with relationships:

> A student said to his teacher: "What am I to do? I am troubled by the people, many of whom pay me visits. By their coming and going they encroach upon my precious time." He replied: "Lend something to every one of them who is poor and ask something from every one who is rich and they will come round thee no more." [1966, p. 131]

In addition to the relations between students and teachers, there is the important relationship between companions on the Sufi path. Al-Ghazzali wrote that real friendship included the following eight responsibilities:

You will not enter Paradise until you believe, and you will not believe until you love another. Let me guide you to something in the doing of which you will love one another: salute all and sundry among you. [Saying of Muhammad]

1. *Material aid.* You have an obligation to help your companions with food, or money, or other things they need for their own survival or development.
2. *Personal support.* "If they are sick, visit them; if they are busy, help them; if they have forgotten, remind them" (1975, p. 33).
3. *Respect.* You should not complain of their faults to them or to others. Also you should not give advice when you know it cannot be acted upon.
4. *Praise and attention.* You should praise the good qualities of your companions and let them know that you care for them.

5. *Forgiveness.* It is helpful to forgive others for their failings.
6. *Prayer.* You should pray for the well-being of your companions with the same fervor as you pray for your own well-being.
7. *Loyalty.* You should be firm in your friendships so that you can be depended on by those who put their trust in you.
8. *Relief from discomfort.* You should not create awkward or difficult situations that involve your companions. You should not be a burden to others.

This straightforward description of the duties of one person toward another was designed to clarify the value and to emphasize the need for mutual support. Sufism suggests that we need other people for our own sake and to help us put into practice the fruits of our own inner work.

Will

Although the term *will* is used in Sufi writings, it is elusive and not subject to a single definition. " 'Will,' to the Sufi, will vary in nature, quality and significance in direct relation to the stage which the aspirant has reached" (Khan, 1974). Every act is made up of the conception, the motivation, and the capacity to carry it out.

Free Will

Free will is assumed to be part of human nature. Humanity is unique in its propensity and capacity to perform actions that are contrary to natural law and incompatible with physical, mental, or spiritual health. Unlike animals, we have the ability to turn away from our own best interests.

. . . The effort of attention by which we hold fast to an idea . . . is the secret of will . . . [James, 1899, p. 91]

Divine Will

In contrast to free will, divine will is described as a fundamental law of nature. A stone falls because it is obeying the divine will manifested as gravity. In this way, one definition of a saint might be one whose every action is in conformity with the divine will. Learning to be a saint is learning to be sensitive and to be "attuned" to natural laws of thought and action, laws as regular as the natural laws of electricity and magnetism. Personal will is capable of directing one's life toward the point of surrender to the divine will.

Thy will be done On earth as it is in heaven. [Lord's Prayer]

Emotions

Emotional states are simply states through which a person passes. One's emotional reactions to a situation can serve as an indicator of one's level of attachment or concern. There is some emphasis on the use and the transformation of emotional states. Emotions orient con-

Three things in life are destructive: anger, greed and pride. [Saying of Muhammad]

sciousness either toward or away from knowledge of reality. A particular emotion is less important than its overall effect on one's behavior. Al-Ghazzali recalls times of bliss and despair, both of which he saw as instrumental in his own realization (1968a).

There is no injunction to suppress or deny one's emotions. Any emotion can serve as a guide or a goad to proper action. For example, al-Ghazzali suggests that, properly used, fear can strengthen one's resolve to overcome the nafs.

Intellect

Al-Ghazzali's description of the intellect foreshadows the developmental models of Piaget and Inhelder (1952, 1958). He distinguishes four stages of development. First there is a drive for understanding, what Western psychology calls curiosity or the need for competence (White, 1959). Second is "axiomatic" intellect, which is the capacity to understand logical relationships. The third element is "empirical knowledge"; it is the aspect that is concerned with external things and events. The last element to appear is the "developed" intellect, which is a higher form of the original drive for understanding. It is this quality of the intellect that guides inner development and allows a person to "conquer and subdue his appetite which hankers for immediate pleasure" (al-Ghazzali, 1966, p. 228).

Knowledge is of two kinds: native and acquired, But no acquired knowledge is of any use
If there is no native knowledge,
Just as the light of the sun is useless
When the light of the eyes is shut off. ['Ali in al-Ghazzali, 1966, p. 228]

Conventional learning can veil or retard the developed intellect if its function is not understood. Al-Ghazzali again and again upbraids his former scholastic colleagues for their unwillingness to use their learning to go beyond it to real knowledge (Watt, 1971). He recounts that he needed to pierce his own intellectual training repeatedly with ecstatic and revelatory states until he understood enough to keep his intellect in balance.

Self

There are two ways to describe the self. The first way is to see the self as a collection of socially determined, changeable roles—the self within society. The second is to see the true self, the core of one's being, distinct yet part of a larger unity. Sufi teaching is one way to learn to shift your identification of who you are from the first point of view to the second. As you identify more and more with your inner self, you do not deny or give up your own personality. What happens is that as you fully accept yourself for who you truly are, the external attributes of personality (how you speak, how you eat, and so forth) are put into a new perspective. They assume their natural place in the totality of your personality.

He who knows himself knows his Lord. [Saying of Muhammad]

Different Sufi teachers have different personalities, both before and after they are able to identify with the divine. It is only the internal point of identification that has shifted. The personal characteristics of individuals (hair color or skin texture, for example) are part of the new integration of the personality and are relatively unchanged.

In the course of training, however, there is often a feeling that one is asked to disown part of oneself, to be different. What is really being asked is that the pupil recognize the part of his or her personality that is an obstacle to a particular period of training. An individual is encouraged to come to terms with the obstacle and reorient his or her own reactions more effectively. If a person sees that the best way to proceed is to eliminate the behavior, he or she may do so. If one sees that the problem can be solved by retaining the behavior but restraining it, that may be equally beneficial.

Teacher

A teacher or guide instructs so that students may move closer to realizing their inner nature. A guide, says al-Ghazzali, teaches out of his or her own fullness. Teaching is in itself an expression of the divine will.

Why is a guide necessary? Mohammed Shafii, a psychiatrist knowledgeable in Sufi tradition, suggests:

> The Sufis feel that maturity cannot be achieved alone. They feel there is a need for guidance and discipline. The path is unknown, the night is dark and the road is full of danger. Dangers include preoccupation with selfishness, false visions, misinterpretations of mystical states, arrest in development, fixation in a particular state, appeal to various drugs to create false mystical experiences and not infrequently overwhelming anxiety and insanity. [1968, p. 11]

It is generally accepted that one cannot progress past a certain point without the aid of a teacher. Among many other qualities, a teacher must possess a *sense of occasion*. This is the capacity to know when a lesson, an experience, or an exercise will help the student. Teaching can only occur at the right time, in the right place, and in the right company, or it will be wasted. Thus a single exercise or story may prove effective when employed by a teacher; but when used by a student on another occasion, it may have no effect at all. "One reason for the institution of a Guide is that he knows when to direct the disciple's effort and work, and when not to direct it. He also knows the kind of effort and work which each individual should do. Only the ignorant mistake any work for useful work . . ." (Palawan-i-Zaif, in Shah, 1970b, p. 229).

Duties of a Teacher

Al-Ghazzali lists eight duties of a teacher (1966, pp. 145–152). They touch on many of the aspects of Sufi teaching but should not be viewed as any kind of standard list applicable to every Sufi teacher.

1. "The first duty of the teacher is to be sympathetic to students and treat them as his own children." The teacher must care about the

But how will you ever know him
as long as you are unable
to know yourself? [Sanai, 1974, p. 10]

With a Guide you may become a real man, without one you will remain an animal. [Rumi, in Shah, 1970a, p. 37]

The Way requires (1) a teacher who has been that way before; (2) an individual whose consciousness is correctly oriented so that he can make use of the material given to him; and (3) a group of such people. [Abdul-Hamid, 1976, p. 57]

students' welfare with the same or greater devotion as a father or mother for his or her own children. The teacher must be constantly aware of their failings but, like a parent, be always able to love the students.

2. "The second duty of the teacher is to follow the example of the Law-giver: he should seek no remuneration for his services . . . and accept neither reward nor thanks." Sufi teachers usually have an occupation and thus do not depend on their students for their livelihood. The teacher should feel gratitude toward the students for their willingness to learn.

3. "[The teacher] should not withhold from the student any advice, or allow him to attempt work at any grade unless he is qualified for it . . ." The teacher, not the student, is the judge of the student's progress.

4. "The teacher, in dissuading the student from his evil ways, should do so by suggestion rather than openly, and with sympathy rather than with odious upbraiding. . . . Open dissuasion destroys the veil of awe, invites defiance, and encourages stubbornness." Before the advent of behaviorism, al-Ghazzali discussed the differential effects of reinforcement and punishment in the learning process. He concluded that punishments inhibit overall learning.

5. "The person who is teaching a certain science should not belittle or disparage the value of other sciences before his students." To attack other teachers is demeaning to the teacher and to the students. The task of a teacher is to teach what he or she knows. It is not to pressure the student into doubting other teachers who may benefit the student at another stage in his or her development. It is usual in Sufi training to be sent to study with others from time to time. The teacher recognizes that the primary goal is the education of the student, not dependence on or adoration for the teacher.

6. "He should limit the student to what the latter is able to understand and should not require of him anything which his mind cannot grasp for fear that he would develop a feeling of dislike for the subject, and his mind would become confused." This admonition is similar to the instructions for structuring programmed learning. Each link is designed to prevent the student from progressing until he or she has completed the preceding lesson correctly.

7. "The teacher should give his backward students only such things as are clear and suitable to their limited understanding and should not mention to them anything about the details that are apt to follow but which he deems fitting for the present to withhold. . . . Everyone usually believes himself capable of mastering every science no matter how complex. . . . Even the most foolish and most feeble-minded among men is usually the most pleased with the perfection of his mind." If one teaches beyond a person's ability to understand, the

> If men had been forbidden to make porridge of camel's dung, they would have done it, saying that they would not have been forbidden to do it unless there had been some good in it. [Saying of Muhammad in al-Ghazzali, 1966, p. 149]

effort is wasted. "A donkey stabled in a library does not become literate" (Hadir in Shah, 1970a, p. 273). Material learned prematurely may be misinterpreted and can in itself become an obstacle later on. Ajmal of Badakhshan comments on the necessity of teaching only what can be learned at the time:

> There are three ways of presenting anything.
> The first is to present everything.
> The second is to present what people want.
> The third is to present what will serve them best.
> If you present everything, the result may be surfeit.
> If you present what people want, it may choke them.
> If you present what will serve them best, the worst is that, misunderstanding, they may oppose you. But if you have served them thus, whatever the appearances, you have served them.
> [In Shah, 1970a, p. 224]

> The Sufi must act and speak in a manner which takes into consideration the understanding, limitations and dominant concealed prejudices of his audience. [Ibn el-Arabi, in Shah, 1970a, p. 33]

8. "The teacher must do what he teaches and not allow his works to give the lie to his words." The teacher is not just a source of information, rather, he or she is a living example of the effect of teaching. The students and the teacher are all working together. "Teachers talk about teachings. Real teachers study their pupils as well. Most of all, teachers should be studied" (Musa Kazim, in Shah, 1970a, p. 221).

EVALUATION

Sufism is difficult to evaluate because it has taken so many forms and adapted its teachings to many different cultural settings. Sufism has been presented here as a theory of personality and a way of self-understanding, rather than as a religious doctrine.

Most descriptions of Sufism characterize it as an integral part of Islam. In our presentation we have placed little emphasis on the Islamic elements. The reasons for this parallel a similar decision made by a current translator of the Sufi poet Sanai. His remarks might well be our own.

> The principles which guided my selection are bound to be highly subjective. . . . Another interpreter might well assemble a very different set. . . . For example, I have soft-pedalled on the traditional Moslem elements which are very much in evidence. . . . Much of Sanai's [and even more so al-Ghazzali's] material caters for an audience imbued with the letter if not with the spirit of the Koran and the *Hadith* [sayings of Muhammad]. There seemed little point in including such material for its own sake, since the conditions which necessitated its inclusion in the first place do not exist here and now. Moreover the effect would be the reverse of what was intended . . . it would simply estrange a Western reader of Christian extraction. Sanai had to present impeccable orthodox credentials in order to be allowed to introduce other materials which, though of essentially greater value, could be and were indeed regarded as heretical by the bigots of his day. [Pendlebury, 1974, pp. 56–57]

Sufism is an ancient tradition; but it has not become so formal, so burdened with old ideas and practices, that it has lost its relevance. It is still responsive to new cultural demands and is still modifying its methods and its message for a new generation of students who can be taught Sufism (Shah, 1981).

There is little use in teaching wisdom. At all events wisdom cannot be taught in words. It is only possible by personal contact and by immediate experience. [Jung, 1973]

It is difficult to accept the emphasis on the need for a living personal teacher. We have become accustomed to the idea that there is nothing that we cannot do for ourselves. Bookstores bulge with shelves of do-it-yourself literature on everything from carpentry to beekeeping, Yoga to childbirth. What Sufism suggests is that you must do the work yourself, but a teacher can help keep you from working unprofitably. It is a common error to think that because you are working hard and diligently your work will lead to some personal benefit. No matter how hard you whip your horse, no matter how hard you kick its sides, no matter how fast it goes; if you are racing around a circular track, you will not go any farther than the point where you started.

One begins to appreciate the Sufi point of view by experiencing the distinctions between knowledge and useful knowledge as illustrated by the following story:

> Nasrudin sometimes took people for trips in his boat. One day a fussy pedagogue hired him to ferry him across a very wide river.
> As soon as they were afloat the scholar asked whether it was going to be rough.
> "Don't ask me nothing about it," said Nasrudin.
> "Have you never studied grammar?"
> "No," said the Mulla.
> "In that case, half your life has been wasted."
> The Mulla said nothing.
> Soon a terrible storm blew up. The Mulla's crazy cockleshell was filling with water.
> He leaned over towards his companion.
> "Have you ever learnt to swim?"
> "No," said the pedant.
> "In that case, schoolmaster, ALL your life is lost, for we are sinking."
> [Shah, 1972d, p. 18]

Not only do humorous tales contain valuable structures for understanding. Their use also helps to weed out people who lack a sense of humour. Sufis hold that people who have not developed or who have suppressed their capacity to enjoy humour are, in this deprived state, also without learning capacity. [Shah, 1981, p. 21]

The story raises some questions: What have you learned that is useful knowledge? What have you learned that is extraneous to your life? What have you learned that may, even now, be holding you back?

Sufism proposes that the more we can sift out the true from the unimportant and the false, the closer we are to being able to see the larger picture of humanity, of which our personality is such a small part.

It has been said that in the West we are able to use only very little of the Sufi teaching. It is all too new to us; it contains too many ideas that we immediately dismiss. It is for this reason that some teachers say they are laying the groundwork for later, more direct teaching experiences. One contemporary teacher has said, "There are different ways of 'awakening.' Man may be asleep, but he must wake in the right way. One necessity is that when he is awake, he will also have the means to profit by his wakefulness. It is the preparation for this profiting as well as the preparation for waking, which is our current endeavor" (Pendlebury, 1974, p. 74).

This chapter is a presentation of unfamiliar materials so that as Sufi ideas become more available to the West, we can more easily accept and understand them.

THE THEORY FIRSTHAND

Stories, one of the many teaching tools of the Sufi tradition, can be studied, extended into exercises, read aloud, or can be simply enjoyed. They are one way that students who know little about Sufism can be exposed to some of its perspectives and a few of its levels, although not its actual operation.

Stories may be used to evoke specific responses in the minds of listeners, to clarify a point in a lesson, or to keep alive some particular aspects of a teacher's work. If a story is entertaining enough, it will be preserved and passed from generation to generation even if the people who tell it have lost the capacity to understand some of its levels of meaning.

Here are a few stories from the works of Idries Shah, a contemporary teacher who has revived the use of teaching stories in both Eastern and Western cultures.

THE TALE OF THE SANDS

A stream, from its source in far-off mountains, passing through every kind and description of countryside, at last reached the sands of the desert. Just as it had crossed every other barrier, the stream tried to cross this one, but it found that as fast as it ran into the sand, its waters disappeared.

It was convinced, however, that its destiny was to cross this desert, and yet there was no way. Now a hidden voice, coming from the desert itself, whispered: "The Wind crosses the desert, and so can the stream."

The stream objected that it was dashing itself against the sand, and only getting absorbed: that the wind could fly, and this was why it could cross a desert.

"By hurtling in your own accustomed way you cannot get across. You will either disappear or become a marsh. You must allow the wind to carry you over, to your destination."

But how could this happen? "By allowing yourself to be absorbed in the wind."

This idea was not acceptable to the stream. After all, it had never been absorbed before. It did not want to lose its individuality. And, once having lost it, how was one to know that it could ever be regained?

"The wind," said the sand, "performs this function. It takes up water, carries it over the desert, and then lets it fall again. Falling as rain, the water again becomes a river."

"How can I know that this is true?"

"It is so, and if you do not believe it, you cannot become more than a quagmire, and even that could take many, many years; and it certainly is not the same as a stream."

"But can I not remain the same stream that I am today?"

"You cannot in either case remain so," the whisper said. "Your essential part is carried away and forms a stream again. You are called what you are even today because you do not know which part of you is the essential one."

When he heard this, certain echoes began to arise in the thoughts of the stream. Dimly, he remembered a state in which he—or some part of him, was it?—had been held in the arms of a wind. He also remembered—or did he?—that this was the real thing, not necessarily the obvious thing, to do.

And the stream raised his vapour into the welcoming arms of the wind, which gently and easily bore it upwards and along, letting it fall softly as soon as they reached the roof of a mountain, many, many miles away. And because he had had his doubts, the stream was able to remember and record more strongly in his mind the details of the experience. He reflected, "Yes, now I have learned my true identity."

The stream was learning. But the sands whispered: "We know, because we see it happen day after day: and because we, the sands, extend from the riverside all the way to the mountain."

And that is why it is said that the way in which the Stream of Life is to continue on its journey is written in the Sands. [Shah, 1970b, pp. 23–24]

THE TALE OF MELON CITY

The ruler of a certain city one day decided that he would like a triumphal arch built, so that he could ride under it with all pomp, for the desirable edification of the multitude. But when the great moment came, his crown was knocked off: the arch had been built too low.

The ruler therefore ordained, in his rightful wrath, that the chief of the builders should be hanged. Gallows were prepared, but—as he was being taken to the place of execution—the Master-Builder called out that it was all the fault of the workmen, who had done the actual construction job.

The king, with his customary sense of justice, called the workers to account. But they escaped the charge by explaining that the masons had made the bricks of the wrong size. And the masons said that they had only carried out the orders of the architect. He, in turn, reminded the king that his Majesty had, at the last moment, made some amendments of his own to the plans, changing them.

"Summon the wisest man in the country," said the ruler, "for this is undoubtedly a difficult problem, and we need counsel."

The wisest man was carried in, unable to stand on his own feet, so ancient (and therefore so wise) was he. "It is evident," he quavered, "that in law the actual culprit must be punished, and that is, in this case, quite evidently, none other than the arch itself."

Applauding his decision, the king ordered that the offending arch be carried to the scaffold. But as it was being taken there, one of the Royal Councillors pointed out that this arch was something which had actually touched the august head of the monarch and must surely never be disgraced by the rope of execution.

As in the meantime, exhausted by his exertions, the venerable wise man had breathed his last, the people were unable to apply to him for an interpretation of this new observation. The doctors of Law, however, decreed that the *lower* part of the arch, which had not touched anything at all, could be hanged for the crime of the whole arch.

But when the executioner tried to put the arch into the noose, he found that the rope was too short. The rope-maker was called, but he soon explained that in his opinion it was the scaffold that was too high. He suggested that the carpenters were at fault.

"The crowd is getting impatient," said the king, "and we must therefore quickly find someone to hang. We can postpone the consideration of finer points like guilt until a later, more convenient, occasion."

In a surprisingly short time, all the people in the city had been carefully measured, but only one was found tall enough to fit the gallows. It was the king himself. Such was the popular enthusiasm at the discovery of a man who would fit, that the king had to conform, and he was hanged.

"Thank goodness we found someone," said the Prime Minister, "for if we had not satisfied the appetite of the mob, they would undoubtedly have turned against the Crown."

But there were important matters to consider, for almost at once it was realised that the king was dead. "In conformity with custom," announced the heralds in the streets, "the first man who passes the city gate shall decide who is to be our next great ruler."

The very next man to wander past the gate was an idiot. He was quite unlike the ordinary sensible citizens with whom we have become familiar, and when he was asked who should be king, immediately said: "A melon." This was because he always said "A melon" to every question. In fact, he thought about nothing else, being very fond of melons.

And thus it came about that a melon was, with due ceremony, crowned.

Now that was years and years ago. Nowadays, when people ask the inhabitants of that land why their king seems to be a melon, they say: "Because of the customary choice. His Majesty evidently desires to be a melon. Certainly we shall allow him to remain one until his further pleasure be known. He has, in our country, every right to be what he wants to be. We are content with that, so long as he does not interfere in our lives." [Shah, 1972b, pp. 83–84]

THE ANTS AND THE PEN

An ant one day strayed across a piece of paper and saw a pen writing in fine, black strokes.

"How wonderful this is!" said the ant. "This remarkable thing, with a life of its own, makes squiggles on this beautiful surface, to such an extent and with such energy that it is equal to the efforts of all the ants in the world. And the squiggles which it makes! These resemble ants: not one, but millions, all run together."

He repeated his ideas to another ant, who was equally interested. He praised the powers of observation and reflection of the first ant.

But another ant said: "Profiting, it must be admitted, by your efforts, I have observed this strange object. But I have determined that it is not the master of this work. You failed to notice that this pen is attached to certain other objects, which surround it and drive it on its way. These should be considered as the moving factor, and given the credit." Thus were fingers discovered by the ants.

But another ant, after a long time, climbed over the fingers and realised that they comprised a hand, which he thoroughly explored, after the manner of ants, by scrambling all over it.

He returned to his fellows: "Ants!" he cried, "I have news of importance for you. Those smaller objects are a part of a large one. It is this which gives motion to them."

But then it was discovered that the hand was attached to an arm, and the arm to a body, and that there were two hands, and that there were feet which did no writing.

The investigations continue. Of the mechanics of the writing, the ants have a fair idea. Of the meaning and intention of the writing, and how it is ultimately controlled, they will not find out by their customary method of investigation. Because they are "literate." [Shah, 1972b, pp. 180–181]

EXERCISES

To ask for a purely intellectual proof of the existence of God is like asking for the privilege of being able to see with your ears. [Baba, 1972]

The exercises have been drawn from authors who have been influenced by Sufi ideas. They are not "Sufi" exercises because Sufi exercises are designed to suit a particular time, place, and group assembled for that purpose. These exercises do not fulfill all of those necessary conditions. No exercises in a book intended for general use could do so. Therefore understand that the exercises are presented to help you "taste" some of the concepts presented in this chapter.

You should not expect from a book what it cannot deliver.

The Key and the Light

Throughout this chapter we have made use of teaching stories—stories that are told by Sufi teachers for more than just entertainment. Here is one famous story and some ways to work with it (adapted from Ornstein, 1972).

MULLA

A man is looking at Nasrudin who is searching for something on the ground.
"What have you lost, Mulla?" the man asked.
"My key," said the Mulla.
So they both went down on their knees and looked for it.
After a time the man asked, "Where exactly did you drop it?"
"In my own house."
"Then why are you looking here?"
"There is more light here than inside my own house." [Shah, 1972d, p. 26]

The joke is well known in American vaudeville as well as in Sufism. If one begins to work with it, it can be more than a joke, more than a story about a simpleton.

Read the story over a few times. Now imagine that you are searching desperately for something.

1. What are you looking for? (Allow an answer, no matter how unusual, to form in your mind.) Where are you looking? Is there a lot of light

there? What kinds of associations did these questions evoke? How do you feel now?

2. Now think about a key. What is a key for? What is the key for your life right now? (Again, allow an answer, an image, or an idea to form; take your time.)

3. Now say to yourself, "I have lost my key." What does this evoke in you?

4. Now think that "my key is in my own house." What are your thoughts and feelings?

5. Then put the whole story together: "I am looking for my key—which I really know is in my own house—in places where I know the key is not, but where there is more light." Spend a little more time with the story.

In addition to the personal associations called up by the story, I offer another. . . . Two areas of the mind are opposed, the light, or "day," and the dark, or "night." The key is inside the house, in the dark, unexplored area of our house, of the mind, of science. We are normally attracted and a bit dazzled by the light of the day, since it is generally easier to find objects in daylight. But *what we are looking for may simply not be there,* and often we may have to grope around somewhat inelegantly in the dark areas to find it. Once we find what we are looking for in the dark, we can then bring it into the light, and create a synthesis of both areas of the mind. [Ornstein, 1972, pp. 174–175]

Do You Know What You Like, Do You Like What You Do?
Here is an exercise to investigate your own heedlessness. Are you constantly aware of the choices and decisions you make?

You wake up in the morning and propose to get up. Ask yourself whether you really wish to get up, and be candid about it.

You take a bath—is it really because you like it or would you dodge it if you could?

You eat your breakfast—is it exactly the breakfast you like in kind and quantity? Is it just *your* breakfast you eat, or simply breakfast as defined by society? Do you, in fact, wish to eat at all?

You go to your office . . . or you set about domestic and social duties of the day—are they your native tastes? Would you freely choose to be where you are and do what you do? Assume that, for the present, you accept the general situation. Are you in detail doing what you like? Do you speak as you please to other persons? Do you really like or only pretend to like them? (Remember that it is not a question yet of *acting* on your likes and dislikes but only of discovering what they really are.)

You pass the day, every phase offering a new opportunity for self-questioning—do I really like this or not? The evening arrives with leisure—what would you really like to do? What truly amuses you: theater or movies, conversation, reading, music, games, and which ones in particular?

It cannot be repeated too often that the doing of what you like comes later. In fact, it can be left to take care of itself. The important thing is to know what you like. [Orage, 1965, p. 112]

A Question of Priorities
You have died. You have pleaded with the Angel of Death to be allowed to return to life. There are so many things you have yet to do. The Angel of Death grants you one additional day—no more.

Imagine that tomorrow morning is the morning of that extra day. What will you do? How will you spend the day?

ANNOTATED BIBLIOGRAPHY

Al-Ghazzali. *The revival of religious sciences.* Farnham, Surrey: Sufi Publishing, 1972. The best translation of the most important of Al-Ghazzali's major works.

———. *Ghazzali's Lhya Ulum-id-din* (Alhaj Maulana Fazlul Karim, Trans.). Dacca, Bangladesh: Mission Trust, 1971. Only full translation of the *Revival* available.

———. *The alchemy of happiness.* Lahore, Pakistan: Muhammad Ashraf, 1964. Part of his own abridgment of *The Revival of Religious Sciences.* It is a short vivid book with very few references to purely Islamic ideas.

Bakhtiar, Laleh. *Sufi: Expressions of the mystic quest.* 1976. A different approach; symbolic, geometric, and with beautiful illustrations. New York: Avon

Burke, Omar M. *Among the dervishes.* New York: Dutton, 1975. Burke traveled and lived in Sufi communities in the Near and Middle East. Since he speaks several Oriental languages he was able to experience and report on how contemporary Sufi communities carry on the teachings today.

Muzaffer, Ozak Al-Jerrahi, *The unveiling of love* (Muhtar Holland, New York: Inner Traditions, 1981.

Shah, Idries. *The Sufis.* New York: Doubleday, 1971. The best single overall book on Sufism. Shah discusses all the major Sufi teachers, Sufism's major influences on Western thought, and some of the central ideas of Sufi practice.

———. *Tales of the dervishes.* New York: Dutton, 1970.

———. *The way of the Sufi.* New York: Dutton, 1970.

———. *The pleasantries of the incredible Mulla Nasrudin.* New York: Dutton, 1971. Three collections of traditional Sufi materials brought together by Shah. *Tales of the Dervishes* is a series of traditional teaching stories. *The Way of the Sufi* is a collection of sayings, sermons, meditations, questions and answers, and stories from the major figures and schools of Sufism. *The Pleasantries of the Incredible Mulla Nasrudin* is a collection of short funny stories about the Mulla, a folk hero who is the subject of numerous Sufi stories. Of the three collections, this is the easiest to understand.

REFERENCES

Abdul-Hamid, Sufi. First statement. In L. Lewin (Ed.), *The elephant in the dark.* New York: Dutton, 1976.

Al-Ghazzali. *Mishkat al-anwar (the niche for lights)* (W. H. T. Gairdner, Trans.). Lahore, Pakistan: Muhammad Ashraf, 1952.

———. *The foundations of the articles of faith* (Nabih Amin Faris, Trans.). Lahore, Pakistan: Muhammad Ashraf, 1963.

———. *The alchemy of happiness* (Claud Field, Trans.) Lahore, Pakistan: Muhammad Ashraf, 1964.

———. *Ghazzali's book of counsel for kings* (F. R. C. Bagley, Trans.). London: Oxford University Press, 1964.

———. *The book of knowledge* (Nabih Amin Faris, Trans.). Lahore, Pakistan: Muhammad Ashraf, 1966.

———. *The confessions of Al-Ghazzali* (Claud Field, Trans.). Lahore, Pakistan: Muhammad Ashraf, 1968a. Also, *The Faith and Practice of Al-Ghazzali* (correctly translated as "Deliverance from Error") (W. Montgomery Watt, Trans.). London: Allen & Unwin, 1953.

———. *The mysteries of fasting* (Nabin Amin Faris, Trans.). Lahore, Pakistan: Muhammad Ashraf, 1968b.

———. *The revival of religious sciences* (Bankey Behari, Trans.). Farnham, Surrey: Sufi Publishing, 1972. (Selections drawn primarily from the last half of Ihyā'Ulum Ad-dīn.)

———. *On the duties of brotherhood* (Muhtar Holland, Trans.). London: Latimer, 1975.

———. *Letters of al-Ghazzali* (Abdul Qayyum, Trans.). Lahore, Pakistan: Islamic Publications, 1976.

Ali, Syed Nawab. *Some moral and religious teachings of Al-Ghazzali* (2nd ed.). Lahore, Pakistan: Muhammad Ashraf, 1944.

Arasteh, A. Reza. *Final integration in the adult personality.* Leiden, Holland: Brill, 1965.

———. *Rumi, the Persian: Rebirth in creativity and love.* Tucson, Ariz.: Omen Press, 1972.

———. Psychology of the Sufi way to individuation. In L. F. Rushbrook Williams (Ed.), *Sufi studies: East and West.* New York: Dutton, 1973, pp. 89–113.

Arberry, A. J. *Sufism: An account of the mystics of Islam.* New York: Harper & Row, 1970.

———. *The Doctrine of the Sufis.* Kashmiri Bazar, Lahore, Pakistan: Sh. Muhammad Ashraf. 1966. Also Cambridge, England: University Press, 1977.

Attar, Farid, Ud-Din. *The conference of the birds* (C. S. Nott, Trans.). London: Routledge & Kegan Paul, 1961.

Baba, Meher. *Listen, humanity.* New York: Dodd, Mead, 1967.

———. *Life at its best.* New York: Harper & Row, 1972.

Beg, Moazziz Ali. A note on the concept of self, and the theory and practice of psychological help in the Sufi tradition. *Interpersonal Development,* 1970 *1,* 58–64.

Behari, Bankey. *The revival of religious sciences* by Al-Ghazzali. Farnham, Surray: Sufi Publishing, 1972, Introduction.

Burckhardt, Titus. *An introduction to Sufi doctrine.* Kashmiri Bazar, Lahore, Pakistan: Sh. Muhammad Ashraf, 1968.

Burke, Omar. Travel and residence with dervishes. In Roy Davidson (Ed.), *Documents on contemporary dervish communities.* London: Hoopoe, 1966.

———. *Among the dervishes.* New York: Dutton, 1975.

Dallas, Ian. *The book of strangers.* New York: Warner Books, 1973.

Dawood, N. J. (Trans.). *The Koran* (3rd Rev. ed.). Baltimore: Penguin Books, 1968.

Deikman, Arthur. Sufism and psychiatry. In Seymour Boorstein, (Ed.), *Transpersonal psychotherapy.* Palo Alto, Calif.: Science and Behavior, 1980, pp. 200–216.

El-Qadiri, Imdad Hussein. *The secret garden.* Introduction by Mahmud Shabistari (Johnson Pasha, trans.). New York: Dutton, 1974.

Erikson, E. *Insight and responsibility.* New York: Norton, 1964.

Farzan, Massud. *Another way of laughter.* New York: Dutton, 1973.

———. *The tale of the reed pipe.* New York: Dutton, 1974.

Foster, William. *Sufi studies today.* London: Octagon, 1968.

Gurdjieff, G. I. *All and everything, the first series: Beelzebub's tales to his grandson.* New York: Dutton, 1950.

———. *Meetings with remarkable men.* New York: Dutton, 1968.

Harman, W. W. Old wine in new wineskins. In James Bugental (Ed.), *Challenges of humanistic psychology.* New York: McGraw-Hill, 1967, pp. 321–334.

Hujwîrî. *Kashf al-mahjub.* (R. A. Nicholson, Trans.). London: Luzac, 1959.

Ibn 'Arabi, Muhyiddin. *Journey to the lord of power*. New York: Inner Traditions, 1981.

Inhelder, B., & Piaget, Jean. *The growth of logical thinking from childhood to adolescence*. New York: Basic Books, 1958.

James, William. *Talks to teachers on psychology and to students on some of life's ideals*. New York: Holt, Rinehart and Winston, 1899. Unaltered republication, New York: Dover, 1962.

Jung, C. G. *C. G. Jung's letters* (Gerhard Adler, Aniela Jaffe, & R. F. C. Hull, Eds.) (Vol. 1). Princeton, N.J.: Princeton University Press, 1973, pp. 1906–1950.

Kabir. *The Kabir book. Versions by Robert Bly*. Boston: Beacon Press, 1977.

Khan, Pir Vilayat. *Toward the one*. New York: Harper & Row, 1974.

MacDonald, Duncan Black. The life of Al-Ghazzali, with special reference to his religious experience and opinions. *The Journal of the American Oriental Society*, 1899, *20*, 71–132.

———. Al-Ghazzālī. In *Development of Muslim theology jurisprudence and constitional theory*. Lahore, Pakistan: Premier Book House, 1903, pp. 215–242.

———. *The religious attitude and life in Islam*. Chicago: University of Chicago Press, 1909.

Nicholson, R. A. *The idea of personality in Sufism*. Lahore, Pakistan: Muhammad Ashraf, 1964a.

———. *Rumi, poet and mystic*. London: Allen & Unwin, 1964b.

Nurbakhsh, Javad. Sufism and psychoanalysis (Parts 1 and 2). Unpublished papers, Department of Psychiatry, University of Tehran, Tehran, Iran, nd.

———. *In the tavern of ruin*. New York: Khaniqahi-nimatullahi, 1978.

———. *In the paradise of the Sufis*. New York: Khaniqahi-nimatullahi, 1979.

———. *Sufism: Meaning, knowledge and unity*. New York: Khaniqahi-nimatullahi, 1981.

Orage, A. R. *Psychological exercises and essays* (Rev. ed.). London: Janus, 1965.

Ornstein, Robert E. *The psychology of consciousness*. San Francisco: Freeman, New York: Viking Press, 1972.

Ouspensky, P. D. *In search of the miraculous*. New York: Harcourt, Brace Jovanovich, 1949.

Ozak, M. al-Jerrahi. *The unveiling of love* (Muhtar Holland, Trans.). New York: Inner Traditions, 1981.

Pendlebury, D. L. Afterword to *The walled garden of truth*, by Hakim Sanai (D. L. Pendlebury, Trans. and abridged). London: Octagon, 1974.

Perry, Whiteall N. *A treasury of traditional wisdom*. New York: Simon & Schuster, 1971.

Piaget, Jean. *The origins of intelligence in children*. New York: International University Press, 1952.

Qayyum, Abdul. *Letters of Al-Ghazzali*. Lahore, Pakistan: Islamic Publications, 1976.

Rice, Cyprian. *The Persian Sufis*. London: Allen & Unwin, 1964.

Rumi, Lalal al-Din. *Discourses of Rumi* (A. J. Arberry, Trans.). New York: Weiser, 1972.

Sa'di, Muslih-uddin Shirazi. *The gulistan or rose garden of Sa'di* (Edward Rehatsek, Trans.). New York: Capricorn Books, 1966.

Salinger, J. D. *Raise high the roofbeam, carpenters and Seymour, an introduction*. New York: Bantam Books, 1965.

Sanai, Hakim. *The walled garden of truth* (D. L. Pendlebury, Trans. and abridged). London: Octagon, 1974.

Shafii, Mohammad. The pir (Sufi guide) and the Western psychotherapist. *R. M. Bucke Memorial Society Newsletter Review,* 1963, *3,* 9–19.

———. Developmental stages in man in Sufism and psychoanalysis. Unpublished paper, 1974.

Shah, Idries. *The Sufis.* New York: Doubleday, 1964.

———. *The way of the Sufi.* New York: Dutton, 1970a.

———. *Tales of the dervishes.* New York: Dutton, 1970b.

———. *The dermis probe.* New York: Dutton, 1971a.

———. *The pleasantries of the incredible Mulla Nasrudin.* New York: Dutton, 1971b.

———. *The magic monastery.* New York: Dutton, 1971c.

———. Interview with Pat Williams. In L. Lewin (Ed.), *The diffusion of Sufi ideas in the West.* Boulder, Col.: Keysign Press, 1972a.

———. *Caravan of dreams.* Baltimore: Penguin Books, 1972b.

———. *Wisdom of the idiots.* New York: Dutton, 1972c.

———. *The exploits of the incomparable Mulla Nasrudin.* New York: Dutton, 1972d.

———. *Thinkers of the East: Teachings of the dervishes.* Baltimore: Penguin Books, 1972e.

———. First statement. In L. Lewin (Ed.), *The diffusion of Sufi ideas in the West.* Boulder, Col.: Keysign Press, 1972f, pp. 133–145.

———. *Learning how to learn.* San Francisco: Harper & Row, 1981.

Shah, Sirdar Ikbal Ali. *Islamic Sufism.* London: Rider, 1933.

Shea, D. (Trans.). *The Dabistan.* London: Oriental Translation Fund, 1943.

Siraj-Ed-Din, Abu Bakr. *The book of certainty.* New York: Weiser, 1970.

Smith, Jane. Women in Islam: Equity, equality, and the search for the natural order. *Journal of the American Academy of Religion,* 1980, *47* (4), 517–537.

Smith, Jane, & Haddad, Yvonne. Women in the afterlife: The Islamic view as seen from Qur'an and tradition. *Journal of the American Academy of Religion,* 1975, *43* (1), 39–50.

Smith, Margaret. *Rabia, the mystic A.D. 717–801 and her fellow saints in Islam.* San Francisco: Rainbow Bridge, 1977. (Originally published, 1928, Cambridge University Press, England.)

Trimingham, J. Spencer. *The Sufi orders in Islam.* New York: Oxford University Press, 1971.

Tweedie, Irina. *The chasm of fire.* England: Element Books, 1979.

Watt, W. Montgomery. *Muslim intellectual: A study of al-Ghazzali.* Edinburgh: University Press, 1971.

White, Robert W. Motivation reconsidered: The concept of competence. *Psychological Review, 66,* 297–333.

NAME INDEX

SUBJECT INDEX

87   88   89   10   9   8   7   6   5